# The Biblical Basis for MODERN SCIENCE

### The Revised and Updated Classic!

# Henry M. Morris

Master Books

First printing: May 2002
Second printing: November 2002

Copyright © 1984, 2002 by Henry M. Morris. All rights reserved. No part of this book may be used or reproduced in any manner whatsoever without written permission of the publisher, except in the case of brief quotations in articles and reviews. For information write: Master Books, Inc., P.O. Box 726, Green Forest, AR 72638.

ISBN: 0-89051-369-4
Library of Congress Number: 2001098885

**Printed in the United States of America**

Please visit our website for other great titles:
www.masterbooks.net

For information regarding author interviews,
please contact the publicity department at (870) 438-5288.

# ACKNOWLEDGMENTS

The scope of this book is broad, dealing with many fields of science, so it was essential that it be reviewed for scientific accuracy by scientists in various disciplines. I am very grateful for this important service to the following members of the Institute for Creation Research Technical Advisory Board and the scientific staff of the Institute for Creation Research.

Steven A. Austin (Ph.D. in geology, Pennsylvania State University), associate professor of geology, ICR.

Richard B. Bliss (Ed.D. in science education, University of Sarasota), professor and head of Department of Science Education, ICR. Deceased

Kenneth B. Cumming (Ph.D. in ecology, Harvard University), professor and head of Biology Department, ICR.

Carl B. Fliermans (Ph.D. in microbiology, Indiana University), consulting scientist in microbial biology.

Duane T. Gish (Ph.D. in biochemistry, University of California at Berkeley), vice president, ICR.

Donald Hamann (Ph.D. in engineering mechanics, Virginia Polytechnic Institute), professor of food science, North Carolina State University. Deceased.

John R. Meyer (Ph.D. in zoology, University of Iowa), director, Van Andel Research Center, Creation Research Society.

John N. Moore (Ed.D. in science education, Michigan State University), Professor Emeritus of Natural Science, Michigan State University. Retired.

Jean S. Morton (Ph.D. in cell biology, George Washington University) science writer and consultant.

John W. Oller Jr. (Ph.D. in linguistics, University of Rochester), professor and head of communicative disorders, University of Louisiana, Lafayette.

Harold S. Slusher (Ph.D. in physics, Columbia Pacific University), assistant professor of physics, University of Texas (El Paso).

All of these scientists read the entire manuscript for the original edition, and made many valuable suggestions, most of which were incorporated into the text. Additions and changes for the revised edition were reviewed by Dr. John Morris, now president of the Institute for Creation Research. Nevertheless, the writer must accept full responsibility for all expositions, both biblical and scientific, as finally published.

Special appreciation is expressed to Dr. John Oller, who not only provided a very thorough review and critique, but also the foreword. Thanks are also due the staff at Baker Book House for their fine editorial work and for a number of very helpful suggestions, as well as Master Books.

Various portions of the original manuscript were typed by Mrs. Mary Louise Morris, Mrs. Mary Smith, Mrs. Judy Strom, and, especially, Mrs. Becky Nichols. Most of the illustrations were prepared by ICR art director Marvin Ross. Mrs. Mary Thomas typed various portions of the new edition, and Mrs. Mary Smith typed and edited the entire second edition.

# CONTENTS

# LIST OF FIGURES

# LIST OF TABLES

# FOREWORD

In his treatise on "Physics and Reality" in 1936 Albert Einstein remarked that it "is a miracle" that "the world of our sense experiences is comprehensible." He said, "The setting up of a real external world would be senseless without this comprehensibility."[1] Thus, the physicist who helped to precipitate the destruction of Hiroshima and Nagasaki with the abstract formula that $E = Mc^2$ also realized that the existence of the physical world is by no means the greatest mystery faced by science. Even the existence of living things pales in comparison to the fact that the world is comprehensible, that it can be represented truly. Surprisingly, in Darwin's materialistic attempt to explain the existence of living organisms, he failed even to ask the deeper question: How is it possible for any of our representations of the world to be true?

C.S. Peirce[2] agreed with Galileo before him and with the world's most quoted living intellectual, Noam A. Chomsky, all of whom supposed that the human mind is designed to comprehend just the sort of world that presents itself. Einstein said, "The very fact that the totality of our sense experiences . . . can be put in order . . . is one which leaves us in awe."[3] This awesome reality is grounded in the fact that *some of our representations are true*. Thus, truth itself is revealed not only in some propositions of the sciences, but also in many of the representations of ordinary experience. While we must guard against errors, illusions, hallucinations, and outright lies, it is nonetheless true that many of the representations in our experience are true. It was for this reason that Einstein (1936) said, "The whole of science is nothing more than a refinement of everyday thinking."[4]

The essential question of science, therefore, is: "What is truth?" This was the question, according to the Gospel of John, that Pilate asked of Jesus Christ. In fact, if the Gospels are true reports, the answer was standing before Pilate in a visible human body. Jesus had said,"'I am the way, the truth, and the life" (John 14:6). Evidently Pilate neither needed nor received any answer other than the one standing before him. The next thing we see Pilate doing is reporting to the

---

1. Albert Einstein, "Physics and Reality," in *Out of My Later Years* (Secaucus, NJ: Citadel Press, 1956), p. 61.
2. C.S. Peirce, "A Neglected Argument for the Reality of God," *Hibbert Journal* (1908): 90–112. Also in C. Hartshorne and P. Weiss, eds., *Collected Papers of C.S. Peirce*, Vol. VI (Cambridge, MA: Harvard University Press, 1935), p. 311–339.
3. Einstein, "Physics and Reality," p. 61.
4. Ibid., p. 59.

Jewish leaders,"'I find in him no fault at all" (John 18:38).

Science repeats Pilate's question: "What is truth?" It is an abstract question. In mathematics, it is supposed that wherever truth may be found, it will at least be self-consistent. That is, the truth cannot contradict itself. All mathematical proofs rely ultimately on this foundational premise, and yet, a perfectly complete mathematical system has not yet been found in mathematics or anywhere in the sciences. Neither can perfect consistency be found in experimental or empirical measurements. In fact, perfect consistency has never been found in the material world or in the sciences, excepting the life of Jesus Christ. The only source for the concept of absolute consistency (truth), as far as I know, is the one pointed to by Dr. Morris in this book: namely, the God who is the same, yesterday, today, and forever (Heb. 13:8); the God whom no one can cause to lie (Num. 23:19); and who has determined the course of events leading to redemption before the world ever was (Matt. 13:35; 25:34; Luke 11:50; John 17:5, 24; 1 Cor. 2:7; Eph. 1:4; 2 Tim. 1:9; Titus 1:2; Heb. 4:3; 9:26; 1 Pet. 1:20; Rev. 13:8; 17:8).

Nevertheless a good definition of truth can be found in the sciences. The best and most complete definition of truth does not come from pure mathematics, but rather from that esoteric branch of mathematical logic known as theoretical semiotics — the grand science that seeks to discover the basis for all possible meaning. The answer is of the logicomathematical kind developed in strict proofs.[5] It comes out that truth is exclusively a formal property of representations. It consists of the agreement between words (or abstract concepts), acts of observation, and facts (physical things and events as related in space-time).

The purest form of truth is also the simplest sort. It is the kind found in true reports of known facts. For instance, if it is true that Jesus Christ appeared before Pilate as reported in all four of the Gospels, the Book of Acts, and Paul's first letter to Timothy, then, these reports not only qualify as true but each contains three critical and necessary elements that must be found in any true report. First, there are the material facts of history that are reported. Second, there are faithful and competent observations that link the material facts in question with certain representations (e.g., the words of some language). Third, there are the words (i.e., the actual representations themselves) used to report the events. A simple triadic structure emerges consisting of (1) facts, (2) linking acts, and (3) representations. If these three are in agreement relative to each other, we say that the narrative is true of the facts reported. To be true in this way, it is only necessary that the facts

5. C.S. Peirce, "The Logic of Relatives," *The Monist*, 7 (1897): 161–217; A. Tarski, "The Concept of Truth in Formalized Languages," in J.J. Woodger, ed. and trans., *Logic, Semantics, and Metamathematics* (Oxford: Oxford University, 1936, translated in 1956), p. 152–278; A. Tarski, "The Semantic Conception of Truth," (1944), in H. Feigl and W. Sellars, eds., *Readings in Philosophical Analysis* (New York, NY: Appleton: 1949), p. 341–374; J.W. Oller Jr., (1996). "Semiotic Theory Applied to Free Will, Relativity, and Determinacy: Or Why the Unified Field Theory Sought by Einstein Could Not be Found" *Semiotica*, 108, no. 3/4 (1996): 199–244.

deliver all that the narrative claims, and that the narrative claims nothing not delivered by or contained in the material facts. It turns out upon logical examination of the formal structure of any true narrative representation that the three elements in question stand in more than a mere triadic relation: they form what logically may be called a trinity of the biblical kind. That is, each element contains and is contained by the others such that if one of the three elements is fully known, the other two are also known.

Thus, it comes out that the simplest and purest form of truth is the sort found in any true narrative. Interestingly, the Bible is a narrative and represents itself to be true. If the Gospels are true, and if Jesus Christ is the Creator God as He claimed to be in saying, "Before Abraham was, I am" (John 8:58), it follows that the biblical narrative must be the most complete account ever rendered about the material world. If true, it reaches from the beginning of the universe until the end of what we know as time. If Jesus is "the Alpha and Omega, the beginning and the end"(Rev. 1:8, 11; 21:6; 22:13), then the book which He came to fulfill must be the best account there has ever been, is now, or ever will be. What if there is a day of judgment and the principal question on that day should be: "What is truth?" We know now that the simplest and most solid kind of truth involves a trinitarian relation between (1) actual material facts, (2) competent observations by one or many reliable witnesses, and (3) representations faithfully mapped into those facts.

During Darwin's heyday, in the 19th century, it became popular to suppose that the material things and living beings in the real world could come about by pure chance and without any assistance whatever from God. In the 20th century, the rage was to question human knowledge of the existence of an external world. In effect, Bertrand Russell, for instance, tried to raise doubt as to whether we can know for sure that there is a real world. Now, in the 21st century, intellectuals have become so mature and advanced that they no longer put the issue in the form of a question. They look so far beyond modern times that they call themselves "postmodern." They deny not only the existence of God, miracles, and knowledge of an external world, but are now (supposedly) certain that no one has the power to know anything for certain, excepting of course that it is certain that nothing can be known for certain. Alistair Pennycook wrote: "We cannot know ourselves or the world around us in any objective fashion."[6] So, according to the postmodernist perspective we must abandon hope of knowing anything. We are reminded of the inscription that William Blake placed over the gates of hell in his drawing to illustrate Dante's Inferno: "Abandon all hope, ye who enter here."

I believe that the day will come when men will look back on this period and be astonished that so many weeds could have grown up in the same fields where good wheat was also thriving. Let it be noted, however, that the existence of

---

6. A. Pennycook, "Incommensurable Discourses?" *Applied Linguistics,* 15, no. 2 (1994): 134.

fictions, errors, and lies alongside true representations are themselves evidence of the existence of truth. If truth did not exist, no fantasy, mythology, illusion, hallucination, or error of any kind, not even a deliberate lie, could ever be discovered. Science, contrary to a lot of nonsense, thrives on the biblical principle of non-contradiction. Science seeks truth in every aspect and part of the universe. It aims to test hypotheses to see which ones can stand up under scrutiny. It requires publication of results so that they may be examined critically, not by literary types who boast of their own inconsistencies, but by persons of integrity seeking to know which representations (which hypotheses and theories) are consistent with observable facts and which are not.

The U.S. federal government has recently issued a policy statement banning falsification, fabrication, and plagiarism in sponsored scientific work. The policy says, "Fabrication is making up data or results and recording or reporting them. Falsification is manipulating research materials, equipment, or processes, or changing or omitting data or results such that the research is not accurately represented in the research record. Plagiarism is the appropriation of another person's ideas, processes, results, or words without giving appropriate credit."[7] Why was such a policy issued? Because truthful reporting is essential to the very existence of scientific inquiry.

The second edition of *The Biblical Basis of Modern Science* shows that science has no other basis than the principle of non-contradiction which is manifested historically only in one God: that is the God of Abraham, Isaac, and Jacob — the one who chooses not to lie and whose power is sufficient to overcome those who would prefer to have Him be other than as He is. The apostle Paul put it well when he said, "Let God be true, but every man a liar" (Rom. 3:4). He went on to paraphrase the Hebrew Psalmist: "That thou mightest be justified in thy sayings, and mightest overcome when thou art judged" (from Ps. 51:4).

*The Biblical Basis for Modern Science* leaves no room for the myth that science is grounded in material philosophy. Materialistic philosophy has no grounding other than fiction, and science, as practiced by persons of integrity has only one basis and that basis can only be found in the Judeo-Christian God who is never inconsistent with himself. Here is an updated version of the book I recommended to readers almost 20 years ago and am glad to recommend again in its revised and updated edition. It shows better than any other that I know of why science can only prosper in contexts pervaded by the Judeo-Christian outlook of the God who cannot lie. It is my pleasure and honor to commend it to readers again.

John W. Oller, Jr.
Head and Professor of Communicative Disorders
at the University of Louisiana at Lafayette

---

7. Federal Policy on Research Misconduct, (December 6, 2000), *Federal Register,* 65, no. 235 (Dec. 6, 2000): 3.

# INTRODUCTION

> If I have told you earthly things, and ye believe not, how shall ye believe,
> if I tell you of heavenly things? (John 3:12).

The Christian witness frequently is confronted with the problem of the alleged scientific mistakes of the Bible, especially in its first 11 chapters. Many Christians have been so intimidated by the supposed weight of modern opinion that they respond merely by a faint-hearted protest that "the Bible is, after all, not a textbook of science but of religion; it merely tells us the fact of divine creation, not the method or the chronology; the Bible is infallible in matters of religion and morals, but we should not expect it to speak precisely on irrelevant data of science and history."

It is obvious, of course, that the Bible is not a scientific textbook in the sense of giving detailed technical descriptions and mathematical formulations of natural phenomena. If it were merely that kind of a textbook, it would quickly become outdated, like other science textbooks. Nevertheless, it does deal extensively with a broad variety of natural phenomena, as well as with numerous and varied events in history. It especially deals with the basic principles of science and the key events in history, and many of its revelations in spiritual and moral matters are keyed to its revelations on scientific and historical matters.

It is logically unsatisfactory and evangelistically unfruitful to try to retain the one without the other. How could an inquirer be led to saving faith in the divine Word if the context in which that Word is found is filled with error? How could he trust the Bible to speak truly when it tells of salvation and heaven and eternity — doctrines which he is completely unable to verify empirically — when he is taught that biblical data that are subject to test are fallacious? Surely if God is really omnipotent and omniscient, and the Bible is really His revelation (and all true Christians at least profess to believe these basic Christian doctrines), then He is able to speak through His Scriptures as clearly and truthfully with respect to earthly things as He does when He speaks of heavenly things.

Men have too rapidly jumped to the conclusion that the Bible is unscientific (or "prescientific," as some would say). The biblical cosmology has never been disproved, it has simply made men uncomfortable and been rejected. Nevertheless the actual facts of observation and experience can be shown to correlate with the biblical view of the world and history in a highly satisfying way.

The Bible authors claim to have written the very Word of God, and it has been accepted as such by multitudes of intelligent people down through the centuries. This is more true today than ever in the past, and there are now thousands of qualified scientists around the world who quite definitely believe in the full verbal inerrancy of the Holy Scriptures. It is thus absurd for anyone to say that "science" has disproved the Bible.

Whenever a biblical passage deals either with a broad scientific principle or with some particular item of scientific data, it will inevitably be found on careful study to be fully accurate in its scientific insights. Often it will be found even to have anticipated scientific discoveries. The Bible is indeed a book of science, as well as a book of history, literature, psychology, economics, law, education, and every other field. It does not use the technical jargon of particular disciplines, of course, but speaks in the universal language of human experience. As the Word of God, it is altogether "profitable . . . that the man of God may be perfect" (2 Tim. 3:16–17), meeting every need, either by direct instruction on specific subjects or by broad guidance in research and decision-making.

The great field of natural science is particularly significant. We are living in a "scientific age," and the proliferation of scientific knowledge and the resulting technologies seem almost boundless. Scientific discoveries and developments, however, can be a danger as well as a blessing to mankind. Not only has the arrogance of the so-called scientific mind tended to subvert religious faith and confidence in the Scriptures, but is also threatening civilization with its nuclear armaments, environmental pollutants, biochemical weaponry, genetic manipulations, and other products of scientific research.

The modern world is desperately in need of God's own wisdom with respect to the purpose and meaning of true science. The Bible will be found not only to reveal a thoroughly modern perspective on the real facts and principles of science but also to provide wisdom and guidance concerning its proper role in human life and in the eternal counsels of God.

It is the purpose of this book to bring together in systematic, useful, and meaningful fashion these key biblical insights and instructions related to all the natural sciences. It should serve effectively as a textbook in courses on science and the Bible, whether formal classroom courses or informal study groups in home and church. It can also be used for reference purposes and is organized and indexed with such use in mind. Most of all, however, it is intended for individual — even inspirational and devotional — reading by men and women and young people in all walks of life. It is the writer's desire to help implant in the heart and mind of every reader a greater appreciation for God's inspired Word than ever known before, along with a greater confidence in the absolute truthfulness of every verse of Scripture, leading to implicit trust in its promises and obedience to its instructions in all things.

This concept of the Bible became the conviction of the writer back in the days of World War II, after an intensive study of both the Scriptures and the writings of evolutionists and other Bible critics. I had trusted Christ as my Savior as a very young boy, but had later become a theistic evolutionist during my undergraduate years studying engineering at Rice Institute (now Rice University). After graduation, as a young engineer working with the International Boundary and Water Commission in Texas, I became active in a strong Bible-believing church and also joined the Gideons International, a lay organization seeking to spread the Scriptures widely and to win people to saving faith in Christ.

This experience solidified my conviction that the Bible was truly effective in changing lives and meeting human needs. When I returned to Rice three years later to teach engineering to the students then being trained as prospective naval officers for the war effort, it also became my burden to influence them for Christ and eternity as well. Therefore, I began an intensive study of Christian evidences and doctrines, as well as anti-Christian literature, in order to do this more effectively.

This study has continued every year since, from youth to maturity to the status of senior citizen, and my conviction that the Bible is God's inerrant Word has become stronger and more confident every year. I taught engineering for almost 30 years, at five different secular universities, trying to maintain an active Christian witness among the students and faculty at each school, and so had many challenges and tests of faith, as well as many wonderful confirmations of the power of the Word. Since getting into Christian education in 1970 (at Christian Heritage College and then the Institute for Creation Research), there have been many fulfillments of God's ancient promise in Jeremiah 33:3 ("Call unto me, and I will answer thee, and shew thee great and mighty things, which thou knowest not"). Although there is still need for research on certain unresolved problems, the positive evidence for the scientific and historical accuracy of the Bible, as well as its validity in human experience, is so abundant and overwhelming as to justify an unshakable faith in its truth.

In this present book, I have continued to use the standard King James text, unless otherwise noted, whenever referring to specific Bible passages. This was, indeed, the standard English version for most Christians for over four hundred years until the sudden explosive proliferation of new translations beginning about 25 years ago. I am aware of these new versions, of course, and have over 40 of them at hand in my own library, using them for study purposes and citing them when helpful. Nevertheless, I still prefer the old standard King James, as the most beautifully written, spiritually powerful, and generally most reliable of all of them, and therefore continue to use it in my own writing and speaking. The evidences and arguments for the scientific accuracy of the Bible apply, of course, regardless of the particular version preferred by the individual reader.

Regardless of the problem, and regardless of the version preferred, one can always find in the Bible a true and satisfying answer to every need. Its statements are true and its promises sure. "Thy testimonies have I taken as an heritage for ever: for they are the rejoicing of my heart" (Ps. 119:111).

PART 1

# SCIENCE AND TRUE CHRISTIANITY

# 1

# QUEEN OF THE SCIENCES

*Biblical Theology*

## The Importance of Theology

Most scientific disciplines have been given English names compounded from two Greek roots, one meaning "organized study," the other referring to the object of study. Biology is the study of life, geology is the study of the earth, hydrology is the study of water, and so on. The ending of each of these words is from the Greek *logos*, meaning "word," also translated "answer," "saying," etc. As a proper name, it is identified in Scripture with the Lord Jesus Christ, as the living Word of God, the Creator of all things (John 1:1–3).

Whether or not men intended it that way, it is at least providential that Jesus Christ should be thus indirectly identified with the study of His creation. Biology is the science of life, and Christ himself is "life" (John 14:6). Geology is the science of the earth, and He is the Creator of the ends of the earth (Isa. 40:28). Hydrology is the science of water, and from Him flows the "water of life" (Rev. 22:1). We also could speak of the sciences of meteorology, zoology, psychology, sociology, climatology, physiology, and many others, but all must ultimately be ascribed to Christ, for in Him "are hid all the treasures of wisdom and knowledge" (Col. 2:3). "By him were all things created" (Col. 1:16), and He "uphold[s] all things by the word of his power" (Heb. 1:3), so it follows inescapably that true knowledge of any component of His creation must depend ultimately on the knowledge of Christ and His Word.

Therefore, the most important of all sciences, or objects of study, is theology, the study of God. In a special sense, this discipline becomes also Christology, since God was in Christ, and since the Lord Jesus Christ is the Word made flesh (John 1:14). Theology, in fact, once was honored as "the queen of sciences," though it has lost this position of public esteem in our modern scientific age. To many it has now become merely a branch of philosophy, known as "philosophical theology," or "the philosophy of religion." Scholars speak of different forms of theology — natural theology, rational theology, dogmatic theology, empirical theology, and so on. Latter-day radical theologians are even promoting such concepts as what they call "liberation theology," equating Christian action with Marxism and revolution.

Since this is not a treatise on theology, however, no attempt will be made to discuss and critique these various theologies. Our interest here is solely in biblical theology, especially the relation of biblical theology to the natural sciences. Biblical theology, of course, is the systematic codification of what the biblical authors, inspired by the Holy Spirit, teach about God — His person, His attributes, His revelation, His works, and His purposes. Other sources of information about God — in nature and in religious experience, for example — can supplement and illumine the biblical data, but only the latter are normative for Christian doctrine. In particular, it is important in the context of this chapter to establish what the Bible teaches about the existence of God and His purposes for man and the universe — created, sustained, and redeemed by Him — in relation to the other sciences as understood today.

## Science and the Existence of God

Although it is not possible to develop a completely rigorous proof for the existence of God (after all, Heb. 11:6 says that "without faith, it is impossible to please him"!), the Scriptures do indicate that it is utter foolishness not to believe (Ps. 14:1; Rom. 1:22; et al.). Although there may exist certain philosophical arguments by which one can avoid acknowledging God's existence, the great solid weight of scientific and statistical evidence, when rationally evaluated, clearly balances the scales heavily in favor of God. One rejects God only because that is the choice of his will, not because of the evidence.

It is superficial to say (as many have said) that since science is based on observation and since God cannot be "observed" with the physical senses, therefore God's existence is an unscientific belief. There are many scientific entities that cannot be seen with human eyes but whose existence is not doubted in the least by scientists (e.g., electrons). The famous assertion by the first Russian astronauts that they had proved God did not exist since they could not find Him in space was a prime example of the irrational rationalizing by which unbelievers justify their unbelief. Scripture itself says, "No man hath seen God at any time" (John 1:18). "God is Spirit, and they that worship him must worship him in spirit and truth" (John 4:24). The very essence of God's revelation of himself precludes evaluation by the experimental procedures of the scientific method. Nevertheless, the most basic principles of science (which are themselves assumed in the application of the scientific method) point directly to the exceedingly high probability that God is the true cause of all causes.

Even though it is not possible to prove God's existence by rigorous scientific demonstration, it is even more impossible (if there were such a category) to prove His nonexistence! One cannot prove a "universal negative." To prove that there is no God anywhere in the universe or at any time in the universe, would require omniscience and probably omnipresence as well, which are themselves attributes of deity. That is, one would have to be God, in order to prove there is no God! Dogmatic atheism, therefore, is self-contradictory foolishness.

One may lodge certain moral arguments against God if he wishes. For instance, he may ask why a holy God condones evil in the world if He is able to prevent it. Some would say that God must be either unrighteous or impotent, or both, and thus not really God.

But such arguments assume that man has the right and the ability to judge God, and thus that man himself is really God. They ignore the possibility that God may have a good reason, consistent with His holiness, to allow evil to exist for a brief time and that He will eventually destroy it forever. According to Scripture, God will eventually judge and purge all evil from His creation (2 Pet. 3:10–13), but in the meantime He is calling men to repentance (2 Pet. 3:9), having created them not as unthinking machines but as volitional beings in His divine image, responsible for their own moral and spiritual choices, and having also himself paid the full price for their redemption (1 Pet. 1:18–20).

At the very best, such anti-theistic arguments are specious and self-serving, arrogating to the creature the right to judge the motives and actions of his Creator. "Shall the thing formed say to him that formed it, Why hast thou made me thus?" (Rom. 9:20).

All but the most presumptuous, therefore, must acknowledge at least the possibility that God exists and that we are His creatures. We can, furthermore, examine that possibility in terms of its probability. If we do happen to be His creatures, then our minds and reasoning capabilities are likewise created by Him, and we can use these very entities and experiences as instruments with which to evaluate this probability. If these were not created by Him and if, indeed, there is no God, then it is quite absurd to believe that we can trust our minds and reasoning faculties at all. They are then merely the products of chance and randomness. Victor Weisskopf, while president of the American Academy of Arts and Sciences, reminded his fellow scientists of the amazing "fact" that non-thinking "Nature" has, as they believe, generated intelligent beings and intelligible systems. "Einstein considered this development to be the great miracle of science; in his words, 'the most incomprehensible fact of nature is the fact that nature is comprehensible.'"[1] Weisskopf perhaps used the term "miracle" inadvertently, but such a development — the evolution of intelligence and intelligibility by random

---

1. Victor F. Weisskopf, "The Frontiers and Limits of Science," *American Scientist,* 65 (July–Aug. 1977): 405.

processes from unthinking atoms — would indeed require a mighty miracle.

Dr. Lewis Thomas, former chancellor of the Sloan Kettering Cancer Center in Manhattan, has commented, "We know a lot about the structure and function of the cells and fibers of the human brain, but we haven't the ghost of an idea about how this extraordinary organ works to produce awareness."[2] In another article this distinguished scientist has noted that "we do not understand a flea, much less the making of a thought."[3] With respect to the idea that complex and comprehensible systems could ever evolve from random process by chance, Thomas rather wistfully laments: "Biology needs a better word than *error* for the driving force in evolution. . . . I cannot make my peace with the randomness doctrine; I cannot abide the notion of purposelessness and blind chance in nature. And yet, I do not know what to put in its place for the quieting of my mind."[4]

With all due respect, Christian theism provides a clear answer to such a query. An omnipotent, omniscient, personal Creator God provides perfect peace of mind and soul to all who come to Him in faith. Theism does not oppose true science. All the great laws and principles of science lead directly to God as their only adequate source and explanation.

In a modern treatment of this fascinating subject, two authorities have pointed out the almost infinite complexity of the human brain.

> The human brain is the most astonishing and mysterious of all known complex systems. Inside this mass of billions of neurons, information flows in ways that we are only starting to understand. The memories of a summer day on the beach when we were kids; imagination; our dreams of impossible worlds. Consciousness. Our surprising capacity for mathematical generalization and understanding of deep, sometimes counterintuitive questions about the universe. Our brains are capable of this and much more. How? We don't know: the mind is a daunting problem for science.[5]

The amazing phenomenon of consciousness is perhaps the most mysterious of all the mysteries of the human brain. Anthropologist Matt Cartmill, in a Phi Beta Kappa message, has noted this.

> The phenomenon of consciousness is the source of all value in our lives. As such, it should be at the top of the scientific agenda. Yet despite its fundamental importance, consciousness is a subject that most scientists are reluctant to deal with. We know practically nothing about either its mechanisms or its evolution. . . .
>
> If consciousness is not algorithmic, then how is it produced? We don't know. The machineries of consciousness are an almost perfect mystery.[6]

2. Lewis Thomas, "On Science and Uncertainty," *Discover*, 1 (Oct. 1980): 59.
3. Lewis Thomas, "On the Uncertainty of Science," *Key Reporter*, 46 (Autumn 1980): 2.
4. Ibid.
5. Richard Sole and Brian Godwin, *Signs of Life* (New York, NY: Basic Books, 2000), p. 119.
6. Matt Cartmill, "Do Horses Gallop in their Sleep?" *Key Reporter* (Autumn 2000): 6, 8.

The answer — indeed the only possible answer that makes sense — is that we were *created* in the image of God!

## Biblical Backgrounds of Science

The basic compatibility of science with Christian theism is even more obvious when it is realized that modern science actually grew in large measure out of the seeds of Christian theism. It is absurd to claim, as modern evolutionists often do, that one cannot be a true scientist if he believes in creation. As outlined in figure 1, most of the great founders of science believed in creation and, indeed, in all the great doctrines of biblical Christianity.

Men such as Johann Kepler, Isaac Newton, Robert Boyle, David Brewster, John Dalton, Michael Faraday, Blaise Pascal, Clerk Maxwell, Louis Pasteur, William

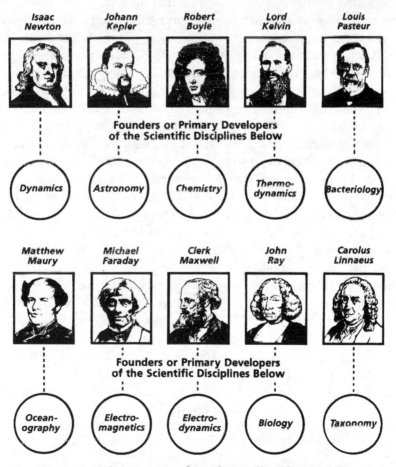

*FIGURE 1 — Christian Founders of Key Scientific Disciplines*
*The humanistic claim that scientists cannot believe the Bible is refuted by the fact that many of the greatest scientists of the past were Bible-believing creationist Christians. See appendix 1 for an extensive listing of these men.*

Thomson (Lord Kelvin), and a host of others of comparable stature[7] were men who firmly believed in special creation and the personal omnipotent God of creation, as well as believing in the Bible as the inspired Word of God and in Jesus Christ as Lord and Savior. Their great contributions in science were made in implicit confidence that they were merely "thinking God's thoughts after Him," and that they were doing His will and glorifying His name in so doing. They certainly entertained no thoughts of conflict between science and the Bible. A tabulation of the names and contributions of many of these great Bible-believing scientists of the past is incorporated in appendix 1.

Some skeptics might say that such men were merely products of their times — that everyone believed in God and the Bible at the time.

But that's exactly the point! It was no coincidence that it was in the milieu of the Reformation and the Great Awakening that modern science first grew and began to thrive. Fruitful scientific research almost demands a biblical world view, either consciously or subconsciously, a world view in which like causes produce like effects, where natural phenomena follow fixed and intelligible natural laws, and where we can have confidence that we can think rationally and meaningfully. Such a world presupposes no random, chaotic origin but an origin under the control of a great mind and will, an intelligent and volitional First Cause, a great lawgiver who can enact, implement, and enforce His created laws.

Many recent scientists, even though they themselves are not creationists, are still willing to recognize the Christian, creationist origin of modern science. Entomologist Stanley Beck, an articulate anti-creationist, has acknowledged this fact: "The first of the unprovable premises on which science has been based is the belief that the world is real and the human mind is capable of knowing its real nature. . . . The second and best known postulate underlying the structure of scientific knowledge is that of cause and effect. . . . The third basic scientific premise is that nature is unified."[8]

Christian creationists certainly would agree with all these premises, although such concepts were largely either unformulated, ignored, or rejected by the pagan philosophers of antiquity. Beck acknowledges that they are essentially Christian in origin and nature. "These scientific premises define and limit the scientific mode of thought. It should be pointed out, however, that each of these postulates had its origin in, or was consistent with, Christian theology."[9]

Why, then, should there be a conflict between Christian theology and true

---

7. See Henry M. Morris, *Men of Science — Men of God* (Green Forest, AR: Master Books, 1988), for brief biographies and testimonies of over 107 of these great Bible-believing scientists of the past.

8. Stanley D. Beck, "Natural Science and Creationist Theology," *Bioscience,* 32 (Oct. 1982): 739.

9. Ibid. See also E. M. Klaaren, *Religious Origins of Modern Science* (Grand Rapids, MI: Eerdmans, 1977); Stanley L. Jaki, *The Origin of Science and the Science of Its Origin* (South Bend, IN: Regnery/ Gateway, 1978); R. Hooykaas, *Religion and the Rise of Modern Science* (Grand Rapids, MI: Eerdmans, 1972); Alfred North Whitehead, *Science and the Modern World* (New York, NY: Macmillan, 1926).

science? The fact is that there is no conflict, but the problem lies with modern evolutionary scientists, who have arbitrarily superimposed an additional, extraneous postulate in their current definition of science. Here is how Beck puts it: "Scientific thought soon parted from theology, because no assumption is made concerning any force outside or beyond natural measurable forces."[10] That is, science is assumed to be, not only rational and causal and unified, but also naturalistic, banning by definition even the possibility of a supernatural First Cause of the rationality, causality, and unity of the universe with which science deals. But such an assumption is purely arbitrary (even emotional, as Isaac Asimov had admitted)[11] and was certainly not held by the great scientists of the past, nor is it indicated by any actual scientific data.

On such a basis, the possibility of true creation is excluded, not because of facts, but because of anti-creationist prejudice. Natural causes are invoked not only to explain the operation of present processes and systems but also the origin of all such processes and systems!

Such a definition of science was not held by the original founders of science or by anyone else until recently. The once-revered definition of "science" was as follows: "'Science,' n. (Fr. from L. *scientia*, from *scio*, to know) 1. In a *general sense*, knowledge, or certain knowledge; the comprehension or understanding of truth or facts by the mind. The *science* of God must be perfect."[12] Thus *science*, as originally defined and intended, meant "truth" or "facts" or "knowledge." The essence of the time-hallowed scientific method has heretofore been claimed to be observation, experimentation, falsifiability, repeatability. But modern evolutionists have prostituted it to mean "naturalism" or "materialism" or even, in effect, "atheism." Such a definition, of course, is a convenient dodge to get away from having to consider creationism.

> Is scientific creationism scientific? Obviously, it is not. Creationism involves acceptance of a premise that lies outside of science. . . . If separated from its origin in a religious tradition, might not the creationist view of life on earth be offered as a scientific theory? . . . The answer is an unequivocal "no," because the creationist theory requires the belief that some force, some factor has created and, in so doing, has bypassed the natural forces and mechanisms by which the physical universe operates.[13]

Such an evaluation ignores the fact that, insofar as any real proofs or unequivocal evidences go, evolution also bypasses any observed natural forces or mechanisms. However, it is considered "scientific" purely because it is "naturalistic."

Scientists like to project an image, for public consumption and admiration,

---

10. Beck, "Natural Science," p. 739.
11. See chapter 4.
12. *An American Dictionary of the English Language*, 1st ed., s.v. "science." This first edition of Webster's famous dictionary was published in 1828.
13. Beck, "Natural Science," p. 740.

of detached objectivity, or searching for truth. Yet that search for truth seems to stop abruptly whenever it begins to lead in the direction of supernatural creation, and the vaunted objectivity of scientists quickly deteriorates to irate emotionalism whenever evolution is questioned on scientific grounds. If evolutionary scientists are going to continue to insist that science is pure naturalism, then they ought to be honest enough to admit that such a position requires at least as much faith as that of the Bible-believing creationist. A discerning article in the journal of the Society for the Study of Evolution has some very appropriate comments in this vein:

> By a metaphysical construct I mean any unproved or unprovable assumption that we all made and tend to take for granted. One example is the doctrine of uniformitarianism that asserts that the laws of nature, such as gravity and thermodynamics, have always been true in the past and will always be true in the future. It is the belief in that doctrine that permits scientists to demand repeatability in experiments. I like the word doctrine in this case because it makes clear that matters of faith are not restricted to creationists and that in the intellectual struggle for citizen enlightenment we need to be very clear just where the fundamental differences between science and theology lie. It is not, as many scientists would like to believe, in the absence of metaphysical underpinnings of science.[14]

Thus we conclude that true science is fully consistent with Christian theology in general and creationism in particular, certain modern scientists to the contrary notwithstanding. Indeed, modern science had its origin in the creationist world view of biblical Christianity. Modern scientism, on the other hand, is based on the arbitrary incorporation of eternity-to-eternity naturalism into the establishmentarian definition of science. As we shall see, however, the basic principles of science (such as causality) are fully consistent with theism and a supernatural creation.

## The Law of Cause and Effect

Probably the most universal and certain of all scientific principles is the principle of causality, the law of cause and effect. This concept has been argued extensively, pro and con, in philosophical treatises, with respect to its possible theological implications, but there is no question of its universal acceptance in the world of experimental science, as well as in ordinary personal experience.

The subtle refinements of philosophical argumentation relative to causality require such a specialized educational background that non-specialists in philosophy (or philosophical theology) find them extremely tedious either to appreciate or evaluate. Such learned disputations are beyond the scope of the practical

---

14. Walter M. Pitch, "The Challenges to Darwinism since the Last Centennial and the Impact of Molecular Studies," *Evolution*, 36, no. 6 (1982): 1138–1139. See also Henry M. Morris, "The Splendid Faith of the Evolutionist," *Acts and Facts* (Sept. 1982), p. 4.

implications in science and human experience, which we seek to explore here.

Since God does exist, it seems very unlikely that He would make the evidence of His existence so tenuous as to require either expertise in philosophy to discern it or blind credulity to appropriate it. "Be ready always to give an answer [Greek *apologia*, an 'apologetic,' a systematic objective evidential defense of the Christian faith] to every man that asketh you a reason of the hope that is in you" (1 Pet. 3:15), wrote the apostle Peter as he was inspired by the Holy Spirit. This is not a suggestion to intellectuals, but a command to all believers! Thus, the evidence must be real and it must be clear, to all who "sanctify the Lord God in their hearts" and who approach such study and witness with meekness and with fear. The Christian should be neither ignorant nor arrogant, though emotional religion by itself tends to the one and intellectual religion to the other. Both heart and mind must somehow be involved together, not in opposition but in fellowship.

It is this need for balance that is met so fully by the principle of cause and effect. Both rigorous science and everyday human experience function within its framework. One speaks to the mind, the other to the heart, but both speak in terms of causality and both lead ultimately to God.

In ordinary daily experiences, one knows intuitively that nothing happens in isolation. Every event can be traced to one or more events which preceded it and which, in fact, cause it. We may raise such causal questions about it as: "*How* did this happen?" "*What* caused this?" "*Where* did this come from?" "*When* did it start?" Or, more incisively, "*Why* did this happen?"

When we try to trace the event to its cause, or causes, we find that we never seem to reach a stopping point. The cause of the event was itself caused by a prior cause, and so on back. Eventually we must face the question of a possible uncaused First Cause.

This situation is equally true in the rigorous system of formal scientific logic. A scientific experiment specifically tries to relate effects to causes, in the form of quantitative equations if possible. That is, for example, if so much of component A is combined with so much of component B, then such an event will result with so much of product C being developed. If one repeats the same experiment with the same factors, then the same results will be reproduced.

Once again, the causal logic can be carried backward in time through a chain of effects and their sequential causes. And again, one must confront the question of either an infinite chain of "second causes," or else, finally, of a primary cause, the uncaused First Cause.

As to the precise definition of a "cause," one could hardly improve on the definition formulated by the great 19ᵗʰ century apologist, C.A. Row: "A cause is a thing previously existing, which has not only the power to bring into existence something not previously existing, but which has actually produced it."[15] Everything with which

---

15. C.A. Row, *Christian Theism* (London: Thomas Whittaker, 1880), p. 49.

we are acquainted in the physical or moral spheres can be thought of as either an effect or a cause. In turn, each cause is itself an effect of some antecedent cause. "Whatever exists in the effect, exists either actively or in potency, in the cause. Otherwise it must either have produced itself, which is absurd, or some other cause must be invoked to account for the existence of such things in the effect which did not exist either actively or potentially in the cause."[16]

If someone objects to using a definition formulated by a theologian, consider the discussion by Dr. Abraham Wolf, former professor and head of the Department of the History and Method of Science at the University of London, one of the greatest philosophers of science in modern times: "Except among believers in magic, at the one extreme, and among thorough-going skeptics, at the other extreme, it is usually assumed either explicitly or at least implicitly, that every event has a cause, and that the same kind of cause has the same kind of effect. This assumption is commonly known as the Postulate or Principle of Universal Causation."[17]

Some intellectuals have eschewed such a definition, regarding it as "anthropomorphic," maintaining that natural phenomena should be described simply in terms of empirical sequences rather than causes and effects. Wolf, however, pointed out the fallacy in such a formulation:

> It would certainly be extravagant to project into the caused sequences of inanimate phenomena anything analogous to the sense of effort or of constraint that is experienced in human activity or passivity respectively. But that is no reason for discarding causality altogether. Carried through consistently, this can only end in the conception of the world as a series of independent miracles — a view even more irrational than the anthropomorphism which it is intended to correct. The principle of conservation of matter and energy would lose all significance without the idea of causal continuity, according to which certain successive events not only *follow*, but *follow from*, one another. In fact, mere laws of sequence are only intelligible in the last resort, when they can be shown to result from direct or indirect causal connections.[18]

The very basis of the highly reputed "scientific method" is just this law of causality — that effects are in and like their causes, and that like causes produce like effects. Even the famous "principle of indeterminacy" involves causality expressed statistically. Science in the modern sense would be altogether impossible if cause and effect should cease.

Oddly enough, however, some modern cosmogonists are indeed trying to deny causality at the quantum level. An astrophysicist at the University of Hawaii has written as follows:

> Let me start by saying that many people believe that everything in nature has to have a causal explanation. Although this may be true at the macro-

16. Ibid., p. 50.
17. *Encyclopaedia Britannica*, 1949 ed., s.v. "Causality, or Causation," by Abraham Wolf.
18. Ibid., p. 62.

scopic level, it is not necessarily the case at the microscopic level, as quantum physics has demonstrated. . . . Similarly, the universe itself does not require a cause.[19]

Quantum physics has *demonstrated* nothing of the sort. The so-called proofs are merely mathematical speculations. This idea is discussed further in chapter 5, but it should be obvious that its main purpose is to account for the universe without God. To do that, it has to be assumed either that the universe suddenly just happened, without a first cause, or else that it has always existed, never beginning at all. For if causality is real, then clear logic implies a first cause, and *that* implies God!

Granted that the law of cause and effect is a universal law, applicable in all science and in all human experience, it still may not be obvious how this points to God's existence. In fact, there have been many attempts to use this very principle to discredit the supernatural of biblical Christianity. The philosophy of scientific determinism has been invoked to disprove biblical miracles, for example. Such arguments miss the point. The occurrence of a miracle does not contravene causality but merely invokes a higher cause, a cause quite adequate to produce the miracle.

Rather than discrediting the possibility of the supernatural, the law of causation offers strong testimony to the existence of a personal, omnipotent God. As noted above, the law leads inevitably to a choice between two alternatives: (1) an infinite chain of nonprimary causes; (2) an uncaused primary Cause of all causes.

Although again it is impossible to prove rigorously that the second alternative is the true one, it surely is more satisfying to all logic and experience. An endless chain of nonprimary causes is all but inconceivable, offering no "mental rest" as a supposed description of reality. Furthermore, this supposed endless chain of finite links can itself be regarded as an effect. Since every component of the chain is a finite effect, the whole series is itself a combined effect, but since the number of links is infinite, its cause must be infinite. Still further, each antecedent link in the chain is "greater" than the one before it, since something is always lost in the transmission from cause to effect.[20] Thus, eventually, in the infinite chain of nonprimary causes, a nonprimary cause must finally be reached that is essentially infinite. And since nothing can be "more infinite" than infinite, this finally must be a primary cause — the infinite First Cause.

There are not really two alternatives after all. If the law of cause and effect applies to the universe as a whole, as it surely applies now to every finite part of the universe, then there must be a great uncaused First Cause of the universe. The First Cause must be adequate to produce and explain every single entity in the universe, as well as the universe itself.

And the only adequate First Cause is the God of the Bible! That is, the First

19. Richard A. Crowe, "Is Quantum Cosmology Science? *Skeptical Inquirer* (March/April 1995): 54.
20. See discussion on the entropy principle in chapter 7.

Cause must be infinite, eternal, and omnipotent (as required by the effects of boundless space, endless time, and the array of various phenomena of energy and matter occurring everywhere through space and always through time). The First Cause must also be living, conscious, volitional, and omniscient, in view of the phenomenal effects of life, consciousness, will, and intelligibility in the universe. Similarly the First Cause of the concept of righteousness — and the universal conviction that righteousness is "better" than unrighteousness — must be a moral Cause. The First Cause of the concepts of beauty, of justice, of spirituality, of love, and other such qualities (all of which, though abstract, are nonetheless real effects in this universe) must, by the principle of causation, be an esthetic, just, spiritual, loving Cause.

Finally, the inexorable conclusion to which we are driven by the scientific law of cause and effect — the foundational principle upon which all true science is built and which all human experience confirms — is that this universe was brought into existence by a great uncaused, self-existing First Cause. As noted in figure 2, that First Cause must be an infinite, eternal, omnipotent, omnipresent, omniscient, living, conscious, volitional, moral, spiritual, esthetic, loving being! Further, since the universe[21] is not a "multi-verse," the God who created it could only have been one God, not two gods or many gods. Neither dualism, polytheism, nor pantheism will satisfy causality, but only monotheism.

The only assumptions involved in arriving at this conclusion are: (1) that our mental processes are real and meaningful, not illusory dreams; (2) that causal reasoning is valid, not only when dealing with finite systems in the present but also when extrapolated toward infinity; (3) that the basic principles which are known to describe all present phenomena (e.g., law of cause and effect, laws of thermodynamics) have also been in operation throughout the past, since the close of creation.

While the above assumptions cannot be proved, they are surely the most reasonable assumptions that could be made based on all known observations and experience. No scientist would ever question them in any circumstance, except perhaps on this question of origins. No exception to any of them has ever been noted, except in the case of miracles (which, as noted above, can also be incorporated within them by allowing the activity of a divine Cause when occasion and evidences warrant).

Thus the basic premise of all biblical theology — that "in the beginning God created the heaven and the earth" (Gen. 1:1) — can be considered proved, as well as anything beyond the immediate reach of experimental demonstration can ever be proved. At this point, the method and time and other particular features of His creation are yet to be discussed, but the fact of the God of the Bible, as the one First Cause of all things, can and should be accepted, on the basis of overwhelming evidence throughout His creation.

---

21. A recent atheistic suggestion is that there may be an infinite number of universes, and that we just happen to be in the one that seems accidentally to support life. There is no evidence for such a notion, except the desire to eliminate God.

**FIGURE 2 — *Principle of Cause and Effect***

*The most basic scientific principle, and the criterion that governs all human experience, is the law of causality. This law states that although one cause can have many effects, no effect can be either quantitatively greater than or qualitatively superior to its cause.*

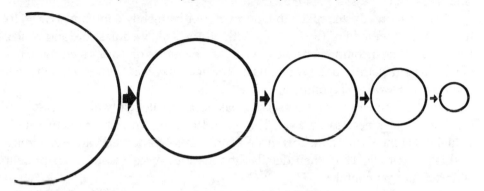

*An effect can never be greater — and, in fact, will always be less — than its cause. Thus, a chain of effects and their causes must eventually trace back to an essentially infinite First Cause.*

**The First Cause of limitless space must be infinite.**

**The First Cause of endless time must be eternal.**

**The First Cause of boundless energy must be omnipotent.**

**The First Cause of infinite complexity must be omniscient.**

**The First Cause of love must be loving.**

**The First Cause of life must be living.**

**Thus, the First Cause of the universe must be an infinite, eternal, omnipotent, omniscient, omnipresent, personal, volitional, holy, loving, living being!**

## God's Purpose in Creation

Apart from the fundamental issue of First Cause, probably the most vital theological question is that of purpose. There is nothing in the essential existence of God that requires Him to create. The universe had a beginning — even time had a beginning — but God is eternal. He existed for endless "ages" (whatever the meaning of such a term before the creation of time) without creating.

Whatever He is, God is not capricious, nor can He be surprised. There must, therefore, be good and sufficient reason why He created the universe and man to live in the universe. Our minds are finite, however, and it is vain and presumptuous for us to attempt to enter into His counsels, except to the extent that He has been pleased to reveal them in His Word. "For who hath known the mind of the Lord? or who hath been his counsellor? . . . For of him, and through him, and to him, are all things" (Rom. 11:34–36).

The Scriptures do reveal that man is at the center of His purpose. Only man (including woman) was created in God's image (Gen. 1:26–27), only man was given dominion over all the earth (Gen. 1:26, 28), and only man will dwell with God forever (1 Thess. 4:17; Rev. 21:3).

Furthermore, this eternal habitation will not be merely contemplative. "His servants shall serve him" (Rev. 22:3). With all the joys of endless life and peace, and with all the incomprehensible (1 Cor. 2:9) blessings of "the exceeding riches of his grace" that are to be shown to us in "the ages to come" (Eph. 2:7), there will still be much work to accomplish.

But the nature of this future service has been revealed only in the most general way. Details necessarily await His second coming. In fact, the actual individual assignments are somehow given as "rewards," associated with our service in this present life. Thus, their details cannot yet be revealed, since our present service is not yet complete.

Since God, who created time as well as space, knows the end from the beginning, His ultimate purpose in creation must be centered on these eternal ages to come and on man's role in these future ages. Since He did not immediately proceed to such a future economy right from the beginning, however, we must conclude that this present economy is tentative and probationary and that this phase also involves good and sufficient reasons on God's part.

The need for a period of probationary service clearly suggests the need for a time of testing and training. As beings created in God's image, men and women are not robots, capable of doing only what they are designed and commanded to do. Neither are they infinite in wisdom and ability, for then they would be not in God's image, but as God himself. They were freely responsible for what they might do, though not yet ready for all God had ultimately planned for them to do. Thus the need for a time of preparation and probation.

Furthermore, God chose not to create a whole population of people directly, but indirectly, through the marvelous process of reproduction. Adam was "the first man" (1 Cor. 15:45) and Eve was "the mother of all living" (Gen. 3:20), and it would take thousands of years before an adequate number of people could be produced and prepared for God's eternal plan.

Not only were human beings created to live forever, but so was the physical universe which God had created. The earth and the sun, the moon and the stars, have been established forever (Ps. 148:1–6, et al.). The universe, in fact, is man's home. Though his physical body may die, it must ultimately be resurrected and become immortal, no longer subject to death (1 Cor. 15:52–53).

As a part of his probationary training, therefore, man must learn the nature of God's universe, for he must live in it and serve his Creator in it forever. He must not only learn to understand it, but also to control and utilize its processes. And what he learns, he must transmit to others, both of his own generation and of subsequent generations, in order that the human race as a whole, as it grows in both knowledge and number through the years, may serve God most effectively.

Initially, of course, even though the entire physical universe was created as man's home, his population would be small and his knowledge and experience very circumscribed. Therefore, God prepared a special part of the universe, a place called earth, that could serve as mankind's home during this growth and learning period. For the time being, the "heavens" were reserved by the Lord for other purposes (Ps. 115:16).

God himself also chose to enter His physical universe and to establish "his chambers" there (Ps. 104:2–3). Having created the universe, He is not, of course, bound by it. He is "transcendent" — outside of space and before time — but He is also "immanent," everywhere "here" in space and always "now" in time.

God has not revealed just where, in relation to earth, His heavenly throne room is located, except that it must be at a tremendously great distance from earth (2 Cor. 12:2–4; Eph. 4:10). It is the place from which Christ came into the world and to which He returned (Ps. 110:1; Hos. 5:15) after His death and resurrection. It is evidently there that He is preparing a place for His disciples (John 14:3) and to which He will receive them when He returns. It is probably also to this "house not made with hands, eternal in the heavens" (2 Cor. 5:1) that the spirit of believers are carried at death, there temporarily to rest and await the resurrection.

Also in the heavens reside "an innumerable company of angels" (Heb. 12:22). These are mighty spirit beings, created not in God's image like man, but created as "ministering spirits" (Heb. 1:14). As "servants," they serve both God (Ps. 103:20–21) and man (Heb. 1:14). They do not share the human capacity of reproduction, having been created initially in adequate numbers for them to accomplish God's purpose for them. They are called "the host of heaven" (2 Chron. 18:18), a term also associated with the stars (Jer. 33:22).

Not very much else has been revealed concerning the matters discussed in this section, and we need to be careful not to draw unwarranted inferences and conclusions. Nevertheless, what is revealed is fascinating, creating in us a yearning to know more, and is beautifully harmonious with all we know in science about the universe and in our hearts concerning God.

## The First Great Commission

When Christ ascended to heaven after His resurrection, He left His disciples what has long been known as the Great Commission, a mandate to all Christian believers to take the gospel to the whole world, commanding them to try to bring all people everywhere to submit to Jesus Christ as Lord and Savior. It is a worldwide, age-long mandate, given to all those who have been saved through His mighty work of redemption. It has never been rescinded, nor will it be, until He sets up His eternal kingdom, composed only of those who have been redeemed.

But long before that another great commission was given to all men, whether saved or unsaved, merely by virtue of being men created by God in His image. It also had worldwide scope, and has never been rescinded. It had to do with implementing God's purpose in His work of creation, just as Christ's commission was for implementing His work of salvation and reconciliation. The first is an obligation for all people, the second an obligation for all Christians.

This primeval commission was transmitted by their Creator to the very first man and woman and, through them, to every man and woman who have descended from them. It has never been withdrawn, and all indications are that it will continue to be applicable forever, since it involves the very purpose of God in creation.

In its primeval form, this mandate (called by some "the cultural mandate," or more appropriately, the "dominion mandate") is found in Genesis 1:26 and 28. "And God said, Let us make man in our image, after our likeness: and let them have dominion over the fish of the sea, and over the fowl of the air, and over the cattle, and over all the earth, and over every creeping thing that creepeth upon the earth. . . . Be fruitful, and multiply, and replenish the earth, and subdue it; and have dominion over the fish of the sea, and over the fowl of the air, and over every living thing that moveth upon the earth."

Man's "dominion," of course, is as God's steward, not as one that is given license to "destroy the earth" (Rev. 11:18). "The earth is the LORD's, and the fullness thereof; the world, and they that dwell therein" (Ps. 24:1). Nevertheless, although God retains ownership, man has been placed in charge of the earth and all its systems, living and nonliving. This is a great responsibility.

The command to "subdue the earth," although couched in military terminology, should be understood to mean bringing all earth's systems and processes into a state of optimum productivity and utility, offering the greatest glory to God and benefit to mankind. Thus, the primeval commission authorizes — in fact, commands — those human enterprises that we now denote as science and technology, or research and development. First we are to learn to understand the full nature of earth's processes, and then we are to organize them in useful and beautiful systems and products. Note figure 3.

The creative acts by which God brought His universe and its inhabitants into existence are reflected now in the major divisions of science, as man continues year after year seeking to subdue the earth. There are only three specific acts of *ex nihilo* (out of nothing) creation recorded in Genesis, indicating three fundamentally different entities in God's universe. These acts are indicated by the use of the verb "create" (Hebrew *bara*):

> 1. "In the beginning God *created* the heaven and the earth" (Gen. 1:1).
> 2. "God *created* . . . every living creature that moveth" (Gen. 1:21).
> 3. "God *created* man in his own image" (Gen. 1:27).

The first use relates to the physical world, the second to the living world, the last to the human world. Research and development related to these three "universes" can be divided into the physical sciences, the life sciences, and the

## Figure 3 — The Dominion Mandate

The first great commission to mankind was to "Be fruitful, and multiply, and replenish the earth and subdue it . . ." (Gen. 1:28). This commandment is still in effect, and is our fundamental warrant for research, development, education, and all other legitimate activities of mankind.

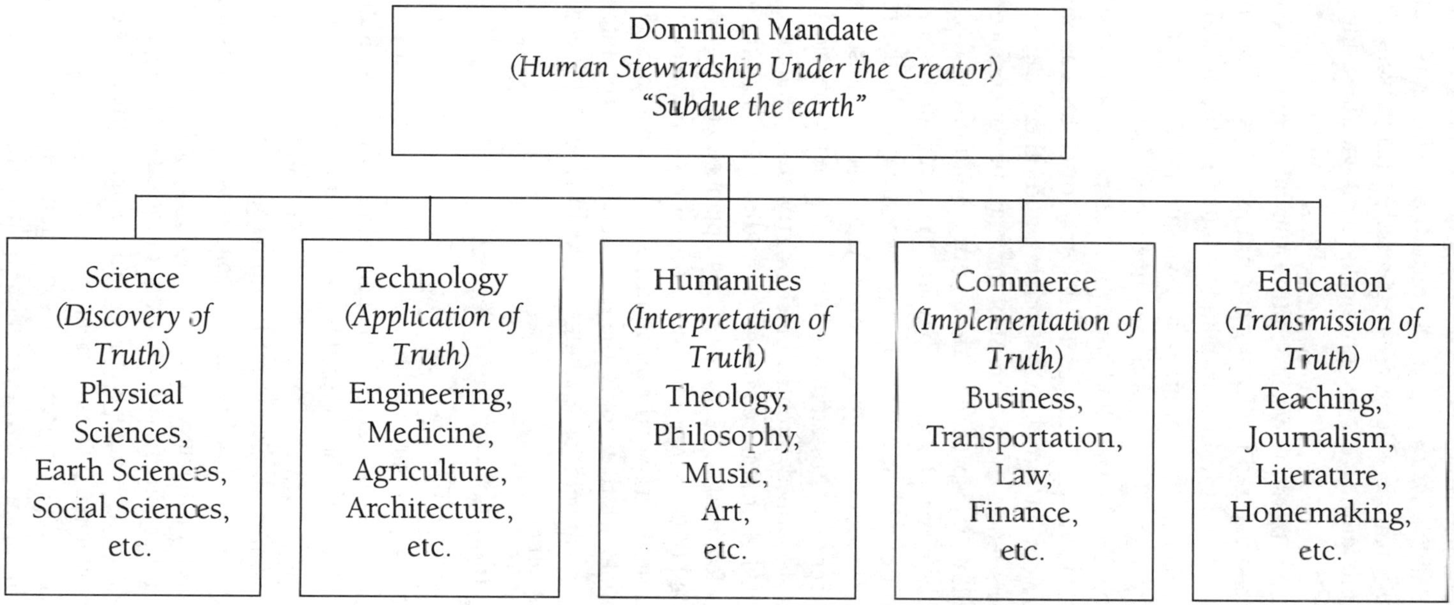

**Dominion Mandate**
(Human Stewardship Under the Creator)
"Subdue the earth"

**Science**
(Discovery of Truth)
Physical Sciences,
Earth Sciences,
Social Sciences,
etc.

**Technology**
(Application of Truth)
Engineering,
Medicine,
Agriculture,
Architecture,
etc.

**Humanities**
(Interpretation of Truth)
Theology,
Philosophy,
Music,
Art,
etc.

**Commerce**
(Implementation of Truth)
Business,
Transportation,
Law,
Finance,
etc.

**Education**
(Transmission of Truth)
Teaching,
Journalism,
Literature,
Homemaking,
etc.

socio-humanistic sciences (or the social sciences and humanities), respectively.

Purely physical materials constitute the fundamental basis of all systems. The "living creature" (Hebrew *chay nephesh*) "that moveth" (that is, *animals*, creatures that are "animated") is a physical system with life added. Similarly, a human being is a living system with God's "image" added. Animals are qualitatively different from physical systems, no matter how complex (plants, although they are highly organized replicating chemical systems, do not possess life in the biblical sense). Similarly, human beings, though both physical and animal, are qualitatively distinct from mere living systems, possessing the divine image, with all its implications. Thus, it is these three types of systems — physical, animal, human — that are the specific objects of God's primeval commission to man.

The physical sciences include such disciplines as physics, chemistry, geology, hydrology, meteorology, astronomy, and others. The technologies that build on these sciences include most of the branches of engineering (civil, electrical, mechanical, aerospace, chemical, petroleum, industrial, etc.). The life sciences utilize the physical sciences, but add to them data that are peculiar to the phenomenon of living and reproducing, becoming such disciplines as biology, physiology, genetics, and others. Since living systems must build on a physical base, a number of interdisciplinary fields between the physical sciences and life sciences have developed, such as biochemistry, paleontology, oceanography, and so on. The fields of botany and other studies related to the plant kingdom could be included in this category; although plants do not possess "life" (Hebrew *nephesh*) in the biblical sense, they nevertheless, as highly complex biochemical systems, do exhibit many of the attributes of life, such as reproduction and variation. The technologies that apply the life sciences and the interdisciplinary sciences include such fields as medicine, agriculture, bioengineering, food technology, and many others.

## The Image of God

The social sciences and humanities include all the disciplines that relate peculiarly to mankind and human society. Theologically, they relate to those aspects of human life and activity that go beyond the laws of physics and biology, associated with what the Scriptures call "the image of God" in man. Since most human activities do involve more than physics and biology, the vocations of most men and women in relation to the primeval commission can be included in this category. The study of theology itself, as well as philosophy and the disciplines of literature, language, music, and art belong here, for example. The transmission and utilization of the knowledge of the data developed in the sciences, as well as the products developed in the technologies, in all the categories of man's dominion, involve activities of great numbers of people in the fields of education, communication, commerce, transportation, and even recreation.

In this area, however, more than in the others, an additional factor has entered the picture, one which was not present when the primeval mandate was given to man by God. This is the "sin-factor," which has profoundly affected man's relation to God and to other men. Although the "image of God" is still present in all men (note Gen. 9:6; James 3:9; et al.), it has been profoundly marred, desperately needing renewal and restoration (Col. 3:9–10). Therefore, all the social sciences and humanities, as well as all human activities which involve interpersonal communication, must now give full cognizance to this factor if they are to be developed and used effectively.

## The Effects of Sin

The entrance of sin into man's nature, through Satan's rebellion and Adam's fall, had pervasive spiritual effects in all areas of life, even bringing God's curse on the earth and death into the world (Gen. 3:17–19; Rom. 5:12). Our immediate purpose here, however, is only to note sin's effect on man's responsibility under the dominion mandate. What changes have been introduced in man's relation to the earth concerning his dominion and his commission to subdue it for God's glory and man's good?

In one sense there has been no change. That is, man still is responsible to "subdue the earth" and to "have dominion" over it. Not only after Adam's sin but even after the worldwide sin of the antediluvians and the cataclysmic judgment of the Flood, God renewed the commission. To Noah and his sons (of whom "was the whole earth overspread," according to Gen. 9:19) was given the same command as to Adam: "Be fruitful, and multiply, and replenish the earth" (Gen. 9:1; Gen. 1:28). Furthermore, man's dominion over the earth and its animal inhabitants was reaffirmed — "into your hand are they delivered" (Gen. 9:2). This dominion mandate was still in effect in David's day. He wrote, "Thou madest [man] to have dominion over the works of thy hands; thou hast put all things under his feet" (Ps. 8:6). It was not withdrawn in the apostolic period (Heb. 2:6–8) nor is there any indication in Scripture that it has ever been withdrawn. Thus all men everywhere are still held accountable to God for its accomplishment.

There is one major difference, however. Before sin came into the world, there was no need for men to exercise dominion over one another. All were in the image of God, so there should have been no need for organized study of man's nature or control of his activities. Such disciplines as psychology, sociology, criminology, politics, jurisprudence, military science, and many others would never have developed if man had not sinned. Neither would there have been any need for doctors or hospitals or mortuaries. The vast insurance industry and numerous other enterprises related to life's uncertainties, as well as vast segments of the entertainment and other industries which cater to man's lust and greed, would never have developed.

But since sin did come in, God has modified and extended His primeval mandate to include the fundamental institution of human government. Instead of the simple patriarchal system of authority, which involved training children until such time as they could establish their own homes (Gen. 2:24), social systems must be established which would maintain order between men. "Whoso sheddeth man's blood, by man shall his blood be shed" (Gen. 9:6).

The responsibility of administering capital punishment is the greatest responsibility of human government. It implicitly entails the obligation also to control those human actions which, if unchecked, could easily (and often do) lead to murder (e.g., robbery, adultery, slander, greed). The dual role of government is that of both protection and punishment — protection of the lives, property, and freedoms of its citizens, and just retribution on those citizens who deprive other citizens of life, possessions, or liberty. When, later at Babel, different languages and nations were established (Gen. 10:5; 11:9), this command was naturally extended to relations between nations as well as between individuals and groups within each nation. Neither has this new dimension of the primeval mandate — that of human governmental responsibility — ever been withdrawn, any more than the command to have dominion over the earth and the nonhuman inhabitants of the earth. The classic proof-text (supported by many others) is Romans 13:1–7, affirming that God has ordained governmental authorities, and that these have the responsibility "to execute wrath upon him that doeth evil" and also to collect "their dues" for their necessary support.

Sin has not only corrupted human relationships, but even the study of God's creation. The natural sciences have been reorganized around the concept of evolution instead of creation, and the Creator has been pushed further and further away in both space and time until, for many, He no longer even exists. The origin of the universe has been attributed to a primordial explosion of unknown cause, the origin of life to unknown processes in a primeval soup, and the origin of man to supposed naturalistic evolution from an unknown animal ancestry. The social sciences and humanities likewise, instead of glorifying God, seek to exalt man as the godlike product of animal evolution. Their economic and social theories, their educational methodologies, and their amoral literature, music, and art similarly assume that man has a naturalistic animal ancestry and purely humanistic goals.

Though all men are still under the Adamic/Noahic mandate to exercise a faithful and productive stewardship over the earth to the glory of God, the truth is that "all have sinned, and come short of the glory of God" (Rom. 3:23). To a tragic degree, man's science and technology, even his theology, philosophy, and fine arts, seem to have taken him further and further away from God. He is not subduing the earth for God's glory, but destroying the earth (Rev. 11:18) for man's lust.

The Christian believer, however, can and should lead out in fulfilling God's first great commission as well as the second. Though the image of God has indeed been badly marred, he can "put on the new man, which is renewed in knowledge after the image of him that created him" (Col. 3:10), and thus he has great divine resources at hand.

## God's Revelation in Nature

Certain faint-minded Christians (Heb. 12:3), alarmed at the dominance of humanistic evolutionary thought among modern scientists and unwilling to stand forthrightly against this untoward philosophy, have propounded what they call the Double Revelation Theory. According to this idea, God has provided two revelations to man, one in Scripture, the other in nature. Both of these, they say, are equally valid when rightly interpreted. The theologian is the interpreter of God's Word, dealing with matters of faith and conduct; the scientist is the interpreter of God's world, dealing with matters of fact in science and history. When these two revelations appear to conflict, the scientist must defer to the theologian if it is a matter of faith, but the theologian must defer to the scientist if it is a supposed matter of fact.

This Double Revelation Theory must, however, be unequivocally rejected by Bible-believing Christians. The writers of Scripture deal abundantly with real matters of fact in science and history (unlike the sacred writings of Buddhism, Confucianism, Hinduism, and other world religions, which do, indeed, deal almost exclusively with faith and conduct). To take the position that the Bible is unreliable when it deals with verifiable data of science and history will almost inevitably cause thinking inquirers to reject its teachings on theological beliefs and right behavior. Jesus said, "If I have told you earthly things, and ye believe not, how shall ye believe, if I tell you of heavenly things?" (John 3:12).

The Bible must be accepted as absolutely inerrant and authoritative on all matters with which it deals at all. Otherwise, it is not really the Word of God! If any man, or group of men, are empowered to tell us authoritatively what God's Word means, then we may as well entrust them with a commission to write the Bible altogether. Man seeks to become God if he (whether he is a theologian or scientist or anyone else) insists that *his* word must be accepted authoritatively as to what *God's* Word means.

We do not question that God "speaks" through His creation, but such natural revelation must never be considered equal in clarity or authority to His written revelation, especially as it often is "interpreted" by fallible human scholars, many of whom do not even believe the Bible. The Scriptures, in fact, do not need to be "interpreted" at all, for God is well able to say exactly what He means. They need simply to be read as the writer intended them to be read, then believed and obeyed. This applies to their abundance of "factual" information as well as to their religious and practical instructions.

By the same token, we must also recognize God's world must always agree with God's Word, for the Creator of the one is author of the other, and "he cannot deny himself" (2 Tim. 2:13). God's revelation in nature can often amplify and illustrate His Word, but His written revelation must always inform and constrain our interpretation of nature.

With such premises to caution us, we soon see that the Bible contains numerous statements affirming that God does, indeed, speak to us through His creation. A few of these, for example, are abstracted from such Scriptures as the following:

> But ask now the beasts, and they shall teach thee; and the fowls of the air, and they shall tell thee: Or speak to the earth, and it shall teach thee: and the fishes of the sea shall declare unto thee (Job 12:7–8).

> By his spirit he hath garnished the heavens; his hand hath formed the crooked serpent. Lo, these are parts of his ways: but how little a portion is heard of him? but the thunder of his power who can understand? (Job 26:13–14).

> The heavens declare the glory of God; and the firmament sheweth his handywork. Day unto day uttereth speech, and night unto night sheweth knowledge (Ps. 19:1–2).

> The heavens declare his righteousness, and all the people see his glory (Ps. 97:6).

> Nevertheless he left not himself without witness, in that he did good, and gave us rain from heaven, and fruitful seasons, filling our hearts with food and gladness (Acts 14:17).

> God that made the world and all things therein, seeing that he is Lord of heaven and earth, dwelleth not in temples made with hands; Neither is worshipped with men's hands . . . seeing he giveth to all life, and breath, and all things . . . that they should seek the Lord, if haply they might feel after him, and find him, though he be not far from every one of us: For in Him we live, and move, and have our being (Acts 17:24–28).

> For the invisible things of him from the creation of the world are clearly seen, being understood by the things that are made, even his eternal power and Godhead; so that they are without excuse (Rom. 1:20).

These and other similar passages clearly show that God has spoken to men through His creation. Therefore, the proper use of science and technology not only helps to implement the Edenic commission but also teaches men more and more about the person and work of the great Creator God.

God's revelation in nature, therefore, must always supplement and confirm His revelation in Scripture. It cannot be used to correct or interpret it. If there is an apparent conflict, one that cannot be resolved by a more careful study of the relevant data of both science and Scripture, then the written Word must take priority. This is not the place for an exposition of the evidences for the inerrancy of Scripture, but these are impregnable and compelling, and many works setting these forth are available to the open-minded searcher. In this study, it is assumed that the Bible is completely true and authoritative.[22]

With this assumption, it will soon become clear that the numerous biblical references to science are not only compatible with the known facts of science but that they often even anticipate scientific discoveries. Even though the Bible is not a scientific textbook, it does speak authoritatively on the fundamental principles of science. Furthermore, it speaks correctly even on details of science whenever it refers to them at all.

These relationships will be explored and discussed in the subsequent chapters of this book.

---

22. See, for example, the writer's book, *Many Infallible Proofs* (Green Forest, AR: Master Books, 1996), 396 p.

# CHRIST AND THE COSMOS

*Biblical Cosmology*

### Testimony of Christ in Creation

In the previous chapter, we examined the evidence for an ultimate First Cause of the universe, showing that there is overwhelming scientific and logical support for the biblical doctrine of a personal Creator God. Neither atheism nor polytheism, pantheism nor dualism, will suffice to explain the universe as science knows it. Only monotheism satisfies the one criterion that is basic to all science and human experience, namely the law of cause and effect.

However, biblical monotheism is more than the monotheism of Islam or Orthodox Judaism. The God of the Bible is a triune God, one God in three persons — Father, Son, and Holy Spirit. Furthermore, God is not only an omnipresent Spirit; He has also been revealed in the person of His incarnate Son, the Lord Jesus Christ. The doctrine of the Trinity and the doctrine of the God-Man are unique and fundamental doctrines of Christianity. Both are profoundly offensive to non-Christians and both seem superficially to be contrary to sound logic and modern science.

But a closer study of the scientific evidence will show these doctrines to be beautifully compatible with the fundamental nature of the cosmos. Instead of contradicting the biblical doctrine of God, the very nature of the physical universe will be seen to provide amazing evidence of the validity of that doctrine. Not only so, but the doctrines of God's grace and salvation also are implicit in the nature of the living universe. The Lord Jesus Christ, both Creator and Savior, is clearly revealed in the cosmos.

"For the invisible things of him from the creation of the world are clearly seen, being understood by the things that are made, even his eternal power and

Godhead, so that they are without excuse" (Rom. 1:20). According to this remarkable verse of Scripture, there is a clear witness to the God of creation to be seen in the created cosmos ("world" in this verse is the Greek *kosmos*). Thus, there is no difference; every man who has ever lived has been confronted with this testimony of creation to the nature of the God who made it. Whether or not he ever opens the pages of Holy Scripture, or whether he believes what he reads therein, he cannot escape confrontation with the Christ of creation! He is without excuse.

But how can this be? "No man hath seen God at any time" (John 1:18). How is it possible that the "invisible things" of God can be made visible so that they are "clearly seen"?

These "invisible things," according to Romans 1:20, are summed up in two great concepts, those of His "eternal power" and His "godhead." Or, one might say, His work and His person. That He is a God of infinite and eternal omnipotence, one of "eternal power," is revealed plainly, according to this verse, in the created universe. Furthermore, His very nature, His "godhead," is also revealed in creation. And this means that Christ is revealed in creation, for the very essence of the godhead is found in Jesus Christ. "For in him dwelleth all the fulness of the Godhead bodily" (Col. 2:9).

The very godhead that is clearly revealed in nature by the "things that are made" (Greek *poiema*, the word from which we transliterate our English word "poem," thus signifying His "poetic handiwork," a word only used elsewhere in Scripture in Ephesians 2:10, where it is said that we who are redeemed by His grace are similarly His "workmanship") is thus summed up in all its fullness in the Lord Jesus Christ. There can therefore be no question that Christ has been revealed in the creation. He is himself the Creator (John 1:3; Col. 1:16). He now sustains and upholds the creation by the word of His power (Heb. 1:3; Col. 1:17), and He is the light that "lighteth *every* man that cometh into the world" (John 1:9, italics mine).

It should be emphasized that no man could recognize and receive Christ through this witness of creation unless the Holy Spirit so draws him that, through a heart made open and willing, he is enabled to see and believe. For if such a preparation of heart by the Spirit is necessary before a man will receive the Lord, even when revealed through the much brighter light of the Scriptures, far more essential must it be if he is to see and believe the fainter light diffused throughout the creation. Nevertheless, the light is surely there for those who really desire to see and know their God! So when a man of any time or culture fails to glorify Him as God and is not thankful, but becomes vain in his reasonings, he is without excuse. When he changes the glory of the incorruptible God into an image like that of corruptible man (whether that image be the wooden idol of the savage or the humanistic, pantheistic, evolutionary philosophy of the intellectual), he is thereby changing the revealed truth of God into a lie and serving the creation more than the Creator, and God must give him up (Rom. 1:21–25).

FIGURE 4 — *Implications of the Two Laws of Thermodynamics, Governing All Natural Processes*

*The first law of thermodynamics states (in accordance with Gen. 2:1–3) that none of the tremendous energy (or "power") of the universe is now being created, so that the universe could not have created itself. The second law (in accordance with Rom 8:20–22, as well as Gen. 3:17–19) states that the available energy of the universe is decreasing, indicating that sometime in the past all the energy (including matter) was available and perfectly organized, like a clock that had just been wound up. This shows that the universe must have been created, even though it could not create itself. The two laws thus point inexorably back to Gen. 1:1.*

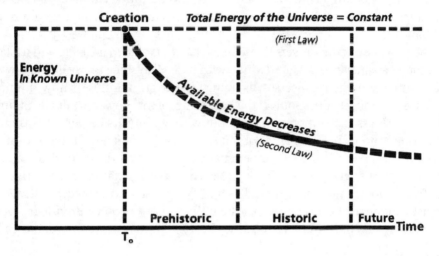

## His Eternal Power

The reservoirs of power in the created universe are so vast as to be completely incomprehensible in their fullness. The earth's energy, for all its physical and biological processes, comes from the sun. But only an infinitesimal fraction of the sun's power is thus utilized by the earth. And there are uncountable billions of suns scattered throughout the universe. The more intensively and thoroughly man probes the universe — whether the submicroscopic universe of the atomic nucleus or the tremendous metagalactic universe of astronomy — the more amazingly intricate and grand are God's reservoirs of power revealed to be.

In these chapters we will frequently refer to the two great principles of thermodynamics,[1] which describe the basic ways physical power in the universe is manifested. These two all-embracing laws of science affirm that none of this power is now coming into existence, even though its form is continually changing and is, in fact, continually being degraded into less useful and available forms. These principles of conservation and decay are common to everyday experience and are likewise substantiated by the most precise scientific measurements. See figure 4 for a better understanding of these relationships.

---

1. See especially chapter 7 for a comprehensive exposition of their significance.

The continual degradation of power (or, better, energy) in the universe is inseparably associated with the progress of time. That is, as time goes on, the energy of the universe becomes progressively less available for maintenance of its processes. The universe is gradually becoming more and more disordered as its entropy inexorably increases. So inextricably is time now associated with the law of entropy, that Sir Arthur Eddington many years ago gave the second law of thermodynamics the graphic name of "time's arrow." The universe is decaying toward an eventual "heat death." However, since it is far from "dead," it must have had a beginning! Thus, by the second law, the universe must have been created somehow at some finite time in the past, since otherwise it would have died long ago.

The processes of the universe, insofar as science is able to measure and understand them, are inextricably intertwined with time. And since the available power for continuance of these processes, as tremendously great as it is, is now running down, it is obvious that the source, the beginning, of this power is outside of time — that is, it is associated not with time, but with eternity. Its beginning was outside of time, and its possible renewal must likewise be outside of time. It cannot be "temporal" power. It is therefore eternal power. And all these "things that are made" continually give witness to God's "eternal power," exactly as the Scripture says. Every process the scientist studies and every system designed by the technologist continually bear witness that the ultimate power source driving the process or the system must ultimately be the Creator of power, the Omnipotent One.

## The Godhead

Not only does the creation testify concerning God's eternal power, but our text also indicates that it speaks plainly of "his Godhead." This term has always been associated by theologians with the Trinity. The godhead is said to be the revelation of God as Father, Son, and Holy Spirit, one God in three persons.

The English word "Godhead" occurs in three places in the King James Version — Acts 17:29; Romans 1:20; and Colossians 2:9 — as a translation of three slightly different but related Greek words, *theion, theoites*, and *theotes*, respectively. Although the connotations of the three may be very slightly different, the essential meaning in all three cases is that of Godhood — the fullest essence of that which makes God what He is. It might be translated as "divinity" or "deity," provided it is understood that the term in every case is to be uniquely applied only to the one true God of creation.

The passage in Acts makes it emphatically clear that no representation made by men, whether physical or mental, can possibly depict the godhead. Since man was created in the image of God, man is entirely unable to make an image or model that will depict God. God, as Creator, is infinitely above that which He created, and the creature can only know and understand the nature of God insofar as God may will to reveal himself.

Nevertheless, Romans 1:20 assures us that the "Godhead" may be "clearly seen" and may be "understood by the things that are made." Not by the things man has made, but by the things God has made. Man cannot make a model of the godhead, but God himself has done so in His creation.

The essence of the "godhead" may be comprehended even more fully through the final passage where the word occurs. In Colossians 2:9 the Holy Spirit has recorded through the apostle Paul the amazing fact that in Jesus Christ "dwelleth all the fulness of the Godhead bodily." Though no man has seen God at any time, the only-begotten Son has declared Him. Jesus Christ is the eternal Word made flesh. He who has seen the Son has seen the Father. All that God is has been manifested bodily in Jesus Christ. This is the great God, our Savior, Jesus Christ!

Both the essence and the attributes of God are incorporated in the godhead, and these are manifest to our understanding especially in the Son. The godhead conveys the omnipresence, the omnipotence, the love, the truth, and the grace, as well as all other aspects and attributes, of God in His fullness. Although the term may not in itself precisely mean the Trinity, yet it is clear that the older theologians were on the mark when they thought of it in this way. The biblical revelation of God and His nature has been just this. God is Father, Son, and Holy Spirit, one God in three persons. The Father is the eternal source of all being; the Son is the eternal presence of God, proceeding everlastingly from the Father through the Son into all creation. Both the Father and the Spirit, being omnipresent, are invisible yet are continually manifest bodily in the Son. God is revealed in time and space, temporally and corporally, in Jesus Christ. It is not accidental that the Scripture says not that in Jesus Christ once "dwelled" the godhead, but that "in Him dwelleth all the fulness of the Godhead bodily." Eternally, Jesus Christ manifests all that God is. He is the everlasting "I Am," the "Word" that was in the beginning and without whom not anything was made that was made (John 1:1–3).

The Christian doctrine of the Trinity has long been a prime object of skepticism — even ridicule — by non-Christians in general and even by such pseudo-Christian groups as the Unitarians, Jehovah's Witnesses, and others. It does seem paradoxical, at best, that God could be both one and three, and even true Christians have often said that this doctrine can only be appropriated on faith. It cannot be understood, they say, but must be believed simply because the Bible teaches it.

However, the Bible never asks for blind faith in its teachings. The Christian gospel must be appropriated by faith, but it is a reasonable faith based on solid evidence, not a credulous faith. A key passage is 1 Peter 3:15: "Be ready always to give an answer to every man that asketh you a reason of the hope that is in you with meekness and fear." The word for "answer" is the Greek *apologia*, meaning "apologetic" or "defense," a legal term referring to a systematic objective defense of the faith. The word for "reason" is *logos*, meaning "word," but conveying also the idea of "logic," or "definitive statement."

It should, of course, be understood exactly what the Bible teaches and does

not teach about the Trinity. The Trinity is not a sort of triumvirate of three different Gods. There is only one God, not three. Nevertheless, there are three divine
persons in the godhead. Each person — Father, Son, and Spirit— is that one
God, equally eternal, equally omnipotent. At the same time, the relation is always
indicated to be in a logical, causal order. The Father is the unseen source of all
being, manifest bodily in the Son, experienced and understood in human life
through the Spirit.

## The Triune God

When, therefore, the writers of Scripture tell us that the things created are so
designed as to reveal the godhead, we must understand this to mean that Jesus
Christ himself is to be seen in the creation as well as the full Trinity. Not only the
Son, but also the Father and the Spirit, must be discernible in the creation. Both
the fact of God and the nature of God are "plainly understood" by the "things that
are made."

That God is a great person should be clearly evident to all whose hearts and
minds are open and willing to learn of Him. Each person is supremely aware of
his own existence as a person, even if he knows nothing else. That there must be
a great person who has made man's personality and to whom man must therefore
somehow be responsible is intuitively recognized by everyone. And the modern
scientist, above all men, should be able to recognize the implications of his own
fundamental scientific principle of cause and effect. Only a person could be the
great First Cause of the individual personalities which constitute mankind. This
great truth was elaborated more fully in chapter 1.

That God is one is evident from the fact that creation is one. There is one
humanity and, as noted earlier, one universe (not a "multi-verse"). Modern scientists recognize this in their continual search for universal laws, unifying principles, underlying unities. And yet, in its unity, the universe is nevertheless one of
great diversity and variety. One mankind, but many men — one basic reality, but
innumerable interrelationships. And should not these facts lead any man, perhaps quite subconsciously, to think of God also as a unity in diversity — as a
person who is one and yet who somehow manifests himself as more than one?

At first it might indeed seem that this concept would lead one directly into
polytheism or pantheism or dualism. The almost universal drift of the early nations into a pantheistic dualism or polytheism may well be understood in these
very terms. Even more fundamentally, this drift may represent a corruption of an
original insight into the triune nature of the Creator. For the universe is ultimately a tri-universe, bearing in a remarkable way the reflection of the triune
nature of its Maker.

First, however, note that polytheism is not reasonable. If there is more than
one God, then none of the "gods" can be either omnipotent or omnipresent, as
we have seen the true God must be. Furthermore, the universe is not a multi-

verse. Its intrinsic unity as a vast and glorious space-mass-time "continuum" is explicable only in terms of a unified First Cause, not as a conglomerate of First Causes. The very notion of a vast assemblage of individual "gods" gathering together to apportion out their several segments of creative responsibility is its own refutation.

In fact, polytheism in practice is usually merely the popular expression of pantheism, which identifies God with the universe, and is experienced primarily as animism. A god who is essentially synonymous with the universe and its varied components could never be the cause of the universe.

What about dualism, the philosophy of two equal and competing gods, one good and one evil? In effect, this elevates Satan to the position he desires, equality with God. In this belief, Satan is equally eternal with God and is the same intrinsic type of being, except that in his moral attributes, he is the opposite of God. Where God is love and holiness, Satan is hatred and evil, and the two are supposed to be eternally in conflict. Such a philosophy does have a superficial appearance of reasonableness. Evil is a very powerful force in the world; one could almost believe that evil is more potent than good and Satan the more powerful and prominent of the two gods.

Nevertheless, there can really be only one First Cause, as we have already seen. The same arguments that militate against polytheism likewise apply against dualism. Even though there may be two competing principles in the universe, it is still a universe! And for a universe, there must be a universal First Cause. Either, therefore, God created Satan and he later became evil, or Satan created God and He later became good. They could not both be equally the cause of the universe.

Now even though we may believe that "truth is forever on the scaffold, wrong forever on the throne," we still have to reckon with the strange fact that we know that truth is "better" than deception, and right is "better" than wrong. If Satan is really the creator of all men and if, indeed, he has the world mostly under his own control, how is it that all men feel they ought to do right even when they find it so much more natural to do wrong? Somehow there is built into every man the deep awareness that love and justice and holiness constitute a higher order of reality than do hate and injustice and wickedness. Even men who do not believe in a God of love and righteousness seem to be continually troubled at the hatred and cruelty that abound in the world. The only reasonable explanation for such phenomena is that the true creation is "good" with "evil" only a temporary, though powerful, intruder. This in turn means, by cause-and-effect relationship, that God is the First Cause of all reality and Satan is only a late-coming disturber of God's creation. The biblical authors, of course, teach exactly this.

In summary, therefore, neither polytheism nor pantheism nor dualism can meet the requirements for the First Cause. Polytheism (in practice, pantheism, or "many gods") is inconsistent with the causation of the universal awareness that "good" is better than "bad." Monotheism (one God, both immanent and transcendent) is alone consistent as the First Cause. The latter must be one God, perfect in power and holiness, and none else. "I am the first, and I am the last; and beside me there is no God" (Isa. 44:6). The law of cause and effect, properly applied, thus not only leads to a primary cause, but to the concept of one eternal, personal Creator God.

How, then, can God be a Trinity? To understand this, one must remember that this doctrine does not mean three gods. "Three gods" is as impossible and false a concept as any other form of polytheism. There can be only one God, and He is the great First Cause, the author of all reality.

But if God exists only in His ineffable unity, He could never be truly known. He is fundamentally the eternal, omnipresent, transcendent God, the great First Cause, the source of all being. Being present *everywhere*, however, He could never be seen or heard or sensed *anywhere*. Yet since He could not be frivolous in His creation, He must have a purpose therein and that purpose must be communicable. He must therefore somehow be seen and heard. He must be a God who is both infinite and yet finite, who is omnipresent and eternal and still comprehensible locally and temporally. He must paradoxically be both source and manifestation, both Father and Son.

Not only must the invisible and inaudible God be seen and heard objectively, however, He must also be experienced and understood subjectively. The life of the creation must be maintained in vital union with that of the Creator. The Spirit of God must move over the creation and must indwell it and empower it. The activity of the Spirit is distinct from that of the Son and from that of the Father, and yet is indissolubly one with both.

God, therefore, is one God, and yet He must be Father, Son, and Spirit. God is Father in generation, Son in declaration, Spirit in appropriation. The Son is the only begotten of the Father, and the Spirit is eternally the bestower of both the Father and the Son.

The doctrine of the Trinity, rather than being unnatural and self-contradictory, is thus deeply implanted in the very nature of reality and in man's intuitive awareness of God. Man has always felt and known in his heart that God was "out there," everywhere, that He was somehow the invisible source of all things. But this deep consciousness of God as eternal and omnipresent Father, he has corrupted into pantheism and then eventually into naturalism.

Similarly, man has always recognized that somehow God must and does reveal himself in human dimensions, so that man can see and discern the nature and purpose of His Creator. But this glorious truth of God as Son and Word, man has distorted into idolatry, seeking continually to erect some kind of model of God to his own specifications, either from material substance or metaphysical reasonings.

Finally, man has always desired to know God experientially and thus has sensed that God indwells His creation, manifesting himself in actual vital union with man in particular. This is the reality of God the Holy Spirit, but once again man has corrupted this glorious truth into mysticism and fanaticism and even demonism.

Man has thus always sensed, and could have understood had he desired, that God is Father, Son, and Spirit, but instead he has corrupted the true God into pantheistic naturalism, polytheistic paganism, and demonistic spiritism. "Lo, this only have I found, that God hath made man upright; but they have sought out many inventions" (Eccles. 7:29). "When they knew God, they glorified him not as God, neither were thankful; but became vain in their imaginations, and their foolish heart was darkened" (Rom. 1:21).

The doctrine of the triune God is thus not only revealed in Scripture, but is intrinsic in the very nature of things as they are. Since God is the Creator and sustainer of all things, it is reasonable to expect also to find built into the structure of the creation a clear testimony of His character. "The heavens declare the glory of God; and the firmament sheweth His handywork" (Ps. 19:1). This, of course, is the claim of Romans 1:20.

## The Tri-universe as a Model of the Godhead

For thousands of years, men have recognized that the universe is a space-matter-time universe. The common phenomena of universal experience are always related to just three — and no other — physical entities. All phenomena, including all forms of matter and all types of physical and biological processes, take place in space and through time. The modern relativistic union of space and time in a space-time continuum, as well as the recognition that matter itself is basically one form of energy, with energy in some form manifest everywhere throughout time and space, merely verifies and crystallizes this fact of universal experience. The perspective of modern science is clearly that of the universe as a space-mass-time continuum, with each of the three entities essentially indistinguishable from, and coterminous with the other two.

One universe, manifested in terms of three conceptual forms, each of which is equally universal, obviously is remarkably analogous to the character of the triune God as revealed in Scripture. One God, yet manifest in three persons — Father, Son, and Holy Spirit — each equally God, and ultimately inseparable. Furthermore, the interrelationships between the three persons of the godhead are closely similar to the relationships between the three entities of the physical universe. As the Son manifests and embodies the Father, so the phenomena of matter represent, as it were, intangible space in a form discernible to the senses. Though space is everywhere, it is itself quite invisible and seemingly unreal, were it not that phenomena of all kinds are continually and everywhere taking place in space and thus manifesting its existence. The phenomena themselves when observed closely, are found to be essentially nothing but space (the atomic structure of matter, for example, whether conceived as particles or waves, consists almost wholly of space). And yet the phenomena (matter and energy) are most definitely real and discernible to the senses and to measurement.

The Holy Spirit proceeds from the Son, again invisible and omnipresent, with the function of interpreting and applying the nature and work of the Son and the Father. Likewise, time is the universal concept within which the significance of space and matter must be interpreted and applied. Time itself only becomes meaningful in terms of the phenomena and material and processes that are everywhere manifest in space. But at the same time, these phenomena are quite inconceivable except in terms of time and the individual segments of time during which they are manifested.

The physical universe as we know it, therefore, is in its nature wonderfully analogous to the nature of its Creator. The continuum of space and matter and time — each distinct and yet inseparably interrelated with the other two and occupying the whole of the universe — is remarkably parallel in character to what has been revealed concerning the nature of God as Father, Son, and Holy Spirit, each distinct and yet each inseparably identified with the other two, and each equally and eternally God.

Space is the invisible, omnipresent background of all things, everywhere displaying phenomena of matter and/or energy (which are interconvertible) that are, in turn, experienced in time. Just so, the Father is the invisible, omnipresent source of all being, manifested and declared by the eternal Word, the Son, who is, in turn, experienced in the Spirit.

It is not that the universe is a *triad* of three distinct entities which, when added together, comprise the whole. Rather each of the three is itself the whole, and the universe is a true trinity, not a triad. Space is infinite and time is endless, and everywhere throughout space and time events happen, processes function, phenomena exist. The tri-universe is remarkably analogous to the nature of its Creator.

But there is more. Each of the three universals of the physical universe is itself a triunity, so that the universe may even be described as a trinity of trinities!

## Triunity of Space

Consider space, matter, and time in turn. As far as space is concerned, the universe is a space-universe of three dimensions, no more and no less. There is no true reality in a line or in a plane; these are mental concepts that have no real existence. Reality requires space, and space is three-dimensional. Furthermore, each dimension of space occupies the whole of space, in like fashion as each person of the godhead is equally and fully God.

From the natural viewpoint of a man considering the created universe, we could say that the three dimensions, or directions, are the north-south, east-west, and the up-down directions. Or, for brevity, call them respectively length, breadth, and height. Each is infinite in extent and each occupies the whole of space. In imagination, if only one dimension existed (e.g., length), even though this dimension be infinitely great, it is impossible even to comprehend or visualize what this would be like. "No man has seen a line at any time." If one tries to draw a line, be it ever so thin, it nevertheless must have some width to it in order to be discernible, and then it is no longer a line, but a plane! Thus, the existence of one dimension can only be demonstrated by a construct in two dimensions. The second dimension must be present in order for the first to be revealed. The reality of "length" can only be demonstrated by the simultaneous presence of "breadth."

When both length and breadth are available for representation of physical truth, then visualization is possible. The "two-dimensional" method of representing physical reality is universally used and, in fact, it is far easier to visualize things in two dimensions than in three. Pictures are painted in two dimensions, construction plans (even for three-dimensional buildings) are drawn in two dimensions, and so for nearly all representations of physical reality. The typical engineering student, for example, in learning how to make engineering drawings, finds it far easier to visualize in two dimensions than in three. And, though it is easy enough to visualize one dimension, he finds it essentially impossible to represent any reality by only one dimension. The two-dimensional representation is necessary and sufficient for the perception of both one dimension and three dimensions.

Analogously, the reality of both the one God, the eternal Father, and of the omnipresent Spirit of God is demonstrated and represented visibly by the incarnate Word, the Son of God, the Second Person. Nevertheless, the experimental reality of the godhead requires more than the recognition of the true existence of the Father as revealed in and by the Son. There must also be experienced the real presence of God by the Holy Spirit. Paul wrote, "If any man have not the Spirit of Christ, he is none of his" (Rom. 8:9); and "For through [Christ] we . . . have access by one Spirit unto the Father" (Eph. 2:18).

So also spatial reality requires the presence of depth, as well as length and breadth. Although reality can be convincingly manifested and represented by means of a two-dimensional visualization, the actual existence of that which is so represented requires all three dimensions.[2] Although a plane can be seen, it cannot be experienced! The real world is a world of three dimensions, no more and no less.

In summary we can say that the existence of the length dimension can only be manifested in terms of the breadth dimension and experienced in terms of the depth dimension. Though all space is one, yet it can only be visualized in terms of two of its dimensions and only "lived in" in all three dimensions. Space is "identified" in terms of one dimension, "seen" in two dimensions, "experienced"

---

2. Some theoretical cosmologists think there may be ten or more dimensions in space. This strange notion is based on the so-called "string theory" of physics, for which there is no evidence except speculative mathematics.

in three dimensions, just as the godhead is identified in the Father, seen in the Son, and experienced in the Holy Spirit. Further, it should be noted that space in its fullness is measured in terms of its volume, obtained by multiplying its three dimensions together. Just so, the "mathematics" of the trinity is not $1 + 1 + 1 = 1$ (which would be a contradiction), but $1 \times 1 \times 1 = 1$, which is profoundly true.

## Triunity of Time

The next in order of the three universals of the physical world is matter. However, since the proper comprehension of matter involves an understanding of both space and time, we shall by-pass it for the moment and pass on to notice the fundamental triune character of time.

It is wonderful to realize that time consists of future time, present time, and past time. Each is quite distinct in meaning, and yet each is the whole of time. All time has been future and will be past. And in the process whereby future time becomes past time, it passes through the present. The future is the unseen and unexperienced source of all time. It is made visible and manifest, moment by moment, in the present. It then moves into the past, into the realm of experienced time. Man's consciousness of time pertains only to the present, but this does not lessen the reality or the significance of both the past and the future in his experience and understanding. He is enabled to understand the present, and even to some extent the future, in terms of the past. But both his recollection of past time and his anticipation of future time are visualized in terms of his consciousness of present time.

And again all these relationships and functions are closely parallel to those of the persons in the godhead. The Father is the unseen source. From Him proceeds the Son, in whom He is visibly revealed. From the Son in turn proceeds the Holy Spirit, who interprets and makes meaningful in actual experience the Son and the Father.

## Triunity of Matter

The last entity to be considered, though the second in natural order, is matter. As noted before, space is embodied and revealed in matter, and both are understood and applied in terms of time. It is clear that matter can only be understood and considered in relation to that portion of space it occupies and that duration of time when it functions. Matter in the broadest sense, of course, is synonymous with energy. Matter and energy are interconvertible. Energy includes light, heat, sound, electricity, radiation, and all other manifestations of energizing phenomena, capable of producing motion and accomplishing work. And of course it also includes what we commonly think of as matter, with its atomic and molecular structure and its characteristics of density and inertia.

Every manifestation of energy or matter in the universe takes place in space and time. For any finite phenomenon, the particular manifestation has a particular location and particular duration, a beginning and ending, both spatially and temporally. It is also profoundly significant that every manifestation of energy necessarily involves some form of motion. Light, heat, sound — all have velocities. The atomic structure of matter is essentially tremendous motion in space. In fact, it may quite accurately be said that the very presence of energy is necessarily manifest in motion. If energy is present, it will beget motion. It accomplishes work. There are many different forms of motion that may be produced, and the particular form will determine the particular phenomenon that is experienced — whether light, electricity, hardness, or whatever it may be. This may, in fact, be said to be the basic triunity of matter. First, there is energy, the unseen but powerful source, begetting and manifesting itself in motion (evidenced by a velocity, passing through a certain space in a certain time), and finally experienced in terms of the phenomenon produced. Each — energy, motion, phenomenon — is inseparably related to the other two and each is universally present wherever there is matter; in fact, each is matter. Matter invariably is equivalent to energy, and energy is invariably manifested in motion, and motion invariably produces phenomena.

But there is even a more general way of understanding the triunity inherent in matter or energy. Since every phenomenon has a beginning and end, both in space and in time, let us call each such occurrence an event. In this sense a flash of lightning, a fire, a musical sound, or any other phenomenon is an event that takes place in space and time. The duration may be brief or great and the space occupied may be small or large. Even a mountain or a planet or a star may thus be considered an event, occupying a certain part of space for a certain length of time. We can include under this term not only physical phenomena but also biological, mental, and spiritual phenomena. An animal, a meditation, a prayer — all are events, each with a beginning and end in space and time.

But, after all, it is not quite correct to say that any such event really has a definite beginning, although its specific manifestation does appear to have such. But associated with the event is its immediate cause, and the cause of the cause, and so on back through a chain of causes to the very beginning of the creation itself. Similarly, the event seems to have a definite ending, but actually the consequences of that event continue to spread out through space and time, causing other events as long as the universe endures. Each event, therefore, is inseparably linked to its cause and its consequence. The cause is the unseen source of the event, and the consequence is that which proceeds from it. And here again is the basic triunity that pervades all nature.

Thus, in a most remarkable way, the universe is a tri-universe. The universe as a whole is a space-matter- (or energy) time continuum. Space is length, breadth, and depth. Time is future, present, and past. And matter, in the broadest sense, is cause, event, and consequence (or energy, motion, and phenomenon). Throughout the universe we see this recurring relationship of source, manifestation, and

FIGURE 5 — The Tri-universe

*The physical universe is an amazing trinity of trinities. The only adequate cause to account for this remarkable effect is that it was created to reflect the triune nature of the God who created it.*

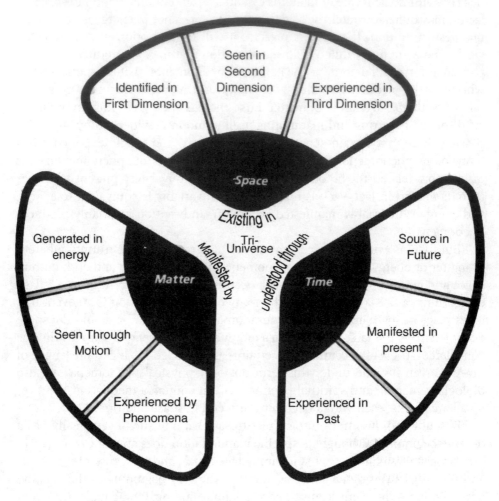

meaning. These relationships are so basic and obvious that we find it difficult even to wonder about them. They seem axiomatic, part of the necessary structure of things, things that are almost too "clearly seen."

These remarkable relations are illustrated in figure 5.

Admittedly, this does not prove that the Creator of this tri-universe is a triune God. But with all these worldwide reflections of the triune nature of the godhead "clearly seen, being understood by the things that are made," men should certainly not stumble over the biblical revelation of a triune God. This should be the most natural way, and undoubtedly was the originally revealed way, of understanding the nature of "His eternal power and Godhead." There must be a cause for every effect, and the physical universe has somehow been caused to be a magnificent trinity of trinities! Certainly a highly adequate and appropriate cause for such a remarkable effect would be that its Creator designed it in His own likeness.

Thus, the basic laws of nature, and the triune dimensionality of natural processes, rather than discrediting God and His primeval creation, emphatically witness to the fact of creation and the nature of the Creator.

## Triunity in Modeling and Dimensional Analysis

This universal continuum of dimensions is the basis of one of the most basic and useful tools of scientific research — namely, that of modeling and dimensional analysis. Since all processes must function within a space-time-mass dimensional framework, a quantitative expression of that process must involve units of space, time, and mass. In the English system these units traditionally constitute the so-called foot-pound-second system. It is possible to use units of energy, power, or force — instead of mass — since these are all directly related to each other, but always there are three (no more, no less) basic units.

A given process under scientific study (e.g., the sedimentary activity of a flooding river) may be difficult or impossible to study quantitatively by direct measurements under field conditions. However, it can be simulated by constructing a small-scale model of the system in a laboratory, and then studying the characteristics of the process as it functions on its laboratory model. The model measurements can then be converted to corresponding quantities (say of water flow, hydro-dynamic forces on structures, erosion of river bed, etc. as they would occur under real conditions in nature, using the principles of similitude and dimensional analysis. Equations derived on the model may be used to solve problems on the prototype, or even to serve as general equations for similar processes operating anywhere. Furthermore, "model studies" can often be made even without recourse to actual laboratory replicas. Processes can be simulated by computer modeling, by mathematical modeling, or even by purely mental models.

It is the nature and structure of God's laws and processes, along with their reliability, that make such modeling and analysis (and indeed all true scientific research) possible. All processes operate within a space-time-mass (energy) dimensional continuum. The two basic laws of nature point to the fact of God as omnipotent Creator and the structure of natural processes in their dimensional framework to His triune nature. Even if scientists fail to see these theological implications, they must use them in their scientific research, every day.

## The Hypostatic Union

Even as there is profound scientific truth in the mystery of the triune nature of God, so also there is profound scientific truth in the great mystery of the incarnation. That Jesus Christ was both man and God, each in the full substance (hypostasis) of reality — fully human and yet very God — has been the foundation of Christian doctrine since the time of Christ himself. The perfect and complete union of the divine and human natures in Christ is so fundamental that its denial is the very identification of the doctrine of Antichrist (1 John 4:2–3, 15). Many have distorted or denied the truth of the genuinely human nature of Christ, especially in ancient times; many more have questioned the true deity of the man Jesus, especially in modern times. Both heresies stress the supposed impossibility of two such completely distinctive natures being consubstantially united in one person.

And yet essentially the same paradox is reflected throughout the creation in a marvelous way. That is, each of the three basic entities of the physical creation itself manifests a paradoxical, complementary duality of essentially the same characteristics as that wherein the Son reveals himself.

The paradox of the Second Person of the godhead (in whom dwells all the fullness of the godhead bodily) lies in the apparent contradiction between the concept of an omnipresent, eternal being confined within the finite bounds of a human body and the temporal duration of a human life. These terms seem contradictory by very definition.

But it is in the very semantics of this apparent contradiction that we find a remarkable analogy in the nature of the physical creation. That is, space is both finite and infinite; and time is both temporal and eternal. These are the very terms we use to describe the paradox of the divine-human nature of Christ. Although space is essentially infinite in conceptual extent (we cannot conceive of an end of space, because what could be outside that except more space?), we can only understand and measure it in terms of finite distances. And though time, insofar as we can conceive it (what could be before or after time?) is essentially flowing eternally, we can only measure and understand it in terms of finite, temporal durations.

In like fashion, though God is essentially infinite and eternal, He can only be understood by finite, temporal man in the terms of finitude and temporality with which man is able to reason and react. In these terms has God revealed himself to man, in the person of the Son of Man, Jesus Christ.

The central triune reality of the physical creation has been described as consisting of the events that take place in space and time. Such events occur in great variety, including all the phenomena of matter, of light, heat, sound, radiation, electricity, and even of life itself. Greatly diverse though these and all other phenomena of nature may appear to be, there is a single underlying unity pervading all of them. Each is essentially some form of motion (and of course motion necessarily takes place in space and time), and further, each is basically a manifestation of some form of energy. Thus, energy is the basic cause of every particular event and its associated motion. The phenomena which proceed from it (heat, sound, materiality, etc.) are the effects, or consequences, as discussed in the preceding section.

"Energy" may be defined as the capacity for accomplishing work. Heat, sound, electricity, chemical energy, mechanical energy, and many other forms of energy exist. Matter itself is essentially a form of energy and can, under the proper conditions, be converted into other forms of energy. But undoubtedly the most basic form of energy is light. It is the light, or radiant energy, from the sun that is the source of all the varied forms of energy that maintain the earth's physical and biological processes. The sun's radiant energy, in turn, is believed to be derived from thermonuclear reactions involving the conversion of matter into energy. Matter is related to other forms of energy in terms of the famous equation of Einstein, the conversion factor involving the square of the velocity of light. That is, $E = mc^2$.

The velocity of light in a vacuum is the most remarkable number in all the physical universe. It is believed to be constant under all possible conditions and is the greatest velocity possible in the physical universe, so far as we know. It is thus the motion to which all other lesser motions in the universe must be referenced.

We come then to this, that the third great reality of the universe, which we have described under the comprehensive term of the events taking place in space and time, can finally be described simply as energy, and energy in turn ultimately as light! More than by any other aspect of the physical creation, the Creator, Jesus Christ, is shown forth by the very fact of light. The first Word of the Creator, uttered in the primeval darkness, was: "Let there be light" (Gen. 1:3). He is the "light of the world" (John 8:12), the "true Light, which lighteth every man that cometh into the world" (John 1:9).

One of the most profound discoveries of modern science has been that physical light (and, therefore, also matter, in its basic atomic structure) has two natures, apparently contradictory and yet perfectly real and harmonious! Under certain conditions light manifests all the characteristics of wave motion; in other situations it seems to behave as a stream of particles.[3]

This dual nature of light (and of the atomic structure of matter) has been the greatest paradox of modern science. Some physicists maintain that this is a contradiction and are hoping that further study will eventually be able to determine whether light is really propagated as waves or as particles. But most scientists are convinced that this duality — they call it "complementarity" — of light is real, even though beyond understanding. It has become the basis of the famous "principle of indeterminacy," which says that it is forever impossible, in the very nature of things, to determine completely the behavior of the subatomic particles which constitute the ultimate basis of matter. The distances are so small, and the velocities so great, that physical measurements, even in imagination, are incapable of precise determination and decision. The powerful tools of mathematical physics known, respectively, as wave mechanics and quantum mechanics, likewise reflect this fundamental "complementarity" of nature, the one being the means

---

3. "In problems where the propagation of light is concerned, it behaves *as if* it were an electromagnetic wave, while in the interaction of light with matter, it behaves *as if* it were an assemblage of particles." H. Heilman, "What Is the E.M. Spectrum?" *Science Digest,* 57 (June 1965): 77.

of studying wave motions, the other of motions of particles, or "quanta," each having its own regime of application.

Thus, both the wave nature of light and the particle nature of light are accepted as scientifically valid descriptions of the basic nature of light (and therefore of all matter). Now one, and now the other, is manifest, but both are real. One might even think of this remarkable reality in terms of a "hypostatic union" of the two natures of light. Analogously, He who is the spiritual light of the world manifests, in perfect union and complementarity, characteristics of both the perfect man and the infinite God! In this remarkable way also does the physical universe — the "things that are made" — witness to the Lord Jesus Christ, in "his eternal power and Godhead," since it is He alone in whom "dwelleth all the fulness of the Godhead bodily."

This remarkable "principle of complementarity" has been formalized in physics through the work of such men as Niels Bohr and Max Born, but it was anticipated in Scripture and in theology long before the development of modern physics. The apparent paradoxes and contradictions of Scripture are beautiful examples of this principle. Not only the paradox of the divine-human nature of Christ, but also the paradox of election versus free will, salvation by grace or works, God's immutability versus His response to prevailing prayer, and others, all illustrate this principle of complementarity. What seems to be apparent contradiction in each case really represents a greater underlying reality, both sides of the same coin, as it were.

It is noteworthy that some of the greatest of these modern scientists have recognized this correlation. Max Born, for example, considered the chief author of the scientific principle of complementarity, has discussed these relations as follows:

> But a real enrichment to our thinking is the idea of complementarity. The fact that in an exact science like physics there are mutually exclusive and complementary situations which cannot be described by the same concepts, but need two kinds of expressions, must have an influence; and I think a welcome influence, on other fields of thought. . . . In biology the concept of life itself leads to a complementary alternative: the physicochemical analysis of a living organism is compatible with its free functioning and leads in its extreme application to death. In philosophy there is a similar alternative in the central problem of free will. Any decision can be considered on the one side as a process in the conscious mind, on the other as a product of motives, implanted in the past or present from the outside world. If one sees in this an example of complementarity, the eternal conflict between freedom and necessity appears to be based on an epistemological error.[4]

Probably even the relation between energy and matter could be considered a further example of this principle. These two basic entities are apparently com-

---

4. Max Born, "Physics and Metaphysics," *Scientific Monthly* (May 1956): 235.

pletely distinct in nature, and yet are fully equivalent to each other in essence. The factor that relates the one to the other is the square of the velocity of light. Here again, He who is "the light of the world" (John 8:12) is suggested. It is Jesus Christ who upholds all things by the word of His power (Heb. 1:3). He who created all things is also the one by whom all things consist (Col. 1:16–17).

## The Grace of God

The Scriptures, of course, reveal God not only to be a God of "eternal power," but also to be the "God of all grace"(1 Pet. 5:10). Since Jesus Christ has manifested not only God's power and holiness, but even more His infinite love and grace, and since He is the bodily incarnation of the whole fullness of the godhead, which in turn is said to have been clearly revealed in the physical creation, it is reasonable to ask also whether there may be evidence in nature of the gospel of the grace of God.

The message of the apostle Paul to the pagans in Lystra speaks of this witness of God in nature concerning His grace. He said, "We also are men of like passions with you, and preach unto you that ye should turn from these vanities unto the living God, which made heaven; and earth, and the sea, and all things that are therein: Who in times past suffered all nations to walk in their own ways. Nevertheless he left not himself without witness, in that he did good, and gave us rain from heaven, and fruitful seasons, filling our hearts with food and gladness" (Acts 14:15–17).

Thus, according to Paul, there is a witness of God in nature, not only to His power in creation, but also to the fact that He "did good." He is a God of goodness, and this is evident by His continual provision of the rain and the seasons and all that is necessary for the continuance of life on earth.

But this provision of life's necessities must also be understood against the background of God's curse on the earth. God had provided "food and gladness" in spite of the fact that He had long ago said, to the very first man, that "in sorrow shalt thou eat of it all the days of thy life" (Gen. 3:17). The whole creation is under the bondage of decay and "groaneth and travaileth in pain together . . . until now" (Rom. 8:21–22).

Both the witness of a "cursed" earth, which yields thorns and thistles, and from which a living may be extracted only at the cost of sorrow, sweat, and tears, and the witness of an accusing conscience (Rom. 2:15), continuously unite in their reminder to man that something is wrong in the world. There is a great gulf between himself and the great God of creation, whose eternal power and godhead should be clearly seen in the things that were made. Above all there is the great enemy, death, which men and women always seek to escape, but which inexorably overtakes them in the end.

Still there is the ever-recurring testimony of hope that is revealed in the creation. Although the earth is reluctant and requires labor and sweat to yield its increase, the fruit does come. God year by year sends the rain from heaven and the corn grows in its mysterious way. The winter comes, and life seems almost to die away as the Curse becomes more and more evident. But then once again God sends His "fruitful seasons" and the earth is renewed.

In fact, every day there is a reminder of death and darkness and sin: "The night cometh, when no man can work" (John 9:4). The light that is so utterly essential to life vanishes away each evening, and there is a long night of darkness. But that which might be the source of terror and hopelessness and death becomes instead a time of rest and restoration, because everyone knows that the sun will rise again the next day. And though we may not know its significance, apart from the biblical revelation, we sense that the rising of the sun is a testimony to God's provision of healing and life.

Each day, in the sunrise, and each year, in the coming of spring, there is a recurring witness to the hope of victory over sin, the Curse, and death. Someday the "Sun of righteousness [shall] arise with healing in his wings" (Mal. 4:2). There will come a time when the world can say: "For, lo, the winter is past, the rain is over and gone; The flowers appear on the earth; the time of the singing of birds is come" (Song of Sol. 2:11–12).

Thus there is in nature a wonderful testimony to the grace of God. Though the whole creation is groaning under the bondage of corruption, and death is the common experience of all animate life, yet there is always the hope of life out of death. Furthermore, the fact that earth's orbital revolution and its axial rotation, which are the physical mechanisms responsible for the annual return of spring and the diurnal return of light to the world, entirely outside of man's ability to produce, should cause him to offer up continual thanks and praise to the God who in grace provides these gifts. They should be perpetual reminders that man is unable to save himself; he is helpless in a hostile environment apart from the grace of his Creator. The great Creator must also be his Savior, or he is utterly lost.

## The Witness to Redemption in the Biological World

But there is another important aspect to God's grace. God is the God of all grace, but He can only exercise His grace and mercy and love in such a way that His holiness and righteousness are maintained in full integrity. He cannot merely wink at sin. Death is not just an accident, but is inherent in the very nature of a world that is in rebellion against its Maker. Salvation and light and life can only be provided when sin and the Curse and death have been overcome. But man himself is no more able to overcome sin and make himself righteous than he is able to defeat the night and cause the sun to rise or to conquer death and rise from the dead.

Only life can vanquish death, and only righteousness can conquer sin, but this is absolutely impossible for any mere human being to accomplish. If it is done, it must be accomplished for him by someone else. He must have a substitute, one who can completely take his place before God, who can suffer in his stead for his sins, and who can also attain full victory over sin and death on his behalf. This is impossible for anyone other than God himself to accomplish. God must be redeemer as well as Creator and sustainer. Before true and lasting life can be provided for dying mankind, God himself must bear the earth's curse and die for the sins of the world.

Is there a witness to this greatest of all gospel truths in creation? Yes, there is, though as with all reflections, it is far less than the reality. The fact that only out of sacrificial death can come forgiveness and life seems to have been recognized since the beginning of human history. All tribes and nations have, in some way or another, recognized that reconciliation with God requires substitutionary and propitiatory sacrifice. To what extent the universal custom of sacrifice, distorted and corrupt though it may be, reflects a remnant of knowledge of God's primeval revelation of a coming Redeemer, we do not know. But the practice is too universal to have been accidental.

Perhaps it also is partially a reflection of the universal experience that even natural life can come into the world only when one is willing to experience unique suffering and possibly death itself. Human birth, even the birth of all higher animals, only comes by way of intense travail, and perhaps even at the cost of the death of the mother.

A most intriguing illustration of this is found in Psalm 22, that marvelous prophetic description of the suffering and death of Christ on the cross, written a thousand years before its fulfillment. In the midst of His sufferings, the Lord Jesus cries in His heart: "But I am a worm, and no man; a reproach of men, and despised of the people" (Ps. 22:6). In the parallel prophecy of Isaiah, it was said that "his visage was ... marred [in fact, according to a literal rendering, "*Corruption*," personified] more than any man, and his form more than the sons of men" (Isa. 52:14), so that truly He seemed like "no man." And Isaiah also said that He was "despised and rejected of man" (Isa. 53:3). But in what sense could He have been said actually to be a "*worm*"?

In ancient Israel, as in the modern world, there were many types of worms, and several different kinds are mentioned in the Bible. But the worm referred to in Psalm 22:6 was a particular worm known as the "scarlet worm." It was from this worm that a valuable secretion was obtained with which to make scarlet dyes. The same word is sometimes translated as "scarlet" or "crimson" (Isa. 1:18).

When the female of the scarlet worm species was ready to give birth to her young, she would attach her body to the trunk of a tree, fixing herself so firmly and permanently that she could never leave again. The eggs deposited beneath her body were thus protected until the larvae were hatched and able to leave and enter their own life cycle. As the mother died, the crimson fluid stained her body and the surrounding wood. From the dead bodies of such female scarlet worms, the commercial scarlet dyes of antiquity were extracted.

What a picture this gives of Christ, dying on the tree, shedding His precious blood that He might bring "many sons unto glory" (Heb. 2:10)! He died for us, that we might live through Him!

Similarly, in greater or lesser measure, wherever there is birth in the animal kingdom, there is also first a period of travail or even death. One must suffer in order for another to live. When this universal truth of experience is combined with all the other great witnesses God has left in His creation, we are not far from seeing in "the things that are made," not only the godhead revealed in His infinite power and triune nature, but even in His eternal sacrificial grace and love.

This is especially true in connection with human birth. In fact, it was by means of a human birth that God himself had promised from the beginning to come into the world to bring redemption and salvation. In the very midst of the primeval curse that He was forced to pronounce on the earth because of man's sin, He also gave the gracious promise of the coming seed of the woman, who would someday crush the head of Satan and restore man's lost estate. This First Gospel, as it has been called, given in Genesis 3:15, is also the everlasting gospel to which God has witnessed through the ages in His physical creation and in His written Word.

Whenever a babe is born, there is "sorrow in . . . conception" (Gen. 3:16), because of the reign of sin and death. But as the Lord Jesus said, "A woman when she is in travail hath sorrow, because her hour is come: but as soon as she is delivered of the child, she remembereth no more the anguish, for joy that a man is born into the world" (John 16:21).

The birth of a babe is a time of joy and thanksgiving everywhere. And everywhere it bears witness to the promised Son, the seed of the woman, who one day would come and would "see of the travail of his soul, and . . . be satisfied" (Isa. 53:11). It also speaks of the glorious fact that, though "the whole creation groaneth and travaileth in pain together until now," it also "shall be delivered," and a new earth shall be born "into the glorious liberty of the children of God" (Rom. 8:21–22).

God indeed has not left himself without witness! To the eye of faith and hope and love, surely even the "invisible things of him are clearly seen," and everywhere one looks in the world he sees an abundance of evidence of Christ in creation.

# 3

# MIRACLES AND THE LAWS OF NATURE

*Biblical Supernaturalism*

## The Fact of Universal Law

Thoughtful scientists have frequently called attention to the remarkable fact that the whole universe can be described by the same set of natural laws, and the same chemical elements are found in every galaxy. The forms of matter, the varieties of energy, and the laws that apply to both are the same throughout the whole universe. This amazing situation is implicit in the very name; it is a universe, not a multi-verse. Despite its tremendous apparent size and duration, it seems essentially the same through all space and time. This is really a strange thing, if indeed the universe had a chaotic, random, unguided origin and development, as evolutionists believe. No naturalistic explanation seems adequate.

> In 1873, J. Clerk Maxwell wrote: "In the heavens we discover by their light . . . stars so distant that no material thing can ever have passed from one to another; and yet this light . . . tells us that each of them is built up of molecules of the same kinds that we find on earth. . . . No theory of evolution can be formed to account for the similarity of the molecules. . . . On the other hand, the exact equality of each molecule to all others of the same kind gives it . . . the essential character of its being eternal and self-existent."
>
> . . . So far as we know, the result is still the same as Maxwell inferred: all electrons are everywhere the same, all protons are the same, and so on. We should expect a sufficiently sophisticated theory to tell us why this is so.[1]

---

1. W.H. McCrea, "Cosmology After Half a Century," *Science,* 160 (June 21, 1968): 1298.

One does not need a sophisticated theory to explain these things, however. The reason why the universe functions as a universe is because it was so created by the one true God. There is no adequate naturalistic theory. The great physicist J. Clerk Maxwell, cited above, fully concurred in such a conclusion.

Even more amazing to the naturalistic philosopher is the fact that the structures and processes and laws of the universe are capable of formulation in mathematical equations and descriptive theories of great elegance. As noted in chapter 1, Einstein felt that the most incredible thing about the universe was that it is intelligible, capable of being described in ways intelligible to men and women.[2] How could random, non-intelligent primeval particles evolve themselves into orderly, intelligible systems?

Another great physicist and mathematician, P.A.M. Dirac, frankly acknowledged the impossibility of mechanistic explanations for the orderly beauty of the universe:

> There is one other line along which one can still proceed by theoretical means. It seems to be one of the fundamental features of nature that fundamental physical laws are described in terms of a mathematical theory of great beauty and power, needing quite a high standard of mathematics for one to understand it. You may wonder: Why is nature constructed along these lines? One can only answer that our present knowledge seems to show that nature is so constructed. We simply have to accept it. One could perhaps describe the situation by saying that God is a mathematician of a very high order, and He used very advanced mathematics in constructing the universe. Our feeble attempts at mathematics enable us to understand a bit of the universe, and as we proceed to develop higher and higher mathematics we can hope to understand the universe better.[3]

The difficulty of explaining such an orderly universe by natural processes is, of course, infinitely compounded by the fact that those processes, always constrained as they are by the second law of thermodynamics, are now causing the universe to proceed inexorably toward greater and greater degrees of disorder. Leading British astronomer Paul Davies has said, "The greatest puzzle is where all the order in the universe came from originally. How did the cosmos get wound up, if the second law of thermodynamics predicts asymmetric unwinding towards disorder?"[4] The great puzzle is easily resolved. "In the beginning God created the heaven and the earth." These are the simplest, yet most profound, words ever written, as well as probably the first words, and certainly the truest words, ever written. The entire universe and all its laws and processes provide clear and unequivocal assurance of this foundational fact.

---

2. Victor F. Weisskopf, "The Frontiers and Limits of Science," *American Scientist,* 65, July–Aug. 1977: 405.

3. P.A.M. Dirac, "The Evolution of the Physicists' Picture of Nature," *Scientific American,* 208 (May 1963): 53.

4. Paul C. W. Davies, "Universe in Reverse: Can Time Run Backwards?" *Second Look* (Sept. 1979): 27.

## Uniformity in the Present Cosmos

Biblical theologians have traditionally made a distinction between God's works of creation and His works of providence. This distinction is completely scriptural and also thoroughly scientific. Scientific study of natural processes in the present world has shown them to be, without exception, conservative processes. That is, all things are being conserved, but nothing is now being created. God's work of creation, insofar as the natural world is concerned, was completed in the creation week and since that time His providential care has been "upholding all things by the word of his power" (Heb. 1:3).

Although the doctrine of uniformitarianism is invalid if applied either to the period of creation or the period of the Deluge, there is ample scriptural support for uniformity in the present cosmos. This is clear in a key passage of Scripture, 2 Peter 3:3–7. Immediately after noting that "the [cosmos] that then was, being overflowed with water, perished," Peter says, "but the heavens and the earth, which are now, by the same word are kept in store" (2 Pet. 3:7). Thus, the present cosmos is being "stored up," or "conserved."

This cosmos is the only one accessible to scientists for study and measurement, and it is thus not surprising that scientists have been led to believe that all processes operate within the framework of uniform law. Nature is reliable and can be studied and described effectively by means of the scientific method. This very fact, of course, is a witness to the power and wisdom of God and makes meaningful and reasonable God's command to man to "subdue the earth" and to "have dominion" over it (Gen. 1:28). The world is a *cosmos*, not a *chaos*. Science, which seeks to understand the processes of nature, and technology (e.g., engineering, medicine, agriculture, etc.), which seeks to utilize them in the service of mankind, are thus legitimate and necessary aspects of man's stewardship under God's providence.

The prevailing uniformity in the present cosmos is thus quite biblical. As emphasized previously, all processes operate within the framework of the first and second laws of thermodynamics. According to the first law, nothing in the physical realm is now being created or destroyed — even though continually changing in form. The operation of this principle apparently dates from the end of the period of creation (Gen. 2:1–3; Exod. 20:11; Isa. 40:26; Heb. 4:3, 10; et al.). According to the second law, all things tend to decay and die, a situation that evidently dates from the imposition of God's Curse on the earth (Gen. 3:17; Ps. 102:25–27; Isa. 40:6–8; Rom. 8:20–22; et al.). See chapter 7 for a full discussion of these matters.

The almost infinite variety of physical and biological processes that exist in the world are all thus fundamentally conservative and disintegrative processes. Science is basically the study of these processes — the various factors that affect them and the rates at which they operate.

The second law describes all processes as, ultimately, decay processes, but it says nothing concerning the rate of decay. Process rates are determined by the various factors that affect the process, and may vary widely if one or more of these factors change. For example, the process of flow of water down a river channel is affected by the size and shape of the channel, the nature of the watershed, vegetation, rainfall, infiltration, temperature, and many other factors. If any of these change, the rate of flow may change substantially. Similar controls affect all other earth processes without exception. In general, every process rate varies statistically around some average rate, and the range of variation depends on the nature and number of the different entities that influence the particular relationship.

At the time of the Flood, such cataclysmic changes took place in the earth and its atmosphere that most geophysical process rates probably were vastly accelerated for a time, and the resulting visitation of disorder and death on the earth was the greatest it has ever experienced. However, at the termination of that awful year, God made a far-reaching promise: "While the earth remaineth, seedtime and harvest, and cold and heat, and summer and winter, and day and night shall not cease" (Gen. 8:22).

Thus, the basic processes of the earth's axial rotation and its orbital revolution about the sun were not to be affected significantly during the present age. These in turn exert primary influence on most other geophysical and biological processes, so that God was in effect promising the essential uniformity, not only of basic laws, but now also of processes, in the postdiluvian cosmos. The uniformity of natural law is thus a valid and powerful interpretive principle, in terms of both basic laws and processes, for the present world.

## The Problem of Miracles

What, then, are we to think about miracles, especially the miracles of the Bible? Is there room in a cosmos under the rule of naturalism for supernaturalism?

The answer of the modern scientific establishment has, in general, been that miracles are impossible. For well over a hundred years, most scientists and philosophers have held that no amount of evidence could ever be sufficient to prove the occurrence of a miracle.

An observed event that seems to have no immediately apparent naturalistic explanation can thus always be rationalized away on one of the following grounds: (1) the observations may have been incomplete or mistaken; (2) the inexplicable character of the phenomenon may be due, not to supernatural forces, but to our very limited and incomplete understanding of natural processes: (3) the statistical nature of natural processes means that very unusual occurrences can always be explained in principle as statistical oddities, without recourse to the supernatural.

These appear to be weighty restrictions and undoubtedly possess much validity. Probably the great majority of supposedly miraculous occurrences can legitimately be questioned on one or more of these grounds. The "miracles" of modern technology — airplanes, televisions, nuclear energy, lasers, and others without number — would surely have been counted as miraculous by our ancestors if they had encountered them. Furthermore, the unreliability of even eyewitness testimony, especially when attempting to retrace events that occurred in an atmosphere of suspense or excitement, is notorious.

And yet there is no doubt that the Bible tells of real miracles! It was by means of the seven great miracles recorded in the Gospel of John, for example, that men were expected to come to believe that Jesus is the Son of God (John 20:30–31). Similarly it was through "signs and wonders and divers miracles" that the Lord confirmed the spoken word of the apostles prior to the inscripturation of His written Word (Heb. 2:3–4). Other periods of supernatural visitations occurred especially during the Exodus, and during the ministries of Elijah and Elisha. In these and other records of biblical miracles, there is always an emphasis on the testimonial value of the particular miracle, validating the power of God and the word of His prophet.

This latter observation reinforces the previous observation concerning the essential uniformity of nature in the present cosmos. The miraculous can only have significant testimonial value if it is extremely rare — so rare, in fact, as to be beyond reach of the types of rationalizations noted previously. Miracles that can be repeated at the whim of a practitioner, or that can be generated by means of certain specific techniques or incantations are perforce brought within the domain of empirical knowledge by these very facts, and thus are not true miracles at all.

## Cosmic Law and Natural Processes

A true miracle must be defined in terms of its relation to the basic laws and processes of the present cosmos that are now being sustained by God himself in Christ (Col. 1:17; Heb. 1:3; 2 Pet. 3:7). Thus, a miracle must be an event outside the scope of either the fundamental laws of nature or of the normal operation of natural processes.

We have already noted that the basic laws of nature are the two laws of thermodynamics, the laws of conservation and decay. "Mass-energy" must always be conserved and "entropy" must always increase. These two entities are the basic concepts common to all phenomena occurring in our space-time universe, and the two laws constitute the constraining framework within which all such processes apparently function.

Not only do all processes conform to the two laws, but they also have still another fundamental feature in common. Though each process may be affected by many different forces of nature and properties of matter, and thus its rate may vary over a wide range, it must ultimately be measurable and described in terms of only three basic categories — units of space, units of energy or mass, and units of time. This is because every process functions in the physical universe and because the universe is a continuum of space and mass and time, with mass understood as interchangeable with and thus essentially synonymous with energy.

Every natural process in the present cosmos operates within the uniform framework of the basic laws of conservation and decay and is capable of formulation and description in terms of the three basic dimensions of space, mass, and time. This is the fundamental structure of the present cosmos (the only one accessible to scientific observation, be it again noted) and it is this cosmos that seems to be under the dominion of uniformity.

It is remarkable that, even viewed in the perspective of naturalism and uniformity as above, the cosmic framework gives clear witness to the "eternal power and Godhead" of its Creator, as noted in Romans 1:20. The fact of God and creation is unequivocally affirmed by the two basic laws, and the nature of the godhead is clearly reflected in every process of that universe which is His creature. These relationships have been detailed in chapter 2.

Even if scientists fail to see or accept the theological implications, they must use these foundational premises, in all their scientific research, every day, as basic in their scientific methodology, making it possible for them to develop reliable scientific descriptions and predictions. God's laws are good and reliable, and this is the very fact that makes all science and technology possible.

## Miracles of Providence

Yet there can be no doubt that miracles are possible. The God who established the cosmos in its framework of basic law and its three-dimensional structure of natural processes is clearly transcendent thereto and thus can intervene when and how He will. Such interventions we call "miracles."

With the basic nature of the cosmos in mind, it is immediately evident that *two* kinds of miracles are possible — those that intervene in the operation of natural processes and those that contravene basic law. For purposes of discussion, we may call these, respectively, miracles of providence and miracles of creation, or, more informally, "Grade B" miracles and "Grade A" miracles.

A Grade B miracle is accomplished strictly within the framework of the two basic laws but involves special control or adjustment of one or more natural processes for a specific purpose at a particular time. It will be recalled that all process rates are subject to statistical variation, the range of which depends on the various factors that may affect the process. If the occurrence is near the statistical limits of the process, it may be a miracle. An example would be the three-and-one-half-year drought, and the subsequent rain, given in answer to the prayers of Elijah (James 5:17–18). Similar biblical examples of providential miracles are the Philippian earthquake (Acts 16:26), the destruction of the army of Sennacherib (2 Kings 19:35), and many others. None of these miracles required intervention in the basic laws, but each required that the particular process be made to occur at an extremely unlikely time or at extremely improbable rates.

Every believing Christian knows from experience that God answers prayer, often in most remarkable and unlikely ways. Such experiences may often come under this category of providential miracles. Most validated instances of physical healing received in response to prayer, for example, can be understood in terms of an unusual, but not impossible, acceleration of the body's innate recuperative powers, or perhaps as a retardation of previously overactive decay processes.

As to the agency which God utilizes in thus intervening in natural processes, the Scriptures suggest that angels may be involved, at least on many occasions. Note, for example, the ministry of angels in the destruction of Sodom (Gen. 19:1, 13), the protection of Daniel from the lions (Dan. 6:22), the deliverance of the apostles from prison (Acts 5:19; 12:7), the host surrounding Elisha and smiting his enemies (2 Kings 6:17–18), and many others.

According to the Scriptures, God has created an "innumerable company of angels" (Heb. 12:22), who are "sent forth to minister for them who shall be heirs of salvation" (Heb. 1:14). They "excel in strength" and "do his commandments" (Ps. 103:20). Scripture indicates that angels possess all the necessary power and wisdom to constrain natural agents that influence natural processes and modify them as may be needed at a particular time and place to do the will of God and to answer the prayers of His people. The Book of Revelation especially describes angels as capable, under God, of unleashing terrific natural phenomena — hail, fire, meteorites, or other heavenly bodies, even of controlling the rate of nuclear processes on the sun (Rev. 8:7–12; 16:8), as well as physical plagues on human flesh (Rev. 16:2, 10). It is not unreasonable, therefore, that God might choose to accomplish His miracles of providence, controlling and modifying natural processes over as extreme a range of statistical improbabilities as may suit His desire, through the instrumentality of His mighty angels.

It should not be forgotten that there also exist a lesser host of *evil* angels, following Satan (himself perhaps the mightiest of all created angels) in his rebellion against God. These also, or at least many of them, are beings of great intelligence and strength, even though fallen. They may also be quite capable of great juggling of the world's natural processes, and thus able to accomplish true Grade B miracles. But such demonic miracles are counterfeit as far as their intended testimonial value is concerned; Paul called them "lying wonders" (2 Thess. 2:9).

## Miracles of Creation

There are those occasions, however, when God has seen fit to set aside even His basic laws of conservation and decay, and to perform special acts of creation of matter or energy (in contradiction to the first law) or special acts of instant increases of order in closed systems (in contradiction to the second law). Such works require creative power and are thus beyond the reach of natural processes and of created angels[5] alike. Only God can create! These, therefore, are creative miracles — Grade A miracles, if you will.

It may not always be clear whether a particular Bible miracle is a miracle of providence or a miracle of creation. But there are some that are clearly miracles of creation. The creation itself, for example, is a tremendous complex of creative miracles. All the immense reservoirs of matter and power and order in the universe have been brought into existence by the Almighty Creator.

Only God is able to perform miracles of creation. He has on occasion done so even in the present cosmos. An obvious example is found in the several instances of restoration of the dead back to physical life, and another is in the daily creation of the manna for the Israelites wandering in the wilderness, and there are many others.

It is significant that the seven great signs in the Gospel of John were all Grade A miracles. The following summary shows this clearly:

1. *Water transmuted into wine* (John 2:1–11). The simple molecular structure of water instantly was converted into the far more complex molecular structure of freshly created wine, indicating a special creation of complexity, or information.
2. *The dying son healed* (John 4:46–54). An instantaneous reversal of the decay process, restoring to full vigor and activity the cellular structure that had been destroyed by a mortal illness, was accomplished merely by a spoken word uttered over ten miles away.
3. *The crippled man made whole* (John 5:3–9). A man unable to walk for 38 years instantaneously received strong, firm legs at Jesus' command, involving the creation of new bone, muscle, and other components in place of the atrophied, dead members.
4. *The multitude fed* (John 6:5–13). The law of mass conservation was suspended while Jesus multiplied five loaves and two fishes into bread and meat more than sufficient for five thousand men.
5. *Gravity superseded* (John 6:16–21). The law of energy conservation was set aside as the Lord Jesus created an anti-gravitational force of unknown nature, enabling Him to walk on the surface of a stormy sea.
6. *The blind made to see* (John 9:1–7). Both matter and complexity were instantly created when a man blind from birth suddenly possessed perfectly functioning eyes in his previously useless eye sockets.

---

5. The apparent miraculous ability of the Egyptian magicians to turn their rods into serpents (Exod. 7:10–12) cannot really be an exception to this principle. Their efforts were actually deceptions of some kind, as is evident from their inability a few days later to produce such a much simpler form of life as lice (Exod. 8:18–19). The "enchantments" which they produced were perhaps hypnotic illusions, and Exodus 7:12 could be read, "For they cast down every man his rod, and they became [as] serpents."

7. *The dead restored to life* (John 11:33–44). Not only were the limbs and eyes dead, but the whole body in this case, and for four whole days, so that putrefaction had set in. Nevertheless, at the creative word of Christ, all cells and functions were instantly restructured and reprogrammed, and even the departed spirit summoned again to the body, so that Lazarus lived.

Since all of these were mighty miracles of creation, and since only God can create, the testimony of John 20:30–31 is an understandably strong assertion of the deity of Christ: "And many other signs truly did Jesus in the presence of his disciples, which are not written in this book: but these are written that ye might believe that Jesus is the Christ, the Son of God; and that believing ye might have life through his name."

Many of the Bible miracles (though not all, by any means) are similar miracles of creation, requiring the suspension of one or both of the two laws of thermodynamics and testifying to the direct power of God the Creator. Examples from the Old Testament, drawn more or less at random, might include the following:

1. *Creation of mass*: the miracle of the increasing oil (2 Kings 4:1–6).
2. *Creation of energy*: the restrained walls of water at the Red Sea crossing (Exod. 14:29).
3. *Creation of complexity*: the multiplied languages, with corresponding physiological modifications relating to the varied grammatical systems introduced at the Tower of Babel (Gen. 11:1–9).

Another form of creative miracle is the impartation of divine "information" to man. Sometimes this information has come through dreams or visions, sometimes by direct theophanic revelation. More commonly, it came by less immediate and obvious ways, but no less real and effective, as "holy men of God spake as they were moved by the Holy Ghost" (2 Pet. 1:21).

Many of the healings described in the Bible (though not all) seem to have involved divine creative activity and thus to have been real miracles of creation. An example would be the healing of Naaman's leprosy after he had dipped his body seven times in the Jordan (2 Kings 5:1–14). There are no medicinal powers to cure leprosy, either in river water or in psychosomatic suggestion. What amounted to new flesh must have been created for Naaman by God in answer to Elisha's prayer.

But the greatest of all miracles of creation was the creation itself, when God brought into existence and completion all the matter and energy and complexity of the entire universe. And the greatest of all delusions is the belief that all of this could be accomplished by anything other than creation! If evolution is true, there must have been a miracle of creation interjected at every stage of evolutionary growth from one level of complexity to the next. Natural processes are described by the second law of thermodynamics, which stipulates that these processes normally proceed in a direction exactly opposite to the direction required by evolution. They go downhill instead of uphill, and this can be reversed only on a limited basis under special conditions never satisfied by any evolutionary processes ever observed (e.g., innate evolutionary programming and "negentropy" generators).

By and large, in the present cosmos God's laws are adequate, His written Word is complete and sufficient, and miracles of creation are rarely warranted. Providential miracles are not uncommon today, but creative miracles must surely be justified by highly unusual and urgent circumstances if at all.

One glorious exception is described in 2 Corinthians 5:17: "If any man be in Christ, he is a new creature." The miracle of regeneration is a Grade A miracle in every sense of the word. A person who is a "closed system" spiritually, utterly inadequate and self-centered, suddenly becomes an "open system," integrated and centered in the omnipotent Creator. He who was spiritually deteriorating day after day — in fact, already "dead while [he] liveth" (1 Tim. 5:6), suddenly experiences "joy and peace in believing . . . through the power of the Holy Ghost" (Rom. 15:13) and becomes "quickened . . . together with Christ" (Eph. 2:5). His life was a chaos and is now a cosmos, with order and meaning and goal. He is "born again," a miracle of grace, a living testimony to the great power of the God of creation, who also is the God of salvation!

## Miracles of the Bible

Recognizing that there are two basic categories of divine miracles — miracles of creation and miracles of providence — we can now take a more comprehensive look at the miracles described in the Bible. Since miracles must be regarded, even by atheists, as at least possible, there is certainly no reason for the Bible-believing Christian to question the historicity of any of the Bible miracles. In a later section of this chapter we shall note the criteria for determining whether or not an alleged miracle is genuine, and it will be evident that all the miracles of the Bible meet these criteria.

At the risk of oversimplification, we can say that creative miracles require suspension or reversal of the basic laws of nature, whereas providential miracles require only manipulative control of the factors that determine the manner in which natural processes function within those laws. In the first case (a Grade A miracle), creative power is required and thus the Creator himself must be involved. In the second case (a Grade B miracle), some agent is required to manipulate the process to the desired end. The Creator in such a case may be involved, but such controls may also be applied by angelic agents (or even, in some cases, by demonic powers). Even men, of course, can to some degree manipulate natural processes and utilize them in manmade systems, but then we call it "science" instead of "miracle."

In categorizing the Bible miracles (table 1) we may sometimes be unable to decide whether a given miracle is creative or providential. In most cases, how-

TABLE 1 — *Summary of Specific Recorded Miracles in the Bible*

*All the miracles recorded in Scripture are based on sound
evidence and were performed for specific divine purposes.
See appendixes 2, 3, and 4 for complete listing.*

|  | Old Testament | New Testament | Total |
|---|---|---|---|
| **Miracles of Creation** | | | |
| Creation of matter | 9 | 2 | 11 |
| Creation of energy, force, or power | 21 | 8 | 29 |
| Creation of order, information, or complexity | 11 | 14 | 25 |
| Creation of biological life | 9 | 7 | 16 |
| Creation of renewal of spiritual life | 2 | 7 | 9 |
| *Total number of creative miracles* | 52 | 38 | 90 |
| **Miracles of Providence** | | | |
| Control of physical processes | 33 | 9 | 42 |
| Control of biological processes | 11 | 2 | 13 |
| Acceleration of decay processes in people | 20 | 6 | 26 |
| Acceleration of human healing processes in people | 11 | 14 | 25 |
| Casting out of demons | 1 | 9 | 10 |
| Control of timing of natural events | 11 | 1 | 12 |
| *Total number of providential miracles* | 87 | 41 | 128 |
| **Satanic and Demonic Miracles** | | | |
| Counterfeit miracles of creation | 7 | 1 | 8 |
| Counterfeit miracles of providence | 7 | 1 | 8 |
| *Total number of satanic miracles* | 14 | 2 | 16 |
| *Total number of recorded specific miracles* | 153 | 81 | 234 |

ever, a reasonable judgment can be made and such a listing will provide many insights into God's economy. So far as known, this is the first such attempt to do this, so there will undoubtedly be some omissions, as well as doubtful inclusions and questionable assignments. The lists are not presented dogmatically but only to indicate the scope and variety of ways in which God has used His laws and processes to accomplish His purposes.

It should again be emphasized, of course, that miracles are rare, not common — especially miracles of creation. One of the main purposes of the biblical miracles was that of testimony. Such a purpose would be defeated if miracles were common or capricious. Their testimonial value is meaningful only against a normal background of uniformity and naturalism.

On the other hand, if every alleged miracle could be quickly "explained" in terms of scientific laws and processes, then it would be pointless to offer it as a testimony of God's presence. In fact, the very concept of "miracle" would become redundant. One might even define a miracle as an event that is scientifically impossible but that God nevertheless causes to happen for His own higher purposes.

Even in the Bible, miracles are relatively rare. The greatest man who ever lived, other than Christ, was John the Baptist, according to the testimony of Christ himself (Matt. 11:11). Yet "John did no miracle" (John 10:41). The Scriptures record no miracles performed by Noah, Job, Nehemiah, or many of the other great saints of God. The Bible miracles seem to be specially clustered about great times of crisis (the Exodus, the days of Elijah, the Apostolic Age, etc.), with only occasional other examples. A summary of all Bible miracles is given in table 1.

Thus, there seem to be approximately 234 specific miracles recorded in the Bible. However, this does not include the many miracles that were said to be performed by Christ (e.g., John 20:30) or the apostles (e.g., Heb. 2:4), but are not described specifically in the Scriptures.

Also completely excluded were several other particular types of divine activity, as follows:

1. Theophanies — that is, appearances of God (or of angels) to man in visible human form.
2. Visions and/or dreams, by which God revealed certain truths to His prophets or other chosen men or women.
3. Prophecies of things to come, later verified by fulfillment.
4. The divine process by which the Holy Scriptures were given by inspiration, thus guaranteeing their accuracy and authority.
5. The oft-repeated miracle of regeneration, by which a believer becomes a new creation in Christ Jesus (2 Cor. 5:17).
6. The miracles prophetically recorded as yet to take place in the future, especially those in the Book of Revelation.
7. "Ordinary" answers to prayer or divine guidance, where no particularly unusual or statistically rare circumstances were involved.

The 234 listed miracles break down percentagewise as follows: 38 percent creative; 55 percent providential; 7 percent demonic. These basic categories can be still further subdivided, as discussed in the following sections, and as listed in appendixes 2, 3, and 4. These subdivisions are somewhat arbitrary, but they do seem to be reasonable inferences from both Scripture and science.

## The Unique Works of Creation

It is appropriate to categorize the Bible's Grade A miracles to accord with God's successive acts of creation in Genesis. These are particularly identified by use of the Hebrew *bara*, "create."

The first and fundamental act of creation was of the creation of the physical universe, consisting of time, space, and matter. "In the beginning God created the heaven and the earth" (Gen. 1:1).

The second act of creation was the creation of life. "And God created . . . every living creature that moveth" (Gen. 1:21). The word "creature" is the Hebrew *nephesh*, often translated "life" or "soul," referring essentially to moving animal life as distinct from mere physico-chemical phenomena or even stationary plant growth.

The third and final act of primeval creation was the creation of man in the image of God. "So God created man in his own image, in the image of God created he him; male and female created he them" (Gen. 1:27).

Thus there are three basic categories of created entities — matter (in space and time), conscious life, and spirituality. The first of these, however, also includes the entities we now call energy and structure. When God first created matter, it was in elemental form and completely static. The "earth" (which, at the time of initial creation, comprised all the "matter" in the universe) was at first "without form and void." That is, the created matter was not yet structured into complex systems and neither was it activated and energized. This situation was only an initial stage, however, and it was soon changed. The unformed, static elements in their watery matrix, with darkness everywhere "in the presence of the deep" (Gen. 1:2) all were soon transformed into a great variety of living creatures and then with man and woman in the image of God.

This transformation was initiated by the "moving" (literally "vibrating") of the Holy Spirit throughout the created universe in the pervasive presence of the waters. As if generated by a cosmic wavemaker, waves of electromagnetic energy streamed forth throughout the universe. "Let there be light" (Gen. 1:3), God commanded. Electromagnetic energy (light, heat, sound, electricity, magnetism, x-rays, etc.), as well as gravitational energy and the nuclear energies in the atoms themselves, all began to function. To all intents and purposes, a mighty infusion of divine energy had taken place and the entire cosmos was activated.

This was not all, however. All of the created elements and energies next were organized into a vast array of complex systems — molecules and compounds, stars and planets, lands and seas, plants and animals, and finally into human bodies, the most complex of all. This work was spread over six days before it was completed.

These activities were not identified as "creative" acts of God, since creation proper is creation *ex nihilo*, and the basic elements in all these systems had already been created on the first day. They are denoted particularly by the verbs *asah* ("make") and *yatsar* ("form"). In one sense, the work of making and forming is of a lesser order than that of creation. ("God" is the only subject ever connected with the verb *bara*, whereas man can make and form things.) Nevertheless, the peculiar formative works of God during creation week are works that man cannot duplicate — the making of continents and stars and planets, for example. Thus, God's work of "creating" and His work of "making," during that first great week, are both unique to God alone. They are not the same as His work of maintaining His creation through the present processes of nature nor are they works that can be duplicated either by nature or man or angels. "Only God can make a tree," the poet recognized, and the same applies to every aspect of the work of creation week.

Thus, even though the word *bara* was not used in this connection, for our purposes it is appropriate to speak of these works of structuring, organizing, making, and forming, as another great and unique work of creation — the creation of order and structure and complexity in the vast variety of systems in the universe. The physical creation thus can be considered as three correlated works of creation — the creation of matter, the creation of energy, and the creation of structure.

Then, secondly, there is the biological creation, the creation of animal life — the moving creature. The key Hebrew works are *nephesh* ("soul," "life," "creature," etc.) and *ruach* ("breath," "spirit," etc.). These words are applied to both men and animals but not to plants. Even though plant bodies are reproduced by mechanisms similar to those of animal bodies, controlled by complex biochemical reactions centered in the so-called DNA molecule, they are not "alive" in the biblical sense, possessing neither animation, blood, breath, or consciousness. Thus, life in this biblical sense required a new act of creation. It could never be produced merely by a complex — even a reproducing — system of chemical elements. God created every one of the numerous "kinds" of animals, each with its own *nephesh* and *ruach* — the air and water animals on the fifth day, the land animals on the sixth day. Within each kind was implanted its own particular reproductive system and genetic code, enabling it to reproduce biologically strictly "after its own kind."

The third great act of creation was that of man and woman "in the image of God." Each human being has a very complex physical body — more complex than any other creature — and the ability to reproduce other human beings. In addition, each man and woman is specially created in God's own image. Each person possesses a body and soul, transmitted by genetic inheritance from his or her first parents, Adam and Eve. Each person, also, however, possesses an entity called "God's image." Since this required a special act of creation (in addition to the creation of the physical elements and life-principle that were designed to be transmitted by genetic reproduction) it must be assumed that this creation is not transmitted by genetic inheritance and thus that each person's "share" of God's image was individually created for him or her. This creation took place for everyone not at the time of conception, when the mere transmission of physical and biological components takes place, but apparently at the time of the very first creation of this entity (with each "image," as it were, reserved in God until it is sent forth at the time of conception). The details of this marvelous transaction have not been clearly revealed, of course.

In any case, it is clear that each human being possesses an eternal spiritual personality, specially created for him or her in the everlasting image of God, capable of knowing and loving God and forever sharing His fellowship and purposes.

When God had finished all these works, as described in Genesis 1, He "rested from all his work which God created and made" (Gen. 2:3). Therefore, He is no longer, in the normal course of things, creating matter, energy, structure, life, or spiritual personality. He ceased to create and began His work of upholding His creation. Jesus Christ once created all things (Col. 1:16), but now sustains all things (Col. 1:17). He upholds all things by the word of His power (Heb. 1:3). In *Him* (not in inviolable natural laws), we live and move and have our being (Acts 17:28).

These present works are God's works of providence, as distinct from His primeval works of creation. The revealed fact that He is no longer creating, but is simply "conserving" His creation, is of course supported by the most universal and basic law of science — the law of conservation. Energy is conserved, matter is conserved, the biological "kinds" are conserved, and each human being in God's image is conserved.

In the original economy, each individual life was also conserved. Death came into the world only when sin entered. By reasonable extension we could infer that there was then operating a law of conservation of structure as well as a law of conservation of matter and energy. Any breakdown of structure (or order or information, etc.) in one system would be exactly balanced by a compensating increase of structure, order, or information in a related system, so that the net amount of structure in the universe remained unchanged from that originally created.

This conservation principle was drastically changed, however, with the imposition of God's curse on the world. Thenceforth, not only did death come in, with all living organisms destined eventually to disintegrate and go back to their basic elements, but so do all other structures tend to become unstructured. Instead of a law of conservation of structure, there now prevails a universal law of breakdown of structure (morpholysis). Not only is there no more creation of order, but the reverse is taking place, a universal decrease of order (or increase of entropy). Whenever, by special circumstances, a given system experiences an increase of order or structure, it is "overcompensated" by a greater decrease of order or structure in a related system.

The present order of things, described by so-called natural laws and processes (actually God's works of "providence") thus dates from the end of the creation period, and, as far as death and the entropy law are concerned, from the Curse. In the Bible, this primeval period is covered by the first three chapters of Genesis. The removal of the Curse and the establishment of the new heaven and earth are described in the last two chapters of Revelation. The entire Bible in between is occupied with the present order of things, governed by God's works of providence, conservation, redemption, salvation, and reconciliation. His works of creation and formation "were finished from the foundation of the world" (Heb. 4:3).

That does not mean, of course, that God is no longer able to create and make things. It is just that, when He does, it requires an act that we call a "miracle." For Him to so intervene in nature would, of course, require good reason on His part, and for us to believe such an intervention would require good evidence.

## Creation Miracles in the Bible

Although miracles of creation are quite unusual, they have taken place. The Bible records approximately 89 such Grade A miracles. (This number could be somewhat reduced or enlarged, depending on which miracles are identified as creative and which as providential.) The greatest such miracles, of course, were the original creation of the universe and life and man in God's image, as described in Genesis 1. Other subsequent miracles can be compared to these and placed in appropriate corresponding categories.

For example, the provision of manna from heaven for the Israelites for 40 years in the wilderness (Exod. 16:35) required a daily creation of matter and structure. The feeding of the two multitudes by Christ, five thousand and four thousand men, respectively, besides women and children, from a few loaves and fishes in each case, required a similar massive creation of matter and structure.

A creation of some tremendous invisible force, balancing the forces of gravity and hydrostatics, was necessary to erect and maintain two gigantic walls of water to form a path for the Israelites through the Red Sea (Exod. 14:29). Another apparent suspension of energy conservation took place at Christ's baptism, when mighty sound waves proceeded from heaven, identifying Christ as the Son of the Heavenly Father.

Many miracles of healing involved a supernatural retardation or reversal of decay processes, thus superseding the principle of increasing entropy and creating a sudden increase of order and structure in a disintegrating human body. An Old Testament example is the healing of Naaman's leprosy (2 Kings 5:14) and a New Testament example is the simultaneous hearing, eyesight, and liberation given the demoniac of Matthew 12:22.

The miraculous conception of Isaac in a "dead" womb (Gen. 21:1–2) and the revival of the dead son of the Shunammite woman (2 Kings 4:33–36) are examples of the miraculous creation of biological life, as is the restoration of dead Eutychus by the apostle Paul (Acts 20:9–12).

The climactic event of creation — that of spiritual life, God's image in man — can be paralleled in the miraculous coming of God's Spirit into Ezekiel (Ezek. 2:2). The miraculous conception of Christ involved not only special creation of his physical body and biological life but also the miraculous entry of himself, as the very personification of the image and likeness of God, into that human body.

The resurrection of Christ also involved not only the miraculous restoration of His biological life but also, since His death was above all a spiritual death, the suffering of separation from the Father because of sin borne in His body on the tree, a miraculous restoration of His own spirit to full fellowship with His Father.

All of the other Bible miracles of creation, subdivided according to these five categories of Grade A miracles, are listed in Appendix 2. One that is not listed (except for the special case of Saul's conversion) is the great miracle of regeneration (2 Cor. 5:17). Because of its frequent occurrence (whenever a sinner truly repents and opens his mind and heart to the saving grace of Christ) its miraculous character may be overlooked. Nevertheless, it is a true miracle of creation, accomplished directly by God himself, in the believer's life.

## Miracles of Providence in the Bible

In general, miracles of creation represent exceptions to the basic laws of nature, within which all processes normally function. The processes themselves, on the other hand, may and do vary quite substantially in their rates and models of operation, though always within the framework of these basic laws. For example, water may flow slowly or rapidly, depending on circumstances, but it always flows downhill (unless forced uphill by a pump or other special energy source). A man may live 20 years or 100 years, but he eventually dies.

Every process, without exception, thus varies around some average rate and manner of operation. The specific rate and manner depend on many factors, and if one or more of these factors change, then the rate or other characteristics of the process will change. For example, the frequency of earthquakes in a given region will depend on the character of the rocks, the rates of movement of different rock masses, existence of previous fractures, flow of heat from the earth's interior, and many other factors. Specific earthquakes are almost impossible to predict because so many variables affect their frequency. The same is true with every other process; all are variable to one degree or another.

As long as a process operates within its ordinary range of variation, this variability is expected. If, however, a given process in a given situation occurs at a highly unusual rate or in a very unusual manner, it might very well be recognized as a secondary class of miracle — a Grade B miracle. It would function within the basic laws of nature, operating in accord with God's providential ordering of its processes, but might be so nearly unique as to require some special explanation, more than mere statistical shuffling of influencing factors.

Many of the Bible miracles seem to fit this definition. Appendix 3 shows a listing of these, totaling approximately 127 in number. In some cases, the assignment of a particular miracle to Grade B instead of Grade A is open to question, so the reader may feel free to reassign it if he prefers. Similarly, the subdivisions discussed below are somewhat arbitrary, but it is helpful at least to attempt to organize the data in this fashion.

All such providential miracles involve very unusual, if not unique, rates or timing of processes or events that otherwise could not be considered quite natural and that, in any case, do not require intervention in the basic laws of science. Some of these (e.g., healing miracles) are sufficiently alike in character to form a convenient subdivision. All are more than just normal "coincidences" and more than just normal variations in processes, suggesting that there is some intelligent agent involved, able to understand and manipulate one or more of the factors that can control the rate or timing of the event.

That intelligent agent could, of course, be God himself, but it also could be one of God's angels. As noted before, a number of these miracles are specifically said to be due to angelic intervention; and it could well be that most of them (except those done directly by Christ himself) involve angels, all, of course, acting under divine direction "hearkening unto the voice of his word" (Ps. 103:20). That angels have great understanding of natural processes is indicated by such Scriptures as 2 Samuel 14:20, in the words of the "wise woman of Tekoah": "according to the wisdom of an angel of God, to know all things that are in the earth." That they have the ability to manipulate natural processes is indicated by Psalm 103:20: ". . . his angels, that excel in strength."

There are many of these providential miracles that quite clearly indicate such unusual control of some natural process. An example is the case of Gideon's wet fleece on the dry ground and then the dry fleece on the wet ground (Judg. 6:38, 40). A New Testament example is Peter's release from prison by the angel (Acts 12:5–7).

The above involved physical processes. A control of biological processes is indicated by the migration of animals to Noah's ark (Gen. 6:20) and by the remarkable catch of fishes in Luke 5:6.

Numerous examples are given of the drastic acceleration of decay processes in human bodies. These miracles could be considered as the reverse of the healing miracles. The plague of boils on the people of Egypt (Exod. 9:10) is one of the numerous Old Testament examples. The sudden death of Ananias and Sapphira (Acts 5:5, 10) is one of the relatively few New Testament examples.

As noted before, many healing miracles apparently require the direct creative power of God. More of them, however, seem merely to suggest an effect on the body's normal healing processes. The miraculous healing of the serpent bites (Num. 21:8) and the removal of Zacharias's dumbness (Luke 1:64) are examples.

A special type of healing miracle is that of curing demon possession. Quite a number of these cases also involve healing physical infirmities caused by the demons. Apparently the only Old Testament example is that of the evil spirit of Saul who was cast out when David played the harp (1 Sam. 16:23). The most spectacular case in the New Testament was the expulsion by Christ of a legion of demons from two men in the Gadarene tombs (Matt. 8:28–32).

A final type of Grade B miracle is what, for want of a better name, we can call the providential timing of events. The remarkable account of Rebekah's meeting with Abraham's servant (Gen. 24:14–15) is a good case in point. Apparently the only specific New Testament example — at least in which a more direct intervention in natural processes was not also involved — was the catching of a fish that had swallowed a coin needed for tribute money (Matt. 17:27).

## Satanic and Demonic Miracles

The Bible authors, of course, do recognize still another type of miracle, speaking of "the working of Satan with all power and signs and lying wonders" (2 Thess. 2:9). Such miracles cannot be considered miracles of creation, of course, since only God can create. They would have to be analogous to providential miracles, although certainly they have nothing in common with God's providential care of His creation, nor with the purpose of other providential miracles.

Satan and his angels, however, still have great ability to affect natural processes, just as do God's holy angels. These evil spirits are also able in some cases even to enter human bodies and human minds, controlling to a greater or lesser degree their physiological and mental processes.

The purpose of demonic miracles, of course, is exactly the opposite of that of true providential miracles. They are "lying wonders," intended to turn men away from God and His will.

Some satanic miracles seem superficially to require creative powers, but it is not possible that Satan or his demons could truly create anything. There is only one true God and Creator of all things. Therefore, we can be sure that such apparent satanic miracles of creation are counterfeit miracles, miracles of deception, contrived to work on human minds or eyes to produce the appearance of creation, but not genuine creation.

For example, the Egyptian magicians were seemingly able to duplicate Moses' feat of turning rods into serpents (Exod. 7:11–12). These, however, could not have been true serpents. They seemed to be so, but were evidently an "enchantment" or illusion generated in the minds of the watchers. Read the passage "they became [as] serpents." The rods were, in reality, still rods, for the next verse says that "Aaron's rod swallowed up their *rods*" (not their "serpents").

Similarly these magicians were able by some form of mental or genetic manipulation to make the waters seem as blood (Exod. 7:22) and to imitate Moses' miracle of bringing the frogs into the land (Exod. 8:7), though only Moses could rid the land of the frogs (Exod. 8:13). What should seem to have been much easier than producing frogs — namely, producing lice — these magicians were completely unable to duplicate (Exod. 8:18–19).

In the wilderness temptation, Satan was somehow able seemingly to transport Christ to the pinnacle of the temple and to a high mountain (Matt. 4:5, 8). Again, however, this must have been some form of mental projection or vision rather than an actual physical transportation. Christ might have gone with him "in the Spirit" to these places, but to move His human body there would have required creative powers that Satan does not possess.

A list of these counterfeit miracles — apparent miracles of creation and apparent miracles of providence — is given in appendix 4.

## Criteria for Testing Alleged Miracles

The essential criterion for distinguishing between divine miracles and demonic miracles, of course, is always the fidelity of the teaching of the miracle-worker to the Word of God. During the days of the Exodus, when the Israelites were encountering the idolatrous demonism of the Canaanites, Moses gave them this rule: "If there arise among you a prophet, or a dreamer of dreams, and giveth thee a sign or a wonder, And the sign or the wonder come to pass, whereof he spake unto thee, saying, Let us go after other gods, which thou hast not known, and let us serve them; Thou shalt not hearken unto the words of that prophet, or that dreamer of dreams" (Deut. 13:1–3).

Similarly, in the days of the apostasy of Judah under King Ahaz, both the king and the people were turning increasingly to idolatry and all its demonic associations. Finally the prophet Isaiah came with this warning: "And when they shall say unto you, Seek unto them that have familiar spirits, and unto wizards that peep, and that mutter: should not a people seek unto their God? for the living to the dead? To the law and to the testimony: if they speak not according to this word, it is because there is no light in them" (Isa. 8:19–20). Similarly, Paul warned that even "ministers of righteousness" and "angels of light" should be repudiated if they preached "another Jesus" or "another gospel" than he had preached (2 Cor. 11:4, 14–15).

Entirely apart from this question, of course, is the important question of determining whether or not any alleged miracle (be it either demonic or divine) is really a miracle at all, or is strictly a natural phenomenon. As stressed already, true miracles — especially miracles of creation — are quite rare, even in the Bible. Most members of the scientific establishment would deny their existence altogether.

Nevertheless, if God exists, miracles can happen and, if the Bible is true, they have happened. Therefore, the question devolves simply upon the character of the evidence for the miracle and the existence of an adequate purpose for the miracle.

God does not leave himself without witness (Acts 14:17) nor does He expect us to follow cunningly devised fables (2 Pet. 1:16). If a true divine miracle has occurred, we can be sure the evidence for it will be quite adequate for anyone who is willing to believe God.

At the same time, God is not capricious, going about performing miracles either to satisfy carnal curiosity or to compel people to believe on Him against their wills. Jesus, in fact, gave a stern rebuke to such as these. He said: "An evil and adulterous generation seeketh after a sign" (Matt. 12:39); and, "Except ye see signs and wonders, ye will not believe" (John 4:48).

There are, then, two questions that should be asked and critically analyzed in the case of any supposed miracle: (1) Is there adequate evidence, both circumstantial and testimonial, that the miracle really occurred? (2) Is there adequate reason, consistent with God's character and purposes, for Him to interfere in such a way with His established and good laws?

If both of these questions can be answered positively and unequivocally in the affirmative, then there is no reason further to question that a true miracle of God has taken place.

If both questions must be answered negatively or doubtfully, then one is warranted in rejecting the miracle. The same is true even if only the first answer is negative, since we can know the real purposes of God only to the extent that He has revealed them in His Word. It would be quite presumptuous to affirm that our will must be His will and that, therefore, a miracle is warranted in some given situation.

If there does exist good evidence for the miracle, but its purpose is equivocal, raising questions about God's Word rather than supporting it, then the possibility of a demonic miracle must be considered.

Now in the case of the divine miracles of Scripture, both questions can always be answered positively. There is always indicated a clear reason for every miracle — either to confirm the spoken word of God or His prophet, to meet some serious human need, or to advance the purposes of God on earth. Never is a miracle performed carelessly or cruelly or deceptively.

As far as evidence is concerned, the mere fact of its being recorded in the Bible should be sufficient. The authority and integrity, the reliability and historicity, of the Scriptures — not to mention their divine inspiration — have been documented and demonstrated over and over again in countless books on Christian evidences written down through the centuries. The internal claims, the fulfilled prophecies, the archaeological confirmations, the impact on human lives — these and many other evidences continually proclaim the truthfulness of the Bible.

Furthermore, many of the more significant and hard-to-believe miracles — the great Flood, the long day of Joshua, the preservation of Jonah in the whale, the virgin birth of Christ, the resurrection of Christ, and others — are also supported by extra-biblical evidences. A few of these key miracles will be discussed in later chapters, in the context of these sciences they are supposed to contradict. In any case, Christian believers are on solid ground when they insist on the absolute historicity of every one of the 230 or so miracles of the Bible.

## Extra-biblical Miracles

There have, of course, been great numbers of miracles claimed through the centuries. All of these alleged miracles, as well as those that supposedly occur today, can be evaluated by the criteria of the previous section. None can begin to compare with the Bible miracles.

There are several groups of miracles that are typical of these particular phenomena: (1) the miracles claimed in ancient and modern paganism, (2) the miracles reported in early Christian apocryphal literature, (3) the miracles of the medieval church, (4) the miracles of witchcraft and occultism, and (5) the miracles of modern charismatic Christianity.

Each of these groups could warrant extended study, but that is not within the scope of our purpose here. As far as the miracles of paganism, witchcraft, and occultism are concerned, it is obvious from the biblical perspective that all such miracles, if genuine, were and are demonic, since all are done in the name of systems diametrically opposed to biblical Christianity. Actually, it is highly probable that the great majority of such miracles are not true miracles at all.

The same is true of the many miracle stories of the apocryphal literature associated with the apostolic and post-apostolic periods. Many of these have to do with the childhood and juvenile exploits of the boy Jesus, as well as His supposed travels to other lands and the wonders performed therein. Miracles of this sort, of course, completely fail the test of conforming to the character and purposes of God, as well as the test of witness reliability.

The miracles of the medieval church and of the modern charismatic movement must be considered more carefully, since they often do claim to satisfy our two criteria. The Roman Catholic Church professes always to make a thorough and critical investigation before accepting an asserted miracle in its system as authentic, and modern charismatic Christians have accumulated a vast array of testimonies supporting their claims of healings and other miracles. As professedly Christian groups, they maintain that a good purpose is also served by these miracles, encouraging the faithful and winning converts to Christianity. These are significant arguments and must be taken seriously.

On the other hand, while there is little doubt that Grade B miracles have occurred among these groups, there does remain considerable room for skepticism about alleged Grade A miracles (for example, claims of raising the dead, instantaneous restoration of broken limbs, and other phenomena that would require miraculous creative intervention to set aside either the law of conservation of mass/energy or the law of entropy or both). Though some alleged miracles of this sort have been reported, it almost inevitably turns out that the testimonial and other supporting evidences are much weaker, and the possibilities of mistake or demonic deception much greater, than for the commoner Grade B miracles.

Also, it should be remembered that, with the completion of the New Testament, one of the main reasons for the apostolic miracles had been removed. They were for "confirming the word with signs following" (Mark 16:20), "God also bearing them witness, both with signs and wonders, and with divers miracles" (Heb. 2:4). Until the inspired New Testament Scriptures were available for the churches, the early Christians had to be guided largely by their own teachers and prophets, the validity of whose teaching was discerned and confirmed by the existence of miraculous gifts in the church — including miracles, healings, speaking in different tongues, interpreting tongues, prophecy, inspired knowledge, etc. (see 1 Cor. 12:8–12, 28). It had also been clearly taught by the apostle Paul that, eventually, these miraculous gifts would cease (1 Cor. 13:8), "when that which is perfect is come" (1 Cor. 13:10). Whether the timing of this withdrawal would be the completion of the Scriptures at the end of the apostolic period or the return of Christ at the end of the church age has, not surprisingly, become a point of contention between different groups of Christians.

It is not within the purpose of this book to attempt to settle this particular question. In the interest of both sound doctrine and sound science, however, Christians should remember several basic truths related to the question of modern-day miracles, as follows:

1. Miracles — even Grade A miracles — are certainly possible today, since God exists.
2. Miracles — especially Grade A miracles — must nevertheless be rare today, since God's "laws of nature" are good laws and since the main need for such miracles ceased with the completion and dissemination of the New Testament Scriptures.
3. Satanic deceptions are prophesied to increase in the last days, so there is an ever-increasing need for very critical testing (in terms of both evidence and purpose) of any alleged miracle before ascribing it to God.
4. Phenomena which are reproducible by standard techniques (e.g., many psychosomatic healings and modern-day ecstatic utterances) fall within the scope of the scientific method by that very fact, and hence do not require a supernatural explanation.
5. Jesus rebuked those of His own generation who were seeking miraculous signs and such a rebuke would apply even more urgently today, since the completed Scriptures are "profitable" for every need, adequate to make the man of God "perfect, throughly furnished unto all good works" (2 Tim. 3:16–17).

With all these cautions, however, we still must not close this discussion on a negative or skeptical note. Miracles do occur today. As pointed out before, the new birth is a true miracle of creation, whereby a lost sinner is regenerated and made a new creation in Christ Jesus (2 Cor. 5:17). Although the created "image of God" was not destroyed or annihilated by Adam's fall or each individual's sin, it died, so that each unregenerated person is spiritually "dead in trespasses and sins (Eph. 2:1). God's direct creative power, through the Holy Spirit, must be exercised before a person can become "alive unto God through Jesus Christ our Lord" (Rom. 6:11). The dormant "image" is then quickened, and the person "put[s] on the new man, which is renewed in knowledge after the image of him that created him" (Col. 3:10). This is a Grade A miracle in every sense of the word, completely inexplicable by the processes of psychology or any other science.

Furthermore, Grade B miracles can and do occur in the lives and experiences of countless Christians. The angels of God are "ministering spirits" for the "heirs of salvation" (Heb. 1:14) and are well able to modify process rates, to provide providential guarding and guiding of their assigned charges, to organize participants in the timing of particular events, to speed up or to retard the innate decay and/or healing processes in the human body, and to manipulate many phenomena short of actual creation. As directed by God, in answer to believing prayer by obedient Christians, "great and mighty things" (Jer. 33:3) can be accomplished on our behalf through these faithful and powerful servants.

4

# SCIENCE FALSELY SO CALLED

*Biblical Evolutionism*

In spite of the fact that the true scientific world view is fully compatible with the world view of biblical Christianity, and in spite of the fact that modern science is actually founded on this biblical view of the world, with most of the great founders of modern science having been Bible-believing, God-fearing, creationist Christians, most people today have come to believe that the Bible is either antiscientific or ascientific. Decades of classroom indoctrination in a purely secular world view have produced a secularized society, with most men and women still professing a nominal belief in God but living their lives in what they consider the "real" world — the world of science and technology, history and politics, business and economics, amusement and recreation — as though God was so long ago and far away as to be of no practical concern to people today.

This was not the way it used to be. The American colonies were founded by people to whom God was very real and whose lives were ordered by His biblical commands. The schools they established were based on biblical principles and priorities, and later the Declaration of Independence itself was framed in terms of human rights and responsibilities with respect to their Creator. As the historian Ostrander has reminded us: "The American nation had been founded by intellectuals who had accepted a world view that was based upon biblical authority as well as Newtonian science. They had assumed that God created the earth and all life upon it at the time of creation and continued without change thereafter. Adam and Eve were God's final creations, and all of mankind was descended from them."[1]

Such beliefs naturally generated great respect for the Ten Commandments

---

1. Gilman M. Ostrander, *The Evolutionary Outlook, 1875–1900* (Clio, MI: Marston Press, 1971), p. 1.

and the moral teachings of the entire Bible. Generations of instruction in the McGuffey Readers then produced not only a highly literate nation but also a nation of the highest morality and spirituality to be found anywhere among the nations of the world.

## The Impact of Evolutionary Thought

Why, then, the great difference between then and now? The fundamental reason is the supposed triumph of evolutionism in the 19th century, which displaced America's former God-centered view of the world with a man-centered humanism.

> . . . . after a generation of argument, educated Americans in general came to accept the fact of evolution and went on to make whatever intellectual adjustments they thought necessary. . . .
>
> In a nation that was undergoing a tremendous urban, industrial, and technological revolution, the evolutionary concept presented itself to intellectuals as the key to knowledge. And beyond that, the technical needs of industry called for a revolution in higher education away from the traditional classical and moral orientation and toward the sciences . . . which were reclassifying man and society in evolutionary terms. In general, the concept of education from kindergarten to graduate school was reoriented from the teaching of a fixed body of knowledge to the teaching of methods of inquiry to be applied to the continually changing facts of existence.[2]

Evolutionary philosophy had been increasingly influential in the so-called Christian world, for many decades before Charles Darwin, but his famous book *The Origin of Species by Natural Selection* became the great watershed. Before 1859, creationism and the biblical world view still dominated western thought. Within one decade after its publication, however, Darwinism was widely accepted in England and, not long afterwards, in continental Europe and the United States, and the world has never been the same since.

> Before Darwin, the adaptations and the diversity of organisms were accepted as facts without an explanation, or, more frequently, they were attributed to the omniscient design of the Creator. God had created birds and butterflies in the air, fish and coral reefs in the oceans, trees in the forest, and most of all, He had created man. God had provided man with eyes so that he might see and had given gills to fish to breathe oxygen in water. Theologians frequently argued that the functional design of organisms evinces the existence of a wise Creator. . . . Darwin . . . provided a natural explanation for these facts — the theory of natural selection . . . substituting a scientific teleology for a theological one.[3]

---

2. Ibid., p. 2.
3. Francisco J. Ayala, "Biological Evolution: Natural Selection or Random Walk?" *American Scientist,* 62 (Nov.–Dec. 1974): 692.

For the devout of past centuries such perfection of adaptation seemed to provide irrefutable proof of the wisdom of the Creator. For the modern biologist it is evidence for the remarkable effectiveness of natural selection.[4]

By the time of the Darwinian centennial in 1959, this naturalistic view had prevailed so pervasively that its keynote speaker, Sir Julian Huxley, could make the following pronouncement: "Charles Darwin has rightly been described as the 'Newton of Biology'; he did more than any single individual before or since to change man's attitude to the phenomena of life and to provide a coherent scientific framework of ideas for biology, in place of an approach in large part compounded of hearsay, myth, and superstition. He rendered evolution inescapable as a fact, comprehensible as a process, all-embracing as a concept."[5]

As Sir Julian pointed out, evolutionism was not merely a biological theory, it was an all-embracing concept. This same point has been stressed by many others, from the time of Darwin on. A typical expression of this claim was made in a Sigma Xi lecture at Virginia Tech by a Wisconsin University professor: "Twentieth century biology rests on a foundation of evolutionary concepts. . . . The evolutionary basis is also apparent in peripheral independent fields such as chemistry, geology, physics and astronomy. No central scientific concept is more firmly established in our thinking, our methods, and our interpretations, than that of evolution."[6] Once "evolution" was considered to have been proved by science, it was inevitable that it would be applied in the social sciences, the humanities, economics, business, politics, and indeed, in every area of life — even religion. And, as Ostrander said, it quickly caused a complete reorientation of education, from kindergarten through graduate school, stressing the "continually changing facts of existence."

Even religion was considered to be the product of "evolution," to be interpreted and applied strictly in an evolutionary context, with little or no reference to biblical criteria. Dr. Theodosius Dobzhansky wrote, "Man has evolved from ancestors that were not human. . . . The creation of God's image in man is not an event but a process, and therefore the moral law is a product of an evolutionary development."[7] Now if morals are merely the products of evolution,[8] they will no

4. Ernst Mayr, "Behavior Programs and Evolutionary Strategies," *American Scientist*, 62 (Nov.–Dec. 1974): 650.

5. Julian Huxley, "The Emergence of Darwinism," in *The Evolution of Life*, vol. 1 of *Evolution after Darwin* (Chicago, IL: University of Chicago Press, 1960), p. 1. Sir Julian, grandson of Thomas Huxley (colleague and protagonist of Charles Darwin), was probably the most influential evolutionist of the 20th century, the first Director General of UNESCO, and the main developer and propagator of neo-Darwinism.

6. Stanley D. Beck, "Natural Science and Creationist Theology," *Bioscience*, 32 (Oct. 1982): 738.

7. Theodosius Dobzhansky, "Ethics and Values in Biological and Cultural Evolution," *Zygon, the Journal of Religion and Science*, as reported in the *Times* (Los Angeles) (June 16, 1974), part 4, p. 6.

8. In this book, unless otherwise noted, the term "evolution" is used only in the sense of "macroevolution," or "mega-evolution." So-called "micro-evolution" is, despite the claims of many evolutionists to the contrary, really only "variation" within limits, at the same level of complexity.

doubt continue to evolve to conform to the ever-changing facts of existence. Rather than being determined by the eternal standards of God's Word, they will be whatever the great cause of continuing evolution may warrant. On this, Dobzhansky wrote, "Natural selection can favor egotism, hedonism, cowardice instead of bravery, cheating and exploitation, while group ethics in virtually all societies tend to counteract or forbid such 'natural behavior,' and to glorify their opposites: kindness, generosity, and even self-sacrifice for the good of others of one's tribe or nation and finally of mankind."[9] Dobzhansky, one of the world's greatest geneticists, was a professing Christian, but the god in which he believed was a pantheistic god, certainly not the God of Scripture. To him, God was essentially the grand process of "evolution": "Evolution on the cosmic, biological, and human levels are parts of one grand process of universal evolution."[10] Thus, evolution pervades everything and, in fact, is everything!

If even religion and morality are products of evolution, then, for all practical purposes, evolution is religion and morality. The only legitimate world view, the only scientific philosophy of life and meaning, is general evolution, according to doctrinaire evolutionists. Julian Huxley said, "The whole of reality is evolution — a single process of self-transformation."[11] And the notorious Jesuit priest-anthropologist de Chardin rhapsodized, "[Evolution] is a general postulate to which all theories, all hypotheses, all systems must henceforward bow and which they must satisfy in order to be thinkable and true. Evolution is a light which illuminates all facts, a trajectory which all lines of thought must follow."[12]

Not all evolutionists regard evolution in such a universalistic and religious light as do these men, of course. Nevertheless, the leaders of evolutionary thought, for the most part, do. Julian Huxley, Teilhard de Chardin, and Theodosius Dobzhansky were, by any standard, the leading evolutionists of the 20th century, and this was their point of view. The same is true of John Dewey, the architect of our public school system, who consciously built his curricular philosophy on Darwinism and evolutionary pantheism, and whose educational methodology has infected schools all over the world.

The modern crop of leading evolutionists, men such as Carl Sagan, Stephen Jay Gould, Isaac Asimov, and others, tend to be more frankly atheistic in their approach (many, such as Gould, are admittedly Marxists). For example, the most

---

9. Dobzhansky, "Ethics and Values," p. 6. Dobzhansky was probably, next to Julian Huxley, the most influential evolutionist of the 20th century.

10. Ibid.

11. Julian Huxley, "Evolution and Genetics," in *What Is Science?* J.R. Newman, ed. (New York, NY: Simon and Schuster, 1955), p. 278.

12. Pierre Teilhard de Chardin, as cited by Francisco Ayala, " 'Nothing in Biology Makes Sense Except in the Light of Evolution': Theodosius Dobzhansky, 1900–1975," *Journal of Heredity*, 68, no. 3 (1977): 3. This article was written as a tribute to the recently deceased Dobzhansky, who had adopted de Chardin's evaluation of evolution as his own belief. The original statement was written by de Chardin in his book *The Phenomenon of Man* (New York, NY: Harper and Row, 1965), p. 219.

prolific science writer of our times — probably any time — was Isaac Asimov, and he had stated his position as follows:

> I am an atheist, out and out. It took me a long time to say it. I've been an atheist for years and years, but somehow I felt it was intellectually unrespectable to say one was an atheist, because it assumed knowledge that one didn't have. Somehow it was better to say one was a humanist or an agnostic. I finally decided that I'm a creature of evolution as well as of reason. Emotionally I am an atheist. I don't have the evidence to prove that God doesn't exist, but I so strongly suspect he doesn't that I don't want to waste my time.[13]

It is clearly evident from the above testimony that atheism is every bit as "religious" as theism. Atheism is not based on scientific proof, but on emotion! No wonder atheistic evolutionists become so emotional in their objections to creationism, no matter how coolly and objectively creationists try to present their scientific evidence for creation.

That evolution itself is basically a religion is acknowledged by leading evolutionist Michael Ruse. "Evolution is promoted by its practitioners as more than mere science. Evolution is promulgated as an ideology, a secular religion — a full-fledged alternative to Christianity, with meaning and morality. . . . That was true of evolution in the beginning, and it is true of evolution still today."[14]

Again, it is readily acknowledged that not all evolutionists are atheists. Most evolutionists are probably theistic evolutionists of one variety or another. The writer himself was a theistic evolutionist throughout his college years.

Nevertheless, the evolutionary model of origins and development is itself fundamentally atheistic (or possibly pantheistic, which is merely a semantic variant of atheistic, for if God is everything in general, He is nothing in particular), since it purports to explain everything without God. If God is imposed on the evolutionary process at all, it is purely arbitrary. He is not *needed* and therefore is actually redundant.

This, of course, is why all the leaders of evolutionary thought are atheists (or pantheists, humanists, or agnostics — softer words that really mean the same thing).

## Evolutionary Religions

It is significant, and not too surprising despite the common claim that creationism is religion while evolution is science, that most of the world's religions are based on evolution rather than creation. This is true not only of atheism and humanism, which are certainly religious systems rather than sciences, but also of the various

---

13. Isaac Asimov in Paul Kurtz, ed., "An Interview with Isaac Asimov on Science and the Bible," *Free Inquiry*, 2 (Spring 1982): 9.
14. Michael Ruse, "Saving Darwin from the Darwinians," *National Post* (May 13, 2000): B-3. Ruse is a prominent philosopher of science and ardent Darwinist, author of many books and articles defending evolution.

ethnic religions such as Buddhism, Confucianism, Taoism, and others. None of these religions involve belief in a personal Creator God who created the universe. To them the universe itself is the ultimate reality and the only eternal entity. Men and women, like all other forms of life, are mere products of the forces of the universe.

In this connection, an interesting relation has been noted between the Taoist concept of evolution and modern "revolutionary evolutionism," the idea that evolutionary advance is sudden rather than gradual and that it is generated by violent perturbations in the environment. This concept is now widely associated with neocatastrophism in geology and punctuationism in biology. "The new systems biology shows that fluctuations are crucial in the dynamics of self-organization. . . . The idea of fluctuations as the basis of order, which Nobel laureate Ilya Prigogine introduced into modern science, is one of the major themes in all Taoist texts. The mutual interdependence of all aspects of reality and the non-linear nature of its interconnections are emphasized throughout Eastern mysticism."[15]

Modern Buddhists, Hindus, Confucianists, Shintoists, Lamaists, and advocates of other great ethnic religions, as well as Taoists and other Eastern mystics, all maintain that their religions are "scientific" because they harmonize so well with modern evolutionism. In fact, the only world religions that assume a primeval special creation of all things, including that of the universe itself, are those based on the Bible and thus, ultimately on the first chapter of the Bible, namely Christianity, Judaism, and Islam. Even these, of course, are now mostly "liberalized," with large segments of each of these faiths now promoting theistic evolution rather than real creation (see sections later in this chapter).

The same reliance on some form of evolution has also characterized all the great religions of the past. For example, one of the most ancient nations is that of Egypt. That the religion of the early Egyptians was one of pantheistic evolutionism was pointed out by one of the greatest Egyptologists, Wallis Budge. Referring to the ancient Egyptian myth of origins entitled *The Book of Knowing the Evolutions of Ra*, this author says, "Returning to our narrative we find that the god continues, 'I came into being from primeval matter, and I appeared under the form of multitudes of things from the beginning. Nothing existed at that time, and it was I who made whatsoever was made.' "[16]

Note that this "god" of Egypt, the great Ra, was not an eternal god, but had come into existence "from primeval matter," indicating therefore that only matter is eternal, with everything — including the "gods" — having somehow evolved from primeval matter. Furthermore, it is significant that the dominant aspect of this primeval matter was *water*. In the narrative, the god continues as follows: "I made all the forms under which I appeared by means (or out of) the god-soul which I raised up out of Nu [i.e., the primeval inactive abyss of water]."[17]

15. Fritjof Capra, "The Dance of Life," *Science Digest,* 90 (Apr. 1982): 33.
16. E. A. Wallis Budge, *The Gods of the Egyptians*, vol. 1 (New York, NY: Dover, 1969), p. 302.
17. Ibid.

The only civilization more ancient than that of Egypt was in Sumeria, centered around Babel, which was built and ruled originally by the great Nimrod (Gen. 10:8–10). The original cosmogonic myth of the Sumerians was the *Enuma Elish*. "Specifically, *Enuma Elish* assumes that all things have evolved out of water. This description presents the earliest stage of the universe as one of watery chaos. . . . Then, in the midst of this watery chaos two gods came into existence — Lahau and Lahamu."[18] Again, it was the universe alone that was believed to be eternal and, as in Egypt, its earliest form was that of omnipresent water.

According to the Bible, all the ancient nations developed from the different families radiating out from Babel after the confusion of tongues. Even though their languages were different, they all still retained the same false concept of cosmogony taught them by Nimrod, the great rebel against God. This false religion, with its false cosmogony and its false pantheon of gods (the "host of heaven"), thus became the progenitor of all the world's religion systems. The gods and goddesses (with different but equivalent names in the different languages) became the objects of worship in the polytheistic popular religions of the nations. The equivalent host of heaven in the cosmic constellations became the basis of the ubiquitous system of astrology, which also assumed an important role in the various religions. The true host of heaven, the true gods and goddesses, were the evil spirits, the demons, the vast host of fallen angels who had followed Satan in his primeval rebellion against his Creator. These were the real spiritual entities possessing the idols and oracles, as well as the mediums and witch doctors of the spiritists and animists. But all were mere manifestations — or evolutionists — of the primeval matter from which they had been derived by the forces of the cosmos. Thus, it is the universe itself that is the god and maker of all things, according to the world's great religions, both ancient and modern, except the monotheistic faiths (such as Judaism, Islam, and Christianity) who accept the Genesis cosmogony. It is true also of modern atheism and evolutionary humanism.

The real author of this vast religious complex — this great world religion of pantheistic, polytheistic, demonistic, astrological, occultistic, humanistic evolutionism — can be none other than the one who is called in the Bible the "god of this world" (2 Cor. 4:4), the one "which deceiveth the whole world" (Rev. 12:9). The Lord Jesus called him "a liar, and the father of it" (John 8:44). He is "the dragon, that old serpent, which is the Devil, and Satan" (Rev. 20:2).

Satan once was Lucifer (Isa. 14:12), God's "anointed cherub" (Ezek. 28:14), the highest of all created angels. However, desiring to be the chief god himself, he rebelled against the true God, leading a third of the angels with him (Isa. 14:12–15; Ezek. 28:15, 17; Rev. 12:3–4, 7–9). God, therefore, cast him and his followers (now the evil spirits, or demons) to the earth, and will eventually consign them to the lake of fire (Matt. 25:41; Rev. 20:10).

---

18. Thorkild Jacobsen, "Enuma Elish — the Babylonian Genesis," in *Theories of the Universe*, Milton K. Munitz, ed. (Glencoe, IL: The Free Press, 1957), p. 9.

In the meantime, Satan is seeking to turn men away from God by every means he can devise. He tries to persuade men that there is no real Creator God who created the very universe itself. The lie of modern humanism is the same ancient lie with which he deceived Adam and Eve — "ye shall be as gods" (Gen. 3:4–5). Whatever the particular deception may be in the particular case (there are, according to 1 Cor. 8:5–6, "gods many, and lords many," though only "one God, the Father, of whom are all things"), his common tactic is to persuade people to "change the truth of God into a lie, and worship and serve the creature more than the Creator, who is blessed for ever" (Rom. 1:25).

Such universal slander against the Creator is, of course, necessary before Satan can ever hope to replace Him on the throne of the universe. He must persuade both men and angels that, since there is no real Creator, they can worship and obey whomever they choose — idols, animals, angels, spirits, other men, or even themselves. Eventually they will come to worship Satan (Matt. 4:8–10; Rev. 13:4).

Modern humanistic evolutionists, of course, scoff at such notions. They believe in neither God nor Satan, worshiping only themselves. So the idea that Satan invented the evolutionary concept and is using it as his vehicle to deceive the nations and to turn men away from God is to them naive foolishness. Our purpose here, however, is not to court the humanists, but to show Christians the great dangers in compromising with evolution. If such compromising Christians have a better explanation for the amazing fact that evolution can be so all pervasive among mankind without resting on a shred of scientific or biblical evidence, let them present it. A universal effect requires a universal cause, and the Scripture says that Satan has deceived the whole world (Rev. 12:9).

And he seems even to have deceived himself! He is bound to know, of course, that he did not create the universe or life or men, though no doubt he can perform great signs and wonders. If he really believes he can vanquish God, it must be that he has somehow persuaded himself that God is not really God.

It is not surprising, therefore, that both ancient and modern extra-biblical cosmogonies all start with "primeval matter," rather than God. Nor is it surprising that the most ancient of such cosmogonies, in Sumeria and Egypt, describe that primeval matter as being a watery chaos, out of which the first gods evolved. Indeed, God did first create a watery matrix when He created the space-mass-time cosmos (Gen. 1:2; 2 Pet. 3:5). It would be in the midst of these waters that the created angels first came into consciousness when God created them (Ps. 104:1–5), and it would be such an environment that would constitute Satan's earliest memories. Therefore, if he is determined to reject God's Word that He created him (which Satan must do if he is to rationalize his own ambition to dethrone God), he must necessarily attribute his "creation" to the waters where he was born.[19]

---

19. For a detailed study of the evolutionary basis of all ethnic religions, ancient and modern, as well as their origin in the evolutionary deceptions of Satan, see the writer's book *The Long War Against God* (Green Forest, AR: Master Books, 1989, 2000).

It is only to be expected, then, that evolutionary thinking is found at the root of not only most of the world's religions, but also of all sorts of humanistic philosophies and systems. The evolutionary basis of Nazism and racism, for example, is briefly but cogently documented in chapters 15 and 16. It is so well known that laissez-faire capitalism, communism, and both economic and military imperialism have been based on evolutionism that no documentation is even necessary.[20] Animalistic psychologies (e.g., Freudianism, behaviorism, the psychologies of B.F. Skinner, Carl Rogers, and others) are based squarely on evolution, as are the animalistic amoralities of recent years (e.g., homosexuality, promiscuity, abortion, drug-induced sensory experiences). When men worship the creature instead of the Creator, it is not surprising that they give way to "vile affections" and "a reprobate mind" (Rom. 1:26–32).

## Theistic Evolution

It is very remarkable, and very sad, that Christian people have always been so quick to compromise with such an atheistic philosophy as evolution. The biblical authors clearly reject such a notion, so there is no such thing as biblical evolution. The Lord Jesus Christ clearly taught special creation and accepted the literal historicity of the Genesis record, so there can be no such thing as Christian evolution. One can, indeed, be a Christian evolutionist (as the writer well knows from personal experience), but evolution itself can never be Christian.

Charles Darwin himself provides an ideal case study of the ultimate impact of evolutionary belief on Christian faith. As a young divinity student, preparing for the Christian ministry, Darwin was fully convinced of the truth and authority of the Scriptures, and of the strong evidence from design and causality for the existence of God as Creator. As he increasingly came to believe in evolution and natural selection, he increasingly lost his faith, finally becoming an atheist. Ernst Mayr, one of the top evolutionists today, tells the story: "It is apparent that Darwin lost his faith in the years 1836–39, much of it clearly prior to the reading of Malthus. In order not to hurt the feelings of his friends and of his wife, Darwin often used deistic language in his publications, but much in his Notebooks indicates that by this time he had become a 'materialist' [more or less = atheist]."[21] In other words, Mayr is telling us that Darwin's copious notes (only published in full in recent years) prove that he had become an atheist some 20 years before he published *The Origin of Species by Natural Selection*. Many modern apologists for Darwin have stressed that his book allowed for the special creation of the first living cell, but apparently this was just to avoid offending his Christian wife and friends.

Darwin also says in his book that evolution is "this grand view of life," and

---

20. Ibid. Full documentation of the multitudes of evil practices and philosophies based on evolutionism is also provided in Volume 3, *Society and Creation*, of the *Modern Creation Trilogy*, by Henry M. Morris and John D. Morris (Green Forest, AR: Master Books, 1996).

21. Ernst Mayr, "Darwin and Natural Selection," *American Scientist*, 65 (May–June 1977): 323.

many of his followers have likewise waxed eloquent about the majestic panorama of evolution, with the beautiful unfolding of higher and higher forms of life over the ages. Many theologians wrote about evolution as God's "method of creation," forgetting conveniently that it was all supposed to be accomplished by a brutal struggle for existence, with the weak perishing and only the fittest surviving. Darwin well understood all this, and despite the window dressing in his book, such beliefs surely contributed heavily to his becoming an atheist. "Nevertheless, it is highly probable that Darwin had been gradually conditioned by his reading to a far less benign interpretation of the struggle for existence than that held by the natural theologians. . . . By necessity, accepting evolutionary thinking undermined a continued adherence to a belief in a harmonious universe."[22]

Darwin became an invalid soon after abandoning his faith in God, the Bible, and creation. He realized the devastating impact he was having and would continue to have as he developed and published and promoted his God-dishonoring theories, and it made him a chronic invalid. But worse by far than the destructive effect on his own life was the awful legacy he left the world. Mayr points out that Darwin's own apostasy is still reflected in the very structure of Darwinism:

> One of these shifts has been rather consistently sidestepped by all those who have occupied themselves with the history of the theory of natural selection. It is the question of the extent that Darwin's loss of Christian faith affected the conceptual framework on which the theory of natural selections rests. . . . Adopting natural selection rather than the hand of God as the active factor responsible for all that was formerly considered evidence for design was, of course, the last step. However, even the acceptance of evolution was already a fatal undermining of natural theology.[23]

The decline and fall of Darwin's faith has been echoed in the experiences of multitudes of others since his day. One of the top modern-day evolutionists, founder and chief protagonist of the popular system known as sociobiology, has given this testimony: "As were many persons in Alabama, I was a born-again Christian. When I was fifteen, I entered the Southern Baptist Church with great fervor and interest in the fundamentalist religion; I left at seventeen when I got to the University of Alabama and heard about evolutionary theory."[24]

The writer spent over 28 years teaching in secular universities and saw this sad tale repeated in many lives. Philosopher Huston Smith also notes the connection between evolution and loss of faith: "Martin Lings is probably right in saying that 'more cases of loss of religious faith are to be traced to the theory of evolution . . . than to anything else.' "[25]

In spite of this record, however, there are multitudes of professing Christian

22. Ibid., p. 324.
23. Ibid., p. 327.
24. E.O. Wilson, "Toward a Humanist Biology," *The Humanist* (Sept.–Oct. 1982): 40.
25. Huston Smith, "Evolution and Evolutionism," *Christian Century* (July 7–14, 1982): 755.

people who think they can believe both the Bible and evolution — that evolution is merely God's method of creation. One can only say that anyone who believes this (as the writer once did himself) simply does not understand either evolution or the Bible or both.

A few of the many reasons why evolution cannot be harmonized with the biblical record of creation follow.

1. No less than ten times in the first chapter of Genesis God's dictum is recorded: "after his kind" (Gen. 1:11–12, 21, 24–25). Although the biblical "kind" (Hebrew *min*) is undoubtedly more flexible than the biological "species" (see chapter 13), this restriction certainly limits all variation to variation within the kind. Some may call this "microevolution," but "macroevolution" is clearly precluded (see also 1 Cor. 15:38–39).

2. At the end of the creation period, "God ended his work, which he had made; and . . . rested from all his work which God created and made" (Gen. 2:2–3; see also Heb. 4:3, 10). Consequently, present-day biological processes (variation, mutation, even speciation) could not be processes of creation or development, as theistic evolutionists must allege.

3. God pronounced all His work of creation to have been "very good" at the end of the six days of creation. Such an evaluation by an omniscient, loving God would be grotesquely inconsistent with a system of nature ruled by tooth and claw, a grinding struggle for existence, with only the fittest and more prolific surviving.

4. The Lord Jesus Christ, who is himself the Creator of all things (John 1:3), plainly taught that the Genesis record of creation, in both Genesis 1 and 2, was intended to be taken historically and literally (see Matt. 19:4–6; Mark 10:6–9). Note in particular His statement that "from the beginning of the creation God made them male and female" (Mark 10:6); not from the tail-end of evolutionary history, after four billion years, but from the beginning, God had made man and woman to have dominion over His creation. Otherwise the command to have dominion (Gen. 1:26, 28) would have been irrelevant for most of the creation.

5. Evolution is the most wasteful, inefficient, and heartless process that could ever be devised by which to produce man. If evolution is true, then billions upon billions of animals have suffered and died in a cruel struggle for existence for a billion years, and many entire kinds (e.g., dinosaurs) have appeared and then died out long before man evolved. The God of the Bible could never be guilty of such a cruel and pointless charade as this!

## Progressive Creation

Among evangelicals, a popular semantic variant of theistic evolution is a system called progressive creationism. There are many Christian intellectuals who feel it inexpedient to adopt a full-blown evolutionary position, and so they allow for a number of acts of special creation interspersed at various points throughout the long evolutionary process. That is, they suggest that perhaps God supernaturally created the first protozoan, then later possibly the different phyla, and eventually the first man and woman. Depending on the particular writer, there may have been few or many acts of special creation inserted by God at strategic stages in evolutionary history, but the overall process was still evolution. In progressive creationism, the same system of evolutionary geological ages and the same mechanisms of evolution (whatever they may be) are accepted as those used by the theistic evolutionist, or even by the atheistic evolutionist. The only differences are these occasional interjections of creation. This system allows its proponents to say that they believe in "special creation" instead of evolution, without experiencing the intellectual opprobrium attached to belief in "six-day creationism" or "flood geology."

Such a semantic game, however, is rightly repudiated by most scientists, who consider it unworthy of the scientific world view, a mere "god-of-the-gaps" device. That is, wherever there currently seems to be a significant gap in the fossil record or in the mechanism of evolutionary progress, then this might have been a point, they would say, where God stepped in to create something. As the gaps are filled in, however, by further paleontological collections or genetic manipulations, then God's role becomes progressively smaller and evolution's role progressively greater. Thus, progressive creation eventually yields to progressive evolution. In the final analysis, it is almost impossible, either scientifically or biblically, to distinguish between progressive creation and theistic evolution.

In fact, if one were forced to choose between only these two alternatives, theistic evolution would surely be the better choice. Not only would it be more acceptable to the scientific establishment, but it would also be less dishonoring to God. That is, the theistic evolutionist at least gives God credit for being able to design and energize the entire evolutionary process right from the beginning. The progressive creationist, however, visualizes a bumbling sort of god, one who has to come down at intervals to redirect the evolutionary process whenever it veers off target, or to re-energize the process whenever it begins to play out. Furthermore, the same objections we have already lodged against theistic evolution can also be lodged against progressive creation. Nothing whatever is gained — except semantic dissimulation — by advocating progressive creation instead of theistic evolution.

## Chronology of Genesis 1–11 and Geologic Time

Apart from the basic evolution/creation issue, the most serious area of tension between the Bible and the modern world view is that of the chronological framework of history. According to a straightforward reading of the biblical record, the world was created in six days only a few thousand years ago. On the other hand, modern cosmologists insist that the earth and the solar system developed about five billion years ago, that primitive life forms evolved from nonliving chemicals about four billion years ago, that all other forms of life have gradually developed during the subsequent geologic ages, and that, finally, man evolved into essentially his present form about one or two million years ago.

Thus, the biblical chronology is about a million times shorter than the evolutionary chronology. A millionfold mistake is no small matter, and biblical scholars surely need to give primary attention to resolving this tremendous discrepancy right at the very foundation of our entire biblical cosmology. This is not a peripheral issue that can be dismissed with some exegetical twist, but is central to the very integrity of scriptural theology.

The short biblical chronology depends primarily on three chapters, Genesis 1, 5, and 11. Chapter 1 deals mainly with pre-human chronology, chapter 5 with pre-Flood human chronology, and chapter 11 with post-Flood human chronology. The question to be settled is whether or not these chapters have been understood properly. Can chapter 1 possibly be reconciled with a 5-billion-year earth history and chapters 5 and 11 with a 1- or 2-million-year human history?

One hesitates even to consider the unfortunate type of exegesis that treats Genesis 1–11 as allegorical or mythical, rather than historical. Nevertheless, there seems to be an increasing number of evangelical scholars today who are advocating the notion that this section is only a great hymn, or liturgy, or poem, or saga — anything except real history! They seem unaware or unconcerned that this type of interpretation inevitably undermines all the rest of Scripture. If the first Adam is not real, and if therefore the Fall did not really take place, then neither is the Second Adam real, and there is no need of a Savior.

Genesis 1–11 is certainly recorded as serious and sober history, and it leads directly and naturally into Genesis 12 and the rest of Genesis. Genesis, in turn, is the necessary foundation for all the rest of Scripture. If these first 11 chapters are not historical, then our entire biblical foundation has been removed.

If we are permitted to interpret Genesis in this fashion, what is to prevent our interpreting any other part of Scripture in the same way! Thus, the Virgin Birth may, after all, be only an allegory, the Resurrection could be only a myth of suprahistory, the Ten Commandments only a liturgy, the crucifixion only a dream. Every man may interpret Scripture as suits his own convenience, and thus every man becomes his own god!

Such hermeneutical irresponsibility is condemned by the clean-cut acceptance of the records of Genesis 1–11 as historical by all the rest of Scripture and especially by Jesus Christ himself! Not surprisingly, this allegorical type of interpretation leads eventually and inevitably to the rejection of belief in biblical inspiration and, finally, of the gospel itself.

Recognizing that Genesis 1–11 does give us a truly historical record, there are only three possibilities for reinterpreting biblical chronology: (1) the day-age theory, which more or less equates the "days" of Genesis 1 with the "ages" of geology, thus placing the geological ages *during* the six days of creation; (2) the

## TABLE 2 — *Spectrum of Interpretive Theories About the Biblical Record of Creation*

*The straightforward biblical record of a literal six-day creation week contradicts the evolutionary geologic-age interpretation of the fossil record. However, all other interpretations of the Genesis account, designed to accommodate the "geologic ages," encounter irreconcilable theological, biblical, and scientific difficulties.*

| Theory of Interpretation | Relation Between Geologic Ages and Genesis Record of Six-Day Creation | Nature of Creation | Proponents | Explanation of Fossil Record and Geologic Column | Typical Difficulties | | |
| --- | --- | --- | --- | --- | --- | --- | --- |
| | | | | | Theological | Biblical | Scientific |
| *Naturalistic* | Geologic ages are historically true. Genesis is only a Hebrew legend. | Atheistic Evolution | Humanists | Actual record of the history of life. | Suffering and death before sin entered the world. | All things in six literal days (Exod. 20:11). | Universally missing transitional fossils illustrate complete lack of evidence for evolution. |
| *Framework* | Geologic ages are literally true. Genesis is a mere literary framework. | Theistic Evolution | Religious Liberals | Actual record of the history of life. | Suffering and death before sin entered the world. | All things in six literal days. (Exod. 20:11) | Universally missing transitional fossils illustrate complete lack of evidence for evolution. |
| *Day-Age* | Geologic ages occurred *during* the six days of creation. | Progressive Creation | Neo-Evangelicals | Actual record of the history of life. | Suffering and death before sin entered the world. | All things in six literal days. (Exod. 20:11) | Numerous contradictions between the order of events in the Genesis record and geologic-age system. |
| *Gap* | Geologic ages occurred *before* the six days of creation. | Irrelevant Creation | Pietistic Fundamentalists | Record of extinct life prior to supposed pre-Adamic cataclysm. | Suffering and death before sin entered the world. | All things in six literal days. (Exod. 20:11). | Geologic-age system precludes supposed pre-Adamic cataclysm. |
| *Literalist* | Geologic "ages" are merely taxonomic. Genesis days are literally true. | Special Creation | Biblical Theists | Primarily due to Noahic deluge and its residual effects. | None | None | Numerous difficulties with geologic-age system, but none with real scientific facts. |

pre-Adamic gap theory, which inserts a 5-billion-year gap between Genesis 1:1 and 1:2, thus placing the geological ages *before* the six days of creation; (3) the post-Adamic gap theory, which assumes one or more gaps in the genealogical lists of Genesis 5 and 11, thus permitting a human history of more than six thousand years. There are slight variants as well as the basic theories (see table 2). Each of these three theories will now be briefly considered.

### The Day-Age Theory

The Hebrew *yom* is occasionally used to mean "time" in an indefinite sense (e.g., the "day of the Lord") and this, together with a superficial correspondence between the order of events in Genesis 1 and in historical geology, has served as the basis for taking the Genesis account to mean six "times" of creation rather than six "days." However, there are numerous objections to this theory, some of which are as follows:

1. *Yom* never means a definite period of time, such as required in Genesis 1 by the circumscribing adjectives ("*first*[26] day," "*second* day," etc.), and terminal references ("evening and morning")[27] unless that period is a solar day.

2. The word is clearly defined the first time it is used (Gen. 1:5), where it says, "God called the light *yom*. . . . and the evening and the morning were the first *yom*." Thus, the "day" is defined as the "light" period in the succession of periods of "light" and "darkness." Even though the "lightbearer" may not have been set in its present form until the fourth *yom*, this passage plainly requires something essentially identical with the present axial rotation of the earth and the corresponding solar day. On the fourth day, the meaning is obviously literal, since the very purpose of the sun and moon is said to be to rule the "day" and "night."

3. When the word "days" appears in the plural (Hebrew *yamim*, as it does over seven hundred times in the Old Testament, it always seems to refer to literal days. Thus, in Exodus 20:11, when the Scripture says that "in six days the LORD made heaven and earth, the sea, and all that in them is," there can be no doubt that six literal days are meant. This passage also clearly equates the week of God's creative work with the week of man's work, and is without force if the two are not of the same duration.

4. If the intent of the writer had been to write of long ages of creation, he could certainly have done so. For example, the Hebrew word *olam* (meaning "long, indefinite time") should have been used instead of *yom*. The ancient people to whom he was writing were quite familiar with the idea of long ages and gradual development out of chaos, since all ancient cosmogonies involved great aeons of time and some kind of evolutionary development. But if his intent were to tell of

---

26. The use of a numeral or ordinal to modify "day" occurs over one hundred times in the Pentateuch alone and always indicates a real solar day.

27. The Hebrew words for "evening" and "morning" over one hundred times each in the Old Testament and always in the literal sense.

a literal creation in six solar days, it would be impossible to express this concept any more clearly than in the account as we actually have it.

5. The main purpose of the day-age theory is to try to fit the geological ages into the six days of creation. But even if the biblical exegesis would permit it, there are so many contradictions in the details of the two supposedly parallel accounts that the attempt is utterly futile. More than 20 of these contradictions are noted below.

a. Geologists say that the earth's waters gradually oozed out of its interior over long ages. Genesis says that the earth was covered with water right from the beginning (Gen. 1:2).

b. Genesis 1:7 speaks of a firmament (or "expanse" — evidently the atmosphere) separating two great reservoirs of water. Historical geologists completely reject this concept.

c. Geologists say that life originated in the primeval oceans. Genesis 1:11 says the first life was on the land.

d. Orthodox geologists believe that fish and other marine organisms developed long before fruit trees. (Genesis 1:11, 20, and 21 directly contradict this order.)

e. Evolutionary geology teaches that the sun and moon are at least as old as the earth, whereas Genesis 1:14–19 says they were made right in the middle of the period of creation, on the fourth day.

f. Genesis 1:16 says God made all the stars on the fourth day. Modern astronomers think the stars and galaxies evolved at different times, and most of them far earlier than the midpoint of the geologic ages!

g. Genesis says that plant life, even in such an advanced form as the fruit tree, was made one "day" before the sun and stars, but this would have been impossible if the day were really an aeon, since plants must have sunlight.

h. The standard system says insects came before birds, but the Bible says the "creeping things" (defined as insects in Lev. 11) were made on the sixth day and birds on the fifth day.

i. According to the Bible, birds and fishes were created at the same time (Gen. 1:21), but geologists believe that fishes evolved hundreds of millions of years before birds developed.

j. The evolutionist maintains that the first marine life was a minute blob of complex chemicals, but the Bible says that God caused an abundance of marine life (Gen. 1:20–21) in great variety when He first created it.

k. According to the Bible, the first animal *created* (implying the origin of sentient life, as distinct from plant life) was the "great whale," the largest animal that ever lived! Evolutionists postulate a long growth from the small trilobite and other marine organisms through fish to amphibians to mammals, and then finally to whales (Hebrew *tannin*: great sea monsters).

l.  The Bible stresses ten times that the entities created were to reproduce "after their kinds." Evolutionists postulate the slow ascent of all organisms from a common ancestor.

m. The Bible says God made man in His own "image" (Gen. 1:26), forming his body out of the "dust of the ground" (Gen. 2:7), not out of the body of an animal as anthropologists claim. Man, at his death, returns to this same "dust" (Gen. 3 :19), which is not back to an animal existence.

n.  God created woman subsequent to His forming man, out of man's body. Evolutionary anthropology requires man and woman to have developed simultaneously and, in fact, the first true man (like all subsequent men) to have been formed in the woman's body.

o.  God told men to exercise dominion over every organism He had created on the previous days (Gen. 1:28). According to the geologic-age system, the vast majority of such organisms were already extinct for ages before man appeared.

p.  Man was originally a vegetarian according to Scripture (Gen. 1:29); anthropologists maintain that the earliest men were not only hunters and meat-eaters, but probably cannibals.

q.  According to the Bible, there was no rain on the earth at least until the time of man's appearance (Gen. 2:5); uniformitarian geologists say rains have existed since the earth first cooled.

r.  In the Bible, Adam gave names to all the land animals God had formed. Geologists claim that most of them were extinct long before man was on the earth.

s.  According to Genesis, plants appeared on the third day, and insects only on the sixth. This would be impossible if the days were ages, since plants require insect pollination for their continued survival.

t.  The Bible author divides the history of the world's development up into six "days" of creation. However, there is no such six-fold division of geologic time even remotely comparable to this, either in order of events or length of subdivisions.

u.  On the seventh day God "rested" from His completed work of creation and formation, as a pattern for man's weekly rest day (though He of course continues His work of providence and redemption). According to the day-age concept, God has never "rested" at all from His work of "creating" and "making," thus the seventh "day" has not yet even begun.

v.  God saw "everything" He had made as "very good" at the end of the creation. Geologists claim that most of these things did not even survive to that point, and the groaning world that did survive until man's appearance was certainly far from perfect.

w. The summary of Genesis 2:1–3 says that "all the host" of things God "created and made" was "finished" after the six days, and that God stopped any further work of creation or development. Modern geologists and biologists say that the same processes used to bring the world to its present form are still in operation, and "creation" is still continuing.

## The Pre-Adamic Gap Theory

It has also been suggested that the primeval creation of Genesis 1:1 may have been followed by 5 billion years of geologic history and then a great worldwide cataclysm, as a result of which the earth "became" without form and void (Gen. 1:2). Most advocates of this theory suggest that the cataclysm was the result of Satan's rebellion against God in heaven. This theory likewise encounters numerous problems. For example:

1. The "was" of Genesis 1:2 is translated "was" in all the standard translations (and not "became") for the very good reason that this is its meaning. When the context requires, it *can* be used with the meaning "became," but this is found in only 22 of its 1,522 occurrences in the Pentateuch. It is the regular Hebrew verb of being (*hayah*), not the normal word for "became" (*haphak*). There is no indication in the immediate context that a drastic change of state is intended by the verb. In fact, the use of the *waw* connective ("and") at the beginning of verse 2 seems to emphasize that the action of verse 2 follows immediately after the actions of verse 1, with no "gap."

2. According to the summaries of Genesis 2:1–3 and Exodus 20:11, the "heavens," as well as the "earth," were made in six days. The heavenly bodies occupying the heavens were made on the fourth day. Since the only mention of the "heavens" in Genesis 1 is in the first verse, it is necessary to conclude that Genesis 1:1 itself is a part of the six days and thus there can be no gap of any consequence thereafter.

3. According to Genesis 2:3, absolutely all of God's work of both creating and making all things — the heavens and the earth and all the host of them ("all that in them is," according to Exod. 20:11) — was accomplished in the six days. There is no room therefore for any remnants of a supposed earlier creation to have been preserved as metamorphosed or fossilized components of the re-creation.

4. There is no scriptural evidence that Satan's fall in heaven produced a cataclysm on earth. Satan was only cast to the earth (Ezek. 28:17) after his rebellion and fall, and thus he had no connection with the earth when it was first created. In fact, God's estimate of "everything" in the earth as "very good" after His six days of creative activity would seem plainly to show that Satan was not yet on the earth at that time. Quite probably his fall and expulsion to the earth occurred sometime between Genesis 1:31, when all things were still "good," and Genesis 3:1, when he appeared to Eve, in the body of a serpent. How long this period may have been, the Scriptures do not say.

5. Instead of accommodating the geological ages in the supposed "gap" between Genesis 1:1 and 1:2, and thus satisfying science, as its advocates had

hoped, the theory introduced numerous scientific difficulties and contradictions, just as the day-age theory does. Some of these are as follows:

a. According to the gap theory, a worldwide cataclysm occurred in very recent geologic time, but there is no evidence of this in the standard system of geology which the theory purports to accommodate. The Ice Age, for example, which some have identified with the description of Genesis 1:2, occupied only a relative small part of the earth's surface.

b. The gap theory attributes most or all of the fossil record to the pre-world; however, most of the plants and animals of the present world are essentially identical with corresponding kinds found in the fossils, including some of the supposedly most ancient strata.

c. The gap theory does not in any wise resolve the problem of evolution, but merely pushes the five-billion-year history of evolution, as supposedly revealed in historical geology, back into a pre-Genesis world. This implies that God used evolutionary methods in the pre-world, and then changed to direct creative activity in the six days of "re-creation."

d. If the geologic column itself is all attributed to the pre-Adamic cataclysm, with all the fossils thus deposited contemporaneously, then the geologic ages have themselves been effectively eliminated, as they are essentially synonymous with the geologic column and its fossil record. The gap theory can hardly hope to harmonize the geologic ages with the Bible by merely erasing them!

e. If, in fact, a worldwide cataclysm is admitted which embraces the whole geologic column, then there is no room for the worldwide cataclysm of the great Flood, which does the same thing. Orthodox geologists, of course, reject any such cataclysm at all, so that it is fruitless to try to accommodate the standard system of geologic ages in either case. However, the Bible does clearly teach, and in considerable detail, that the Flood was a world-destroying cataclysm, whereas it is completely silent with respect to a possible pre-Adamic cataclysm.

f. The gap theory requires the existence of pre-Adamite men to explain the fossils of men and various "hominid" forms that have been found in the geologic column, but the Bible teaches that Adam was the "first man" (1 Cor. 15:47, et al.). These fossil men are believed in many cases to have used tools and fire, buried their dead, and shown many other human characteristics, so it is altogether arbitrary to assume they had neither souls nor the hope of salvation.

g. Finally, several of the scientific difficulties noted in connection with the day-age theory apply with almost equal weight to the gap theory. These need not be repeated here, but may be noted as listed on previous pages in this chapter under topics e, f, o, q, r, v, and w.

### The Theological Impossibility of the Geologic Ages

There are many other fallacies to be found in both the day-age theory and the gap theory; furthermore, the handful of proof-texts that have been suggested for each can easily be shown to have been taken out of context and to yield other, preferable, interpretations. But the one overriding and overwhelming objection to both theories is that they make God out to be the author of evil and confusion! This is because they both accept the historical reality of the so-called geological ages.

The geological ages are identified explicitly in terms of the forms of life supposedly characteristic of those ages as revealed by the fossils found in the rocks representing them. This is evident in the very names given the basic systems — Proterozoic ("before life"), Paleozoic ("ancient life"), Mesozoic ("intermediate life"), and Cenozoic ("recent life").

These sedimentary rocks and the multiplied millions of fossils found in them testify with great clarity and force that they were formed at a time when storms, floods, volcanic eruptions, great earth upheavals, disease, fighting, struggle, and above all *death*, existed in the world. All of these are still in the world today and are evidence of a creation that "groaneth and travaileth in pain together," and in "the bondage of corruption" (Rom. 8:20–22). The fossil world of the geological ages is to be understood as the same basic kind of world that now exists.

This can only mean that, since all of this supposedly took place before man had sinned (and, for that matter, even before Satan had sinned), sin was not the cause of death and disorder in the world. Consequently, God himself must have deliberately and willfully instituted this system of decay and death in His creation as a process finally leading up to man's appearance. Therefore, God would then be the direct author of confusion, suffering, and death.[28]

But such a conclusion as this is theological chaos! The Scriptures explicitly condemn such ideas. "God saw every thing that he had made, and, behold, it was very good" (Gen.1:31). "By man came death" (1 Cor. 15:21). "God is not the author of confusion" (1 Cor. 14:33).

Therefore, our attempts to harmonize the Genesis record with the geological ages are completely inhibited by the intransigence of the biblical record. Furthermore, the geologic ages as understood by modern geologists and paleontologists are of such character as to preclude the very existence of the God described in the Bible. Since God is truly omnipotent and perfect in righteousness and love, then the so-called geologic ages can have had no existence except in the realm of speculative evolutionary philosophy.

### The Intelligent Design Theory

Beginning about 1990, an ostensibly new compromise theory has been having wide influence among evangelicals. Its proponents call it the "intelligent design movement" or "more creationism." It has also been called "neocreationism," especially by traditional anti-creationists and Darwinists.

---

28. God of course does *permit* suffering and death — occasionally even great catastrophes — in the present world, but this is a part of the Adamic curse, and is ultimately to be removed when God's work of judgment and redemption is finished.

In essence, this movement stresses the evidence for intelligent design and "irreducible complexity," especially in living systems and with respect to the first origin of life. However, most of its spokesmen (though not all) accept the geological ages and its evolutionary framework, and many accept theistic evolution. They insist, quite properly, that there is strong evidence for design in the world, but in general refuse to insist that the "designer" is the God of the Bible. In fact, they try to leave the Bible out of their discussion altogether.

Yet many of them (not all) profess to be Bible-believing Christians. They believe that this approach, which is called the "wedge strategy," will gain a hearing for them in the scientific and academic worlds, which would be closed to them if they were committed to biblical literalism and recent creation. The hope is that if intellectuals can be persuaded that there is real evidence for design in the world, they will then be open to a presentation of the Christian message as a whole.

They do get invited to speak on college campuses, but they seem to get few if any converts, either to creationism or to Christ. What they do seem to get in considerable numbers are converts from biblical creationism to the intelligent design compromise. They forget that this is primarily a spiritual issue, not just scientific. "The entrance of thy words giveth light," the Bible says (Ps. 119:130), not the scientific evidence of design.

The design argument is nothing new. It was strongly advocated by William Paley and others long before the days of Charles Darwin. In fact, it was specifically to negate the design argument that Darwin introduced the concept of natural selection, and this is still the escape hatch used by evolutionists whenever presented with some new evidence for intelligent design. Current evolutionists tend to dismiss the new return to the old design argument as merely a roundabout way of getting creationism back into the schools.

The organization devoted entirely to opposing creationism, representing the evolutionary community as a whole, is the National Center for Science Education, whose director is anthropologist Eugenie Scott. Dr. Scott comments on this movement as follows:

> The anti-evolution movement evolved in some new directions, primarily in the avoidance of any form of the word creation or "creationism." Phrases like "intelligent design theory," "abrupt appearance theory," "evidence against evolution," and the like, have sprung up, although the content of many of the arguments is familiar. This view can be called "neocreationism." . . . Prominent among the neocreationists is a recently emerged group of scholars who call themselves "design theorists." . . . Most of them are progressive creationists.[29]

We have already discussed the fallacies of progressive creationism, as well as theistic evolutionism, so we do not need to repeat that analysis here. The point is

---

29. Eugenie C. Scott, "Creationists and the Pope's Statement," *Quarterly Review of Biology,* 72 (December 1997).

that even this further compromise, avoiding reference to the Bible or even the creation, is no more successful (less in fact) in winning people to Christ and creation than true and uncompromising literal biblical creationism.

Another very influential evolutionist is Dr. Ken Miller, of Brown University, considered by many creationists (including this writer) as the most charismatic and effective of all debaters against creationism. Dr. Miller claims to be a practicing Catholic, but he is, nevertheless, a thorough believer in totally naturalistic evolution. He is not an atheist, like Dr. Scott and most leading evolutionists, but nevertheless believes in total evolution by random chance processes, this being the method God used, according to his personal theology. He has no more respect for the intelligent design movement than any atheistic biologist would have, since he sees clearly the fallacy of trying to fit divine creation into the assumed geologic column and its fossil sequences.

> Like it or not, intelligent design requires us to believe that the past was a time of magic in which species appeared out of nothing. That magic began with the dawn of life on this planet and continued unabated for more than a billion years, bringing a grand parade of living things into existence. Throughout this time, novel organisms spring into existence one after another, transforming the earth and producing eras in which organisms now extinct dominated the planet.[30]

Why would God do such a thing? The whole scenario seems unnecessary and cruel if the creation and redemption of man is really God's ultimate purpose in it all. Miller goes on to say:

> Finally, whatever one's view of such a designer's motivation, there is one conclusion that drops cleanly out of the data. He was incompetent. . . . In simple terms, the designer just can't get it right the first time. Nothing he designs is able to make it over the long term.[31]

Ken Miller also notes another of the same objections that we had already pointed out many times.

> Why did this magician, in order to produce the contemporary world, find it necessary to create and destroy creatures, habitats, and ecosystems millions of times over?[32]

Although (not surprisingly) Dr. Miller fails to point out the deadly blow the geological-ages concept strikes against the saving gospel of Christ, that impact is very real. If suffering and death existed for a billion years before man appeared on earth, then death is not really "the wages of sin" after all, and it was not by man that death "came" into the world (Rom. 6:23; 1 Cor. 15:21), despite what the

---

30. Kenneth R. Miller, *Finding Darwin's God* (New York, NY: Harper Collins Publishers, 1999), p. 100.
31. Ibid, p. 103.
32. Ibid, p. 128.

Bible says. Therefore, the cruel death of Christ on the cross, ostensibly to pay the penalty for sin and to defeat death, was a pointless charade.

Those who advocate theistic evolution or progressive creation — or any system involving the geological ages and the fossils of billions of dead animals (and human-like forms) embedded in the sedimentary rock beds of the earth — may not realize the lethal implications of this compromise, but it is a very real problem. It is far better to assume God is able to speak clearly, and that the biblical record is literally true.

### The Genealogical-Gap Theory

It is now generally accepted by evolutionary anthropologists that man in essentially his present form (*Homo erectus* and possibly even *Homo sapiens*), has been in existence for at least a million years. It would seem that the only possibility for harmonizing the biblical record of man's early history with this chronology is to assume one or more gaps in the genealogical lists in Genesis 5 and 11.

Since Adam is beyond doubt said in Scripture to have been the first man (Gen. 2:4–7; Mark 10:6; Rom. 5:12–14; 1 Cor. 15:45; et al.), there can have been no man before Adam. There are 20 names listed in Genesis 5 and 11 for the span of Adam to Abraham. For this period, the total time (using the numbers given in the Masoretic Text for the age of each father at the birth of the son next in the messianic line) is less than two thousand years.

To explain a discrepancy between 1 million and 2,000 years, for the time from the first man to the time of Abraham (about 2,000 B.C. by secular chronology) in terms of genealogical gaps means that the average such gap between each pair of names in Genesis 5 and 11 is more than 50,000 years! Each "gap" is therefore more than eight times as long as the entire period of recorded history.

The patriarchal lists of Genesis 5 and 11 become, by this device, the ultimate in irrelevancy! Not only does their chronological information become useless, but their genealogical information becomes equally pointless. What conceivable purpose can there have been, for example, in carefully recording the age of each father at the birth of some unknown son who was then to be the ancestor of the next individual named on the list some fifty thousand years in the future? Who ever heard of such a genealogy as this? And yet it is recorded not only in Genesis, but also in 1 Chronicles and Luke.

There seems to be no reasonable conclusion but that the patriarchal compilers of these lists (under the guidance of the Holy Spirit) intended them to be understood as essentially complete records of the messianic line leading from Adam through Noah to Abraham, and finally to the founder of that nation through whom one day the promised "seed of the woman" would appear. It gives us not only the genealogical line that is central in human history but also the true chronological framework within which the history of redemption is being accomplished.

This does not deny the possibility that minor "gaps" may occur in the lists.

There is possible warrant for this idea in the analogy of certain other genealogical lists in Scripture. But such gaps, if they exist, must be relatively small, as is certainly true of the other genealogies in the Bible. It is significant that the reliable recorded history of all ancient civilizations (Egypt, Sumer, etc.) invariably begins only a few thousand years ago, as the biblical chronology of Genesis 5 and 11 would imply. The question of whether the earth's population of 4 billion people could have been produced in the few thousand years since the first pair (Noah and his wife, since the antediluvian population was all destroyed in the great Flood) will be answered affirmatively in chapter 15.

We conclude, therefore, that the biblical chronology must be taken at face value and that no comparison with the standard evolutionary chronology, either for the earth as a whole or for man in particular, is possible at all. The geologic age concept and its evolutionary framework are thereby proved false, since the Bible is the Word of God.

## Supposed Biblical Problems

The arguments in the foregoing section have been frequently presented, and they have never been answered biblically. Christians who reject them do so because of what they consider to be scientific hindrances to the recent literal creation doctrine of Genesis. Thus, these at least intended to teach that the creation of all things took place in six literal days only a few thousand years ago. To interpret any passage of Scripture in a manner contrary to the intent of the author is unsound hermeneutically and dangerous theologically, opening the door to all kinds of arbitrary teaching and transmuting the inspired Word of God into whatever message the reader prefers to receive. He becomes in effect his own god.

These supposed scientific problems with recent creationism will be discussed and answered in later chapters. The real facts of science, as distinguished from various evolutionary interpretations imposed on those facts, all point to the recent special creation of all things, not long ages of evolutionary uniformitarianism.

There are, however, a few biblical problems that have been raised by Christian uniformitarians. These are discussed briefly below. It should be emphasized, of course, that even if we don't yet have complete answers to every problem that might be conceived, the overwhelming biblical evidence for literal-day creationism has still not been refuted thereby in any way. One does not solve the problem of a missing button by discarding the garment. But let us look at these so-called problems.

## Different Meanings of "Day" in Genesis 1

A common complaint against the literal-day view is that the Hebrew word for "day" (yom) has two non-literal meanings even in the first chapter of Genesis, being applied to the "days" before the sun was placed in the heaven, and also used (in Gen. 2:4) to apply to the entire creation week.

The burden of proof for such non-literal interpretations, however, is on those who would advocate them. The context neither precludes the literal meaning nor requires a non-literal meaning.

The meaning of *yom* in the context is specifically defined the first time it is used (Gen. 1:5). "God called the light Day." In the cyclical succession of light and darkness that began on the first creative day and has continued regularly ever since, the period of light — when God was working — was defined as "day." The light was followed by "evening," then the darkness by "morning," and this cyclic sequence was identified as "day 1," "day 2," etc. Whether the light was produced by the sun (as it certainly was after day 4) or by some temporary light source, or even by God himself on the first three days, is irrelevant. Unless one is willing to argue for half-billion year cycles of day and night for the first three periods, such a non-literal interpretation here is not only forced but also of no use whatever in accommodating the geological ages.

As far as Genesis 2:4 is concerned, this also is best taken literally. It refers to "the day that the Lord God made the earth and the heavens." The Lord did not, however, make the earth and the heavens throughout the six days. He made them on the first day, and Genesis 2:4 obviously is a reference to Genesis 1:1 (no other verse in Genesis 1 mentions either "the heavens and the earth" or "the earth and the heavens").

God placed the stars in the heavens on the fourth day, and the birds in the heavens on the fifth day, but the heavens were already there when this was done. Similarly the earth emerged from the waters on the third day and brought forth cattle on the sixth day, but it had been created on the first day.

But even if one insists on taking "day" in Genesis 2:4 as referring to all six days of God's creating and making works, this would in no wise detract from the unequivocal teaching that the six days themselves were literal days.

## God's Rest Day

Another common argument is that, since the seventh day of the creation week is still continuing, with God still "resting" from His work of creation, the other six days of the creation week could be long periods of time as well. This argument also is based in part on the absence of the "evening and morning" formula at the end of the seventh day.

Such an interpretation, however, introduces a serious contradiction in the day-age argument. If the seventh day is still continuing, then God is still resting from His works of creating and making. Consequently, the present processes which maintain the creation are not the processes that produced it and brought it to its present form. But this inference denies the premise of the uniformitarianism and the continuity of the geologic ages with the present. The very existence of the geologic ages (which both the day-age theory and the gap theory hope to accommodate) is based on the assumption of uniformitarianism, the idea that present processes were operating in past ages just as they do today. This could not be, if the seventh day — God's rest day — is still going on.

The fact is, of course, that the seventh day was a literal day just like the other six. There was no need to record its "evening," since no work had been done on it, and it would be pointless to talk about what God did on the eighth or ninth days, since the completion of all His work had already been noted on the seventh day.

He did do one thing on the seventh day, of course: He "blessed the seventh day, and sanctified it," thus setting it in a special category as a divine memorial of His completed work of creation. This would be odd, indeed, if the world was still groaning in pain from the long geological ages of struggle and suffering, and still more odd if this seventh day were still continuing, with its thousands of years of human wickedness and slaughter.

That the seventh day was a literal day is proved every week when one day in seven is observed as a day of rest and worship, just as it has been ever since the beginning. This was, in fact, written down in stone, in the Ten Commandments in a well-known passage that is crystal clear and that really ought to settle the question for anyone who believes in the Bible. This is in the fourth commandment: "Remember the sabbath day, to keep it holy. Six days shalt thou labour, and do all thy work: But the seventh day is the sabbath of the Lord thy God . . . For in six days the Lord made heaven and earth, the sea, and all that in them is, and rested the seventh day: wherefore the Lord blessed the sabbath day, and hallowed it" (Exod. 20:8–11).

Man is to work six days because the Lord worked six days; he is to keep the seventh day holy because the Lord hallowed the seventh day. The same words are used ("day" = *yom*; "days" = *yamim*) for both God's week and man's week. Everything is parallel. If the two weeks are not composed of the same kinds of days, then it would seem that intelligible words cannot be used to convey intelligible meanings. There is no possible way that better or more precise words could be used to say that God's week was the same as man's week, if that were indeed the intended meaning. If that were not the intended meaning, then why would God use these words, especially in the Ten Commandments and especially as the basis of His rigorously enforced Sabbath day? All of the Bible is divinely inspired, but his portion was divinely inscribed, written with God's finger on a table of stone (Exod. 31:18). It is irreverent, to say the least, to deny that Scripture means what it plainly says, just to accommodate the imaginary ages of evolutionary geology in the Genesis record.

It is extremely significant that nations of all times and places have used the week as their basic unit of time, even though it has no basis in astronomy — as do the day, the month, and the year. The only explanation that fits the facts is that people have continued to organize their work cycle around the week because God did. Even those who don't believe in God or creation still take their weekly day of rest!

## Events of the Sixth Day

One other biblical argument that has been advanced with all seriousness by certain competent biblical scholars who ought to know better is the contention that the events recounted in the Genesis narrative for the sixth creative day could not all have been accomplished in just one day. These events included the creation of man and the higher land mammals, the planting of the Garden of Eden, Adam's naming of the animals, and finally the forming of Eve from Adam's side. Especially is it deemed impossible for Adam to have named all the animals in, say, a 12-hour period. The other events could perhaps be allowed in the early morning and twilight hours, they say.

However, the Bible does not say he named *all* the animals, but only the "cattle" and the "fowl of the air" and "every beast of the field" (Gen. 2:20). The great hosts of "creeping things" and "fish of the sea" were excluded. Only those animals with whom Adam would be likely to have close contact as he exercised his dominion over them were to be named by him. At the most this would include only the birds and the higher mammals. Furthermore, as noted in chapter 13, the created kinds undoubtedly represented broader categories than our modern species or genera, quite possibly approximating in most cases the taxonomic family. Just how many kinds were actually there to be named is unknown, of course, but it could hardly have been as many as a thousand. Although even this number would seem formidable to us today, it should be remembered that Adam was newly created, with mental activity and physical vigor corresponding to an unfallen state. He certainly could have done the job in a day and, at the very most, it would only have taken a few days even for a modern-day person, so there is nothing anywhere in the account to suggest that the sixth day was anything like a geological age.

## What About the Geological Ages?

If the evolutionary ages of geology cannot be fitted into the Genesis record, either before the six days of creation (gap theory) or during the six days (day-age theory), and if the Bible is indeed true and perspicuous, then where do we put the geological ages? The answer, of course, is that they don't need to be put anywhere, since they never existed in the first place.

This may seem to evolutionists like an extreme statement, but the biblical record leaves no alternative. As we have just seen, the Word of God explicitly states that all things were created and made in just six days several thousand years ago. Therefore, there is simply no room for the geological ages in its histories, nor for the long, sad spectacle of evolution that they represent.

But how, then, can we explain all the supposed scientific evidences for evolution? In particular, what about the great thicknesses of sedimentary rocks and the tremendous number of fossils contained in them — especially the dinosaurs and other exotic animals that seem to have lived in former ages? These fossil assemblages have even been used to identify the various ages, and they comprise the main evidence for evolution. It is well and good to insist that the Bible precluded evolution and the geological ages, but then what about people who don't believe the Bible, and what about all the supposed scientific evidence for evolution and the ages?

Actually, the Bible itself gives the answer to this question, though not in Genesis. In the last chapter written by the apostle Peter before his martyrdom, the Holy Spirit enabled him to see this great intellectual conflict of the last days: "Knowing this first, that there shall come in the last days scoffers, walking after their own lusts, And saying, Where is the promise of his coming? for since the fathers fell asleep, all things continue as they were from the beginning of the creation (2 Peter 3:3–4). This is a remarkable prophecy, in effect predicting that the intellectual dogma of the end times in Christendom would be evolutionary uniformitarianism, and that this philosophy would be the intellectual rationale for repudiating all of God's purposes and promises in creation and redemption. According to the prophecy, even "creation" would be conceived by latter-day scoffing intellectuals as still "continuing," like all other processes ever since the "*beginning*" (not just the termination) of creation. This prediction has, of course, been precisely and pervasively fulfilled in the decades since Darwin, with practically the entire intellectual world now committed to uniformitarianism and evolutionism.

But then Peter, by the Holy Spirit, reveals the false basis of this philosophy, thereby guiding us in the proper way to answer and refute it. It is not to be accomplished by some compromising system of exegesis but is to be repudiated and corrected. "For this they willingly are ignorant of, that by the word of God the heavens were of old, and the earth standing out of the water and in the water: Whereby the world that then was, being overflowed with water, perished" (2 Pet. 3:5–6).

That is, this latter-day commitment of the intellectual establishment to evolutionary uniformitarianism will be based on willful ignorance of what is evidently clear and satisfactory evidence against it. This evidence, refuting evolution and uniformitarianism is at the same time positive evidence for creation and catastrophe, which are opposites. Specifically, Peter is telling us that the scientific evidence requiring special creation of the primeval heavens and earth, combined with the scientific evidence for the great cataclysmic flood that destroyed the earth in the days of Noah, is abundantly adequate to disprove the humanistic world view, as built on evolution and the uniformitarian ages of geology.

This chapter has focused essentially on the biblical and theological fallacies in evolution and the long-age concept. Of course, there are not many who would ever even suggest that the Bible teaches such things, were it not for the fact that they have been told that science teaches them. The fact is, however, that the real scientific facts (as opposed to theories and speculations) do not prove evolution and the geologic ages at all. Instead, they clearly point to special creation and the worldwide flood, just as the Bible teaches. The true sciences of astronomy, physics, chemistry, biology, and especially thermodynamics, all give strong witness to the primeval special creation of all things, whereas the sciences of geophysics, geology, paleontology, and others similarly give clear testimony to the great Deluge. The fossil record, in particular, commonly alleged to provide the strongest evidence of evolution and the geological ages, instead can be understood much better in the framework of the Flood. All of this will be elaborated in later chapters, as we consider the confirming testimony of the various sciences in turn, to the truth of creation and the inerrancy of the written Word of God.

As will be seen, the evolutionary system has been invested with an altogether spurious cloak of scientific authority. Generations of students have been indoctrinated with belief in evolution, having been misled by their teachers to think that science has proved evolution and that all scientists today accept it as fact. The real facts, however, are otherwise. There is no scientific evidence for evolution that is not at least as well explained by creation, and there are now thousands of modern scientists[33] who have abandoned evolution and become creationists. Furthermore, at least in part because of the increasing influence and persuasive arguments of these scientific creationists, the evolutionists themselves are arguing more than ever among themselves, and the case for evolution is in greater disarray than ever in its history. Dr. Keith Thompson, former professor of biology and dean of the graduate school at Yale University, has published the following evaluation of the situation at that time: "Twenty years ago Mayr, in his *Animal Species and Evolution* seemed to have shown that if evolution is a jigsaw puzzle, then at least all the edge pieces were in place. But today we are less confident and the whole subject is in the most exciting ferment. Evolution is both troubled from without by the nagging insistence of anti-scientists and nagged from within by the troubling complexities of genetic and developmental mechanisms and new questions about the central mystery — speciation itself."[34]

It is an amazing thing that evolutionists continue to be so sure about the "fact" of evolution and yet, 145 years after Darwin was believed to have solved the problem of its mechanism, they still don't have any idea how it works! The origin of species is, as Thompson says, still the "central mystery." No one has ever seen any example of real evolution taking place today, no one has any real evidence that it took place at any time in the past, and no one knows how it could possibly work even if it does take place.[35] Yet they call this science!

---

33. For example, there are over six hundred scientists in the Creation Research Society alone, each of whom has one or more postgraduate degrees in science. Furthermore, the writer has spoken to over three thousand audiences in the past 40 years (since the Creation Research Society was formed) and has encountered in those audiences several times more creationist scientists who are not members of the society than scientists who are members.

34. Keith Stewart Thompson, "The Meanings of Evolution," *American Scientist,* 70 (Sept.–Oct. 1982): 529. The term "antiscientists" is, of course, Thompson's self-serving euphemism for creationists.

35. For a recent summary of the conflicts in the evolutionary camp, see Henry M. Morris, *Evolution in Turmoil* (San Diego, CA: Creation-Life, 1982).

The relevant scientific evidences from different fields will be discussed in later chapters. In the meantime, the admonition of Paul to young pastor Timothy is applicable: "O Timothy, keep that which is committed to thy trust, avoiding profane and vain babblings, and oppositions of science falsely so called: Which some professing have erred concerning the faith. Grace be with thee. Amen" (1 Tim. 6:20–21). To Christians today has been committed the great foundational truth of special creation, and God expects us to keep, or "guard," it against all the "naturalistic and vacuous speculations and oppositions of this self-serving pseudo-science" of evolution. In Paul's day, the dominant humanistic philosophies were Gnosticism, Stoicism, Epicureanism, and others — all based on evolution. In our day, it may take the form of Darwinism or punctuationism, but it is still the same old pagan evolutionary philosophy, and believers must still avoid being influenced by it if we are to be effective witnesses to our own generation.

PART 2

# THE PHYSICAL SCIENCES

# 5

# CREATION OF THE WORLD
## Biblical Cosmogony

Cosmogony is the study of ideas about the origin of the cosmos. The term is closely related to cosmology, which is the study of the cosmos in all its aspects. Cosmogony purports to be that division of cosmology having to do with its beginnings. The cosmos, in simplest terms, is the space-mass-time universe and all its arrays of complex systems.

Most evolutionary cosmogonies, ancient and modern, have assumed that the space-mass-time cosmos is the ultimate reality, self-existent from eternity. However, a bizarre modern notion advanced by certain mathematical astrophysicists is that the universe evolved out of nothing, via a quantum fluctuation of the primeval nothingness, into the first infinitesimal particle of space-time, which then evolved into the cosmos.

The fundamental creation model, on the other hand, assumes creation *ex nihilo* instead of evolution *ex nihilo*. God alone is the ultimate reality. Space and time, as well as matter, did not exist until God brought them into existence out of nothing by His omnipotence.

This primeval act of special creation, of course, is recorded in the very first verse of divine revelation. God created the heavens (i.e., "space") and the earth (i.e., "matter") in the beginning (i.e., "time"). The cosmos is a *continuum* of space, matter, and time, with all three entities essential to a meaningful cosmos and with all three therefore coming into existence simultaneously.

## Ubiquity of the Evolutionary Cosmogony

It is significant that the only real creationist cosmogony is found in the Bible. All other cosmogonic systems, both ancient and modern, begin with the space-mass-time universe already in existence, either from eternity or from the imagined quantum fluctuation of nothing into the first particle. The ancient Babylonians began their system in a primeval water chaos; modern evolutionary cosmogonists start the universe in a highly explosive chaos of elementary particles. There have been many other concepts throughout the history of human philosophy, but the common feature of all of them is the tacit assumption that the cosmos itself is the ultimate reality. Many of them also envision the universe as going through perpetual cycles of growth and decay. This particular notion is strong in both the ancient Hindu cosmogony and in the modern oscillating universe theory, as well as others.

In any case, all of these systems are evolutionary in all their essential features. None allow the concept of an eternal, transcendent Creator who spoke the universe into existence. Some are more scientifically sophisticated than others — those of the Greek atomists and the ancient Chinese philosophers, for example. Some are grossly idolatrous and polytheistic, involving hordes of demonic spirits and the worship of stars and winds and other objects and forces of nature, but even these represent mere outward expressions of an all-embracing pantheism that equates the creation with the Creator. As summarized in the cogent clause of Romans 1:25: "[They] worshiped and served the creature more than the Creator, who is blessed for ever. Amen."

Since this is not a textbook of comparative religions, we will not attempt to survey all these ancient cosmogonies. Those great religions that are extant today have largely become adapted to modern "scientific" cosmogonies. Buddhism, Confucianism, Taoism, Shintoism, and Shamanism, for instance, are all essentially man-centered religions, either ignoring or rejecting the idea of a transcendent Creator. Thus, they are basically atheistic and have easily accommodated Darwinism and other modern evolutionary concepts into their systems. The same is true of modern pseudo-intellectual occult religions such as spiritism, witchcraft, astrology, theosophy, and all the other imported Eastern cults. The list goes on — scientology, the Unification church, transcendental meditation, Hare Krishna, the cargo cults of the Pacific, etc. — "gods many, and lords many," "false Christs, and false prophets" (1 Cor. 8:5; Matt. 24:24). None of these believe in an omnipotent, personal God, and all have adjusted to one or another of the modern evolutionary cosmogonies.

The Bible alone, of all ancient or modern books claiming divine revelation and authority, tells of the actual creation of the universe. As we shall see, this teaching is repeated again and again, all throughout Scripture, completely precluding any legitimate attempt to harmonize it with either an ancient or a modern evolutionary cosmogony.

Not only the Christian religion, of course, but also a few other religions have accepted the Old Testament as divine Scripture. These include Judaism, Islam, and an assortment of smaller cults, ancient and modern. To the extent that these have retained their faith in the Book of Genesis, adherents of these religions have held creationist cosmogonies. There are creationist Jews and creationist Moslems, for example.

Unfortunately, the non-Christian creationist religions as a whole have refused to acknowledge that the Creator's purpose for His creation can only be accomplished through His own personal redemptive work on its behalf. They retain a humanistic emphasis by presuming that man can redeem himself. Thus, Jesus Christ is recognized as a great man, perhaps even as the highest created being, but not as the Creator. With the absolute deity of Christ thus denied, God in His essence becomes unknowable, and the awareness of a sovereign, personal, omnipotent (yet loving) God retreats further and further away in their consciousness. Even in Judaism and Islam, therefore, true creationism becomes diluted, and compromises with evolution become easy and common. The same is true of such cultic offshoots of these faiths as Bahaism, which has long been fully adjusted to an evolutionary cosmogony.

Even more tragically, many segments of so-called Christianity have likewise accommodated evolution in their cosmogonic systems, denying either the creative or redemptive work of Christ, or both. This is true of both "main-line" Christianity and cultic Christianity. There are many pseudo-Christian cults (e.g., Christian Science, Unity, Divine Science, Unitarianism, Universalism) for which this fact is most obvious. Others (e.g., Mormonism, Christadelphianism, Jehovah's Witnesses) maintain in some cases an anti-evolutionary stance (most Mormons, however, probably now accept evolution; this is believed by many to be quite consistent with their doctrine of an eternally existing cosmos). The rejection by such cults of the Trinity and the full deity of Christ fatally undermines the full biblical revelation of an absolute Creator who is also absolute Redeemer and coming sovereign King of all creation.

The mainstream denominations of the Christian world — Catholic, Protestant, and Independent alike — have traditionally upheld the doctrines of special creation of the cosmos and the absolute deity of Jesus Christ, including his threefold work (past, present, and future) of a complete creation, redemption of that by His substitutionary sacrifice, and future reconciliation of the creation to himself.

Sadly, however, even these orthodox denominations have largely capitulated to evolutionism in the century following Darwin. In almost every such denomination there has been great tension between creationists and evolutionists, and in most cases, the evolutionists and liberals have come to dominate the seminaries and other educational institutions. Some great denominations have even become largely humanistic in theology and socialistic in soteriology as a result, though most have maintained at least a nominal commitment to basic Christian doctrine (including creation) sufficient to placate the conservative component of their membership.

Thus, even the major portions of Christendom have followed the other religions and philosophies of the world in adapting to some form of evolutionist cosmogony. This defection has been tragically premature. Not only is general evolution completely contrary to Scripture, but also it is completely unscientific. Because of supposed scientific intimidation, theologians have felt impelled to try to accommodate Scripture and biblical theology to some form of evolutionary cosmogony. One after another, however, these evolutionary cosmogonies have been abandoned by the very scientists whose aura had captivated the theologians. The time is long past due for a full return of all true Christians to the straightforward creationist cosmogony taught in the Bible.

## Cosmogony According to the Bible

We shall take a critical look at the important current evolutionary cosmogonies later on in this chapter, but it is desirable first to establish the basic teachings of Scripture on the origin of the universe. On such a subject as this, it is transparently obvious that no theory can ever be *proved* scientifically. No scientist was present to observe the origin of the cosmos, nor can any scientist reproduce or even simulate the process in his laboratory. The universe is essentially infinite in size and complexity, and attempts of finite men to speculate as to its origin are merely presumptuous and arrogant.

The only way we can possibly know anything about cosmic beginnings is through divine revelation. As already shown, the only adequate cause to explain the universe is that of a personal, omnipotent God, and the only way we can know how He did it is by means of revelation.

The most basic fact of this revelation, of course, is that the universe as we know it has not existed forever in the past, though it will exist forever in the future. It had a beginning! Even time had a beginning.

It is impossible for time-bound minds such as ours to conceive of anything "before" time began, but this is a necessary component of the concept of an omnipotent God. That is, if time has existed eternally, then time is co-equal with an omnipotent God, and this is impossible, by definition.

Furthermore, the universe is a "continuum" of time, space, and mass/energy. None can have real existence without the others, and each merges imperceptibly into the others. The beginning of time must be concurrent with that of space and that of mass/energy. The universe is a universe, not a multi-verse.

As discussed in chapter 7, the fact that time must have had a beginning point is also the testimony of the second law of thermodynamics. The universe is now dying. Time's arrow points downward and, if the second law continues to function, the universe will "die" in time. Since it is not dead, time had a beginning. If time stretched back eternally, the universe would already be dead.

The second law thus indicates that the universe must have been created — otherwise it would be dead. But the first law indicates that the universe could not create itself, since in the present structure of nature energy can neither be created nor destroyed. Consequently, the universe must have been created, at some beginning point of time, by an external cause adequate to the task of creating a complex, infinite, eternal universe.

Thus, the first verse of the Bible states the most profound — yet most simple — and most fundamental fact every conceived or spoken. "In the beginning God created the heaven and the earth."

The subject of this inexhaustible declaration is "God" (Hebrew *elohim*, the uniplural name for the omnipotent God of creation). The object is the universe, "the heaven and the earth in the beginning" — that is, space and matter in a framework of time. The action of the subject on the object is "created." This is a completed action, not a continuing action. God is not continually "creating" the universe; He created it — once and for all — in the beginning. Thenceforth, the physical universe of space and matter and time would never cease to be. "I know that, whatsoever God doeth, it shall be for ever" (Eccles. 3:14). God is the Creator, not the Annihilator. Thereafter, space and time, matter and energy will forever be "conserved."

Some translators and commentators have argued that Genesis 1:1–2 could legitimately be translated in some such fashion as this: "In the beginning of God's creating the heaven and the earth, the earth was without form and void . . ." as though the universe already was existing in some chaotic state when God first began to "create" it.

Hebrew scholars disagree among themselves as to whether or not this is a legitimate translation linguistically, but it is certainly not a legitimate translation contextually. The whole purpose of Genesis 1 is so clearly to describe the beginning of the universe — including even the sun, moon, and stars — that no one could ever even imagine another meaning were he not predisposed to try to find a device for elongating the Genesis chronology and somehow to accommodate the evolutionary cosmogonic requirement for no real beginning.

Furthermore, this is not the only verse in the Bible that speaks of an absolute beginning of the universe. Only God is eternal. "In the beginning was the Word, and the Word was with God, and the Word was God" (John 1:1). The triune God alone existed eternally, and He spoke all things into being. "All things were made by him; and without him was not any thing made that was made" (John 1:3).

To emphasize the weight of this biblical testimony, many passages setting forth this theme are quoted and briefly discussed in the following pages.

## God's Pre-existence

The fundamental fact that irrevocably distinguishes true creationism from true evolutionism is the pre-existence of God. In no way can God be conditioned by an externally existing cosmos, since He alone brought the whole cosmos into existence at "time zero." The universe, the laws controlling the universe, the basic systems and processes of the universe, and the basic kinds of living creatures in the universe (including even the angels) were simply called into being by God, who alone is eternally omnipotent. Consider, for example, the following Scriptures:

> Before the mountains were brought forth, or ever thou hadst formed the earth and the world, even from everlasting to everlasting, thou art God (Ps. 90:2).

> The LORD possessed me [that is, the divine Wisdom, the eternal Word, the pre-incarnate Christ — see entire context] in the beginning of his way, before his works of old. I was set up from everlasting, from the beginning, or ever the earth was (Prov. 8:22–23).

> Knowing this first, that there shall come in the last days scoffers, walking after their own lusts, And saying, Where is the promise of his coming? for since the fathers fell asleep, all things continue as they were from the beginning of the creation. For this they willingly are ignorant of, that by the word of God the heavens were of old, and the earth standing out of the water and in the water (2 Pet. 3:3–5).

Note the explicit denial here of eternal "things," continuing from "the beginning" (not the "end") of the creation, and the explicit affirmation of special creation of the heavens and the earth by the divine Word. "For by him were all things created, that are in heaven, and that are in earth, visible and invisible, whether they be thrones, or dominions, or principalities, or powers: all things were created by him, and for him: And he is before all things, and by him all things consist" (Col. 1:16–17).

The context of the above passage specifically names Jesus Christ as the Creator, who was before all things. All things in heaven and earth owe their very existence to Him.

There are many other Scriptures that likewise affirm the pre-existence of the Creator, but these surely suffice to demonstrate this truth. The fundamental premise of evolutionist cosmogony — that is, the eternal existence of matter and the universe in some form — is thus clearly falsified by Scripture.

## The Completed Creation

That creation is not a continuing process, but a completed event of the past, is another biblical truth that pointedly refutes evolutionary cosmogony. In that type of cosmogony (whether the big-bang theory, the steady state theory, or others), the processes that existed at "the beginning of the creation" are still "continuing" (2 Pet. 3:4), so that stars, galaxies, life, etc., are continually being generated at various points throughout the universe by those evolutionary processes.

The Scriptures cited in the previous section on God's pre-existence all clearly affirm a completed creation. Many other passages do the same, as is evident from the fact that they all use the past tense of the relevant verb ("created," "made," etc.). The following are a few additional examples.

Thou, even thou, art LORD alone; thou hast made heaven, the heaven of heavens, with all their host, the earth, and all things that are therein, the seas, and all that is therein, and thou preservest them all; and the host of heaven worshippeth thee (Neh. 9:6).

The sea is his, and he made it: and his hands formed the dry land (Ps. 95:5).

Lift up your eyes on high, and behold who hath created these things, that bringeth out their host by number: he calleth them all by names by the greatness of his might, for that he is strong in power; not one faileth (Isa. 40:26).

For thus saith the LORD that created the heavens; God himself that formed the earth and made it; he hath established it, he created it not in vain, he formed it to be inhabited: I am the LORD; and there is none else (Isa. 45:18).

He was in the world, and the world was made by him, and the world knew him not (John 1:10).

God that made the world and all things therein, seeing that he is Lord of heaven and earth, dwelleth not in temples made with hands; Neither is worshipped with men's hands, as though he needed any thing, seeing he giveth to all life, and breath, and all things (Acts 17:24–25).

Thou, Lord, in the beginning hast laid the foundation of the earth; and the heavens are the works of thy hands (Heb. 1:10).

Thou art worthy, O Lord, to receive glory and honour and power: for thou hast created all things, and for thy pleasure they are and were created (Rev. 4:11).

## Fiat Creation

The Scriptures teach not only that creation was completed in the past, but also that it was essentially an instantaneous act — or, more precisely, a series of acts, spread over a six-day period. Some pseudo-creationists have tried to call evolution the "method of creation," alleging that the entire evolutionary cosmogonic history is somehow equivalent to creation. The Bible teaches unequivocally, however, that creation is not evolution. Creation was accomplished *ex nihilo* merely by the spoken, instantaneously obeyed, word of the Creator. Note Hebrews 11:3: "Through faith we understand that the worlds were framed by the word of God, so that things which are seen were not made of things which do appear."

This important verse, in the great "faith chapter" of Hebrews, shows that the foundation of all true faith is faith in God's special creation of all things and also stresses the fact that God did not utilize pre-existing materials at any point of His making of all these things. "By the word of the LORD were the heavens made; and all the host of them by the breath of his mouth. He gathereth the waters of the sea together as an heap: he layeth up the depth in storehouses. Let all the earth fear the LORD: let all the inhabitants of the world stand in awe of him. For he spake, and it was done; he commanded, and it stood fast" (Ps. 33:6–9).

Whether making the heavens or storing up the waters of the great deep, God's Word was instantly obeyed. At each act, He merely said, "Let there be. . . ." And it was! The Psalmist wrote: "Praise ye him, sun and moon: praise him, all ye stars of light. Praise him, ye heavens of heavens, and ye waters that be above the heavens. Let them praise the name of the LORD: for he commanded, and they were created" (Ps. 148:3–5).

"Remember the sabbath day, to keep it holy. Six days shalt thou labour, and do all thy work . . . for in six days the LORD made heaven and earth, the sea, and all that in them is, and rested the seventh day" (Exod. 20:8–11). This definitive verse makes as clear as words can express the fact that man's work week of six days is based explicitly on God's work week of six days. There is no legitimate way in which these divine "days" can be interpreted as anything but literal days. If they are six ages, or merely an elliptical expression for the geological ages or for six ages of revelation or anything but a work week of six real days, then God's very rigidly enforced weekly Sabbath is based on nothing but a vague and hollow pun. Any such conclusion surely is preposterous. God's work of creating the cosmos and all things therein certainly did not require the long imaginary ages of evolutionary cosmogony — at least not if the Bible is true and perspicuous. The only apparent reason, in fact, why the creation took six days was to provide an example for man's obedience. "The sabbath was made for man," Jesus said (Mark 2:27). God knew man would need a weekly rest and would need the divine pattern and commandment for its implementation. Otherwise, the entire creation could have been completed in an instant.

## Conservation of the Creation

In summary, the biblical creationist cosmogony reveals that God is not a part of the cosmos, but antecedent and transcendent to it, that the creation was accomplished not by process but by fiat, that it was completed in the past, and that it was produced *ex nihilo*. In all these aspects, it is in direct conflict with evolutionist cosmogony.

Furthermore, the cosmos, once completed is to be conserved forever. The laws of the cosmos are immutable, and the multitudes of heavenly bodies are to be maintained, each with its own peculiar structure for its own divine purpose. "One star differeth from another star in glory" (1 Cor. 15:41). The earth itself is uniquely different from all heavenly bodies, stars and planets alike. "The glory of the celestial is one, and the glory of the terrestrial is another" (1 Cor. 15:40).

God is not capricious. He does nothing without a purpose, and that purpose will be accomplished. Although we cannot, at this particular state of history, discern the distinctive purposes and functions of each of the stars and planets of the cosmos, we can be confident that these will all be revealed in the course of the ages to come. The fact that the universe is eternal, with all its myriads of stars, is revealed in such Scriptures as the following:

Thou hast made heaven, the heaven of heavens, with all their host . . . and thou preservest them all (Neh. 9:6).

And he built his sanctuary like high palaces, like the earth which he hath established for ever (Ps. 78:69).

Who laid the foundations of the earth, that it should not be removed for ever (Ps. 104:5).

Praise ye him, sun and moon: praise him, all ye stars of light. . . . He hath also stablished them for ever and ever: he hath made a decree, which shall not pass (Ps. 148:3–6).

One generation passeth away, and another generation cometh: but the earth abideth for ever (Eccles. 1:4).

I know that, whatsoever God doeth, it shall be for ever: nothing can be put to it, nor any thing taken from it; and God doeth it, that men should fear before him (Eccles. 3:14).

Thus saith the LORD, which giveth the sun for a light by day, and the ordinances of the moon and of the stars for a light by night. . . . If those ordinances depart from before me, saith the LORD, then the seed of Israel also shall cease from being a nation before me for ever (Jer. 31:35–36).

And they that be wise shall shine as the brightness of the firmament; and they that turn many to righteousness as the stars for ever and ever (Dan. 12:3).

. . . and upholding all things by the word of his power (Heb. 1:3).

These and other Scriptures clearly witness to the fact of a completed, eternally conserved creation. As already noted, this tremendous truth is likewise attested by the law of mass/energy conservation — the most universal and best-substantiated law in science. This is a law of physical science, but if this is true of the lesser, it must be true of the greater, which means that all created spirits are likewise eternal.

It may be recalled that the creation record in Genesis 1 mentions three distinct events of *ex nihilo* creation: (1) creation of the space/mass/time universe, with the "matter" in elemental form (Gen. 1:1); (2) creation of the "life" principle, referring not to mere preprogrammed genetic replication but to the entity of consciousness, as in animals (Gen. 1:21); (3) creation of man and woman in the "image of God," clearly a reference to the "godlike" qualities of mankind not shared with animals, especially the moral and spiritual attributes of human nature (Gen. 1:27).

The conservation principle may be understood with reference to these three categories of creation in some such fashion as follows. The law of conservation of mass/energy does not imply that every particular aggregation of matter or manifestation of energy must be conserved, but that the totality of matter, the totality of energy and/or the totality of matter/energy be conserved in any phenomenon.

In addition, certain systems of matter and energy (e.g., sun, earth, stars), as well as certain types of substances (e.g., water, gold) and even certain types of plants (e.g., tree of life) are specifically revealed in the Bible as present in the new earth and thus as existing forever. Although these statements are not detailed enough to warrant firm conclusions, they do at least imply that all the basic types of material entities originally formed by God out of the created matter and energy will also be preserved (or reformed) in the new heavens and new earth. This is also implied by the mere fact of God's purposiveness, and the perhaps as yet incompletely fulfilled accomplishment of His primeval purposes in all these material systems.

In analogous fashion, the conservation principle with respect to the created entity of conscious life does not require that each individual animal "soul," or "life," be preserved, but rather that each category be conserved. That is, the created entity of cat life, or horse life, or bear life, and so on, must be preserved intact. The genetic design for cats, for example, could not be transmuted into a system producing dogs. Each kind, whose seed was in itself, could only replicate after its own kind. The created pattern for each kind would be maintained without basic change forever. In each original created pair (and also, as far as land animals are concerned, in each pair on Noah's ark) was contained genetically the "lives" of all subsequent animals of that kind, so that the total *nephesh* of each kind, whether concentrated in the primeval pair or proliferated in all their progeny, has been maintained within fixed limits ever since.

Even in those cases where an entire kind has faded into extinction, the pattern or code for that kind exists forever in principle, as a permanently designed category. This may well encourage us to believe — although the Bible writers are not explicit on this point — that each kind of land animal, at least, may well be re-established by God's creative power in the new earth. Since, however, there will be "no more sea" in the new earth (Rev. 21:1), the created *nephesh* for the marine kinds will presumably persist thereafter only in pattern rather than in operation. In any case, the conservation principle guarantees that no created type of *nephesh* can ever evolve into some other type of *nephesh*.

With respect to the creation of individual men and women, the conservation law is applied far more comprehensively and specifically than is the case either for matter/energy or for the life principle. Each single "person," with his or her particular identity, must be preserved eternally. This is so because each person is created "in the image of God" (Gen. 1:27) and this requires individual personality — not only possessing conscious life but self-conscious life, capable of abstract thought, of understanding right and wrong, of giving and receiving love, of spiritual worship. This category — that of personhood — is meaningful only in terms of individuality, and thus each person (like God, in whose image he or she was created) must continue to exist forever — somewhere, somehow.

Although the person could in principle exist apart from a physical body (composed of material elements like the earth) and from biological life processes (like those of animals) — and, in fact will so exist between the time of physical death and the resurrection — God has promised someday to restore both to the person, an incorruptible form when Christ returns. He will, indeed, preserve our whole spirit and soul and body (1 Thess. 5:23) and restore them all together as one indissoluble unit in that day.

This great principle of conservation is thus marvelously pervasive. God was not capricious in His great work of creation, and His great work of redemption and restoration assures that all His purposes in creation will be fulfilled. What God does, is forever!

## Fallacies in the Evolutionary Cosmogonies

The clear biblical testimony of special, fiat, completed and conserved creation of the cosmos is, of course, explicitly supported by the two great laws of thermodynamics, the most secure generalizations about the universe that exist in science. These two laws are universal laws, if there is such a thing. No exception to either of them has ever been found. The first, the universal law of conservation, we have just discussed. The second, also known as "time's arrow," is the universal law of *deterioration*, and will be discussed in detail later.

Both of these laws, individually and jointly, clearly contradict the evolutionist cosmogony. Evolutionists purport to describe a cosmos in which all things come into existence and build themselves up into higher, more complex levels of existence by purely natural processes in a universe that is self-contained and self-sufficient. That is, evolution is a universal *principle of innovation and integration*, functioning in a closed-system universe. The laws of thermodynamics, on the other hand, describe a universal *principle of conservation and disintegration*, functioning in a universe that must, at least in its beginning, have been an open-system universe, created and energized by a Creator/energizer transcendent to it. That is, the two universal laws of science yield exactly the same conclusion stated in Genesis 1:1: "In the beginning God created the heaven and the earth."

The first law states, in effect, that the universe could not have created itself. The second law states, in effect, that it must have been created or else it would already have completely disintegrated. The arrow of time points downward and, if these present laws continue to operate, the universe will eventually "die," with the sun and all its reservoirs of useful energy completely depleted. It will not cease to exist (by the first law), but it will be dead (by the second law). Since it is not yet dead, it must have had a beginning; if it were infinitely old, it would already be dead.

By the evolutionary presupposition, there is no external agent available to rejuvenate it. It is a closed system, operating all by itself. But by the second law, a closed system must proceed toward disintegration: it cannot organize itself into higher levels of integration or organization, as the evolutionary concept requires.

Thus, the two most certain laws of science flatly and explicitly contradict the evolutionary cosmogony. The only way the evolutionary cosmogony could be valid would be at some time or place where the laws of science were not valid.

The cosmos is a continuum of space and time, and the laws of thermodynamics apply to all systems of mass and energy that have ever been observed and measured in space and time, with no known exceptions. But it may be conceivable that in some portions of space and time that cannot be observed and measured the laws don't apply. If so, an evolutionary cosmogony might then be conceivable.

This situation has already been discussed, but is also mentioned here because of its profound importance. There are only two basic types of evolutionary cosmogony that might be devised to overcome the laws of thermodynamics. One makes use of nonobservable space, the other of nonobservable time. Note figure 6.

In the first instance, the continual "death" of those portions of the cosmos accessible to observation can be offset by postulating a continual "birth" of corresponding portions of the universe which are not accessible to observation. Far out in nonobservable space, there is a continual evolution (out of nothing!) of mass/energy in some form, which then enters into the cosmic process to keep it all in balance somehow as the observable cosmos decays. This is the famous

**FIGURE 6 — *Creationist Cosmogony (Based on Laws of Thermodynamics) Versus Evolutionary Cosmogonies***
*The two laws of thermodynamics, as based on all observable scientific data, point back to special creation of the universe. The two basic evolutionary cosmogonies, on the other hand, must be based on nonobservable processes, simply to avoid the implication of creation.*

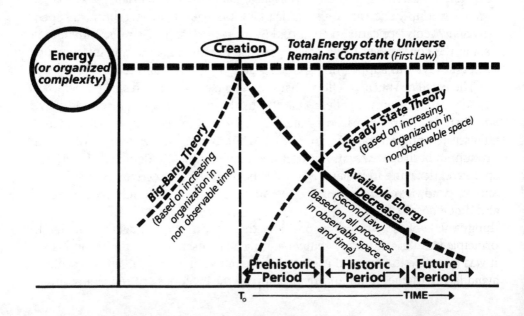

steady state theory, originated and popularized over 50 years ago by the great British astronomer, Sir Fred Hoyle.

In the second instance, the matter and energy of the cosmos were in some unknown fashion brought into existence and into complex organization at a primeval discontinuity in time. This is the even more famous big-bang theory, according to which the matter, energy, and organization of the cosmos somehow evolved in a very brief period of nonobservable time, just before the beginning of the present order of things — the present order being described by the laws of thermodynamics.

Thus, an evolutionary cosmogony is supposedly able to overcome the creationist cosmogony demanded by the two laws of science, simply by denying the cosmic validity of the laws. Either in nonobservable space or nonobservable time, the laws don't apply. But it should be remembered that in observable space and time they do apply! This is the domain of science; the other is sheer metaphysical speculation. It seems that, in cosmogony at least, the application of sound science points to the special creation of the cosmos; an evolutionary cosmogony can be held only at the cost of repudiating true science.

In addition to this most basic fallacy of the two types of evolutionary cosmogonies — namely, their conflict with the most important and basic laws of science, the first and second laws of thermodynamics — both cosmogonies have repeatedly encountered other serious problems, and neither can point to any real unequivocal supporting evidence.

## Abandonment of the Steady State

The steady state theory, or as it used to be called, the continuous creation theory, has largely been abandoned even by its former advocates. There never was any real evidence for it. Imagine basing an entire cosmology on hydrogen atoms suddenly appearing out of nothing, coming from nowhere! These imaginary atoms could never have appeared to anyone, since their supposed materialization always was supposed to have occurred at such times and places as never to be detectable. The only reason for postulating such an absurdity was the necessity to escape the creationist implications of the laws of thermodynamics. Hoyle and his followers merely invented what they called the "perfect cosmological principle," stating that the large-scale structure of the universe must always be uniform in both space and time. Since the universe appeared to be expanding in space and decaying in time, this principle was held to require a continuous creation (actually evolution) of matter or energy out of nothing throughout space and time in order to compensate for these apparent changes, thus keeping everything in a "steady state." The fact is, of course, that their perfect cosmological principle was not in any way based on scientific observation or experimentation. It was metaphysical speculation, pure and simple, deemed necessary in order to avoid facing the necessity of creation and a confrontation with the Creator.

Interestingly, Sir Fred eventually abandoned his original steady state theory and, with a few other very competent astronomers, had been trying to revise it. His death in 2001 leaves its future uncertain at best. The big-bang theory is currently the accepted evolutionary cosmogony, believed almost as an orthodoxy by evolutionists in all fields.

## Contradictions of the Big Bang

A number of astrophysicists are beginning to have their doubts about the big-bang theory, too. One prominent astronomer, after discussing the various evidences, concludes, "These arguments should indicate to the uncommitted that the big-bang picture is not as soundly established, either theoretically or observationally, as it is usually claimed to be — astrophysicists of today who hold the view that 'the ultimate cosmological problem' has been more or less solved may well be in for a few surprises before this century runs out."[1]

One eminent astronomer at Dartmouth College, after discussing various problems with the big-bang theory, made the following observation: "In the light of all these problems, it is astounding that the big-bang hypothesis is the only cosmological model that physicists have taken seriously."[2]

The main evidence for the big bang has been the so-called 3°K background radiation, supposed to be the uniform low-energy remnant of the primeval cosmic explosion. However, Jayant Narlikar and others have shown that this radiation can be explained in various other ways as well as by the hypothetical explosion.

There are several other serious problems with the big bang. Some of these are listed below.

1. The primordial explosion should have propelled all the matter/energy of the cosmos out radially from its center, and by the principle of conservation of angular momentum, none of it could ever thereafter have acquired any kind of curvilinear motion. Yet there are all kinds of curving and orbiting motions of the stars and galaxies of the cosmos, a situation that seems quite impossible if the universe began with the big bang.
2. Sensitive measurements in recent years have increasingly been showing that the background radiation is not homogeneous and isotropic (that is, the same in all directions), as it should be if it had been produced by the big bang, but is "anisotropic" in all directions.
3. The universe is anything but uniform in large-scale structure, as both the big-bang and steady state theories require, but instead is full of huge agglomerations of matter in some regions and vast empty spaces in others, scattered around the cosmos in far from any uniform manner. Some astronomers are now trying somehow to justify a primeval lumpy big bang!

1. Jayant Narlikar, "Was There a Big Bang?" *New Scientist*, 91 (July 2, 1981): 21.
2. Robert Oldershaw, "What's Wrong with the New Physics?" *New Scientist*, 128 (Dec. 22–29, 1990): 59.

4. In the context of the primeval fireball, it is hard to justify the accumulation of any amount of matter in any one location such as a star. If the explosion is driving all galaxies apart in the resulting expansion, how could it fail to drive all atoms apart before they came together in galaxies?

5. The most serious objection comes back again to the second law of thermodynamics. Explosions produce disorder, not order! The primordial superexplosion surely would have produced absolute chaos and the most utter disorder. If the universe is indeed a closed system, as evolutionary cosmogonists allege, then how in the name of sense and science could this primeval chaotic disorder have possibly generated the beautifully organized and complexly ordered universe that we now have? The big-bang idea, viewed in this light, is as absurd as the steady state idea.

## Cosmogonic Fantasia

Even the big-bang theory, with all its obvious physical impossibilities, does not mark the outer limit of the evolutionist's faith. Since this cosmic atom and its primeval explosion constitute such a flagrant contradiction of the laws of thermodynamics, a few astrophysicists (e.g., Robert Jastrow and Paul Davies) have suggested that some kind of divine miracle may have been involved and this may even have been the primeval act of creation by God. Naturally, theistic evolutionists and progressive creationists have likewise incorporated the big bang into their own compromising interpretations of Genesis, proposing that the declaration of Genesis 1:1 refers to this explosive irruption of energy and matter into the universe at the beginning.

Most scientific advocates of the big bang, however, have tried to incorporate even this unique event within the framework of evolutionary naturalism. Isaac Asimov, the most prolific science writer of our generation, is typical of these. As an atheist, he could not allow himself to think that the cosmos had an ultimate beginning, and therefore an ultimate cause. "The Bible describes a Universe created by God, maintained by him, and intimately and constantly directed by him, while science describes a Universe in which it is not necessary to postulate the existence of God at all."[3] Asimov recognized there is an apparent problem with the second law of thermodynamics, but by-passes this by assuming that somehow the primeval cosmic egg was very highly ordered, so that although it must become increasingly disordered with time, it could still generate all the ordered systems of the universe. "The cosmic egg may be structureless (as far as we know), but it apparently represented a very orderly conglomeration of matter. Its explosion represented a vast shift in the direction of disorder, and ever since, the amount of disorder in the Universe has been increasing."[4]

---

3. Isaac Asimov, *In the Beginning* (New York, NY: Crown, 1981), p. 13.
4. Ibid., p. 24. It is amazing that an atheist such as Asimov would write a verse-by-verse commentary on the first 11 chapters of Genesis, but that is what this book purports to be!

Exactly how the primeval universe could be both completely without structure and also possess a high degree of order at the same time is mind-puzzling. In
ordinary usage, "structure" and "order" are essentially synonymous. But even if
we overlook this anomaly, there is still the problem of explaining the high initial
order without an "orderer." Asimov at least acknowledges the problem. "The existence of the cosmic egg is, however, itself something of an anomaly. If the general movement of the universe is from order to disorder, how did the order (which
presumably existed in the cosmic egg) originate? Where did it come from?"[5] Since
Asimov cannot admit a supernatural cause of order, he must postulate a naturalistic ordering agent. But since the basic law of nature says that disorder increases
with time, he must assume a different basic law of nature before time — that is,
before the instant of the big bang. And so he assumes (as do most other modern
cosmogonists) that the second law was reversed before the big bang. This means
he must believe the universe is eternally oscillating: when it contracts, order increases; when it expands (as at present), order decreases.

This notion, of course, is sheer imagination. It has not even been proved that
the present universe is expanding, although this is certainly the most common
interpretation of the famous "red-shift," the so-called Doppler effect, the shift of
the light rays from distant galaxies toward the red end of the optical spectrum. To
speculate that a universe that perhaps now is expanding and gaining entropy was
long, long ago possibly contracting and losing entropy (that is, gaining order)
may be permissible as fantasy but scarcely qualifies as science! Even if the universe were to start contracting, there is not the slightest reason to think that the
entropy law would ever be reversed in such an operation. Much more likely, the
more it contracted, the more its components collide and become fragmented into
utter disorder.

Even if this problem is ignored, the only force available to cause the galaxies
to come together is gravity, but the force of gravity depends on mass, and the total
mass of all galaxies plus intergalactic dust is many times too small to support such
a gravitational collapse. Asimov also recognized this problem, but he ignored it. "I
have a hunch that the 'missing mass' required to raise the density to the proper
figure will yet be found and that the universe will yet be discovered to oscillate."[6]
Thus, Isaac Asimov offers us a "hunch" as the reason why we should reject the
overwhelming evidence that the universe must have been created by God.

The missing mass has more recently proliferated into hot dark matter, cold
dark matter, and even dark energy, none of which have ever been seen or measured, but all of which seem necessary to explain the inferred nature of our naturalistic cosmos without God. The very first two affirmations of the famous Humanist Manifesto[7] are as follows: "*First*. Religious humanists regard the universe

    5. Ibid.
    6. Ibid., p. 25.
    7. American Humanist Association, "Humanist Manifesto I," *The New Humanist* 6 (May–June 1933).

as self-existing and not created. *Second.* Humanism believes that man is a part of nature and that he has emerged as the result of a continuous process." An influential Harvard biologist has bluntly expressed this remarkable "particles-to-people" philosophy as follows:

> It is a fundamental evolutionary generalization that no external agent imposes life on matter. Matter takes the form it does because it has the inherent capacity to do so. . . . This is one of the most remarkable and mysterious facts about our universe; that matter exists that has the capacity to form itself into the existence of a vital force or entelechy or universal intelligence, but just to state an attribute of matter as represented by the atoms and molecules we know."[8]

Thus, to the consistent evolutionist, self-existent and self-organizing matter, operating by random natural processes over eternal eons of time, has replaced God as ultimate reality.

Exactly *how* matter does this, despite the law of increasing disorder in the universe (second law of thermodynamics), is apparently to be left as an article of faith in the evolutionist's creed. No evidence or explanation is necessary, since the only alternative is God, and the concept of God is unscientific!

> The more statistically improbable a thing is, the less can we believe that it just happened by blind chance. Superficially the obvious alternative to chance is an intelligent Designer.
>
> . . . I am afraid I shall give God rather short shrift . . . as an explanation of organized complexity he simply will not do. It is organized complexity we are trying to explain, so it is foolish to invoke in explanation a being sufficiently organized and complex to create it.[9]

This remarkable statement, by the Oxford University zoology professor who invented the equally remarkable concept of "selfish genes" was apparently written in all seriousness! It is foolish, he says, to try to explain a given effect by a cause adequate to produce the effect. It is more scientific, presumably, to explain effects by causes that are not adequate to produce them. It must be such reasoning that the apostle Paul had in mind when he wrote about people who, "professing themselves to be wise . . . became fools" (Rom. 1:22). Perhaps God is unacceptable to such men, but they certainly have no better (in fact, no *other*) explanation to offer for the complex cosmos.

## Modifications of the Big Bang

The basic big-bang theory, as inferred from the assumed expansion of the universe, starts with an infinitesimal particle of space-time (not a particle *in* space, but *of* space!), which has evolved into our complex cosmos, with its incredibly

---

8. P.J. Darlington, *Evolution for Naturalists* (New York, NY: John Wiley, 1980), p. 233.

9  Richard Dawkins, "The Necessity of Darwinism," *New Scientist,* 94 (April 15, 1982): 130. In context, Dawkins here is defending neo-Darwinism against other forms of evolution.

numerous stars and galaxies, and its eventual animal and human inhabitants.

However, the concept has encountered many difficulties, and so is being frequently modified and extended. One of the more widely accepted modifications has been the "inflationary hypothesis," advanced by Alan Guth of M.I.T. in the early 1980s. According to this now fairly widely accepted notion, the primeval infinitesimal universe first went through a rapid inflation to about the size of a grapefruit in $10^{-35}$ second, doing this with a speed vastly exceeding the velocity of light! It then proceeded to go through the whole alleged scenario of the big bang, eventually evolving into our present cosmos.

And where did the initial point universe come from? It came — they say — from nothing! As Guth says, "So, in the inflationary theory the universe evolves from essentially nothing at all, which is why I frequently refer to it as the ultimate free lunch."[10]

Evolutionists used to criticize Christians for believing in *ex nihilo* creation, but now they want us to believe in *ex nihilo* evolution! Actually, we never believed in creation out of nothing at all, but rather creation by God — creation *ex deo*! But now they want us to believe that quantum theory actually allows for quantum fluctuations of nothing into something — which in turn, in billions of years becomes our amazing universe. Remarkable!

> If this theory is correct, then seeds of structure are nothing more than patterns of quantum fluctuation from the inflationary era. In a very real sense, quantum fluctuations would be the origins of everything we see in the universe.[11]

"Very real!" he says? But at least he does hedge this conclusion with the assumption that the inflation theory is correct. And *that* is the big question. As another astronomer says:

> Even so, there is no proof that inflation is correct: and, to add to the uncertainty, distinct versions of the theory have proliferated, as physicists grapple with the problem of finding an inflation that could have produced the universe but is also compatible with known laws of physics.[12]

He goes on to recite still more modifications that have been tried.

> The theory now comes in varieties called old, new, chaotic, hybrid, and open inflation, with numerous subdivisions like super symmetric, supernatural, and hyper-extended inflation, each a vision of just how the inflation might have touched off the birth of the universe we see today.[13]

Still another astrophysicist, after trying to sort through all the problems, expostulated, "But then nobody knows whether inflation actually happened any-

10. Alan Guth, "Cooking up a Cosmos," *Astronomy,* 25 (Sept. 1997): 54.
11. Rocky Kolb, "Planting Primordial Seeds," *Astronomy,* 26 (Feb. 1998): 43.
12. James Ganz, "Which Way to the Big Bang?" *Science,* 284 (May 28, 1999): 1448.
13. Ibid.

way."[14] In spite of all this, the inflationary theory has become widely accepted by cosmogonists, because the big bang needs it!

But there are still other fantastic ideas floating in the cosmogonic market-place. There is the remarkable theory of Andre Lind, of Stanford, who thinks that each universe generates other universes, so there are multiple universes out there, with ours happening to be the one that allowed life to evolve. A variant of the multiple-universe idea assumes that all are clones of each other, so that there are actually multiple versions of you and me and everyone else out there, too.

Needless to say, there is no observational evidence of any such thing — just imaginative mathematical manipulation. And how about the so-called "string theory" of the cosmos, which comes up with 10 or 11 or so dimensions of space, rather than the three-dimensional real space in which we live? But as Eric Chaisson of Tufts University cautions, "And although the theory of super strings is now causing great excitement in the physics community, there is to date not a shred of experimental or observational evidence to support it."[15]

The same author has the same cold water to throw on the oscillating universe theory. "Alas, there is not a shred of observational evidence to favor an oscillating universe. . . ."[16]

In addition to these speculations, modern cosmo-philosophy seems to non-initiates to be a strange fantasyland, not only of big bangs and oscillating universes, but also of black holes, curved space, time reversals, antimatter, quarks, space-time warps, and an assortment of other weird and wonderful phenomena derived from relativistic mathematics. Whether or not such abstractions have any physical reality in the cosmos is a matter of controversy even among evolutionist astrophysicists, but none have ever been observed!

In any case, there is no need to discuss such problematical phenomena in an exposition of biblical cosmogony. Whatever merit these far-out speculations may have in relativistic mathematical metaphysics, they seem forever outside the realm of anything that could be studied experimentally, and the Bible certainly has nothing to say about any of them.

In conclusion, the straightforward biblical record of cosmic creation can be accepted in its most natural and literal sense, in full confidence that all the speculations of evolutionary cosmogony are unproved and unprovable. The real facts of physics and astronomy are all perfectly consistent with the biblical revelation of special, recent, fiat, complete creation of the universe.

---

14. Peter Coles, "The End of the Old Model Universe," *Nature*, 393 (June 25, 1998): 743.
15. Eric J. Chaisson, *Cosmic Evolution* (Cambridge, MA: Harvard University Press, 2001), p. 246.
16. Ibid., p. 10.

# THE HOST OF HEAVEN
*Biblical Astronomy*

"*The heavens declare the glory of God*" (Ps. 19:1). The Bible writers frequently mention the starry heavens, always with a sense of awe of their beauty and precision and majesty. While we may wonder at the divine function commissioned by God for each individual star out of the almost infinitely great number of stars in the universe, one major purpose of all of them is certainly that of praising their Creator. In the preceding chapter, it was shown that, according to the Bible, the universe has not evolved into its present form; it was created in its present form! In this chapter the various components of the heavenly universe will be examined in relation to the biblical references. Why did God create stars in such great profusion and variety? Are there other solar systems out there with planets like ours? What does the Bible say about our own solar system, with its sun and moon, planets and comets, asteroids and meteorites? Is there any reference in the Bible to extraterrestrial life? Do the facts of modern scientific astronomy support the various biblical passages dealing with the heavens? These and other such questions will be discussed in this chapter.

## The Number of the Stars

The most obvious question about the stars is, "How many are there?" A glance at the heavens on a clear, starry night immediately impresses one with their great number in all parts of the sky. Yet only about four thousand or so stars can actually be seen without a telescope, and this would hardly seem to warrant what seem to be many extravagant claims in Scripture about their numbers. For example: "That in blessing I will bless thee, and in multiplying I will multiply thy seed as the stars of the heaven, and as the sand which is upon the sea shore" (Gen. 22:17). "As the host of heaven cannot be numbered, neither the sand of the sea measured: so will I multiply the seed of David my servant" (Jer. 33:22).

However one wishes to interpret the "seed" mentioned in such passages (whether as spiritual seed, or in terms of the impossibility of physically counting a greatly multiplied number of physical descendants, or in some other way), the point in this connection is that the number of stars and the number of grains of sand are considered to be equivalent measures of quantity for comparison purposes. Since one could easily count to four thousand (or whatever the actual number of visible stars may be), this can only imply that there were such multitudes of stars (although invisible to men in ancient times) as to make the job of counting ("numbering") them as impossible as counting all the grains of sand. God also told Abraham it would be as difficult to count his ultimate seed as it would be to number the stars (Gen. 15:5)[1] or to number the dust of the earth (Gen. 13:16).

Now, although no one can say for sure what these numbers are, they are at least comparable in magnitude. With the giant telescopes now available (note figure 7), astronomers have statistically estimated that there are about $10^{25}$ stars (that is, 10 million billion billion) in the known universe. One can also calculate that this is about the number of grains of sand[2] in the world. In any case, it is not possible to count either number. If one could count even as many as 20 numbers per second, it would still take him at least 100 million billion years to count up to $10^{25}$!

And there may actually be even an infinite number of stars! Since God is infinite, and He is the Creator of the universe, there is no reason to assume that either our telescopes or our relativistic mathematics have penetrated to its boundaries. What could be beyond the "boundary" of space, except more space? "For as the heavens are higher than the earth, so are my ways higher than your ways, and my thoughts than your thoughts" (Isa. 55:9). Since the ratio of God's omniscience to man's wisdom is infinite, so apparently is the ratio of the size of the universe to that of the earth, according to this assertion by God himself.

Even though no man could count all the stars, God of course can do it. In fact, He has even assigned names to each one of them. "He telleth the number of the stars; he calleth them all by their names" (Ps. 147:4, see also Isa. 40:26). Just as Adam named the animals in accordance with their distinctive characteristics (Gen. 2:19–20), so God has named the stars. This can only mean that, despite the

---

1. There are many other biblical references comparing the number of children of Israel to the number of stars. These include Genesis 26:4; Exodus 32:13; Deuteronomy 1:10; 10:22; 28:62; 1 Chronicles 27:23; Nehemiah 9:23; and Hebrews 11:12. Although some of these refer to Israel's numbers at the time of writing and thus to numbers only in terms of millions, even these numbers were vastly more than the number of visible stars, indicating divinely given knowledge that there were multitudes of stars that could not be seen.
2. See *The Genesis Record*, Henry M. Morris (Grand Rapids, MI: Baker, 1976), p. 384.

*FIGURE 7 — **The Number of the Stars***

This typical photograph of a section of the starry heavens, taken through a modern giant telescope, pictorially emphasizes the biblical teaching of the tremendous number of stars, anticipating modern astronomy by three thousand years.

immensity of their number, each has been created for a particular purpose, with distinctive characteristics and attributes of its own, to be discovered or revealed in God's good time.

## Variety of the Stars

To the untrained, unaided human eye, all the stars look just about the same, except for difference in brightness, and this difference could easily be assumed to be simply a matter of distance. Even with a telescope, all seem to be merely points of light in the sky. Yet the Bible indicates that all are distinct. Not only has God given them all individual names, but also "one star differeth from another star in glory" (1 Cor. 15:41). The word translated "glory" (Greek *doxa*) can also be translated "dignity," "honor," "praise," or "worship." It thus does not refer merely to the star's brightness, but seems to indicate again that every star has its own divinely designed structure for its own particular divinely ordained function.

That every star is different is indicated scientifically by the fact that each will plot at a different location on a standard astronomical graph known as a Hertzsprung-Russell (HR) diagram. The horizontal axis of the HR diagram is the temperature of the star (with values decreasing toward the right). The vertical axis is the brightness (measured in relation to the sun's brightness), increasing upward. See figure 8.

Although every star will have its own unique position on the diagram, astronomers have tried for convenience to group them by generic names, depending on the region of the diagram in which they fall. Most stars fall somewhere within a broad band that drops gently to the right. These are called main-sequence stars. In general, the bright, hot stars are also larger and heavier. Furthermore, as one proceeds down the slope on the main-sequence band, the spectral type of stars tends to change, from blue-white on the left (bright, hot stars) to red on the right (cool, dim stars). These spectral varieties have been arbitrarily classified into seven classes shown in table 3.

Most of the information that can be learned about stars comes from spectroscopic analysis of their light, as tabulated above. Detailed analysis of stellar spectra can determine a star's surface temperature, its chemical composition, the nature of its magnetic field, and many other properties.

The above categories do not by any means exhaust the different types of stars. Some of the others are red giants, supergiants, white dwarfs, variable stars, pulsars, binaries, planetary nebulae, neutron stars, black holes (possibly), and others. Stars are also classified as Population I stars (containing considerable amounts of heavy elements) and Population II stars (made up almost entirely of the light elements hydrogen and helium).

There are also various types of massive star groupings, or galaxies. These include the elliptical nebulae, the normal spiral nebulae, the barred spirals, the dwarf galaxies, and the irregular galaxies. Our own solar system is part of the

FIGURE 8 — Hertzsprung-Russell Diagram and Stellar Variety
*The standard HR diagram has been interpreted as representing an evolutionary hierarchy of stars. In actuality it stresses the biblical teaching of an infinite variety of stars, each star plotting at its own distinctive point on the diagram.*

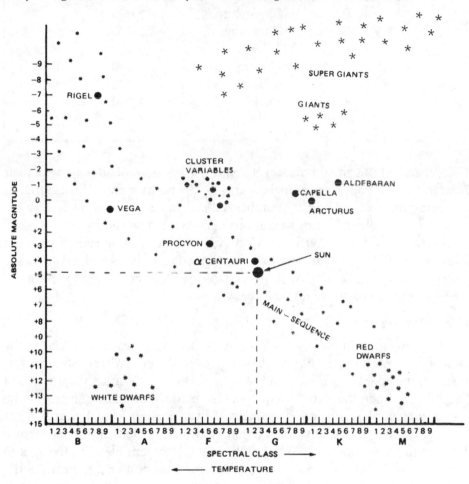

Milky Way galaxy, which is apparently one of the spiral galaxies. Within a galaxy, as in the Milky Way, there are various subgroupings of stars, including the galactic clusters and the globular clusters. The galaxies also are joined in various groupings, known as clusters of galaxies. The Milky Way is associated with over 20 other galaxies called the Local Group. Then there are clusters of clusters, known as superclusters.

Since this is not a textbook on astronomy, and since the Bible mentions nothing about this array of stars and galaxies (actually none of the galaxies, except the Milky Way, can even be seen without a telescope), we shall not attempt to define and discuss these various components of the heavens. The fact of an almost infinite number and variety of great objects in the heavens is what is stressed by the

| TABLE 3 — Seven Classes of Spectral Varieties of Stars | | |
|:---:|:---:|:---:|
| Spectral Class | Color | Typical Temperature |
| O | Blue-white | 35,000°K |
| B | Blue-white | 21,000 |
| A | White | 10,000 |
| F | Creamy | 7,200 |
| G | Yellow | 6,000 |
| K | Orange | 4,700 |
| M | Red | 3,300 |

Bible, and all of this should cause us to rejoice at the power and majesty of their Creator. "Lift up your eyes on high, and behold who hath created these things, that bringeth out their host by number: he calleth them all by names, by the greatness of his might, for that he is strong in power; not one faileth" (Isa. 40:26). Even though we do not yet know God's reasons for creating such a vast and diverse array of stars, we can be sure there are good reasons. As pointed out in the preceding chapter, the stars have been established forever, so there is plenty of time in the ages to come to find out these things.

## The Solar System

By far the most important of all the $10^{25}$ stars of the heavens, at least in the present order of things, is the sun. Although only a rather ordinary star in terms of size or intrinsic brightness, its mission "to divide the day from the night" and "to give light upon the earth" (Gen. 1:14–15) marks it as unique among all the host of heaven. In God's created economy and divine purpose, the earth is not only the home of men and women uniquely created in God's image, but is also destined to be the home of God himself, in the New Jerusalem, in the ages to come. The sun, with its tremendous output of radiant heat energy, provides the physical power to sustain all of the earth's physical and biological processes. It is physically speaking, "the light of the world" (John 8:12), and on the earth, "there is nothing hid from the heat thereof" (Ps. 19:6).

The sun is mentioned specifically at least 175 times in the Bible, almost three times as often as all the rest of the stars put together. Next in importance to the sun, also because of its relation to the earth, is the moon, specifically mentioned 40 times in the Bible (not including the very numerous references to "months"). From the point of view of both God and man (by whom and for whom, respectively, the Word of God was revealed), of all the physical bodies in the universe, the earth is most important, then the sun and moon, then the stars. Therefore, the earth was created first (Gen. 1:1), then the two great lights to rule the day and night (Gen. 1:16), then finally "the stars also" (Gen. 1:16).

This is the reverse of both the importance and chronological order imagined by evolutionists, according to whom the universe evolved first, then its galaxies of stars, and finally the solar system, with the earth and moon somehow spinning off from the sun in the process. Although it is clearly impossible to prove scientifically which of these two sequences is correct, the biblical order is far more logical. The earth is the most complex body in the physical universe, so far as known. The moon is much less complex than the earth, and the sun (consisting mostly of hydrogen and helium) is very much less complex than the moon. The various stars are probably even less complex than the sun. Intrinsic value, of course, is measured by organized complexity — by "information" — rather than mere size.

The Genesis record indicates that the original act of creation brought into existence the basic space-mass-time universe (Gen. 1:1), with space identified as "heaven," mass (matter) as "earth," and time as "beginning." The second act of creation was that of "living creatures" or "life" (Gen. 1:21), the third that of man "in the image of God" (Gen. 1:27). In addition to the basic acts of creation (that is, of calling into existence) were numerous divine acts of "making" and "forming" the created entities into complex systems. This apparently means that all the matter in the universe was originally part of the earth. From these elements, God formed all the earth's complex physical and chemical systems, including even the replicating chemical systems called plants. Then, from the abundance of matter still remaining, He made the sun and stars, igniting their vast reservoirs of light elements to provide lights for the universe by some remarkable, but still uncertain process. Possibly the moon, as well as the planets and their satellites, were constituted of some of the earth's more complex "left-over" inorganic systems.

This biblical order — earth, sun, moon, stars — will seem shocking to evolutionists, of course, but there is nothing either impossible or illogical about it in the context of God's creative power and purpose. It must be remembered that God's work of creation and making all things was "finished" at the end of the six days (Gen. 2:1–3), so that present-day natural processes are not the same as the processes of the creation period. Consequently, it is illegitimate and actually impossible to determine the order or duration of the events of the creation period by extrapolation of present processes. The earth is the center of God's interest in the universe, with the sun, moon, and stars merely providing various essential services for the earth and its inhabitants.

The solar system is not mentioned in the Bible as an organized system, of course, since the various planets could not have been recognized as planets until the invention of the telescope. To the naked eye, the planets appear simply as stars and, as far as their function is concerned, they serve along with all of the other stars of heaven, as well as the sun and moon, "for signs, and for seasons, and for days, and years" (Gen. 1:14). However, there seem to be a number of allusions in the Bible to some of the individual planets, since these "stars" were indeed recognized as "wandering stars" (Jude 13) against the background of the more slow-moving regular stars.

During biblical times, only five of these planets (a name derived from a Greek word meaning "wanderers") could actually be seen. These were the three "terrestrial planets" — Mercury, Venus, and Mars — so called because of their solid construction, like Earth, and the two closest "Jovian" planets, Jupiter and Saturn. The most distant planets — Uranus, Neptune, and Pluto — were not discovered until more modern times.

The five visible planets were well known to ancient astrologers, and were associated with important deities in the various systems of pagan polytheism practiced in antiquity. There are a number of equivocal references to these planets in the Bible — not in their role as planets, but as the gods or goddesses associated with their names. The brightest object in the heavens, except for the sun and moon, is the planet Venus, also called both "morning star" and "evening star." Since it is the only "star" bright enough to be seen in the daytime, it is also called the "day star."

This beautiful star is referred to in the Scriptures as a symbol of Christ no less than three times. Christ is called "the day star" in 2 Peter 1:19 and "the bright and morning star" in Revelation 2:28 and 22:16. In each case, the rising of the morning star is evidently taken as symbolic of the return of Christ.

Satan, as the great usurper and deceiver, the one who would dethrone Christ and make himself king of the universe, is also symbolized by this star when he is called Lucifer. Isaiah 14:12 says, "How art thou fallen from heaven, O Lucifer, son of the morning!" The name "Lucifer" means "day star," and is so rendered in some translations. Satan's counterfeit star may seem to be rising in this age, but Christ is the true day star. "Lucifer" will eventually prove to be a falling star (Rev. 9:1) rather than the true rising morning star.

To the naturalistic astronomer, Earth is merely one of the planets, all of which are in orbit around the sun. In the Bible, however, Earth is more important than all of them put together and even than the sun itself. When the earth is made new, there will be "no need of the sun" in the New Jerusalem (Rev. 21:23).

At present, however, the sun is absolutely indispensable. All of the processes of life on earth, as well as its inorganic processes, derive their energy ultimately from the sun. The biblical eulogies of the sun are well merited. The classic example is Psalm 19. "In them hath he set a tabernacle for the sun, which is as a bridegroom coming out of his chamber, and rejoiceth as a strong man to run a race. His going forth is from the end of the heaven, and his circuit unto the ends of it: and there is nothing hid from the heat thereof" (Ps. 19:4–6). In this passage, the phrase "going forth" refers not so much to the sunrise as to that which is perpetually "going forth" from the sun — that is, its "heat," its radiations. It is the same word as in Psalm 65:8: "Thou makest the outgoings of the morning and evening to rejoice." It is used also in connection with the gushing forth of water from a spring and other similar uses.

These prodigious outgoings of the sun, only a minute percentage of which actually reach the earth to sustain all the processes thereon, are still quite mysterious as to their actual nature. Most astrophysicists believe they are derived from the energy released by thermonuclear fusion processes deep in the heart of the sun.

The moon, of course, was created "to rule the night" (Gen. 1:16) and it does so by reflecting the light of the sun to that portion of the earth which has turned away at night from the direct light of the sun. The moon is now known, as a result of the space program and the lunar landings, to be completely void of life (just as the Bible had indicated all along) but to be composed of similar rocks and minerals to those on the earth. At the same time, the structure of the moon, as well as the proportions of the different rocks and minerals, is so vastly different from the corresponding attributes of Earth as to make it almost certain that the two could not have had a common evolutionary origin.

It is remarkable that the sun's diameter is about four hundred times that of the moon and its distance from the earth is also about four hundred times that of the moon. This means that the moon is just exactly large enough to precisely cover the sun's disc, from the point of view of an observer on the earth, at the time of a total eclipse of the sun. The exact reason why God designed it this way is not yet evident, but the relationship is too precise to be accidental.

Skeptics have frequently alleged that the Bible teaches a pre-Copernican astronomy, with the earth fixed at the center of the universe and the sun, moon, and stars all revolving around it each day. It is true that there are many references to "sunrise" and "the going down of the sun." But this is common terminology even today — the "language of appearance." Such expressions are used every day even by astronomers, surveyors, and navigators who know full well that the earth rotates on its axis, and that the heavenly bodies only "appear" to orbit the earth. It is common practice in these sciences to assume that the earth is at the center of a great celestial sphere, with the sun, moon, and stars moving along the surface of the sphere. The measurements and calculations based on this assumption can quite accurately determine latitude, longitude, solar time, and sidereal time anywhere on earth. It is only the more esoteric data of astronomy that require other more sophisticated assumptions and computations.

It is quite difficult even today to prove that the heliocentric theory is true, and there is a small body of scientists, including some competent astronomers, who are advocating a reconsideration of the geocentric theory. The Bible, however, does not teach the geocentric theory any more than modern textbooks on navigation teach the geocentric theory. The celestial sphere concept implied by both simply utilizes the scientific principle of relative motion which, since it works best, is the most "scientific" assumption to use in such calculations or descriptions. Since the universe is, so far as we can tell, infinite in size, there is no possible way to locate its stationary center. How could one even define the center of an infinitely large space? Any point could be used as the center, and the best point to use is the one that provides the easiest description and the simplest calculations to achieve a desired result. In most cases, this would be the location of the observer. It is thus not only the most appropriate assumption, but also the most scientific, to use (as the Bible writers do) the earth's surface at the location of the observer as the assumed fixed point, with all motions measured relative to that point.

The passage quoted previously from Psalm 19:6 may even be taken in the fullest Copernican sense, if desired. The sun's path, it says, "is from the end of heaven, and his circuit unto the ends of it." It is now believed that the sun moves in a gigantic orbit around the center of the Milky Way galaxy, an orbit that would take 230 million years to complete, with a tangential speed of 600,000 miles per hour, relative to the central point. Furthermore, it is believed that our galaxy is similarly moving with respect to other galaxies. One could say, quite literally, that the sun's circuit is from one end of heaven to the other. The sun is no more "fixed" than the earth. Although David himself may have known little of modern astronomy, the Holy Spirit led him to choose words which would be consistent both with the everyday language of appearance yet also with the most scientific concepts of galactic astronomy.

Even the rotation of the earth is implied in Job 38:14: "[The earth] is turned as clay to the seal." The figure, in context, is of a clay vessel being turned on a wheel to receive the design impressed upon it by a seal or signet, like the earth as it turns into the dawning sun, gradually revealing the intricate features on its surface. In summary, there is no observational fact of modern solar system astronomy which contradicts any biblical statement, but many such facts correlate beautifully with the Scriptures.

## Stellar Evolution

In the preceding chapter, the dominant theories of cosmic evolution were briefly discussed, and it was pointed out that none of these are on sound footing today. There is no reason at all not to believe that the universe was simply called into existence by God, just as the Bible says.

Apart from this question of the primeval origin of the universe, however, modern naturalistic astronomers have also developed various ideas of stellar evolution, trying to account for the great variety of stars and galaxies as some sort of an evolutionary hierarchy. An attempt is made, starting with the hydrogen atoms of the big bang, to develop a scenario which can show how these primeval atoms and energies coalesced into protostars and then proceeded through various stages from young, growing stars into old, dying stars. All of the various types of stars and galaxies are believed to constitute different stages in this speculative evolutionary process, rather than an array of divinely created objects as the Bible teaches.

There is much gas and dust in interstellar space, and astronomers assume that stars have somehow condensed out of such clouds. The Population III stars, which are almost entirely hydrogen and helium, supposedly form first. Population I and Population II stars presumably cannot form until much later, after heavier elements are dispersed into the interstellar dust clouds from supernova explosions in which presumably the elements have been built up by fusion processes in the hot interiors of the stars. Thus, the composition of the interstellar medium is believed to have evolved into a higher proportion of heavy elements during astronomic time. This is purely an evolutionary assumption, however, as no evidence exists that this change in composition has actually occurred. That there are no known Population III stars as yet is confirmed by the following authorities. "The first generation of stars likely formed when the universe was only a few million years old (though these 'Population III' stars have not yet been identified)."[3]

Equally arbitrary is the assumed sequence in the life history of stars. A cluster of stars supposedly begins to form from a hydrogen cloud, with each star getting hotter as it contracts under its own gravity. The protostar (supposedly recognizable by being associated with a surrounding gas cloud) becomes a "main sequence" star when its interior becomes hot enough to convert some of its hydrogen to helium. Eventually the star begins to burn out and becomes a "red giant." After that it may become a "planetary nebula" and eventually cool and contract enough to become a "white dwarf."

Occasionally an old star, if large enough, may explode and become a supernova. This in turn may leave an extremely small but extremely heavy object called a neutron star. If it collapses beyond a certain point, it may even become a strange entity called a "black hole," with essentially infinite gravity condensed into a point which swallows up everything near it, even light, and where time itself stands still. Whether such a thing exists at all is very uncertain, since it is deduced solely from relativistic mathematics.

Now all of this is pure speculation, since no one has ever observed one type of star evolve into another. No one has ever observed any kind of evolutionary changes in stars at all, except for the rapid disintegration process which produces an occasional nova or (very rarely) a supernova.

The initiation of the whole imaginary process — the contraction of hydrogen atoms by gravity to form a protostar — seems clearly impossible in the first place. How are atoms propelled out explosively in the primeval big bang going to reverse themselves and come together again? Thermodynamic calculations will always show that the entropy in such a coalescing body of gas would have to be decreasing, and this is impossible. The radially outward pressures of the gaseous body tending to cause expansion will always exceed the gravitational forces promoting contractions, keeping the contraction process from ever starting in the first place.

---

3. Fred Adams and Gregory Laughlin, "The Future of the Universe," *Sky and Telescope*, 96 (Aug. 1998): 34.

The constellation Orion, brightest in the heavens, is frequently cited as an example of the active formation of new stars from the interstellar gas which permeates the surrounding region. The fact is, of course, that Orion has always looked exactly as it does now, throughout all human history, so that no evolution has actually been observed. Furthermore, recent studies have raised real doubts about the traditional interpretation. The bright young protostars in Orion, instead of growing from the surrounding dust cloud, are actually losing mass to the cloud!

> The discovery that at least some of the infrared sources once thought to be protostars are more probably very young, massive stars dramatically shedding mass has some important implications for the understanding of how new stars form. First of all, it means astronomers may have to start afresh for the precursors of typical main-sequence stars. Second, the wind from a large luminous star may have a strong influence on the creation of smaller stars, such as those resembling the sun. . . . the wind could so badly disrupt the cloud surrounding it that further star formation would be impossible. . . . Third, if a strong wind is a feature of the early evolution of all stars, not just massive ones, it could adversely affect the formation of planetary systems.[4]

Thus, studies of the best example of so-called stellar evolution in the heavens — the mighty Orion nebula (see figure 9) — seem to show that massive young stars are losing rather than gaining mass, that smaller young stars are inhibited from forming at all, and that even if stars do get started, they cannot get planetary systems. This sounds like stellar evolution is going in the wrong direction, if it is taking place at all!

Neither is there any evidence as to how galaxies evolve, even though it is assumed always that they must do so somehow. "So even though we cannot watch a galaxy evolve the way we watch a flower grow, the operative question is, not whether galaxies evolve, but how. How they form and how they change is one of the primary questions in astrophysics."[5]

The fact is, that no real evidence exists that stellar or galactic evolution occurs at all. The only satisfactory explanation for the beautiful starry heavens is special creation.

## Origin of the Solar System

If, as we have shown, there is no evidence that the universe could have evolved, that galaxies could have evolved, or that stars could have evolved, then there is surely no evidence that the solar system could have evolved. The sun is a star and, like any other star, it could not possibly have developed from some kind of protostar which in turn grew out of an interstellar gas cloud of some kind. The second law of thermodynamics, if nothing else, would completely preclude such a sequence of events from a cold cloud of individually isolated molecules to a vast

---

4. Gareth Wynn-Williams, "The Newest Stars in Orion," *Scientific American*, 245 (Aug. 1981): 55.
5. Dietrick E. Thomsen, "Astration and Galactic Evolution," *Science News*, 110 (Nov. 6, 1976): 299.

### FIGURE 9 — *The Orion Nebula and Stellar Evolution*

*The bright constellation of Orion is specifically mentioned in Scripture, but is believed by evolutionary astronomers to be the best example of evolution in action. Later studies have indicated, however, that its "evolution" is more likely disintegration.*

flaming orb of tremendous energy. And it would be still more impossible to develop — either from the gas cloud or the sun itself — by any naturalistic process, the very complex accumulation of complicated chemical and physical systems called planets, especially the earth.

There have been many speculative ideas presented for the origin of the earth since La Place and Kant proposed their famous "nebular hypothesis," but each one in turn — the "planetesimal hypothesis" of Chamberlin, the "tidal hypothesis" of Jeans, the "dust-cloud hypothesis" of Whipple, and others — inevitably is found to have insuperable obstacles, and the search is still going on for a plausible model.

There are so many complex and diverse phenomena that characterize the solar system that it would seem impossible ever to devise an evolutionary scheme which could explain them all. Some of these include:

1. The fact that the distances of the different planets from the sun conform to a remarkable mathematical function known as Bode's law.[6]

---

6. Bode's law states that, if a series is formed of the numbers 0, 3, 6, 12, 24 . . . (doubling each time) and then another series formed by adding 4 to each successive number and then dividing the sum by 10, the resulting series (.4, .7, 1.0, 1.6, 2.8, 5.2, 10.0, 19.6, 38.8) gives the distances from the sun to the various planets in "astronomical units" (one AU = distance of Earth from the sun).

2. The planets contain 98 percent of the angular momentum of the system (approximately, the amount of "spin" in the system), even though the sun contains 99 percent of the mass of the solar system.
3. Some planets rotate in one direction, some in another, and the same is true of their various satellites.
4. There are vastly differing chemical compositions of the sun and the various individual planets and their satellites.

There are a great many other difficulties with all theories, as well as many special difficulties with each individual theory.

The NASA space program was supposed to have helped solve this problem, but its discoveries have only complicated it. One of the world's greatest geophysicists, Sir Harold Jeffreys, concluded, "To sum up, I think that all suggested accounts of the origin of the Solar System are subject to serious objections. The conclusion in the present state of the subject would be that the system cannot exist."[7]

More recently, the astronomer William Metz has said:

Speculations about the origin of the solar system have been proposed, modified, buried, and resurrected many times in the last three centuries. The best suggestion still seems to be the "nebular hypothesis" of La Place, who theorized that the solar system formed from the contraction of an interstellar cloud. But the laws of celestial mechanics, hydrodynamics, modern chemistry, and thermodynamics require that many steps take place before a diffuse cloud forms into a lumpy solar system with a few heavy planets.[8]

Each one of those steps encounters physical and thermodynamic barriers which are still unremoved. Metz concludes: "Judging from the diversity of assumptions, models, and predispositions among those hardy scientists who venture to try to outguess the course of evolution of the nebula that presumably predated us all, more constraint is precisely what is needed."[9]

An official publication of NASA voiced a similar conclusion: "It is important to be aware that there is no one theory for the origin and subsequent evolution of the Solar System that is generally accepted. All theories represent models which fit some of the facts observed today, but not all."[10] In addition, the great astronomer Herman Bondi has said, "As an erstwhile cosmologist, I speak with feeling of the fact that theories of the origin of the Universe have been disproved by present day empirical evidence as have various theories of the origin of the Solar System."[11]

7. Harold Jeffreys, *The Earth: Its Origin, History, and Physical Constitution* (Cambridge, England: University Press, 1970), p. 359.
8. William D. Metz, "Exploring the Solar System: Models of the Origin," *Science,* 186 (Nov. 29, 1974): 814.
9. Ibid., p. 818.
10. National Aeronautics and Space Administration, "Mars and Earth" (Washington, DC: U.S. Government Printing Office, NF-61, Aug. 1975), p. 1.
11. Herman Bondi, "Letters Section: Reference to Quote by Karl Popper," *New Scientist,* (Nov. 21, 1980): 611.

One theory enjoying increasing popularity, mainly because nothing else is left, is the impact theory, which has to do with randomly colliding and accreting planetoids. Presumably this is as good an *ad hoc* way of explaining the great variety of materials and motions in the planets and their satellites as any. It is not susceptible of proof, however, or any kind of testing.

Other than the earth, the body in the solar system that has generated most attention is the earth's moon, with astronauts actually walking on its surface. Even so, its origin is still mysterious. "Many models have been proposed for formation of the moon, but no one has succeeded in showing the formation satisfactorily."[12]

In summary, there is not the slightest scientific evidence that any object in the universe has developed into its present form and structure by any naturalistic evolutionary process from any previous simpler structure. The earth, moon, planets, sun, stars, galaxies, and universe all came into existence essentially just as they are now by special creation, exactly as stated in the Bible. "By the word of the LORD were the heavens made; and all the host of them by the breath of his mouth. . . . For he spake, and it was done; he commanded, and it stood fast" (Ps. 33:6–9).

## The Expanding Universe

One of the most fascinating aspects of astronomy is the concept of the expanding universe. Astronomers generally believe that the distant galaxies are all receding from us — or, better, that all galaxies in the cosmos are receding from each other. The universe as a whole is rapidly expanding, according to this view, with the velocity of recession of the different galaxies increasing with their distance from us.

The evidence for this remarkable state of affairs is the famous Doppler effect, the "red shift," in the light spectra from distant galaxies. A source of light which is moving toward us will emit light waves with a shorter wave-length than will a light source moving away from us. In the first case, this would make the light bluer, in the second, redder, than the light spectrum from a stationary source. Actually this shows up as a shift in the spectral lines of the elements toward the blue end of the spectrum in the one case and toward the red end in the other.

Some would even interpret the expanding universe to mean that space itself is expanding, whatever that means. Surprisingly, there are even some Scripture verses that seem to correlate with this idea. For example:

> Who coverest thyself with light as with a garment: who stretchest out the heavens like a curtain (Ps. 104:2).

---

12. Shigero Ida, Robin M. Canup, and Glen R. Stewart, "Lunar Accretion from an Impact-Generated Disk," *Nature*, 389 (Sept. 25, 1997): 353.

It is he . . . that stretcheth out the heavens as a curtain, and spreadeth them out as a tent to dwell in (Isa. 40:22).

I, even my hands, have stretched out the heavens, and all their host have I commanded (Isa. 45:12).

. . . the LORD, which stretcheth forth the heavens, and layeth the foundation of the earth, and formeth the spirit of man within him (Zech. 12:1).

See also Job 26:7; Isaiah 42:5, 44:24, 51:13; Jeremiah 10:12, 51:15; et al.

Such passages, of course, do not necessarily imply an expanding universe, but such a concept, if it is actually a valid physical phenomenon, could be correlated with them. The same is true of the word for "firmament" in Genesis 1:6–8, which God called "heaven." The Hebrew is *raqia*, meaning "expanse," or, perhaps better, "spread-out thinness," or simply "space." The idea of an expanding space may well be implied by the term "expanse."

On the other hand, all such verses and terms could apply just as well to a static, but unbounded, space that had been initially "spread out" by God at the time of creation. There are problems with the expanding universe idea, and some astronomers do question it. Just how an infinite, unbounded universe can grow larger is difficult to conceive. More directly pertinent is the fact that the recession velocities of some of the quasars (stars of exceptionally high energies) are so high as to make the whole Doppler interpretation of the red shifts very questionable. There are many other examples of discordant red shifts besides those of the quasars. There are, for example, galaxies so closely associated with each other that they are actually "connected" by luminous filaments of gas. Yet their red shifts are vastly different. There are also binary stars whose two members show different red shifts.

These and other problems make the expanding universe concept at least open to serious question. Some have suggested that the red shifts are due to light losing some of its energy as it crosses the vast reaches of space. In any case, the expanding universe concept (and therefore the big-bang theory which depends on it) must be considered improbable at best. Even if the universe is actually expanding, it would still be most plausible to assume that God had created it at a certain ongoing stage in the process of expansion, as the Scriptures cited above might imply. There is certainly no reason to believe that it started in the primeval explosion of a cosmic egg, as modern cosmologists like to imagine. It is salutary to recall again that, as long as men have been observing the stars, they have always looked just as they do now, exactly as stated in the biblical record of primeval special creation.

## The Height of the Stars

Rather than describing the sky as a vaulted dome, with the stars attached to its surface, at a relatively small distance from the earth — as many people in antiquity believed, and as critics have alleged to be the biblical teaching — the Scriptures often imply the vastness of space and the extreme distances of the stars from the earth.

> Canst thou by searching find out God? canst thou find out the Almighty unto perfection? It is as high as heaven; what canst thou do? deeper than hell; what canst thou know? (Job 11:7–8).

> Is not God in the height of heaven? and behold the height of the stars, how high they are! (Job 22:12).

> For as the heavens are higher than the earth, so are my ways than your ways, and my thoughts than your thoughts (Isa. 55:9).

Since God is infinite in power, it is reasonable that the universe He would create would be a universe of boundless space and endless time. In fact, our minds are so constituted (by creation) that we cannot even conceive of anything else. That is, what could be outside the boundaries of space, except more space? What could be after time, but more time? Relativistic mathematics may involve such things as curved space and warped time, but the real world of human experience and observation is one of unbounded three-dimensional space and unending one-dimensional time. And, as the above Scriptures imply, this space is as high as the infinitude of God himself.

Thus, the biblical cosmology is quite consistent with the idea that some of the distant galaxies may be billions of light years from the earth. On the other hand, there is no way that astronomers can measure such distances directly. The greatest distance that can be measured directly by methods of triangulation, using the two extremes of the earth's orbit as end points on a base line, is about three hundred light years.

Greater distances than this require a series of esoteric assumptions related especially to certain stars known as Cepheid variables, in particular the relation between the frequency of their pulsations and their brightness, both apparent brightness and intrinsic brightness. Still greater distances involve similar assumptions about novas. The red shifts associated with distant galaxies have been used, but still other assumptions are involved here.

All these assumptions are very questionable, but it would serve no relevant purpose to critique these here, since it is perfectly compatible with Scripture to believe that many stars are at almost infinite distances from the earth.

But then comes a very obvious question: if some stars are billions of light-years away (a light-year being the distance light travels in a year, moving at a speed of over 186,000 miles per second), then by definition that light must have been traveling across space for billions of years. If that is the case, then the universe must be billions of years old, regardless of the contrary testimony of Genesis. This is a very common objection raised by those who question the biblical teaching of recent creation.

Creationists have suggested various ways of resolving this problem. One possibility is that light travels in a type of curved space called Riemannian space even though geometric space is flat.[13] Calculations for this type of geometry have indicated that light coming from an infinitely distant source would reach the earth in less than 16 years. These conclusions resulted from a study almost 50 years ago by two very competent evolutionary astrophysicists and electrodynamicists, P. Moon and D. E. Spencer, associated at the time with the Massachusetts Institute of Technology. However, most astronomers have rejected this idea because of its compatibility with a young universe.

Another suggestion has been that the velocity of light has been decreasing since light was first created, having settled down to its present speed (which seems to be constant) only recently. An Australian amateur astronomer, Barry Setterfield, has pointed out that some measurements gave higher values for the velocity of light about a century ago than measurements made more recently. By extrapolation, he showed that light could have had almost an infinite velocity at the time of its creation just a few thousand years ago. Again, however, very few astronomers have accepted this analysis, pointing out that the relevant scientific data are too scattered and equivocal to justify the conclusion that light is really decelerating.

In any case, the very fact that such possibilities can at least be defended by competent scientists means that they are scientifically feasible, at least in the context of primeval special creation. In order for the stars to perform their intended function of indicating signs and seasons, days and years (Gen. 1:14), they would need to be visible on earth essentially as soon as Adam and Eve were created. Since even the nearest star is four light-years distant, it would be necessary for God somehow to make their light available on earth practically as soon as they were created. Possibly He did this either by giving the light an exceedingly high velocity at first or by causing it to travel initially in Riemannian space or by some other special device.

Any such explanation is, to all intents and purposes, tantamount to the simplest solution of all — namely, the assumption that the whole universe was created fully functioning right from the start. Adam and Eve were created as a full grown man and woman, fruit trees were created already bearing fruit, and the light rays from the stars were created already in transit through space. The whole universe was created "full grown," ready to function according to the divine plan and purpose intended for it by its Creator. Thus, Adam and Eve could have seen all the visible stars the first night they were together, even though the stars had only been placed in the heavens two days earlier.

There are two main objections that have been placed against this very reasonable concept. One is that it would be deceptive on God's part to make the uni-

---

13. See Richard Niessen, "Starlight and the Age of the Universe," ICR Impact Series, *Acts and Facts,* 12, no. 121 (July 1983).

verse look "old" when it was really young. This objection completely begs the question, however, since it implies that nothing whatever could really have been created. If God ever really created anything at all — that is, called it into existence out of nothing — that object would appear to have been there before, and thus would necessarily have an "appearance of age." To say that God could not create something with an appearance of age is the same as saying He could not create anything at all. Such an assertion is tantamount to atheism. Furthermore, there is no warrant whatever for the charge that this would be "deceptive." God has revealed in His own inspired Word exactly what He did and how long it took, and He said it took just six days for Him to create and make everything in the universe (see Exod. 20:8–11). There would be a deception, however, if He had made such a plain assertion of recent creation, when He knew that the universe was really old. It is patently wrong for men today to try to study what happened in the creation week by uniformitarian extrapolation of present processes (even such a process as the propagation of light across space), when God has repeatedly told us that He "rested" after He "finished" all His work of creating and making everything in the universe in the six days. Processes then were different than processes now, by God's own clear statement of that fact (Gen. 2:1–3). Are we going to believe Him, or call Him a liar? That is the question!

The other objection is more difficult to answer. Certain stars have dramatically increased in brightness to become novas or supernovas at various times during human history. Some of these are in distant galaxies, and so are commonly interpreted as events that happened on the stars perhaps millions of years ago, with their light just recently reaching the earth. If the universe is young, the stars were not even in existence that long ago. How can this paradox be reconciled?

The Riemannian space concept mentioned above would be one means of doing so, of course, and so would the concept that the velocity of light is now much slower than it was at the time of creation. Also, it should be remembered that astronomic distances greater than three hundred light years cannot be measured at all by direct geometric methods; furthermore, even the largest stars (except for our sun) appear only as points of light even through the largest telescopes.

There have also been a number of attempts to equate the six literal days of Genesis on earth with the billions of years of astronomic time in the distant reaches of the cosmos, using relativistic mathematics and the assumed phenomenon of gravitational time dilation implied in Einsteinian relativity theory. The most impressive of these studies, both biblically and scientifically, is believed to be the treatment in the book *Starlight and Time*, by Dr. Russell Humphreys.[14]

---

14. D. Russell Humphreys, *Starlight and Time* (Green Forest, AR: Master Books, 1994). Dr. Humphreys for many years served as a physicist at the Sandia National Laboratories in Albuquerque. Since 2001, he has been a professor of physics in the Institute for Creation Graduate School in Santee, California.

The fine points of Humphreys' arguments are difficult to understand without knowledge of advanced mathematical physics, and the reaction from specialists in this field, both Christian and non-Christian, has been mixed. Dr. Humphreys has apparently responded effectively to criticisms, so his theory should at least be seriously considered.

In any case, this minor unresolved problem of the light from distant stars should not cause us to reject the clear and unequivocal biblical teaching of recent special creation of the whole universe and all its parts.

## Joshua's Long Day

A number of remarkable astronomical miracles are recorded in the Bible, the most amazing of which is the notorious long day, as recorded in the tenth chapter of Joshua. The account is as follows:

> Then spake Joshua to the LORD in the day when the LORD delivered up the Amorites before the children of Israel, and he said in the sight of Israel, Sun stand thou still upon Gibeon; and thou moon, in the valley of Ajalon. And the sun stood still, and the moon stayed, until the people had avenged themselves upon their enemies. Is not this written in the book of Jasher? So the sun stood still in the midst of heaven, and hasted not to go down about a whole day. And there was no day like that before or after it, that the LORD hearkened unto the voice of a man: for the LORD fought for Israel (Josh. 10:12–14).

This event was indeed a remarkable miracle. The earth stopped rotating (no doubt very gradually, so that no great tectonic disturbances would occur) and the moon simultaneously slowed down and stopped its orbital revolution about the earth. In describing this event, the author obviously used the proper scientific terminology of relative motion (as scientists, surveyors and navigators commonly do when describing movements of the sun and stars relative to the earth as a reference point).

As a miracle, the discussion of miracles in chapter 3 is relevant, as given in the section "Criteria for Testing Alleged Miracles." There was certainly adequate justification for the miracle from the divine point of view. This was the beginning of the long-promised invasion, and conquest of the land of the Canaanites, and it was vital that God demonstrate in no uncertain terms that "the iniquity of the Amorites" finally was "full" (compare Gen. 15:16), and their land was to be given to worshipers of the true Creator God. The Amorites, who were pagan pantheistic sun-worshipers and did not believe in God or primeval creation at all, were the most influential, and probably most wicked morally, of all the Canaanite tribes, and Joshua had been commanded by God to destroy this combined five-kingdom Amorite horde. This could only be done with supernatural help, and God seems to have chosen to use the sun (which was worshiped as the greatest god by these Amorites) to complete their defeat.

As far as the test of historical confirmation is concerned, the "histories" of that ancient period are now found mainly in the legends and traditions of the earliest nations. It is significant that tales of a long day (or "long night") are indeed found all over the world — in the legends of the Hindus, the Greeks, the Chinese, the ancient Mexicans, the American Indians, and the Polynesians, among others,[15] in addition to the record in the divinely inspired account by Joshua himself, who was there!

No true miracle can be tested experimentally, of course, especially a global miracle such as this, but that is not adequate reason to reject it, since God does exist! He who established the laws of nature, so-called, can change them if He so desires. The only question is whether there is adequate reason for Him to do so in a given situation, and then whether there is sufficient testimonial or other evidence that He actually did so. The long day of Joshua satisfies both criteria.[16]

There are other astronomical miracles recorded in the Bible, such as the reversed shadow on the dial of Ahaz (2 Kings 20:8–11) and the supernatural darkening of the sun at the time of the crucifixion (Matt. 27:45; Luke 23:44–45). These also could be shown to satisfy the necessary criteria for acceptance. Their very inclusion in the Bible ought to be enough, because the Bible is God's Word, whether men wish to believe His inspired words or not.

The very special case of the star of Bethlehem will be considered shortly, along with the prophetic role stars are yet to play in respect to the earth.

## Constellations

As long as men have been observing the stars, they have been associating them together in groupings called constellations. The remarkable thing about this is that, although these constellations bear little or no resemblance to the creature whose names they bear (Balances, Goat-Fish, Bull, etc.), the same constellations and figures seem to have been used everywhere in the ancient world. This is still as true today among modern astronomers as it has always been true among astrologers. Even more remarkably, this same system seems to have been recognized in the Bible, with the implication that it was of divine origin.

There are a number of specific references to the constellations, as in the following Scriptures.

---

15. The following works, among others, have discussions of these extra-biblical traditions of the long day:

    (1) T.W. Doane, *Bible Myths* (New York, NY: Truth Seeker Co., 1882);

    (2) M.W. Stirling, *Annual Report* (Smithsonian Institution, 1945);

    (3) Immanuel Velikovsky, *Worlds in Collision* (New York, NY: Macmillan, 1950). These books are probably all out of print, but possibly available in college libraries.

16. The widely circulated report that NASA computer studies showed a missing day about the time of Joshua, unfortunately is not true. The book *Joshua's Long Day*, by Charles Totten, also argued for a missing day in astronomic history, but the premise on which the calculation was based was entirely arbitrary, thus rendering the calculation essentially meaningless.

Which alone spreadeth out the heavens, and treadeth upon the waves of the sea. Which maketh Arcturus, Orion, and Pleiades, and the chambers of the south (Job 9:8–9).

By his spirit he hath garnished the heavens; his hand hath formed the crooked serpent (Job 26:13).

Canst thou bind the sweet influences of Pleiades, or loose the bands of Orion? Canst thou bring forth Mazzaroth in his season? or canst thou guide Arcturus with his sons? Knowest thou the ordinances of heaven? canst thou set the dominion thereof in the earth? (Job 38:31–33).

For the stars of heaven and the constellations thereof shall not give their light: the sun shall be darkened in his going forth, and the moon shall not cause her light to shine (Isa. 13:10).

Seek him that maketh the seven stars and Orion, and turneth the shadow of death into the morning, and maketh the day dark with night: that calleth for the waters of the sea, and poureth them out upon the face of the earth: the LORD is his name (Amos 5:8).

In addition to these explicit references, there are numerous passages whose imagery may have been drawn from the constellations (e.g., Isa. 27:1; Rev. 12:1–4, 15). For example, the protoevangelic prophecy of the conflict between the serpent and the seed of the woman (Gen. 3:15) seems to be depicted in a number of constellations.

Such data seem clearly to indicate some kind of divine origin for the constellations and the strange figures of men and beasts that have been associated with them. At the same time, the practice of astrology as based on these phenomena is sharply rebuked in the Bible, in such verses as: "Thou art wearied in the multitude of thy counsels. Let now the astrologers, the stargazers, the monthly prognosticators, stand up, and save thee from these things that shall come upon thee. Behold, they shall be as stubble; the fire shall burn them; they shall not deliver themselves from the power of the flame" (Isa. 47:13–14). The impotence of the astrologers to understand God's ways is repeatedly emphasized in the Book of Daniel (Dan. 1:20; 2:27; 4:7; 5:7–8; et al.). There are also many Scriptures that rebuke the worship of "the host of heaven" (see Deut. 4:14–19; et al.).

This phrase, "the host of heaven" is used in the Scriptures in a very intriguing way, being applied both to the angelic hosts and also to the starry hosts, apparently interchangeably. In reference to the stars, for example, note verses such as 2 Kings 23:5: "And he put down . . . them also that burned incense unto Baal, to the sun, and to the moon, and to the planets, and to all the host of heaven." However, angels are clearly in view in verses such as 2 Chronicles 18:18: "Again he said, Therefore hear the world of the LORD; I saw the LORD sitting upon his throne, and all the host of heaven standing on his right hand and on his left." Both meanings appear together in Nehemiah 9:6: "Thou, even thou, art LORD alone; thou hast made heaven, the heaven of heavens, with all their host, the earth, and all things that are therein, the seas, and all that is therein, and thou preservest them all; and the host of heaven worshippeth thee." The very first use of the term, at the end of the creation period, is probably intended to embrace both meanings together. "Thus the heavens and the earth were finished, and all the host of them" (Gen. 2:1). The angels, as well as the stars, had all been created by God during the creation week — the angels probably on the first day (see Ps. 104:1–5), the stars on the fourth day.

The reason for this interchangeable usage of "the host of heaven" is obviously because the ancients worshiped both stars and angels. Baal, for example, was a "god," but he was the "sun-god." Angels (or which amounts to the same things, "gods") were identified with stars. Jupiter and Saturn and Venus were planets, for example, but also considered to be gods. This association is too close to be accidental, and was the same in all the ancient nations. The Bible likewise frequently associates stars and angels. The "stars of heaven" of Revelation 12:4, for example, are identified as the "angels" of Revelation 12:7–9.

Although we cannot be certain, it seems likely that this close correspondence of meanings is because the realm of the stars is the realm of the angels. Both are said to be innumerable (Jer. 33:22; Heb. 12:22).

Angels, of course, were created to be "ministering spirits" (Heb. 1:14), not "gods." The New Testament, no less than the Old, condemns the worshiping of angels (Col. 2:18; Rev. 22:8–9), but many of the angels, led by Satan, "kept not their first estate" (Jude 6). Satan, the highest of all angels, "the anointed cherub" (Ezek. 28:14), rebelled against God, seeking to exalt his own throne above that of God (Isa. 14:13), and led a third of the angels with him in his rebellion (Rev. 12:3–9).

It is these who now comprise the "angels," "principalities," and "powers" (Rom. 8:38) who seek to estrange men from God, and whose sphere of operations in this age is in the heavens, constituting "spiritual wickedness in high places" (Eph. 6:12). It is these fallen angels, or demons, who seek to usurp the worship due to God alone and to persuade men to worship and serve the creature more than the Creator (Rom. 1:25).

With such tremendous forces moving in the invisible world behind the scenes, as it were, one can understand the great hold that astrology has exercised over the minds and lives of people through the ages. It is not just the physical stars whose movements and "emanations" influenced mankind, but the powerful spirits who roamed the heavenly places and were identified with the stars. The corruptible men, and birds, and four-footed beasts, and creeping things (Rom. 1:23), whose images were associated with the stars and their constellations, were modeled on earth in the form of idols, and these also were often energized by other evil spirits, so that the whole monstrous complex of astrology, pantheism, polytheism, idolatry, animism, and spiritism became an extremely powerful and pervasive system that has enslaved multitudes of lost men and women through the ages.

## The Gospel in the Stars

There thus seems at first to be a contradiction in the biblical perspective on the stars and constellations. On the one hand, the Bible unequivocally condemns astrology, idolatry, and everything associated with worshiping the host of heaven. On the other hand, many Scriptures indicate that God not only created the stars to glorify himself (Ps. 19:1) but that He even formed and identified the various constellations, investing them with names and symbols which bore no obvious resemblance to the actual physical star groupings at all. In fact, one of the intended purposes of all the heavenly bodies was to "be for signs" (Gen. 1:14). The Hebrew word used for "sign" is the same as used for the "mark" upon Cain (Gen. 4:15) and for the rainbow as a "token" of the Noahic covenant (Gen. 9:13). It is frequently used in the phrase "signs and wonders" (e.g., Exod. 7:3). Thus, the meaning here seems to be more than that of calendar markers.

A very significant verse in this connection is Job 38:32: "Canst thou bring forth Mazzaroth in his season?" This obviously was a rhetorical question, to which the only answer is, "No, only God can bring forth Mazzaroth in his seasons."

The Hebrew word *Mazzaroth* apparently means literally "constellations," but all scholars agree that it refers in particular to the zodiacal constellations, the 12 so-called "signs of the zodiac." Thus, God himself was evidently the one who invested the constellations with their original form and meaning. These ancient signs are sketched in figure 10.

If so, however, their present meanings in astrology must have been badly corrupted from their original meanings, in view of the strong biblical condemnation of such astrological interpretations. This would not be surprising, since Satan is "a liar and the father of it," and the one who "deceiveth the whole world" (John 8:44; Rev. 12:9). It would be a master stroke of Luciferian duplicity for him to transform a primeval revelation of truth into a seductive counterfeit that would turn men away from the true Creator God.

Assuming that the present astrological system, structured around the signs of the zodiac, is indeed a destructive counterfeit, is there any way of getting back to the original meanings? One should remember that, whatever that primeval message may have been, it is no longer needed. We have the complete Word of God now, inscripturated, providing absolutely all the guidance we need for faith and life today.

This was not always true, of course. For at least the first third of human history, from Adam to Abraham, the only known Scriptures available to mankind were the brief records of the primeval patriarchs, now preserved for us by Moses as the first 11 chapters of Genesis. Except for the Jewish nation, to whose prophets were then revealed the rest of the Old Testament, the nations of the world had no written revelation throughout at least two-thirds of human history.

Thus, it may well be that the "signs" placed by God in the heavens, "declaring the glory of God," were originally intended as a great visual aid to all the peoples

**FIGURE 10 — The Ancient Constellations of the Zodiac**

The "signs of the zodiac" are mentioned in the Bible as having a divine origin. They were also known by all the ancient nations. Although now satanically corrupted into astrology, there is some indication that their original meaning was a primeval revelation of the gospel. See table 4.

of the world, supplementing the primeval protoevangelic promise of the coming Redeemer, the seed of the woman, who would finally crush the serpent's head (Gen. 3:15). Such a message would survive even the devastations of the great Flood, and the eventual confusion of languages at Babel, since it was indelibly written in the heavens. It is significant that the most important constellations, the

12 that come forth month by month along the heavenly ecliptic (the apparent path of the sun), that is, the 12 signs of the zodiac, have always been recognized as the same in every nation, since the dawn of history, as they are today.

There may have been a certain body of divine laws available to earlier true believers in God, since both Abraham and Job are said to have obeyed them (Gen. 26:5; Job 22:22; 23:12). Whether these had been written down, or simply spoken and memorized, is not known. In any case, we now have all of God's written words, and need no more until Christ returns.

Even though the great symbolic figures may still be the same, the message has been drastically distorted. Gleams of the original meanings may perhaps still be dimly discerned, since so many of the constellations do seem to reflect biblical themes. There have been a number of books written on this subject, each indulging in considerable speculation, but nevertheless showing that there probably was such a primeval revelation inscribed in the heavens. The writer has a brief treatment of the subject in the book *Many Infallible Proofs*,[17] which indicates that the original message of the 12 signs might have been something like that shown in table 4.

In any case, whether the above deductions are correct or not, the correct understanding of the heavenly signs is certainly not as important as it may once have been in the primeval world. Nevertheless, this gospel in the stars does contribute in some measure to the field of Christian evidences and to the fuller understanding of God's dealings with the nations throughout history.

### The Star of Bethlehem

The stars were created to be "signs," as well as to measure "seasons, days and years" (Gen. 1:14). In addition to their possible use as signs in the sky commemorating God's primeval promises, one particular star was destined to be a very special sign, announcing the birth of the promised Savior. "There shall come a Star out of Jacob, and a Sceptre shall rise out of Israel," said the ancient prophet Balaam. "Out of Jacob shall come he that shall have dominion" (Num. 24:17, 19).

The star prophecy was given almost 15 centuries before its fulfillment, but at the proper time it appeared in its divinely appointed place and time, directing the watching Magi in faraway Persia to Israel, and finally to Bethlehem, where they could worship the newborn King.

Many have been the theories since that day concerning the nature of the Bethlehem star and how it was able to lead those Eastern wise men to Christ in Bethlehem. Probably the most frequent explanation, especially by secularists, liberals, and even some evangelicals, is that it was a conjunction of planets. The great astronomer Johann Kepler in 1605 suggested that a conjunction of Saturn, Jupiter, and Mars had occurred in 7 B.C., and that *this* was the promised star.

---

17. Henry Morris, *Many Infallible Proofs* (Green Forest, AR: Master Books: 1990), p. 367–376).

## TABLE 4 — The Gospel in the Stars

The possible message of the zodiac signs is elaborated on in appendix 5.

| Sign | Theme |
|---|---|
| 1. Virgo, the Virgin | Promised Seed of the Woman |
| 2. Libra, the Balances | Scales of divine justice |
| 3. Scorpio, the Scorpion | Sting to be inflicted on the promised Seed |
| 4. Sagittarius, the Archer | Corruption of the human race through demonism |
| 5. Capricornus, the Goat-Fish | Utter wickedness of mankind |
| 6. Aquarius, the Water Pourer | Destruction of the primeval world by water |
| 7. Pisces, the Fishes | Emergence of the true people of God |
| 8. Aries, the Ram | Sacrifice of an innocent Substitute for sins |
| 9. Taurus, the Bull | Resurrection of the slain Ram as the mighty Bull |
| 10. Gemini, the Twins | The dual nature of the reigning King |
| 11. Cancer, the Crab | Ingathering of the redeemed from all ages |
| 12. Leo, the Lion | Destruction of the fleeing serpent by the great King |

Others have suggested that a conjunction of Jupiter and Venus in 3 B.C. was the Christmas star. Some have thought a comet might have been the star.

Probably most evangelicals and fundamentalists have argued that the "star" was a specially created guiding light in the sky, that moved along in front of the wise men to guide them to Bethlehem — possibly an angel or something like the Shekinah glory cloud.

However, it is difficult to see how the Magi, the most well trained and observant of all ancient scholars in astronomy, could have mistaken any of these phenomena for a star! None of the suggested conjunctions were ever close enough together to be mistaken for a single star. And surely these very capable astronomers were able to tell the difference between a fixed star and a special light moving along in the atmosphere above them. Apparently, Matthew's record of the star must have come originally from these wise men (or else by direct inspiration from God) and they did not call it a guiding light or a comet (which, with its tail, would never be mistaken by such experts for a star) or a conjunction between two or three planets which never even touched each other — but a star!

The Greek word for "star" is aster (occurring some 24 times in the New Testament) or, sometimes, astron (occurring four times). Occasionally, angels are symbolized by stars (e.g. Rev. 1:20; 12:4, 7) and so even are human beings (Jude 13). It is also true that planets, comets and meteorites were called stars by the ancients, and even by the Lord Jesus himself (Matt. 24:29). But such usages are always apparent in the context, whereas there is nothing in the context of this record to indicate such a metaphorical meaning.

The account of the wise men, however, is given as a simple historical record, and these Magi (who certainly knew what a star was as well as anybody in that day) called it a star (in fact, *His star*). If we really wish to take the Bible *literally*, then it would seem best to agree with the record of the wise men (as well as the Holy Spirit, who inspired Matthew's account of it) that the star of Bethlehem was a real star, and nothing else.

And there *is* a certain type of star that does seem to fit all the specifications of the account. This would be a *nova* (meaning "new star") or, even more likely, a rare supernova.

These stars are believed to be sudden, unpredictable explosions of existing stars. What seems to be an ordinary star suddenly increases tremendously in brilliance, continuing so for several months until it fades away.

There have been only a few visible supernovas in historical times. The oldest of which we have any clear record occurred in A.D. 1054. However, there may well have been one or more in earlier times. In fact, certain early Bible scholars (Ignatius, Eusebius, and others) apparently took a deep interest in the peculiar Bethlehem star. They did some research on their own on this possibility and concluded that there had indeed been a uniquely brilliant new star in the heavens about the time of Jesus' birth. A more recent writer, Robert McIver, has written a book[18] giving various evidences that such a unique new star had actually been observed all over the world about the time of the birth of Christ.

Assuming that the star of Bethlehem was a real star, probably a supernova, how would the magi recognize its significance? That is perhaps best explained in terms of their familiarity with the prophecies of Daniel, who had been an adviser to the great Persian emperor Cyrus, as well as their familiarity with the stars and the primeval message intended to be carried by these divinely intended "signs." They were also familiar with the ancient prophecy of Balaam, who had himself very probably been a member of the Magi — some have argued that he was their founder. Putting all these clues together, they became convinced that this bright new star was indeed *His* star, and that God's promised Savior had finally come.

The impression that the star actually "led" the wise men to Bethlehem does not come from the biblical account. The account says merely that they saw the star twice — once while they were at home "in the east," then later as it "stood over where the young child was" (Matt. 2:2, 9). The first observation of the star convinced them to go to Jerusalem, where they seem to have assumed the child

18. Robert McIver, *Star of Bethlehem, Star of Messiah* (Canada: Overland Press, 1998), 207 p. See also this writer's summary of the evidence in his booklet *When They Saw the Star* (San Diego, CA: Institute for Creation Research, 2000).

would be by the time they arrived there, gladly welcomed by the Jewish leaders as their long-promised King.

Instead, they found only ignorance at the court and troubled concern among the religious leaders, who sent them on to Bethlehem, where Micah 5:2 had predicted he would be born. There the Magi again saw the star, now standing vertically over Bethlehem, thus confirming their conviction that it really *was His star!* It had been in the sky all during the months in between the two sightings, but out of their nighttime sight as the earth had been moving along in its orbit around the sun.

We cannot be dogmatic, of course, but the supernova explanation does seem to meet all the biblical and astronomical data as well as or better than any other. In any case, as science writer Mullaney has said, after examining the various theories and then concluding that the star was a brilliant supernova, "Truly, here is a celestial announcement card above all others worthy the birth of a king."[19]

## Heavenly Catastrophism

The NASA space program has revealed one important phenomenon that might seem to be a problem to biblical creationism. Photographs of the surfaces of the moon, Mercury, Mars, and the satellites of the various planets have all revealed heavily cratered surfaces, with every indication that these craters were caused by bombardment with meteorites, asteroids, or comets at some time in the past. These discoveries have stimulated closer study of the earth's surface for such blemishes, and more of these have indeed been found, largely masked now by erosion and plant growth, but nevertheless indicative of significant terrestrial meteorite impacts in the past. All of this speaks clearly of catastrophism in the heavens.

Furthermore, the very existence of meteorites and asteroids seems to be evidence of catastrophism. The asteroids, in particular, give evidence of being the fragmented remains of a former planet that once orbited the sun between the orbits of Mars and Jupiter.

The problem is how to fit such phenomena into the context of biblical teachings about the stars and planets. Everything was "very good" at the end of the creation period (Gen. 1:31), even among the host of heaven (Gen. 2:1), so it is difficult to believe that God created these bodies in this condition. If not, then something must have happened subsequent to their creation. The Bible, however, has no direct statement about any such astral catastrophe. To the biblical writers, all heavenly bodies, except the sun and moon, appeared as stars and so are called stars. Planets were called "wandering stars" and meteorites "falling stars," but these along with the relatively "fixed stars" all were fulfilling the same purpose, serving for "signs and seasons, days and years."

19. James Mullaney, "The Star of Bethlehem," *Science Digest* (Dec. 1970): 65.

Although the Bible includes no specific references to historical astral catastrophes,[20] it does predict future catastrophes of this sort, when stars will be falling from heaven (e.g., Matt. 24:29; Rev. 6:13; 8:8, 10, 12; 16:21). These predicted events seem to refer to meteorite, asteroid, or comet impacts on the earth in the last days.[21]

Entirely apart from the Bible, many secular writers have discussed the possibility of future (or past) cataclysmic encounters of the earth with swarms of meteorites or other bodies. Two astronomers at the Royal Observatory in Edinburgh, for example, have published a book[22] in which they maintain that the earth goes through such a bombardment every few thousand years, and that those periodic catastrophes have been the key factors in organic evolution. They believe that the most recent of these took place well within the period of human history. "The current overabundance of planetary particles, fireball activity and meteor streams in Apollo orbits all seem to bear witness to a sky that must have been exceedingly active within the past few thousand years. We see today the remnants of what must have been larger and most impressive pieces of cometary debris. . . . The breakup of a huge comet in Earth-crossing orbit in the middle of the third millennium B.C. would explain much of this evidence, and was probably a watershed for humanity."[23]

Whatever the precise nature of the objects impacting on earth may have been, there is indeed much geological evidence that impacts have occurred.[24] Furthermore, since the orbits of all the planets about the sun lie in essentially the same plane, it is quite possible that such impacts from the debris of a giant comet or other hurtling objects would affect them all at about the same time.[25] Thus, most of the impact craters on the planets and their satellites, as well as those on the earth, could well have been formed at essentially the same time, in a great catastrophic event several thousand years ago.

Why, then, does the Bible not mention such an earth-shattering event? The answer may be that it took place before the writing of most of the Bible, in the very early days of the human race.

The early chapters of Genesis, of course, do describe a great worldwide cataclysm on the earth, the great Flood. The overwhelming evidence for the Flood is

20. Actually there is one such reference, "the image which fell down from Jupiter" (one word in the Greek, meaning "from the sky"), in Acts 19:35.

21. Despite these biblical references, modern astronomers only began to acknowledge the existence of meteorite impacts in the early 19th century.

22. Victor Clube and Bill Napier, *The Cosmic Serpent: A Catastrophist View of Earth History* (London: Faber, 1982).

23. Victor Clube and Bill Napier, "Close Encounters with a Million Comets," *New Scientist,* 92 (July 15, 1982): 150.

24. These evidences include such phenomena as impact craters, meteorite fragments, shatter cones, breccia ejecta, high-pressure minerals, and others.

25. Astronomers estimate there are perhaps one thousand asteroids more than one kilometer in diameter which may cross the earth's orbit.

discussed in a later chapter. Although the Bible does not mention falling stars in this connection, it does speak of the opening of the windows of heaven (Gen. 7:11; 8:2). This phrase undoubtedly refers mainly to the torrential rains falling from heaven, although it is just possible that it might imply other objects also raining from the sky. In fact, the passage of a cloud of cometary debris through the earth's primeval protective blanket of water vapor might even have served to trigger the condensation and precipitation of the canopy.

There may be another possibility. The Scriptures occasionally refer to the fall of Satan and his angels from heaven in what appears to be the symbolic language of stars falling from heaven (see Isa. 14:12; Luke 10:18; Rev. 9:1; 12:4). Could it be that this is more than mere symbolism? Was the expulsion of Satan and his angels from heaven accompanied by a corresponding devastating blast of heavenly bodies from outer space through the solar system? If so, this would have taken place soon after the creation period, before Adam and Eve had sinned, and so would possibly not have affected the earth itself, but only the planets and satellites.

There are still many unanswered questions related to ancient heavenly catastrophes, of course, and much need for further research. However, all the known scientific facts are thoroughly in accord with the biblical perspective on astronomy, so that we can have confidence that these minor unresolved questions will all be answered eventually in full conformity with everything written in the inspired Word.

# THE POWER OF HEAT
*Biblical Thermodynamics*

## The Universality of Thermodynamics

It might be supposed at first thought that thermodynamics is a rather obscure and specialized scientific discipline, of little significance in a biblical discussion. Nothing, however, could be further from the truth. As a matter of fact, thermodynamics could practically be considered as synonymous with science, since its concepts and laws embrace all scientific processes in all scientific disciplines.

The term itself came into use at the beginning of the industrial revolution. When men first discovered that heat could be converted into mechanical work, and thereby invented the first steam engine, our modern age of science and technology was born. From that great discovery, the old age of man-powered and horse-powered civilization was soon at an end. The principles that were then developed to quantify the conversion of heat into work were called the principles of *thermodynamics* (a word coined from two Greek words — often used in the New Testament — meaning "heat power"). As scientific investigation continued, it soon became obvious that there were other sources of power in nature that could also be converted into work. There is electricity, for example, as well as magnetism, sound, light, chemical energy, gravity, elasticity, and other types of force, all of which can now be utilized as energy sources in various types of mechanical devices. Nineteenth-century physicists and engineers soon discovered that the principles of thermodynamics actually described all such energy conversion phenomena and contrivances. Thus, the principles of thermodynamics have come to be recognized as universal in scope and applicability.

As already emphasized, instead of the many scientific mistakes and anachronisms alleged by its enemies, the Bible actually contains a remarkable number of passages with modern scientific insights. Of these, none are more significant than the two principles commonly acknowledged to be the most important and most universal of all known scientific generalizations. These are the so-called first and second laws of thermodynamics.

Several of the other chapters of this book deal with certain aspects of the scientific nature of the two laws, especially their implications with respect to the creation/evolution issue. In this chapter the biblical and theological aspects are treated, with only enough scientific background to point up their significance.

Like every other scientific "law," these two laws are merely empirical generalizations based on agreement with a broad range of scientific data. In principle they might even have to be modified or rejected if data should later turn up contradicting them. Nevertheless, they are based on such a tremendous number of supporting measurements, on such a wide variety of types of physical systems, that practically all knowledgeable scientists would recognize them as the most secure of all scientific laws. If there is such a thing as a real law in science, these two laws would be the best examples. Despite this fact, however, their importance and profound implications are commonly ignored or misunderstood by most scientists.

## First Law of Thermodynamics

The first law is commonly considered as synonymous with the law of conservation of energy.[1] By "energy" is meant "an entity which does, or has the capacity to do, work." "Work" is the product of a force and the distance through which that force operates. The nation's most prolific science writer, the humanistic biochemist Isaac Asimov, defined the first law as follows:

> To express all this, we can say: "Energy can be transferred from one place to another, or transformed from one form to another, but it can be neither created nor destroyed." Or we can put it another way: "The total quantity of energy in the universe is constant."

This law is considered the most powerful and most fundamental generalization about the universe that scientists have ever been able to make.

No one knows *why* energy is conserved, and no one can be completely sure it is truly conserved everywhere in the universe and under all conditions. All that anyone can say is that in over a century and a quarter of careful measurement scientists have never been able to point to a definite violation of

---

1. For general discussions, as in this book, energy and power are qualitatively similar. Technically, power is defined by scientists as the time-rate of energy, whereas energy is equal to the work done. For example, if a 100-pound weight is lifted a distance of 25 feet in two seconds, the work done is equal to the energy expended, and each is equal to 2,500 foot-pounds. The power utilized was 1,250 foot-pounds per second.

energy conservation, either in the familiar everyday surroundings about us, or in the heavens above or in the atoms within.[2]

If one regards *mass* as being a type of entity different from energy, then the law can be modified to apply to "the total quantity of energy and mass in the universe," thus allowing for the possibility of energy/mass conversions, as in nuclear reactions. Except for the latter, of course, mass also is universally conserved.

In addition, there are other conservation laws in physics (e.g., momentum, electric charge), not to mention the universally observed principle in biology that "like begets like" (that is, the basic kinds of plants and animals reproduce only their own kinds, never some new kind). It seems beyond question that the world as science knows it is a world in which existing entities are always conserved, never created or annihilated. (The phenomenon of extinction in biology may seem to be an exception, but it should be remembered that in genetics, it is the code that is conserved, not the individual or even the "kind" built up around that code.)

## Second Law of Thermodynamics

The second law is expressed in a number of different ways, all of which are essentially equivalent to each other. Again calling on Asimov (no creationist or theist, but an atheist and evolutionary humanist) for an unbiased definition, he spoke of it this way:

> We can say: "No device can deliver work unless there is a difference in energy concentration with the system, no matter how much total energy is used."
>
> That is one way of stating what is called the Second Law of Thermodynamics. It is one of many ways; all of them are equivalent although some very sophisticated mathematics and physics is involved in showing the equivalence.[3]

Asimov then went on to give another very picturesque definition:

> Another way of stating the Second Law, then, is: "The universe is constantly getting more disorderly."
>
> Viewed that way, we can see the Second Law all about us. We have to work hard to straighten a room, but left to itself, it becomes a mess again very quickly and very easily. Even if we never enter it, it becomes dusty and musty. How difficult to maintain houses, and machinery, and our own bodies in perfect working order; how easy to let them deteriorate. In fact, all we have to do is nothing, and everything deteriorates, collapses, breaks down, wears out, all by itself — and that is what the Second Law is all about.[4]

---

2. Isaac Asimov, "In the Game of Energy and Thermodynamcis, You Can't Even Break Even," *Smithsonian* (June 1970): 6.

3. Ibid., p. 8.

4. Ibid., p. 10.

These words were written many years ago, and Asimov himself is now deceased. Yet the universality of the second law still holds. "No exception to the second law of thermodynamics has even been found — not even a tiny one. Like conservation of energy (the 'first law'), the existence of a law so precise and so independent of details of models must have a logical foundation that is independent of the fact that matter is composed of interacting particles."[5]

The second law obviously is no less universal than the first. *Everything* deteriorates — all by itself! Furthermore, just as with the first law, no one knows why this is true; it just always works that way. Asimov was referring specifically to the "universe" as getting more disorderly, just as he had said it was for the universe that the total quantity of energy was a constant.

In any so-called "open system" of size less than the universe, there can for a while, of course, be an influx of energy or mass or order into that system, at the expense of decreased energy, etc., outside the system, but this is superficial. The conditions under which such a superficial appearance of exception to one of the laws can occur will be discussed later. For present purposes, we can stipulate the range of application of the two laws as follows:

1. To the universe as a whole, applicable without exception, so far as any scientific observation can determine.[6]
2. To a local (theoretically) isolated system within the universe, applicable without exception, so far as all scientific measurements have shown.
3. To a local "open" system, directly applicable in most situations and always applicable as a normal tendency in the system, with exceptions possible only under certain special conditions as described elsewhere, and then only at the cost of offsetting external conditions which maintain the integrity of the two laws in the universe as a whole.

In connection with the second law, it is necessary also to define the term "entropy." The entropy of a system is usually expressed mathematically, and so it is difficult to define precisely without reference to the mathematical description of a particular system. In general, however, entropy can be defined as a mathematical function which quantifies the "disorder" or "unavailable energy" (other terms might be used, depending on the type of problem) in the system. In any case, the second law states that the entropy of any system either increases (if isolated or universal) or tends to increase (if local and open).

Furthermore, as Asimov noted, there are several ways to describe the second

---

5. Elliott H. Lieb and Jakob Yugvason, "A Fresh Look at Entropy and the Second Law of Thermodynamics," *Physics Today,* 53 (Apr. 2000): 32.
6. Speculations of evolutionary cosmogony, such as the big-bang theory and the steady state theory, have attempted to get around the second law. Such attempts, as shown in chapter 5, are always metaphysical, not scientific. Evolutionists maintain that the universe is a closed system — not controlled by a transcendent God — and the second law applies specifically and unequivocally to closed systems.

law (or its measure, entropy) all of them equivalent and interchangeable. In physical systems, for example, it is commonly expressed in three ways.

1. As a measure of the increasing unavailability of the energy of the system for useful work (*classical thermodynamics*).
2. As a measure of the increasing disorder, randomness, or probability of the arrangement of the components of the system (*statistical thermodynamics*).
3. As a measure of the increasingly confused information in the transmission of the coded message through a system (*informational thermodynamics*).

Entropy thus is a measure of the useless energy in a working system, the disorder in a structured system, or the "noise" in an information system. All use the same types of mathematical formulations, so all are essentially equivalent.

The concept can be extended still further. In biological systems, the phenomena of sickness, death, and extinction represent ourworkings of the Curse. In social and economic systems, the tendency of once-vigorous societies to atrophy and disintegrate is another example. In religious systems, the tendency of faiths which were once strong and dynamic to become lethargic and apostate is still another.

Thus, it is evident that the first and second laws of thermodynamics are exceedingly important universal principles. Far from being limited to the study of heat engines, as the name might imply, they represent broad categories of phenomena throughout the whole of human experience — and a universal effect requires a universal cause!

## Theological Implications

Consider, for the time being, only the theological implications of the two laws for the universe as a whole. A superficial application of the first law would conclude that the mass/energy of this universe is eternal, since none is being either created or annihilated within the natural processes that obey the law. A superficial application of the second law would imply a future death of the universe (not its annihilation, but the cessation of all processes and maximum disorder), since the universe is now proceeding inexorably in that direction.

But the real meaning of the two laws is profoundly teleological. If matter had really been functioning eternally in the manner described by the two laws, the universe would already be dead. Its present unrestrained progress in the direction of decay has been called "time's arrow," and the arrow points down! The future fate of the universe has frequently been called its inevitable eventual "heat death," when the sun and stars have all burned out and all the high-level energy in the cosmos has been degraded to heat at a uniformly low temperature throughout all space. The energy will not have been annihilated, but will be at a constant level everywhere, so that no more work can be done.

Now since the universe is not yet "dead," and since it is going to die in time, it is obvious that time had a beginning! If time had extended infinitely into the past, the universe would already be dead. Thus, the second law testifies conclusively that the universe of time, space, and matter (the universe is a "continuum," so space and matter must be contemporaneous with time), in its present form at least, must have had a beginning at "zero time."

The first law, on the other hand, unequivocally stipulates that the universe could not have begun itself! The second law says there must have been a creation, but the first law says the universe could not create itself.

The only way out of this impasse is to recognize that "in the beginning God created the heaven and the earth." Genesis 1:1 is the most profoundly scientific statement ever written, with all the systems and processes of the cosmos uniting in asserting its truth. The two laws of thermodynamics, the best-proved, most universal generalizations of science, embrace all the processes of nature within their framework, standing as a continuing testimony that the universe as it now exists must have had a beginning and that the cause of the universe must have been transcendent to it, capable of creating an entire universe, infinite in extent, unending in duration, and boundless in variety and complexity.

This great First Cause must have been able to create all the complex of effects permeating the space-mass-time cosmos. These include an endless array of intelligible complex systems, stars and suns in almost infinite number and power, a tremendous variety of living organisms, and human beings who think, feel, will, and love. The two laws can thus be sublimated into the great law of cause and effect, with a clear testimony that the uncaused First Cause of the universe must be an infinite, eternal, omnipotent, omniscient, living, willing, loving person.[7]

## Escape from Science

The universal theistic implications of the two laws thus clearly confirm the profound assertion of Genesis 1:1. Since both science and Scripture unite in pointing to a transcendent God as primeval Creator of all things, one can escape from this conclusion only by appealing to evolutionary metaphysics.

It is one thing, however, to repudiate Scripture with philosophy, and quite another to reject science at the same time. In a science-oriented society, this can only be done by so masking the metaphysics as to make it appear scientific. This is exactly what evolutionary "cosmogonists" have essayed to do with their steady state and big-bang cosmogonies.

The problem is the second law. All observed processes and systems operating in space and time conform to the second law, which thus points back to a creative origin of all such *natural* processes and systems (or, more fundamentally, energy and mass), as well as space and time themselves, by what must have been a *supernatural* event of process.

This unwelcome conclusion can be avoided, however, by postulating that

---

7. See chapter 1.

some process or system operating in either *nonobservable space* or *nonobservable time* may be able by "naturalistic" means to overcome the second law. The first assumption (second law negated by a naturalistic process functioning in nonobservable space) leads to some form of the so-called steady state theory. The second assumption (second law negated by a naturalistic process functioning in nonobservable time) leads to some form of the so-called big-bang theory.

By their very nature, these so-called theories cannot really be scientific theories, since the processes on which they depend cannot possibly be observed. In all observable space and time, all natural processes conform to the second law. To negate the second law requires, therefore, processes that are anti-natural. Evolutionary metaphysicians may enjoy playing semantic games in order to escape from the conclusion of primeval creative supernatural processes but all they have in their place is imaginary unnatural processes!

It is encouraging that at least some evolutionary cosmogonists acknowledge this aspect of their speculations, though most of them continue to mask their antiscientific presuppositions with an imposing mathematical apparatus to make their efforts seem scientific.

The steady state theory in its original form (then also called the continuous creation theory, since it postulated a continuous "creation" of hydrogen atoms out of nothing somewhere deep in interstellar space) is currently out of favor by most cosmologists, even by Fred Hoyle, its originator.

However, Hoyle and a number of other cosmologists also reject the big-bang theory. In later years they have tried to develop a modified steady state concept, which they called the quasi-steady-state cosmology.

> Since 1993, we have been developing an alternative cosmology, beginning from an action principle, by which we seek to explain how matter and radiation appeared in the universe.[8]

In the process of developing this new cosmology, Hoyle and his colleagues continued to be vigorous opponents of the big bang. Although Hoyle died in 2001, there will no doubt continue to be a number of capable cosmologists opposing it and promoting alternative views — all of which, in the very nature of things, will somehow have to ignore or distort the laws of thermodynamics. Another well-known astronomer and writer on cosmogony, Paul Davies, has tried to face this problem.

> The greatest puzzle is where all the order in the universe came from originally. How did the cosmos get wound up, if the Second Law of Thermodynamics predicts asymmetric unwinding toward disorder? There is good evidence that the primeval universe was not ordered, but highly chaotic: a relic

---

8. Geoffrey Burbidge, Fred Hoyle, and Jayant V. Narlika, "A Different Approach to Cosmology," *Physics Today*, 52, April 1999): 39. This article is an introduction to a new book by Fred Hoyle, with the same name as the article and presenting his tentative quasi-steady-state cosmology.

of the primordial chaos survives in a curious radiation from space, believed to be the last fading remnant of the primeval heat, and the characteristics of its spectrum reveal that in the earliest moments of the universe the cosmological material was completely unstructured.[9]

Thus, not only is the primeval explosion not scientifically observable but also the very data (e.g., expanding universe, background radiation, energies available for nucleosynthesis, etc.) that seem to offer a quasi-scientific rationale for postulating the big bang, still further support the inferences of the second law, and so offer little prospect of energizing the entire future evolutionary development of the cosmos.

The problem is further compounded by the modern notion advanced by some that the universe (or at least the initial mini-particle of space/time) evolved out of nothing by a "quantum fluctuation" of the primeval nothingness. This concept makes nothingness out of the laws of thermodynamics themselves!

The only hope apparently lies in the first few minutes of the expansion, when the energies and densities were (possibly) sufficiently high as to act in opposition to the second law. Davies continues his analysis thus: "To discover the cosmic winding mechanism, one has to investigate the processes that occurred between about one second and ten minutes after the bang. Unfortunately, the expansion is now too sluggish to have much invigorating effect, so the universe seems doomed to steadily unwind again until all organized activity ceases; the interesting and varied world of our experience will be systematically destroyed."[10] But how can we deduce a naturalistic winding-up process for the universe when all observable naturalistic processes are unwinding processes? Well, as a matter of fact, admits Davies, we can't!

> So far it has been supposed that the shuffling process is *random*. But how do we know that the universe which emerged from the big bang was truly chaotic so that subsequent collisions and interactions between subatomic particles are overwhelmingly likely to disintegrate any order which may appear? If the miracle of the big bang included *miraculously* organized subatomic arrangements too, then random shuffling would have to be replaced by *organized* rearrangement.[11]

*There* is the answer! We must have the "*miracle* of the big bang" and "*miraculously* organized subatomic arrangements," with "*organized* rearrangment" of the subatomic particles!

Yes, a sufficiently comprehensive miracle of supernatural creation and integration might make the big-bang concept workable, but there is no naturalistic way it can be done. And if we are going to acknowledge a miraculous creation at

---

9. Paul C. W. Davies, "Universe in Reverse: Can Time Run Backwards?" *Second Look,* 1 (1979): 27.
10. Ibid.
11. Ibid.

the beginning of things, by what possible logic (even metaphysical dissimulation) can we preclude a miraculous Creator?

If we acknowledge a supernatural Creator, why not allow Him to do the work of creating and organizing the cosmos all at once, getting right to the implementation of His purposes for creating it in the first place? Why force Him to drag it out over tortuous aeons, merely in order to accommodate evolutionary speculations for which there is not one iota of either scientific or scriptural evidence? If the Creator actually employed unknown billions of years of universal decay, after first using a primordial ten minutes of miraculous integration, to eventually produce man "in his own image," then He certainly selected the most wasteful, inefficient, and cruel process that could be conceived to accomplish His goal.

The fact is that absolutely all the solid data of both true science and true logic coincide perfectly with the biblical premise: "In the beginning God created the heaven and the earth" (Gen. 1:1). Supporting this clear foundational statement are many other unequivocal assertions of Scripture:

> In six days the LORD made heaven and earth, and on the seventh day he rested, and was refreshed (Exod. 31:17).

> By the word of the LORD were the heavens made; and all the host of them by the breath of his mouth. . . . For he spake, and it was done; he commanded, and it stood fast (Ps. 33:6–9).

> For he commanded, and they were created (Ps. 148:5).

> Through faith we understand that the worlds were framed by the word of God, so that things which are seen were not made of things which do appear (Heb. 11:3).

> By the word of God the heavens were of old, and the earth . . . (2 Pet. 3:5).

## Origin of the Two Laws According to Scripture

As admitted by Isaac Asimov (see earlier in this chapter), "No one knows *why* energy is conserved." Neither does anyone know why entropy increases. All we know is that in all scientific measurements and observations, energy is conserved and entropy increases, and there are no known exceptions. These are the two best-substantiated and most universally applicable generalizations of science, but no one knows why!

That is, scientifically, no one knows why. Theologically and biblically, however, the reasons why are clear and definite. Not only did Scripture long anticipate the fact of the two laws, but also the reasons why they are laws.

Consider the first law. The reason why no energy is now being created is that "on the seventh day God ended his work which he had made. . . . in it he had rested from all his work which God created and made" (Gen. 2:2–3).

Similarly, the reason why nothing is being annihilated in the present cosmos is that the Creator (none other than the eternal Son of God, the Lord Jesus Christ) is now "upholding all things by the word of his power" (Heb. 1:3).

During the six days of creation, God was creating and making all things. Obviously, therefore, the first law was not yet "enacted." When God "ended His work," however, the whole universe was "very good" (Gen. 1:31). Nothing further needed to be added, nor did anything need correction. Consequently, on God's first great rest day (the Hebrew *sabbath* means "rest"), God, as it were, legislated His law of conservation, and the processes of the cosmos have obeyed it ever since!

As a matter of fact, not only were the created energy and matter intended for conservation following the creation week, but so was entropy. Everything was "good," so the entities measured by entropy (disorder, lost energy, noise, disintegration, confusion, death, etc.) could not have been increasing then as they are today. Decay and death are not good.

During the creation period, God was "forming" (Hebrew *yatsar*) and "making" (*asah*) things, as well as "creating" (*bara*). Thus, His processes then were explicitly opposite to those now constrained by the two laws. His processes then were processes of *creation* and *integration*; now all processes are processes of *conservation* and *disintegration*. God was producing order and complexity, as well as energy and matter, during creation week, and all of these were certainly intended to be conserved following creation week.

This fact in no way implies, however, that there was to be no decrease in order in individual systems. For example, God specifically prepared the grasses, herbs, and fruits of the plant kingdom to serve as foods for both people and animals (Gen. 1:29–30; 2:9, 16). The eating of these foods did, of course, involve the various processes of ingestion and digestion with a corresponding disintegration of the structure of the particular fruit or vegetable (fruits, incidentally, do not "die," when eaten, since they do not possess the *nephesh*, or "soul," or "life," as usually translated from the Hebrew). Only men and animals were invested with *nephesh* (see Gen. 1:21; 2:7).

In the primeval creation, however, even though what we might call "decay" processes certainly existed (e.g., digestion, friction, water erosion, wave attenuation, etc.), they must all have balanced precisely with "growth" processes elsewhere either within the individual system, or perhaps more commonly, in an adjacent system, so that the entropy of the world as a whole would stay constant. The entropy of the universe now is increasing, but ideally it should be conserved along with energy. Every process and machine would then have 100 percent efficiency, with all input energies being converted completely into useful work. Even the heat energy employed in processes necessitating the force of friction for their operation would be completely productive, with no energy being "lost." No parts would wear out, no organism would "age" past the point of maximum vigor and productivity, and everyone could easily design and build perpetual motion machines!

The above is obviously imaginative, and no doubt imprecise and incomplete, but it could not be too far off. Everything was designed by an omniscient, omnipotent God to be "very good." The first law would have stated, as at present, the conservation of mass/energy in all systems and the second law of conservation of entropy in all systems.

But there has been a drastic amendment to the second law! No death of sentient life, either animal or human, was intended in God's original creation. Animal flesh as well as human flesh — and indeed all things in God's physical creation — had been formed by God out of the "dust of the earth" (the basic elementary particles that function in the space-time universe) into a tremendous variety of complex systems, the most complex of all being man's body and brain.

But now everything is proceeding back again to the dust, according to the second law of thermodynamics. "For we know that the whole creation groaneth and travaileth in pain together until now" (Rom. 8:22).

The question why once again can only be answered theologically, and the biblical answer is man's sin and God's curse. God had warned Adam and Eve that death would result from disobedience to His word (Gen. 2:16–17), but they chose to believe Satan's word rather than God's word, and thus brought death into the world. The formal announcement of the second law in its post-Fall form is found in Genesis 3:17–19: "Cursed is the ground for thy sake; in sorrow shalt thou eat of it all the days of thy life; Thorns also and thistles shall it bring forth to thee; and thou shalt eat the herb of the field; In the sweat of thy face shalt thou eat bread, till thou return unto the ground; for out of it wast thou taken: for dust thou art, and unto dust shalt thou return."

The curse extended in like form to all of man's dominion. Man had brought spiritual disorder into his own dominion; God appropriately imposed a principle of physical disorder on that dominion as befitting its spiritual condition.

The divine curse was not only punitive, but also pedagogical. It was "for man's sake." A world in which there was no judgment for sin, no struggle to survive, and no contemplation of suffering and death would be suitable only for beings wholly in fellowship with their Creator. For creatures who had deliberately broken that fellowship, however, such a perfect world could only encourage them to persist in that rebellion and even to intensify it, forever.

Thus, as best we can understand both Scripture and science, we must date the establishment of the second law of thermodynamics, in its present form at least, from the tragic day on which Adam sinned, and when "by man came death" (1 Cor. 15:21). "Wherefore, as by one man sin entered into the world, and death by sin; and so death passed upon all men, for that all have sinned" (Rom. 5:12).

Not only is the curse pedagogical but also eschatological. Although it points forward to a future heat death of the universe, it also points backward to a purposeful Creator who would never allow the universe to die! "For the creature was made subject to vanity [or better, 'futility'], not willingly, but by reason of him who hath subjected the same in hope, Because the creature itself also shall be delivered from the bondage of corruption [literally 'decay'] into the glorious liberty of the children of God" (Rom. 8:20–21).

There is a great day coming when "there shall be no more curse" (Rev. 22:3). In the present age, however, ever since Eden, "the whole creation groaneth and travaileth in pain" (Rom. 8:22).

## Biblical References to the First Law

In additional to the fundamental statements already cited from Scripture, establishing the completeness and permanence of the creation, there are numerous other references in the Bible to the principle of conservation of energy. These are not couched in technical jargon, of course, since this would change from generation to generation, but in terms of the timeless concept that God safeguards His finished creation, enabling it to accomplish His purposes in every part. Listed below are a few of the passages asserting one or another aspect of the great principle of the conservation of God's finished creation.

### Passages Asserting God's Rest from a Finished Creation

Thus the heavens and the earth were finished, and all the host of them. And on the seventh day God ended his work which he had made; and he rested on the seventh day from all his work which he had made. And God blessed the seventh day, and sanctified it: because that in it he had rested from all his work which God created and made (Gen. 2:1–3).

For in six days the LORD made heaven and earth, the sea, and all that in them is, and rested the seventh day: wherefore the LORD blessed the sabbath day: and hallowed it (Exod. 20:11).

For in six days the LORD made heaven and earth, and on the seventh day, he rested, and was refreshed (Exod. 31:17).

The works were finished from the foundation of the world. For he spake in a certain place of the seventh day on this wise, and God did rest the seventh day from all his works (Heb. 4:3–4).

For he that is entered into his rest, he also hath ceased from his own works, as God did from his (Heb. 4:10).

To the above texts could be added a very large number of references referring to God's works of creation, *all of which are in the past tense* (e.g., Col. 1:16). It is significant that the Bible never refers to the creation of either the physical universe or the living creatures in it as a work that is continuing today. It is always presented as completed in the past, exactly as implied by the laws of thermodynamics.

### Passages Indicating God's Preservation of the Finished Creation

Thou hast made heaven, the heaven of heavens, with all their host, the earth, and all things that are therein, the seas, and all that is therein, and thou preservest them all (Neh. 9:6).

He hath also stablished them for ever and ever: he hath made a decree which shall not pass (Ps. 148:6).

Lift up your eyes on high, and behold who hath created these things . . . for that he is strong in power; not one faileth (Isa. 40:26).

And he is before all things, and by him all things consist [literally "are sustained"] (Col. 1:17).

Who being the brightness [literally "out-radiating"] of his glory, and the express image of his person, and upholding all things by the word of his power (Heb. 1:3).

Every good gift and every perfect gift is from above, and cometh down from the Father of lights, with whom is no variableness, neither shadow of turning (James 1:17).

The heavens and the earth, which are now, by the same word are kept in store (2 Pet. 3:7).

## Passages Asserting Permanence of Created Kinds of Organisms

God said, Let the earth bring forth grass, the herb yielding seed, and the fruit tree yielding fruit after his kind, whose seed is in itself, upon the earth: and it was so (Gen. 1:11).

And God created great whales, and every living creature that moveth, which the waters brought forth abundantly, after their kind, and every winged fowl after his kind (Gen. 1:21).

And God made the beast of the earth after his kind, and cattle after their kind, and every thing that creepeth upon the earth after his kind (Gen. 1:25).

That which thou sowest, thou sowest not that body that shall be, but bare grain, it may chance of wheat or of some other grain: But God giveth it a body as it hath pleased him, and to every seed his own body. All flesh is not the same flesh: but there is one kind of flesh of men, another flesh of beasts, another of fishes, and another of birds (1 Cor. 15:37–39).

Can the fig tree, my brethren, bear olive berries? either a vine, figs? so can no fountain both yield salt water and fresh (James 3:12).

Whether or not the scientific principle of conservation of mass/energy can eventually be demonstrated to incorporate the principle of conservation of the genetic code for each created "kind" is a subject for future creationist research, but the principle of divine conservation of the completed creation beautifully covers both, and all known facts of either physical or biological science agree.

## Passages Summarizing Both Completion and Permanence

The thing that hath been, it is that which shall be; and that which is done is that which shall be done: and there is no new thing under the sun. Is there any thing whereof it may be said, See, this is new? It hath been already of old time, which was before us (Eccles. 1:9–10).

I know that, whatsoever God doeth, it shall be for ever; nothing can be put to it, nor any thing taken from it; and God doeth it, that men should fear before him. That which hath been is now; and that which is to be hath already been; and God requireth that which is past (Eccles. 3:14–15).

Who hath measured the waters in the hollow of his hand, and meted out heaven with the span, and comprehended the dust of the earth in a measure, and weighed the mountains in scales, and the hills in a balance? (Isa. 40:12).

## Biblical References to the Second Law

The decay principle is referred to almost as often as the conservation principle. The basic passage, as noted earlier, is Genesis 3:14–19, recording the divine curse on the whole creation because of the rebellion of its human masters, Adam and Eve.

As noted earlier, the entropy principle is very broad, referring to the loss of useful energy, the loss of order, or the loss of information. It applies to all processes, both inorganic and living, and many are applying it today to social and economic systems as well. Similarly the Bible indicates that the process of decay is universal.

### Passages Referring to Decay of the Whole Cosmos

Of old hast thou laid the foundation of the earth: and the heavens are the work of thy hands. They shall perish, but thou shalt endure: yea, all of them shall wax old like a garment; as a vesture shalt thou change them, and they shall be changed: But thou art the same, and thy years shall have no end (Ps. 102:25–27; see also Heb. 1:10–12).

Lift up your eyes to the heavens and look upon the earth beneath: for the heavens shall vanish away like smoke, and the earth shall wax old like a garment, and they that dwell therein shall die in like manner: but my salvation shall be for ever, and my righteousness shall not be abolished (Isa. 51:6).

Heaven and earth shall pass away [literally "are passing away"], but my words shall not pass away (Matt. 24:35; see also Mark 13:31; Luke 21:33).

For the creature was made subject to vanity, not willingly, but by reason of him who hath subjected the same in hope, Because the creature itself also shall be delivered from the bondage of corruption into the glorious liberty of the children of God. For we know that the whole creation groaneth and travaileth in pain together until now (Rom. 8:20–22).

And this word, Yet once more, signifieth the removing of those things that are shaken, as of things that are made, that those things which cannot be shaken may remain (Heb. 12:27).

And the world passeth away [literally "is passing away"], and the lust thereof: but he that doeth the will of God abideth for ever (1 John 2:17).

## Passages Indicating Decay of All Living Organisms

Man that is born of a woman is of few days, and full of trouble. He cometh forth like a flower, and is cut down: he fleeth also as a shadow, and continueth not (Job 14:1–2).

As for man, his days are as grass: as a flower of the field, so he flourisheth. For the wind passeth over it, and it is gone; and the place thereof shall know it no more (Ps. 103:15–16).

For that which befalleth the sons of men befalleth beasts; even one thing befalleth them: as the one dieth, so dieth the other; yea, they have all one breath; so that a man hath no preeminence above a beast: for all is vanity. All go unto one place; all are of the dust, and all turn to dust again (Eccles. 3:19–20).

All flesh is grass, and all the goodliness thereof is as the flower of the field: The grass withereth, the flower fadeth: because the spirit of the LORD bloweth upon it: surely the people is grass. The grass withereth, the flower fadeth: but the word of our God shall stand for ever (Isa. 40:6–8; see also 1 Pet. 1:24–25).

## Passages Asserting Personal Decay

For all our days are passed away in thy wrath: we spend our years as a tale that is told. The days of our years are threescore years and ten; and if by reason of strength they be fourscore years, yet is their strength labour and sorrow, for it is soon cut off, and we fly away (Ps. 90:9–10).

Even the youths shall faint and be weary, and the young men shall utterly fall: But they that wait upon the LORD shall renew their strength (Isa. 40:31).

But I see another law in my members, warring against the law of my mind, and bringing me into captivity to the law of sin which is in my members. O wretched man that I am! who shall deliver me from the body of this death? (Rom. 7:23–24).

Then when lust hath conceived, it bringeth forth sin: and sin, when it is finished, bringeth forth death (James 1:15).

It will be noted that in many of the above passages the decay of the particular system in view (be it cosmic, biological, or human) is often set in contrast with the stability and permanence of its Creator and the spiritual gifts He provides. The one who enacted the law of decay is, by that very fact, not bound by it himself.

## Aging and Death

Although not usually associated with thermodynamics, which most people regard as a physical science exclusively, even living systems are governed by physical and chemical processes insofar as their bodies are concerned. Consequently, the principles of thermodynamics are perpetually at work in living organisms as well as inorganic systems. There is much indication that they somehow control even social systems, and a number of present-day sociologists and economists, for example, are diligently trying to apply the entropy principle in the study of human societies.

It should be noted in passing that natural processes are conveniently divided into three categories: physical, biological, and sociological. This corresponds to the threefold division of the sciences into the physical sciences (physics, chemistry, geology, engineering, astronomy, etc.), the life sciences (zoology, physiology, medicine, etc.), and the behavioral sciences (psychology, sociology, anthropology, economics, etc.). The two laws of thermodynamics, being universal laws, apply to all three realms and to all three categories of processes.

Both laws also correspond to the three great acts of *ex nihilo* creation recorded in Genesis 1, as marked by use of the Hebrew verb *bara*. These are: the physical universe (Gen. 1:1), the universe of life (Gen. 1:21), and the universe of "spirit" — or better, the image of God in man (Gen. 1:27). The inorganic realm is that of the "body," the animate realm is that of "body and soul" (Hebrew *nephesh*), and the human realm is that of "body, soul, and spirit."

As far as man is concerned, the entropy law impinges more directly and painfully upon him in the phenomena of aging and death. Biological aging and death are, of course, also the destiny of all animals as well. Theologically, death is the result of man's sin (Rom. 5:12) and God's resulting curse on the whole creation (Gen. 3:17–19; Rom. 8:20–22), but the actual physical mechanisms which induce aging and death are still rather obscure. There have been many theories and much scientific study devoted to this important subject, but relatively little is known about it yet. Whatever the details may turn out to be, the basic tendency itself must somehow be related to the fateful second law of thermodynamics. As far as individual organisms are concerned, even though they appear to grow and thrive for a time, the aging process which is implicit in the second law eventually causes them to decay and die.

The process of aging, though naturally an object of much interest and study, is thus still not well understood. Furthermore, there seems to be nothing that can be done to change it. "One continually hears that the life span of the average American has been dramatically increased in recent years through advances in medical science, and this is perfectly true. However, the maximum life span of man has apparently not changed since biblical times, and all modern medicine has done is to allow a larger fraction of the population to have a life span close to the maximum."[12]

One rather reasonable theory suggests that aging is primarily related to mutations in the various cells of the body, or "somatic" mutations. These are sudden, random changes in the cell structure of the tissues and organs of the body (other

---

12. Howard J. Curtis, "Biological Mechanisms Underlying the Aging Process," *Science,* 141 (Aug. 23, 1963): 688.

than the germ cells), caused by radiations or other environmental influences. Since mutations are random changes in the highly ordered cell structure, they naturally result in a decrease of efficiency of the cell's intended activities. As such mutations accumulate, some vital organ, or the body as a whole, eventually ceases to function altogether and death ensues. Curtis says, "Certainly the vast majority of mutations must be deleterious, so if the organs of older animals contain appreciable numbers of cells which are carrying mutations, it is a virtual certainty that the organs are functioning less efficiently than they otherwise would."[13]

It has been shown experimentally that environmental radiations both cause mutations and also accelerate the aging process, and it seems probable that the two effects are directly related. Thus, until the general radiation penetrating the earth's atmosphere from outer space — mostly from the sun, of course — can be greatly reduced, it is probably impossible for man's maximum life span to be greatly increased.

Thus, although the radiant heat from the sun provides the energy for the maintenance of life processes, it seems also to insure that death must overtake each individual!

If death eventually accrues to the individual because of the accumulation of mutations in the body cells, it seems likely that it will also eventually overtake the entire species, as a result of accumulation of mutations in the germ cells. The latter are much better protected than the body cells, and therefore much less affected by environmental radiations, so that the species is continued even though individuals die. Curtis concludes by saying, "It is suggested that the mutation rates for somatic cells are very much higher than the rates for gametic cells, and that this circumstance insures the death of the individual and the survival of the species."[14]

The species thus survives longer than the individual. Nevertheless, mutations also occur in the germ cells occasionally and these also are deleterious. Since these effects are hereditable, the eventual result must inevitably be a deterioration of the species itself, and perhaps even its eventual demise. This principle may account in some measure for the extinction of many kinds of animals that once lived on the earth and for the fact that most modern kinds are represented in the fossil record by larger, evidently more vigorous, ancestors.

That such genetic mutations are actually almost always harmful to the animals experiencing them is indicated by the following summary.

> The process of mutation ultimately furnishes the materials for adaptation to changing environments. Genetic variations which increase the reproductive fitness of a population to its environment are preserved and multiplied by natural selection. Deleterious mutations are eliminated more or less rapidly depending on the magnitude of their harmful effects. High-energy radiations,

---

13. Ibid.
14. Ibid, p. 694. Curtis was chairman of the biology department at the Brookhaven National Laboratory.

such as x-rays, increase the rate of mutations. Mutations induced by radiation are random in the sense that they arise independently of their effects on the fitness of the individuals which carry them. Randomly induced mutations are usually deleterious. In a precisely organized and complex system like the genome of an organism, a random change will most frequently decrease, rather than increase the orderliness or useful information of the system.[15]

In spite of this, evolutionists have hoped that rare beneficial[16] mutations may occur in a population of organisms and will be preserved, by natural selection, gradually resulting in a higher, better organized, and more complex kind of organism. This is a remarkable type of reasoning, apparently acceptable in evolutionary speculations, though not permitted in more prosaic statistical and scientific analyses.

It ought to be obvious that mutations are a perfect illustration of the entropy principle in operation. An accumulation of mutations, in either an individual or a population, must inevitably result in a decrease of organization in that individual or species and, if continued long enough, in its death. Thermodynamics surely applies at all levels of biological systems and processes.

These radiation-induced somatic mutations are of interest in another application as well. If environmental radiations do, indeed, accelerate the process of aging and death, then it seems possible that an environment that was free of such radiations might have profound implications for slowing down the rate of aging and therefore for increasing longevity.

Genesis 5 records that before the great Flood people typically lived for hundreds of years, with the average age of the antediluvian patriarchs (not including Enoch, who was taken into heaven without dying) being 912 years. The Bible also records (Gen. 1:7) that in the primeval age there were "waters . . . above the firmament." This antediluvian watery blanket was most likely a vast expanse of invisible water vapor above the earth's atmosphere and (probably) stratosphere. See chapter 10 for further discussion of this possibility.

Such a vapor canopy, among other things, would have served as a highly efficient radiation filter, keeping most of the cosmic rays, ultraviolet rays, and other forms of radiation from ever reaching the earth, and thus effectively inhibiting the production of mutations. Some laboratory tests have confirmed that radiations do decrease longevity, so this may be at least a partial explanation of the long lives of the antediluvian patriarchs.

## Entropy Verses Evolution

It is obvious that there is at least an apparent conflict between evolution and the second law of thermodynamics. Both are considered to be universal principles, applying to all systems and processes in the cosmos, yet each is the opposite of the

---

15. Francisco J. Ayala, "Genotype, Environment, and Population Numbers," *Science,* 162 (Dec. 27, 1968): 1436.

16. It should be noted that no truly beneficial mutations have ever been demonstrated.

### FIGURE 11 — The Evolution Model

Evolution, whether in terms of Darwinism or some other concept, requires a vast increase in organized complexity over the ages, from primeval chaotic particles to present-day complex people.

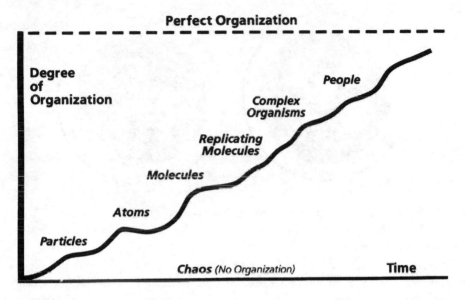

### FIGURE 12 — Entropy and the Creation Model

The entropy principle in science can be considered as a "prediction" from the biblical doctrines of special creation and the subsequent divine curse on the creation.

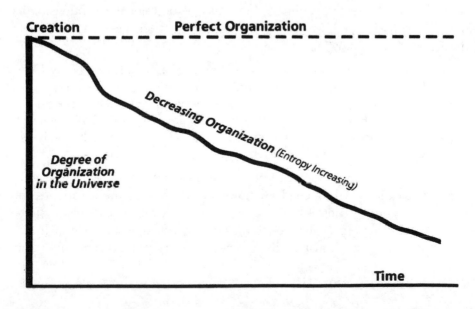

*FIGURE 13 — Increase of Entropy in a Closed System*
*In all real processes inside a closed system, the entropy (measuring the lack of structure or organization) must always increase. Even when the system is opened, the tendency toward disorganization is still present and may even increase.*

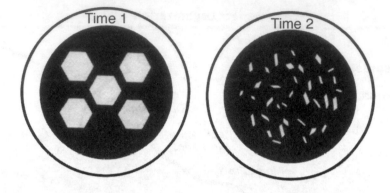

other! One describes a universal process of upward change (see figure 11), the other downward change (figure 12). How can the universe go up and down at the same time?

Creationists maintain, of course, that a law of science (entropy) should take precedence over a scientific belief (evolution). Evolution, being nonobservable and nonrepeatable, cannot even be tested. The entropy principle, on the other hand, has been tested and proved, as thoroughly and effectively as any law of science ever could be proved.

Evolutionists, of course, are completely unwilling to face up to the obvious conclusion that they should abandon their evolutionary beliefs and so have tried to find some way of getting around the second law. One way is to say that the law is only statistical in essence, and so there may be occasional exceptions, when things go up instead of down. That this possibility is sheer speculation, however, is indicated by the following:

> Being a generalization of experience, the second law could only be invalidated by an actual engine. In other words, the question, "Can the second law of thermodynamics be circumvented?" is not well-worded and could be answered only if the model incorporated every feature of the real world. But an answer can readily be given to the question "Has the second law of thermodynamics been circumvented?" Not yet.[17]

A much more common device of evolutionists for avoiding the antievolutionary implications of the second law, however, is to say that the law applies only to "isolated systems" (note figure 13), whereas the earth is an "open system." Somehow they think that even though the entropy principle may eventually win out and the universe ultimately die, the evolutionary process can still operate

---

17. Frank A. Greco, "On the Second Law of Thermodynamics," *American Laboratory* (Oct. 1982): 88.

effectively on the earth throughout geologic time. The excess energy reaching the earth from the sun, they say, is more than adequate to drive the evolutionary engine for billions of years, even though it must eventually run down.

But merely having energy coming into an open system (such as solar energy entering the earth) will not increase the order of that system (that is, decrease its entropy). In fact, exactly the opposite is true.

The most basic equation of thermodynamics, expressed in words rather than symbols, is as follows: The total influx of heat energy into a system, divided by its absolute temperature, is equal to the *increase* of the entropy of the system.

Thus, the more energy that goes into a system (other things remaining equal), the more will be the disorder produced!

It is true that, for increases in order to be produced in systems, the systems must be open and external energy must enter them. But that is not enough! Just having energy come in, unless carefully directed and utilized, would be like a bull entering a china shop! Nevertheless, the "open-system" argument is almost always the naïve answer that evolutionists will give to the entropy problem when it is raised by creationists.

But this argument, with which evolutionists are inclined to impatiently dismiss the antievolutionary implications of the second law, is quite superficial and does not really face the issue at all. In the first place, most evolutionists insist that evolution is a universal law, and not just a temporary perturbation occurring for a billion years or so on a minor planet. The wistful anxiety with which the scientific establishment keeps grasping for the minutest evidence of extraterrestrial life (this was one of the main reasons for the billions of dollars poured into the space program, for example) is symptomatic of this attitude. But surely nothing could be more obvious than that the evolutionary process and the entropy principle cannot both be universal laws. Each is exactly the converse of the other!

Even if evolution is understood as limited to the process of organic evolution on the earth, the second law is a strong witness against it. Although the laws of thermodynamics are defined in terms of an idealized isolated system, there is actually no such thing in the real world. But this does not prevent our applying the laws to open systems. In addition to the requirements of available energy and open system (which are "necessary," but not "sufficient," conditions), two additional criteria must be satisfied before increased order can be produced in any system. There must also be a "program" to direct the growth and a storage/conversion "mechanism" to implement the growth.

The evidence demonstrating the universal applicability and scope of the two laws has, in fact, been derived solely from experimentation on open systems, since it is impossible to set up a system that is isolated (from all effects of the environmental radiations from the sun and other sources, for example). Thus, the experimental support for the two laws is founded on measurements from systems of the same basic kind as the earth system itself. Certainly the implications of the second

### FIGURE 14 — Increase of Entropy in an Open System

*The thermodynamic equation for influx of heat-energy into an open system (e.g., solar radiation onto the earth, Mars, or Venus) indicates that the entropy of the system will increase more rapidly than if it had remained closed, unless certain special conditions are present in the system. Thus, energy entering into an open system is not a sufficient cause to increase the organized complexity of the system.*

law of thermodynamics apply to open systems and it is obscurantism for evolutionists to claim otherwise! In fact, as shown in figure 14, disorder will usually increase more rapidly when the system is opened up than when closed.

This, of course, does not preclude temporary increases of order in specific open systems. The seed does develop into a tree, the embryo does grow into an adult, the village expands into a city, and so on.

Even during such growth periods, the basic decay processes are at work in the system, and these eventually overcome the temporary growth process. The tree dies, the adult dies, and even the city eventually dies. It is thus the growth process that is basically unnatural and that must be sustained, if at all, by a continuing excess influx of ordering information and energy from outside the system.

A person doesn't just naturally grow, for example, but he does naturally and inevitably die. To grow and develop, there must first of all be two parents who come together in a highly complex process of sexual union; there must then be accomplished the amazing mechanics of conception with its intricate embroidering of the molecular strands from the parental germ cells; and there must be present the incredibly complex genetic structure of both cells, with all the encoded information necessary to initiate and regulate the future development of the organism. And then the growth process has just begun!

One can hardly write of the further development of the embryo in the womb, the process of birth, and all the necessary processes of metabolism — digestion, blood circulation, respiration, etc. — without frequent use of such words as "complex," "remarkable," "fantastic," or even "miraculous." However, they do not simply sustain themselves automatically. Food, water, air, sunlight, parental instruction, and much else is continually required from outside the system. If left to function "naturally," it will decay and die. And eventually it will decay and die regardless of how much care and external input are devoted to it. The *natural* tendency is disintegration and death; the *unnatural* process of growth and development is initiated and sustained only with much effort and difficulty, and then only temporarily.

And this principle is found true wherever any appearance of growth and development is seen. In addition to the required conditions of an open system and available energy (both of which are satisfied by all systems on earth), some underlying ordered structure must always be available (e.g., the genetic code in the seed, the molecular structure for the growing crystal, the blueprint for the building, etc.) and then some remarkable complex of natural or artificial processes must be available to build on that structure (e.g., photosynthesis, digestion, construction equipment, etc.), or else no growth can take place, regardless of whether or not the system is an open system!

It is utterly naïve to think that the contradiction between evolution and the second law can be resolved simply by saying that the earth is an open system and evolution is maintained by the sun's energy. The unanswered (and unanswerable) question is "*How* is evolution sustained by the sun's energy?" Where is the underlying informational code directing the evolutionary process? What is the marvelous mechanism that converts the sun's energy into the age-long growth process from some "simple" replicating chemical in a primeval ocean to the present complex world of organic life, including man? These questions must be answered before the evolutionist has the right to expect men to believe his philosophy. In the absence of such a directing structure and implementing mechanism, the evolutionary process is utterly contrary to scientific law and can be sustained only by faith in pure magic!

Imagine, for example, a construction site on which are scattered piles of steel beams, bags of cement, bricks, and other construction materials. No blueprint for the desired office building has been prepared, no work crew has been assembled, no erection equipment provided, no electricity or other power source made available. None of these things are necessary, of course, since the construction site and materials constitute an open system! Every day they are literally bathed in the sun's energy, not to mention the energy of the rains and winds that frequently occur at the site. Obviously, there is far more than enough energy entering the site to do the work of erecting the building.

It is foolish, therefore, to go to the trouble and expense of providing engineers, construction workers, machinery, and electrical power to build the building. Let some evolutionary process do it, since we are in no hurry! The sun's energy will gradually draw the materials together into the proper arrangement, fasten them all together, and then provide furnishings for the offices. Of course all this may take a hundred million years or so, but it will be completed eventually.

Or at least it is infinitely more probable that this will happen than that the

## TABLE 5 — Testing Systems for Possible Natural Increase of Organization

The four criteria for increasing organization are satisfied by living organisms and certain artificial systems, but according to evidence are not satisfied by any supposed evolutionary system.

|  | Real System | | Evolutionary System | |
| --- | --- | --- | --- | --- |
| Criteria | Growing Plant | Building Construction | First Living Cell | Population of Complex Organisms |
| Open System | Seed | Materials | Complex Inanimate Molecule | Population of Simple Organisms |
| Available Energy | Sun | Sun | Sun | Sun |
| Directing Program | Genetic Code | Blueprint | None | None (Natural Selection?) |
| Conversion Mechanism | Photosynthesis | Workmen | None | None (Mutations?) |

sun's energy, without direction or ordering mechanism, will build the entire world of organic life this way. A man, or a tree, or even a simple cell, is infinitely more complex than an office building. Note the examples in table 5.

For the evolutionist to proffer chance mutations and natural selection (and this is the best he has been able to come up with so far) as the mechanism for accomplishing this marvelous conversion is only an ironic commentary on his frantic attempt to escape confrontation with his Creator. For chance is the very antithesis of structure, mutations constitute a perfect example of a disordering mechanism, and natural selection is a prime example of a stabilizing principle at work in nature! Such things as these reinforce and support the two laws and could not possibly provide the vehicle for offsetting or overturning them.

## Order Out of Chaos?

A relatively new science, called "chaos theory" has received some attention in recent years. Systems that seem to be "chaotic" in highly ordered systems can arise through very small perturbations that are gradually magnified as their effects spread through the systems. The study of such apparently chaotic systems with a view to determining the underlying order in them does have a number of useful applications.

However, the increasingly common notion that such systems can somehow go in reverse and become ordered systems seems to be another futile attempt to negate the entropy law. Much of this emphasis has stemmed from the publications of Belgian scientist Ilya Prigogine. He and a co-author have even written a book entitled *Order Out of Chaos*. In it, they say, "In far from equilibrium conditions, we may have transformation from disorder, from thermal chaos into order."[18]

And just how are such magical changes wrought? The answer is by means of what Prigogine calls "dissipative structures."

> In classical thermodynamics, the dissipation of energy in heat transfer, friction, and the like was always associated with waste. Prigogine's concept of a dissipative structure introduced a radical change in this view by showing that in open systems dissipation becomes a source of order.[19]

The idea is that, in certain open systems where there is a large and continuing flow-through of energy, especially if it occurs in pulsations, there may well be a large amount of dissipation of energy, in accordance with the second law of thermodynamics. However, in the region of dissipation, there may actually be generated an ordered sub-structure of some kind. Prigogine's classic example is the generation of vortices in a coffee cup, as heat from a source below the cup flows through the liquid. This, according to Prigogine, is a "dissipative structure," and supposedly represents a generation of order out of chaos.

Perhaps an even better example is the generation of a tornado, as incoming solar heat stirs up the atmosphere.

> Tornadoes are paragons of order-through-fluctuations. Small, naturally occurring wind shear effects, under conditions of severe non-equilibrium and strong pressure gradients, can amplify into massive energy flows that, though superbly (and locally) constructed can be utterly (and globally) destructive, ravaging the environment to feed the sustaining storm with ever more energy.[20]

A tornado is a highly "dissipative structure," all right, but just how such a structure — or a vortex in a coffee cup or any other kind of dissipative structure could contribute to some even more highly organized structure and even to produce evolution itself is not yet known, to put it mildly.

Eric Chaisson, the author of the book from which the above quote was taken, was so impressed with the idea of dissipative structures and order through perturbations and far from equilibrium conditions (which was Prigogine's idea, though Chaisson gives only minimum recognition to that fact) that his entire book is built on the theme that all aspects of the universe and life have evolved in this way!

As brilliant as Prigogine and his idea may be, however, that author does acknowledge that he has not proved any of it, nor does he really understand how it could work to produce evolution, even at the simplest level.

---

18. Ilya Prigogine and Isabelle Stengers, *Order Out of Chaos* (New York, NY: Bantam Books, 1984), p. 12.
19. Fritjof Capra, *The Web of Life* (New York, NY: Anchor Books, 1996), p. 89. Dr. Capra is a physicist at U. C. Berkeley, active in new-age philosophy.
20. Eric J. Chaisson, *Cosmic Evolution: The Rise of Complexity in Nature* (Cambridge, MA: Harvard University Press, 2001), p. 62.

The problem of biological order involves the transition from the molecular activity to the super molecular order of the cell. This problem is far from being solved.[21]

Eric Chaisson (who is a professor of physics at Tufts University) has to make a similar admission with respect to his very ambitious ideas about cosmic evolution.

Our treatment of cosmic evolution set forth in the book is by no means complete or comprehensive, especially regarding the devilish details.[22]

Those devilish details include any explanation whatever as to how any stage in evolution was actually accomplished by dissipative structures, or any other process that could increase organized complexity naturalistically. "In short, chaos theory cannot explain complexity."[23]

And neither can any other attempt to get around the anti-evolution conclusions of the second law of thermodynamics.

## Thermodynamics and Human Behavior

There remains to be considered the realm of man and his cultures and institutions as formally studied in the social or behavioral sciences. It may not be immediately obvious how thermodynamics may affect this domain of the spirit. Yet Scripture says: "There is *nothing* hid from the heat thereof" (Ps. 19:6, emphasis mine).

The sun is, of course, only a physical creation and the heat by which it energizes the earth is physical energy. Nevertheless the ultimate source and sustainer of this energy is Christ himself (John 1:3, 4) who is also the source and sustainer of our spiritual life and energy (John 1:9; 1 John 1:7).

Man understands very little yet about the physiologic mechanisms associated with his spiritual decisions, though there undoubtedly is some relation. The intensely sophisticated electric circuitry built into man's brain and nervous system does have a bearing on his memory, his ability to assimilate knowledge and to make choices. Everyone is aware that his own physical condition may affect his emotions, and vice versa. Furthermore, damage to the brain or the nervous system may result in a complete change in personality, usually for the worse. Evidence has accumulated in recent years that there are definite biochemical factors involved in the tendency toward delinquency and criminality. Genetic studies have demonstrated that hereditary factors influence not only physical characteristics but also the ability to learn and reason, and perhaps even the ability to comprehend spiritual truths.

Though much remains to be discovered about these intriguing subjects, there appears to be no doubt that physical mechanisms influence in some way our spiritual and moral attitudes and decisions, just as they do our biological pro-

---

21. Prigogine and Stengers, *Order Out of Chaos*, p. 175.
22. Chaisson, *Cosmic Evolution*, p 131.
23. Per Bak, *How Nature Works: The Science of Self-Organized Criticality* (New York, NY: Springer-Verlag, 1996), p. 31.

cesses. If this is so, since all such mechanisms are ultimately powered by the sun's energy, then the sun may even be the indirect source of the energy for our spiritual lives. And of course this finally comes from the Lord Jesus Christ! "In him we live, and move, and have our being" (Acts 17:28). When Jesus said, "I am the light of the world" (John 8:12), this was more than a statement of a spiritual truth — though it certainly includes that. In the fullest and most ultimate sense, He is the source, through the sun which reflects His glory, of all physical, biological, and spiritual power.

It is significant that man normally works during the day and rests at night. It is also significant that the "unfruitful works of darkness" (Eph. 5:11) are normally done at night. "They that sleep sleep in the night; and they that be drunken are drunken in the night" (1 Thess. 5:7). Somehow, the presence of the warmth and light of the sun seems to stimulate productive and beneficial activities, whereas its absence seems to lead to lethargy and sleep and often to "rioting and drunkenness," "chambering and wantonness," "strife and envying" (Rom. 13:13). The exact cause-and-effect relation of the sun's energy to all these characteristics of man's behavior is not yet fully known, but there is *something* there.

On the other hand, the sun's energy may also cause disintegration and death! Too much exposure to its ultraviolet radiations or its heat or its light may cause cancer or sunstroke or blindness. As already noted, solar radiation may even be the primary agent in somatic mutations, aging, and death. Though absolutely necessary for life, it eventually leads to death! In like manner, the Lord Jesus Christ is the "Sun of righteousness . . . with healing in his wings" (Mal. 4:2) to them that fear His name. But He is "consuming fire" (Heb. 12:29) to the wicked and the proud, and the "day that cometh shall burn them up" (Mal. 4:1). There is a future day when the sun will "scorch men with fire" (Rev. 16:8). When "the curse [hath] devoured the earth . . . the inhabitants of the earth are burned, and few men left" (Isa. 24:6).

In any case, whatever agency the physical sun may ultimately be shown to exercise in man's spiritual and moral life, there is no doubt that this life is also under the reign of the universal principles of conservation and decay. That is, man's spirit is both unending and degenerating, just as is the physical energy comprising his body. Though its temporary body may go through physical death, the spirit will continue to exist and to decay forever: "He that is unjust, let him be unjust still" (literally "yet more"; Rev. 22:11). Other Scriptures bear this truth: "And the smoke of their torment ascendeth up for ever and ever" (Rev. 14:11); ". . . their worm dieth not, and the fire is not quenched" (Mark 9:48). Every individual knows by experience that if he simply lets himself go, he goes down. He doesn't get better or do better if he simply "turns inward" on himself — or, literally, "entropies." Even a man such as the apostle Paul had to say, "But I see another law in my members, warring against the law of my mind, and bringing me into captivity to the law of sin which is in my members" (Rom. 7:23).

And if this condition is true of individual men, it is bound to be true also of his institutions. Just as a baby grows into an adult who thrives for a time but eventually ages and dies, in like manner cities, nations, cultures, languages, and whole civilizations rise and fall. In a generic sense, "life" and "language" and "civilization" are conserved, but individual languages, civilizations, and empires decay and die.

Thus, man's entire dominion — body, soul, and spirit — his physical, biological, and social world — is under the "bondage of corruption," "groan[ing] and travail[ing] in pain together until now" (Rom. 8:21–22). A universal effect requires a universal cause and that cause beyond doubt is God's curse on man and his domain because of sin (Gen. 3:17–19). The entrance of spiritual disorder into God's perfect creation (Gen. 1:31) led to the imposition of a universal and age-long reign of physical and biological decay and death as well. Nevertheless, God's law of conservation is still in effect and the world and life go on.

Hope also goes on, because God has promised a Redeemer! Some day this groaning creation will be delivered from the bondage of corruption and "there shall be no more curse" (Rev. 22:3). In that day the sun will be replaced by the one whom it now only feebly represents: "The city had no need of the sun, neither of the moon, to shine in it: for the glory of God did lighten it, and the Lamb is the light thereof" (Rev. 21:23).

Even in this present time, the same coming Redeemer has made possible individual deliverance from bondage to the law of decay and death. He has borne the full penalty and suffering of the Curse himself, on the Cross, dying for our sins and rising for our justification.

"For the law of the Spirit of life in Christ Jesus hath made me free from the law of sin and death" (Rom. 8:2). This tremendous gift is imparted by the Holy Spirit, in response to individual faith in the Lord Jesus Christ and His Word.

In order to set aside the principle of decay and death in the spirit (and ultimately in the body and soul as well), there must be an infusion of new life — a regeneration — and this of course can come only from that which is not itself subject to the same principle.

There is only one thing in this present world that meets this criterion! Since we are still in the flesh, it must be physically accessible and intelligible to the mind, as well as operational in the spiritual realm, yet it cannot be subject to the universal law of decay. The only thing that can fulfill these requirements is the Word of God. This Word has been revealed and inscripturated to be accessible to man but is also eternal and incorruptible and thus able to mediate salvation to lost men. "The Word of God is quick, and powerful" (literally "living and energizing"; Heb. 4:12). "Heaven and earth shall pass away, but my words shall not pass away" (Matt. 24:35). "All flesh is as grass . . . but the word of the Lord endureth for ever" (1 Pet. 1:24–25). "All scripture is given by inspiration of God . . . that the man of God may be perfect" (2 Tim. 3:16–17). "The engrafted word . . . is able to save your souls" (James 1:21). Over and over again we are reminded in the

Bible that God's Word is uniquely incorruptible and everlasting, in contrast to everything else in the world, which is under the bondage of corruption and death. "Thou hast magnified thy word above all thy name" (Ps. 138:2).

Although the second law presents the whole universe in a state of decay, the one who created the universe and established its laws is above the universe and not bound by its laws. The grass withers, but the Word of God stands. Though the earth shall wax old like a garment, God's salvation shall be forever. The world is passing away, but they who do the will of God abide. Even the young men faint, but those who wait on the Lord renew their strength.

There is a succinct and wonderful passage in the Bible describing the primeval "winding-up" of the cosmos. The universe has been "running down" ever since Adam's fall, but this required that it first be powered by God before it can be dissipated. The beautiful order of the creation must be designed and structured before it can run down to disorder. The infinite complexity of the cosmos and the information required for its operation must be planned and encoded before it can become distorted and confused. All three of these aspects of the cosmos are summarized in Isaiah 40:26: "Lift up your eyes on high, and behold who hath created these things, that bringeth out their host by number: he calleth them by all names by the greatness of his might, for that he is strong in power; not one faileth." Note that God brings out the host of entities in the cosmos by "number" — that is, in perfect *order*. He identifies them all by specific *names* appropriate to their intended functions — with complete *information*. And He invests them all with unfailing *power* — renewable *energy*.

In this present world, systems may become confused and disordered and feeble. But not their Creator! "Hast thou now known? hast thou not heard, that the everlasting God, the Lord, the Creator of the ends of the earth, fainteth not, neither is weary? there is no searching of his understanding" (Isa. 40:28).

And then, in one of the most beautiful passages ever written, the chapter closes with the assurance that this same infinite energy, order, and information are available to all those men and women who, as "open systems" open their hearts and lives to Him: "He giveth power to the faint and to them that have no might he increaseth strength. Even the youths shall faint and be weary, and the young men shall utterly fall: But they that wait upon the Lord shall renew their strength; they shall mount up with wings as eagles; they shall run, and not be weary; and they shall walk, and not faint" (Isa. 40:29–31).

## Thermodynamics and Eschatology

If the first and second laws of thermodynamics were to continue functioning as universal laws into the eternal future, the eschatological future would be dismal indeed. Time's arrow points down, and the cosmos is proceeding inexorably toward an ultimate "thermodynamic death." The sun and all the stars will burn away, and eventually all the available energy of the universe will be unavailable;

uniformly low-level heat energy, at the same temperature everywhere, will exist throughout the universe. The universe will (according to the first law) never cease to exist, but it will *die!*

That is, it would die if there were no Creator. The Creator who made it in the first place, and wound it up, and who in fact imposed on it the very decay principle which now seems to predict its death, will yet accomplish all His original purposes — and these do not include the uncreation of His creation! Note again the tremendous promises of Romans 8:20–22.

Nevertheless, a traumatic change still awaits the earth. The decay/death principle which now afflicts "the whole creation: is active because of sin, and thus cannot be removed until sin and all its effects have been purged.

The prophetic Scriptures foretell many profound changes scheduled for the earth and the heavens in the days ahead. They are to be climaxed by a chaotic intensification of the normal decay processes which have operated ever since the Curse was pronounced by God on His creation. The apostle Peter describes it thus: "The heavens shall pass away with a great noise, and the elements shall melt with fervent heat, the earth also and the works that are therein shall be burned up. . . . the heavens being on fire shall be dissolved, and the elements shall melt with fervent heat" (2 Pet. 3:10–12).

This passage has been variously interpreted, but obviously describes a profound and ultimate disintegration of "the heavens and the earth, which are now" (2 Pet. 3:7). The cosmos is not to be annihilated, but it is possible that atomic disintegrations are involved, which will convert mass into heat, sound, and other forms of energy. The total mass/energy in the cosmos will be unchanged, so that the first law remains inviolate. The second law also continues to operate, except that rates of disintegration will operate more pervasively and catastrophically than at any time since the world began. The universe did not begin with a "big bang," as evolutionists allege, but its present form will end with a big bang (not with a "whimper," as some have predicted), and the cosmos will die its "heat death" — not of old age but by divine execution: "Nevertheless we, according to his promise, look for new heavens and a new earth, wherein dwelleth righteousness" (2 Pet. 3:13).

After God's great white throne judgment (Rev. 20:11–15), He will *create* and *make* new heavens and a new earth (Isa. 65:17; 66:22), so that His creative power will once again be exercised throughout the entire universe.

All the age-long effects of sin (e.g., the fossils in the earth's sedimentary crust) will have been purged from the very elements, and there will be "no more curse" (Rev. 22:3). These will be "the times of restitution [or, better, 'restoration'] of all things" (Acts 3:21). The perfect conditions of pristine Eden will be restored and no doubt vastly enlarged and varied as well. The second law of thermodynamics will be repealed, and "there shall be no more death" (Rev. 21:4) in all the universe throughout all the ages to come.

# THE DUST OF THE EARTH

*Biblical Chemistry and Physics*

## The Nature of Matter

The sciences that are probably further advanced than any others, in terms of human understanding of their data and relationships, are the so-called "hard" sciences of physics and chemistry. Their phenomena have proved more amenable to mathematical analysis and precise description than any others, primarily because of the smaller number of variables that affect them than in the life sciences and earth sciences. Astronomy, already discussed in a separate chapter because of its prominence in the Bible, is often considered a branch of physics. Thermodynamics, likewise treated in a separate chapter, is an important branch of both chemistry and physics, and also (as we have noted) is directly involved in all other sciences in one way or another.

Chemistry deals with the basic structure of matter in terms of its atomic elements, molecules, and compounds, as well as with exchanges and reactions between them. Physics deals especially with the forces and energies exerted by and upon various aggregations of matter, as well as the resulting behavior of these material objects in response. Particularly at the subatomic level, the two disciplines tend to merge together, so that nuclear chemistry and nuclear physics are more or less synonymous.

Both sciences deal with matter and energy, the totality of which, according to the law of conservation of mass/energy, is always conserved. Matter can change its state (gas, liquid, or solid) and can become either very dense or very dispersed, but its total mass never changes. Energy can change its form (gravitational, elastic, compressive, viscous sound, heat, light, chemical, electrical, magnetic, etc.), but never its totality. The only exception in both cases consists of nuclear reactions, wherein mass changes to energy, or vice versa, in which case the total amount of mass plus energy is constant. As discussed in the preceding chapter, this principle is the most universal and best-proved law of science, the law of conservation of mass/energy, or the first law of thermodynamics. It is supported, in nontechnical terms of course, in many passages of Scripture (see preceding chapter for listing), all of which were recorded many centuries before the law was enunciated and proved by modern scientists.

The structure of all material objects is made of the same basic elements, whether those objects are living or nonliving. That is, both our human bodies and the rocks on the mountain are composed of hydrogen, carbon, oxygen, and other such elements. Altogether there seem to be 96 naturally occurring elements, plus a number of heavier elements produced in giant laboratory accelerators. Everything in the earth, as well as in the stars and planets, is composed of some combination of these elements, with the particular properties of the object (density, hardness, inertia, crystalline structure, etc.) being determined by the particular combination.

It is significant that, long before men realized this universality of material structure, the Bible had indicated that all things, including even human bodies, were made of the dust of the earth.

These basic elements were originally created (Gen. 1:1) as the fundamental components of matter in the space/matter/time cosmos ("heavens"/"earth"/"beginning") called into existence by the omnipotent Word of God (John 1:1–3). This basic "unformed" earth material (Gen. 1:2) was then "made" or "formed" by God into complex systems. Originally suspended and dispersed in a vast matrix of water (Gen. 1:2; 2 Pet. 3:5), all other elements were built up into a vast array of terrestrial and celestial bodies (1 Cor. 15:40) and, on the earth, both inorganic and living systems.

The gases of the atmosphere were made on the second day of creation (Gen. 1:6–7) from these elements, and the solids of the earth planet on the third day (Gen. 1:9–10). Also on the third day from these elements God built complex self-replicating chemical systems called plants, which "the earth brought forth" (Gen. 1:12). He then made the sun, moon, and stars, from the same elements. The bodies of all kinds of animals were "brought forth" from the waters and from the earth on the fifth and sixth days (Gen. 1:21, 24), and all of these were made from the same elements as well.

Finally, the bodies of human beings also were formed "of the dust of the ground" (Gen. 2:7). Long before men had any idea that everything in the physical cosmos was made of the same "dust," the unique statement of primeval creation of matter in the very first verse of the Bible had revealed that the creation was of *earth*. No other material substance was ever later said to be "created," but only "formed" or "made." Thus, the elements brought into existence by divine fiat as the basic earth materials when the universe was first created by God are the elements He then used to form all substances on earth, both living and nonliving, as well as in all the stars of the cosmos. This basic doctrine of Scripture was only confirmed by science in the past century.

These elements apparently constitute the biblical "dust of the ground," and it is significant that the great Curse was pronounced on "the ground" (same Hebrew word as "earth") when Adam sinned (Gen. 3:17). The outworking of the Curse involves final dissolution of all things — including the most complex structure of all, the human body — back again to "dust" (Gen. 3:19). This principle, as we have seen, is now formulated scientifically as the second law of thermodynamics.

## Chemical Reactions

It is remarkable that the relatively small number of different basic elements — the dust of the earth — can unite into such a very large number of molecules, compounds, and mixtures, comprising all the different types of substances and materials in the world, living and nonliving. These combinations and interchanges are not random, however, but, especially in the case of compounds, proceed only in accordance with their increasing atomic numbers (from 1 to 96) and beyond, which is also roughly in order of their increasing atomic weights. They are then further organized in a remarkable table of cyclically similar groups of elements (that is, similar in terms of their types of chemical activities) known as the periodic table. This table has proved extremely useful in describing and predicting the different ways that different elements can, and cannot, combine with each other. The number and arrangement of orbital electrons in the outermost ring of the atom of each element determines a number called the *valence* of that element, which is always an integral number and measures the relative ability of that type of atom to combine with the other types of atoms. The valence number itself is the number of hydrogen (or equivalent) atoms with which the particular element can combine (e.g., two in the case of oxygen, to form water) or can displace.

Such properties as these made chemistry a quantitatively predictable, "exact" science. They constitute a testimony to the wisdom and forethought of the Creator who formed these elements and whose sustaining power maintains their integrity.

There is a beautiful reference to this integrity, and even to the numerical nature of the valency property, in the magnificent 40th chapter of Isaiah: "Who hath measured the waters in the hollow of his hand, and meted out heaven with the span, and comprehended the dust of the earth in a measure, and weighed the mountains in scales, and the hills in a balance?" (Isa. 40:12). The Creator has very precisely determined all the components of His created universe, from the fantastic dimensions of interstellar space to the broad dimensions of the oceans and lands of earth, and even to the carefully controlled elements — the dust, the smallest particles known to the ancients. This passage clearly implies that these elemental particles are precisely ordered. Verse 26 says that the Creator of all things "bringeth out their host by number," indicating that God precisely and numerically orders the structure and size and activities of even the elements of the earth.

All the interactions between these elemental particles, the dust particles of God's creation, are controlled by their structure. They have been numbered and comprehended by their Creator, and now can even be controlled by man, who was primevally commanded to "subdue" the earth (Gen. 1:28).

Such interactions — or chemical reactions, as they are called today — are very numerous, and yet limited in number by the valence structure of each atomic element. Some of these reactions (e.g., fermentation, as in the case of bread and wine) are described in the Bible, and always accurately (note, e.g., Matt. 9:17; 1 Cor. 5:6).

Many of the elements, especially the metals, are mentioned explicitly in the Bible — iron, tin, gold, silver, sulphur (brimstone), copper, and others. Likewise, many minerals — that is, stable, inorganic compounds of two or more elements which occur in the earth in various locations and quantities — are mentioned. These include many of the precious stones such as amethyst, ruby, emerald, and others.

The most common and important of all chemical compounds is water. In fact, all other elements were originally created and constituted in a vast matrix of water (Gen. 1:2). Water continues to be the most useful chemical substance known, participating in more types of reactions and processes than any other. Water not only fills the vast oceans of the world, but is also by far the most abundant component in all living substances. All nutrition and digestion processes are carried out by means of a water medium. Practically all important chemical and biological processes involve water in one way or another.

This remarkable fact is intimated in 2 Peter 3:5, where Peter refers to the primeval special creation of heaven and earth and then says that "the earth [was] standing out of the water and in the water." The word "standing" (Greek *sunistemi*) is the word from which our English word "sustaining" is derived, and conveys the thought of being "held together," or "constituted" (the same word is used in Col. 1:17, where the King James Version translates it as "consist"). Thus, the earth — that is, all its materials and processes — was created to be constituted and maintained through the primeval substance of water. This verse, along with numerous others in the Bible dealing with water (see chapters 9 and 10), seems in this way to have anticipated the later development of the sciences of chemistry, geology, hydrology, meteorology, and others, as men would increasingly learn how to subdue the earth and the watery environment in which it was constituted.

## Power and the Word

Since everything in the physical universe is energy and everything that happens involves energy exchange, it is not surprising that courses or curricula in physical science commonly are subdivided and identified according to various types of energy — thermodynamics, electricity and magnetism, elasticity, optics, mechanics, etc., even nuclear energy. And, of course, closely associated with the concept of energy is the concept of power, the work or energy per unit of time. All scriptural references to energy and power, as we should expect, will be found to be consistent with scientific knowledge, even though these concepts, in the technical sense, are modern discoveries.

Christians often speak, and rightly so, of the power of the Word of God, thinking of such a text as Hebrews 4:12: "For the word of God is quick [i.e., "living"], and powerful, and sharper than any twoedged sword, piercing even to the dividing asunder of soul and spirit, and of the joints and marrow, and is a discerner of the thoughts and intents of the heart." There are numerous illustrations in Scripture, and in the life of every soul-winning Christian, of the power of the Word of God to convict and to illumine the mind and heart of a lost man and to bring him to Christ.

But it is not often realized how intimately associated is the concept of the power of God, not only in the spiritual sense but even in the physical realm, with the Word of God. Of course, the term "the word of God" is used in more than one sense in Scripture. It is used of the Scriptures themselves, the written Word. It is also used to refer to any form of communication from God to man, whereby God reveals himself to man, whether by an audible voice, by vision, through conscience, or even in the phenomena of nature. And it is one of the great titles of the Lord Jesus Christ himself, as the living Word of God, the one through whom God has been most clearly and completely revealed to man, in all the perfection of His love. But wherever the term is used, it brings to view in some way the fact that God is speaking and making himself known in man's experience.

## The Word of His Power

In Hebrews 1:3 we have a striking intimation that God's Word is associated with physical power. The first two verses of Hebrews bring to view both the written Word and the living Word: "God, who at sundry times and in divers manners spake in time past unto the fathers by the prophets, Hath in these last days spoken unto us by his Son."

Then the tremendous assertion is made not only that the Son, the living Word: "made the worlds," but also that He is "upholding all things by the word of his power," that is, that all the matter and physical phenomena of the universe are being sustained by "the word of his power."

The striking implications of this verse could only have been understood (and then only in very slight degree) in recent decades, when it has been discovered that everything in the physical universe is basically energy. All phenomena that affect the senses, such as light, sound, and heat, as well as matter itself, are merely different forms of energy. Energy is measured by the ability to perform mechanical "work," and all natural processes involve utilization of energy in some form. Einstein formulated the equation that describes the equivalence of matter and energy, which, as is well known, has served as the basis of modern discoveries in the field of nuclear energy. Matter, composed of molecules, atoms, electrons, protons, neutrons, and numerous submicroscopic particles, is now known to be nothing really substantial at all, but composed fundamentally of tremendous energy. When some of this energy is released, either through nuclear fission or thermonuclear fusion, the physical effects are also tremendous. The mysterious "binding energy" that normally holds the atom together, in opposition to the tremendous forces that are always acting to disintegrate it, is apparently somehow related to the primal and basic energy of creation.

Energy can manifest its presence in different phenomena, depending upon the nature and velocities of the motions which embody it. Whether it appears as matter or as light, heat, or in some other form is governed by the particular motions that occur.

The Scripture quoted above (Heb. 1:3) says that the Lord Jesus Christ is the ultimate source of the infinite power (or energy) that, revealing itself through its outworking (the Word), is the agency by which all the physical universe is "upheld." Here is the modern discovery of the equivalence of matter and energy, expressed more than 1,900 years ago, and, further, teaching that it is the living Word of God that supplies the power for keeping the matter of the universe from disintegrating, and for enabling it to manifest all the multitudinous physical phenomena that constitute God's creation.

## Power in the Scriptures

Several different Greek words are translated in the New Testament by our English word "power," and each gives a slightly different shade of meaning, but all are legitimately included under our concept of power. It is significant that each word is used with reference to the Word of God.

One of the words is the Greek *exousia*, meaning "authority." This word is used by Jesus in Matthew 28:18: "All power is given unto me in heaven and earth." This word is also used in Luke 4:32: "his word was with power."

Another Greek word frequently translated "power" is *dunamis*, from which we derive our English word "dynamic," and which means "strength" or "might." This word is found in Hebrews 1:3: "the word of his power," and also in Matthew 22:29, where the "scriptures" and "the power of God" are used essentially as equal terms.

Another interesting Greek word is *energes*, from which we get our English word "energy." This word is used in Hebrews 4:12, where the Word of God is said to be "quick, and *powerful*" (italics mine). The meaning in this verse is that the Word of God is full of energy; it is *energizing*; it produces work resulting from the energy contained therein.

In the Old Testament, the word most frequently translated "power" is the Hebrew *koach*. In Psalm 29, the great "Psalm of the Voice of the Lord" (and, therefore, the psalm of the Word of God), verse 4 states, "The voice of the Lord is powerful; the voice of the Lord is full of majesty." God's Word, therefore, is said to be filled with power, in both the Old and New Testaments, and by each of the major words which are used to convey the different connotations of the concept of power.

## Modern Technical Concept of Energy and Power

The concept of power or energy is extremely important in modern science and technology, and it is striking to note our technical meaning of these terms is so similar to their meaning as given in Scripture. Energy is not a substance but is a concept meaning the property of matter or phenomena that has the capacity of performing useful work, in the moving of forces through distances — in "making the wheels go around." In fact, the term "work" is practically equivalent to "energy," each amount of work done being numerically equal to the energy expended in doing the work.

Power is a similar concept, being the rate or speed with which the energy is used or the work is performed. Our familiar unit of horsepower, for example, represents 550 foot-pounds of energy being used up each second. (A foot-pound is the amount of work required to lift a one-pound weight a distance of one foot.)

This concept of energy is of absolutely paramount importance in all of the great modern advances in science and engineering that have contributed so immensely to modern civilization. R.B. Lindsay, long-time professor of physics, director of the ultrasonics laboratory, and dean of the graduate school at Brown University, described it as follows: "Of all unifying concepts in the whole field of physical science, that of energy has proved to be the most significant and useful. Not only has it played a major role in the development of science, but, by common consent, it is the physical concept which has had and still has the widest influence on human life in all its aspects."[1]

The importance of this concept of power and energy is seen in the fact that the most generally accepted definition of engineering (by engineers, at least) is that it is the "art and science by which the properties of matter and sources of power in nature are made useful to man in structures, machines, and manufactured products." This study of the properties of matter (and matter is now itself a "source of power") and the sources of power has resulted in more than a hundredfold increase in per capita power in our country in the past one hundred years. That is, each individual can now, on the average, accomplish one hundred times as much as one could one hundred years ago, by means of machines and methods developed by aid of the energy concept, and this of course is the reason for our modern high standard of living.

---

1. R.B. Lindsay: "Concept of Energy in Mechanics," *Scientific Monthly*, (Oct. 1957): 188.

## The Two Energy Laws

As noted before, this powerful scientific concept of energy is embodied in the two great laws, which are the most basic, universal, and important laws of all science, the first and second laws of thermodynamics. Although the name arose from the fact that, historically, they were first discovered in the study of thermodynamics, the science of heat power, their applicability has since been shown to extend to literally every branch of human scientific knowledge. The great Harvard physicist P.W. Bridgman, said, for example, "The two laws of thermodynamics are, I suppose, accepted by physicists as perhaps the most secure generalizations from experience that we have. The physicist does not hesitate to apply the two laws to any concrete situation in the confidence that nature will not let him down."[2]

Probably all of the basic formulas and methods in every branch of science and engineering are ultimately either based on, or intimately related to, these two great principles. These have already been discussed in detail in chapter 7.

## Analogy of the Word and Physical Power

In view of the close biblical connection between the concepts of the Word of God and the power of God, it is not surprising to find in searching the Scriptures that the effects of the Word upon the hearts of individuals are often compared to the physical phenomena associated with the various forms of energy. One might even see a relation between the fact that the originally created energy can neither be destroyed nor augmented with the revealed fact that God's written Word is likewise now completed, and is neither to be added to nor taken from (Rev. 22:18–19).

There is no corresponding analogy with the second law of thermodynamics, of course, since this law represents a state of things in the physical universe resulting from the Fall and God's resulting Curse on the whole creation. The law of energy deterioration is a continual reminder that the creation is under the bondage of corruption, departing ever further from its originally intended state of everlasting perfection. The Word of God, on the other hand, is completely perfect and eternally pure. "The law of the Lord is perfect . . . the testimony of the Lord is sure. . . . The statues of the Lord are right . . . the commandment of the Lord is pure" (Ps. 19:7–8).

## The Energy of Light

The most basic of all forms of energy is light energy, including not only visible light but all forms of radiant energy, from the very short wavelength rays such as x-rays and cosmic rays at one extreme, to the long wavelength rays manifested by heat and the electromagnetic rays used in radio and television communications. All these forms of light move in waves at a tremendous rate of speed known as the velocity of light. Furthermore, the energy of radioactivity — whereby mat-

---

2. P.W. Bridgman, "Reflections on Thermodynamics," *American Scientist*, (Oct. 1953): 549.

ter is disintegrating — and even the energy of the atom itself are also associated with light energy. The Einstein equation relates matter and energy by a simple constant, and that constant is the velocity of light.

Light energy is thus the primal form of energy, and the spiritual analogy is that, through the Word of God, the sin-darkened soul must first of all be enlightened before he can manifest any other form of spiritual energy in his life. Psalm 119:130 says, "The entrance of thy words giveth light."

Second Corinthians 4:6 says, "For God, who commanded the light to shine out of darkness, hath shined in our hearts, to give the light of the knowledge of the glory of God in the face of Jesus Christ." It is significant that the very first creative command of God recorded in Scripture (and therefore the first mention of God speaking, i.e., of the Word of the God), was that of the appearance of light. "And God said, Let there be light: and there was light" (Gen. 1:3). Another significant statement is made in Genesis 1:17 when, in describing the establishment of the sun, moon, and stars, their function was said to be "to give light upon the earth."

The light, or radiant energy coming from the sun to the earth, is now known by scientists to be the source of practically all of the earth's energy by which the processes of nature and life itself are maintained upon the earth. In fact, all of the earth's energy, except that of its own motion through space, its axial rotation, and the atomic energy of its matter, has come originally from the sun. It has been calculated that all of the earth's energy stores — its coals, oil and gas reserves, its timber and other burnable material, even its uranium and other fissionable atoms — could supply a total amount of power equal only to that which reaches the earth from the sun in just three days' time.[3]

Truly, with respect to physical phenomena and biological life on the earth, the sun is "the light of the world."

These facts intensify the significance to us of the tremendous claim made by the Lord Jesus, the living Word, when He said, "I am the light of the world: he that followeth me shall not walk in darkness, but shall have the light of life" (John 8:12). As the sun is the source of earth's physical energy, so Jesus is the source of the spiritual illumination and power of the believer. The written Word is likewise said to be the source of light for the divinely energized individual. "Thy word is a lamp unto my feet, and a light unto my path" (Ps. 119:105). "We have also a more sure word of prophecy; whereunto ye do well that ye take heed, as unto a light that shineth in a dark place" (2 Pet. 1:19).

## Atomic Energy

We have mentioned that atomic energy is itself intimately related to the energy of light. All the matter of the universe is basically energy and therefore in one sense is light energy. However, it normally appears not as light at all but as physical matter,

---

3. Eugene Ayres and Charles A. Scarlott, *Energy Sources* (New York, NY: McGraw-Hill, 1952), p. 186.

characterized by weight, hardness, etc. This form of energy likewise was created and is sustained by the Word of God: "By the word of the Lord were the heavens made; and all the host of them by the breath of his mouth" (Ps. 33:6). And Hebrews 11:3 says, "Through faith we understand that the worlds were framed by the word of God, so that things which are seen were not made of things which do appear."

Not only were the worlds brought into being through the Word of God but they are sustained by His Word. Hebrews 1:3 has already been mentioned in this connection. Another significant passage is found in 2 Peter 3 where, in describing the antisupernaturalistic scoffers of the last times, Peter says, "For this they willingly are ignorant of, that by the word of God the heavens were of old, and the earth standing out of the water and in the water . . . But the heavens and the earth, which are now, by the same word are kept in store, reserved unto fire against the day of judgment and perdition of ungodly men" (2 Pet. 3:5–7).

Second Peter 3:10 prophesies that at the coming Day of the Lord this maintaining power of the Word of God will be withdrawn from His present activity of holding together (Col. 1:17) all material things, the binding energy will be withdrawn, and all the atomic structures of the earth permitted to disintegrate instantly into other forms of energy — sound, heat, and fire.

> But the day of the Lord will come as a thief in the night; in the which the heavens shall pass away with a great noise, and the elements shall melt with fervent heat, the earth also and the works that are therein shall be burned up. Seeing then that all these things shall be dissolved [literally "released," or "unloosed"], what manner of persons ought ye to be in all holy conversation and godliness, Looking for and hasting unto the coming of the day of God, wherein the heavens [i.e., the atmospheric heavens], being on fire shall be dissolved, and the elements shall melt with fervent heat? (2 Pet. 3:10–12).

And just as the Word of God, through atomic power, has created and maintained the structure of the physical universe, so does His Word create and sustain the spiritual life of the one who believes after receiving the light from the Word. The following verses convey this truth:

> But he answered and said, It is written, Man shall not live by bread alone, but by every word that proceedeth out of the mouth of God (Matt. 4:4).

> Verily, verily, I say unto you, He that heareth my word, and believeth on him that sent me, hath everlasting life, and shall not come into condemnation; but is passed from death unto life (John 5:24).

> Being born again, not of corruptible seed, but of incorruptible, by the word of God, which liveth and abideth forever (1 Pet. 1:23).

## The Energy of Sound and Heat

Sound is another form of energy, moving out as a wave from its source. The sound of thunder was the most awe-inspiring sound known to the biblical writers, and was often compared to the voice of God. For example, "The voice of the Lord is upon the waters: the God of glory thundereth: the Lord is upon many waters" (Ps. 29:3).

For the one who has been illumined, redeemed, and kept by the Word of God, the energy thus imparted to his spirit must make itself manifest in a spoken witness so that through him the Word of God sounds out to others, ultimately over many waters and to the ends of the earth, in fashion analogous to the spreading of sound waves out from their source. "So then faith cometh by hearing, and hearing by the word of God. But I say, Have they not heard? Yes verily, their sound went into all the earth, and their words unto the ends of the world" (Rom. 10:17–18).

This passage is quoted by Paul from Psalm 19:4. The latter part of the verse refers to the sun and calls attention to the heat energy radiated from the sun to all the earth, providing the warmth necessary for life to be sustained. The same energy source also produces thunder associated with the rains. Thus, the heat energy from the sun is almost as important as the light energy therefrom and, of course, we have already noted that heat is really a form of light. It is significant that in this 19th Psalm the mention of the sun's heat is immediately followed by a declaration of the converting power of the Word of God. "His [the sun's] going forth is from the end of the heaven, and his circuit unto the ends of it: and there is nothing hid from the heat thereof. The law of the Lord is perfect, converting the soul" (Ps. 19:6–7).

Therefore, heat energy, like sound energy, is pictured to us as analogous to the process whereby the Word of God through the testimony of Christians, both individually and corporately, is used to witness and convert. The sounded witness alone, while permitting men to hear the gospel, will not convert the soul unless presented in warmth and zeal, earnestness and sincerity. But the Word of God sent forth in the warmth of a heart of love for Christ and lost men will melt cold hearts. "He sendeth out his word, and melteth them" (Ps. 147:18).

## Electrical and Chemical Energy

Since people in biblical times knew nothing about electricity and chemistry, one might think at first that these two very important forms of power could not be mentioned in the Bible. However, they are mentioned, and once again we find that they, too, are compared to the Word of God. Electrical energy, now as well as in ancient times, appears most vividly in the form of lightning. In Scripture both the lightning and thunder are symbols of the voice of God. "Hear attentively the noise of his voice, and the sound that goeth out of his mouth. He directeth it under the whole heaven, and his lightning unto the ends of the earth" (Job 37:2–3; see also Job 38:35). "The Lord also thundered in the heavens, and the Highest gave his voice; hail stones and coals of fire. Yea, he sent out his arrows, and scattered them; and he shot out lightnings, and discomfited them" (Ps. 18:13–14).

God is thus seen to speak in the lightning to defeat and rout the enemy. It is like a great arrow in His hand. Similarly, the Word of God is the sword of the Spirit, wielded by the Christian in resisting the devil and defeating him (see Eph. 6:17; Heb. 4:12).

Great stores of chemical energy are locked in the earth's reserves of coal, oil, peat, timber, gas, etc. This has originated from the sun's light energy, which through the marvelous process of photosynthesis has caused the growth of plant life, and this in turn has been used to sustain animal life. When the plants and, at least in some cases, animals have died and been buried, the energy stored up in their cell structure has been preserved in the ground over many years.

This energy remains chained up, so to speak, until released through the process of burning. When set on fire, however, chemical energy in its various forms provides a great portion of the power used in industry and transportation. The Word of God is like this form of power. Jeremiah wrote, "Wherefore thus saith the Lord God of hosts, Because ye speak this word, behold, I will make my words in thy mouth fire, and this people wood, and it shall devour them" (Jer. 5:14). "Then I said, I will not make mention of him, nor speak any more in his name. But his word was in mine heart as a burning fire shut up in my bones, and I was weary with forbearing, and I could not stay" (Jer. 20:9).

## Stress and Strain: Weight

Chemical energy is one form of potential energy in which the capacity for doing work is stored up, motionless and ineffective until released. Another type of potential energy is that contained in an elastic material which is held under restraint; that is, it has been either compressed or stretched and if released would revert to its original dimensions and accomplish work in so doing. Examples might include a compressed or elongated spring, water held behind a dam or kept under pressure in a pipe system, or compressed air, or steam under pressure. One of the laws of physics states that the stress is proportional to the strain; that is, the amount of potential force that could be exerted by the material is directly in proportion to the amount of distortion that it has undergone. And the amount of stored energy is essentially the product of the stress and strain.

There seems to be an implication, spiritually speaking, of this form of power released by the Word in Luke 16:16–17. "The law and the prophets were until John: since that time the kingdom of God is preached, and every man presseth into it. And it is easier for heaven and earth to pass, than one tittle of the law to fail." In this passage it is noted that as the Word is preached it exerts a pressure upon its hearers, causing them to "press" into the kingdom, or to "take it by force" according to the parallel passage in Matthew 11:12. Only when the "tension" or "pressure" resulting in the heart of the hearer of the Word is relieved by his permitting the Spirit's conviction to press him into the kingdom is he truly set "free from the law" (Rom. 8:2).

Gravitational energy, which manifests itself in the weight of objects, is a related form of potential energy. It appears as the capacity of an object which has been lifted against the force of gravity to fall when released. This energy is measured by the product of the weight of the object and its height above the ground or other surface to which it could fall. Similarly, the Word of God is a great weight, burdening those who resist it. As an example, some of the Corinthian church members ridiculed the physical appearance and speech of the apostle Paul, but his divinely inspired epistles, embodying as they did the very Word of God, were not so easily shunted aside. "For his letters, say they, are weighty and powerful; but his bodily presence is weak, and his speech contemptible" (2 Cor. 10:10).

## Mechanical Energy

Most of the various forms in which energy can appear are but preparatory to the accomplishment of the work of which they are capable. Electrical energy, chemical energy, strain energy, etc., all must be converted into mechanical energy in order to accomplish the work that needs to be done. Mechanical energy is the energy of motion, the turning of wheels, the moving of loads, the driving of hammers. It is also called kinetic energy.

This energy of movement and mechanical work is implied in such passages as the following, speaking of the spiritual effects of the Word. "He sendeth forth his commandment upon earth: his word runneth very swiftly" (Ps. 147:15). "Is not my word like as a fire? saith the Lord; and like a hammer that breaketh the rock in pieces?" (Jer. 23:29).

The accomplishment of God's work through the Word is also taught, analogous to the way in which the physical work of the world is accomplished through the conversion of other forms of energy into the kinetic energy of useful work. "So shall my word be that goeth forth out of my mouth: it shall not return unto me void, but it shall accomplish that which I please, and shall prosper in the thing whereto I sent it" (Isa. 55:11).

Furthermore, as has been noted, all energy is fundamentally manifested in motion. The various forms of energy basically are exhibiting different kinds and rates of motion. The most obvious form is the mechanical energy just mentioned, but even the primal form of energy, light, is associated with the ultimate in motion, that of the velocity of light, over 186,000 miles per second.

It is significant, then, that the origin of God's Word is associated with motion. Prior to the first spoken command in creation, when the Word of God was first heard, the Scriptures say that ". . . the Spirit of God moved upon the face of the waters." The process by which God inspired His written Word, mysterious and diversified though it may have been, was likewise fundamentally characterized by motion. "For the prophecy came not in old time by the will of man: but holy men of God spake as they were moved [literally 'carried along'] by the Holy Ghost" (2 Pet. 1:21).

## The Eternal Word

These many analogies between the spiritual power associated with God's Word and the different forms of physical power of His universe are too numerous to be accidental. They bear a dual witness both to the divine inspiration of the Scriptures which record them and to the divine origin of the physical creation at the hand of the author of Scripture.

We have seen that this is more than an analogy. The source of the physical power of the universe is itself the Word of God, upholding all things thereby.

But there is one sense in which this resemblance is incomplete. The law of energy conservation teaches that the total energy of creation is finite and unchanging, and the law of energy deterioration teaches that the universe is growing old and wearing out. The Word of God, on the other hand, is not finite but is infinite; it has no bounds. And it is not temporal, subject to aging and decay, but is eternal.

> For ever, O Lord, thy word is settled in heaven (Ps. 119:89).

> Thy word is true from the beginning [i.e., eternity past]: and every one of thy righteous judgments endureth for ever [eternity future] (Ps. 119:160).

> Thou hast magnified thy word above all thy name (Ps. 138:2).

> The grass withereth, the flower fadeth: but the word of our God shall stand for ever (Isa. 40:8).

> Heaven and earth shall pass away, but my words shall not pass away (Matt. 24:35).

> The word of God is not bound (2 Tim. 2:9).

## Biochemistry and the Origin of Life

At the borderland of the physical sciences and the life sciences lies the field of biochemistry, the chemistry of living systems. The study of the *origin* of living systems on the primeval earth brings in the earth sciences as well, so that the question of the origin of life is a truly interdisciplinary topic. The laboratory studies related to this subject, however, use the techniques of chemistry and physics, since they must at least start with inorganic materials and energies.

Belief in spontaneous generation, the idea that living organisms could emerge from nonliving materials, is very ancient. The Greek philosopher Aristotle believed in spontaneous generation, as indeed did most other ancient philosophers, and people continued to believe in it until the late 19th century. Finally, however, through a series of carefully planned and executed experiments, the great creationist chemist/biologist Louis Pasteur demonstrated once and for all that spontaneous generation does *not* occur, and the doctrine of "biogenesis" (life only from life) became the reigning doctrine of biology.

Evolutionary biologists could not long be satisfied with such a creationist position and diligently searched for other ways to explain life naturalistically. If complex creatures such as mice and maggots (or even bacteria) do not evolve from nonliving substances in the present age, then perhaps certain very simple protocells of some sort had emerged in some previous age. Consequently, many theoretical and experimental studies were devised to try to see how some such imaginary scenario might have been played out in the primeval world.

The most widely accepted concept during the 20th century was that of the Russian communist chemist O.A. Oparin, whose theory of *abiogenesis* postulated in 1938 that the first life forms arose in a primordial soup of complex chemicals through reactions with electrical discharges under an assumed reducing (no-oxygen) primeval atmosphere.[4] The famous experiment of Stanley Miller, published in 1953, supposedly demonstrated that this indeed could have happened and, this soon became the standard textbook presentation of how life began. The Miller demonstration utilized a laboratory apparatus which repeatedly circulated a mixture of heated gases (water vapor, methane, ammonia, and hydrogen) past an electric corona discharge. Each cycle produced a minute amount of liquid containing certain amino acids and other compounds, which were collected in a trap at the bottom of the apparatus. It took a week to accumulate enough material for significant measurement but, since amino acids are constituents of proteins, this achievement has been widely heralded as an experimental confirmation of at least the probability of primeval abiogenesis, in the manner theorized by Oparin.

The necessity of Miller's trap, together with the fact that no such trap would have been available in the primitive atmosphere to shield the amino acids from immediate disintegration by the same electrical discharges supposed to have generated them, is always systematically ignored in such textbook discussions. So are the facts that a few simple amino acids are almost infinitely less complex than the simplest protein molecule and that the simplest known living systems, the protozoa, are composed of great numbers of highly organized, specifically functioning enzymes and other proteins of many complex forms.

In more recent years, the nature of the information coding system in the living cell, centered in the double-helical structure of the DNA molecule and all its appurtenant systems, has been at least partially elucidated through research, and the extreme complexity of its "genetic code" is beginning to be appreciated. Since life even at the simplest level depends on this system, any assumed evolutionary origin of life must require that this whole system somehow be developed by natural processes from the assumed primordial soup, and such a development seems beyond all possibility. One of the nation's top men in this field has concluded, "We do not yet understand even the general features of the origin of the genetic code. . . . The origin of the genetic code is the most baffling aspect of the

---

4. Recent studies have shown that the primeval atmosphere could not have been a reducing atmosphere.

origins of life and a major conceptual or experimental breakthrough may be needed before we can make any substantial progress."[5]

At present, the genetic information in an organism is itself specified by the genetic codes of its parents, and there is no other way to do it. But how did the whole process start? The only plausible answer is, by creation!

Studies in later years have revealed that the genetic code indeed is far too complex to have originated naturalistically.

> Roughly $10^{20}$ genetic codes are possible, but the one nature actually uses was adopted as the standard more than 3.5 billion years ago. . . . the natural code is far better than the vast majority of randomly generated codes at minimizing the errors caused by genetic mutations. . . . it is extremely unlikely that such an efficient code arose by chance.[6]

Instead of the obvious conclusion that such an efficient code was created by God, however, most biochemists assume that natural selection operating on these multiplied billions of different possible codes somehow chose the right one. As Sir Fred Hoyle once said, however:

> The notion that . . . the operating program of a living cell could be arrived at by chance in a primordial organic soup here on the Earth is evidently nonsense of a high order.[7]

The basis of Hoyle's opinion was his calculation of the improbability of even the simplest form of life arising by chance. The common idea that natural selection can somehow overcome such chance probabilities is not supported by any actual tests, of course.

> At present all discussions on principal theories and experiments in the field either end in stalemate or in a confession of ignorance. . . . hypothetical arguments often dominate over facts based on experimentation or observation.[8]

A frequent participant in creation/evolution debates is Dr. Massimo Pigliucci. Even such a doctrinaire anti-creationist as he, however, has admitted that the origin of DNA and the genetic code by naturalistic means seems intractable.

> If the proteins appeared first, so that they could eventually catalyze the formation of nucleic acids, how was the information necessary to produce the proteins themselves coded? On the other hand, if nucleic acids came first, thereby embodying the information necessary to obtain proteins, how were the acids replicated and translated into proteins?[9]

---

5.  Leslie Orgel, "Darwinism at the Very Beginning of Life," *New Scientist*, 94 (Apr. 15, 1982): 151.
6.  Jonathan Knight, "Top Translator," *New Scientist*, 158 (April 18, 1998): 15.
7.  Fred Hoyle, "The Big Bang in Astronomy," *New Scientist*, 92 (November 19, 1981): p. 527.
8.  Klaus Dose, "The Origin of Life: More Questions Than Answers," *Interdisciplinary Science Reviews*, 13, no. 4 (1988): 348–349.
9.  Massimo Pigliucci, "Where Do We Come From?" *Skeptical Inquirer*, 23 (Sept.–Oct. 1999): 24.

One very unlikely way out of this impasse had been suggested by Dr. Leslie Orgel and others.

> We proposed that RNA might well have come first. . . . This scenario could have occurred, we have noted, if prebiotic RNA had two properties not evident today: a capacity to replicate without the help of proteins and an ability to catalyze every step of protein synthesis.[10]

These two seemingly impossible conditions mark this suggestion to be almost like belief in magic. No wonder Pigliucci concludes his analysis thus:

> The origin of life is one question that science will be pondering for some time to come, and skeptics should be wary of oversimplified answers found in introductory biology textbooks.[11]

There are many other aspects of living substances which seem impossible to explain by chance. One of the most baffling is the universal "left-handed" orientation of amino acids in living forms, whereas in nonliving substances, these amino acids occur equally in "left-handed" and "right-handed" orientation with respect to their optical activity. No explanation as to how this remarkable system could have evolved has been forthcoming.

> Since the time of Louis Pasteur, the origin of optical activity in biological systems has attracted a great deal of attention. Two very different questions must be answered. First, why do all amino acids in proteins or all nucleotides in nucleic acids have the same handedness? Secondly, why are the amino acids all left handed (L-) and the nucleotides all right-handed (D-)? We do not know the answer to either question.[12]

When an organism dies, its amino acids gradually "racemize," that is, they gradually decay from their left-handedness until there are an even number of left- and right-hand molecules, just as in all nonliving situations where amino acids are found. Stanley Miller's laboratory-produced amino acids were already racemized, of course. But the problem is, how did all living organisms come to have only left-handed amino acids, when both their imaginary inorganic progenitors and their decadent descendants (after death) both have equal amounts of left- and right-handed amino acids? Again, the only answer seems to be that they must have been specially created that way.

Even the simplest imaginary replicating protein molecule, if there ever were such a thing, would have to be so incredibly complex — in order to be able to code and direct its own replication from the constituents of the surrounding "soup" — as to be completely beyond the range of chance assemblage. The previously agnostic scientist Sir Fred Hoyle was driven to become a creationist of sorts when

---

10. Leslie E. Orgel, "The Origin of Life on the Earth," *Scientific American*, 271 (Oct. 1994): 78.
11. Pigliucci, "Where Do We Come From?" p. 27.
12. Leslie Orgel, "Darwinism at the Very Beginning of Life," p. 151.

he tried to calculate the probability of such a chance assemblage. "Precious little in the way of biochemical evolution could have happened on the earth. If one counts the number of trial assemblies of amino acids that are needed to give rise to the enzymes, the probability of their discovery by random shufflings turns out to be less than 1 in $10^{40,000}$."[13]

This number is so minuscule as to be equivalent to zero. That is, there is no chance whatever that it could have happened by chance. A similar calculation was performed by information scientist Marcel Golay. Such a system, according to Golay, would require 1,500 successful chance events in succession, each with a one-half chance of success. Thus, the probability that any series of 1,500 successive chance events will generate life at the simplest level would be:

$$(1/2)^{1500} = 1 \text{ chance out of } (10)^{450}$$

Assume that the universe is 3 trillion years old, or $10^{20}$ seconds. Assume also that the universe is 5 billion light-years in radius, and thus could hold a maximum of $10^{130}$ electron-sized particles. Assume each particle can act in $10^{20}$ events per second. Then the maximum number of events that could ever have taken place in the entire history of the universe would be:

$$(10)^{20}(10)^{130}(10)^{20} = (10)^{170}$$

The maximum number of 1,500-event sequences is as follows:

$$(10)^{170} \div (10)^3 = (10)^{167}$$

Thus, the probability that any one of the required 1,500-event sequences will be the only correct sequence to generate life is:

$$(10)^{167} \div (10)^{450} = 1 \text{ chance out of } (10)^{283} = 0! \text{ [since less than 1 in } (10)^{170}]$$

The chance that the simplest imaginable replicating system could be formed naturalistically from non-living chemicals, even with the most generous allowances, turns out to be essentially zero. Life can come only from life.

The upshot of such calculations is that Sir Fred Hoyle, as well as Dr. Orgel, Dr. Frances Crick (co-discoverer of the structure of the DNA molecule), and others have felt it necessary to infer that life must have arisen somewhere else in the universe and then been translated to earth, since it could not have formed on the earth.

This, of course, is the refuge of desperation, since there is not the slightest evidence of extraterrestrial life anywhere in the universe, as discussed in chapter 5. In fact, many studies have shown that the requisite conditions for sustaining life are found to be so rare in the cosmos that they could not have "evolved" more than once, at most. "There is a deeply ingrained conviction in the great majority

---

13. Fred Hoyle and Chandra Wickramasinghe, "Where Microbes Boldly Went," *New Scientist*, 91 (1981): 412–15. See also the book by these two authors, *Evolution in Space* (New York, NY: Simon & Schuster, 1982).

of mankind, to which the appeal of science fiction and fantasy bears witness, that the universe is so constituted that, if an opportunity exists for hominids to evolve, that too will be actualized. Whatever may be the basis for such convictions, it clearly must be sought outside the domain of science."[14]

It is a welcome relief to escape from the sterility of such foolish speculations about the origin of life to the certainty, clarity, and rationality of God's Word. The only way there can be life is for one who has life to produce life. The first life on earth must have come from the living God in heaven. On the fifth day of the creation week, the Scripture says, "And God created great whales, and every living creature that moveth, which the waters brought forth abundantly, after their kind, and every winged fowl after his kind: and God saw that it was good" (Gen. 1:21).

This is the second creative act of God, the first being the creation of the basic space-mass-time cosmos in Genesis 1:1. The entity first created was physical; the entity here created is biological, the "living *creature*" (Hebrew *nephesh*, also commonly translated "soul" or "life"). The adjective "living" (Hebrew *chay*) is evidently intended here to be synonymous with "moving" in Genesis 1:20, stressing that these living creatures were moving creatures — that is, *animals*.

Thus, in the Bible, "life" required a special act of creation, and it is therefore completely impossible that nonliving chemicals could ever evolve into living animals. It is no wonder that biochemists and other scientists have found all attempts to generate life in the laboratory mere exercises in utter futility!

The entity of conscious life, life sustained by the breath of life (Gen. 2:7) and the life of the flesh, which is blood (Gen. 9:4), is a special creation, completely incommensurate with the phenomena of chemistry and physics. Plants, on the other hand, do not possess life in this sense. They are not animate (though they grow), they do not breathe (though they "transpire"), they do not have blood (though they are nourished by means of water and nutrients conveyed through the root system) and, above all, they do not possess sentient life. They are extremely complex chemical systems, programmed to replicate themselves via the marvelous DNA molecular genetic code, but they are not "alive" in the biblical sense, and so cannot "die" in the biblical sense. They were created specifically to provide a continually replenishable food supply for men and animals. "And God said, Behold, I have given you every herb bearing seed, which is upon the face of all the earth, and every tree, in the which is the fruit of a tree yielding seed; to you it shall be for meat. And to every beast of the earth, and to every fowl of the air, and to every thing that creepeth upon the earth, wherein there is life, I have given every green herb for meat: and it was so" (Gen. 1:29–30).

The general distinction between plants and animals is thus clear enough, at least as far as the "higher" animals are concerned, but the exact boundary may be hard to define, pending further research. In any case, the Scriptures do make the

---

14. William G. Pollard, "The Prevalence of Earthlike Planets," *American Scientist*, 68 (Nov.–Dec. 1979): 659.

point that there is a distinction. Plants were *formed* from the dust of the earth, and do not possess *nephesh* life, whereas the *nephesh* possessed by animals was specially *created*. The bodies of animals are similar in many respects to those of plants, being constructed of essentially the same chemical elements and with genetic reproduction and development coded by the DNA molecule. Though similar, the bodies of animals are far more complex than those of plants, of course, but the truly essential difference is the created *nephesh*, the "life" or "soul." We can be absolutely certain that the sentient animal life not only *did* not evolve from nonliving chemicals, but *could* not evolve from nonliving chemicals. They are two different spheres of reality.

Furthermore, as we have already seen, even though all organisms are composed of the same chemical elements, the "dust of the earth," the complexity of the body of even the simplest one-celled bacterium is far too great to have ever become organized originally by chance or by any known process in nature.

Not only is the origin of life a biochemical process, so is the reproduction of life. The marvelous process of reproduction and embryonic growth is not yet fully understood, but is known to be centered in part around the remarkable double-helical structure of the DNA molecule and the genetic information programmed therein. The double helix serves as a "template" upon which and around which the body of the embryo is built up, step-by-step and cell-by-cell.

This process long ago was poetically and beautifully described by David in Psalm 139:

> For thou hast possessed my reins: thou hast covered me in my mother's womb. I will praise thee; for I am fearfully and wonderfully made: marvelous are thy works; and that my soul knoweth right well. My substance was not hid from thee, when I was made in secret, and curiously wrought in the lowest parts of the earth. Thine eyes did see my substance, yet being unperfect; and in thy book all my members were written, which in continuance were fashioned, when as yet there was none of them (Ps. 139:13–16).

To appreciate this passage properly, as quoted above from the King James Version, we must look more closely at several of the key words. In verse 13, the word "possessed" (Hebrew *qanah*) has the basic meaning of "erected" — that is, the Lord "possesses" by virtue of the fact that He was the one who "formed" the human body. The word "reins," of course, refers specifically to the kidneys, but is commonly used in the Old Testament to refer to the inward parts of the body in general, especially as being the seat of one's deep emotional nature. The word "covered" (Hebrew *sakak*) means "entwine about and over, for protection." It conveys the idea, not only of shielding the fragile fetus in the womb, but also of overshadowing and overseeing each stage in its development, providing a secure interlocking pattern for its gradual growth in strength and complexity.

The words "wonderfully made" in verse 14 are one word in the original, the Hebrew *palah*, which means "uniquely made." That is, God has designed a wonderful system for reproduction and for generating new bodies, so that even though the basic process and pattern (e.g., the DNA molecule) is the same for every person, yet the genetic system is so structured that every single individual is unique. A prominent geneticist[15] has calculated that there is sufficient potential diversity in the genes of a single human couple to allow for $10^{2017}$ different children without any identical twins. This number is inconceivably large — it would take at least 100 billion billion universes the size of the entire cosmos just to cram in that many people. No wonder the Psalmist says that every person is distinctly, wonderfully made!

Then the passage speaks of "my substance." The word is the Hebrew *ostem*, meaning "body substance," probably referring especially to the bone structure. Before it could be seen by human eyes, even before the male and female cells had united in conception, the future body is seen by God, not just in prophetic foresight, but in terms of all the individual atoms of carbon and calcium and oxygen and other elements which He knows will eventually be organized by His created program in the DNA to come together to form the complete body.

One of the most fascinating aspects of the process is the template action of the genes in the intricately coiled double helix of the DNA molecule, which somehow brings all the necessary atoms together as they are received in the womb and directs their fashioning into the component parts of the growing body. It is like a beautiful piece of embroidered silk, with the design taking shape, stitch-by-stitch in glorious color, on the basis of the pattern hidden within the cloth. The text uses the graphic expression "curiously wrought," which is one word in the Hebrew, *raqam*, and which actually means "embroidered"! It is frequently translated as "needlework" or "embroiderer."

The phrase "lowest parts of the earth" is enigmatic. It occurs eight other times in the Old Testament, translated either as "low parts of the earth," "lower parts of the earth," or "nether parts of the earth." In all these other occurrences, the context clearly indicates that it is speaking of the great pit in the interior of the earth which housed the spirits of dead men and women, both those who died in faith and those who died as unrepentant sinners. The equivalent Greek expression is used in Ephesians 4:9, where we are told that, before His ascension, Christ "also descended first into the lower parts of the earth." In this passage, we learn that, as He ascended, He "led captivity captive," speaking of the spirits of Old Testament period believers, set free by His work on the cross to be henceforth with Him in paradise.

But how can such a phrase be applied to the embryo being sewn together in the womb? It may simply be, as most commentators interpret, that the utter darkness of the deep pit in the center of the earth is being compared figuratively to the darkness and security of the womb. There is another possibility, however,

---

15. Francisco Ayala, "The Mechanisms of Evolution," *Scientific American*, 239 (Sept. 1978): 63.

perhaps more in keeping with the actual wording of the declarative statement of the verse. That is, even though the living fetus is actually being "embroidered" in the womb, the elements which are being added one by one to its structure originally came from the depths of the earth. Also, the "information" stored in its DNA had been transmitted generation after generation through the ancestral family line from Noah and ultimately from Adam and Eve. At the time of David's writing, all of his own ancestors had already departed in spirit to these lowest parts of the earth, but their genetic inheritance (and perhaps even their spiritual intercessions) continued to influence the development of their yet unborn descendants on the earth.

Thus, God has seen the developing embryo at each stage since even *before* conception. The words "my substance yet being unperfect" are all just one word in the original (Hebrew *golem*) and mean "a wrapped and unformed mass," clearly referring explicitly to the embryo. Even his "days" were written in God's book ahead of time. The words "in continuance" actually use the Hebrew *yamim* ("days"). The phrase "my members" has been inferred, as indicated by the King James Version italics, and so can be omitted, but the developing embryo would certainly contain all the developing members of the body. Even one's *days* are planned ahead somehow by God, and are all in some mysterious way set by the biological clock coded within the genetic system. These were actually "fashioned" ahead of time, it says, and the word is the Hebrew *yatsar*, the same word as used in Genesis 2:7, when God "formed" man of the dust of the ground.

Now although this passage is written in exalted, poetic language, it still is remarkably harmonious with all that is known scientifically about the amazing biochemical process established by God for propagation of the human family. God first created matter (the earth, unformed), next "the dust of the earth" (the basic elements), then formed man's body of these elements (as well as all other material objects), and finally established in that body a system of reproduction and coded recombinations that would suffice for its indefinite multiplication until the earth was filled with human inhabitants. This most important of all biochemical processes is not yet fully understood and even less appreciated, but it is a marvelous evidence of the power, wisdom, and love of our heavenly Father, "of whom the whole family in heaven and earth is named" (Eph. 3:15).

PART  3

# THE EARTH SCIENCES

# FOUNDATIONS OF THE WORLD

*Biblical Geophysics*

## Uniqueness of the Earth

The earth has been designed by God to be man's eternal home, and so is unique among all the planets and stars of the cosmos. Although the earth at present has been ravaged by the effects of man's sin and God's judgment, it was designed by the Creator for man, and was originally "very good" (Gen. 1:31). One day its elements will have to be melted and purified (2 Pet. 3:10), but from the energies and gases of the great conflagration, God will renew the earth and its atmosphere by once again exerting His great creative and formative powers. Thenceforth, the "[renewed] heavens and [renewed] earth" will serve as the home of redeemed men and women forever (see Isa. 65:17; 66:22; 2 Pet. 3:13; Rev. 21:1). The adjectives translated "new," in both the Old Testament and New Testament references here cited, have the connotation of "fresh" or "renewed," rather than "young." That is, the conservation law will continue to apply even in the fiery disintegration described by Peter; the earth's solids and liquids will be converted to vapors, and perhaps through nuclear disintegration even into pure energy, after which God will presumably use these same energies and elements, now purified, to establish the new heavens and new earth.

That the earth was uniquely designed for man is indicated in such Scriptures as, "The heaven, even the heavens, are the LORD's: but the earth hath he given to the children of men" (Ps. 115:16). And, "God that made the world and all things therein, seeing that he is Lord of heaven and earth . . . hath made of one blood all nations of men for to dwell on all the face of the earth, and hath determined the times before appointed, and the bounds of their habitation" (Acts 17:24–26).

This is still further, and conclusively, demonstrated by the fact that the Lord

Jesus Christ will live and reign forever in the new Jerusalem on the new earth (Rev. 22:3–5).

The fact of the earth's unique suitability for life is also confirmed by all known scientific facts concerning the character of other heavenly bodies and, in contrast, the essential ingredients to sustain life. Astrophysicist William Pollard discussed this subject in some detail in an important article. As far as other planets in the solar system are concerned, the nation's space program has shown consistently that life neither does exist nor could exist on any of them. "It is almost certain that no other planet in our solar system now supports the phenomenon of life."[1] As far as distant stars and galaxies are concerned, there is no evidence, either in science or Scripture, that any of them have earth-like planets. It cannot be proved that they do not have such planets, of course, since they are far beyond the reach of either telescopes or spaceships, and it is not possible to prove a universal negative.

Pollard (and many others, for that matter) has shown that the requirements for life are so restrictive and so finely tuned on earth that it is extremely improbable that such conditions could have evolved anywhere else in the universe on any naturalistic basis. Especially vital is the presence of liquid water in sizable amounts. "Even more essential than Earthlike land masses is the presence of sizable bodies of liquid water throughout the history of the planet. A full evolutionary development of complex organelles and organisms is not conceivable apart from an ample continuous marine environment."[2] Although there is some evidence of water ice or water vapor on other planets, none of them have any significant amount — probably none at all — of liquid water. The astronauts commented rapturously on the beautiful appearance from space of our "water planet," and the Bible appropriately speaks of the initial creation of the earth as abundantly associated with water (Gen. 1:2; 2 Pet. 3:5).

In a similar study to that of Pollard, who was a theologian as well as an eminent astrophysicist, another astronomer later summarized the evidence thus: "The sobering reality is that there is no observational evidence whatsoever for the existence of other intelligent beings anywhere in the universe."[3]

## Size and Shape of the Earth

Critics of the Bible have been saying for centuries that the Bible authors describe a flat and stationary earth with four corners, resting on giant pillars, with sun, moon, and stars orbiting it daily along the surface of a great celestial sphere. Nothing, however, could be further from the biblical facts. Such a cosmology may have been the teaching of the medieval church, strongly influenced as it was by Greek and Roman philosophy, but the Bible teaches no such thing. As a matter

---

1. William G. Pollard, "The Prevalence of Earthlike Planets," *American Scientist,* 67 (Nov.–Dec. 1979): 653.
2. Ibid.
3. Robert Naeye, "OK, Where are They?" *Astronomy,* 24 (July 1996): 42.

of fact, the Scriptures were far in advance of modern science in their assertion of the size, shape, support, and rotation of the earth.

To the people of antiquity, the earth must have seemed much larger than either the sun or the moon, and certainly than the stars. Without telescopes, the stars were mere points of light, and even the sun seemed like merely a "great light" which circled the earth each day. Yet the Psalmist somehow had the correct perspective on the relative sizes of earth and heaven. "When I consider thy heavens, the work of thy fingers, the moon and the stars, which thou hast ordained; What is man, that thou art mindful of him?" (Ps. 8:3–4). In asking this question, David was anticipating the question that would later be raised by great numbers of people in the modern era, who do realize how insignificant the earth is in relation to the vastness of the astronomic universe. Many have doubted that, even if there is a God, He would take any interest in a speck of dust in a remote corner of the immense cosmos.

It is not size that measures importance, however, but complexity, and the human brain is, as Asimov put it, "the most complex and orderly aggregation of matter in the universe."[4] Even in terms of size, man stands about halfway between the microscopic world of the atom and the telescopic view of the universe. In any case, the biblical view, both of the size of the cosmos and of the importance (that is, the organized complexity) of mankind, is thoroughly appropriate scientifically. "Thou madest him to have dominion over the works of thy hands; thou hast put all things under his feet" (Ps. 8:6).

The Bible describes a spherical earth suspended in space, not a flat earth supported on pillars. Note the following Scriptures. "When he prepared the heavens, I was there; when he set a compass upon the face of the depth" (Prov. 8:27). "It is he that sitteth upon the circle of the earth, and the inhabitants thereof are as grasshoppers; that stretcheth out the heavens as a curtain, and spreadeth them out as a tent to dwell in" (Isa. 40:22).

The word "compass" in Proverbs 8:27 and the word "circle" in Isaiah 40:22 are both translations of the same Hebrew *chuwg*, an excellent rendering of which is "circle." It could well be used also for "sphere," since there seems to have been no other ancient Hebrew word with this explicit meaning (a sphere is simply the figure formed by a circle turning about its diameter).

Note that both verses also refer to the "heavens" above this sphere of the earth and the deep ("depth" is the same Hebrew word as "deep"). These are apparently the atmospheric heavens that have been "prepared" for the earth's inhabitants as "a tent to dwell in." Isaiah, of course, had no firsthand knowledge that the atmosphere was of only limited extent, not having any vehicle with which to ascend into the atmosphere for measurements. Nevertheless, he is led to compare the upper boundaries thereof to a curtain or a tent, within which earth's inhabitants

---

4. Isaac Asimov, "In the Game of Energy and Thermodynamics, You Can't Even Break Even," *Smithsonian* (June 1970): 10.

must dwell. Outside the "tent" it is dark and cold and deadly. Inside, with the sun's radiation scattered, reflected, and dispersed, there is light and warmth and life-sustaining oxygen.

That the earth is suspended in space, not supported on pillars, is evident from Job 26:7: "He stretcheth out the north over the empty place, and hangeth the earth upon nothing." The word actually is rather emphatic — "nothing whatever." The earth is neither resting on pillars nor suspended from some heavenly ceiling. It is maintained in an orbit about the sun by the force of gravity, but that really explains nothing, since gravity — "action at a distance" — is merely a name used to describe phenomena of this sort. No one really understands gravity, or why it works as it does.

The first part of the above verse has been variously interpreted. Many have taken it to mean that there is a region in the northern sky that is void of stars. As a matter of fact, there may indeed be such a void.

> The recently announced "hole in space," a 300 million-light-year gap in the distribution of galaxies, has taken cosmologists by surprise. . . . But three very deep core samples in the Northern Hemisphere, lying in the general direction of the constellation Bootes, showed striking gaps in the red shift distribution. In each, the gaps extended from roughly 360 million to 540 million light-years; moreover, each showed a marked enhancement of galaxies on the inner and outer edges of the void.[5]

This void could not be detected by the naked eye, so Job could not have known about it by observation. However, it may well be that this is not what the verse means anyway. The words "empty space" are one word in the original, the Hebrew *tohu*, which is the word translated "without form" in Genesis 1:2. As we have pointed out, the elemental earth material was originally unformed when God called it into existence. But then the Spirit of God energized the creation; electromagnetic and gravitational energies began to function throughout the cosmos. The planet earth was formed out of "earth" elements, held together now by gravity, in spherical form ("the circle of the earth" and "the compass on the deep"), and the earth began to rotate, so that a cyclical succession of day and night could thenceforth prevail over its surface. In order to rotate, a polar axis must be established, with a "north" and a "south." Thus the "north" was first "stretched out" as an endless line, around which the day/night cycle would alternate, over the unformed earth elements, some of which then were drawn together by gravity into global form, and suspended by God in the infinite vastness of the cosmos.

The rotation of the earth has already been discussed in chapter 5 in reference to Job 38:14. The remarkable prophetic statement of Christ concerning the instantaneous and unexpected nature of His second coming also implies both the roundness and rotation of the earth. "I tell you, in that night there shall be two

---

5. M. Mitchell Waldrop, "Delving the Hole in Space," *Science,* 214 (Nov. 27, 1981): 1016.

men in one bed; the one shall be taken, and the other shall be left. Two women shall be grinding together; the one shall be taken, and the other left. Two men shall be in the field; the one shall be taken, and the other left" (Luke 17:34–36). In other words, the great event will take place instantaneously at night, in the morning, and in the afternoon. Such a combination would be possible only on an earth in which day and night could be occurring simultaneously, and that means a rotating earth suspended in space.

The charge that the Bible refers to an earth with four corners is easily answered. The phrase "the four corners of the earth" only occurs in Isaiah 11:12 and Revelation 7:1. The same word is translated as "four quarters of the earth" in Revelation 20:8, and this is really a more precise meaning, in both the Hebrew (*kanaph*) and Greek (*gonia*). The division of all geography into four quadrants (northeast, northwest, southwest, and southeast), with the "origin of coordinates" at the location of the observer, is standard practice in all surveying and navigation. The Greek word *gonia* literally means "angle" and provides the suffix in English words as *polygon, hexagon*, etc. The "four angles" of the earth means simply the four directions. To take this obvious meaning of the phrase and distort it into teaching a square earth is inexcusable special pleading.

As a matter of interest, although this is clearly not the meaning of these verses, modern geodetic studies surprisingly have shown that the earth actually does have four "corners," or protuberances, that disrupt the normal curvilinear shape of the geoid (the actual "figure of the earth" is not precisely spherical, but what is called an oblate spheroid, slightly bulging at the equator and flattened at the poles, responding to the centrifugal forces of the earth's rotation). These four protuberances on the geoid have been located as follows; in terms of latitude and longitude.[6]

1. 55° N, 10° W (near Ireland)
2. 50° S, 48° E (near South Africa)
3. 15° N, 140° E (near the Philippines)
4. 18° S, 80° W (near Peru)

Thus, if one wishes to press the point, earth actually does have four corners! However, the clear meaning of the expression as used in the Bible is simply one meaning all parts of the earth — the four directions, or four quadrants, or four angles, or four quarters. People quite commonly even today use the expression "to the four corners of the earth" as a picturesque way of saying "to the uttermost parts of the earth," and that is the way it was intended to be understood in the Bible.

## Pillars of the Earth

But what about the expression "pillars of the earth," or "foundations of the earth"? Does the Bible teach that the earth rests on pillars? Or on foundations

---

6. W.H. Guier and R.R. Newton, "The Earth's Gravity Field — Doppler Tracking of Five Satellites," *Journal of Geophysical Research,* 70 (Sept. 15, 1965).

supporting its corners or edges? Of course not. A pillar is a column supporting a structure, in the strictly literal sense. The figurative analogy is obviously to the moral support or spiritual foundation of a doctrine or an institution.

The phrase "pillars of the earth" is actually used only once in the Bible (1 Sam. 2:8), although the term "pillars" is used in the same context in Job 9:6 and Psalm 75:3. The first usage is interesting: ". . . for the pillars of the earth are the LORD's, and he hath set the world upon them" (1 Sam. 2:8). This is in Hannah's famous prayer at the birth of her son Samuel, and the verse contains the first mention of the word "world" in the Bible. Two verses later, in the same prayer, occurs the first mention of the name "Messiah" (or "the anointed one") in the Bible: "The LORD shall judge the ends of the earth; and he shall give strength unto his king, and exalt the horn of his anointed" (1 Sam. 2:10). That is, just as God set His created world upon "firm summits" (literal meaning of "pillars") belonging to himself, and thus impregnable, so He will give the same sure strength to His coming King Messiah.

The "pillars of the earth," therefore, primarily refers to the divine strength of God himself as He is "upholding all things by the word of his power" (Heb. 1:3). There is another more physical sense in which the words can be taken, however, as the earth's continental surfaces are indeed being supported by great mountainous roots extending deep below the surface. In this sense — as well as in the figurative sense — the term is essentially synonymous with "foundations of the earth," which occurs quite frequently (2 Sam. 22:16; Job 38:4, 6; Ps. 18:15; 82:5; 102:25; 104:5; Prov. 8:29; Isa. 24:18; 40:21; 51:13, 16; Jer. 31:37; Mic. 6:2; Zech. 12:1; Heb. 1:10). In the New Testament, the phrase "foundations of the world" occurs in Matthew 13:35; 25:34; Luke 11:50; John 17:24; Ephesians 1:4; Hebrews 4:3; 9:26; 1 Peter 1:20; and Rev. 13:8; 17:8.

In the latter case, "foundation of the world" is always clearly used in the sense of "founding of the world" as it was completed by God, giving no suggestion at all of any specific physical foundation. The Greek word is *katabole*, from roots meaning "to cast down" (as one would do to lay a masonry foundation), and some writers have, unfortunately, tried to interpret this as referring to a speculative pre-Adamic "casting-down" of the primeval world, as in the so-called gap theory of Genesis, whereby a global cataclysm is supposed to have terminated the geologic ages and the pre-Adamic world just before the six days of creation.

The gap theory is quite impossible to harmonize with either science or Scripture as shown in chapter 4. In the present connection, it is obvious from a mere reading of the above references that *katabole* has no reference whatever to such a primeval catastrophe. For example, consider the following: ". . . the works were finished from the foundation of the world" (Heb. 4:3). This is a clear reference to God's works of creation, which only *began* after the imaginary cataclysm, and were not finished unto the end of the creation period (Gen. 2:1–3). The "foundations of the earth," as used in the Old Testament, however (and as quoted from

Ps. 102:25 and Heb. 1:10), often do seem to have at least an implicit reference to the physical construction of the earth. Note the following in particular:

> Where wast thou when I laid the foundations of the earth? declare, if thou hast understanding. Who hath laid the measures thereof, if thou knowest? or who hath stretched the line upon it? Whereupon are the foundations thereof fastened? or who laid the corner stone thereof; When the morning stars sang together, and all the sons of God shouted for joy? (Job 38:4–7).

> Who coverest thyself with light as with a garment: who stretchest out the heavens like a curtain: Who layeth the beams of his chambers in the waters: who maketh the clouds his chariot: who walketh upon the wings of the wind: Who maketh his angels spirits; his ministers a flaming fire: Who laid the foundations of the earth, that it should not be removed for ever (Ps. 104:2–5).

> When he prepared the heavens, I was there: when he set a compass upon the face of the depth: When he established the clouds above: when he strengthened the fountains of the deep: When he gave to the sea his decree, that the waters should not pass his commandment: when he appointed the foundations of the earth (Prov. 8:27–29).

From the above passages appear several important truths.

1. The earth does have a solid structure resting upon foundations that assure its eternal endurance and final stability.
2. Immediately after God's appearance in His newly created universe, He covered himself with His light, established His personal residence in primeval waters He had made, and then called His mighty angelic hosts into existence and into His presence.
3. Before the foundations of the earth were laid, the heavens were stretched out, the waters above the heavens ("clouds above") and waters below the heavens ("fountains of the deep") were positioned, and the spherical sea level established.
4. Following the laying of earth's foundations, the angels (called both "sons of God" and "morning stars," in the Hebrew poetic parallelism employed) all sang together in a mighty hymn of praise to the Creator, with a joyful noise that must have resounded throughout the universe.

From all of the above, it becomes obvious that the foundations of the earth were laid only on the third day of the creation week, when God called the waters all into a common bed and caused the solid materials that heretofore had been dispersed throughout the watery matrix to come together and form solid land. Since this was constructed out of the earth elements created in the beginning (Gen. 1:1), the dry lands now aggregated together were called earth.

And the foundations of the earth were clearly those subterranean roots that maintained the land surfaces as solid, stable bodies, capable of sustaining the land animals and people who soon would be dwelling there.

Now exactly what these foundations are, modern geophysicists still do not know, since it has so far proved impossible to dig a hole deep enough to observe them. The Bible, in fact, assures us that this will never be possible. "Thus saith the LORD; If heaven above can be measured, and the foundations of the earth searched out beneath, I will also cast off all the seed of Israel for all that they have done, saith the LORD" (Jer. 31:37). Men have tried to dig such holes, but so far all such attempts have been unsuccessful. The famous Mohole project of the early 1960s was the most ambitious such attempt, trying to drill down through the earth's crust at the bottom of the ocean to reach the so-called Mohorovocic Discontinuity at the top of the earth's mantle. However, the project encountered so many problems and became so costly that it had to be abandoned long before reaching its goal.

Estimates of the earth's internal structure can be made by using the methods of seismology and geodesy, and geophysicists are confident they have at least a reasonably good model for its major components. The earth's radius is about 3,959 miles. The central core, which has long been assumed to be composed mostly of nickel and iron, is about 2,100 miles in radius. Outside of that is a region called the mantle, approximately 1,800 miles thick. There are two or more subdivisions in both core and mantle, and the detailed structure is far from settled. At least a portion of the lower mantle is believed to be in a plastic state, with the crust above it, and possibly some of the mantle attached to it as a lithospheric "plate" more or less "floating" on it. The earth's crust in the traditional sense is the solid rock above the Mohorovocic Discontinuity (or "Moho") with its pronounced change in density, affecting earthquake waves. It averages only about 25 miles in thickness, being thicker under the continents and thinner under the oceans. The continental rocks are believed to be less dense than the crustal rocks beneath the oceans, so that the total weight per unit area above the Moho is supposed to be more or less constant. That is, a small thickness multiplied by a larger density under the ocean balances the large thickness times the smaller density in continental areas.

This rough balance is known as the principle of isostasy (equal weights), and is one of the key principles of geophysics, being used to explain and predict various types of earth features and movements. It seems to be anticipated in some measure in certain Bible verses. For example: "Who hath measured the waters in the hollow of his hand, and meted out heaven with the span, and comprehended the dust in the earth in a measure, and weighed the mountains in scales, and the hills in a balance?" (Isa. 40:12).

In this single verse there are emphasized the high precision of the water balance of the earth, the dimensions and composition of the atmosphere, the valency relationships and quantities of the chemical elements, and even the isostatic adjustments in the earth's crust (the foundations of the sciences of hydrology, meteorology, chemistry, and geophysics, respectively) — all of which are essential for the maintenance of life.

Returning to the earth's foundations, we have to acknowledge that we do not yet know their precise nature, and perhaps we will never be able to know their nature, at least in this present age. That the earth's solid crust does have foundations is indicated both by Scripture and by the fact that it is at least relatively stable. That the foundations have been disturbed in the past — especially at the time of the great Flood — and will be profoundly disturbed again in the last days is also indicated in a number of the passages listed above. The fact that the earth throughout this present era has experienced many great earthquakes and volcanic eruptions is indication enough that the perfect isostatic balances designed by God from the primeval "very good" world as He created and made it were drastically upset at the time of the Flood, even though it still is sufficiently well adjusted to support life in great abundance.

## The Center of the Earth

It is remarkable that the central focus of divine activity and of biblical history on the earth has always been in the region where the three great continents of Europe and Asia and Africa meet, the land of Israel, with its neighbors — Egypt, Greece, Rome, Babylonia, Persia, and the other countries of the Near East. Medieval traditions held that Jerusalem was the center of the earth, and the Bible in fact speaks of the land of Israel as "the midst (literaly *navel*) of the earth" (see Ps. 74:12; Ezek. 38:12).

Remarkably enough, this designation has been confirmed by a modern computer study, in which all the earth's land areas were divided into small increments. The sum of the distances from each incremental area to all other areas was determined and averaged. The geographical center of the earth was defined as that point for which the average distance to all other points is the smallest.

The three locations on the earth which might be candidates for most appropriate geographical center would be as follows:

1. Mount Ararat, the center of dispersion for men and the animals from Noah's ark after the Flood, and thus the best location from which to "fill the earth," as God had commanded (lat. 39°, long. 44°).

2. Jerusalem, the capital of the world during the coming reign of Christ, and the center of God's redemptive work in the world (lat. 32°, long. 35°).

3. Babylon, the capital of both the first and last anti-God world kingdoms (Gen. 11:9; Rev. 17:5, 18), the center of world commerce and religion (lat. 33°, long. 44°).

As it turned out, the computer study showed the earth's center to be at a point of 39° latitude and 34° longitude, near the present city of Ankara, Turkey.[7]

---

7. Andrew J. Woods and Henry M. Morris, *The Center of the Earth* (San Diego, CA: Institute for Creation Research, 1973), p. 18.

*FIGURE 15 — The Center of the Earth*

*According to an Institute for Creation Research computer study, the geographical center of the earth is near Ankara, the present capital of Turkey, indicating that God providentially directed the ark to the most convenient location for repopulating the earth, and established Jerusalem at the most strategic location for evangelizing and ruling the earth.*

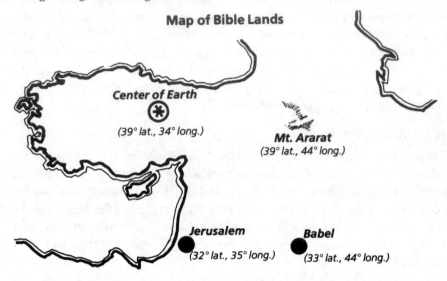

**Map of Bible Lands**

This is the same latitude as Mount Ararat and essentially the same longitude as Jerusalem. Thus, as shown in figure 15, the four locations are roughly at the corners of a square 550 miles on the side. It would make little practical difference in terms of relative advantage for the center of the earth to be located anywhere in this square. In any case, the important point is that, of all the land areas of the earth, the geographical center of the earth is located in the Bible lands.

## The Earth Divided?

In the mid-1960s a revolution took place in the earth sciences. Within a few years, most geologists and geophysicists (with a few notable exceptions) had abandoned the stable-continent framework of geophysical interpretation and become proponents of drifting continents. It is now widely accepted in earth science that the sea floors are spreading, continents are drifting apart, and the structure of the earth is built around the tectonics of vast moving plates of rock. New rock materials are believed to be continually emerging from the earth's upper mantle (the asthenosphere) through the sea floor, especially at the Mid-Atlantic Ridge, with old rock material being subducted back into the mantle below or through great oceanic trenches.

Because of the wide acceptance of this concept, many Christians have felt that they must find some means to accommodate it in their biblical interpretations. For those who accept either theistic evolution or progressive creation, with the uniformitarian philosophy and the standard geological-age system that go with these concepts, there is no problem. They accept whatever notion the geologists may be currently promoting at any given time.

For those who hold to strict biblical creationism, however, there seems to be only one passage of Scripture which might possibly be interpreted as referring to continental drift. This is a somewhat cryptic reference in the chapter known as the Table of Nations. "And unto Eber were born two sons: the name of one was Peleg; for in his days was the earth divided" (Gen. 10:25). The name Peleg means "division," so the verse seems to suggest that his name was given to him by his father Eber in order to commemorate a great event of division that took place shortly before he was born.

The most natural interpretation of this verse, in context, is that the particular event was the division of the people into different languages and tribes by the confusion of tongues at the Tower of Babel. This "division" is mentioned three times in the same chapter (Gen. 10:5, 25, 32) and described more fully in Genesis 11:1–9.

However, since the word for "divided" used in connection with the division by languages (Hebrew *parad*) is slightly different from that used at the time of Peleg (Hebrew *palag*), there does exist the possibility that two different dividings are in view, one being that of the nations, the other a physical splitting of the continents. If this is the case, then both dividings must have taken place at essentially the same time. Perhaps the splitting asunder of the original continent (called "Pangea" by the geologists) helped to implement the rapid dispersal of people and animals into all parts of the world.

This, however, seems to be a rather far-fetched scenario to be imposed on the simple biblical account of the dispersion of the nations at Babel, especially since it all seems to hang on a single verse of somewhat uncertain meaning. If the currently popular plate tectonics/continental drift model is ever really substantiated as an actual fact of history, then this may indeed turn out to have been a biblical reference to the event of rifting that initiated the drifting.

On the other hand, it would be premature at this time for Christians to climb on this particular geological bandwagon when it is still quite possible that the geologists themselves may eventually abandon it. One should remember that no one has ever actually observed the sea floor spreading or the continents drifting. No geological measurements, even by satellite, have been able yet to detect any such motion at present. The tectonics of the great crustal rock plates have been inferred, not measured. Like the evolution model, the plate-tectonics model is so broad and flexible that practically everything can be explained in its framework.

An earth-science professor at the University of Texas pointed this out a number of years ago. "Strictly speaking, then, we do not have a scientific hypothesis, but rather a pragmatic model, reshaped to include each new observation. The model is highly versatile, even able to incorporate quite easily such out-of-character behavior as 'behind-the-arc' spreading. Obviously, this kind of model is not testable in any rigorous scientific sense."[8]

Although it is true that many phenomena can be explained in terms of the drift hypothesis, it is also true that most of these phenomena had previously been explained quite satisfactorily by the stable-continent hypothesis. The apparent "fit" of transoceanic continents, as well as parallel biota and stratigraphy on the opposite sides of the Atlantic — which seemed to be the most obvious indicators of a previous single continent — had been well known for many years, and early proponents of the drift (Wegener, du Toit, et al.) had stressed these evidences, but they were unconvincing, both because of the many exceptions to this superficial fit and parallelism, and also because of the strong evidences for stable continents, so continental drift was considered as only an aberrant notion of a few geologic eccentrics until about 1968 or so.

The one event that suddenly persuaded most geologists to abandon the stable-continent model in favor of the drifting-continent model was the finding of supposed paleomagnetic "stripes" on the two sides of the Mid-Atlantic Ridge on the bottom of the Atlantic Ocean. These were interpreted to correspond to a series of global reversals of the earth's magnetic field, at intervals in the past history of the world. Magmas are considered to be emerging through crustal fissures at the ridge, then moving east and west from there as the sea floor spreads and the continents drift apart. Those minerals in the magma that are subject to magnetization presumably align themselves in accordance with the north magnetic pole at the time and are "frozen" with that orientation as the magma solidifies into rock. When the polarity reverses, the alignment is reversed in the fresh lavas then emerging. Parallel alignments on the two sides of the ridge, formed as the magmas flow in both directions from the ridge, are thus taken to prove that the sea floor is spreading.

The fact is, however, that these supposed "stripes" have never been directly observed on the sea floor. They were merely inferred from cyclic patterns on certain magnetometer surveys taken just below the ocean surface. A tremendous amount of geological interpretation has since been erected on this fragile foundation. From the start, many top-flight scientists have pointed out the highly equivocal nature of this evidence, showing that the supposed magnetic stripes were quite variable in detail and could easily be explained by other causes than reversal of the earth's dipole magnet. Nevertheless, the great majority of earth scientists soon became committed advocates of plate tectonics and continental drift. For several years now, it has become essentially a test of geological orthodoxy.

However, data more recently have been obtained from actual corings in the

---

8. John C. Maxwell, "The New Global Tectonics," *Geotimes,* 18 (Jan. 1973): 31.

Atlantic sea floor, which bring the magnetic-stripe concept into serious question. "An unexpected result of drilling is the almost complete lack of lateral lithologic and stratigraphic continuity in the crust. . . . This lack of stratigraphic continuity suggests that eruptions onto the sea floor are very local, building accumulations directly over the vent."[9]

These drill holes showed almost complete heterogeneity in the actual magnetic orientation of the sea floor rocks. The cores penetrated 600 meters (over one-third of a mile) into the rocks, and yet failed to find any evidence whatever of the supposed magnetic stripes. "It is clear that the simple model of uniformly magnetized crustal blocks of alternating polarity does not represent reality. Clear reversals of polarity with depth are observed in a number of the deeper holes."[10] These reversals were supposed to show up laterally, not vertically! It became obvious that the actual observed reversals must be attributed to *local* magnetic effects, not global. The situation was well summarized in a review article several months later.

> Somewhat to the chagrin of paleomagneticians, when they examined the rocks recovered by the Deep Sea Drilling Project from the crust of the Atlantic Ocean, the magnetic stripes were nowhere to be found. The recovered rocks not only were too weakly magnetized to account for the observed stripes, but their directions of magnetization were sometimes wrong. Instead of being constant down a drill hole, the magnetization sometimes jumped between normal and reversed or even gradually rotated with increasing depth.[11]

A consulting geologist in Texas has stressed that these magnetic stripes cannot legitimately be used any longer either for dating purposes or as evidence of sea-floor spreading.

> . . . these several vertically alternating layers of opposing magnetic polarization directions found in cored oceanic crust disproves one of the basic parameters of sea-floor spreading theory, namely that the oceanic crust was magnetized entirely as it spread laterally from the magnetic center. . . . It appears today that oceanic magnetic stripes have no value for age determinations of oceanic crusts.[12]

Thus, the key "proof" of continental drift was seen to prove no such thing at all. Exactly how to explain the magnetometer data in the context of the core data is highly uncertain. The most likely explanation probably has to do with alternating global catastrophes during or soon after their formation. "It is apparent that crustal drilling to date has shown that the processes of generation and modification of

9. J.M. Hall and P.T. Robinson, "Deep Crustal Drilling in the North Atlantic Ocean," *Science,* 204 (May 11, 1979): 578.

10. Ibid.

11. Richard A. Kerr, "How is New Ocean Crust Formed?" *Science,* 205 (Sept. 14, 1979): 1115.

12. J.C. Pratsch, "Petroleum Geologist's View of Oceanic Crust Age," *Oil and Gas Journal,* 84 (July 14, 1986): 115.

oceanic crust are much more complex than originally thought."[13] This evidence does not disprove sea-floor spreading, of course, but it does indicate that any substantiation thereof will have to come from other data than paleomagnetism. Since the latter had been assumed to be the key evidence, it at least means that the whole subject is still very much an open question. Most geologists still favor it, but majorities have often been wrong in the past on key scientific issues. In any case, it is clearly premature for Christians to try to adapt their biblical exegesis to this fragile hypothesis of continental drift.

## Fractured Crust

Although there is still much reason to question current ideas of plate tectonics and continental drift, there is certainly no doubt that the earth's crust has been subject to tremendous stresses and strains in the past, and that these have resulted in complex features of terrestrial topography. Great faults and folds, tremendous mountain ranges, belts of metamorphosed rocks, abundant volcanic activity, earthquakes, and other such phenomena (great meteorite impacts of the past have been mentioned in a previous chapter, for example) all bear witness to intense and unusual geophysical phenomena in ancient times.

Many of these seem inconsistent with — if not incompatible with — the divine revelation of a primeval perfect creation prepared by a loving, omniscient Creator for man's dominion and the glory of God, as the following verses show:

> And God saw every thing that he had made, and, behold, it was very good (Gen. 1:31).

> He hath made every thing beautiful in his time: also he hath set the world [or, better, "eternity"] in their heart, so that no man can find out the work that God maketh from the beginning to the end (Eccles. 3:11).

> Thou are worthy, O Lord, to receive glory and honour and power: for thou hast created all things, and for thy pleasure they are and were created (Rev. 4:11).

In the biblical context, the original perfection of the created world was first contaminated by sin and God's curse, but it remained outwardly much the same until the onset of the great Flood 1,656 years later (the number of years calculated from the chronologies of Genesis 5, assuming they are complete and have been transmitted accurately via the Masoretic Text of the Old Testament). Then, however, the structure of the earth's surface — no doubt including much of its crust and its atmosphere — was catastrophically and completely changed.

> And God said unto Noah, The end of all flesh is come before me; for the earth is filled with violence through them; and, behold, I will destroy them with the earth (Gen. 6:13).

---

13. Hall and Robinson, "Deep Crustal Drilling," p. 586.

And it came to pass after seven days, that the waters of the flood were upon the earth. In the six hundredth year of Noah's life, in the second month, the seventeenth day of the month, the same day, were all the fountains of the great deep broken up, and the windows of heaven were opened (Gen. 7:10–11).

Whereby the world [literally "cosmos"] that then was, being overflowed [literally "cataclysmically overthrown"] with water, perished (2 Pet. 3:6).

These passages, as well as others, indicate that the earth's primeval perfections, including its isostatic and climatologic equilibrium, were all devastated and rearranged during the Flood and its aftermath. The simultaneous "cleaving open" of all the fountains of the great deep implies not only the onset of great masses of subterranean waters, previously stored in pressurized reservoirs, but also of gigantic outpourings of volcanic lava and debris, as well as associated tectonic upheavals of unimagined immensity.

The entire event was so uniquely cataclysmic and nonreproducible as almost to defy any attempt to decipher all the phenomena that must have been involved. In any case, a great amount of research is still needed before the details can be confidently determined.

The Bible does tell us that one of the most important questions of geophysics — that is, the question of orogeny, of how and when the mountains were formed — must be answered specifically in terms of the great Flood. There were, of course, mountains in the originally created world, but they were relatively low and of gentle slope, not the rugged, uninhabitable ridges of the present world. The waters of the Flood covered these mountains to at least 15 cubits (probably 22.5 feet), so that the fully loaded ark, with a total height of 30 cubits, could float freely over all the mountains at the peak of the Flood (Gen. 7:19–20). Once the antediluvian topography had been leveled by the devastating flood waters, however, and the world completely inundated, then great mountain uplifts began to take place. "Thou coveredst [the earth] with the deep as with a garment: the waters stood above the mountains. At thy rebuke they fled; at the voice of thy thunder they hasted away. They go up by the mountains; they go down by the valleys [or, as in the NASV, 'The mountains rose; the valleys sank down'] unto the place which thou hast founded for them. Thou hast set a bound that they may not pass over; that they turn not again to cover the earth" (Ps. 104:6–9).

Thus, the present mountain ranges of the world were formed during and following the Flood. This biblical teaching is supported by the fact that most of the great mountainous areas are considered even by uniformitarian geologists to be quite young, uplifted since man has been on the earth. That they have been under water is clear from the fact that they are formed largely of marine strata near their summits, often containing recent marine fossils. The mechanism that has produced orogenies is still a matter of considerable controversy among geophysicists, but the tremendous energies associated with the eruptions and erosions of the great Flood provide the most likely model within which to find the true answer.

The great mountain uplifts, and corresponding ocean basin depressions, would necessarily be accompanied by an abundance of other tectonic activities — faults, folds, thrusts, and earth movements of many kinds. The present earthquake belts and continuing earthquake activity around the world can best be understood as remnant effects of the great postdiluvian uplifts.

The same applies to the earth's still significant volcanism. The eruption of the fountains of the great deep, as already noted, almost certainly included great volcanic outpourings. The post-Flood isostatic readjustments, especially the mountain uplifts, would surely have triggered the release of additional floods of magma, and these are reflected in the tremendous recent lava plains and plateaus around the world, as well as the great numbers of only recently extinct volcanoes, not to mention the considerable number still active.

Thus, a great portion of the earth's recent and continuing geophysical activity — especially its earthquakes and volcanic eruptions — can be attributed to the cataclysmic upheavals initiated by the Flood and its residual effects. Even the plate-tectonics concept, if it eventually proves to be valid, could best be understood in terms of the Flood and its after-effects. That is, the tremendous energies required to break continents apart and translate them on great lithospheric plates for thousands of miles could be explained in terms of the energies released at the Flood but otherwise are still completely enigmatic to uniformitarian geologists.

## Age of the Earth

It should be obvious to even the most casual reader that when the Bible is taken naturally and literally, it teaches that the earth is only a few thousand years old. Abraham lived about 2000 B.C., a date which is confirmed archaeologically as well as biblically, and the chronologies of Genesis 5 and 11 add up to about two thousand years from Adam to Abraham, with the universe created six days before Adam. Even if it could be demonstrated that gaps exist in the Genesis 5 and 11 chronologies, they could only be stretched out for a reasonable number of generations, possibly allowing for a date for Adam of, say around 10,000 B.C. at the most. In Chapter 4 we discussed the various possibilities for stretching out the creation week itself and found it obvious that the natural and proper interpretation is the literal interpretation (or, better, *no* interpretation), which thus implies recent creation.

This biblical implication is confirmed by all real history — that is, by the actual written records of early men. It is significant that all of these are invariably of the same order of magnitude as the Bible chronology. Even the most ancient nations — Egypt, Sumeria, Syria, China, etc. — have historical records going back only a few thousand years.

It should be remembered that *science* means "knowledge." Science deals with systems and processes we can observe now, whereas history deals with what earlier generations have observed in the past and recorded for posterity. Once we go beyond the earliest historical records, however, we are outside the scope of human observations and, therefore, outside the scope of real science. We can speculate about prehistorical chronologies, basing our speculations on some physical process, but these can never be more than estimates, whose accuracy depends entirely on the assumptions on which they are based.

There are, indeed, a number of natural processes that have been, or could be, used as chronometers, recording the age of the earth. Since the most important of these are geophysical processes, it is appropriate to consider some of them in this chapter. First, however, it is appropriate to stress the arbitrary assumptions that must be made before any such process will actually yield an apparent age for the earth. Note the summary outline in figure 16.

These assumptions are as follows:

1. The process used must always have operated at the same rate at which it functions today.
2. The system in which the process operates must always have functioned as a closed system throughout its history.
3. The initial condition of the various components of the system, when it first began to function at a constant rate in a closed system, must be known.

In addition, the system and process must be essentially worldwide in scope to give a meaningful age of the earth as a whole. If it is local, then at most it can only give a local apparent age. Furthermore, it should be a process whose components and rate can be accurately measured as they exist at present. There are a goodly number of such processes that seem to meet these two criteria, of course.

However, the assumptions listed above are not so easily satisfied. In fact, there is no such thing in the real world as a process whose rate is always constant or a system that is truly closed. Neither is there any way the initial conditions can be determined, since no one but the Creator himself was present to observe them at the beginning. If one assumes that the "daughter component" of the process is entirely the product of the process itself, so that its "initial value" was zero, then he can at least calculate an "upper limit" for the apparent age of the system, but this may have little relevance to the much smaller "true age."

Even though it is never possible to verify these three basic assumptions, one can at least use his best judgment in selecting processes that at least reasonably seem to conform to the assumptions. For example, consider briefly the testimony of two such worldwide processes in the following:

## Decay of the Earth's Magnetic Field

It has been known for many years that the earth functions as a dipole magnet, with its north magnetic pole varying slightly and changeably in its "declination" from the geographic pole. The strength of its field (its "magnetic moment")

### FIGURE 16 — False Assumptions in Age-Dating Calculations

*Any calculated age based on a prehistoric physical process must be based on at least three unprovable and unreasonable assumptions. Any published geological date can only be as valid as those arbitrary assumptions on which it is based.*

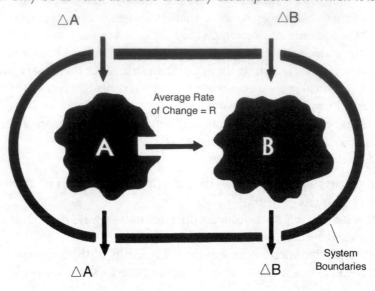

## Natural System Changing with Time

$$T = \frac{(A_O - A_T) + (B_T - B_O) \pm A \pm B}{2R}$$

1. Assume R = Constant    i.e., Uniformitarianism
2. Assume A = B = 0    i.e., Isolated System
3. Assume $B_O = 0$    i.e., Initial Conditions
4. Assume $A_O = A_T + B_T$    i.e., Conservation

(Only Assumption 4 is valid!)
Then $T = B_T / R$

can be determined only by making magnetometer measurements at many points over the earth's surface, extending over a considerable period of time. This would then "average out" the effects of local magnetic influences, which are many and significant.

This procedure has been followed for over 135 years, ever since the days of the great physicist Karl Gauss, whose name is now used as the actual unit of measurement for magnetic field intensity. When these data for average worldwide magnetic intensity are plotted against time, the curve of best fit turns out to be a typical exponential decay curve with a "half-life" of approximately 1,400 years.

That means that the magnetic field was twice as strong 1,400 years ago, four times as strong 2,800 years ago, and thirty-two times as strong 7,000 years ago.

From these data Dr. Thomas G. Barnes has calculated an upper limit of about 10,000 years for the age of the earth,[14] since the magnetic field would have been impossibly strong before that time. The constant rate-closed system assumptions seem to be more nearly valid for this process than for others, since the magnetic field is produced by phenomena deep in the earth's core. If any process is impervious to external influences which might change it, this one should be!

### Growth in Radiocarbon Assay

Radiocarbon (Carbon 14) seems to be increasing in the earth's biosphere. This radioactive isotope of natural carbon (Carbon 12) is formed in the earth's upper atmosphere by a complex process involving atmospheric nitrogen and the cosmic radiation impacting the earth from outer space. It then proceeds to decay, at the rate of 5,730 years per half-life. However, the total amount decaying is less than the amount being formed, so that the amount in the world as a whole is still building up.

> We note in passing that the total natural C-14 inventory of $2.16 \times 10^{30}$ atoms . . . corresponds to a C-14 decay rate of $1.63 \times 10^4$ disintegrations per second per square meter of the earth, considerably below the estimated production rate . . . of $2.5 \times 10^4$ atoms per second per square meter. . . . The source of the discrepancy is therefore unknown unless the present day production rate is indeed significantly higher than the average production rate over the last 8,000 years, the mean life of C-14.[15]

Thus, the formation rate is about one and a half times greater than the decay rate. As time goes on the two will approach equilibrium. This would be essentially at the time when all the very first atoms of radiocarbon formed from nitrogen have decayed back to nitrogen — five or six half-lives, or about 30,000 years. After this time, if the amount being formed still continues at the same rate, the radiocarbon assay would thenceforth be in a steady state. Because it is still about 50 percent deficient from this condition, the process has been going on much less than 30,000 years. Allowing for the exponential relationships involved, it turns out that the upper limit for the earth's age as based on this process once again is about 10,000 years.

These two examples are typical of many such worldwide processes that will yield similar results on the age of the earth. The alpha-decay process, by which

---

14. Thomas G. Barnes, *Origin and Destiny of the Earth's Magnetic Field*, 2nd ed. (San Diego, CA: Institute for Creation Research, 1983), p. 64. Dr. Barnes is Professor Emeritus of Physics at the University of Texas (El Paso) and former dean of the Institute for Creation Research Graduate School. He has directed many important research projects on terrestrial magnetism and atmospheric physics, and is author of a textbook in this field.

15. A.W. Fairhall and J.A. Young, "Radiocarbon in the Environment," *Advances in Geochemistry,* 93 (1970): 401–18.

helium atoms are released into the environment by the radioactive decay of uranium and thorium, is causing a worldwide build-up of helium, and this also indicates a very young age for the atmosphere. So does the influx of each of the many dissolved chemicals into the ocean through erosion and river inflow. Scores of processes, in fact, indicate relatively young ages, far too young to accommodate the supposed evolutionary history of life on earth. Appendix 6 provides a tabular listing of many such processes, with the indicated ages and a reference source providing further information on each.

A study of this table will quickly show a wide variety of "apparent ages" for the earth, though none are large enough to accommodate evolution. The reason for the spread, of course, is because all of them must necessarily be based on the assumptions listed at the beginning of this section and all of these assumptions are unprovable, untestable, and, in most cases, unreasonable. Nevertheless, other things being equal, the assumptions are more likely to be valid for a short period of time than for a long period of time, and this means that processes yielding young ages are probably more nearly accurate than those giving older ages. Thus, it is reasonable to conclude that the earth is actually quite young and that, therefore, human civilizations are almost as old as the earth itself. This conclusion certainly is more compatible with the character of God, who would hardly occupy billions of years in a tortuous spectacle of evolution, if His purpose were the creation and redemption of man.

It will be noted in this tabulation that almost half of the 68 processes listed have to do with the accumulation of various chemical elements into the ocean through influx from rivers. Assuming that the ocean was composed of nothing but pure water in the beginning and also assuming that river transport of the respective chemicals has always been as it is now, then the apparent age of the ocean in each case is calculated simply by dividing the present amount of each chemical by the annual increment being added each year from rivers.

This calculation would usually yield an upper limit for the age rather than the true age, because of the assumptions. The ocean surely contained at least some of each chemical at the beginning in order to provide a suitable marine environment for its animal inhabitants. Also, the present influx is probably much lower than the average, especially in view of the vast erosional activities on the continents during and soon after the Noahic flood.

On the other hand, it is also true that some of the chemicals could be recirculated back to the land through evaporation, uplifts, or other processes. In fact, if the annual amount being recirculated should happen to be equal to the annual influx, then the oceanic chemical content would be in a steady state and the type of calculation noted above would yield the "residence time" of each chemical in the ocean before being recirculated. That, in fact, is the arbitrary assumption usually made by geochronologists. The truth is that there is very little evidence of significant recirculation at all, except for a minor amount of precipitation on the ocean bottom.

The most significant oceanic chemical, of course, is sodium. Extensive studies by Austin and Humphreys (ICR geologist and physicist, respectively) have shown compellingly that the absolute upper limit for the age of the ocean is approximately 62 million years.[16] They made maximum allowances for all possible sodium output processes (sea spray, bottom precipitation, etc.), but made no allowance for initial salt content or other factors that would lower the age calculation. Thus, 62 million years is the maximum possible age of the ocean (in reality it is much less than that) whereas evolutionists need it to be billions of years old. But if the ocean had accumulated salt under these conditions for even a billion years, it would be so choked with salt that life would have long been impossible.

Somewhat similar calculations can be made from the studies of Salman Bloch on the ocean's content of uranium. He also made allowance for all possible processes affecting this content, both input and output processes. Although Bloch did not calculate it himself, it is easily possible to use his measured values of uranium influx and efflux to calculate that the age of the ocean is no more than 1,260,000 years.[17]

It is almost certain that one would obtain similar results for all other oceanic chemicals. The figures in the table, therefore, are *not* residence times, but upper limits for the ocean's age (based on the assumptions of no chemical content at the start and uniform annual rates of net influx since that beginning). However, some of these "ages" (e.g., for aluminum) are much too small to be either upper limits or residence times, reflecting as they do recent high influx rates due to industrial activity in the watershed.

Of course, the only way we could really know the age of the earth is for God to tell us, and He has, in fact, done just that, as we have shown in chapter 4. It is only to be expected, therefore, that His world will agree with His Word, so that nature itself would indicate that the earth is young, just as the Bible says.

But what about the various geophysical processes that supposedly do point to an earth much older than the age based on the Bible? Although there are only a few of these, they have received an inordinate amount of publicity and promotion, and many people have been led to believe they actually have proved that the earth is old. Those that are most important include the radiocarbon, uranium-lead, potassium-argon, and rubidium-strontium methods. All of them involve radiometric decay processes, which are supposed to be constant in rate regardless of such environmental variables as temperature and pressure.

As far as radiocarbon is concerned, it has been used especially for artifacts at

---

16. Steven A. Austin and Russell D. Humphreys, "The Sea's Missing Salt: A Dilemma for Evolutionists," *Proceedings of the Second International Conference on Creationism*, 2 (1991): 17–33.
17. Salman Bloch, "Some Factors Controlling the Concentration of Uranium in the World Ocean," *Geochemica et Cosmochimics Acta* 44 (1980): 373–377. For the calculation, see *What is Creation Science?* by Henry M. Morris and Gary E. Parker (Green Forest, AR: Master Books, 1987), p. 283–284.

archaeological sites and other organic remains less than about 50,000 years old. The ratio of radiocarbon to natural carbon in the dead material, compared to what it would be if it were still alive and in equilibrium with its environment, is taken as an index of the time since its death. Its results check with reasonable accuracy events which occurred within the last 3,000 years, so it has generally been assumed legitimate to extrapolate its range of application.

As noted above, however, the usual steady state assumption in the radiocarbon method is badly in error. If the more accurate nonequilibrium equation is used, then all radiocarbon dates will adjust themselves downward within the past 10,000 years. This would, of course, be quite unacceptable to evolutionary archaeologists who, in recent years, have been complaining that radiocarbon dates are too small, rather than too large. There are so many other possible sources of error in carbon dating, especially such phenomena as contamination and selective absorption, that the method itself may soon be abandoned.

> The troubles of the radiocarbon dating method are undeniably deep and serious. Despite 35 years of technological refinement and better understanding, the underlying *assumptions* have been strongly challenged, and warnings are out that radiocarbon may soon find itself in a crisis situation. . . . It should be no surprise, then, that fully half of the dates are rejected. The wonder is, surely, that the remaining half come to be *accepted*.[18]

> No matter how "useful" it is, though, the radiocarbon method is still not capable of yielding accurate and reliable results. There are *gross* discrepancies, the chronology is *uneven* and *relative*, and the accepted dates are actually *selected* dates.[19]

The other three methods mentioned above (uranium-lead, potassium-argon, rubidium-strontium) all have very large half-lives, and so give very great ages, often in the billions of years. They cannot date the age of the earth directly (as do the methods discussed previously) but only the apparent age of particular minerals in particular rocks.

The apparent ages obtained, however, are actually quite meaningless, in view of the assumptions that have to be made to obtain them. In the first place, radioactive decay rates could change, especially during times of major atmospheric upheavals, such as might be caused by nearby supernovas: "There has been in recent years the horrible realization that radiodecay rates are not as constant as previously thought, nor are they immune to environmental influences. And this could mean that the atomic clocks are reset during some global disaster, and events which brought the Mesozoic to a close may not be 65 million years ago but, rather, within the age and memory of man."[20] In particular, the tremendous atmospheric

18. Robert E. Lee, "Radiocarbon Ages in Error," *Anthropological Journal of Canada,* 19, no. 3 (1981): 9.
19. Ibid., p. 29.
20. Frederic B. Jueneman, "Secular Catastrophism," *Industrial Research and Development* (June 1982): 21.

upheavals at the time of the Flood, as well as the possible astronomic catastrophes that may have occurred then or earlier (as discussed in chapter 6), may well have caused tremendous increases in all radioactive decay rates for a time.

However, a more common and more likely source of error in radiometric ages arises from the closed system assumption, an assumption which could almost never be really valid. These radioactive methods are always applied only in igneous rocks, and these have all been affected by numerous tectonic, metamorphic, and hydrologic forces. It is almost inconceivable that any mineral could remain a closed system for a billion years of fracturing, folding, solvent action, and other such phenomena. Geochronologists recognize this to be a serious and common problem, but they say that when dates from two or more independent methods agree for a given formation, it proves that both have been in closed systems and so are reliable.

The problem with this is that such agreement is really so rare as to be explainable, when it occurs, as either statistical coincidence, redundancy, or preferential selection of data.

> In conventional interpretation of potassium-argon age data, it is common to discard ages which are substantially too high or too low compared with the rest of the group or with other available data such as the geological time scale. The discrepancies between the rejected and the accepted are arbitrarily attributed to excess or loss of argon.[21]

> In general, dates in the "correct ball park" are assumed to be correct and are published, but those in disagreement with other data are seldom published nor are discrepancies fully explained.[22]

Whenever apparent ages from different methods really do agree with each other for a given formation, this is only what would be expected in terms of primeval creation. That is, the creation of the elements was most likely a synthesis process, in which the elements were built up from hydrogen to uranium, probably in amounts and at rates corresponding in reverse to the decay chains and quantities which would be operating after the creation period, and especially after the imposition of the great decay principle in the world at the time of the Curse. Barring later disturbances, especially during the Flood period, these would therefore all tend to be in equilibrium and in agreement with one another right from the beginning.

However, this is still not the main source of error in these very high calculated apparent radiometric ages. The main problem is the assumption that the

---

21. A. Hayatsu, "Potassium-Argon Isochron Age of the North Mountain Basalt, Nova Scotia," *Canadian Journal of Earth Sciences*, 16 (1979): 974.

22. P.L. Mauger, "Potassium-Argon Ages of Biotites from Tuffs in Eocene Rocks of the Green River, Washakie, and Uinta Basins, Utah, Wyoming, and Colorado," *University of Wyoming Contributions to Geology*, 15, no. 1 (1977): 37.

amount of radiogenic daughter element present — lead, argon, or strontium — has all been formed by radiometric decay from the parent element — uranium, potassium, or rubidium. The probability is strong, however, that all these radiogenic "daughter" isotopes were either formed *in situ* with their "parents" at the time of creation, or else incorporated with them at the time of magma emplacement, so that the "apparent ages" were built into the radioactive minerals right from the time they were formed.

It is significant that all three of these dating methods (as well as others of lesser importance) have been found useful only in igneous rocks such as granites and basalts, etc. They are not used to date sedimentary rocks. Igneous rocks were evidently all formed originally by the flow of magma up from the mantle, either carrying the radioactive minerals with them as they flowed, along with their radiogenic "daughter" products, or else incorporating the daughters from the magmatic mix in which they were being transported, so that the igneous rocks formed by the cooling magmas might already seem to have an "apparent age" of millions or billions of years at the moment when their true age was zero years!

That this must have been the case is shown by the fact that all modern igneous rocks, formed in historic times by lava flows from active volcanoes (essentially the same process as envisioned for the great igneous rocks of the past) exhibit this phenomenon. That is, all such modern rocks will show very ancient radiometric ages, as calculated from the uranium, potassium, or rubidium inclusions which they contain. Since this is true in all such rocks of known age, and since igneous rocks of unknown age were formed by the same process, it is almost certainly the case in all these other rocks as well.

For example, potassium-argon dates, commonly employed for deep-sea basalts in paleomagnetic studies, probably have all been greatly enlarged by the incorporation of environmental argon, which is an abundant and easily available gas in such environments. "Potassium-argon dates of these rocks may be subject to inaccuracies as the result of sea-water alteration. Inaccuracies may also result from the presence of excess radiogenic Argon-40 trapped in rapidly cooled rocks at the time of their formation."[23] Similarly, there is an abundance of radiogenic strontium available for easy assimilation into rubidium minerals at the time of emplacement, as well as so-called "common" lead, containing a mixture of lead isotopes.

In the case of uranium and rubidium minerals, however, it is probably more common that lead and strontium, respectively, are carried with them all the way from their original locations in the mantle. In this case (and this is so typical as to be the rule, rather than the exception), the problem then has nothing to do with the age of the rocks where they are found, but rather with the processes of nucleosynthesis and the primeval formation of the earth that brought these ele-

23. David E. Seidemann, "Effect of Submarine Alteration on Potassium-Argon Dating of Deep-Sea Igneous Rocks," *Geological Society of America Bulletin*, 88 (Nov. 1977): 1660.

ments together in the first place. The original creation of the earth and all its elements in a balanced, equilibrium condition is, of course, an adequate explanation, if people would only accept it.

However, modern geochronologists are currently placing much emphasis on such devices as isochron diagrams (used especially with rubidium-strontium dating) and discordia curves (used especially with uranium-lead dating) as means for eliminating the problem of the "initial conditions." Such plots are made for a "whole rock," or even an entire region, using isotope ratios from many different minerals in the rock. From such plots it is alleged that the initial components in each can be eliminated and the true age determined, if only these points all plot on a straight line.

Without going into the technicalities of this argument, which are beyond the intended scope of this book, it can be shown quite definitely that straight-line plots of such data do not eliminate this problem at all. The same initial error can be common to all the points, or else alternatively, subsequent mixing of rock components from various sources can produce "pseudo-isochrons" which will give vastly erroneous readings of age. Both problems are recognized by geochronologists and are used by them whenever the radiometric age so determined does not agree with the "geologic age" (as determined essentially by fossils in adjoining sedimentary rocks). That is, either "inherited age" as transported by the magma, or "varied-source mixing" resulting from some later convulsion, are frequently invoked to explain why the radiometric age is so vastly different from the assumed true age. Since this is a very common situation, there seems no reason why such phenomena could not have occurred in every case, thus making all radiometric ages, even when determined by isochrons, immensely greater than the true age. In any case, it is certainly impossible to prove that this was not the case. It is eminently reasonable and is supported by all the data available on rocks of known age, as pointed out above.

In recent years, a number of creationist geologists and geophysicists have been devoting much critical attention to this subject, recognizing its key importance in relation to understanding the true history of the earth. For example, ICR adjunct geologist John Woodmorappe has written a detailed critique of many radiometric dating publications.[24] Uniformitarian geologists frequently claim that, even though some indicated dates may be erroneous, most of them agree, thereby confirming the validity of the assumptions on which they are based.

Woodmorappe has shown this is not true. There is abundant evidence of arbitrary data selection, discordancy in dating by different methods on the same rock, and many other fallacies and discrepancies, leaving very little basis for confidence in the validity of any radiometric date.

Dr. Steve Austin and Dr. Andrew Snelling, of the ICR Geology Department,

---

24. John Woodmorappe, *The Mythology of Modern Dating Methods* (El Cajon, CA: Institute for Creation Research, 1999), p. 108.

have made very significant field observations in the Grand Canyon, collecting many samples for radioisotope dating from rocks in the canyon walls, then having them dated by professional dating labs. The fascinating result was that the apparently "young" rocks at the top of the canyon were (as based on the radiometric dates) much "older" than those that had been laid down supposedly much earlier at the bottom. Details are provided in a Grand Canyon study book edited by Dr. Austin.[25]

Even more striking have been the dating results obtained by Dr. Austin on the volcanic rocks resulting from the eruption at Mount St. Helens in 1980. These very "young" rocks were found to give radiometric "ages" (potassium-argon) of up to 2.8 million years on the 1986 dacite flow from the lava dome there.[26]

This clear-cut result surely demonstrates that the "apparent ages" of igneous rocks have practically nothing to do with their true age. They are actually "inherited" from relationships already present in the earth's mantle where the rocks originated. And these may well be a function either of the creation itself or the profound geophysical and atmospheric disturbance in the earth at the time of the Flood.

In that connection, an important committee was formed in 1997 by earth scientists from the Creation Research Society and the Institute for Creation Research. All members of the committee have earned terminal degrees in geology, physics, or geophysics, and their mission is to do the necessary library, laboratory and field research to determine the true significance of the large radiometric "ages" seemingly obtained from radioisotope dating.

Much has already been accomplished, and one very significant book has been published,[27] which should certainly be read by both evolutionists and creationists concerned with this key subject. The fallacies of the standard methods are fully exposed, and much progress indicated toward the ultimate goal. Research is continuing at this writing.

We may conclude that dates obtained by radiometric means are interesting geophysical exercises but prove nothing as far as the age of the earth is concerned. Such processes as the decay of the earth's magnetic field are much more meaningful, but not even these can give conclusive information. The only way to know when the earth was created is for the Creator to tell us when. He has done this in His Word, very clearly and forcefully, and we are on good ground when we simply believe what He says!

---

25. Steven A. Austin, ed., *Grand Canyon: Monument to Catastrophe* (El Cajon, CA: Institute for Creation Research, 1994), p. 120–131.

26. Steven A. Austin, "Excess Argon within Mineral Concentrates from the New Dacite Lava Dome at Mount St. Helens Volcano," *CEN Technical Journal* 10, no. 3 (1996): 335–343.

27. Larry Vardiman, Andrew A. Snelling, and Eugene F. Chaffin, eds., *Radioisotopes and the Age of the Earth: A Young-Earth Research Initiative* (El Cajon, CA.: Institute for Creation Research and Creation Research Society, 2000), p. 667.

# 10

# WATER AND THE WORD

*Biblical Hydrology and Meteorology*

Hydrology — "the science of water" — can either be considered as a branch of geology ("the science of the earth") or, better, as a separate scientific discipline of its own. It is a very ancient science, for people have always had to have some means of utilizing the world's water resources for their own needs. Dams, irrigation canals, water conduits, and other such hydraulic structures have been found preserved in the ruins of the world's oldest civilizations.

There are innumerable ways in which water is essential both for individual human life and for the corporate life of mankind. Over 70 percent of the earth's surface is water surface; and, if the earth's land surfaces were smoothed out, there would be enough water to cover the whole world to a depth of over one and three-quarters miles. Water plays a key part in almost all geological and chemical processes, and is especially important in biology. Living flesh, of both men and animals, is made up of about two-thirds water. "The life of the flesh is in the blood" (Lev. 17:11), and the blood serum is 92 percent water. All nutrition and digestion processes and the growth of plant life require water. Life in any higher form would be quite impossible without an abundance of liquid water, and only planet Earth possesses any significant amount of liquid water. It has been called "the water planet," for good reason.

## The Water Cycle

The central fact of hydrology, to which all hydrological data are referenced in one way or another, is the so-called hydrologic cycle, or, as it is also called, the water cycle. This remarkable system only began to be adequately understood within the past few centuries by scientists, but it has always been assumed in the pages of the Bible. Because of the tremendous importance of this remarkable substance called water, in the life and activities of mankind, there are many, many references to it in the Bible. Although the Bible was written in a supposedly "prescientific era," all of these references are completely up-to-date and scientifically accurate, not expressed in the technical jargon of modern science, of course, but nevertheless expressing truth concerning the actual relationships.

The hydrologic cycle is the remarkable "engine" by which solar energy lifts water from the ocean through evaporation, then translates it inland by the winds, whence it condenses and falls to the land as rain, snow, or sleet, after which it runs off through the rivers and groundwater back to the ocean again (see figure 17). Each of these phases is important in its own right. They are all treated in various subdivisions of hydrology. Oceanography deals with the waters of the ocean, meteorology treats the atmospheric phases of the cycle (evaporation, translation, precipitation), potamology is the study of river flow, limnology is the study of lakes, and geohydrology deals with groundwater.

It is remarkable that tremendous quantities of water can be lifted, against the force of gravity, hundreds and thousands of feet into the air and there suspended until it has been moved inland where it is needed. Because there is no agency on the earth sufficiently powerful or ingenious, God has equipped the sun, 93 million miles away, to do it.

Liquid water becomes water vapor, at a rate and to an extent dependent upon the temperature, degree of saturation of the adjacent air, etc., and is carried upward by turbulence and diffusion in the gaseous atmosphere. Since gases, including water vapor, expand with increasing temperature, warmer air near the surface tends to rise. On a large scale, the great warm air masses near the equator tend to rise and flow poleward, where the cold air masses, being dense, have settled nearer the ground. Thus, there tends to be a continual movement of warm, equatorial, moisture-laden air toward the poles, and beneath this a movement of cold, dry air toward the equator.

But that is not all. It would not be sufficient for God to have provided for the evaporation of the waters from the ocean, only to leave them suspended directly above their former bed.

We have mentioned the great air movement from the equator to the poles and back again. The winds of the world cannot be described so simply as this; they are also influenced by the earth's rotation, the topography, and many other things. However, the major air motions of the world are always of the same kind and follow the same circuits, fulfilling, among other things, the essential purpose of bringing the life-giving waters, cleansed of their salts and impurities, back to the land. It is significant that God, as recorded in Jeremiah 10:13, reminds us that "He bringeth forth the wind out of his treasures." Consider also Ecclesiastes 1:6: "The wind goeth toward the south, and turneth about unto the north; it whirleth about continually, and the wind returneth again according to his circuits." This is

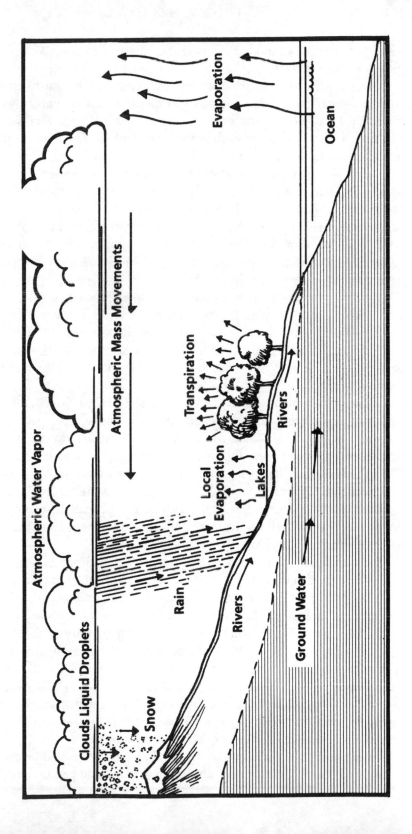

FIGURE 17 — *Hydrologic Cycle*

*The water cycle, which is the basis of the earth's water economy, as well as the basic principle of the sciences of hydrology and meteorology, is anticipated in many passages of Scripture.*

a striking example of modern knowledge, revealed in God's Word nearly three thousand years ago.

An even more interesting biblical reference concerns the construction of clouds. Ordinary water vapor, being gaseous, is transparent and is almost always present, to some extent, in the atmosphere. However, God has made very wonderful provision for its being restored to the earth. After it has been moved inland, it may recondense into liquid water in the form of clouds, dew, fog, etc.

However, the particles of water vapor need to have some solid particle of dust or other foreign matter about which to "congeal" into particles of liquid water. The reference in Proverbs 8:26 to "the highest part of the dust of the world" may be a reference to the meteoritic and other dust particles that exist throughout the lower atmosphere and serve as a sort of hydrological catalyst in inducing the condensation of water vapor into minute opaque particles of liquid water that form clouds (or fog if near the ground).

However, even after their formation as clouds, the particles of water remain aloft, seemingly in complete independence of the law of gravity. The agency that holds them up is the strong upward rush of the same air currents that caused their condensation, overbalancing the weight of the water particles until the smaller particles coalesce into sufficiently large particles to fall in spite of the strong upward currents.

All of this is a marvelous evidence of the skill and wisdom of the Creator. If it were not for this particular provision, once the temperature permitted it, all of the water in the cloud would condense and precipitate at once, in a great, destructive mass. It was a very fitting question that Elihu asked Job 3,500 years ago: "Dost thou know the balancings of the clouds, the wondrous works of him which is perfect in knowledge?" (Job 37:16). Even with all the knowledge of modern science the answer to that question is still far from complete. Consider also Job's statement: "He bindeth up the waters in his thick clouds; and the cloud is not rent under them" (Job 26:8).

Finally, when conditions become right, the small particles of water in the clouds (each averaging about a hundredth of an inch in diameter) combine with other particles until they become of sufficient size to overcome the dynamic force of the uprushing air and fall to the earth as rain (or snow or hail, depending on temperature and updraft conditions). The average raindrop is about one-tenth of an inch in diameter. "By watering he wearieth the thick cloud" (Job 37:11). "If the clouds be full of rain, they empty themselves upon the earth" (Eccles. 11:3). Consider also Job 28:24–27: "For he looketh to the ends of the earth, and seeth under the whole heaven; To make the weight for the winds; and he weigheth the waters by measure. When he made a decree for the rain, and a way for the lightning of the thunder: Then did he see it, and declare it."

After the rain has fallen upon the ground, a part of it will percolate into the ground to become groundwater. This portion will be tapped by wells, may come out in springs, or may be used by plants, but most of it flows slowly through the pores in the soil or rocks toward the handiest surface drain. Some of the falling water is used directly by the plants upon which it falls, some evaporated again, and a large part runs off over the surface to the nearest river or tributary. It is this stage of the hydrologic cycle, in its various aspects, that is of most interest to man, because it is here that he is directly affected by the water, whether for good or bad.

It is interesting that most of the water for precipitation does not come from land evaporation and evaporation from inland water surfaces, as thought only a few decades ago. Quite extensive upper-air soundings of temperature, pressure, humidity, and wind carried out by the United States Department of Agriculture have demonstrated conclusively that oceanic areas are the only significant sources of moisture for precipitation on continents.

In the light of all this, how significant does Solomon's statement in Ecclesiastes 1:7 appear! Immediately after his marvelous scientific statement concerning the wind circuits of the world, he completes an amazingly precise description of the hydrologic cycle in the following words: "All the rivers run into the sea; yet the sea is not full; unto the place from whence the rivers come, thither they return again."

The present balance between land and water, between air and water, the distance of the earth from the sun, the constituents of the atmosphere, the location of mountain ranges and equatorial ocean streams, and many other things that contribute to the workings of the hydrologic cycle all are well known to be so delicately adjusted that any great change in their present relations would result in making life difficult, if not impossible, upon the earth. Isaiah's testimony is particularly appropriate: "Who hath measured the waters in the hollow of his hand, and meted out heaven with the span, and comprehended the dust of the earth in a measure, and weighed the mountains in scales, and the hill in a balance?" (Isa. 40:12).

Isaiah also has another reference to the hydrologic cycle itself, comparing water to the Word of God. "For as the rain cometh down, and the snow from heaven, and returneth not thither, but watereth the earth, and maketh it bring forth and bud, that it may give seed to the sower, and bread to the eater: So shall my word be that goeth forth out of my mouth: it shall not return unto me void, but it shall accomplish that which I please, and it shall prosper in the thing whereto I sent it" (Isa. 55:10–11). That is, just as God's Word accomplishes its divine mission before returning to Him who sent it, so the rain and snow return into the heavens after accomplishing their mission of watering the earth.

There are many other references in the Bible to one or more phases of the hydrologic cycle, and several of these also seem to anticipate modern science. For example, although it is obvious that there is some kind of connection between rain and lightning, it is not so clear as to which is cause and which is effect. Meteorologists and atmospheric physicists are still researching this question, but the weight of evidence now seems to be that an electrical field must be generated in a cloud before its water droplets will coalesce to form drops large enough to fall as rain. The presence of an electric field is, of course, also precursive to actual lightning discharges.

There are several references in the Bible to such a direct relationship. For example, "He causeth the vapours to ascend from the ends of the earth; he maketh lightnings for the rain; he bringeth the wind out of his treasuries" (Ps. 135:7). Practically the same verse is also found in Jeremiah 10:13 and 51:16, except that these verses say that God "maketh lightnings with rain." The important emphasis in each case is that there is a necessary relationship between rain and electricity. Note also that the verse mentions four phases of the hydrologic cycle — evaporation, wind, electricity, and rain. The evaporation phase, one should note, takes place "from the ends of the earth" — evidently referring to the distant oceans where the lands end. As mentioned already, the fact that the rains on land originate in the waters evaporated from the oceans as mentioned also in Ecclesiastes 1:6–7 is definitely a discovery made by scientists only in modern times.

The connection between rain and electricity is further suggested in the following verses:

> When he made a decree for the rain, and a way for the lightning of the thunder (Job 28:26).

> Who hath divided a watercourse for the overflowing of waters, or a way for the lightning of thunder; To cause it to rain on the earth, where no man is; on the wilderness, wherein there is no man; To satisfy the desolate and waste ground; and to cause the bud of the tender herb to spring forth? (Job 38:25–27).

> Canst thou lift up thy voice to the clouds, that abundance of waters may cover thee? Canst thou send lightnings, that they may go, and say unto thee, Here we are? (Job 38:34–35).

Another interesting anticipation of modern knowledge is found in Job 28:25: "To make the weight for the winds. . . ." The idea that "wind" or "air" has weight was unheard of in ancient times, except in the Bible. Now, of course, it is known that "atmospheric pressure" is simply the weight of the column of air above a unit area on the earth's surface.

Finally, consider Job 38:22–23. "Hast thou entered into the treasures of the snow? or hast thou seen the treasures of the hail, Which I have reserved against the time of trouble, against the day of battle and war?"

The ultimate meaning of these verses is yet to be discovered, since God has "reserved" these resources. To some degree, however, modern hydrologists and engineers have already entered into the treasures of the snow, developing the annual winter snow pack in mountainous regions into invaluable water resources for irrigation and water supply during the drier periods of the year.

Hail has been used by God on various occasions in the past as a weapon of war in answer to the prayers of His people for deliverance from their enemies (e.g., Josh. 10:11). This will also be a divine weapon in the latter days (e.g., Ezek. 38:22; Rev. 16:21).

There are many other passages in the Bible that refer to different phases in the hydrologic cycle, all of which are quite compatible with all known science. The cycle itself, necessary as it is for human and animal life in numerous ways, is a marvelous evidence of God's divine forethought.

Yet, wonderfully precise and marvelously providential though the world's present hydrological cycle may be, it was not the one God originally designed for His perfect creation. Nor will it be the final one, for in the new earth, there will be "no more sea" (Rev. 21:1).

## The Canopy Model

"And darkness was upon the face of the deep" (Gen. 1:2). On the primeval earth there was a universal sea; on the new earth there will be no sea. In like manner, a global darkness enveloped the earth at first, but on the new earth "there shall be no night there" (Rev. 21:25).

On the first day of creation, God began to dispel the darkness by command-ing light to shine out of the darkness, dividing the light from the darkness, and day from night. In exactly parallel fashion, on the third day, God began to dispel the universal sea by commanding the dry land to appear, dividing the seas from the land that was prepared as the abode of man.

But between these two activities of division or separation, there was, on the second day, a division of the waters themselves into two great reservoirs, one above the firmament (i.e., the expanse, corresponding probably to our present troposphere) and the other below the firmament.

These were all mighty acts of creation, and we do not know what means or processes God employed in bringing them about. Since God "rested from all his work" at the end of the six days of creation (Gen. 2:3) and since these works included "heaven and earth, the sea, and all that in them is" (Exod. 20:11), we can therefore no longer observe or study these processes of creation. Present-day physical and biological processes must be entirely different; their study, no mat-ter how carefully or scientifically prosecuted, can give us no certain information about God's true creative devices at all. The modern scientific premise of unifor-mity in natural processes cannot be legitimately applied to the creation period.

The remarkable prophetic warning against latter-day scoffers who use the principle of uniformitarianism in exactly this illegitimate fashion (2 Pet. 3:3–6) is accompanied by an equally remarkable statement concerning the primary impor-tance of water in the methods and results of the creation. ". . . by the word of God the heavens were of old, and the earth standing out of the water and in the water" (2 Pet. 3:5). Varying renderings of this verse are found in different translations, and varying interpretations in different commentaries; perhaps the basic reason for so much difficulty with it is a subconscious insistence on interpreting the events of creation in terms of our modern scientific concepts and processes.

The word "standing" is the Greek *sunistemi*, essentially meaning "holding together" or "consisting" (note the same word in Col. 1:17, where it is said that "all things hold together in him"). The created earth, originally "without form" (Gen. 1:2) was "formed" by the Word of God, by the means of water, and now is sustained by the same means. The first lands were undoubtedly molded by the action of water, and life itself was organized to be nourished and held together in and by a water medium. Finally, a portion of the waters was designed to serve as a great protective canopy for the earth, elevated and sustained "above the firmament," also by the Word of God (Gen. 1:7).

In order for these upper waters to be maintained aloft by the gases of the lower atmosphere and also for it to be transparent to the light of the sun, moon, and stars (Gen. 1:14–16), the canopy must have been in the form of a vast blanket of water vapor, extending far out into space, invisible and yet exerting a profound influence on terrestrial climates and living conditions. It would have insured a worldwide warm, mild climate, with only minor seasonal and latitudinal differences. This in turn would have inhibited the great air circulational patterns that characterize the present world, and which constitute the basic cause of our winds, rains, and storms.

There could have been no rain in the form with which we are familiar, and this is exactly the testimony of Scripture (Gen. 2:5–6). But there was a system of rivers and seas (Gen. 1:10; 2:10–14), nourished probably by water that had been confined under pressure beneath the land when the land and water were "divided" as well as by the low-lying vapors that were daily evaporated and recondensed (Gen. 2:6). As far as the record goes, these rivers, especially that which emerged from a great artesian spring in the Garden of Eden (Gen. 2:10), were the main sources of water for Adam and his descendants.

The vapor canopy (see figure 18) also would have served as a highly effective shield against the many powerful and harmful radiations that surround the earth, and which are now only partially filtered by our present atmosphere. Such radiations are now known to be the cause of many physical damages to man's genetic system, tending to cause harmful mutations and general biological deterioration. It is quite possible that the blanket was one major factor contributing to human longevity in those early days.

This postulated vapor canopy should, of course, be considered only as a model. It is not taught dogmatically in Scripture, though it does seem to be the most natural and logical inference from the biblical references to "waters above the firmament" and other related passages. Its implications (greenhouse effect, inhibition of rainfall and storms, radiation filter, etc.) seem to fit many data in both science and Scripture. However, various objections have been raised to it, and further research is needed.

One of the objections has been that the additional water vapor above the

### *Figure 18* — *The Canopy Theory and the Greenhouse Effect*

*Many intriguing aspects of the antidiluvian world as described in the Bible, as well as many geological phenomena preserved in crustal rocks, can be explained in terms of "the waters above the firmament" (Gen. 1:7), taken as a vast canopy of invisible water vapor above the primeval atmosphere. Such a canopy would augment the existing greenhouse effect and thus maintain a more equable worldwide climate than we have now.*

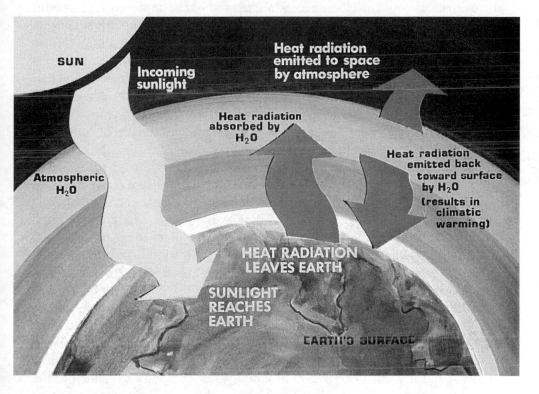

troposphere would increase the barometric pressure to levels which would be lethal to human life. Also, it is said, the greenhouse effect would be so strong as to make the earth's surface temperature unbearably hot.

These objections, however, must be based on some arbitrary assumption as to how *much* water would be stored in the canopy, and this is something we do not know at this point. There is, right now, a greenhouse effect and a pressure effect due to the present vapor content (less than two inches) in the atmosphere, and this obviously could be significantly augmented with no ill effects. As far as pressure is concerned, there is indeed much evidence that so-called hyperbaric pressures could be quite beneficial, rather than harmful. Studies by Dr. Edgar End, at the University of Wisconsin, as well as many others, have shown that inhaling hyperbaric oxygen, administered in a pressure chamber, will restore memory, energy, and zest to many older men and women. "Massive documentation provides overwhelming evidence that hyperbaric oxygenation frequently reverses senility, dramatically helps stroke victims, successfully treats osteomyelitis and gas gangrene, improves eyesight, reduces healing time for severe burns, saves victims of carbon monoxide poisoning. . . . The pressure is raised to the equivalent of anywhere from 49 to 70 feet below the surface of water."[1]

The present very small amount of water vapor in the atmosphere does have a profound greenhouse, or shielding, effect that makes life possible right now, and there can be no doubt that these beneficial effects would be improved if the amount were increased. Just exactly what amount would provide the optimum benefits may be determined by further research. We might assume, at least until further information is available, that the primeval "waters above the firmament" contained this optimum amount, to produce the "very good" environment God had created. The detailed physics of the canopy would surely be quite complex but seem to be perfectly feasible. The most detailed study made to date on this subject was published by Dr. Joseph Dillow,[2] who enlisted the help of competent specialists in thermodynamics, optics, fluid mechanics, and all of the other sciences that bear on the subject. Their conclusion was that, although many details still need to be resolved, the basic vapor canopy model is sound, providing an excellent explanation for a wide range of data in both science and the Bible.

Computer model studies on the assumed vapor canopy have been carried out at the Institute for Creation Research over a period of several years, under the direction of Dr. Larry Vardiman, by a number of his graduate students. Dr. Vardiman has a Ph.D. in meteorology from Colorado State University as well as many years experience in atmospheric physics with the U.S. Weather Bureau and the Bureau of Reclamation. The work is continuing as time and resources allow. [3]

The computer simulations did, indeed, confirm that there was a serious heating problem at the earth's surface, if a large vapor canopy was postulated. However, tentative studies have also shown that, if this large canopy was significantly reduced, and if a small component of liquid water in clouds was added to the atmosphere, then the canopy model becomes feasible. In addition, it is noted that there are so many potential variables in a canopy scenario that it is impossible to take all of them adequately into account in a computer model study. The canopy model becomes very realistic, for example, if the solar constant was different before the Flood.

In summary of the present situation, the canopy model has not been "proved" — and probably never can be — but it is certainly not precluded as at least a scientific possibility. In view of its ability to correlate the biblical data so well, it is proper

---

1. Paul Martin, "Can Hyperbaric Oxygen Add Years to Your Life?" *Consumer's Digest* (Mar.–Apr. 1975): Pt. 2, p. i.

2. Joseph C. Dillow, *The Waters Above* (Chicago, IL: Moody, 1981), p. 479.

3. Larry Vardiman and David Rush, "Pre-Flood Vapor Canopy Radiative Temperature Profiles," *Proceedings of the Second International Conference on Creationism* II (1990): 231–240. See also Dr. Vardiman's monograph, *Climates Before and After the Genesis Flood* (El Cajon: CA: Institute for Creation Research, 2001), p. 116.

to continue citing it as a viable scientific model of the pre-Flood atmosphere.

Closely associated with the waters above the firmament, of course, were the waters below the firmament. These had been separated from each other by the atmospheric expanse on the second day of creation (Gen. 1:6–8), and were to be brought together again later at the time of the great Flood. During the antediluvian period, however, they provided the basis for a hydrologic system even more beneficial to the earth than the present water cycle.

The original world was created with such a remarkable climate control system that "the LORD God had not caused it to rain upon the earth" (Gen. 2:5), and there is no suggestion that this regime changed at the time of the Curse (Gen. 3:17–19) or, indeed, until the time of the Flood. The best explanation for such a state of affairs is the antediluvian canopy which, by maintaining uniform global temperatures, would inhibit the establishment of an atmospheric circulation to bring ocean water to the land as rain. Each day/night cycle would cause a daily evaporation of local waters, with their reprecipitation at night as dew, ground fog, or mist (Gen. 2:6 speaks of "a mist from the earth" that "watered the whole face of the ground").

Nevertheless, there were both rivers and seas, as in the present world. The various seas of the world were all "gathered together unto one place" (Gen. 1:9), referring to interconnecting beds and a common sea level, not to one single ocean (the term "seas," in Gen. 1:10, is in the plural). Four rivers are named in Genesis 2:10–14 and, even though they all have a common source, each was evidently a large and important river, watering a broad geographical area.

Since there was no rain to feed these rivers, either through surface runoff or through a subsurface water table, their flow could only have come from deep-seated springs of some kind, functioning like an artesian well, with water flowing from pressurized reservoirs far below the surface. These reservoirs and pressures must have been very substantial to supply four major rivers in this way. The Bible indicates the surface outlet to have been in Eden, with its first purpose that of providing water for the lush garden God had planted for Adam and Eve (Gen. 2:10). Although the Bible does not mention any other antediluvian rivers, it seems necessary to infer that a similar hydrologic system prevailed throughout the world, providing enough water to maintain an abundance of plant life and animal life everywhere.

Thus, the antediluvian hydrologic cycle was a subterranean, earth-controlled cycle, unlike our present atmospheric, sun-controlled cycle. The pressures in the subterranean "deep" would have to be maintained by the earth's own internal heat, continuously applied as it moved upward from the earth's interior. The water leaving the great reservoirs presumably coursed through great natural conduits of some sort, precisely planned by their divine Creator to release the right amounts of warm spring waters at the intended outlets all over the earth. The "fountains of the deep" were "strengthened" (Prov. 8:28) to withstand these pressures and temperatures and thus to serve faithfully as long as their intended function was needed.

As the rivers emptied into the seas, the latter could maintain their levels by pressing the deeper waters, cooled now to a heavier density, back down into the subterranean reservoirs to complete the cycle. In some way, the return conduits were thermally insulated, so that the recycled waters could not be reheated until they were admitted again into the reservoirs, possibly through some kind of natural check-valve system.

The above description is obviously speculative and incomplete, since the Bible gives little specific information on this particular subject. In any event, we can be sure that God was equal to the occasion. Since a human engineer could, at least in principle, design a system of this type that would be workable, God could certainly do it. The key ingredients, of course, were water and energy. There was an ample supply of the first in the great deep, and an abundant supply of the second in the intense heat of the earth's internal furnaces. Speculation is obviously involved here, but some such system as schematically sketched in figure 19 seems likely.

To the skeptic who objects that there are no such pressurized reservoirs, thermal conduits, fountains of the deep, or vapor canopies in the present world, the answer is that the Bible tells us this also: "The world that then was . . . perished" (2 Pet. 3:6).

## The Flood of Waters

Sin had entered into the perfect world, and death by sin, and then followed a long, sad history of deterioration and rebellion against God. Finally, God determined to "bring a flood of waters upon the earth, to destroy all flesh, wherein is the breath of life, from under heaven; and every thing that is in the earth shall die" (Gen. 6:17). To accomplish the earth's cleansing and purification, God chose the very element out of which the earth had been "standing" and by which its very life was sustained. By this same water, the world of the antediluvians was overflowed and perished. The great expanse of waters above the firmament was condensed and plunged to the earth, continuing everywhere at fullest intensity for 40 days and 40 nights (Gen. 7:12). The "great deep," the vast storehouses of the waters under the firmament confined in the seas and under pressure beneath the surface rocks of the earth's crust, also issued forth, as "all the fountains of the great deep [were] broken up" (Gen. 7:11). This latter upheaval must have been followed by the eruption of subterranean magmas, and these by great earthquakes, and these in turn by tremendous tsunami waves in the seas. Destruction beyond imagination must have been wrought on the antediluvian earth!

The Greek terminology is graphic, literally translating as, "The cosmos [the beautifully ordered earth/heaven system] that then was, being cataclysmically overwhelmed with its waters, was utterly destroyed."

Finally, the waters prevailed upon the earth to such a height that "all the high

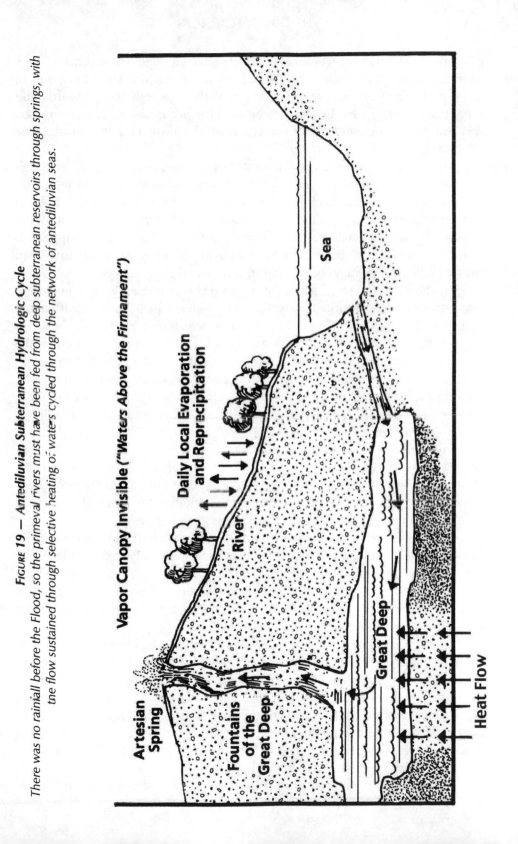

*FIGURE 19 — Antediluvian Subterranean Hydrologic Cycle*

There was no rainfall before the Flood, so the primeval rivers must have been fed from deep subterranean reservoirs through springs, with the flow sustained through selective heating of waters cycled through the network of antediluvian seas.

hills, that were under the whole heaven, were covered," and "the mountains were covered," and "all flesh died that moved upon the earth, both of fowl, and of cattle, and of beast, and of every creeping thing that creepeth upon the earth, and every man" (Gen. 7:19–21). Once again, as in the beginning, there was a universal ocean. The same waters which had sustained the life of the world now became its shroud.

Furthermore, there was again "darkness upon the face of the deep," although not the total darkness that originally was present. When the vapor canopy condensed into liquid water and began to fall as rain, it was necessarily converted into a great mass of cloud, of such vast depths that only very small amounts of the sun's light could penetrate. And although the greatest of the rains and upheavals continued only for 40 days, they continued in some degree of intensity until "restrained" after 150 days (Gen. 7:24–8:2).

But the darkness was not total, nor was death universal. Noah had "found grace," and God had an ark of safety. The same waters which brought death to the "world of the ungodly" (2 Pet. 2:5) were those which bore up the ark, "wherein few, that is, eight souls were saved by water" (1 Pet. 3:20). The Flood portrays the paradox of water and the spiritual realities it typifies. Water is both a vehicle of life and a vehicle of death and judgment. As such, it is used in the Scriptures in many beautiful and instructive passages to symbolize both the life-giving wisdom and love of God, and also the fierce wrath of God poured out on rebellious, unrepentant sinners.

The waters of the Flood were literally poured forth from the windows of heaven by a wrathful God, destroying the whole world that then was. But this tremendous baptism in water was not only a baptism unto death but also a baptism unto life, delivering those who were in the ark from the filth and corruption of the antediluvians that would otherwise have engulfed them.

Consider the remarkable phrase "poured out," or "shed" (both being translations of the Hebrew *shaphak*). This word is used frequently in Scripture of the "pouring out" of the indignation and wrath of God (e.g., Ps. 69:24; Isa. 42:25; Hos. 5:10; et al.). On the other hand, it is also used in connection with great poured-out blessing, as when God says: "And it shall come to pass afterward, that I will pour out my spirit upon all flesh" (Joel 2:28).

But it is used first of all immediately after the Flood had been poured out, in connection with the pouring out, not of water, but of *blood*! "Whoso sheddeth man's blood, by man shall his blood be shed: for in the image of God made he man" (Gen. 9:6). The sacredness of human life, and of the blood maintaining that life, is thus emphasized by God, with the basic reason given being the image of God in man. But undoubtedly there is in view here, ultimately, the one who as Son of man would yet be the "image of the invisible God" (Col. 1:15), and whose precious blood would one day be "shed" by man.

This is the same word that is used again and again of the blood of the sacrificial offerings "poured out" at the base of the altar (e.g., Lev. 4:7, et al.), which was symbolic of the "blood of the new testament, which is shed for many for the remission of sins" (Matt. 26:28).

And finally this is the word used prophetically of Christ's suffering on the cross, when He cried, "I am poured out like water, and all my bones are out of joint: my heart is like wax; it is melted in the midst of my bowels" (Ps. 22:14). Notice how strongly John emphasizes the pouring out of both blood and water. "But one of the soldiers with a spear pierced his side, and forthwith came there out blood and water. And he that saw it bare record, and his record is true: and he knoweth that he saith true, that ye might believe" (John 19:34–35).

We can discern, then, not only something of the physical significance of the waters of the earth, but also of the spiritual. Absolutely essential to physical life, in numerous ways, they nevertheless can be the agent of suffering and death. They are most intimately essential to the life of man through his blood, which is not only made up almost wholly of water but which requires the instrumentality of the water taken into the body to convey the necessary nourishment from all his intake of food. The life of the flesh is in the blood, and the blood is constituted in a matrix of water. And when the blood is poured out, even as the waters of the Flood were poured out, death ensues. But when the blood and water were poured out at the base of the cross, there was somehow released a "well of water spring ing up into everlasting life" (John 4:14). The spiritual reality of which this speaks is nothing less than the outpouring of the Holy Spirit, in a glorious baptism into Christ himself. "Not by works of righteousness which we have done, but according to his mercy he saved us, by the washing of regeneration, and renewing of the Holy Ghost; Which he shed [i.e., 'poured out'] on us abundantly through Jesus Christ our Saviour" (Titus 3:5–6).

Thus do water and the blood and the Holy Spirit all testify of the great fact of death to sin and eternal life in Christ, imparted to us through faith in Him and His atoning death. "This is he that came by water and blood, even Jesus Christ; not by water only, but by water and blood. And it is the Spirit that beareth witness, because the Spirit is truth. . . . And there are three that bear witness in earth, the Spirit, and the water, and the blood: and these three agree in one" (1 John 5:6–8).

With the precipitation of the vapor canopy, there was no longer the worldwide warm climate that prevented the development of winds and storms. Soon great winds began to blow (Gen. 8:1), generating great waves and currents (Gen. 8:3); perhaps these forces also triggered the tectonic forces that must have been acting when "the waters hasted away (the mountains rose, the valleys sank down) unto the place which Thou hadst founded for them. Thou hast set a bound that they may not pass over; that they turn not again to cover the earth" (Ps. 104:7–9; ASV).

An entirely different climatic mechanism henceforth prevailed. Distinct seasons were inaugurated (Gen. 8:22), and the rainbow was established (Gen. 9:13), neither of which was possible with the antediluvian vapor canopy. Furthermore, human life spans began to decline, probably as a result of the increase in atmospheric radiations and the general austerity of climate and living conditions.

But in spite of the loss of many of the favorable aspects of earlier climatic controls, even the present hydrologic cycle is marvelously effective in maintaining life on the earth. Although it is still not understood in many of its details, the broad outlines have been deciphered, and it is significant that the many biblical references to the various phases of the hydrologic cycle are in harmony with the most modern perspectives in this science.

The oceans, of course, are much larger than they were before the Flood, now containing the waters formerly "above the firmament," as well as those released through the "fountains of the great deep." It is these that now constitute the great "storehouses" of water that are essential for the operation of the water cycle (Ps. 33:7). Waters are evaporated from the oceans (Ps. 135:7), carried inland by the winds (Eccles. 1:6), caused to encounter particles of dust and sea salt to serve as nuclei of condensation (Prov. 8:26), condense into liquid water droplets in the form of clouds (Job 26:8), which in turn under the proper conditions coalesce and fall as rain (Job 36:27–28), providing water for maintenance of life on the earth (Isa. 55:10), and finally return by the rivers to the oceans from which they came (Eccles. 1:7).

The waters in the present atmosphere are of much smaller volume than those above the antediluvian "firmament," amounting to an equivalent depth of less than two inches distributed uniformly over the earth, underscoring the fact that there could never be another global rain like that which produced the Flood, in accordance with God's promise (Gen. 9:11). In spite of their relatively small amount, however, the atmospheric water vapors are quite essential, not only as the immediate source of rain but also as a shield against what would otherwise be lethal radiation from space. They also create a thermal blanket for retention and distribution of the light and heat rays coming to the earth from the sun. The water cycle as it now operates is marvelously effective in all essential respects and offers eloquent testimony to the providential care of God for His creature, even in the more rugged environment of the postdiluvian world.

### This Great and Wide Sea

All the waters that once were stored in the prediluvian canopy above the firmament and in the pressurized reservoirs below the earth's crust came together again in the Flood, and then drained into the newly opened ocean basins after the Flood. Thus, the present oceans are much wider and deeper than the seas of the pre-Flood world. This, of course, is the answer to the frequently asked question as to where the waters of the Flood went after the Flood. At the height of the Flood, one could assume that the pre-Flood hills and seas had been roughly evened out, so the solid earth then approximated a smooth sphere, covered by approximately 9,700 feet of water. Since the great orogenies after the Flood, the resulting land surfaces now approximate 30 percent of the earth's surface, with water areas occupying over 70 percent.

The transition period, however, probably lasted many centuries. All over the surface of the earth one finds indications of former water levels higher than now. All internal-drainage lakes and seas (e.g., Caspian Sea, Great Salt Lake) show evidence of old beach lines far up on the adjacent slopes. The same is true of rivers, practically all of which have old river terraces preserved on the valley sides. Furthermore, almost all of the world's rivers are "underfit" streams — that is, they now course through valleys that are much too large to have been carved by the present streams. Not only are the valleys too wide and too deep, but the beds of alluvium under the valleys and under the streams themselves are usually far too extensive to have been laid down by the existing rivers. All of this speaks clearly of a time in the recent past when the lakes and rivers of the world carried much more water than they do today.

The great deserts of the world once were all well watered. The Sahara Desert, the Gobi Desert, the Arabian Desert, the Great Basin of the western United States — all give abundant archaeological evidence that they once carried flowing streams and lakes and supported many communities of people. In other words, the surface of the world everywhere exhibits the character of a world recently and slowly emerging from the waters of a universal ocean. Even today there are some indications that the world is still slowly drying up — lakes falling, water tables dropping, deserts encroaching, etc. All of these evidences constitute strong visual confirmation of the biblical record of the worldwide Flood in the early days of human history.

Even in the time of Abraham, about 2000 B.C., the Bible describes the Dead Sea region, now extremely desolate, in these terms: "All the plain of Jordan . . . was well watered every where, before the LORD destroyed Sodom and Gomorrah, even as the garden of the LORD, like the land of Egypt" (Gen. 13:10).

Archaeological discoveries within recent years have shown conclusively that these cities of the plain were great metropolises, with large populations and complex cultures. Similarly, the barren Negev, in southern Israel, once was interlaced with a complex network of ponds and canals, supporting an extensive agricultural economy. Comparable examples could be cited from ancient settlements all over the world.

The very fact that the Bible speaks of the whole earth as being under water at one time is significant, since this would have been almost inconceivable to early nations living near the great mountain ranges of the world. Yet modern geologists have found incontrovertible fossil and sedimentary evidence near the summits of all these mountains that the waters of the ocean have, indeed, covered them at some time in the past.

The earth's land surfaces are endlessly fascinating to study, but so also are the seabeds. Until modern times, however, men had no real understanding of the sea bottoms, the abundance and variety of living creatures in the deep, the amazing ocean currents, or many other marvels of these great depths of water. They could only see the surface of the ocean, and the general belief was that the sands in the shallows along the shore continued on to form a relatively flat and shallow sandy bottom everywhere, even in the deep ocean.

Modern hydrography has shown, of course, that such a concept was enormously incomplete, to say the least. The Bible, however, does seem to have an accurate perspective on the magnitude and complexity of the seas.

> O, Lord, how manifold are thy works! in wisdom hast thou made them all: the earth is full of thy riches. So is this great and wide sea, wherein are things creeping innumerable, both small and great beasts (Ps. 104:24–25).

> They that go down to the sea in ships, that do business in great waters; These see the works of the LORD, and his wonders in the deep (Ps. 107:23–24).

> Whatsoever the LORD pleased, that did he in heaven, and in earth, in the seas, and all deep places (Ps. 135:6).

These verses speak of the sea as "great and wide," containing innumerable animals of all kinds and sizes, a region in which God does "wonders," and of "deep places" (same word as "deeps") as meaning more than just "the seas," which are also mentioned.

The very emphasis on the word "deeps" (or "depths") so often when referring to the ocean (same as the initial "deep" in Genesis 1:2 — Hebrew *tehom*) indicates that there are, indeed, many "deep places" in the oceans. Just how deep was never even remotely realized until recent decades, when echo sounding and other techniques have made it possible to measure the actual depth of the oceans. Great canyons practically circling the globe have been discovered in the ocean floor, and some of the great trenches reach depths of almost eight miles. The sea-floor topography is far more rugged than on land, with gigantic mountains and great numbers of volcanoes.

Jonah speaks of mountains in the ocean when he cries, in his awful experience of being cast overboard into a stormy sea. "The waters compassed me about, even to the soul: the depth closed me round about, the weeds were wrapped about my head. I went down to the bottoms of the mountains" (Jonah 2:5–6). The mountains Jonah saw (possibly by vision) may have been some of the "seamounts" which are now known to dot the floor of the ocean.

Second Samuel 22 and Psalm 18 both record, in almost identical words, David's song of praise on the occasion of his special deliverance by God from his enemies. The imagery of the psalm is figurative and poetic, but nevertheless seems to suggest actual events that could take place in God's future day of judgment against all the enemies of God's people (or perhaps, events that had taken place at the time of the Flood). In any case, some of the figures provide remarkable insight into certain aspects of the ocean's deep structure. "Then the channels of

waters were seen, and the foundations of the world were discovered at thy rebuke, O LORD, at the blast of the breath of thy nostrils. He sent from above, he
took me, he drew me out of many waters" (Ps. 18:15–16).

Only in recent decades has it been discovered that the ocean floor is lined
with deep channels and canyons, some of which dwarf even such terrestrial features as the Grand Canyon. Yet David somehow knew that, deep down near the
very foundations of the world, at the bottom of the earth's crustal rocks and beneath the floor of the deep ocean, were great channels, below "many waters." It is
also possible, however, that this verse may refer in retrospective vision to the
great subterranean channels of the pre-Flood hydrologic cycle network, which
were broken up at the time of the Flood.

Not only are there great mountains, ridges (e.g., the Mid-Atlantic Ridge),
volcanoes, and canyons on the ocean floor, but also many remarkable springs of
water, whence flow great amounts of rich, warm, fresh waters from deep in the
earth's interior. Others seem to be outlets from sources high in the continental
mountains. In any case, God's message to Job and friends seemed to refer to them
long before modern men discovered them. "Hast thou entered into the springs in
the sea? or hast thou walked in the search of the depth?" (Job 38:16).

One of the most useful of all oceanographic discoveries was made by Matthew Maury, the "father of oceanography," who made extensive hydrographic
surveys of the winds and currents of the Atlantic Ocean. He discovered the cause-
and-effect relations between air circulation systems on the earth and the great
oceanic circulations, and then was able to chart the most effective routes for sea
travel, taking advantage of the regular current systems. As a Bible-believing Christian, he had received his conviction that such relationships existed and such paths
could be discovered from such Scriptures as the following: "The fowl of the air,
and the fish of the sea, and whatsoever passeth through the paths of the seas" (Ps.
8:8); and, "For he commandeth, and raiseth the stormy wind, which lifteth up
the waves thereof" (Ps. 107:25). Maury eventually became known as "the path-
finder of the seas," an ascription which was even engraved on his tombstone.

Water is extremely important in the life of the earth and its inhabitants, and
there are more than two thousand references to various aspects of these waters in
the Bible (water, river, rain, sea, etc.). Surely it is significant that none of these
references have turned out to be incorrect in the light of 20th-century science,
while many of them contained allusions to modern facts of science millennia
before they were confirmed by scientific research.

## Navigation and Noah's Ark

With the earth's surface being 70 percent water as it is, it was natural, and
indeed essential, for early nations to develop the sciences of shipbuilding and navigation. The great cities of the ancient world almost invariably grew up either along
the seacoast or along a navigable river, and merchant ships have carried their

cargoes from one city or nation to another since the beginning of historical records.

The Phoenicians, with their great seaports at Tyre and Sidon on the eastern shore of the Mediterranean and their far-flung colonies at Carthage in North Africa, Cadiz in Spain, and elsewhere, were the most famous navigators of the ancient world. But long before these were the Cretan navies, and more and more evidence is coming in that the early Egyptians and Chaldeans also traveled far and wide in the ancient seas. Ancient India and Malaysia traded by sea with the Babylonians. The Greek legends tell of Ulysses and the Argonauts, and more scholars all the time are becoming convinced that even the Americas were visited by the Phoenicians, Egyptians, maybe even Israelites, and other ancient mariners perhaps thousands of years before Columbus.

In the Bible, Jacob in about 1700 B.C. prophesied that the future home of the tribe of Zebulun would be "an haven of ships" (Gen. 49:13), and Job, perhaps even earlier, had written about "swift ships" (Job 9:26). The most ancient annals of recorded history open on a world of great ships and navies, driven by sails and propelled by oars. King Solomon had a great navy about 1000 B.C. (1 Kings 9:26), and so did Hiram of Tyre (1 Kings 10:22).

But the first and greatest of all ancient vessels — in fact, probably their first prototype — was Noah's ark. It is small wonder that the earliest peoples after the Flood soon developed sea-worthy vessels of their own, since they were direct descendants of the builders and operators of the great ship that had safely transported all the world's primeval inhabitants from the lost world of the antediluvians to the new world that emerged from the global deluge.

The ark is the only ship mentioned in the Bible whose dimensions are actually recorded — and remarkable dimensions they were, making it the largest floating structure ever built until modern times! God himself gave the directions.

> Make thee an ark of gopher wood; rooms shalt thou make in the ark, and shalt pitch it within and without pitch. And this is the fashion which thou shalt make it of: The length of the ark shall be three hundred cubits, the breadth of it fifty cubits, and the height of it thirty cubits. A window shalt thou make to the ark, and in a cubit shalt thou finish it above; and the door of the ark shalt thou set in the side thereof; with lower, second, and third stories shalt thou make it (Gen. 6:14–16).

The ark was thus to be essentially a huge box (the Hebrew word itself implies this), designed essentially for stability in the waters of the Flood rather than for movement through the waters. Assuming the cubit to be 17.5 inches, which is the minimum suggested value, the dimensions of the ark were as sketched in figure 20.

The ark was taller than a normal three-story building and about one and a half times as long as a football field. The total volumetric capacity was equal to 1,396,000 cubic feet. Since the standard railroad stock car contains 2,670 cubic feet effective capacity, the ark had a volumetric capacity equal to that of 522

*Figure 20 — Dimensions of Noah's Ark*
*The figures shown below are based on a cubit of only 17½ inches. Even with such a small cubit, the ark would have had a volumetric capacity equivalent to that of 522 standard railroad stock cars, enough to carry 125,280 sheep-size animals and far more than enough to carry two of every known kind of land animal, living or extinct.*

## Noah's Ark

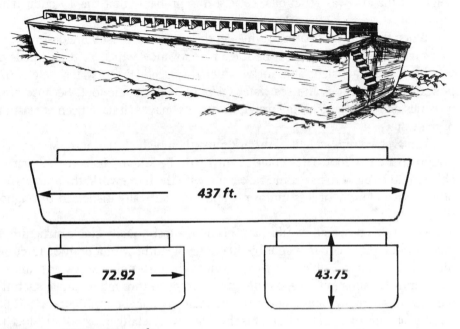

**Volume: 1,396,000 cu. ft.**
**Gross tonnage: 13,960 tn.**

standard stock cars. It obviously could have carried a tremendous number of animals, and was clearly designed to hold representatives from all kinds of animals throughout the entire world. Since a standard stock car can carry 240 sheep, the ark could have carried over 125,000 sheep. The average size of all animals is certainly less than that of a sheep, and there are less than 18,000 species of land animals alive today (that is, birds, mammals, reptiles, and amphibians). There are even a smaller number of known fossil species of extinct land animals, so the ark was certainly large enough.

In the complex of hydrodynamic and aerodynamic forces unleashed in the Flood, it was also necessary that the ark remain afloat for a whole year. The gopher wood of which it was constructed was no doubt extremely strong and durable. The timbers forming the sides and bottom, as well as the floors of the intermediate decks, were probably cut and shaped from great trees that had been growing since the world began, over 1,600 years earlier. The "pitch" (Hebrew *kaphar*, meaning "covering") was evidently an excellent waterproofing material, though we do not now know what it was.

In addition to floating, it must not capsize under the impact of the great waves and winds which might beat against it. The Scripture says the floodwaters rose at least 15 cubits above the highest mountains (Gen. 7:20), evidently to point out that the ark was floating freely wherever the waters might propel it. The height of the ark was 30 cubits, so it seems probable that the 15-cubit figure represents the draft of the ark when loaded.

When the ark was floating at this depth, according to Archimedes principle, its weight must have equaled the force of buoyancy, which in turn equals the weight of the equivalent amount of water displaced. Fresh water weighs 62.4 pounds per cubic foot and sea water 64 pounds per cubic foot. Because of the minerals and sediments in the water, its density may well have been at least that of sea water.

The average unit weight of the ark must then be half that of the water, or 32 pounds per cubic foot. The center of gravity of the ark and its contents presumably would be close to its geometric center, with the framework, the animals, and other contents more or less uniformly and symmetrically dispersed throughout the structure.

The ark as designed would have been an exceptionally stable structure. Its cross section of 30 cubits height by 50 cubits breadth, with a draft of 15 cubits, made it almost impossible to capsize, even in the midst of heavy waves and violent winds. To illustrate this, assume the ark tipped through an angle such that the roof was actually touching the water's edge, as sketched in figure 21. This is an angle of approximately 31°, that is the angle whose tangent is 30/50. Since the weight of the ark continues unchanged, it must still displace an amount of water equal to half its cross section. Thus, the water surface coincides with the diagonal. The buoyant force B continues to equal W, the weight of the ark.

However, the two forces are not now acting in the same line. The weight W acts vertically downward through the center of the ark's cross section. The force B acts vertically upward through the centroid of the triangle LQN, since this is the location of the center of gravity of the volume of water that has been displaced by the ark.

The two forces W and B, equal in magnitude but opposite in direction, form a couple, of intensity equal to the product of either force times the distance between them. As long as the line of action of B is outside that of W, in the direction toward the submerged side of the ark, the couple is a "righting couple" and would act to restore the vessel to its upright position. The magnitude of the couple is of no particular interest, but the location of M, the metacenter, is significant. As long as M is above G (the centroid of the entire vessel cross section) on the axis of symmetry of the vessel, then the ship is stable.

*Figure 21 — Stability of the Ark*

The ark's dimensions made it almost impossible to capsize. Even if tilted through any angle less than 90°, the buoyant force tending to right it always acts "outside" the weight force tending to capsize it, thus causing it to return to its normal floating position.

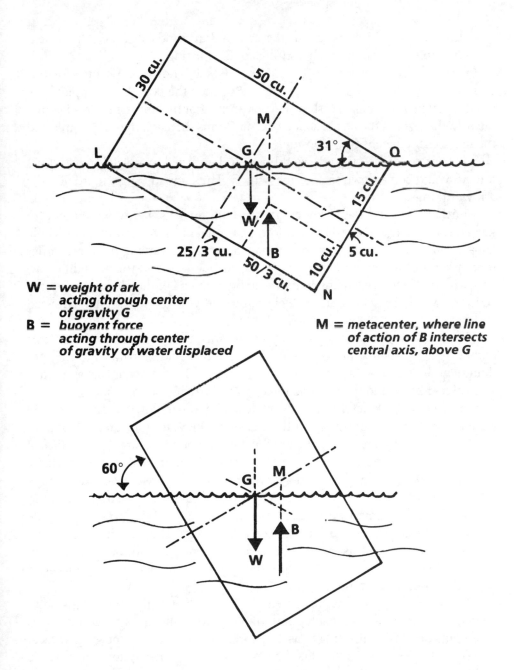

**W** = weight of ark acting through center of gravity G

**B** = buoyant force acting through center of gravity of water displaced

**M** = metacenter, where line of action of B intersects central axis, above G

For the condition shown, M can be calculated to be 8.9 cubits above G on the axis of symmetry (calculated, from dimensions shown on the sketch, as

$$\frac{25/3}{\tan 31°} -5 = \frac{125}{9} -5 = \frac{80}{9} \ \ cu.).$$

This is almost 13.5 feet about the centroid and indicates the ark was extremely stable, even under such a strong angle of listing.

The metacentric height, as the distance GM is known, is positive for this cross section even for much higher angles. Suppose the boat, for example, were tilted through a 60° angle, as shown. The centroid of the immersed area is obviously to the right of the line of action of G, and thus there is a righting couple and the metacentric height GM is positive.

As a matter of fact, the ark would have to be turned completely vertical before M would come down to coincide with G. Thus, for any angle up to 90°, the ark would right itself.

Furthermore, its relatively great length (six times its width) would tend to keep it from being subjected to wave forces of equal magnitude through its whole length, since wave fields tend to occur in broken and varying patterns, rather than in a series of long uniform crest-trough sequences, and this would be particularly true in the chaotic hydrodynamic phenomena of the Flood. Any vortex action to which it might occasionally be subjected would also tend to be resisted and broken up by its large length-width ratio.

The ark would tend to be lined up by the spectrum of hydrodynamic forces and currents in such a direction that its long axis would be parallel to the predominant direction of wave and current movement. Thus, it would act as a semi-streamlined body, and the net drag forces would usually be minimal.

In every way, therefore, the ark as designed was highly stable, admirably suited for its purpose of riding out the storms of the year of the great Flood.

During the filming of the popular Hollywood motion picture film *In Search of Noah's Ark*, produced by Sun Classics, Inc., the above inferences were actually confirmed by testing a scale model of the ark in a large wave tank at Scripps Institute of Oceanography at La Jolla, California. Giant waves were produced in the tank by a mechanical wave generating device, simulating waves on the scale model larger than any ever experienced on a real ocean. The ark did indeed prove impossible to capsize, just as the above calculations had indicated. It was not intended for speed, of course, but for stability, and its divinely given dimensions were ideal for that purpose.

As far as navigation was concerned, God himself evidently steered the ship, keeping its occupants reasonably comfortable inside while the storms and waves raged outside, finally directing it (as noted in chapter 9) to near the geographical center of the postdiluvian world's new land surfaces, a newly formed volcanic mountain, projecting high over the adjacent plains. This mountain, known ever since as Mount Ararat, now rises to 17,000 feet in elevation and is one of the greatest and most majestic mountains of the world.

There are numerous questions that have been raised by skeptics concerning the story of the ark. All such questions are thoroughly answered in a remarkable book by John Woodmorappe.[4]

Soon after the flood waters receded, the ark's inhabitants descended the mountain to begin their lives in the new world, leaving the ark resting high up on the mountain. The climate soon changed and snow began to fall. Eventually the mountain's summit became encased in a permanent ice cap and the ark itself has perhaps been preserved in ice for thousands of years, as a silent monument to God's judgment on a wicked world.

From time to time through the intervening centuries, during times of occasional melt-back, travelers have reported seeing the vessel projecting through the ice-pack. These reports eventually became so numerous and convincing that a long series of expeditions began to venture forth to locate the ark and officially document its existence. These have all proved difficult and dangerous — sometimes fatal — and, so far, unsuccessful.

There is also the possibility that one or more avalanches, of which there have been many on Mount Ararat, especially following volcanic activity, have buried the ark or even broken it and carried part of it to a lower level (most reports of sightings indicate the ark has been at about 15,000 feet).

There have been various reports that the ark is on another mountain altogether. All of these are highly questionable, however. Most sighting reports have been on the traditional Mount Ararat.

## The Water of Life

Because of the all-pervasive importance of water in the life of man in the present world, God often used the figure of water to picture the great spiritual truths associated with eternal life. As physical water is essential for physical life, so spiritual life requires "living water," that water given by the Lord Jesus Christ, so satisfying that he who drinks shall "never thirst" (John 4:10, 14). And this water, which springs up eternally, is none other than the Holy Spirit. "He that believeth on Me, as the scripture hath said, from within him shall flow rivers of living water. But this spake He of the Spirit, which they that believe on Him were to receive" (John 7:38–39; ASV).

The "master of Israel," Nicodemus, had undoubtedly either been in the delegation of Pharisees, or heard their report, when they saw John baptizing in water and heard him say, "He that sent me to baptize with water, the same said unto me, Upon whom thou shalt see the Spirit descending, and remaining on him, the

---

4. John Woodmorappe, *Noah's Ark: A Feasibility Study* (El Cajon: CA: Institute for Creation Research, 1996), p. 306.

same is he that baptizeth with the Holy Ghost. And I saw and bare record that this is the Son of God" (John 1:33–34). And when, a few nights later, he went to Jesus to make further investigation, the Lord reminded him of this symbolic import of John's baptism, saying: "Verily, verily, I say unto thee, Except a man be born of water and [i.e., 'even'] of the Spirit, he cannot enter into the kingdom of God" (John 3:5).

Christian baptism in water is thus rich in its spiritual testimony both to those who submit to it and to those who may witness it. It speaks of death to the old life, as did the waters of the Flood. It thus also speaks of being raised to a new life, as Christ was raised from the dead (Rom. 6:3–5). It also symbolizes cleansing from the filth of sin, as water cleanses the flesh. And in its life-giving character the water portrays the pouring-out of the Holy Spirit into the life of the one who receives Christ and is thereby "baptized into one body . . . by one Spirit," and who has been "made to drink into one Spirit" (1 Cor. 12:13).

And finally, since all these blessings are mediated to us through the Word of God, the latter is also symbolized by water. "Christ . . . loved the church, and gave himself for it; That he might sanctify and cleanse it with the washing of water by the word" (Eph. 5:25–26).

When all the promises of the Word have been fulfilled and when we have entered upon life in all its heavenly fulness, there will no longer be need for the present earth and its atmospheric heavens, and there will be found "no place for them" (Rev. 20:11). "The earth . . . and the works that are therein shall be burned up" (2 Pet. 3:10). And this must include the most prominent feature of the earth, its "great and wide sea" (Ps. 104:25).

But first, "the sea gave up the dead which were in it" (Rev. 20:13). Also, death and Hades delivered up their dead, and then were cast into the lake of fire, and it would have seemed that these two terms should have included all the unsaved dead. Why, then, are the dead in the sea specially mentioned? One immediately recalls the judgment of the great Flood, when the present "sea" was formed, and when "the world that then was, being overflowed with water, perished" (2 Pet. 3:6). Those who perished in the waters of the Flood were wicked in more than the normal sense of the term. "All flesh had corrupted his way upon the earth" (Gen. 6:12), and this corruption was so uniquely pervasive in the soul of antediluvian man that "every imagination of the thoughts of his heart was only evil continually" (Gen. 6:5). The Nephilim, the men of renown, born of the monstrous union of men possessed by the sons of God and the daughters of men, together with their evil progenitors (Gen. 6:4), have apparently been singled out by God for special condemnation and punishment at the judgment of the great day (1 Pet. 3:19–20; 2 Pet. 2:4; Jude 6).

It was specifically the sea which formed the tomb of these beings; in fact, in a sense the sea was formed to be their tomb. It is thus either symbolically or in reality the "prison" of their evil "spirits" (1 Pet. 3:19). But these, along with all those whose unsaved spirits are in Hades and whose bodies are in the grave, will be given up from their prisons and brought before the great white throne for final judgment according to their works. And when the heavens and the earth are made new, there will be no more sea.

There will, of course, be no further need in that day for the sea. Water will no longer be needed for cleansing, for there will be nothing there which is unclean (Rev. 21:27). It will not be needed to preserve life and to renew the body chemistry day by day, as at present, for death and the Curse are no more. No longer will the life of the flesh be in the blood, for flesh and blood do not inherit the kingdom, and the resurrection body will have no need of blood to maintain its structure (1 Cor. 15:50; Luke 24:39). Men will not need water to quench their thirst, for "they shall hunger no more, neither thirst any more" (Rev. 7:16).

Furthermore, all that is now symbolized by water will then have been realized. On the one hand, water has symbolized death and judgment, especially when God's wrath was poured out in the Flood. And this was made a type of the coming judgment by fire at the return of Christ (Matt. 24:37–39; 2 Pet. 3:5–7). As the great sea has been an ever-present reminder of God's judgment by water, so the lake of fire will be an eternal reminder of God's greater judgment by fire.

On the other hand, water has symbolized eternal life and the Holy Spirit and the Word of God. Water has been necessary for life because of the necessity for continual bodily renewal, but this necessity has really arisen only because of the temporal nature of the original creation, and more especially because of the Curse. Under these conditions, characterized by spiritual death and separation from God, it has been perfectly appropriate that water should typify that which would impart spiritual life, the regenerating work of the Holy Spirit, and the Word of God, bridging the great gulf of broken fellowship and communication between God and man.

But in the new earth, the Curse is gone and eternal life is experienced in all its fullness. No longer need men study the written Word of God for knowledge of Him, "for the earth shall be filled with the knowledge of the glory of the Lord, as the waters cover the sea" (Hab. 2:14). In the present time, we can only know "that we dwell in him, and he in us, because he hath given us of his Spirit" (1 John 4:13). But then, "shall we ever be with the Lord" (1 Thess. 4:17).

There is water in the new Jerusalem: "a pure river of water of life, clear as crystal, proceeding out of the throne of God, and of the Lamb" (Rev. 22:1; only one throne, because God is the Lamb, slain from the foundation of the world). The fountain of cleansing, opened in the side of the Lamb on Calvary's cross, when blood and water poured forth, continues eternally, in a figure, to pour forth the pure water of life from the Lamb on His throne.

This is the river foreshadowed by the first river in Eden which went out to water the garden. These are the "living waters" promised the sinful woman of Samaria, which would be in her a "well of water springing up into everlasting life"

(John 4:10, 14). These are the waters offered when Jesus stood and cried, "If any man thirst, let him come unto me, and drink" (John 7:37). And to those who will come out of the great tribulation, the gracious promise is given that "the Lamb which is in the midst of the throne shall feed them, and shall lead them unto living fountains of waters" (Rev. 7:17).

And when Israel shall look in faith upon Him whom they have pierced, there shall be a "fountain opened to the house of David and to the inhabitants of Jerusalem for sin and for uncleanness" (Zech. 12:10; 13:1). During the millennial reign of Christ, a great river of healing waters, apparently really physical in character, will go out from the temple in Jerusalem (Ezek. 47:1–12; Zech. 14:8), but these will also be prophetic of the "pure river of water of life," constituting a visible promise and invitation to those who will inhabit the earth during the thousand years.

At present, God issues a gracious invitation: "Ho, every one that thirsteth, come ye to the waters" (Isa. 55:1). And how wonderfully fitting and compelling it is, that the very latest invitation recorded in the Word of God should come from the lips of the Lord Jesus himself, as He says: "Let him that is athirst come. And whosoever will, take the water of life freely" (Rev. 22:17)!

# 11

# OVERFLOWED WITH WATER

*Biblical Geology*

## Geology in the Bible

The field of science that has probably been most effectively used by skeptics in attempting to discredit the Bible is geology, "the study of the earth." The analysis of the earth's structure, especially the rocks that lie in the upper part of the earth's crust, with their fossil contents, has been built into a rather elaborate naturalistic view of the origin and "history" of the earth — an origin and history vastly different from what is recorded in the Bible.

Yet the processes of geology — physical processes that affect the crust of the earth and the surface features of the earth — are all quite consistent with biblical references to such processes. For example, the most important geological process is that of sedimentation. All the earth's fossil-bearing rocks, which are by far the most important in deciphering earth history, are sedimentary rocks that have been formed by the erosion, transportation, deposition, and lithification of sediments. Sediments are normally composed of rock particles such as clay, silt, sand, pebbles, or boulders. They are eroded usually by water (occasionally by wind or ice), then transported and finally deposited when the water velocity slows enough. With time, and either a cementing agent or long-sustained high pressures, the loose sediments will be converted into solid rock types, such as shale, siltstone, sandstone, conglomerate, or limestone.

The Bible occasionally refers to these processes in such verses as the following: "But as a mountain falls and crumbles away, And as a rock is moved from its place; As water wears away stones, And as torrents wash away the soil of the earth; So you destroy the hope of man (Job 14:18–19; NKJV). "He putteth forth his hand upon the rock; he overturneth the mountains by the roots. He cutteth out rivers among the rocks; and his eye seeth every precious thing" (Job 28:9–10).

The Bible also gives numerous references to more spectacular geological processes, such as earthquakes and volcanic eruptions. The earth's basic physical structure and its geophysical processes, as presented in the Bible, have already been discussed in chapter 8.

However, the aspect of geology most important to biblical studies is the historical aspect. That is, "historical" geologists profess to be able to decipher the supposed long evolutionary history of the earth and its inhabitants from their study of the earth's sedimentary crust and the fossils contained therein. Since this speculative history explicitly contradicts the very first chapters of the Bible, we first need to consider in some detail the actual biblical and scientific evidences related to earth history.

## The Unscientific Nature of "Historical" Geology

The study of historical geology holds great fascination for many people who are neither historians nor geologists. This discipline occupies a uniquely interesting and important position in human thought. Among the humanities, the study of history surely is of singular significance and, among the sciences, geology, dealing as it does with the very earth itself, is similarly of unique interest. When the two are combined in historical geology, which professes to be able to decipher the mystery of the origin and history of the earth and its processes, the resulting panorama is of marvelous interest and significance. Such a picture, in fact, is of far more than historical and geological pertinence. Anything that elucidates origins is necessarily of philosophical and theological interest, with strong implications regarding meanings and purposes and destinies as well.

It is little wonder that historical geology has attracted the intense interest and concern of a great variety of people. As a matter of fact, the basic structure of modern historical geology was worked out over a hundred years ago by such men as James Hutton (an agriculturalist with medical training), John Playfair (a mathematician), William Smith (a surveyor), Charles Lyell (a lawyer), Georges Cuvier (a comparative anatomist), Charles Darwin (a divinity student and naturalist), Robert Chambers (a journalist), William Buckland (a theologian), Roderick Murchison (a soldier and gentleman of leisure), Adam Sedgwick (who, when seeking election to the chair of geology at Cambridge, boasted that he knew nothing of geology), Hugh Miller (a stonemason), John Fleming (a zoologist), and others of like assortment.

Although the basic framework of historical geology as worked out by these men has not changed to the present day, there has now arisen a group of specialists in historical geology who have come to regard this field as their own particular field of science, and who now regard with disdain any who venture to write or speak in this field without giving full allegiance to the accepted system. By its very nature, however, historical geology is not, and can never be, a genuine science, and therefore the dogmatic insistence that one follow the interpretations of its founders and present-day leaders, with all the implications of origins and meanings that are involved, is nothing less than scientism. Since historical geology was founded by men untrained in geology, it seems legitimate for non-geologists as well as geologists to evaluate and critique it.

This is in no way meant to be a reflection upon the science of geology, which is a true science in every sense of the word, and which has made a tremendous contribution to our understanding and application of the laws of nature. When, however, a geologist (or lawyer or surveyor or naturalist or anyone else) seeks to become a *historical* geologist, he must leave the realm of science and enter that of philosophy or religion. The presently accepted system of historical geology is basically nothing else than a philosophy or a religion of evolutionary uniformitarianism. This will become more evident as we consider the true nature of physical processes studied by scientists in general and by geologists in particular.

The word *science* itself, of course, is derived from the Latin *scientia* ("knowledge"), and this is essentially what it means. A more formal definition, as given in the Oxford Dictionary, is: "A branch of study which is concerned either with a connected body of demonstrated truths or with observed facts systematically classified and more or less colligated by being brought under general laws, and which includes trustworthy methods for the discovery of new truth within its own domain."

Science thus involves observed facts and demonstrated laws. The scientific method involves experimental reproducibility, with like causes producing like effects. Science is knowledge, not inference, speculation, or extrapolation.

True science is necessarily limited to the measurement and study of present phenomena and processes. Data that have been observed in the present, or that have been recorded by human observers in the historic past, are properly called scientific data. Laws that have been deduced from these data, that satisfactorily correlate the pertinent data, and that have predictive value for the correlation of similar data obtained from like experiments in the future, are properly regarded as scientific laws.

But there is no way of knowing that these processes and the laws that describe them have always been the same in the past or that they will always be the same in the future. It is possible to make an assumption of this kind, of course, and this is the well-known doctrine of uniformitarianism. The assumption is reasonable, in the light of our experience with present processes, and it is no doubt safe to extrapolate on this basis for a certain time into the future and back into the past. But to insist that uniformitarianism is the only scientific approach to the understanding of all past and future time is clearly nothing but a dogmatic tenet of a particular form of religion.

That uniformitarianism has been the foundational and guiding principle of historical geology is widely recognized. A widely used textbook on the subject said, for example:

> The uprooting of such fantastic beliefs [that is, those of the catastrophists] began with the Scottish geologist James Hutton, whose *Theory of the Earth*, published in 1785, maintained that *the present is the key to the past*, and that, given sufficient time, processes now at work could account for all the geologic features of the Globe. This philosophy, which came to be known as the *doctrine of uniformitarianism* demands an immensity of time; it has now gained universal acceptance among intelligent and informed people.[1]

Real science deals with the data and processes of the present that can be experimentally measured and observationally verified. The principle of uniformitarianism is a philosophy, or faith, by which it is hoped that these processes of the present can be extrapolated into the distant past and the distant future to explain all that has ever happened and to predict all that will ever happen.

But, when viewed in these terms, it is obvious that uniformitarianism is not proved, and therefore is not properly included in the definition of science. There may be any number of other assumptions that might serve as the basis of such extrapolation, and all would similarly be mere acts of faith.

It is perfectly possible and reasonable, on the other hand, to assume that the processes studied by science were created at some time in the past and may be terminated at some time in the future. The processes then could tell us nothing about their creation or termination — this would be outside the domain of scientific investigation. Such information could come, if at all, only by revelation from their Creator.

## True Uniformitarianism

The concept of uniformitarianism, while perfectly valid and proper in its legitimate framework, has thus been applied quite illegitimately in historical geology. True uniformity has to do with the inviolability of natural law (especially, the laws of thermodynamics), and not with the uniformity of process rates. The laws of thermodynamics indicate what the character of all natural processes must be, but they do not indicate how fast or how slow such processes will proceed. And there is certainly never any assurance that the rate of any given process will always be constant.

But it is this assumed uniformity of process rates that is at the very hub of the principle of uniformitarianism as it has been applied in historical geology. This is evident from the following rather typical description of the principle:

> Opposed to this line of thinking was Sir Charles Lyell (1979–1875), a contemporary of Cuvier, who held that earth changes were gradual, taking

---

1. Carl O. Dunbar, *Historical Geology*, 2nd ed. (New York, NY: John Wiley and Sons, 1960), p. 18. Emphasis is his.

place at the same uniform slowness that they are today. Lyell is thus credited with the propagation of the premise that more or less has guided geological thought ever since, namely that *the present is the key to the past*. In essence, Lyell's *doctrine of uniformitarianism* states that past geological processes operated in the same manner and at the same rate they do today.[2]

It is obvious that if geological processes have always been going on at the same slow rates they exhibit today, the earth must be immensely old. Age calculations by certain of these processes — such as radioactive decay, continental erosion, canyon cutting, deltaic deposition, oceanic sodium increments, and others — when based on present rates, are of course bound to give extremely high values, far greater than can possibly be accommodated within the framework of biblical chronology.

But there is clearly no scientific basis for assuming such uniformity of process rates. It is quite valid to assume that running water will erode soil and rock, that radioactive minerals will decay, and that all other such processes will proceed irreversibly, in accord with the second law of thermodynamics, but neither this nor any other scientific law provides any guarantee that such rates will always be slow and uniform. In fact, it is certain that all such real decay processes are so intricately complex and are affected by such a great number of factors (a change in any one of which may drastically affect the process rate) that it will forever be quite impossible to say exactly what the rate will be except under precisely known and experimentally confirmed conditions.

It is encouraging that many geologists in recent years are beginning to recognize and acknowledge this distinction which was long ago urged by creationists and biblical catastrophists. Dr. Stephen Jay Gould, one of the most influential modern evolutionists, was one of the first to distinguish between the true and the fallacious uniformitarianism (calling them methodological and substantive uniformitarianism, respectively): "Uniformitarianism is a dual concept. Substantive uniformitarianism (a testable theory of geologic change postulating uniformity of rates or material conditions) is false and stifling to hypothesis formation. Methodological uniformitarianism (a procedural principle asserting spatial and temporal invariance of natural laws) belongs to the definition of science and is not unique to geology."[3]

With this we would heartily agree. Uniformity of natural laws (since the end of the creation period) is basic in science, and is quite in accord with Scripture

---

2. James H. Zumberge, *Elements of Geology*, 2nd ed. (New York, NY: John Wiley and Sons, 1963), p. 200. Emphasis is his. As a matter of interest, this writer and Dr. Zumberge were graduate students together at the University of Minnesota in the late 1940s and became friends through mutual interest in geology and the Bible. At that time, he thought flood geology was a viable option but asked that this not be mentioned to any of our professors, as it might jeopardize his career. He indeed did have a very successful career, including the chairmanship of a major university geology department and later the presidency of a major university.

3. Stephen Jay Gould, "Is Uniformitarianism Necessary?" *American Journal of Science,* 263 (Mar. 1965): 223.

(always allowing, of course, for the possible miraculous interruption of those laws by the Creator when He so wills). But the type of geological uniformitarianism that has held sway for a hundred years, and which has indeed served as the very foundation of modern theories of evolution, is not only contrary to the biblical record, but is inadequate to explain the actual data of geology. "Substantive uniformitarianism as a descriptive theory has not withstood the test of new data and can no longer be maintained in any strict manner."[4]

Since geological uniformitarianism in the traditional sense can no longer be maintained, and since uniformitarianism in the true sense is in no way a peculiar possession of the science of geology, it is wrong to refer to uniformitarianism as being in some way particularly the possession of geological theory. An illuminating admission giving the reason why this identification continues to be made is revealed in the following: "As a special term, methodological uniformitarianism was useful only when science was debating the status of the supernatural in its realm; for if God intervenes, then laws are not invariant and induction becomes invalid. . . . The term today is an anachronism, for we need no longer take special pains to affirm the scientific nature of our discipline."[5] If one looks beneath the surface of these reasonings, he sees that the real problem is not one of science at all, but of scientism! That is, historical geologists have attempted to defend substantive uniformitarianism (i.e., uniformity of process rates) by citing the undisputed evidences of methodological uniformitarianism (i.e., uniformity of natural law). Whether this fallacy in reasoning has been conscious or subconscious is really immaterial; the basic reason for it in either case has been the innate desire to relegate the position of the Creator and His possible intervention in history as far back in time as possible, and perhaps even to eliminate Him altogether. A full-orbed philosophy — rather, a religion — of origins and development has thus been erected upon a fallacious uniformitarianism.

Although a number of other geologists had begun even earlier to question substantive uniformitarianism, Gould's persuasive writing style seems to have been the catalyst that has triggered a renaissance of catastrophism in geology. This naturalistic "neocatastrophism" has meshed well with the new "punctuated equilibrium" school of thought in evolutionary biology and geology, also strongly promoted by Gould, so that old-style uniformitarianism, involving very slow geological processes along with slow and gradual biological evolution, is now rapidly being relegated by many to the realm of discarded dogma.

In a remarkable article in an official publication of the Geological Society of America, geologist James Shea catalogued a long list of fallacies in the uniformitarianism of his geological forebears. Among other criticisms is the following statement: "Furthermore, much of Lyell's uniformitarianism, specifically his ideas on identity of ancient and modern causes, gradualism, and constancy of rate, has

4. Ibid., p. 226.
5. Ibid., p. 227.

been explicitly refuted by the definitive modern sources as well as by an over-whelming preponderance of evidence that, as substantive theories, his ideas on these matters were simply wrong."[6] Later, he goes on to comment, "The idea that the rates or intensities of geological processes have been constant is so obviously contrary to the evidence that one can only wonder at its persistence."[7]

In a presidential address to the Society of Economic Paleontologists and Min-eralogists, one of the nation's leading geologists, University of Wisconsin Professor Robert Dott, stressed that the geological record, as preserved in the sedimentary rocks, was a record of local and regional catastrophes, not one of slow and uni-form rates of deposition. After giving many evidences and examples, he said, "I hope I have convinced you that the sedimentary record is largely a record of epi-sodic events rather than being uniformly continuous. My message is that episodicity is the rule, not the exception."[8] His reason for using the term "episodicity" rather than "catastrophism" was fascinating, reflecting as it does the growing fear of cre-ationism. " 'Episodic' was chosen carefully over other possible terms. 'Catastrophic' has become popular recently because of its dramatic effect, but it should be purged from our vocabulary because it feeds the neocatastrophist-creation cause."[9] Mod-ern "episodists" or "catastrophists," however, still adhere to the standard system of geologic ages that were originally associated with Lyellian uniformitarianism. They regard the ages as real and long-lasting, even though all the geological formation representing them were formed rapidly. Thus, during most of supposed geological time, no records at all were left, according to these new ideas.

Another modern geological neocatastrophist, Derek Ager, put it this way: "But I maintain that a far more accurate picture of the stratigraphical record is of one long gap with only very occasional sedimentation."[10] Dr. Ager was professor and head of the department of geology and oceanography at the University Col-lege, Swansea, England. He had written extensively on this subject, maintaining that all geological formations and structures are the records of catastrophes. How-ever, he also was sensitive to the possible creationist implications of such a con-clusion, and made it clear he wanted no part of that: "In case this book should be read by some fundamentalist searching for straw to prop up his prejudices, let me state categorically that . . . I find divine creation, or several such creations, a completely unnecessary hypothesis. Nevertheless this is not to deny that there are some very curious features about the fossil record."[11]

---

6. James H. Shea, "Twelve Fallacies of Uniformitarianism," *Geology*, 10 (Sept. 1982): 456. Such an article in an "official" geological journal would have been considered unpublishable heresy until recent years.

7. Ibid., p. 457. Shea was, at the time, editor of the *Journal of Geological Education*, published by the National Association of Geology Teachers.

8. Robert H. Dott, "Episodic View Now Replacing Catastrophism," *Geotimes* (Nov. 1982): 16.

9. Ibid.

10. Derek Ager, *The Nature of the Stratigraphical Record* (New York, NY: John Wiley and Sons, 1973), p. 34.

11. Ibid., p. 19.

In an important book written shortly before his death, Dr. Ager, a man who had done actual field research in geology in 57 countries, summarized his experience by noting that "in all branches of geology there has been a return to ideas of rare violent happenings and episodicity," replacing what he called "the dangerous doctrine of Uniformitarianism."[12]

Modern naturalistic catastrophists such as Dott and Ager desire to retain the geologic-age system because of its vital importance for evolution. Evolution requires long ages to be feasible at all, and so the standard system of geological time is considered inviolable, even though all real geologic formations speak clearly of short time periods of rapid deposition.

## The Evolutionary Framework

The vast ages of earth history that supposedly are implied by the principle of uniformitarianism have been subdivided into a more or less standard series of geological eras and periods, each with a generally accepted name and approximate duration. The whole sequence is known as the Geologic Column, and the corresponding chronology is known as the Geologic Time Scale (see table 6). This, of course, is the very backbone of the so-called historical geology. Any given rock formation must occupy a certain position in the column, and presumably it can be dated as to time of formation in terms of the time scale.

A pertinent question needs to be asked at this point (although it is often considered to be impertinent). On what basis are the various rock types and formations identified and classified? How is one system assigned to say, the Devonian period and another to the Ordovician? How do we know which is older and which is younger? How are the divisions between successive periods recognized?

This problem of stratigraphic classification is clothed in uncertainty and controversy, even though the Geologic Time Scale has been generally accepted in its present form for over a hundred years.

The nonspecialist is inclined to assume that the principle of superposition is the main factor in determining relative age and that equivalent strata in different areas can be recognized by their chemical or physical composition. However, this is not so. The factor that is most important in assigning an age to a given stratum is its biological content — that is, the fossils it contains. "Thus it appears that the only presently available rational geochronological indices are biostratigraphically based — i.e., *biochronologic*."[13] This means plainly that only the fossils can be relied upon as a criterion for determining the time in earth history when a particular formation was deposited. Other data — vertical position, physico-chemical characteristics, and other factors — are essentially insignificant.

---

12. Derek V. Ager, *The New Catastrophism* (Cambridge, UK: Cambridge University Press, 1993), p. xii, xvi.
13. T.G. Miller, "Time in Stratigraphy," *Paleontology*, 8 (Feb. 1965): 119. Emphasis his.

# TABLE 6 — *Standard Geologic Column and System of Geologic "Ages"*

*This standard column, representing the hypothetical vertical cross section through the earth's sedimentary and fossiliferous crust, is actually never found at any one location. It is merely an artifical construct, developed by superposition and interpolation from many locations.*

## Main Division and Events of Geological Time

| Eras | Periods | Characteristic Life | Estimated Years Ago |
|---|---|---|---|
| Cenozoic | Quaternary:<br>Recent Epoch<br>Pleistocene Epoch | Rise of modern plants and animals, and man. | 25,000<br>975,000 |
| | Tertiary:<br>Pliocene Epoch<br>Miocene Epoch<br>Oligocene Epoch<br>Eocene Epoch<br>Paleocene Epoch | Rise of mammals and development of highest plants. | 12,000,000<br>25,000,000<br>35,000,000<br>60,000,000<br>70,000,000 |
| Mesozoic | Cretaceous | Modernized angiosperms and insects abundant. Foraminifers profuse. Extinction of dinosaurs, flying reptiles, and ammonites. | 70,000,000<br>to<br>200,000,000 |
| | Jurassic | First (reptilian) birds. First of highest forms of insects. First (primitive) angiosperms. | |
| | Triassic | Earliest dinosaurs, flying reptiles, marine reptiles, and primitive mammals. Cycads and conifers common. Modern corals common. Earliest ammonites. | |
| Paleozoic | Permian | Rise of primitive reptiles. Earliest cycads and conifers. Extinction of trilobites. First modern corals. | 200,000,000<br>to<br>500,000,000 |
| | Pennsylvanian | Earliest known insects. Spore plants abundant. | |
| | Mississippian | Rise of amphibians. Culmination of crinoids. | |
| | Devonian | First known seed plants. Great variety of boneless fishes. First evidence of amphibians. | |
| | Silurian | Earliest known land animals. Primitive land plants. Rise of fishes. Brachiopods, trilobites, and corals abundant. | |
| | Ordovician | Vertebrates, graptolites, corals, brachiopods, cephalopods, and trilobites abundant. Oldest primitive land plants. | |
| | Cambrian | Earliest vertebrates. All sub-kingdoms of invertebrate animals represented. Brachiopods and trilobites common. | |
| Proterozoic | Keweenawan<br>———————<br>Huronian | Primitive water-dwelling plants and animals. | 500,000,000<br>to<br>1,000,000,000 |
| Archeozoic | Timiskaming<br>———————<br>Keewatin | Oldest known life (mostly indirect evidence). | 1,000,000,000<br>to<br>1,800,000,000 |

The only way in which the fossil contents of a rock could possibly indicate how old the rock might be is if the animals found as fossils were living only at that specific time in earth history. This would mean that there must have been different kinds of life at different periods in history, and that therefore the fossil forms provide an unambiguous index to the chronology.

But how do geologists determine which forms were living when? There must be some systematic way of viewing and classifying the changes of life forms with the passage of geologic time. The key, of course, is evolution! If everything must be explained in terms of uniform laws and uniform processes, this must include the development of the biological world as well as the physical world. All kinds of animals must therefore have gradually developed from earlier and simpler forms. There must have been a slow increase of organization and complexity of living forms during geologic history.

The fossil record thus is of paramount importance in geologic dating. However, many fossils are found in many "ages," so only certain fossils known as "index fossils" are used for dating purposes. "In each sedimentary stratum certain fossils seem to be characteristically abundant: these fossils are known as *index fossils*. If in a strange formation an index fossil is found, it is easy to date that particular layer of rock and to correlate it with other exposures in distant regions containing the same species."[14] The evolutionary significance of the methodology is clearly indicated by the following: "Once it was understood that each fossil represents a biologic entity, instead of a special divinely created life form, it became quite obvious that the plants and animals of each stratigraphic division had simply evolved from those of the preceding epoch through gradual adaptation. They were, in turn, ancestral to those that followed."[15]

This technique might have merit if it were actually known from historical records, from divine revelation, or from some other source, that all living forms had indeed evolved from prior forms. But the actual evidence for evolution on such a scale as this is, as implied by the above quotation, limited to the fossil record itself. In a presidential address before the Geological Society of America, Dr. Hollis Hedberg stressed the evolutionary significance of the fossil record:

> That our present-day knowledge of the sequence of strata in the earth's crust is in major part due to the evidence supplied by fossils is a truism. Merely in their role as distinctive rock constituents, fossils have furnished one of the best and most widely used means of tracing beds and correlating them. However, going far beyond this, fossils have furnished, through their record of the evolution of life on this planet, an amazingly effective key to the relative positioning of strata in widely separated regions and from continent to continent.[16]

---

14. J.E. Ransom, *Fossils in America* (New York, NY: Harper & Row, 1964), p. 43.
15. Ibid.
16. H.D. Hedberg: "The Stratigraphic Panorama," *Geological Society of America Bulletin,* 72 (Apr. 1961): 499–518.

Thus, the primary means of dating rock formations relative to each other, in the Geologic Column, is the evolutionary sequence of life on the earth through geologic time and the preservation of distinctive life forms as fossils deposited in the rocks laid down during each successive period. But, in turn, the history of evolution on the earth has been built up on the basis of the record revealed in the rocks representing the successive geologic ages. In fact, the only genuine historical evidence that might relate to the question of evolutionary history is found in this fossil record. Dunbar says, "Although the comparative study of living plants and animals may give very convincing circumstantial evidence, fossils provide the only historical, documentary evidence that life has evolved from simpler to more and more complex forms."[17]

The evidence for evolution afforded by living plants and animals is, indeed, hardly convincing at all. The almost universally accepted biologic mechanism for producing evolutionary change is supposed to be genetic mutation (a sudden random change in the biochemical structure of the germ cell) preserved, if favorable, by natural selection. Furthermore, it is admitted by all geneticists that the great majority — in fact, almost all — mutations are basically harmful. This is only to be expected, since they represent random changes in highly ordered systems.

As a matter of fact, mutations provide a very fine illustration of the second law of thermodynamics — the universal tendency toward disorder and decay. In any case, truly beneficial mutations are obviously such very rare events, if they occur at all, that it is quite impossible to see real evolution occurring among present plants and animals. There is, of course, a great deal of variation within basic kinds of creatures — in fact, no two individuals are exactly alike — but there are also clear-cut gaps between such basic kinds of creatures.

Since evolution cannot be demonstrated as occurring in the present, and since such evidence as does exist of biologic change in the present seems to be evidence of decay and death, rather than growth and increasing organization, it is obvious that, in the last analysis, the only possible historical evidence for evolution in the broad sense would have to be that contained in the fossil record.

But the fossil sequences are based on the geologic ages, and the geologic ages have been built up as an interpretive framework for earth history on the basis of the implicit assumption of evolution! This is circular reasoning, as shown in figure 22. That in itself does not condemn it, however, since, in the final analysis, all philosophies are based on circular reasoning. One always brings certain innate presuppositions with him when he tries to philosophize on origins and meanings, and these necessarily determine his conclusions. It is only when such circular reasoning is called "science" that it really becomes scientism. As a religious faith, it may be a live option, but not as science! Furthermore, when such a system begins to encounter problems and contradictions, necessitating continual

---

17. Dunbar, *Historical Geology*, p. 47.

*FIGURE 22 — Circular Reasoning in Historical Geology*
*The main evidence for evolution is the fossil record, with the simpler fossils in the older rocks. However, the geologic ages of rocks are determined by the assemblage of time-indexing fossils found in them. The ages assigned to these index fossils are determined by their stage of evolution. The circularity inherent in such reasoning is retained despite the many anomalies and contradictions it entails, apparently only because of the sacrosanct nature of evolution.*

*Stage of evolution of fossils determines geologic age of rocks*

*Sequence of fossils "demonstrates" evolution*

*Geologic age of rocks determines sequence of fossils*

modification or expansion to encompass all the special cases, then it is time to take a critical look at the fundamental premises upon which the system is based. This is the case with the vast, circular structure of the evolutionary geological-ages system.

## Scriptural Geology

If evolutionary uniformitarianism is invalid as a framework for historical geology, there must be a better framework. If the orthodox Geologic Time Scale is really based on circular reasoning and the assumption of evolution, then there must be a better explanation for the sedimentary rocks and their fossil sequences. The biblical record of primeval earth history does, indeed, provide a far more effective model for correlating all the real data of geology, and the main key is the Flood in the days of Noah, described in detail in Genesis 6–9.

Most of the early geologists did believe that the biblical Flood was responsible for the earth's sedimentary rocks and the great beds of fossils. These included such men as Nicolaus Steno, the "father of stratigraphy," John Woodward, who founded the paleontological museum at Cambridge University, and many others. Sir Isaac Newton, probably the greatest scientist of all time, was a close friend of Woodward's at Cambridge, and he also believed in literal creation and flood geology.

By the end of the 18th century, however, the concept of long geological ages and uniformitarianism was being promoted by such men as Buffon, Playfair, especially James Hutton, and then Charles Lyell. At the same time, others were advocating a modified catastrophism. The biblical teaching of one worldwide cataclysm was replaced by the concept of multiple catastrophism strongly promoted by Georges Cuvier.

By the middle of the 19th century, Lyellian uniformitarianism had triumphed over Cuvierian catastrophism, and the way was completely prepared for Darwinian evolutionism. Darwin confidently acknowledged that his theory of gradual evolution by natural selection implicitly depended on the long ages and slow changes supposedly provided by geological uniformitarianism, and soon the whole intellectual world was won over to this system.

Biblical theologians were, unfortunately, quite intimidated by this development, and tried desperately to devise new exegetical systems that would accommodate evolution and the geological ages. Many began to eulogize evolution as "God's method of creation" and the vast time required was incorporated into Genesis by interpreting the six days of Creation as a literary framework that corresponded to the geologic ages. Some theologians simply pigeon-holed the geologic ages into an imagined gap between the first two verses of Genesis. These various devices (theistic evolution, day-age theory, gap theory) were discussed in chapter 4.

The most urgent problem, however, was to get rid of the cataclysmic Flood of the Bible. If such a flood had really occurred, the whole system of uniformitarianism and long ages would be destroyed. Accordingly, the compromising theologians soon were advocating the "local flood theory," with a few suggesting a global "tranquil flood." The fact is, however, the local flood concept is completely anti-biblical, and the tranquil flood concept is an absurdity and a contradiction in terms.

According to Scripture, the great Deluge in the days of Noah was a worldwide catastrophe in which "the world that then was, being overflowed with water, perished" (2 Pet. 3:6). Since the biblical account is reliable and meaningful, then the Genesis Flood was indeed worldwide and cataclysmic.

That the Bible teaches a universal flood rather than a local or regional flood is evident for many reasons, among which are the following:

> 1. The flood waters covered all the high mountains (Gen. 7:19–20) and continued to cover them completely for about nine months (Gen. 8:5). These facts can answer hydraulically to a worldwide flood and to nothing else.

> 2. Expressions of universality in the account (Gen. 6–9) are not scattered and incidental (as is the case elsewhere in Scripture when apparently universal terms are used in a limited sense), but are repeated and emphasized again and again, constituting the very essence of the narrative. There are at least 30 times in which this universality ("all flesh," "every living thing," "all the high hills under the whole heaven," etc.) is mentioned in these chapters.

> 3. The worldwide character of the Flood is also assumed in later parts of Scripture. See especially the testimony of the Psalmist (Ps. 104:7), of Peter (1 Pet. 3:20; 2 Pet. 2:5; 3:5–6), and of the Lord Jesus Christ (Matt. 24:37–39).

4. The primary purpose of the Flood was to destroy all mankind. This is seen not only in the numerous statements in Genesis to that effect but also in those of Peter (2 Pet. 2:5) and of Christ (Luke 17:26–27). This could never have been accomplished by anything less than a global catastrophe. The wide distribution of early man is indicated by anthropological studies, but of even greater significance is the biblical testimony concerning the extreme longevity and productivity of the antediluvians, who had been filling the earth for hundreds of years (Gen. 1:28; 6:1, 11).

5. The tremendous size of the ark (which, according to the most conservative calculations, had a volumetric capacity equivalent to that of over five hundred standard railroad stock cars) is an eloquent witness that far more than a regional fauna was to be preserved therein. Its purpose was "to keep seed alive upon the face of all the earth" (Gen. 7:3), quite a pointless provision if the Deluge was local.

6. There would obviously have been no need for an ark at all if the Flood were anything other than universal. Noah and his family could far more easily have migrated to some distant land during the 120 years it took to build the ark. Similarly, the birds and animals of the region could much more simply have been preserved by a process of migration. The Flood narrative is thus made entirely ridiculous by the local-flood hypothesis.

7. God's thrice-repeated promise (Gen. 8:21; 9:11, 15) never again to "smite every thing living" by a flood clearly applies only to a universal catastrophe. If the promise referred only to a local flood, it has been repeatedly broken every time there has been a destructive flood anywhere in the world. The local flood notion therefore not only charges Scripture with error, but maintains that God does not keep His promises![18]

Biblical Christians tread on dangerous ground when they allow so-called scientific difficulties to dilute this plain and emphatic Bible teaching of the historical fact of a universal flood in the days of Noah. Rejecting or neglecting this fact means rejection of not only the Genesis record but also the New Testament's testimony about that record.

On the other hand, acceptance of the Flood as universal immediately leads to scientific implications of profound importance. For instance, the waters for such a flood can only have come from either great upheavals of the ocean basins or from an atmospheric source entirely different from the grossly inadequate vapor content of the present atmosphere. The Scriptures attribute it to both sources. The torrential rains, continuing for 40 days and nights (Gen. 7:12), and in perhaps lesser intensity for 110 more days, in all probability resulted from condensation of the extensive vapor blanket implied by the "waters . . . above the firmament" of Genesis 1:6–8. The simultaneous breaking up of "all the fountains of the

---

18. The seven reasons listed are only a few out of many. In his commentary on Genesis, this writer has given one hundred biblical and scientific reasons why the Flood must be regarded as universal. See *The Genesis Record* (Grand Rapids, MI: Baker, 1976), p. 683–686.

great deep" (Gen. 7:11) undoubtedly involved volcanic and tectonic upheavals of the earth's crust and subterranean waters that continued for 150 days (Gen. 7:24; 8:2–3). This has been discussed in chapter 10.

The apostle Peter wrote that "the world that then was, being overflowed with water, perished." That "world," of which he spoke, included both the earth and the atmospheric heavens (2 Pet. 3:6), and they were evidently completely different from "the heavens and the earth, which are now" (2 Pet. 3:7). According to the Genesis record, not only man but also the earth was destroyed by the Flood (Gen. 6:13; 9:11). This destruction obviously did not mean annihilation, and therefore, must have meant some profound change in its surface and atmospheric features, its geography, hydrology, geology, meteorology, and so on.

Since there was simultaneously taking place an unprecedented destruction of living creatures of all kinds, it is quite certain that hosts of these animals, and plants as well, must have been entrapped and buried in the resulting sediments, later to become lithified and preserved as vast graveyards of fossils. This conclusion is further verified by the biblical record of the Edenic curse. The original creation was pronounced by God to be "very good," but when Adam sinned, God cursed the "ground" (earth) (Gen. 3:17; 5:29), thus introducing the principle of decay and death into the world. The plain implication of both this and the New Testament statements of Paul (Rom. 5:12; 8:20–22; 1 Cor. 15:21) is that death of sentient animal life, as well as human death, was nonexistent in the world before the Curse.

Thus, fossil remains of once living creatures — wherever found in the rocks of the earth — must have come from animals that died *after* man's fall. This can only mean that all fossiliferous deposits have been formed sometime within the span of human history. There seems, therefore, no better explanation for their existence in most cases than the Flood and its associated geological and hydraulic activities.

Consideration of the probable action of the flood waters and the sediments deposited by them leads to the conclusion that, at any given locality, the fossils deposited would tend to assume a certain peculiar order of superposition. That is, there would be a tendency for organisms of heavier specific weight, of simpler structure, of lower-elevation habitats, and of lesser capacity for swimming, running, or flying, to be entrapped earlier and buried deeper in the deluge sediments. More complex and active organisms, with upper-level habitats, would be buried later and higher, if at all. Many exceptions to these rules might be anticipated because of the catastrophic nature of the Flood, but this would certainly be the general order and is exactly what is found in the earth's fossil-bearing sediments. This phenomenon is treated more fully in chapter 12.

## Alternate Theories of Catastrophism

Recognition of the necessity of catastrophism as a legitimate geologic principle, however, of course opens the door to all kinds of imaginative catastrophist

and quasicatastrophist theories. The great advantage and strength of the uniformitarian concept always has been that geologic interpretations are thereby supposed to be developed within the limits of actual known geologic processes as
they exist at present. Even modern neocatastrophism attempts to limits its catastrophes to such as occasionally experienced during historic times.

An unrestrained catastrophism, however, has no such bounds. An arbitrary
catastrophe may be postulated to fit any kind of geologic feature or phenomenon,
and there is no way of scientifically proving or disproving the idea since it involves a nonreproducible event outside the scope of scientific observation or experimentation. The only restraint is the imagination of the theorizer and his ingenuity in adapting his proposed catastrophic mechanism to as wide a variety of
particular geologic features as possible and in making his idea sufficiently flexible
so as to inhibit its refutation through specific tests.

In 1950 Immanuel Velikovsky published the first of several widely publicized books developing a modern theory of catastrophism around the idea of a
series of encounters of the earth with large comets that later became planets. At
the time this aroused a veritable furor of antagonism among uniformitarian scientists, but in recent years a number of similar quasicatastrophic theories have been
published, some by members of the scientific establishment itself. Even Velikovsky's
ideas are now being taken more seriously by many scientists.

In this vein, there have been also the theory of Kelly and Dachille, emphasizing the effect of large meteorites on the earth's past history; the shifting-crust
theory of Charles Hapgood and Ivan Sanderson; the cosmic-encounter neo-
Velikovskian speculations of Donald Patten; the ice-cap hypothesis of Melvin Cook;
the wobbling-axis theory of H.A. Brown; the asteroid-bombardment notions of
J.L. Butler; and numerous other such theories. Most of these writers have added
significant and valuable evidence against uniformitarianism. Each has also been
able to point to a number of physiographic features that could be explained in
terms of the particular form of catastrophism he was championing. Among orthodox geologists, significant levels of support have also appeared in recent years
for such neocatastrophist concepts as shifting poles, drifting and colliding continents, asteroid and cometary encounters, widespread floods, rapid and drastic
changes in sea levels, accelerated orogenies, vast submarine landslides and turbidity flows, and many such phenomena. Catastrophic speculation has become
increasingly more acceptable in recent years and old-style uniformitarianism has
encountered more criticism.

The main trouble with catastrophist theories is that there is no way of sub-
jecting them to empirical testing. One can imagine all sorts of things that might
be accomplished by a wandering comet or shifting poles or swarms of asteroids
or whatever, but there is no way of proving it. Suppose there were ever-so-many
features that might possibly be understood in terms of, say, a trespassing planet
— that hardly constitutes that such an event actually occurred, or even could

occur. There seems to be no restraint on imagination or speculation when catastrophism is espoused, and this is one reason why it has been in such poor repute for over a hundred years.

And yet catastrophism, as we have seen, is necessary! It is not necessary to speculate, however, since the biblical record has provided a clear description of the causes, nature, and results of the true catastrophism. The Noahic flood is the only worldwide catastrophe mentioned and described in the Word of God and is abundantly adequate to account for all the earth's geological and physiographic evidences of catastrophism. Some have suggested the possibility of great geologic activity in the work of the third day of creation (Gen. 1:9–10), but this is uncertain in view of the "finished" nature of the divine activity during the creation period. We cannot verify the Flood experimentally, of course, any more than any of the various other theories of catastrophism, but we do not need experimental verification; God has recorded it in His Word, and that is sufficient.

Actually, catastrophism is not quite the proper word to use in regard to the Flood. A geological "catastrophe" is a natural event of high energy, brief duration, and wide extent, such as a great tidal wave or volcanic eruption. The apostle Peter called the destruction of Sodom and Gomorrah an "overthrow" (Greek *katastrophe*) in 2 Peter 2:6. But for the Flood he used the Greek word *kataklusmos*, from which we transliterate our English "cataclysm" (2 Pet. 2:5). Similarly, the Lord Jesus, speaking of the Flood, said: "The [cataclysm] came, and destroyed them all" (Luke 17:27). This word is never used of a great river flood or of any other kind of geologic catastrophe but solely of Noah's flood!

Thus, the biblical Flood was no local river overflow or any event of only regional significance, but rather a worldwide cataclysmic inundation that completely destroyed the antediluvian order. The true framework for interpretation of earth history is neither uniformitarianism nor catastrophism, but cataclysm-ism!

It is this fact, indeed, by which Peter refutes uniformitarianism, charging proponents of the latter with willful ignorance (2 Pet. 3:5). The clear testimony of the Scriptures to the universal Flood, supported by the worldwide evidence of the rapid burial of the fossils in the sedimentary rocks of the earth's crust, proves that evolutionary uniformitarianism and its purported explanation of "all things" in terms of processes that still "continue" is a false cosmology.[19]

## Hydraulic Deposition of the Strata

If the major geological formations of the earth's crust were really caused by the great Flood, there should be physical evidence as well as biblical evidence. Most of the earth's present sedimentary rock beds, especially those containing fossils, on which the evolutionary geologic-age system is based, do indeed give

---

19. See John C. Whitcomb and Henry M. Morris, *The Genesis Flood* (Philadelphia, NJ: Presbyterian and Reformed, 1961), p., 515 for a detailed discussion of the scriptural framework for historical geology.

much evidence of having been eroded, transported, and deposited by water. In fact, that is why they are called *sedimentary* rocks. Furthermore, as now widely recognized even by evolutionary geologists, these give evidence of rapid deposition and so provide prima facie evidence of flood flows, not quiet deposition in stationary bodies of water. As we shall see, these great sedimentation beds also show strong evidence of essentially contemporaneous, continuous deposition rather than intermittent deposition separated by long ages of quiescence.

To fully appreciate these evidences, one needs to have some understanding of the sciences of hydraulics and sedimentology. Modern-day hydraulic engineers and geohydrologists have made extensive theoretical, laboratory, and field investigations of the phenomena of water flow and sediment transport, and these studies provide valuable insights on the real nature of the geologic column. Not surprisingly, they are fully consistent with the biblical record of the great Flood, and fully inconsistent with traditional uniformitarianism.

As noted in the preceding chapter, hydrology is the science that deals with the phenomena of the earth's natural waters and their distribution, especially in the forms of precipitation, streamflow, and groundwater. Hydraulics is the study of the forces, velocities, and frictional resistances associated with flowing fluids.

One of the most important functions of the earth's natural waters is that of erosion, transportation, and deposition of sediments. Mechanics of sedimentation phenomena control formation and development of river systems. Rivers not only carry the waters back to the ocean whence they came, but also serve to carry off large quantities of sediment eroded from their drainage basins, depositing them finally along their flood plains or in deltas near their mouths. Deltaic sediments are gradually reworked by wave action and by littoral currents until finally deposited more or less permanently along the continental shelves and slopes. Thus, land surfaces are gradually cut down and ocean basins filled.

These sedimentation processes are highly important to both the geologist and the hydraulic engineer. Most geologic processes involve water in one way or another, but the processes of sedimentation are by far the most important, since most of the earth's land surface consists of sediments, either still loose and unconsolidated or else compacted and hardened into sedimentary rocks. In order to understand and explain geologic formations and phenomena, therefore, the geologist should have a thorough understanding of the processes of sedimentation.

The hydraulic engineer has a more immediate and practical need for such knowledge. He is concerned with the silting-up of canals, reservoirs, and harbors; with the stability of structures built along river channels; with erosion of valuable lands; with bank caving and channel shifting in alluvial rivers; and with numerous other practical and costly problems associated with the hydraulics of sedimentation as connected with the design of hydraulic structures and systems.

Hydraulic engineers, therefore, have been engaged for many years in intensive laboratory and analytical studies dealing with the processes of sedimenta-

OVERFLOWED WITH WATER                    297

tion. These phenomena are extremely complex, but much has been learned and will continue to be learned concerning them.

It is obvious that even the 29 percent of the earth's surface that is dry land has in the past been covered with water and that most of the rocks on the surface were originally laid down by moving water. Rock formations are usually classified as igneous, metamorphic, or sedimentary, with the latter formed primarily by deposition of sediments out of water after transportation from some source area. It is significant that most surface rocks are sedimentary rocks. "By volume, sedimentary rocks are about one-tenth as abundant as igneous rocks in the earth's crust; but when it comes to the rocks exposed at the earth's surface, sedimentary rocks or sediments, as they are sometimes called, cover nearly three-fourths of the land surface."[20]

Furthermore, many of the igneous rocks at the earth's surface are underlain by sedimentary rocks, upon which they flowed after eruption through volcanic vents or fissures. Similarly, many of the metamorphic rocks at the surface represent rocks that once were sedimentary rocks (e.g., marble transformed from limestone by processes of metamorphism).

It is evident that the water that at some time covered the earth's surface was profoundly effective in the very formation of rocks themselves as well as the surface features of the earth's physiography. The question is whether the sedimentary processes were slow or rapid, and whether they were intermittent or continuous. This is the traditional conflict between evolutionary uniformitarianism and biblical creationism.

For example (and this is obviously the example most pertinent to our present discussion), sediment erosion, transportation, and deposition is a process that may take place very slowly or exceedingly rapidly. A very large number of variables go into the determination of sedimentation rates. An incomplete list would include:

1. *Hydraulic factors*, such as channel slope, shape, and size; quantity of water available; roughness of channel bed and sides; variability of water flow; and water temperature.
2. *Topographic factors*, such as shape and size of watershed, slope, and aspect of the terrain, nature of the soil and its vegetal cover, tributary network, and groundwater conditions.
3. *Meteorological factors*, such as frequency and intensity of storm rainfall, direction of air mass movements, and duration of rainfall.
4. *Sedimentary factors*, such as size, shape, variability, specific gravity, and chemical character of the sediment being transported.

Other influences could be added, but even this list will indicate how futile it would be to try to establish any kind of average rate of sedimentation, and then to

---

20. James H. Zumberge, *Elements of Geology*, 2nd ed. (New York, NY: John Wiley and Sons, 1963), p. 44.

extrapolate such a rate for hundreds of millions of years into the past to try to explain the immense sedimentary formations of the earth's crust! There is no *a priori* reason whatever why rapid (or catastrophic) formation of these beds would not provide as satisfactory an explanation — and as fully in accord with the assumptions of uniform natural law — as would slow deposition over millions of years.

In principle, one would think it should be possible by induction to examine the character of a given sedimentary deposit; and therefrom to determine (1) the nature of the source area from which the sediment had been eroded initially, (2) the magnitude and nature of the water flow which had transported it, and (3) the character and extent of the basin into which it had finally been dropped. In actuality, however, owing to the excessive number of variables which may have contributed to the phenomenon, as above enumerated, it is normally quite impossible to make such extrapolations with any degree of assurance.

A great many studies have been made in laboratory flumes, and in a smaller number of actual streams, of rates of sediment transport. Numerous empirical formulas have been derived and some have been employed with fair success in engineering problems. One of the simplest of these formulas is the following:[21]

$$G_S = \frac{1.36\, W\, V^4\, n^3}{k^3 d^1 \cdot {}^5 D\, (10^{15})} \tag{1}$$

In this formula, $G_S$ represents the total number of pounds of sediment being transported each second past any given point in the stream. $W$ is the stream width, $V$ is the velocity of flow in feet per second, and $n$ is the channel roughness coefficient, which measures the hydraulic resistance to flow. The depth of flow, in feet, is $D$, and the diameter of sediment particles is $d$, also in feet. The effect of temperature is measured by the kinematic viscosity of the water, $k$. Typical values of $k$ and $n$ might be, respectively, about 0.00001 square feet per second and 0.35, although they can vary over a wide range.

The formula applies only to a uniform channel with flow at constant velocity for sediment composed predominantly of sand grains of only one size. Even with these limitations it is able to give only approximate answers. Many formulas attempt to distinguish between the suspended sediment load, the saltation (rolling and bouncing) load, and the bed load. Also, depending upon the velocity and other factors, the form of dunes on the bed may change materially, thus changing the hydraulic roughness and modifying the flow.

The problem, of course, is compounded if any of the factors become nonuniform.

---

21. For a discussion of the background of this equation, as well as other methods used in sediment calculations, see Henry M. Morris and James M. Wiggert, *Applied Hydraulics in Engineering* (New York, NY: John Wiley and Sons, 1972), p. 448–467. This textbook for senior and graduate courses in hydraulics and hydrology, used at one time in at least 75 colleges and universities, had been continually in print from 1963 to 2001, an unusual record for an engineering textbook.

If there is a change in the channel cross section, velocity, or roughness, or if the sediment is of varying sizes, then it becomes almost impossible to make calculations of sediment transport that are quantitatively accurate, although it may be possible to determine whether there will be scour or deposition.

And calculations become necessarily still more complex if nonequilibrium conditions exist — that is, if material is being eroded or deposited instead of simply transported. It is thus quite clear that any truly quantitative understanding of the processes and rates of sediment deposition, even in the environments of the present, is still far from being attained.

However, one very important inference can be derived from the above formula: if any one of the variables (e.g., flow velocity) changes, then the sediment quantity also changes. This means that the sedimentary stratum (i.e., "layer") being deposited will be terminated and a new stratum initiated. Thus, in any given formation composed of a series of parallel strata, each individual stratum represents a uniform sedimentation process and therefore a constant set of flow variables. In any actual flow situation, however, such uniform conditions usually persist only for a few minutes or hours before at least one of the variables changes. Consequently, each stratum probably was formed in a matter of minutes or hours. As long as successive strata are parallel and similar in structure and composition, the deposition process itself was evidently continuous, which would mean, therefore, that the entire formation was laid down in a period of a few days at the most.

Practically every local geologic column is composed of a relatively small number of stratified sedimentary rock formations, and it is certainly reasonable to conclude that each formation in every region was laid down rapidly — which means catastrophically. No wonder, therefore, that modern geologists are reluctantly returning to catastrophism as the necessary explanation of the great sedimentary rock beds of the earth. This is certainly the testimony of the hydraulic processes that produced them.

## Other Evidences of Hydraulic Catastrophism

In addition to the evidence from sedimentation hydraulics, there are many other indications of catastrophism in the geologic column, often more obvious than the rather subtle and technical testimony of hydraulic processes. The latter is more pervasive and fundamental, but there are others that are more striking. A few of these are discussed below.

### Fossil Graveyards

It is well known that when a living organism dies, especially one of the larger animals, its remains soon disappear because of the efficiency of scavenger organisms and the decay processes that immediately go to work on it. Yet in the earth's sedimentary rocks there are buried vast numbers of plants and animals of all kinds, often in great fossil "cemeteries," where thousands, even millions, of organisms may be found crushed together and buried by the sediments. Even after centuries of collecting great quantities of fossils all over the world, new "graveyards" continue to be found.[22]

It is a matter of the most elementary scientific logic to recognize that phenomena such as these must be attributed to very rapid burial and rapid subsequent lithification, or otherwise they could never have been preserved. And since most such fossil graveyards have been buried in water-laid sediments, they clearly give witness to the fact of aqueous catastrophism.

## Polystrate Fossils

Stratification (or layered sequence) is a universal characteristic of sedimentary rocks. As noted above, a stratum of sediment is formed by deposition under essentially continuous and uniform hydraulic conditions. When the sedimentation stops for a while before another period of deposition, the new stratum will be visibly distinguishable from the earlier by a stratification line (actually a surface). Distinct strata also result when there is a change in the velocity of flow or other hydraulic characteristics. Sedimentary beds as now found are typically composed of many "strata," and it is in such beds that most fossils are found.

Not infrequently, large fossils[23] of animals and plants — especially tree trunks — extend through several strata, often 20 feet or more in thickness. Dutch geologist N.A. Rupke has suggested that these be called "polystrate fossils" and has documented[24] numerous remarkable examples of this phenomenon. Note figure 23.

It is beyond question that this type of fossil must have been buried quickly or it would not have been preserved intact while the strata accumulated around it. And since the strata entombing these polystrate fossils are no different in appearance of composition from other strata, it is obvious that neither was there any significant difference in the rapidity of deposition.

## Ephemeral Markings

Another evidence of very rapid deposition is the preservation of what Rupke[25] calls "ephemeral markings." These constitute a special type of fossil originally formed as a transient marking on the surface of a recently deposited layer of sediment. These include such phenomena as ripple marks, rain prints, worm trails, and bird and reptile tracks.

It is a matter of common observation that such fragile structures, once formed,

---

22. A typical example is described by W.W. Dalquest and S.H. Mammay: "The remains of 400 or more Permian amphibians were found in a series of siltstone channels confined to an area 50 feet square. . . . The fossils are mostly or entirely of heavy-bodied, weak-limbed forms that probably could not walk about on land." "A Remarkable Concentration of Permian Amphibian Remains in Haskell County, Texas," *Journal of Geology*, 71 (Sept. 1963): 641.
23. N.A. Rupke, "Prolegomena to a Study of Cataclysmal Sedimentation?" *Creation Research Society Quarterly*, 3, no. 1 (May 1966): 16–37.
24. Ibid., p. 21–25.
25. Ibid., p. 25–29.

### Figure 23 — Polystrate Fossils

*One of the most obvious proofs of rapid deposition of the sedimentary rocks is the frequent occurrence of polystrate fossils (that is, fossils extending through numerous successive strata). Polystrate fossils cutting through many coal seams, for example, clearly show that such coal deposits were not formed by the slow accumulation of peat deposits in swamps, as evolutionists have claimed.*

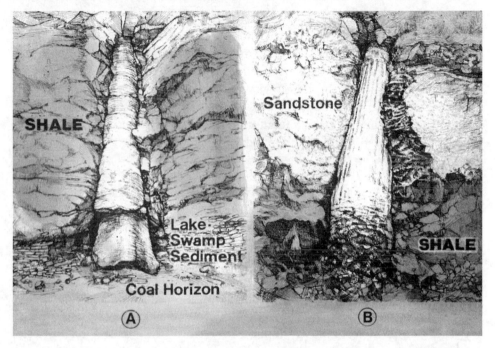

are very quickly obliterated by subsequent wind or air currents or by later erosion and sedimentation. The only way they could be preserved is by means of abnormally rapid burial (without concurrent erosion), plus abnormally rapid lithification.

It would indeed be difficult, it not impossible, to point to examples of such fossils in the process of formation at present. Sudden burial by turbidity currents is frequently suggested. For example, Adolf Seilacher, Geologisches Institut University of Frankfurt, Germany, says, "The postdepositional sole trails of Flysch psammites occur only in thinner beds up to a thickness particular to each species. This proves instantaneous deposition of the individual beds as postulated by the turbidity-current theory. The majority of the sole trails are predepositional mud burrows washed out and sand cast by turbidity currents. Thus, erosion of an unusual type must have preceded every turbidite sedimentation."[26]

The remarkable fact is that ephemeral markings of this type are found in great abundance in the ancient sedimentary rocks of practically all of the so-called

26. A. Seilacher, "Paleontological Studies on Turbidite Sedimentation and Erosion," *Journal of Geology*, 70 (Mar. 1962): 227.

geologic ages, including the most ancient. Furthermore, they appear equally fresh when exposed in the present time, regardless of what the particular geologic age is supposed to be, whether Proterozoic or Tertiary or anywhere in between. Only an overwhelming catastrophic sedimentary phenomenon can account for these markings and their preservation.

## Preservation of Soft Parts

Numerous instances are known where the fossil remains do not consist of petrification or molds or the like, but where the actual soft tissues of the organism have been preserved. This is true even in very "ancient" strata, and often such fossils are found massed together in large numbers.[27] Not only do these deposits speak plainly of very rapid burial by the sediments, but they also make the contention that they have remained unaffected by decay and erosion for many millions of years exceedingly difficult to believe.

## Phenomena of Stratification

Not only do the fossils contained in the sedimentary strata demonstrate the necessity of catastrophic deposition, but the very strata themselves indicate this. As already noted, most of the earth's surface is covered with sediments or sedimentary rocks, originally deposited under moving water. This in itself is prima facie evidence that powerful waters once covered the earth. Furthermore, even under modern conditions most sedimentary deposits are the result of brief, intense periods of flood run-off, rather than slow, uniform silting.

Laboratory evidence that a typical sedimentary deposit may form quite rapidly is found in the work of Alan Jopling at Harvard, who made a long series of studies on delta-type deposition in a laboratory flume and then applied the results to the analysis of a small delta outwash deposit, supposedly formed about 13,000 years ago. His conclusion was as follows: "It may be concluded therefore that the time required for the deposition of the entire delta deposit amounted to several days. . . . Based on the computed rate of delta advance and the thickness of individual laminae, the average time for the deposition of a lamina must have been several minutes."[28]

A number of significant laboratory flume studies on strata formation were later made by Guy Berthault of France,[29] many of them in the large hydraulic laboratory at Colorado State University. He also found that relatively large strati-

---

27. See *The Genesis Flood* by John C. Whitcomb Jr., and Henry M. Morris (p. 159–60) for a discussion of various examples of this phenomenon.
28. Alan V. Jopling, "Some Principles and Techniques Used in Reconstructing the Hydraulic Parameters of a Paleo-Flow Regime," *Journal of Sedimentary Petrology,* 36 (Mar. 1960): 34.
29. Guy Berthault, "Experiments on Lamination of Sediments," *Creation Ex Nihilo Technical Journal,* 3, no. 1 (1988): 25–29; Guy Berthault, "Genesis and Historical Geology," *Creation Ex Nihilo Technical Journal,* 12, no. 2 (1998): 213–217.

fied beds could be formed quickly, with successive strata formed continuously and without intervening periods of erosion or quiescence. There remains no reason at all to accept the notion that a given geologic formation containing many stratified layers took a long period of time to form. Instead, it was probably formed very rapidly, even catastrophically, in a matter of days at most.

The testimony of the eruption of Mount St. Helens in 1980, along with its ongoing effects in subsequent months and years, has provided striking proof that brief geologic catastrophes can produce geologic features resembling those in the geologic column that had been interpreted as requiring long ages to form. For example, extensive sediment layers, individually very thin but adding up to large thicknesses in total, were laid down in a matter of days and hardened into sedimentary rock in just a few years. These and many other phenomena developed rapidly, but they now give a superficial appearance of great age. These remarkable facts are summarized in two ICR publications, and research is still continuing.[30]

The fact that many sedimentary formations in the stratigraphic column consist of gravel or conglomerate, or even boulders, is further testimony to hydraulic activity of high intensity, as is the frequent occurrence of "cross-bedding" phenomena, indicating rapidly changing current directions.

## Alluvial Valleys

Practically all modern rivers course through valleys that once carried far greater volumes of water than they do now. This is indicated not only by the universal presence of old river terraces high on the valley walls but even more by the vast amounts of sand and gravel lying beneath the present flood plains that now fill what were formerly the stream channels.

> Subsurface explorations of meandering valleys in the Driftless Area of Wisconsin, by means of a refraction seismograph, reveal large filled channels similar to those previously determined in English rivers where the augering technique was used. The channels are asymmetrical in cross profile and attain their greatest depths at valley bends. In cross-sectional area at probable bankfull they are some 25 times as large as the present stream channels.[31]

This sort of thing is practically universal. The Mississippi Valley, for example, consists of alluvial deposits extending to depths of six hundred feet. All of this indicates that the rivers of the world, in very recent times (probably during and after the continental uplifts terminating the year of the Flood) carried tremendous volumes of water and sediment.

---

30. Steven A. Austin, "Mount St. Helens and Catastrophism," Institute for Creation Research *Impact* Article 175 (1986); John D. Morris, *The Young Earth* (Green Forest, AR: Master Books, 1994), p. 103, 107, 115–117.

31. G.H. Dury, "Results of Seismic Explorations of Meandering Valleys," *American Journal of Science*, 260 (Nov. 1962): 691.

## Incised Meanders

Another universal characteristic of alluvial streams is the phenomenon of meandering. Many analytical and experimental studies have been made to determine the cause and mechanics of meandering, but these have been only partially successful. It is well accepted, however, that stream meandering requires relatively mild stream gradients and easily eroded banks. If the slopes are steep and the sides resistant, then erosion will occur primarily at the beds and the stream will cut down essentially vertically, forming a canyon section.

Most remarkable, therefore, are the intricate meandering patterns found frequently incised in deep gorges in high plateau and mountainous areas. These would seem to defy any explanation in terms of the ordinary hydraulics of rivers, and geologists' suggestions (superposed meanders, for example) seem to be oblivious of such hydraulics.

Clearly, some kind of catastrophic origin is indicated. Great regions of horizontal sedimentary beds, still relatively soft and erosible when uplifted following the Deluge, riven by great fissures during the uplift process, possibly provide a realistic model of conditions suitable for formation of these structures. The initial cracks could have been rapidly widened and deepened into the present meandering gorges as great volumes of water were being rapidly drained off the rising plateaus.

There are numerous other evidences of catastrophism in the earth's sedimentary crust, and more are being reported in almost every issue of various creationist journals. Dr. John Morris has discussed a number of these in his book *The Young Earth*.[32] These evidences include the following, among others.

1. *Lack of Soil Layers*: If there had been many geological ages, each age should have been marked by a layer of soil. But fossil soil layers and even soil materials are seldom, if ever, found. The so-called "underclays" in coal beds have been shown not to be true soils at all.

2. *Undisturbed Bedding Planes*: Not only in regularly stratified beds, but even at the interface between great formations, there is little if any evidence of weathering features that develop on bedding planes today. Most contacts between formations are almost knife-edge sharp, showing there could have been no great passage of time between them.

3. *Soft-Sediment Deformation*: The existence of complex bending and even overturning of stratified formations is fairly common everywhere, indicating much internal stress in the earth's crust in the past. This must have occurred in most cases while the sediments were still soft and plastic. Otherwise, if they had already hardened into rock (and that process normally requires only a few years at most) the rocks would have become brittle and then broken, rather than retaining their stratigraphic integrity and sequences.

---

32. Morris, *The Young Earth*, p. 93–112.

4. *Clastic Dykes*: A "dyke" is a vertical wall-like structure. A clastic dyke, as distinct from igneous dykes, is composed usually of sandstone, apparently formed by upwelling of sandstone material into cracks in a limestone bed, and coming from a sandstone formation beneath the limestone. However, for this to occur, the material in the dykes must have been a newly deposited and still unconsolidated sandy mud deposited below the limestone.

## Evidence of a Single Depositional Epoch

The above is not of course a complete, but only a representative, list of evidences of aqueous catastrophism. Igneous and metamorphic rocks likewise yield many evidences of rapid formation.

It can be said that, in general, catastrophism provides an adequate framework of interpretation for most, and probably all, the features of the known geologic column. Uniformitarianism, on the other hand, seems utterly inadequate to account for any of them satisfactorily.

As one geologist expressed it:

> Even the most staid of modern geologists are invoking sedimentary surges, explosive phases of organic evolution, volcanic blackouts, continental collisions and terrifying meteoroid impacts. We live in an age of neo-catastrophism.[33]

There is one question, however. Even though admitting the validity of the concept of aqueous catastrophism to explain many of the geologic phenomena, as many geologists readily are doing today, there is still almost universal resistance to the idea of one, single, cataclysmic epoch such as described in the Bible. Historical geologists still prefer a general framework of uniformitarianism and great ages, even though they are willing to recognize any number of intense and widespread floods and other local catastrophes occurring within that framework.

Thus, the question is whether the numerous evidences of catastrophic sedimentation, including those discussed in the preceding pages, were caused by one great cataclysm or by a great number of lesser catastrophes.

If it were not for the religious implications, and were it only a matter of seeking a logical explanation of the actual physical data, the application of the principle of Occam's Razor (which cautions against the unnecessary multiplication of hypotheses) would lead quickly to a decision in favor of the one great cataclysm.

To insist instead that there have been great numbers of geologic catastrophes (in all parts of the world and through all the aeons of geologic time) sufficient to explain the many evidences of catastrophism; and further knowing (1) that many of these catastrophes must have been far greater than anything ever observed in the modern world, and (2) that uniformitarianism is inad-

---

33. Gordon L.H. Davies, "Bangs Replace Whimpers," *Nature*, 365 (September 9, 1993): 115.

equate to incorporate them within any kind of experimentally quantitative frame-work, would surely seem to suggest a strong religious bias against the concept of the biblical record of the great Deluge and favoring an evolutionary interpreta-tion of history.

The various evidences for hydraulic catastrophism cited previously — the fossil graveyards, polystrate fossils, ephemeral markings, and others — are gener-ally found more or less indiscriminately among strata throughout the entire geo-logic column. There is no evidence of progressive change in the characteristics of catastrophism throughout the supposed geologic ages, such as should be expected in response to changing climatic and geophysical regimes as postulated through-out the earth's evolution. Sedimentary deposits of the Proterozoic era have essen-tially the same physical characteristics as those of the Tertiary or any others, the only significant difference being the fossil assemblages, especially the index fos-sils, contained in them.

And of course, the fossil assemblages themselves are better explained in terms of aqueous cataclysm than of evolutionary uniformitarianism. They are supposed to show increasing complexity (and therefore evolution) with the passage of geo-logic time, but this interpretation is belied by the fact of the great gaps between all the major kinds of creatures in the fossil record, which are essentially the same as the gaps between the same kinds of plants and animals in the modern world.

The fact that, in general, the fossils are found segregated into assemblages of similar sizes and shapes is exactly what would be expected as a result of diluvial processes, since turbulent water is a highly effective "sorting" agent. In his flume studies at Harvard, Jopling found that even when the flows were steady and uni-form and the sediments transported were randomly mixed to begin with, the flow would sort them out. "Segregation invariably occurs even when uniform conditions of sediment transport prevail, and where the various size grades of the sediment have been thoroughly mixed to begin with. This segregation occurs on either a plane, rippled, or duned bed, and it is evident in both the transverse and longitudinal direction."[34]

This sorting action is basically produced because the amount of hydrody-namic "lift and drag" forces on immersed objects are directly related to the size and shape of the objects. The same applies, of course, to objects falling vertically through water, so that objects that are simpler in shape (and thus, supposedly more "primitive") would tend to settle out of a decelerating flow more rapidly and be buried more deeply than would objects of complex geometry. This ten-dency would be further augmented by the fact that these simpler organisms (shells, for example) normally are of somewhat greater specific gravity than "higher" or-ganisms.

Other things being equal, since the simpler organisms dwell at lower eleva-

---

34.  Alan V. Jopling, "Laboratory Study of Sorting Processes Related to Flow Separation," *Journal of Geophysical Research*, 69 (Aug. 15, 1964).

tions, it would be expected that they would be buried at lower elevations. And still further, the mobility of animals is rather closely related to their complexity, so that higher animals would escape burial for longer periods.

All of these factors would contribute toward the preservation of fossils in the Flood sediments in just the order in which they are now usually found, whereas the usual evolutionary interpretation is obviously inadequate. These phenomena are discussed further in chapter 12.

These three factors — hydraulic, ecologic, and physiologic — would of course tend to act only statistically, rather than absolutely, so that the numerous exceptions to the usual order that have been found are not particularly surprising. They are an embarrassment to the evolutionist, however, since fossils in the wrong stratigraphic order would indicate a reversal of evolution and thus completely upset the assignment of geologic ages.

It is typical of evolutionary reasoning that such anomalies and contradictions can never be allowed to bring into question the basic assumption of evolution. Consequently, a further multiplication of hypotheses is employed, invoking the possibility of great earth movements as a means of explaining how the fossiliferous strata have been rearranged into the "wrong" order. Vast horizontal "thrust faults" by which great thicknesses of sedimentary strata have been uplifted and then translated horizontally over the adjacent regions, have typically been offered as mechanisms explaining the many areas where "ancient" fossil-bearing formations have been found on top of "recent" formations.

It is interesting that another hydraulic principle has been employed to explain how such movements are possible, since it is well known that ordinary mechanical sliding, even if the sliding planes were lubricated, would be physically impossible on such a large scale without completely destroying the structural integrity of the sliding formations. A common explanation is that the thrust block was "floated" into place by abnormally high internal fluid pressures along the thrust plane.

These pressures, in order to be effective, would have to be far higher than in ordinary ground water and are supposedly caused by compression of water trapped in the sedimentary interstices when the sediments were originally deposited. That is, as the original sediments were gradually compressed and lithified, the "connate water" contained in the soil pores was somehow sealed off from any possible escape channels and was eventually so compressed as to develop elastic pressures capable of actually lifting and "floating" the huge rock overburden above it.

This is indeed a remarkable speculation. The "seal" around the sides of the thrust blocks (not infrequently hundreds or thousands of square miles in extent) must have been quite elastic itself, permitting great vertical and horizontal motions of the block and yet preventing any escape of the highly compressed water in the process. In a cogent analysis of this idea, Platt has pointed out:

Obviously an important factor is the quality of the seal that forms in the clay or shale. No matter how small the permeability in the relatively impermeable layer that effectively seals the connate water beneath the thick sequence, some leakage does occur. . . . Hence, if the fluid support is to be available to "float" the rocks, the thrust movement must occur soon (geologically) after the deposition of the final weight of the thick sediments. If the delay is sufficient, the seal of shale becomes very good, but there is no fluid left to seal off.[35]

This requirement for early flotation of the block, suggested by Platt, of course, is at cross purposes with the long period of time supposedly required for compression and lithification of the sediments before the fluid could develop the required pressures. The even more important problem of how the necessary seal could be maintained during the period of thrust action is not mentioned at all.

A number of more recent writers[36] have raised still further objections to the fluid-flotation overthrust concept. It now seems almost impossible to devise any physically plausible mechanism that would allow great blocks of "old" rocks to move up and on top of "young" rocks, at least on the large scale of the great "overthrusts" of the world. The Alps, the Appalachians, much of the Rockies, the Cascades, and other great mountain ranges of the world are supposed to be in this upside-down condition (as based on the inferred geologic ages of the rock formations involved) and yet there is no way this could have been accomplished, except possibly by some unknown type of catastrophic convulsion. Of course, if the rocks are all of essentially the same age anyhow, as the Bible would indicate, along with the other evidences cited, there is no problem!

Another evidence of contemporaneity is the geological trade secret of anomalous fossils — that is, fossils from one evolutionary "age" found mixed with fossils from another age. This is a fairly common phenomenon but is usually either ignored or explained away as a case of "reworking" or "displacement," whereby fossils somehow migrate from where they were deposited to where they are found!

> We define stratigraphic disorder as the departure from perfect chronological order of fossils in a stratigraphic sequence. Any sequence in which an older fossil occurs above a younger one is stratigraphically disordered. Scales of stratigraphic disorder may be from millimeters to many meters. . . . stratigraphic disorder at some scale is probably a common feature of the fossil record.[37]

It has already been shown that there is no truly objective means of determin-

---

35. Lucien B. Platt, "Fluid Pressure in Thrust Faulting, A Corollary," *American Journal of Science,* 260 (Feb. 1962): 107.

36. See, for example, P.L. Guth, K.V. Hodges, and J.H. Willemin, "Limitations on the Role of Pore Pressure in Gravity Gliding," *Geological Society of America Bulletin,* 93 (July 1982): 606–12, with the many relevant references cited in this paper.

37. Alan H. Cutler and Karl W. Plessa, "Fossils Out of Sequence: Computer Simulations and Strategies for Dealing with Stratigraphic Disorder," *Palaios,* 5 (June 1990): 227.

ing the geologic age of a rock. That is, the age is estimated by the fossils on the basis of their assumed stage of evolution, but the only evidence for evolution is the supposed evolutionary sequence of fossils during the geologic ages. Such circularity and redundancy is brought into further question by the anomalous fossils and flat upside-down age sequences in the so-called overthrusts.

Furthermore, rocks of all types, minerals of all types, metals of all types, structures of all types, and coal and oil are found in rocks of all ages. Many old rocks look young and many young rocks look old, as far as hardness and density are concerned. All types of age sequences and age omissions are found in the various local geologic columns around the world.

In other words, there is no real way to be sure that any given rock formation is older or younger than any other rock formation. Radiometric dating has many fallacies, as noted in chapter 9; and when (as is more often the case than not) it disagrees with the assigned geologic age, the latter always governs (after all, it is based on evolution!). Therefore, for all we can determine otherwise, all the rocks could well be the same age, all formed at the same time. Finally, since each of them was formed rapidly in some kind of geologic catastrophe, they could all have been formed in different phases of the same great worldwide hydraulic cataclysm.

This implication is all but conclusively confirmed when it is realized that there is no worldwide unconformity in the entire geologic record, except at its very base,[38] and except for Pleistocene and other local post-Flood deposits. An unconformity is an erosion surface interfacing between two formations whose strata are not "conformable" with each other. It, therefore, represents a gap in time of unknown duration, between the deposition of the formations below and above. Study figure 24. At best, of course, as mentioned earlier (under "Undisturbed Bedding Planes") it is highly unlikely that any great time could have elapsed between the deposition of the two formations.

It is such unconformities that must provide the long ages between periods of "episodic sedimentation" that produced the actual formations of the so-called geologic column, if the geologic-age system is to be maintained. But, since there is no worldwide unconformity, there is no worldwide time gap in the fossiliferous column. Finally, since every unit in the column represents at least a local catastrophe, and since there is no worldwide time gap, therefore all the local catastrophes must be connected and, therefore, continuous.

In other words, one could start at the bottom of the geologic column — anywhere in the world — and then trace his way up to the surface without ever crossing an unconformity. Whenever he encountered a local unconformity, he would merely have to move laterally to some location where the formation graded

---

38. Between the time of the Genesis Curse (Gen. 3:17–19) and the Genesis Flood, the absence of rainfall and other related phenomena would have inhibited the formation of fossil-bearing sedimentary rocks. If any pre-Flood strata had been formed, they would almost certainly have been eroded away by the violence of the Flood phenomena.

*FIGURE 24 — **Worldwide Continuity of Sedimentary Deposition***
*Since there are no worldwide unconformities (erosion surfaces, representing interruptions in the deposition process, and therefore time gaps), there are no worldwide time gaps represented in the geologic column. Since each stratum, as well as each formation, was formed rapidly, the entire column represents an epoch of continuous, rapid, hydraulic deposition of the rocks of the earth's crust.*

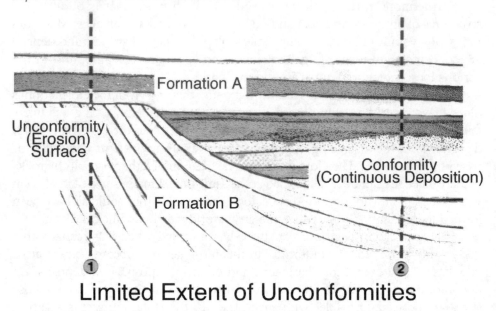

## Limited Extent of Unconformities

*(Formation B, originally horizontal, is uplifted and tilted at section 1, rising above the water surface. At section 2, the deposition process continues uninterrupted, leaving unconformity only at section 1.)*

into another higher formation without an unconformity, and then proceed upward. This would always be possible since no local unconformity extends all around the world. Along such a trace, the deposition process would have been continuous and, since every particular formation is the product of catastrophe, the whole series must represent a continuous series of catastrophes without a time break. A similar process could be followed by starting at any other point on the base of the geologic column. Thus, the entire geologic record represents a vast complex of "local" catastrophes, all interconnected and continuous, the whole thus compromising a worldwide hydraulic cataclysm, in which, as the apostle Peter said, "the world that then was, being overflowed with water, perished" (2 Pet. 3:6).

It should be understood that the very broad field of biblical geology could only be treated in an introductory fashion in a single chapter. The actual data and processes of geology are the same to both biblical creationists and evolutionary uniformitarians, but the interpretations of those data in a historical context are vastly different. Since geology has been so thoroughly oriented toward evolution and great ages over the last hundred years, and since the data of geology are so numerous and so variable, the reorientation of all these data within the context of the true biblical framework (that is, a recent creation and a worldwide cataclysmic flood) will demand a tremendous amount of future study and research by many creationist scientists. In the meantime, a much more detailed discussion of this broad subject can be found in *The Genesis Flood*, a book co-authored by Dr. John C. Whitcomb and this writer.[39] Also, many important articles on different aspects of flood geology can be found in the various issues of the *Creation Research Society Quarterly*, published continually since 1964, as well as in numerous other books and journal articles (see chapter 11 bibliography).

Even though many problems remain to be solved, the broad and basic considerations outlined in this chapter do at least show that the biblical model of earth history fits the facts of geology far better than the standard model of evolutionary geology can ever do. With further research, the remaining questions will eventually be answered within the framework of that model.

---

39. John C. Whitcomb and Henry M. Morris, *The Genesis Flood* (Philadelphia, PA: Presbyterian and Reformed, 1961), 518 p.

# 12

# FOSSILS AND THE FLOOD

*Biblical Paleontology*

Unlike the other sciences we have been dealing with, there are no specific biblical references to the science of paleontology, the study of fossils. There do seem to be a number of references to certain extinct animals that are now known only by their fossil remains (e.g., dinosaurs), but the Bible writers make no mention of fossils as such. For all we can tell, people in Bible times may not even have known there were such things.

Nevertheless, fossils are of prime importance in any study of the Bible and science because of the key role they have played in earth history and because of their central position in the creation/evolution conflict. The fossil record is often claimed to be the main evidence for evolution, supposedly documenting the evolutionary changes in living creatures throughout the geological ages. Creationists, on the other hand, believe that fossils speak of death, and therefore of sin and judgment, most of them having been buried at the time of the great Flood.

Does the fossil record depict the evolution of life over many ages or the destruction of life in one age? That is the vitally important question we consider in this chapter.

In the preceding chapter we examined some of the many biblical and geological evidences for the universal Flood of the Bible, showing that it actually occurred just as recorded there. The real geological column is thus primarily a record of the great Flood, not of the slow accumulation of sediments gradually developed over many ages. For the sake of discussion, however, we can still use the terminology of the standard column and its supposed geological ages as we consider the actual data of paleontology.

## The Problem of the Fossil Gaps

Now even if we take the geological ages at face value, all the way from the Cambrian period of the Paleozoic era to the Pleistocene epoch of the Cenozoic era, the remarkable fact is that there is still not the slightest evidence for evolution in the fossil record. That is, out of all the billions of fossils known and documented in the rocks of the earth's crust — fossils in tremendous variety, representing both extinct and living kinds — there is not a single true transitional evolutionary sequence that has yet been excavated anywhere in the world.

Creationists, of course, have been stressing this fact for many years, but evolutionists — especially the neo-Darwinians — have been teaching the doctrine of slow and gradual evolutionary change for so long that most people have simply assumed that the fossils actually document these imaginary great evolutionary changes of the past. But there are no such transitional fossils, and this fact has finally been acknowledged today even by evolutionary paleontologists. Stephen Jay Gould of Harvard is perhaps the leading representative of this modern school of paleontologists. He makes the following admission: "All paleontologists know that the fossil record contains precious little in the way of intermediate forms; transitions between major groups are characteristically abrupt."[1]

Gould and his colleague Niles Eldredge of the American Museum of Natural History have popularized the concept of what they call "punctuated equilibrium" as a better model of evolution than the "slow-and-gradual" concept of the neo-Darwinists: "Thus, our model of 'punctuated equilibria' holds that evolution is concentrated in events of speciation and that successful speciation is an infrequent event punctuating the stasis of large populations that do not alter in fundamental ways during the millions of years that they endure."[2]

Note that these gaps are said by Gould to apply both to "transitions between major groups" and also to "events of speciation." That is, there are no gradual transitions even between species, let alone the higher categories.

Another leading modern paleontologist is Steven Stanley of Johns Hopkins University. He makes the following observation: "Established species are evolving so slowly that major transitions between genera and higher taxa must be occurring within small, rapidly evolving populations that leave no legible fossil record."[3]

This is a remarkable state of affairs. Evolution is supposed to deal with *change* in organisms, and yet the main factor in evolution is "stasis," which means *no change*!

---

1. Stephen Jay Gould, "The Return of Hopeful Monsters," *Natural History,* 76 (June–July 1977): 24.
2. Stephen Jay Gould, "Is a New and General Theory of Evolution Emerging?" *Paleobiology,* 6, no. 1 (1980): 125.
3. Steven M. Stanley, "Macroevolution and the Fossil Record," *Evolution,* 36, no. 3 (1982): 460.

Barring extinction, a typical established species — whether a species of land plants, insects, mammals, or marine invertebrates — will undergo little measurable change in form during $10^5$–$10^7$ generations.[4]

The implication of the stability of established species is that most evolutionary change occurs rapidly, in local populations. Because the direction taken by rapidly divergent speciation is variable and only weakly predictable for large segments of phylogeny, macroevolution is largely decoupled from microevolution.[5]

The [fossil] record now reveals that species typically survive for a hundred thousand generations, or even a million or more, without evolving very much. We seem forced to conclude that most evolution takes place rapidly, when species come into being by the evolutionary divergence of small populations from parent species. After their origins, most species undergo little evolution before becoming extinct.[6]

The logic employed by evolutionists is amazing. Since species "undergo little measurable change" for at least "a hundred thousand generations," therefore "most evolution takes place rapidly." This is a splendid statement of credulous faith in evolution. Since there is no evidence for evolution, either in the present world of living organisms or in the fossil world of extinct organisms, therefore evolution must have taken place in a hurry and in very small populations so that it left "no legible fossil record."

We have already shown in chapter 8 the complete impossibility of the naturalistic origin of life even at the simplest level. The gap between the nonliving and the living is unbridgeable.

The same turns out to be true at every stage of the supposed evolutionary history. First of all, there are no intermediate forms between the one-celled bacteria of the Precambrian period and the wide variety of complex multicelled marine vertebrates of the Cambrian period. "The evidence is now mounting that most of the major fossil groups of the Cambrian arose by rapid evolution. . . . In the first place, fossil assemblages consisting of the imprints of soft-bodied creatures . . . have been found in many areas of the world, but are never older than latest Precambrian."[7] For the phrase "most of the major groups of the Cambrian" in the above quotation, one should of course read "all of the major fossil groups."

Evolutionists used to claim that the reason for the sudden appearance of complex creatures in the Cambrian, with no fossil precursors, was that their ancestors were all soft-bodied and thus left no hard parts to be fossilized. As Stanley

4. Ibid., p. 464.

5. Ibid., p. 472.

6. Steven M. Stanley, *The New Evolutionary Timetable: Fossils, Genes and the Origin of Species* (New York, NY: Basic Books, 1981), preface.

7. Steven M. Stanley, *Macroevolution: Pattern and Process* (San Francisco, CA: W.H. Freeman, 1979), p. 69.

pointed out, however, many fossils of soft-bodied animals have been found in the Cambrian (and later) rocks, so there is no good reason why soft-bodied creatures could not have been fossilized in the Precambrian, if they existed. It is especially noteworthy that all of the great phyla have been found in rocks of the Cambrian, supposedly the oldest of the fossil-bearing rock systems. Pierre Grassé, who held the Chair of Evolution at the Sorbonne in Paris for over 20 years and was one of Europe's leading zoologists, has pointed out the significance of this fact. "The formation of the phyla or basic structural plans constitutes the most important and, perhaps, the essential part of evolution. Each phylum offers great novelties and its structural plan guides the destiny of the secondary lines . . . paleontology does not shed any light on the genesis of the phyla."[8] The same phyla that "evolved" before the Cambrian have continued unchanged right up to the present. Grassé also noted, "The genesis of the phyla stopped in the Ordovician."[9] The Ordovician is the system immediately "after" the Cambrian. When Grassé wrote his book, it was believed that all the invertebrate phyla had evolved in the Cambrian but that the vertebrates only appeared in the Ordovician. More recently, however, vertebrate fossils have also been discovered in the Cambrian, so that all phyla are now represented there. "Discoveries of fragmentary phosphatic plates, interpreted as pertaining to heterostracans, from numerous localities in Late Cambrian and Early Ordovician marine limestones extend the vertebrate record back to more than 500 million years before the present."[10]

Every one of the animal phyla thus appear suddenly and fully developed in Cambrian rocks. In particular, it is significant that there are no transitional forms between the vertebrates and any of the invertebrates.

> Fossil evidence of pre-vertebrate chordate evolution is still scanty and equivocal.[11]

> All three subdivisions of the bony fishes first appear in the fossil record at approximately the same time. They are already widely divergent morphologically, and they are heavily armored. How did they originate? What allowed them to diverge so widely? How did they all come to have heavy armor? And why is there no trace of earlier, intermediate forms?[12]

These and other authors have offered speculative answers to these questions, but no evidence. Furthermore, each invertebrate phylum is completely separated

8. Pierre P. Grassé, *Evolution of Living Organisms* (New York, NY: Academic, 1977), p. 27.

9. Ibid., p. 70.

10. James A. Hopson and Leonard B. Radinsky, "Vertebrate Paleontology: New Approaches and New Insights," *Paleobiology,* 6 (Summer 1980): 256. For a more recent discovery of vertebrate fossils in the Cambrian, see "Lower Cambrian Vertebrates from South China," *Nature,* 402 (Nov. 4, 1999): 42–46. This article describes two types of agnathan fish found in supposedly early Cambrian rocks.

11. Ibid.

12. Gerald T. Todd, "Evolution of the Lung and the Origin of Bony Fishes — A Causal Relationship," *American Zoologist,* 20, no. 4 (1980): 757.

from all others and, as mentioned above, the various main orders of the fishes, as well as the class of fishes in general, were completely distinct from the start.

Evolutionists believe that some order of fishes, possibly the crossopterygians, evolved into amphibians, with the fins of the fish developing into the feet and legs of the amphibian. Nevertheless, there is no transitional form indicating how this great change came about. "The oldest known tetrapods, the icthyostegid amphibians of the Late Devonian, though first reported on in 1932 and represented by numerous specimens, have never been completely described. No clearly intermediate form in the fish-tetrapod transition has been discovered."[13] The next major evolutionary advance is believed to have been the transmutation of an amphibian into a reptile. Again, however, there is no evidence of it. "Unfortunately not a single specimen of an appropriate reptilian ancestor is known prior to the appearance of true reptiles. The absence of such ancestral forms leaves many problems of the amphibian-reptilian transition unanswered."[14]

Another major class of animals is the insects, but again there is no known evolutionary transition. Grassé wrote, "We are in the dark concerning the origin of insects."[15]

It is not until this point in the evolutionary scenario that evolutionists even claim to have a reasonable candidate for a major evolutionary transitional fossil. Both mammals and birds are assumed to have evolved from reptiles. The famous *Archaeopteryx* is supposed to be the intermediate between reptiles and birds and is often said to be the classic example of a transitional form. The so-called mammal-like reptiles, especially the therapsids, are now also being promoted as transitional between reptiles and mammals.

In both cases, these animals are not transitional forms, but mosaic forms. That is, they possessed no transitional *structures*; all their features were fully developed and fully functional, none being either incipient structures or vestigial structures. As sketched in figure 25, an animal with true transitional structures could not even have survived. *Archaeopteryx* had teeth and claws like a reptile, wings and feathers like a bird, but all were perfectly formed for the needs of the creature. It did not have "sceathers" (half-scales, half-feathers) or "lings" (half-legs, half-wings). The therapsids also were highly efficient in every respect for the time and environments in which they lived, with all their features perfectly designed for their purposes.

Furthermore, the chronologies are all wrong. True birds have existed at least as long as *Archaeopteryx*,[16] so that the latter could hardly have been their ancestor. Similarly, all the mammal-like reptiles died out even before the so-called "age of

13. Hopson and Radinsky, "Vertebrate Paleontology," p. 258.
14. Lewis L. Carroll, "Problems of the Origin of Reptiles," *Biological Reviews of the Cambridge Philosophical Society,* 44 (1969): 393.
15. Pierre P. Grassé, *Evolution of Living Organisms* (New York, NY: Academic, 1977), p. 30.
16. Jean L. Marx, "The Oldest Fossil Bird: A Rival for Archaeopteryx?" *Science,* 199 (Jan. 20, 1978): 284.

*FIGURE 25 — Supposed Reptile-Bird Transition*
Archaeopteryx, the supposed reptile-bird, is almost always cited by evolutionists as the best example of an evolutionary transition. However, this was clearly a mosaic creature, since it contained no transitional structures (such as half-legs/half-wings) as a true transitional creature would have. A real transitional creature would not even survive, as illustrated in the above hypothetical scenario.

reptiles" began, not to mention the age of mammals, and no one knows which mammal-like reptile gave rise to the mammals. Each mammal-like reptile is completely different from all others, with no gradual transitions to other reptiles, to any of the mammals, or to each other.[17]

Two other more recently proposed candidates for transitional creatures are the so-called "feathered dinosaur" and "walking whale." If anything, these animals illustrate the desperate desire of evolutionists to find *some* evidence, no matter how flimsy, for evolutionary transitions in the fossil record.

Several fossils of small dinosaurs were found in China, beginning about 1990, with peculiar structures on their skins, which some evolutionists interpreted as incipient feathers. However, most real specialists in avian evolution have vigorously rejected this idea, pointing out that bird feathers are extremely complex and aerodynamically efficient structures without which bird flight would be impossible. The feathers of *Archaeopteryx* were true feathers, and *Archaeopteryx* was "older" paleontologically than these supposed feathered dinosaurs. The latter not only did not have true feathers, but neither did they have incipient wings. The only such fossil, which *did* have real feathers, and was widely publicized by *National Geographic*, turned out to be a hoax.

The walking whale is also the product of evolutionary wishful thinking. Whales are mammals, of course, but there are a number of other marine mammals (e.g., dolphins) which live in the sea, as well as others that live partly on land also (e.g., seals). God has made a great variety of animals, some of which have become extinct (e.g., *Pakicetus, Ambulocetus*) which may have been at home on both land and sea, although the few remains of these creatures found so far leave this in doubt. In any case, there is no reason to think that any one of them evolved from any other. The differences are too great, and each was well designed by God for its own intended environment.

Thus, there really are *no* true transitional series in the fossil record, any more than in the present world.[18] Stephen Jay Gould once made a very revealing admission, as follows: "The extreme rarity of transitional forms in the fossil record persists as the trade secret of paleontology. The evolutionary trees that adorn our textbooks have data only at the tips and nodes of their branches. . . . In any local area, a species does not arise gradually by the gradual transformation of its ancestors; it appears all at once and 'fully formed.' "[19] Evolutionists may interpret such data in terms of "punctuated equilibrium" if they wish (or "quantum speciation," or "hopeful monsters," as some prefer), but this is arguing not from evidence but from lack of evidence! This is a unique form of scientific "logic" never employed elsewhere in science.

---

17. Tom Kemp, "The Reptiles That Became Mammals," *New Scientist,* 92 (Mar. 4, 1982): 581–84.
18. The most comprehensive recent study of the fossil record from the creationist point of view is *Evolution — The Fossils Still Say No!* by Duane T. Gish (Green Forest, AR: Master Books, 1995), 391 p.
19. Stephen Jay Gould, "Evolution's Erratic Pace," *Natural History,* 86 (May 1977): 14.

Another fascinating admission was made by evolutionist Carlton Brett: "Did life on Earth change steadily and gradually through time? The fossil record emphatically says 'no!' "[20]

Brett, who is a convinced protagonist in favor of punctuated equilibrium, was not about to become a creationist but, consciously or subconsciously, he clearly appropriated the title of Dr. Duane Gish's book (*Evolution — The Fossils Say No*) to apply to the Gould-Eldredge scenario of long ages of "stasis" broken by brief catastrophic "punctuations" of essentially instant evolution the evidence for which is *stasis*! As Gould says, "Stasis has become interesting as a central prediction of our theory."[21]

We creationists have always thought stasis was a central prediction of *our* "theory." How can it also predict sudden evolution?

Except for the inordinate time spans which evolutionists insert between their "punctuations" (presumably caused by mass extinctions following geological catastrophes), these notions of "stasis" and the sudden appearance of new kinds without evolutionary transitions correspond nicely with the Genesis record of creation.

Ten times in the very first chapter of the Bible the phrase "after its kind" is used, implying a firm genetic basis for the reproductive process that would preclude evolutionary transmutations from any one kind into a different kind. The "kind" (Hebrew *min*) may not be equivalent to what modern systematists mean by "species," but it does mean some category beyond which variation is not permitted. And the fact is — both genetically and paleontologically — that there is still no unequivocal scientific evidence that "microevolution" (that is, "variation") ever transgresses even the species boundary!

No wonder there are no transitional forms ever found in the fossils — they never existed! When God programmed creatures to reproduce only according to their own kinds, He intended for this program to be carried out. He is both omniscient and omnipotent. He was able to design creatures the way He, in His omniscience, knew they should be designed, and He was able, in His omnipotence, to build them that way. Therefore, He will see to it that, as long as they exist, they will stay the way He designed and built them. Many varieties could develop within each kind, of course, so that they could adapt to different environments as needed, without becoming extinct, but the kinds themselves could not change.

Since all the evidence, both biblical and scientific, precisely fits special creation, the big question is why people believe in evolution at all. But that is a theological question, not a scientific question.

## Fossils as Evidence for Catastrophism

The very existence of fossils, of course, is prima facie evidence of catastrophism. This is particularly obvious in the case of the great fossil graveyards that are found

20. Carlton E. Brett, "Stasis: Life in the Balance," *Geotimes*, 40 (March 1995): 18.
21. Stephen Jay Gould, "Opus 200," *Natural History*, 100 (August 1991): 16.

### *Figure 26 — Fossil Graveyards*

*Vast fossil beds of fishes, dinosaurs, mammoths, amphibians, and a variety of other animals are found all over the world. These phenomena require catastrophism on an immense scale.*

*Mixed fossils in Nebraska.*

all over the world in the rocks of every so-called geologic age. As noted in the preceding chapter, these ages are determined on the basis of the fossils contained in the rocks, and yet the fossils speak of rapid burial, not slow deposition over long ages. When animals die, their remains quickly decompose on the surface unless they are somehow rapidly covered with sediments that are soon compacted and hardened.

Examples are legion. A fossil graveyard is shown in figure 26. Another such discovery was made in Baja, California. A team of Mexican and American paleontologists reported ". . . the discovery of more than 18 fossil sites on the peninsula. The sites dot a 350-mile stretch of ragged coastal and inland terrain . . . fossils literally cover the ground for miles in some locations where torrential rains have washed away the soil. At other sites, the team found fossil beds thousands of feet thick."[22] Similarly, great beds of fossil fish are found in California, New York, Scotland, and many other places. Dinosaur graveyards abound in the Rockies, in South Africa, in Spitzbergen, in Central Asia, in Belgium, and in every other continent and most other countries. Tremendous fossil beds of pachyderms and other animals are found in the permafrost soils of Alaska and Siberia. Massive deposits of marine invertebrates are found practically everywhere.

Even beds of fossil birds have been found, despite the fact that birds can obviously avoid burial by all but the most violent, widespread, and prolonged catastrophes. "Because most bird bones are hollow or pneumatic as an adaptation for flight, they are not well preserved in the fossil record."[23] Birds not only can fly and perch on eminences when tired, but their bones are light and tend to float even when the birds collapse and fall to the ground or water surface. Nevertheless, "During the early to mid-1970s, enormous concentrations of *Presbyornis* have been discovered in the Green River Formation."[24] This interesting creature is now apparently extinct, but was a large bird that "suddenly" appeared in the Eocene epoch, dated at some 60 million years ago. "*Presbyornis* is an evolutionary mosaic, combining a strange montage of morphological characteristics of shorebirds, modern ducks and allies, and modern flamingoes."[25] Note that it was a *mosaic* form, not a transitional form. Paleontologists do not regard the *Presbyornis* as ancestral to ducks or flamingoes, but contemporaneous with them. None seem to have any evolutionary ancestors in the fossils. In any case, the significant point in this connection is the abundance of its fossils, strangely interpreted by evolutionists as lake-bottom accumulations!

As a matter of fact, this remarkable Green River formation of Wyoming contains many other fossils, too, including "abundant fossil catfish in oil shales."[26] The authors of this study recognize the remarkable nature of this fossil bed that extends over an area of 16,000 square kilometers. The catfish range in length up to ten inches and many even have the skin and other soft parts, including the adipose fin, well preserved, even though they are supposed to be 60 million years old.

Although the exact nature of the processes that formed these famous Green River oil shales has been a matter of considerable controversy among geologists,

---

22. "A Fossil Bonanza in the Baja," *Science News,* 106 (1974): 247.
23. Alan Feduccia, "*Presbyornis* and the Evolution of Ducks and Flamingoes," *American Scientist,* 66 (May–June 1978): 298.
24. Ibid., p. 299.
25. Ibid., p. 300.
26. H. Paul Buchheim and Ronald C. Surdem, "Fossil Catfish and the Depositional Environment of the Green River Formation, Wyoming," *Geology,* 5 (Apr. 1979): 196.

it should be obvious that catastrophism on a vast scale has been involved. Nothing less can account for the extensive fossil deposits. The beds also contain fossil insects and fossil plants in abundance.

Yet, amazingly enough, much of this Green River formation consists of "banded" shale deposits that uniformitarian geologists interpret as varves — that is, cyclic lake-bottom sedimentary accumulations — each band of which is supposed to represent the deposits of one year. The average thickness of each varve is less than a hundredth of an inch, and they extend over vast areas. The idea that these microscopic bands are yearly accumulations of bottom sediments in quiescent lakes, when at the same time they contain vast fossil deposits, is absurd. Whatever the cause of the banding phenomenon might be (and there are several other possibilities), they could not be annual varves! The entire deposit is the product of regional catastrophism, at least.

The Green River formation also contains a wide assortment of inorganic deposits, including thick salt deposits. Although salt beds are commonly called "evaporates," Sozansky and others have shown that they could not have been formed by evaporation from inland seas, as the uniformitarians had supposed, but only by rapid precipitation out of juvenile waters emerging from the mantle below the earth's crust. "Precipitation of salt from highly mineralized thermal brines of juvenile origin that escaped from the mantle along deep faults is the most logical explanation for the origin of salt deposits."[27] There are other indications of igneous activity in the Green River deposits. The entire complex — especially the great fossil deposits — clearly can only be properly understood in terms of catastrophism, even though it is often used as a leading argument for great ages of slow deposition.

Another type of fossil deposit that is frequently cited as evidence for long ages of time is that of the petrified forests in Yellowstone Park, where over 50 successive fossil "forests" have been counted, each one supposed to have grown in the soil developed from volcanic deposits that had destroyed and buried the previous forest. Since each cycle is said to have required a thousand years or more, this formation is often cited as proof that the biblical chronology is wrong.

The fact is, however, that these fossil tree trunks did not grow in place but were transported into place. That is, they were not autochthonous deposits, but allochthonous.

> In view of the fact that the prone petrified logs are often split and fractured, almost always devoid of limbs and bark, and lie well above the root levels of the erect petrified stumps in volcanic breccia showing both normal and reverse grading, the orientation of the horizontal trees is clearly the result of transport by volcanic mud flows (lahars). It is probable that the same lahars removed, transported and deposited the upright stumps (vertical stance generally little

---

27. V.I. Sozansky, "Depositional Environment of the Green River Formation of Wyoming: Discussion," *Bulletin of the Geological Society of America*, 85 (July 1974): 1191.

disturbed). The major roots which usually control the asymmetry of the lower tree bole are acted upon by moving mud. Thus both prone and erect trees are deposited with long axes in the same general direction.[28]

Some of the fossil trees are even standing at a considerable angle with the vertical, providing more evidence that they could not have grown in place. "Besides vertical stumps, logs that are parallel and diagonal to the bedding also occur in abundance."[29] The general aspect of the fossil logs and stumps is thus strong evidence for burial by transport from some location where they were catastrophically uprotted or sheared off at the roots: "In some areas . . . all the trees are horizontal and most of the logs are oriented in a particular direction, as in log jams. The vertical stumps are shorter than horizontal logs and were broken above the root level before burial. Only in a few locations are branches and small roots present, both generally having been broken off during transport before deposition at present sites."[30] Still another evidence of allochtony is the mixture of species involved. "If these identifications are correct, the mixture of temperate and tropical plant remains is extreme even for a Paleogene flora. . . . Although common for transported floras, this mixture seems out of place for 'forests' interpreted as having been buried in place with little or no transportation."[31]

Providentially for the understanding of this type of fossil deposit, the sudden eruption of Mount St. Helens in 1980 seems to have produced deposits very similar to the Yellowstone fossils. "Deposits of recent mud flows on Mount St. Helens demonstrate conclusively that stumps can be transported and deposited upright. These observations support conclusions that some vertical trees in the Yellowstone 'fossil forests' were transported in a geologic situation directly comparable to that of Mount St. Helens."[32]

Thus, instead of being an argument for long ages of uniformitarian growth processes, as frequently claimed, these Yellowstone fossil trees are strong evidences for catastrophism. In the biblical context, they are probably associated with the volcanic upheavals implied in the eruptions of the "fountains of the great deep" (Gen. 7:11; 8:2) that were a primary cause of the Noahic flood.

Many other remarkable fossil deposits are likewise associated with volcanic/hydraulic catastrophism. Sozansky has shown good evidence that the world's great salt deposits were formed in this fashion.[33] Other Russian scientists believe

---

28. Harold G. Coffin, "Orientation of Trees in the Yellowstone Petrified Forests," *Journal of Paleontology,* 50 (May 1976): 542.
29. William J. Fritz, "Reinterpretation of the Depositional Environment of the Yellowstone Fossil Forests," *Geology,* 8 (July 1980): 312.
30. Ibid.
31. Ibid.
32. William J. Fritz, "Stumps Transported and Deposited Upright by Mount St. Helens Mud Flows," *Geology,* 8 (Dec. 1980): 588.
33. V. I. Sozansky, *Geology and Genesis of Salt Formations* (Kiev: Izd. Naukokva Dumka, 1973), p. 200.

that the world's petroleum deposits are also attributable to such causes,[34] although most western geologists still believe oil is a "fossil fuel," derived from the compressed and transformed remains of multitudes of buried marine organisms.

Another amazing effect of volcanic catastrophism is the preservation of the coloration and fine structure of organisms for the imagined millions of years since their burial.

> Thirty million years ago some green leaves from elm trees in Oregon were rapidly buried under volcanic ash. Some of those leaves are still a vivid green today. . . . So far they find the chemical profile of the prehistoric leaves surprisingly similar to that of modern leaves.[35]

> Examination of the ultrastructure of preserved tissue in the abdomen of a fossil fly (Mycetophilidae: Diptera) entombed in Baltic amber revealed recognizable cell organelles. Structures that correspond to muscle fibers, nuclei, ribosomes, lipid droplets, endoplasmic reticulum, and mitochondria were identified with the transmission electron microscope. . . . Baltic amber is believed to have originated in the late Eocene to early Oligocene, or about 40 million years ago.[36]

The fossil fly was practically identical to modern flies, even though "30 millions years" older! It seems really impossible to believe that these assumed millions of years have actually transpired since the leaves and insects were fossilized. These examples are far from unique, as similar intricately preserved organisms have been found in numerous fossil deposits around the world. Only catastrophism — and recent catastrophism at that — can really account for such phenomena. It is not certain how the amber deposits were formed and preserved (this phenomenon is not occurring today), but it is obvious that some form of catastrophism was required.

A very different type of fossil, but one that is very important in geochronology, is the coral reef, composed of the calcified remains of multitudes of marine animals known as corals. Both the living reefs, which are still growing with live colonies of the coral organisms, and the fossil reefs, which have presumably been identified in various limestone formations in the geological column, are often exhibited as evidences of great age. The size of the reefs, in contrast with their assumed slow growth rates, is taken as indication that they require long periods of time to attain their final size.

The fact is, however, that the actual coral growth is merely a relatively thin veneer over a nonorganic substrate, especially in living reefs. Braithwaite has extensively documented this fact, showing that many so-called reefs exist without

34. V.B. Porfir'ev, "Inorganic Origin of Petroleum," *American Association of Petroleum Geologists Bulletin,* 58 (Jan. 1974): 3–33.

35. "Chemistry of Still-Green Fossil Leaves," *Science News,* 3 (June 18, 1977): 391.

36. George O. Poinar Jr., and Roberta Hess, "Ultrastructure of 40-Million-Year-Old Insect Tissue," *Science,* 215 (Mar. 5, 1982): 1241.

corals, and corals often grow without a reef substrate at all. Others have shown that the Florida reefs are only a thin veneer over another limestone formation and that the famous Bikini reefs are also growing on an older surface. The same is true in the Seychelles, Yucatan, and elsewhere. "In summary, present reefs commonly are bedded structures. . . . Coral frames commonly represent only a small part of the volume."[37]

As far as fossil reefs are concerned, probably the most extensive and important is the Permian Reef complex of the Guadalupe Mountains of west Texas. These beds also contain extensive salt deposits as well as fossil graveyards of amphibians and other vertebrates, all of which bear witness of catastrophism. The reef itself gives much evidence of allochthonous origin, although Braithwaite believes it is similar in structure to modern reefs with their surficial veneer of coral.

> There is little doubt that this "reef" had real topographic expression and that it controlled the distribution and character of sediments and organisms in the region. What does seem questionable is that this was an organic reef in which bioconstruction determined the feature. Dunham (1970) stated that the structure was in fact largely the result of inorganic binding, and that organisms, although present, did not provide a rigid framework.[38]

Furthermore, coral can grow much more rapidly than uniformitarians allege if the conditions are suitable (available light, food supply, good population of organisms, space to grow, and warm water — all of which certainly were available in abundance in the pre-Flood world). For example, undersea explorers have found a 5-foot diameter coral growth on a bow gun on a ship sunk only in 1944, as well as a black coral "tree" 15 feet high on the starboard side of a ship 60 feet deep.[39]

Although more research is still in order, there is certainly no reason for concluding that coral reefs, either living or fossil, require more than a few centuries or millennia for their production.

Thus, the paleontological components, as well as all the other components of the geologic column, give clear evidence of catastrophism. Although some no doubt were formed in various local catastrophes after the Flood, the Flood provides the best means of explaining most of these vast fossil graveyards.

Even though the Bible never mentions fossils or their sedimentary rock formations at all, the Flood undoubtedly would have been the greatest producer of fossils since the world began:

---

37. C.J.R. Braithwaite, "Reefs: Just a Problem of Semantics?" *Bulletin of the American Association of Petroleum Geologists,* 57 (June 1973): 1108.

38. Ibid., p. 1105.

39. Sylvia A. Earl, "Life Springs from Death in Truk Lagoon," *National Geographic,* 149 (May 1976): 578–613.

And God said unto Noah, The end of all flesh is come before me; for the earth is filled with violence through them; and, behold, I will destroy them with the earth (Gen. 6:13).

And all flesh died that moved upon the earth, both of fowl, and of cattle, and of beast, and of every creeping thing that creepeth upon the earth, and every man: All in whose nostrils was the breath of life, of all that was in the dry land, died. And every living substance was destroyed which was upon the face of the ground, both man, and cattle, and the creeping things, and the fowl of the heaven; and they were destroyed from the earth: and Noah only remained alive, and they that were with him in the ark (Gen. 7:21–23).

The combination of overwhelming waters and great crustal upheavals, and then the destruction of "every living substance" and the death of "all flesh," as recorded in the Bible, could not fail to have been the greatest producer of thick sediments and entrapped plants and animals in those sediments of any event in world history. If the biblical flood really occurred in the manner recorded in Scripture, then the earth's true geologic column must be primarily a record of that flood, and not of long imaginary ages of evolution.

## Dragons and Unicorns

Although fossils as such are not mentioned in the Bible, it does contain references to various animals that do not appear to exist in the modern world. The best known of these are the dragon and the unicorn, but other such exotic animals as the behemoth, the leviathan, the satyr, the ibis, and the cockatrice also are mentioned. Most liberal commentaries have interpreted these as simply legendary animals, while conservative commentators have tried to identify them as picturesquely describing living animals. Thus, the dragon is said by conservatives to be the jackal or whale or serpent, the unicorn the wild ox or aurochs, the behemoth an elephant or hippopotamus, the leviathan a crocodile, the satyr a wild goat, the ibis an owl, and the cockatrice an adder.

In several cases, however, the specific biblical descriptions of these strange animals do not correspond at all to those living animals with which they have been associated. The biblical writers mention at least 160 different specific animals by name, and always the descriptions seem quite accurate, except for these few equivocal animals. The latter are apparently also intended by the writers as real animals, as real as the many others they describe accurately. Thus, it is more reasonable to regard these animals, in most cases at least, merely as extinct animals, known to the patriarchs as living animals but later known only by their ancient reputations.

Many animals are known to have become extinct in historic times, including the Egyptian ibis. A great host of other extinct animals are now also known from their fossil records. The uniformitarian view, of course, is that practically all the fossil record antedates the evolution of man, so the Bible writers could not possibly have been familiar with any of the extinct animals represented in the fossils.

The fact is, however, that all these fossils represent animals that perished in the Flood, so they were indeed known to the early generations of mankind.

They must also have been included on Noah's ark, so that they became extinct some time after the Flood. Consequently, it seems at least possible that these dragons and unicorns and other animals might actually be identifiable in the fossil record.

Dragons, for example (Hebrew *tannim*), are mentioned at least 25 times in the Old Testament. In one of these, the word is used synonymously with "leviathan that crooked serpent," being called "the dragon that is in the sea" (Isa. 27:1). Ezekiel 29:3 refers to "the great dragon that lieth in the midst of his [that is, Egypt's] rivers." On the other hand, the mountains of Edom are said to have been laid "waste for the dragons of the wilderness" (Mal. 1:3). Other references likewise indicate that there were dragons of the desert as well as dragons in the waters.

A number of physiological attributes of dragons are also mentioned. Dragons made a wailing sound (Mic. 1:8), "snuffed up the wind" (Jer. 14:6), and apparently had poisonous fangs (Deut. 32:33). Seemingly, some were fairly small. Aaron's rod, which is said to have become a "serpent," actually became a *dragon*. The regular Hebrew word for "dragon" (*tannim*) is used (Exod. 7:10). *Tannim* is not translated "serpent" in other passages, at least in the KJV. Moses' rod, on the other hand, had become a snake (Heberw *nahash*; Exod. 4:3; 7:15), but the rods of Aaron and the Egyptian magicians became dragons (*tannim*), presumably small dragons.

Many dragons, on the other hand, were great monsters. The very first use of *tannim* is in Genesis 1:21, which is also the first reference to God's creation of animal life. "And God created great [dragons], and every living creature that moveth, which the waters brought forth abundantly, after their kind, and every winged fowl after his kind; and God saw that it was good." The King James Version translates *tannim* here as "whales," and most other versions use "sea monsters" or "sea creatures," but the word is actually "dragons," and the emphasis is on "great" dragons.

Unfortunately, because of the reluctance of modern translators to commit the Scriptures to teaching the existence of something they regard as purely mythical, modern versions commonly translate *tannim* by "jackals" or "serpents" or "sea monsters," depending on the context in each passage. But how can the same Hebrew word carry such a wide, even contradictory, diversity of meanings? The very idea is a striking testimony to the rationalism of modern translators, who are so committed to the uniformitarian view of earth history that they miss the obvious fact that the *tannim* were simply extinct animals, known in earlier periods of human history but now preserved only (or mainly) in the fossil record.

As a matter of fact, if one will simply translate *tannim* by "dinosaurs," every one of the more than 25 uses of the word becomes perfectly clear and appropriate. The fossil record reveals both terrestrial and marine dinosaurs, small and large dinosaurs, dinosaurs of many different characters living in different environments with one or another of them fitting well into each context where *tannim* is used.

The only problem with such a translation, of course, is that the dinosaurs are supposed to have died out about 70 million years before man evolved, according to the standard evolutionary chronology. Fossils of dinosaurs were first excavated less than two hundred years ago, and it was a contemporary of Charles Darwin, Sir Richard Owen, who coined their name, meaning "terrible lizards."

However, the evolutionary chronology is inconsistent with the Bible, as we have seen, so there is no adequate reason to question the contemporaneity of men and dinosaurs in the early ages of human history. The dragons of the Bible could well be the dinosaurs of paleontology. It is significant that not only in the Bible but also in the ancient records and traditions of most of the nations of the world, tales of dragons abound. Such a universal phenomenon must have a universal explanation, and the best explanation is that all the ancient nations actually had had experiences with dinosaurs. A detailed study[40] of the different dragon "traditions" has pointed out that there were evidently many different kinds of dragons and that these more or less corresponded to the different known kinds of dinosaurs.

In addition to the biblical and ethnological evidences, there is also some good geological evidence of the coexistence of men and dinosaurs. Numerous footprints of various kinds of dinosaurs are well preserved in a Cretaceous limestone formation near Glen Rose, Texas, and the area has actually been set aside as a dinosaur park by the state of Texas. In the same formation many human footprints have been reported over the years, of various sizes, some wearing sandals, and some barefoot.[41] Evolutionists have rejected this evidence, of course, arguing that some of the tracks were actually carvings, many of the originally reported tracks are now missing, and some give evidence of unknown reptilian origin. These questions are still unresolved and research is continuing, but it is doubtful that they would have been raised at all if the same human-like tracks had been found in a geologically "recent" formation, associated, say, with mastodon tracks instead of dinosaur tracks.

There are many other lines of evidence as well, though these also have been ignored or rejected by evolutionists. Two human skeletons were discovered in the same Utah sandstone formation in which, a few miles away, the Dinosaur National Monument had been constructed because of the great number of dinosaur

---

40. Paul S. Taylor, *The Great Dinosaur Mystery and the Bible* (Elgin, IL: David E. Cook Publishing Co., 1989), p. 63. See also Bill Cooper, *After the Flood* (New Wine Press, 1995), p. 256.

41. John D. Morris, *Tracking Those Incredible Dinosaurs and the People Who Knew Them* (San Diego, CA: Creation-Life, 1980), p. 250. This book contains descriptions of all relevant tracks known at time of writing. For the negative evidence, see John D. Morris, "The Paluxy River Mystery," *ICR Acts and Facts,* 15 (Jan. 1986). A site containing similar dinosaur and human tracks has been located in Russia.

### FIGURE 27 — Men and Dinosaurs

*Shown here is one of the supposed human trails crossing a dinosaur trail in the Glen Rose limestone of Texas. These now are considered doubtful. However, humanlike tracks have also been found associated with dinosaur tracks in Russia.*[42]

fossils found there.[43] Dinosaur pictographs made by early tribal artists have been found in Arizona, Siberia, Zimbabwe,[44] and elsewhere. A Mayan carving strongly resembling the ancient bird *Archaeopteryx*, believed to be a contemporary of the dinosaurs, has been described near Vera Cruz, Mexico,[45] indicating that the Mayans were familiar with this bird which, according to evolutionists, was the link between reptiles and birds, and which died out 130 million years ago, during the dinosaur age.

Furthermore, numerous reports[46] have been published in recent years indicating that some of the dinosaurs, both marine and land dinosaurs, may still be

42. Alexander Romashko, "Tracking Dinosaurs, " *Moscow News Weekly: Science and Engineering News*, no. 24 (1983): 10.

43. F.A. Barnes, "The Case of the Bones in Stone," *Desert* (Feb. 1975): 36–39.

44. "Bushmen's Paintings Baffling to Scientists," *Herald-Examiner* (Los Angeles, CA), Jan. 7, 1970. From London Express Service, *Evening News* (London), Jan. 1, 1970.

45. "Serpent-Bird of the Mayans," *Science Digest*, 64 (Nov. 1968): 1.

46. "Living Dinosaurs," *Science-80*, 1 (Nov. 1980): 6–7. This article summarizes the evidence for living dinosaurs like the apatosaurus in the Congo's rain forests. "Dinosaur Found in NT Harbor," *Darwin News* (Australia) (Feb. 2, 1980). Living plesiosaurs (often called marine dinosaurs) have been described in a harbor near Darwin. There are also the tales of the Loch Ness and other monsters, as well as numerous reports of sea serpents. Some such animal was actually caught and photographed near New Zealand by Japanese fishermen — John Koster, "What was the New Zealand Monster?" *Oceans* (Nov. 1977): 56–59. See figure 29.

FIGURE 28 — *Living Fossils*

*There are numerous so-called living fossils — that is, animals supposedly extinct for millions of years that have turned up still living in the present world. Two of these, shown here, are the coelcanth, a fish previously thought extinct for 70 million years, and the beakhead reptile, tuatara, which has no fossil record for the past 135 million years.*

living. Although none of these reports have been confirmed, they at least are being taken seriously by a number of evolutionary scientists. If the existence of living dinosaurs is a viable consideration, then it should not be too unreasonable to accept the evidence of the contemporaneous footprints of men and dinosaurs in the Paluxy River bed near Glen Rose.

Although not as spectacular as living dinosaurs would be, it also should be remembered that many other "living fossils," supposedly extinct since the dinosaur age or before (e.g., the coelacanth fish, the tuatara reptile; see figure 28), have been recently found alive and well in the modern world.[47]

There have been many other "anomalous fossils" reported in the popular literature, but these are rarely taken seriously by the evolutionary establishment.

---

47. R.L. Wysong's *The Creation-Evolution Controversy* (Midland, MI: Inquiry, 1976) has an instructive list of 18 of these living fossils, with photographs of 13 of them (p. 287–294).

*FIGURE 29 — A Modern Dinosaur-like Sea Monster*

*There have been many reports of sea monsters still living in modern oceans. This widely published photograph of a dinosaur-like creature dredged up near New Zealand in 1976 is striking evidence that some marine dinosaurs may still be surviving, like many other "living fossils" supposedly extinct for millions of years. However, most evolutionists argue that this was merely a basking shark.*

There are always devices to explain them away (reworking, displacement, mistaken observations, etc.), so whenever a fossil discovery seems to contradict the standard evolutionary sequence, it is commonly either ignored or "explained." Fossil footprints out of order, of course, cannot be attributed to displacement or reworking, and so are usually dismissed as hoaxes or mistakes.

Nevertheless, there are many examples that have been reported, most of which would never have been questioned at all if they were not out of the evolutionary order. For those who are interested, three collections[48] of these anomalies may be mentioned for further study.

Returning to the biblical record, two other strange animals are mentioned which may well refer to two particular kinds of dinosaurs. These are "behemoth" and "leviathan," described in Job 40 and 41, respectively. Although commentators (including modern Orthodox Jewish scholars) have commonly identified the behemoth with either the elephant or hippopotamus, and the leviathan with the crocodile, it is obvious from the descriptions (in Job 40:15–24 and Job 41:1–34) that these modern animals in no way qualify for such identification.

It is important to remember that Job lived during the early generations after the Flood, and that he no doubt had seen many animals that later became extinct.

---

48. William R. Corliss, *Strange Artifacts: A Sourcebook on Ancient Man* (Glen Arm, MD: Sourcebook, 1976), p. 287; Wiliam R. Corliss, *Ancient Man: A Handbook of Puzzling Artifacts* (Glen Arm, MD: Sourcebook, 1978), p. 786; Erich A. Von Fange, *Time Upside Down* (Published by author, 1981), p. 41.

The description of behemoth seems to fit perfectly what we know about such a land dinosaur as apatosaurus, for example, and leviathan fits what we know about some large marine reptiles, such as the plesiosaur or ichthyosaur, for example.

In the context, Job and his three friends are philosophizing about life and its meaning, going back and forth and apparently getting nowhere, just as people do today. Then God comes down and speaks to them directly, telling them in effect that their basic problem is an inadequate perspective on the greatness and uniqueness of God's creation. "Where wast thou when I laid the foundations of the earth? declare, if thou hast understanding" (Job 38:4). Then, for the next two chapters (Job 38, 39), God asks a series of rhetorical questions concerning different facts of His creation, all indicating a fully accurate scientific perspective, and even suggesting a number of scientific facts millennia before their recognition by modern scientists.[49]

Finally, God comes to the climax of His discourse, describing the two greatest animals He had created, the mighty behemoth (the greatest land animal), and the fearsome leviathan (the greatest sea animal). As one reads these descriptions carefully, it quickly becomes obvious that these animals are not the elephant and the crocodile!

Note the description of behemoth in Job 40:15–24, and observe how impossible it is to apply these words to either the elephant or hippopotamus: "Behold now behemoth." The very word means a uniquely gigantic and powerful beast. An ordinary beast is called *behema* in the Hebrew, but this is a special beast, "the chief of the ways of God." No man could trap this animal: "his nose pierceth through snares." "His strength is in his loins, and his force is in the naval [that is, probably 'cord' or 'sinews'] of his belly. He moveth his tail like a cedar." One should try to visualize the tail of an elephant or a hippopotamus as he reads this! And one should also visualize the mighty apatosaurus or tyrannosaurus or some other great terrestrial dinosaur. Every sentence is appropriate in describing such a huge dinosaur, but no other animal we are aware of, living or extinct, fits the bill (compare figure 30).

The same is true of the leviathan, described in detail throughout Job 41. That leviathan is a type of dragon is evident from Isaiah 27:1. "In that day the LORD with his sore and great and strong sword shall punish leviathan the piercing serpent, even leviathan that crooked serpent; and he shall slay the dragon that is in the sea."

The two other references to the leviathan in Scripture also suggest the great size and ferocity of this sea monster.

> Thou didst divide the sea by thy strength; thou brakest the heads of the dragons in the waters. Thou brakest the heads of leviathan in pieces, and gavest him to be meat to the people inhabiting the wilderness (Ps. 74:13–14).

---

49. See *The Remarkable Record of Job* by Henry M. Morris (Green Forest, AR: Master Books, 1988), 146 p.

*FIGURE 30 — Behemoth and the Dinosaurs*

*The biblical descriptions of two mighty animals called behemoth and leviathan (Job 40 and 41, respectively) do not fit any existing animals, but do seem to describe a land dinosaur such as apatosaurus (shown below) and a marine dinosaur such as plesiosaurus, thus indicating that the people of Job's time were aware of the existence of dinosaurs.*

> So is this great and wide sea, wherein are things creeping innumerable, both small and great beasts. There go the ships; there is that leviathan, whom thou hast made to play therein (Ps. 104:25–26).

In Job 41 he is called "a king over all the children of pride" (Job 41:34). The chapter stresses the impracticability of trying to capture him with a hook or harpoon, like other sea animals. He is described as having heavy, close-set scales (Job 41:15–17, 23), as making the sea "boil" (Job 41:31), as having a heart as "firm as a stone" (Job 41:24), and as breathing fire (Job 41:18–21).

Whatever one may make of such characteristics, they do not describe a crocodile! The obvious allusion to "fire-breathing dragons" is supported by the fact that many of the dragon traditions of the various nations also speak of this phenomenon. Since these animals are apparently now extinct and cannot be examined directly, it is presumptuous merely to write all this off as mythological and impossible. To say that the leviathan could not have breathed fire is to say much more than we know about leviathans (or water dragons or sea serpents). Fire flies produce light, eels produce electricity, and bombardier beetles produce explosive chemical reactions. All of these involve complex chemical processes, and it does not seem at all impossible that an animal might be given the ability to breathe out certain gaseous fumes which, on coming in contact with oxygen, would briefly ignite.

These great dragons, or dinosaurs, of the past are also used in the Bible as symbolic of evil. In particular, leviathan, the monster of the deep, is symbolic of Satan himself. The only reference in the New Testament to the dragon is in

Revelation, where the symbolic dragon is said to be "the great dragon . . . that old serpent, called the Devil, and Satan" (Rev. 12:9; cf. Rev. 20:2).

We cannot discuss the Bible's other exotic animals in as much detail as we have devoted to dragons, but the principle to remember is that they may well be extinct animals, not myths. The unicorn (Hebrew *reem*) is mentioned nine times in the Old Testament; in only one of these is there a possible suggestion that it was single-horned (Ps. 92:10). Psalm 22:21 and Deuteronomy 33:17 speak of "the horns of unicorns." Numbers 23:22 and 24:8 speak of the great strength of unicorns, and Job 39:9–12 stresses the impossibility of domesticating them. Psalm 29:6 alludes to the extreme friskiness of young unicorns.

Most scholars believe the *reem* was the great aurochs, or wild bull, which is now extinct but was well known in ancient times. Isaiah 34:7 seems to directly connect unicorns with bulls. The exact identity of this animal is uncertain, but there is certainly no reason not to think of it as a real animal, though now apparently extinct.

The same is true for the "satyr" (Hebrew *sair*). This word most frequently means simply "he-goat" or "kid," but also occasionally may refer to demons. In Greek and Roman mythology, the satyr (or "faun") was said to be a creature that was half-man/half-goat, but there is no hint that any such meaning is attached to its Old Testament usage. In certain instances, it may possibly refer to wild goats that were demon possessed (like the swine of Gadara in Matt. 8:30–32) and thus to demons worshiped in the form of goat idols (2 Chron. 11:15).

The "cockatrice" (Hebrew *tsepha*) is mentioned five times in the Old Testament (once translated as "adder" in the KJV, usually translated either as "viper" or "adder" in all occurrences in other versions). It was certainly not the mythological snake hatched from a cock's egg, of English mythology, but was some kind of venomous serpent, associated possibly with the "fiery flying serpents" of the Sinai wilderness (Isa. 14:29).

## Order of the Fossils

As we have shown, there are no real transitional forms in the fossils so that, even if the geological ages were real, there is no evidence that evolution was occurring. Similarly, we have shown that all geological formations give evidence of catastrophism in their deposition. Furthermore, since there are no worldwide time breaks in the supposed geologic column, all the major units of the column were formed continuously in a great complex of local catastrophes comprising together a worldwide hydraulic cataclysm.

But if that is so, evolutionists often object, then why do the fossil sequences look like evolution? That is, why are the lowest (Cambrian) fossils only simple marine invertebrates, while the highest (Quaternary) fossils are complex land vertebrates? As one proceeds up the geologic column — from trilobites to fishes to amphibians to reptiles to birds and mammals to man — one certainly gets the impression of orderly evolutionary progress. How can this be if all were buried in the same great cataclysm?

The answer to this question is twofold. First, the supposed order is largely superficial or even nonexistent. Second, any such order that does appear, superficially and statistically, to characterize the fossiliferous rocks is only what would be expected if the rocks were really formed in the worldwide Flood.

First, with respect to the supposed standard order, it should be remembered that the official geologic column occurs only in textbooks, never in the real world. Woodmorappe,[50] who made a thorough study of world geological maps, came to the following remarkable conclusions. Out of the 12 major geological systems (i.e., Cambrian, Ordovician, Silurian, Devonian, Permian, Mississippian, Pennsylvanian, Triassic, Jurassic, Cretaceous, Tertiary, Quaternary), two-thirds of the world's land surface has five or fewer systems represented and one-fifth of the world's land surface has three or fewer systems represented. In many parts of the world (e.g., the Canadian Shield) there is essentially no part of the geologic column, with the "basement rocks" right at the surface. The suboceanic sediments are believed to be almost always represented only by Tertiary and Quaternary sediments with Cretaceous sediments in some places. The geologic column is thus an artificial construct at best.

Furthermore, as we have also seen, the geologic age of a particular formation is determined, not by superposition or lithology or unconformities or radiometry, but by the assumed evolutionary order of fossils. Therefore it is not surprising that the geologic column so constructed should appear to follow the standard evolutionary sequence — it was made that way! Even such a vitriolic anti-creationist as Niles Eldredge has acknowledged this: "And this poses something of a problem: if we date the rocks by their fossils, how can we then turn around and talk about patterns of evolutionary change through time in the fossil record?"[51]

Dr. David Raup, curator of geology at Chicago's Field Museum of Natural History, where probably the nation's largest collection of fossils is housed, has pointed out that the fossil record as it stands is so equivocal in its order (despite the fact that billions of fossils are known to exist) that any interpretation of it is bound to be almost wholly subjective. It is not in a standard evolutionary order or any other kind of order. Raup is an evolutionist, but he acknowledges that one could fit just about any theory he likes to the record. "The fossil record of evolution is amenable to a wide variety of models ranging from completely deterministic to completely stochastic."[52] By "deterministic" he means sequences deter-

---

50. John Woodmorappe, "The Essential Non-Existence of the Evolutionary Uniformitarian Geologic Column," *Creation Research Society Quarterly,* 18 (1981): 46–71.

51. Niles Eldredge, *Time Frames: The Rethinking of Darwinian Evolution and the Theory of Punctuated Equilibrium* (New York, NY: Simon & Schuster, 1985), p. 52.

52. David M. Raup, "Probabilistic Models in Evolutionary Paleo-Biology," *American Scientist,* 166 (Jan.–Feb. 1977): 57. Raup at the time was chairman of the Geology Department at the University of Chicago.

mined by the course of evolution; by "stochastic" he means sequences completely random in occurrence.

Uniformitarians often argue that if the fossils were all buried in the same cataclysm, then the fossils should be randomly distributed rather than in an orderly sequence. Dr. Raup, who knows the fossils probably as well as any living scientist, seems to be saying they *are* randomly distributed!

On the other hand, creationists do recognize that in any real, local geologic column (remember the standard column only exists in textbooks) there often appears a more or less regular order, though with many exceptions. That is, marine invertebrate fossils are usually found in the lower strata, mammal fossils in the higher strata, and so on.

Such an order of deposition is, of course, only to be expected in a worldwide flood; it is the order of environmental associations, of habitat elevation. That is, other things being equal, the order of deposit would be the order of elevation. Organisms living at the lowest elevations would be buried at the lowest elevations, and so on. Thus, the simplest marine invertebrates would be buried first, since they live in the deep ocean. Above them are the free-swimming vertebrates. Then, at the land/ocean interface are found the amphibians and reptiles, and at the higher elevations birds, mammals, and finally man.

This also happens to be the same order as the order of degree of mobility, ability to escape being buried in sediments that would preserve the creatures as fossils. It is also the order, approximately, of numbers of organisms produced, and therefore of probability of eventual discovery by paleontologists.

Finally, within a given sedimentary formation unit, it is the order of hydrodynamic sorting action and velocity of sedimentary deposition. That is, as sediments are transported, each object experiences a certain drag force based on its size, shape, and velocity and thus is sorted out to be with others of similar characteristics. Hydrodynamic sorting is highly efficient, and even a completely heterogeneous assortment of objects will quickly be sorted as the flow moves along. Thus, except in the most violent catastrophic milieu, fossils at any horizon will tend to be fairly uniform. When the flow finally stops and the sediments settle out, the simplest, most nearly streamlined objects (of the same specific gravity) will tend to settle first, with the more complex objects settling last. Thus, in a given formation, the "simpler," less specialized objects would tend to be on the bottom, the more complex (thus, superficially, more "evolved") on the top.

The factor of hydrodynamic sorting, of course, would be effective within a given formation, with the same lithology, source area, etc., and not so much between different formations. For the latter, comprising the major units in the geologic column, the other factors — especially that of environment and elevation of habitat — will be more important. Some evolutionists do recognize the importance of this factor, acknowledging that what appears to be an evolutionary series in time is really only a variational series in habitat. "It is worth mentioning that continuous 'Evolutionary' series derived from the fossil record can in most cases be simulated by chronoclines — successions of a geographical cline population imposed by the changes of some environmental gradients."[53] To the extent that there is any real order in the fossil record, therefore, it can be best explained by the sequence of expected depositions in the Flood. Actually, as Raup has pointed out, there is no clear-cut order in the record. It certainly does not support evolution. "So the geological time scale and the basic facts of biological change over time are totally independent of evolutionary theory. . . . One of the ironies of the evolution-creation debate is that the creationists have accepted the mistaken notion that the fossil record shows a detailed and orderly progression and they have gone to great lengths to accommodate this 'fact' in their flood geology."[54]

In other words, Raup is saying that flood geologists need not bother to work out a Flood model for the order of the fossils, since there isn't any "order" to accommodate!

Two additional commonly suggested difficulties with the Flood model should be mentioned. One is that important marine strata are found throughout the geologic column, not only in the bottom portions. The fact is, however, that marine strata from two or more widely separated geologic ages are very rare in any local column, especially with terrestrial sediments between them. This is merely another artifact of the artificiality of the standard column.

The other difficulty is the rarity of human fossils deposited by the Flood. As discussed in chapter 14, the antediluvian population could well have been at least as large as the present world population. Why, then, do we find so few human fossils and remains of the pre-Flood civilizations? As we shall see in chapter 15, most of the human fossils that have been found (Neanderthal, etc.) are probably post-Flood.

The answer could well be that man is the most mobile of all creatures, and thus would be able to survive the Flood waters by swimming, climbing, rafting, and other means, much longer than other creatures. When finally overtaken and drowned, the bodies of the antediluvian men and women would finally merely decay and be dispersed, never being caught and buried in sediments at all. Except for the "anomalous fossils" occasionally found in coal beds and the like, their civilizations also were apparently completely obliterated in the awful cataclysm.

In such a wide-ranging book as this, seeking to survey all fields of science in light of Scripture, it is not possible to touch on every aspect of all these topics nor to attempt to answer all questions and difficulties that may be put forth. The great Flood in particular is an extremely complex subject in relation to all the accumulated data of the earth sciences. We have tried to establish a general framework for the study of these sciences in terms of the Flood, a framework based on an

53. V. Krassilov, "Causal Biostratigraphy," *Lethaia,* 7, no. 3 (1974): 174.
54. David M. Raup, "Evolution and the Fossil Record," letter in *Science,* 213 (July 17, 1981): 289. See also, by the same author, "Geology and Creationism," *Field Museum Bulletin,* 54 (Mar. 1983): 16–25.

abundance of solid evidence in both science and Scripture. Within this general framework, it is believed that all individual problems can eventually be resolved.

The book *The Genesis Flood*[55] can be referred to for much more extensive treatment of many of the topics surveyed in these four chapters (chapters 9, 10, 11, and 12 dealing with geophysics, hydrology, geology, and paleontology, respectively). Many scholars believe it was this book that catalyzed the modern revival of creationism.[56] Even though it was published in 1961 and is in need of updating, its basic position and data are sound, with little need of correction. The case for creationism and Flood geology is broader and stronger than it was in 1961, but there is very little change required otherwise. Many other more recent books and articles also deal with various aspects of these subjects, some of which are included in the chapter bibliographies.

---

55. John C. Whitcomb, Jr., and Henry M. Morris, *The Genesis Flood* (Philadelphia, PA: Presbyterian and Reformed, 1961), 518 p.
56. Ronald Numbers, "Creationism in 20th-Century America," *Science,* 218 (Nov. 5, 1982): 541–44.

PART

# THE LIFE SCIENCES

# THE LIFE OF THE FLESH

*Biblical Biology*

## The Life Sciences

Thus far we have devoted four chapters to the physical sciences and four to the earth sciences, showing that in every case the biblical perspective on every scientific discipline is sound and accurate, often far in advance of its original time of writing. The same will be found true with respect to the life sciences.

We have already dealt also with the interdisciplinary area between the physical sciences and the life sciences (biochemistry and the origin of life) and the interdisciplinary area between the earth sciences and the life sciences (paleontology and the history of life). In this chapter, we wish to examine the biblical doctrine of life itself — the nature of life, the various forms of life, mechanisms of variation and heredity, specific animals mentioned in the Bible, and so on. In chapter 14, we shall focus on the unique nature of human life. Chapters 15 and 16 will be devoted to the development of human populations, languages, races, nations, and cultures.

The sciences that deal with living matter have not been as fully developed as those that deal with inorganic materials. This is partly due to the more complex character of living forms. Probably it is also partly due to the fact that the physical sciences have been developed (even though unwittingly) around the basic physical principles revealed in Scripture, as discussed in previous chapters. The life sciences, however, have in the past hundred years been seriously retarded by adherence to the antiscriptural and unscientific philosophy of organic evolution. A substantial proportion of the efforts of research workers in these fields has been devoted to fruitless attempts to explain and promote evolution, and these endeavors could have been put to far more productive uses in other aspects of the study of life.

A very interesting anomaly is evident here. Biologists for the most part decry vitalism, vigorously denying that there is any sort of "vital energy" present in organic matter, energy of some radically different nature from the ordinary forms of physical energy. Such concepts as those of "creative evolution," "orthogenesis," "entelechy," and the like are anathema to most life scientists. They contend that all organic processes must be explained in terms of chemistry and physics (notably the first and second law of thermodynamics) must be as determinative in organic processes as they are in inorganic processes. These laws postulate quantitative stability and qualitative deterioration, rather than evolutionary growth and development. And this quite clearly indicates that evolution is invalid as a guiding principle in the study of biologic processes. Certainly there may be mechanisms of biologic change, but these changes must be fundamentally conservational or degradational in nature.

These facts had of course been previously set forth in Scripture. The essential identification of the physical substance of organic and inorganic matter is clearly indicated. The "earth" was to bring forth grass, herbs, and trees (Gen. 1:11), as well as cattle and other living creatures (Gen. 1:24; 29). Finally, man's body itself was formed of the dust of the earth (Gen. 2:7; 3:19). In other words, the elementary materials out of which the earth was made (which we know to be the various chemical elements) were also used to make the bodies of living organisms and of man himself. Another very fundamental fact of biologic science revealed in Scripture is that of biogenesis and stability. This fact is generally denied in evolutionary theory, of course, but is nevertheless borne out by the actual data of science. That is, there is no real evidence that the present clear-cut "gaps" between the basic "kinds" of living creatures have ever been crossed or narrowed. Obviously, there are many types of biologic differences. No two individuals are ever exactly alike, even when born of the same parents. There is tremendous potential for variation around the fixed locus of each basic kind of animal, leading to different varieties, perhaps occasionally even to different species and genera, depending upon how these are defined. But never is there any actual evidence that these variations, in either the present or the past, have resulted in changes beyond the limits of the Genesis "kind." If life scientists would only accept this basic fact of science as revealed in the biblical "textbook," it could be a tremendous boon to further progress in understanding the science of life.

Another important revealed fact, generally rejected by modern anthropologists and psychologists and others dealing with the phenomena of human life, is that man himself is basically distinct from all other types of living creatures. The elements of his body are no different, of course, as we have seen. But man has been created "in the image of God" (Gen. 1:26; 9:6), and this certainly involves more than the "breath of life," that God breathed into man, because this is shared by other creatures (Gen. 2:7; see also Gen. 7:21–22). Perhaps even this much ought to indicate that it will never be possible to understand living matter in terms solely of chemistry and physics. Certainly it seems to imply quite strongly that the "breath of life" is of such a different order of phenomena that any hope of man "creating" life is ill-advised, to say the least. Yet how much scientific talent is being wasted in fruitless efforts in this direction!

Experimentation on animals may yield much valuable information on characteristics of the living matter of which human bodies are composed but cannot yield correct insight into the behavior of man himself. The assumption that it may yield such information is one of the tragic mistakes of modern behavioral and social science, stemming from the erroneous belief that there is an evolutionary continuity between man and other creatures. If only psychologists and sociologists and others in similar fields would be willing to recognize the basically spiritual nature of man and his behavior! Since man is made "in the image of God," his actions must be intrinsically connected with this fact and its implications. He has rebelled against the divine fellowship for which he was created, and the behavior of unregenerate man is fundamentally dependent upon this fact, and not upon chemical and physical phenomena or upon those characteristics of consciousness and intelligence that are shared with animals. A real science of human behavior must necessarily be built upon the great biblical truths of the Fall, redemption, and reconciliation, and certainly the Bible is our only reliable "textbook" on these areas of science!

## Biological Life and the Bible

As already pointed out, the entity of biological life in the Bible is associated with the created *nephesh*, the regular Old Testament word for "soul" but also frequently translated "life" and in various other ways, depending on context. It is first used in connection with God's second great act of fiat creation. "And God created great whales [or as noted in chapter 12, 'dragons'] and every living creature [*nephesh*]" (Gen. 1:21). The word "living" in this passage is the Hebrew *chay*, which also is translated "life" and in various other ways.

The fact that this biological life, or "soul," is not merely a very complex assemblage of inorganic replicating chemical systems, as in the case of plants, is indicated by the fact that its generation required a special act of creation by God — the same mighty power that called into existence the space-mass-time universe in Genesis 1:1.

The *nephesh* is also associated with "the breath of life." In speaking of the formation of man's body, the record says, "And the Lord God . . . breathed into his nostrils the breath of life; and man became a living soul [*nephesh*]" (Gen. 2:7).

That is, in order to have the created *nephesh*, the body must have "breath" (Hebrew *ruach*). This word is the same word as for "wind" or "spirit." That animals other than man possess the breath of life is evident from Genesis 7:21–22 where it is stressed that all having the breath of life — fowl, cattle, beasts, creeping things, as well as man, perished in the waters of the great Flood. Just as the

Spirit (*ruach*) of God was present to energize the created universe (Gen. 1:2), so He gives to every living soul the "breath" (note Ps. 104:29–30). The higher animals, therefore, as well as man, possess both soul and spirit (or "life and breath") as a gift of God's creative love and power.

This does not apply to plants, however, and possibly not to the lower orders of animals either. Plants were formed from the inorganic elements of the earth on the third day of creation week (Gen. 1:11–12), but no act of special creation was involved. Rather, the earth "brought forth" its plant cover. This also was a mighty act of the power of God, as was everything God accomplished in the six days of creation week. But it was "making" or "forming" or "developing," not "creating." Plants have neither soul nor spirit, as do animals, though they are marvelous organisms, designed to provide a continuing food supply for the animate creation (Gen. 1:29–30).

Evolutionists may object at this point that, at the lower levels of plant and animal life — especially the protozoans, not to mention the viruses — there is no clear-cut boundary. In fact, some have proposed a third "kingdom" (in addition to the plant kingdom and the animal kingdom) — the kingdom of the *protista* — for those organisms that cannot be clearly distinguished as either plants or animals.

However, the Scriptures have laid down a very important principle by which to identify animals that possess life in the real biblical sense. "The life of the flesh is in the blood" (Lev. 17:11; see also Gen. 9:3–6).

In this key verse, the word "life" is *nephesh*. The fact that the blood sustains life is a relatively modern concept, especially associated with William Harvey's discovery in 1616 of the circulation of the blood. The blood carries water and nourishment to every cell, transmits hormones as needed, maintains the body's temperature, and removes the waste materials of the body cells. Especially vital is the "breath of life," and it is the blood that carries the oxygen from the lungs to the rest of the body's cells.

The importance of the heart in the blood circulation is also anticipated in Proverbs 14:30: "A sound heart is the life of the flesh." "Life" in this verse is *chay* rather than *nephesh*. The heart/blood system is the vitally essential basis of every "living creature" (*chay nephesh*) that God created (Gen. 1:21).

Plants, of course, do not possess this heart/blood apparatus (though there may appear to be a superficial analogy between the sap and the blood) and so, as already noted, they are not really living creatures in the biblical sense. Some of the simpler invertebrate animals likewise have only rudimentary circulation systems, if any, and so could possibly be regarded as not really having the "blood" that denotes biblical life. This is a matter of speculation at present, but could warrant further research. At least it is interesting that, so far as known, the Bible never uses the term "life" or "death" or their correlatives in connection with either plants or one-celled animals or even the simpler invertebrate many-celled animals.

The vital spiritual importance of blood in the Bible, especially the shedding of blood, is derived indirectly from its scientific importance. Since physical life is maintained by the blood, it is fitting to take the blood as symbolic of spiritual life. Ever since Adam, the divine penalty for sin has been death, with the ultimate death being the "second death," eternal separation from God in the lake of fire (Rev. 20:14–15). Deliverance from the death penalty requires nothing less than the sacrificial shedding of innocent blood, with the life of a sinless substitute being offered up instead of that of the guilty sinner. There is no sinless human blood, however; that is, none except that of the one perfect man, God himself who became man, the Lord Jesus Christ. God could only allow the covering of sin by the shed blood of certain animal sacrifices. Since animals do not have a moral nature, the requirement for innocent blood could only be symbolized and then only by using animals that were physically "without spot or blemish."

The blood of bulls and goats could symbolize spiritual life but could never provide spiritual life, for it could never take away sin. Only Christ's blood could take away sin. As the blood carries away the wastes, and then provides the food and water and air needed for the body's life, so the shed blood of Christ takes away sin and imparts the bread of life, the living water, and the Spirit of God, to the one who receives Him by faith.

## After Their Kinds

That God is the Creator of all things, including all plants and animals, is the unequivocal teaching of Scripture. That these were all established in distinctive groupings called "kinds" (Hebrew *min*) and that there are permanent clear-cut gaps between these kinds (though much potential variation within kinds) is the obvious implication of Scripture. This prescription applies to the complex replicating chemical systems of both plants and animals, as well as man.

The formation of the various kinds is not said to have been a work of creation, but was nonetheless the direct result of unique divine work. Using the "dust of the earth," the basic chemical elements, and a marvelous genetic replication system that scientists are only barely beginning to unravel today, God established a tremendous array of various kinds of organisms to occupy the beautiful world He had made. Each of these was equipped with a perfectly coordinated structure to accomplish its divinely intended mission in the world and also with the will and ability to reproduce itself after its kind.

This meaningful phrase is found no less than ten times in the first chapter of Genesis, referring to grasses, herbs, and trees, fishes and birds, and beasts and creeping things. All were to obey this rule.

> And God said, Let the earth bring forth grass, the herb yielding seed, and the fruit tree yielding fruit *after his kind*, whose seed is in itself, upon the earth: and it was so. And the earth brought forth grass, and herb yielding seed *after his kind*, and the tree yielding fruit, whose seed was in itself, *after his kind*: and God saw that it was good (Gen. 1:11–12, emphasis added).

> And God created great whales, and every living creature that moveth which the waters brought forth abundantly, *after their kind*, and every winged fowl, *after his kind*: and God saw that it was good (Gen. 1:21, emphasis added).

> And God said, Let the earth bring forth the living creature *after his kind*, cattle, and creeping thing, and beast of the earth *after his kind*: and it was so. And God made the beast of the earth *after his kind*, and cattle *after their kind*, and every thing that creepeth upon the earth *after his kind*: and God saw that it was good (Gen. 1:24–25, emphasis added).

In the five verses quoted above, the phrase "after his kind" or "after their kind" occurs ten times, as emphasized. While the broad categories as listed certainly do not enable us to determine the exact meaning of the term "kind" (Hebrew *min*), the principle is clear that distinct categories within the plant and animal kingdoms have existed right from the beginning. Whatever the "kind" may be, it is *something*. Each kind was designed to reproduce after its own kind, not to become some other kind. Creationists insist that these clear statements of God's creative act and purpose absolutely exclude theistic evolution as an option for Christians who really believe the Bible to be God's Word.

Early philosophers tended to believe in a "great chain of being" throughout all life. Many biologists believed that the cell was the fundamental unit in biology with all cells essentially the same. Contrary to this idea, the Bible teaches that all flesh is not the same flesh. This fact that distinct categories of organisms exist, rather than all being connected in an evolutionary chain of existence is confirmed also in the New Testament. "But God giveth it a body as it hath pleased him, and to every seed his own body. All flesh is not the same flesh: but there is one kind of flesh of men, another flesh of beasts, another of fishes, and another of birds" (1 Cor. 15:38–39). Each "seed," therefore, has its own divinely given "body," both to enable it and to constrain it to reproduce after his own kind, and not after some other kind. These distinctive patterns, once impressed by God on the original plants and animals, have remained essentially unchanged since the beginning. "Can the fig tree, my brethren, bear olive berries? either a vine figs? so can no fountain both yield salt water and fresh" (James 3:12).

However, assuming that there really are distinctive created kinds, and that these are fundamentally inviolate, the question is, how do these relate to the standard taxonomic system of biological classification used by biologists today, the so-called Linnaean system? The major categories in this system are as follows in descending order of rank and scope: kingdom, phylum, class, order, family, genus, species, variety. Which of these corresponds to the biblical "kind" (or *baramin*, if one adopts the term suggested by creationist Frank Marsh[1])?

Very few creationists have ever taught (although evolutionists have frequently

---

1. Frank L. Marsh, *Life, Man, and Time* (Mountain View, CA: Pacific, 1957), p. 118. The term *baramin* is constructed of the Hebrew words *bara* ("create") and *min* ("kind") and has been used by various later creationist writers.

alleged they have) that the *species* is the same as the Genesis *kind*. Consequently, creationists do not necessarily hold to the "fixity of species," as evolutionists claim they do. In the early days of biology, practically all biologists were creationists and their purpose in working out the biological classification system was certainly not to show any imagined evolutionary connections, but to identify evidence of order and design in the created kinds. Carolus Linnaeus, in 1735, tried to identify the species as a natural, stable, interbreeding unit, which he assumed to be identical with the Genesis kind. Many years later, after much further research, he decided that this was too narrow a definition, so he then defined the genus as more or less equivalent to the kind.

In recent years, scientific creationists have attempted to define the biblical kind in various ways, though none define it as narrowly as the species category. Probably most would say that no single category always fits, so that sometimes the kind is the species, sometimes the genus, sometimes the family. Even evolutionary taxonomists have differed widely from each other as to the exact nature and limits of a species or genus, for example.

In many ways, the most "natural" of the Linnaean categories (at least among the higher animals) appears to be that of the family (bears, dogs, etc.), so this category may represent approximately the original kind. The family is characterized more by similar behaviors and physiologies than by ease of interbreeding. On the other hand, the species does seem to be a highly stable unit in the present order of things, with very little evidence that it ever changes significantly. In fact, this is the strong base of the modern "punctuated-equilibrium" school of evolutionary thought.

> To a very large extent, the formation of a species is a phenomenon which has occurred in the past, so that the recognition of the events surrounding the actual division of an ancient gene pool cannot be directly observed. . . . The search for truly incipient species has been difficult and, to a considerable degree, frustrating.[2]

> No one has ever produced a species by mechanisms of natural selection. No one has ever gotten near it and most of the current argument in neo-Darwinism is about this question: how a species originates. And it is there that natural selection seems to be fading out, and chance mechanisms of one sort or another are being invoked.[3]

> Ever since Darwin called his book *The Origin of Species*, evolutionists have regarded the formation of reproductively isolated units by speciation as a fundamental process of large-scale change. Yet speciation occurs at too high a level to be observed directly in nature or produced by experiments in most

---

2. Hampton L. Carson, "Chromosomes and Species Formation" (review of *Odes of Speciation* by M.J.D. White), *Evolution*, 32 (1978): 325.
3. Colin Patterson, "Cladistics," interview on British Broadcasting Corporation, Mar. 4, 1982. Interviewer, Peter Franz; producer, Brian Lak.

cases. Therefore, theories of speciation have been based on analogy, extrapolation, and inference.[4]

Evolutionists occasionally cite instances of new species being formed ("events of speciation"), but these are very few and highly equivocal. Paleontological studies, as pointed out in the last chapter, are causing modern paleontologists to conclude that species typically survive unchanged for a hundred thousand generations or more. Furthermore, they seem to appear suddenly and then disappear suddenly, with no transitions.

Thus, modern punctuated-equilibrium advocates argue that speciation must occur in quantum leaps. Most, however, do not propose the "hopeful-monster" idea, where the new form originates in a single leap, probably in one individual (it would take two individuals, of course, to reproduce the new form), but in a few generations in a small population. "Evidence is also mounting that quantum speciation events themselves may span rather few generations. . . . It is generally agreed that quantum speciation takes place within very small populations — some would say populations involving fewer than 10 individuals."[5]

The great Harvard systematic zoologist Ernst Mayr, though generally considered one of the pillars of the neo-Darwinian gradualism school of evolutionary thought, long ago advocated a very similar concept, which he called the "founder principle." Another leading neo-Darwinian, Theodosius Dobzhansky, incisively discussed this principle in connection with his famous studies on speciation in fruit flies.

> The founder principle is "establishment of a new population by a few original founders (in an extreme case, by a single fertilized female) that carry only a small fraction of the total genetic variation of the parental population." Founder events are inevitably followed by inbreeding for one or several generations. The populations descended from the founders are then restructured by natural selection, which operates on a changed gene pool and usually in an altered environment.[6]

This "restructured population" after the "founder event" might be considerably different from the "parental population," and it is examples taken especially from Dobzhansky's fruit flies that evolutionists usually cite when they talk about modern-day events of speciation. These might well be taken also as instances of Stanley's "quantum speciation."

Very small inbreeding populations of other creatures as well (including men) have been observed to develop distinctively new characteristics quite rapidly, in contrast to the quite stable very-slow-drifting characteristics of large populations.

---

4. Stephen Jay Gould, "Is a New and General Theory of Evolution Emerging?" *Paleobiology,* 6, no. 1 (1980): 122.
5. Steven M. Stanley, *Macroevolution: Pattern and Process* (San Francisco, CA: W.M. Freeman, 1979), p. 145.
6. Theodosius Dobzhansky, "Species of Drosophila," *Science,* 177 (Aug. 25, 1972): 667.

Genetic characteristics that tend to be recessive and only latent in large populations have much better opportunity of becoming visibly expressed and dominant in such small founder populations.

The "altered environment" is also an important stimulus to rapid change. This may be true even in large populations. The classic cases of "evolution-in-action" often cited by evolutionists (changed coloration in peppered moths, development of resistance to antibiotics by bacterial strains, etc.) are all simply cases of recombinations of existing genetic characteristics selectively preserved in the changed environment. Another leading neo-Darwinist says, "Hence it is not surprising that whenever a new environmental challenge materializes — a change of climate, the introduction of a new predator or competition, man-made pollution — populations are usually able to adapt to it. A dramatic recent example is the evolution by insect species of resistance to pesticides."[7] Ayala makes it plain that such changes are not due to mutations, as often asserted by evolutionists, but merely to recombinations of factors already present.

Thus, either an altered environment or an isolated, small population can lead to rapid changes in the characteristics of a species, possibly even to a new species, depending on definitions. If both are present, there would be the greatest potential for rapid variation (or speciation). That is, if a small population is somehow placed in a radically different environment and then forced to inbreed to survive, the most favorable constraints possible toward producing new population characteristics — and doing it rapidly — would have been applied. What could well be recognized as a distinctly new and different species would probably soon appear, adapted to the new environment, not even inclined to mate with its relatives from the old population.

These changes do not constitute evolution, however, but simply variation (production of new varieties) or possibly speciation. In some cases even new genera may result. All, however, would merely constitute recombinations of genetic factors already present in the genotype since the original creation of the kinds, but without previous need or opportunity for expression in the respective phenotypes.

Note how perfectly all this coincides with the Genesis record. Assuming that the "created kinds" corresponded in general to our modern taxonomic families, each family of land animals would be represented by a single pair of animals on Noah's ark (the "clean" animals would be represented by three pairs plus an extra animal, presumably for sacrificial purposes).

In the globally uniform pleasant climate and lush environments of the pre-Flood world, each of these kinds would also have been rather uniform in its characteristics and probably large and vigorous physically. Within the genetic system of each kind, however, was an abundant range of potential variation lying dormant until evoked by the changing environmental pressures lying in its unknown future.

---

7. Francisco J. Ayala, "The Mechanisms of Evolution," *Scientific American*, 239 (Sept. 1978): 64.

With the precipitation of the earth's antediluvian vapor canopy, its weather was no longer subtropical everywhere, and a wide assortment of climatic zones had been established. The geography also was vastly altered, with a multitude of new environmental niches that had not existed before. In general, the environments were far more varied and more rigorous than before, and they would continue to change still more for many centuries after the Flood.

When the animals emerged from the ark they were instructed (or "programmed") by God to multiply and fill the earth.

> And God spake unto Noah, saying, Go forth of the ark, thou, and thy wife, and thy sons, and thy sons' wives with thee. Bring forth with thee every living thing that is with thee, of all flesh, both of fowl, and of cattle, and of every creeping thing that creepeth upon the earth; that they may breed abundantly in the earth, and be fruitful, and multiply upon the earth. And Noah went forth and his sons, and his wife, and his sons' wives with him: every beast, every creeping thing, and every fowl, and whatsoever creepeth upon the earth, after their kinds, went forth out of the ark (Gen. 8:15–19).

It is significant that, in this last sentence, the phrase "after their kinds" is not the same as that used ten times in Genesis 1. "Kinds" here is not the usual *min* but rather *mishpachah*, usually translated "families" or "kindreds" and normally referring to human families. For example, it appears next in the account of the post-Flood nations. "By these were the isles of the Gentiles divided in their lands; every one after his tongue, after their families, in their nations" (Gen. 10:5).

The term may be applied either to a man's immediate family in his own household or to all his descendants, depending on context. Its unique use mentioned above in connection with the animal "families" leaving the ark, suggests that the proliferation and multiplication of animals on the earth after the Flood was similar to that of the human family (though only reluctantly followed by mankind after its forced implementation at Babel).

As each animal family migrated away from Ararat, conditions were optimal for proliferation (no competition, with the whole world available for foraging) and rapid speciation (small inbreeding populations, with environments changing rapidly both geographically and temporally). Each family soon divided into an array of species, each with characteristics appropriate for the particular ecological niche into which it had entered. For example, the original bear family on the ark has become the polar bear, the grizzly bear, the brown bear, and all other bears. The original pair of dogs (probably something like the dire wolf) has become the wolf, the coyote, the domestic dog, and all the others in the dog family.

Some such scenario seems to correlate perfectly with all known data of taxonomy and population genetics. It accounts for the present stability of species, since the speciation events took place thousands of years ago and environments are now relatively stable. It also accounts for the similar morphological and behavioral patterns of the various members of each family. Genera may represent either arbitrary groupings of species within the family or else the first generation group of speciation events.

Since the "clean" kinds were represented on the ark by seven animals rather than the single pair that was specified in most cases (note Gen. 7:2), it would be expected that the number of species in their families would now usually be greater than in the case of "unclean" kinds, corresponding to the greater amount of variational potential in three original pairs as compared with one. This, in fact, turns out to be the case.

Not only do the existing unclean kinds exhibit a relatively small number of species and varieties, but great numbers of them (e.g., the dinosaurs, therapsids) have become extinct altogether. The created variational potential within each kind is very great, enabling it to adapt to a wide variety of environmental changes, and this is a testimony to the great conservation principle established by the Creator. However, it is not unlimited. In a world under the Curse and the reign of decay and death, the environment may become so difficult that a given kind of organism may finally become unable to adapt sufficiently to survive at all.

Especially in the early centuries after the Flood, with the climate so drastically different from that of the antediluvian world, and with the environments difficult and changing, many of the animals finally became extinct. There continue to be extinctions taking place even today. (Incidentally, there have been many recorded extinctions of existing animals in historic times, but no recorded evolutionary emergences of new animals. If this is typical, it is amazing that we still have any animals at all after the supposed millions of years of earth history!) But the long list of extinct animals now known only as fossils is mute testimonial to the drastic environmental deteriorations occasioned by the great Flood. The present world is "zoologically impoverished," as the great geologist James Dana used to say, in comparison with the multitudinous variety of great beasts and birds that roamed the antediluvian world.

## Animal Classification in the Bible

At least 160 different specific animals are mentioned in the Bible and the descriptions of the animals that can be identified are all quite consistent with what we know about these animals today. Many, however, are difficult to identify at this time. A few will be discussed briefly in this section.

First, however, it will be helpful to note again that the biblical system of classification has a somewhat different basis than that of the modern Linnaean system. The "kind" is the basic biblical unit; as discussed in the preceding section, the Linnaean equivalent could be anything from the species to the family. It is quite possible that future creationist genetic research will be able to delineate these boundaries more precisely.[8]

---

8. A helpful discussion on this subject is Arthur J. Jones, "A General Analysis of the Biblical 'Kind' (Min)," *Creation Research Society Quarterly,* 9 (June 1972): 53–57.

It is interesting that frequently asked questions about the Genesis "kind" resulted in 1995 in the formation by Dr. Kurt Wise and others of an informal ongoing committee on "baraminology," seeking to determine the limits of the "kind" (Hebrew *min*), among other things. Their research and studies seem to confirm the close correlation of the Linnaean "family" with the "baramin" in many cases, with the ability to produce hybrids the best indicator of related groups within each baramin.

As far as broader categories in the Bible are concerned, plants and animals are distinguished from each other, but the other divisions bear little resemblance to the arbitrary system of modern taxonomy. Plants are divided in the Bible simply into three broad groups: (1) grasses; (2) herbs; and (3) fruit trees (Gen. 1:11–12). All types of plant structures do fit fairly easily into one or the other of these categories.

Divisions of the animal kingdom are somewhat more complex, but again are based on natural, visual groupings for ease of human identification and discussion. The "fowls of the air" were created on the fifth day of creation week, concurrently with all the marine animals (Gen. 1:20–21). Among the latter, the "great whales" (Hebrew *tannim*, "dragons," or probably great marine reptiles) are specifically mentioned. On the sixth day were made the "cattle," the "beast of the earth," and the "creeping things" (Gen. 1:22–25), as well as man. These animals are all then summarized as "fish of the sea," "fowls of the air," "cattle," and "creeping things" (Gen. 1:26). Mentioned separately is the "beast of the earth" (Gen. 1:25), and possibly still another category is "beasts of the field" (Gen. 2:19). The last two, however, may well be synonymous.

Again, these are natural divisions, based on general appearance, and especially on ecology or sphere of life. The "fowls of the air" and "fish of the sea" constitute such obvious divisions that they have been incorporated in the modern Linnaean system as the class *Aves* and the class *Pisces*, respectively. It is probable that "the beasts of the earth" (i.e., "land") include all the larger wild animals of the dry land, and the "cattle" are the domesticable animals, the two groups together being more or less equivalent to land mammals. Also, they may include some of the larger land reptiles and amphibians, especially many that are now extinct.

The "creeping things" seem to cut across many categories of the modern system. There are "flying creeping things" (Lev. 11:21; Deut. 14:19), and a number of small mammals are called creeping things (Lev. 11:29), as well as most small reptiles. Apparently anything that "creepeth upon the earth" (Lev. 11:41) or that "goeth upon his belly" (Lev. 11:42) is included in the term. There are also creeping things in the sea (Ps. 104:25), both "small and great beasts." In fact, the term "moving creature," used to describe the swarms of marine animals created on the fifth day of creation (Gen. 1:20–21), is the Hebrew *sherets*, which is also translated "creeping thing" in many passages that apply specifically to land animals

(Gen. 7:21; Lev. 11:29; et al.). It seems that the "creeping things" include all animals that crawl along close to the ground, whether they are marine, land, or air animals. This group would probably comprise most marine invertebrates, as well as all insects and most amphibians and reptiles (though not the *tannim*, or dinosaurs). Even the smaller land mammals (rats, moles, etc.) are considered to be creeping things.

The above are the broad categories of animals according to the Bible, and these are natural and easily comprehended groupings. The narrower category of the "kind" as already discussed, is evidently also a natural grouping, even though we are not yet certain just how it fits into the Linnaean taxonomy.

Leviticus 11 and Deuteronomy 14 give numerous examples of what the Bible apparently means by "kinds." The problem lies in identifying the particular animals, however, since the Hebrew words are in many cases obscure and controversial. Some that do seem to be fairly well identified are the raven, the hawk, the eagle, the heron, the locust, the grasshopper, the mouse, the ox, the sheep, the goat, the camel, and the pig, among others. These examples at least provide some insight into the general nature of this category called "kind" in the Bible. In the Linnaean nomenclature, the "family" may well be as close as we can come to the biblical kind, at least in the present state of genetic understanding.

There is another very broad classification scheme for animals in the Bible, the twofold division of "clean" and "unclean." These terms are not defined explicitly but seem to be used to identify animals that are suitable for two purposes. That is, clean animals could be eaten by the Israelites and could also be used as sacrifices; unclean animals could not be so used.

This distinction is first noted in the gathering of animals into Noah's ark. Seven of each clean kind were carried in contrast to only two of each unclean kind (Gen. 7:2). The three pairs of each clean animal were presumably specified in order to permit greater numbers to develop, as well as more varieties, since these would be more suitable to domesticate for food and other purposes than would the unclean animals. The seventh animal was apparently intended for sacrifice immediately after the Flood (Gen. 8:20).

The divine decision as to which animals were "clean" and thus suitable for human consumption was, no doubt, based on physiological and health considerations. Carnivorous animals and carrion-eating animals were off limits, as were birds of prey and almost all "creeping things." Among herbivorous animals, only those were defined as clean that had cloven hooves and chewed the cud (Lev. 11:3; Deut. 14:7). Under this rule, the clean animals included cattle, sheep, goats, deer, antelope, and gazelle, but not the pig, the rabbit, and many other animals that were and are commonly eaten by many non-Israelite peoples.

Although the Bible does not mention particular fish by name, fish were a very common food staple. Fish with scales and fins (that is, the bony fishes) were considered clean (Lev. 11:9–12). Other marine creatures such as the cartilaginous fishes (e.g., sharks, eels, catfish) and the shellfish and other invertebrates were excluded by this rule.

Certain insects were considered suitable for food, notably locusts, crickets, and grasshoppers. These are, indeed, a good source of protein and are still eaten regularly in many parts of the world. However, almost all other "creeping things" were considered unclean.

These restrictive classifications are generally recognized in modern medical and nutritional science as well-founded physiologically for various reasons — unclean nature of diet, susceptibility to infection and parasites, etc. The flesh of unclean animals is much more likely to be harmful to humans than that of clean animals.

Only these clean animals could be used as sacrificial offerings on the altar, whereas the ancient pagans commonly sacrificed pigs, dogs, and other unclean animals. As far as the worship of Jehovah was concerned, blood shed on the altar must be "clean" blood, just as the flesh eaten by His people must be clean flesh, as "the life of the flesh is in the blood" (Lev. 17:11).

In the New Testament economy the distinction between clean and unclean has been eliminated as far as dietary prohibitions are concerned (Acts 10:9–16); 1 Tim. 4:3–5), and blood sacrifices have been eliminated altogether. Nevertheless, although there are no longer any theological restrictions as to diet, the health reasons involved are worth considering and are still recognized today as being well-founded.

## Questionable Descriptions

A comparison of the animal names listed in Leviticus 11 as translated in the King James Version and as translated in, say, the New King James Version (both of which are based on the same Hebrew texts and principles) will graphically show that the modern equivalents of the Hebrew animal names are highly uncertain. See table 7.

The same kind of confusion will be noted in other Bible translations and commentaries, as well as throughout the other books of the Old Testament (the New Testament translations do not seem to have this problem). For example, the King James "greyhound" (Prov. 30:31) becomes a "war horse" in the American Standard Version (footnote), a "strutting cock" in the New American Standard, a "peacock" in the Living Bible, and a "greyhound" again in the New King James.

This all seems very strange. Why do Hebrew scholars find it so hard to recognize the names of animals in the Hebrew language when most other nouns seem to cause relatively little trouble?

The answer could well be that it is not the words that have changed, but the animals. The uniformitarian bias with which modern scholars seem almost always to be afflicted impels them to try to identify each Hebrew animal name with some existing modern animal. The fact is, however, that the fossil record (including that of the Pleistocene epoch, which is acknowledged even by evolutionists to be the epoch when modern man appeared) reveals great numbers of fossils of extinct

### TABLE 7 — Uncertainty of Animal Names in the Old Testament

*As indicated in the tabulation below, the Hebrew words for animals in the older books of the Bible are often of very uncertain meaning, indicating that at least some of them may be extinct animals, now known only as fossils.*

| Text | Animal name as translated in | |
| --- | --- | --- |
| | **King James** | **New King James** |
| Leviticus 11:13 | eagle, ossifrage, ospray | eagle, vulture, buzzard |
| Leviticus 11:16 | owl, night hawk, cuckow, hawk | ostrich, seagull, hawk, short-eared owl |
| Leviticus 11:18 | swan, pelican, gier eagle | white owl, jackdaw, carrion vulture |
| Leviticus 11:29 | weasel, mouse, tortoise | mole, mouse, large lizard |
| Leviticus 11:30 | ferret, chameleon, lizard, snail, mole | gecko, monitor lizard, sand reptile, sand lizard, chameleon |
| Deuteronomy 14:5 | hart, roebuck, fallow deer, wild goat, pygarg, wild ox, chamois | deer, gazelle, roe deer, wild goat, mountain goat, antelope, mountain sheep |

animals. If one accepts the biblical chronology as it stands, without trying to distort it to allow for the evolutionary ages of an imaginary historical geology, then all of these fossil animals were at one time contemporaneous with early post-Flood man. They have become extinct because of inability to adapt to the radically altered postdiluvian environments. The rate of extinctions was very high in the early centuries after the Flood, but it eventually slowed down, and the remaining kinds have continued reasonably constant now for two millennia or more.

We have already noted this phenomenon, in the previous chapter, in connection with behemoth (Job 40:15–24). Commentators persist in identifying this mighty creature as a hippopotamus or an elephant, even though such are patently absurd in light of the recorded description of the behemoth, which almost certainly portrays a dinosaur. Surely there should be no such trouble in recognizing this animal, "chief of the ways of God" (Job 40:19), if it were still a living animal. The fact that it is an extinct animal, however, now known only through its fossil record, makes it all very clear. If people could, over many generations, forget the meaning of the name even of this greatest of all animals, it is not surprising that the names of many lesser animals would likewise be forgotten after they become extinct. Translators should quit trying to be interpreters. When they don't know the modern equivalent of the name, they should leave it untranslated, and merely transliterate it as they did with "behemoth" and "leviathan" (Job 41:1).

This situation will go far toward explaining those few instances in which the biblical descriptions of certain animals have been judged mistaken. The most frequently cited case is that of Leviticus 11:6. "And the hare, because he cheweth the cud, but divideth not the hoof; he is unclean unto you." Critics have called this one of the "mistakes of Moses," since hares are not ruminants and thus do not chew the cud. Conservative apologists have usually suggested that the hare appears to chew the cud, or partially chews the cud, but opponents argue that these are equivocations. The Hebrew word is *arnebeth* and the fact is that no one knows any modern animal that really corresponds to *arnebeth*. The probability is that the *arnebeth* is difficult to identify because it is now extinct. The same situation quite likely applies to many other animal names recorded in the Bible's earliest books, such as Job and the Pentateuch.

## Jonah and the Whale

The animal subjected to the greatest amount of ridicule by Bible critics, however, is undoubtedly the great fish that swallowed Jonah. The fish may well have been a whale and the New Testament Greek word (*ketos*) is so translated in the King James Version (Matt. 12:40). However, the word itself simply means a huge fish. The word used in the story of Jonah in the Old Testament (Hebrew *dag*) is the common word for "fish," but it is modified by *gadol*, meaning "great" (Jonah 1:17). In biblical taxonomy, of course, the whale is certainly a great fish (not a "beast of the earth," the term used for other large wild mammals), but there are also other great fish (e.g., the whale shark). It could also have been a now-extinct fish, or even a fish especially prepared by God for this one occasion. In any case, the critics are certainly out of order when they allege that the gullet of the whale is not large enough to permit a man to pass whole into the belly. The gullets of several species of whales, as well as that of the whale shark and probably others, are certainly amply large for this purpose. Furthermore, there have been several modern Jonah-type incidents alleged in the history of the whaling industry, when men were swallowed whole by whales and yet survived.

Nevertheless, the record of Jonah's experience is clearly miraculous, so there is no need to discuss naturalistic parallels at all. His experience was said to be a type of the coming death and resurrection of Christ, and Jonah himself testified that he had drowned and his soul was in Sheol (equivalent to Hades, the place of departed spirits); his body was swallowed by the fish, then later revived by God and delivered from the belly of the fish (Jonah 2:2, 5, 6, 10) in answer to his prayer.

The subject of miracles and the authenticity of those recorded in the Bible has already been discussed in chapter 3. Jonah's deliverance was a mighty miracle of creation, but even greater was the miraculous conversion of the whole city of Nineveh when Jonah preached to its people (Jon. 3:5) the message of repentance and faith toward the true God of creation.

## Modern Genetics and the Flocks of Jacob

A fascinating biological excursus is found in the story of Jacob and the development of his own flocks through genetic manipulation of the flocks of his employer, Laban (Gen. 30–31). Jacob had agreed to continue to work for Laban, with his wages to be any future progeny of Laban's flocks of goats that might turn out to be "speckled and spotted" (that were normally and dominantly black in color) and sheep that might be speckled, spotted, or brown (that were dominantly white). The flocks were mostly solid-colored animals, so this was obviously a very good deal for Laban, whose flocks had already multiplied tremendously under the skillful supervision of Jacob. Furthermore, Jacob offered to separate all the spotted and off-colored animals from the flock initially and not to use any of them for breeding with the solid-colored animals. In fact, Laban's sons were instructed to keep this speckled flock well separated from Jacob. Thus, Jacob's wages were to be only those spotted and streaked animals, as well as the brown sheep, that were born from a flock initially composed only of solid black goats and solid white sheep. When an animal meeting these specifications was born, it would immediately be removed into Jacob's small flock.

These seemed like extraordinarily favorable terms to crafty Laban, and he immediately accepted them, especially since he had been so anxious to retain the services of Jacob that he had given him carte blanche to name whatever wages he wanted. How could Jacob possibly develop an appreciable flock of his own under such restrictive conditions?

Jacob, however, had spent many decades breeding and raising livestock, first for his father and then more than 14 years for Laban. He had a scientific mind and had empirically learned many principles of animal genetics. He knew that even in a flock of solid-colored animals there would be some that were what modern geneticists called "heterozygous" — that is, they had within their genetic endowment the ability to produce a small proportion of off-colored progeny. Many, of course, were "homozygous" and when two homozygous animals mated, they could produce only the dominant coloration in their offspring. The latter were predominant in the flocks, so it was an act of faith on Jacob's part, trusting God to see to it that spotted and off-colored animals would somehow come from an apparently homogeneous flock of normal-colored animals.

God did honor Jacob's faith, as well as his high integrity in dealing with Laban. Though Jacob could not know which of the goats and sheep were heterozygous, God knew, and He saw to it that only these mated with the homozygous animals (or with each other), so that a much greater proportion than normal turned out be ring-streaked, spotted, and speckled. God later revealed to Jacob in a dream that this is exactly what happened (Gen. 31:10–12). These spotted kids and lambs were then placed into Jacob's own breeding flock, where they multiplied. Thus, by sound principles of selective breeding, Jacob was soon able to develop a flock of sheep and goats whose dominant coloration was spotted and speckled, even though he had started with a flock of uniformly solid-colored animals, under conditions that even by Jacob's intent would normally have proved far more beneficial for Laban than himself.

Furthermore, his long experience in animal breeding had taught him how to make sure that the future flocks (both his own and Laban's) would increase in strength and vitality. That is, he would encourage only the stronger animals to mate with each other. He had apparently learned that an effective aphrodisiac device for these species of goats and sheep was to place rods from certain trees, peeled in a striped pattern, in the watering troughs where the flocks came to drink. He divided the animals into two shifts — the stronger and the weaker — using the rods when the strong were drinking, leaving them out otherwise. Thus, the stronger animals were stimulated to mate; the weaker ones were not.

Whether these trees contained a particular chemical component that had an aphrodisiac effect or whether it was merely the sight of the streaked rods (like erotic pictures stimulating the sexual apparatus in human beings) that produced this effect remains for further research to ascertain. Most assuredly it was not a naive belief in prenatal influence (as many critics have charged) on the part of Jacob that persuaded him to try such a device in hopes that the sight of the rods by the ewes would somehow "mark" their offspring. Jacob was far too careful and experienced a student of nature to believe any such old-wives' tale as this.

Jacob's entire approach to this matter was thoroughly honorable[9] and scientific, calculated to benefit Laban even more than himself, but also intended to enable him to become independent of Laban, to care for his own family, and eventually to return to his homeland as God had instructed him to do. God providentially overruled, prospering Jacob far more than he had anticipated and judging Laban in the process. Not only is the account in harmony with known principles of modern genetics, but it may even anticipate discoveries yet to be made in genetic engineering.

## The Virgin Birth

The marvelous process of reproduction and birth has been briefly discussed in chapter 8. However, the greatest birth of all — that of Jesus Christ, when God became man — was not accomplished in this normal way at all. It required a mighty miracle, the miracle of the Virgin Birth.

Actually the miracle was not the birth of Christ, which was a normal birth in every respect, but rather His miraculous conception in the womb of the virgin Mary. Biblical skeptics have long directed many of their most vehement attacks at

---

9. Jacob's character is often unjustly maligned, both in connection with the story of Esau's unwarranted claim on the family birthright and patriarchal blessing (Gen. 25:24–34; 27:1–40), and in his dealings with Laban, but it is significant that God never rebuked Jacob, and unreservedly bestowed the ancestral promises on him and his seed. For a full discussion of these matters, see the writer's commentary, *The Genesis Record* (Grand Rapids, MI: Baker Book House, 1976), p. 411–418, 427–492.

this great Christian doctrine of the Virgin Birth, alleging that such an event was biologically impossible and thus completely unscientific.

There have always been compromising "Christians" who respond (as they do to other attacks of scientism on the Scriptures) by downgrading the importance of the doctrine and by trying to explain the birth of Christ naturalistically or "spiritually." Some have said the divine Incarnation could have been accomplished merely by an infusion of God's Spirit into the human body of Jesus, without regard to whether His birth had been supernatural, or even legitimate. Others say He was the Son of God in the same way all people are children of God, except that He understood it better. Others have cited the phenomenon of parthenogenesis (growth of the mother's egg cell into a complete animal without any paternal contribution), or artificial insemination (implantation of the father's seed into the egg without actual coitus), or even the modern technique of cloning (reproduction from a somatic cell rather than a genetic cell) as examples of how a child might be born of a virgin, suggesting that Jesus himself may have been the product of some such natural process.

All such suggestions, however, are nothing but compromising equivocations, denying the clear record of the Scriptures and dishonoring the unique divine/human nature of the Son of God, destroying the very basis of His great work of salvation. His unique incarnation required an altogether miraculous, supernatural conception, and it is futile and destructive even to attempt to explain or justify it naturalistically. It was a biological miracle — in fact, a mighty miracle of creation, fully comparable to the first great miracle of creation, when (as it says in Heb. 11:3) "the worlds were framed [Greek katartizo] by the word of God." Hebrews 10:5 says, "When he cometh into the world, he saith, Sacrifice and offering thou wouldest not, but a body hast thou prepared [same Greek word, katartizo] me."

For Christ's body to serve as a sacrificial offering for the sins of mankind, it had to meet two conditions. First, physically it had to be "without blemish and without spot" (1 Pet. 1:19), carrying no mutant genes (and their physical defects) inherited from either father or mother. Second, spiritually it had to be "holy, harmless, undefiled, separate from sinners" (Heb. 7:26), with nothing of the sin nature inherited from either parent. "In Him is no sin" (1 John 3:5).

The only way these conditions could be satisfied would be by special creation of the embryonic body in Mary's womb.

Since all genetic inheritance — physical, mental, and spiritual — is transmitted equally from both mother and father, it would be impossible for Christ to be born with a blemish-free body and a sin-free nature if either parent (mother as well as father) contributed genes or other genetic materials to His formation. This must be a special creative act of God himself. "That holy thing which shall be born of thee shall be called the Son of God," the angel told Mary (Luke 1:35).

Nevertheless, from the very instant of conception (when His body consisted only of a single cell) on through gestation, birth, life, and death, Jesus experienced a fully normal human life, for He must be Son of man — man as God intended man to be — as well as Son of God. "Wherefore in all things it behooved him to be made like unto his brethren" (Heb. 2:17). That is, He experienced a fully human life in every way, except for sin! Not only did He have no inherited sin nature (Adam and Eve also had no inherent sin), but also, He "did no sin" (1 Pet. 2:22). He was "made flesh" (John 1:14), but it was only in "the likeness of sinful flesh" (Rom. 8:3). He "knew no sin" (2 Cor. 5:21). He "was in all points tempted like as we are, yet without sin" (Heb.4:15).

Biologically, the Virgin Birth may have been impossible, but after all, that's how we define a miracle of creation, an event that is scientifically impossible but happens anyway!

Some have denied this requirement of the special creation of Christ's body, arguing that the absence of a specific genetic tie to Mary would somehow have precluded Him from being truly human or truly Jewish, as the Scriptures required Him to be.

But such objections are trivial, bespeaking a completely inadequate appreciation of God's ability to create! John the Baptist said, "God is able of these stones to raise up children unto Abraham" (Luke 3:8). According to the Bible, "Jesus Christ . . . was made of the seed of David according to the flesh" (Rom. 1:3), because his legal father was a descendant of David and his biological mother (that is, the one who carried and nurtured him in her womb from the point of conception, and who gave birth to Him) was also a descendant of David. In this way, He was *made* of the seed of David (the word is *ginomai*, and can be translated in many different ways, depending on context) or, as the American Standard Version renders it, He was "born of the seed of David." This assertion, however, is not a whit less true because His body was specially formed in Mary's womb rather than carrying Mary's actual genes.

Nor is Jesus' humanity the least bit lessened by this fact. Adam's body was likewise specially formed (Gen. 2:7) and had no human mother or father. Yet he was fully human; in fact, he was the first man, the prototype man, the father of all men.

But it is also true that all men who were "in Adam" are thereby innately sinners, and it is inescapable that Jesus was "in Adam" if he had any genetic inheritance from Mary. Jesus Christ is called the "last Adam" (1 Cor. 15:45) and, as such, it is not only possible, but appropriate and necessary, that His body (like that of the first Adam) should be directly formed by God. Not only does this not preclude Him from being, like Adam, fully human, but it is the only way by which He could be truly human, without sin, as God had intended man to be. At the very least, a special miracle would have to be performed by God on Mary's genetic apparatus, in order to purge the "sin-factor" (whatever that may be), as well as the accumulated defective mutations of all the generations since Adam. To all intents and purposes, this would amount to a special creation of the newly formed body in Mary's womb.

# IN THE IMAGE OF GOD

*Biblical Anthropology*

## Ape or Angel

According to the Bible, man stands uniquely alone with respect to all the animate creation. He is made in the image of God and has been given dominion over all the earth (Gen. 1:26). When the Psalmist asked the question, "What is man?" (Ps. 8:4), the answer immediately came that man was made "a little lower than the angels" (Ps. 8:5).

To the evolutionist, on the other hand, man is merely "a little higher than the apes." Man is nothing more than a higher animal, more complex in brain structure than other animals but not distinct from them in any qualitative sense. The tenets of the Manifesto of the American Humanist Association express it as follows:

> Humanism believes that man is a part of nature and that he has emerged as the result of a continuous process. Holding an organic view of life, humanists find that the traditional dualism of mind and body must be rejected. . . . It follows that there will be no uniquely religious emotions and attitudes hitherto associated with belief in the supernatural.[1]

> I use the word "humanist" to mean someone who believes that man is just as much a natural phenomenon as an animal or plant; that his body, mind and soul were not supernaturally created but are products of evolution, and that he is not under the control or guidance of any supernatural being or beings, but has to rely on himself and his own powers.[2]

---

1. American Humanist Association, "Humanist Manifesto I," *The New Humanist,* 6 (May–June 1933), tenets 2 and 10.
2. Sir Julian Huxley, quoted in a standard American Humanist Association promotional brochure. Huxley, one of the founders of the A.H.A., was probably the most influential scientific evolutionist of the 20th century, chief founder and promoter of neo-Darwinism, as well as first director-general of UNESCO.

The question to be considered in this chapter is whether the real scientific facts support the biblical view of man or the humanistic view. If one were to judge from the teachings of the colleges, universities, museums, public schools, and the news media, there would be no doubt at all. All of these institutions are dominated by evolutionary humanism.

Nevertheless, even though establishment science and education are committed to the concept of human evolution, all the fossil evidence and other data of physical anthropology are fully consistent with the Bible teaching that man is completely unrelated to the apes or any other animal ancestor. Man (and this term, of course, is used generically, including both male and female human beings) was created in God's image and is destined for eternity. True anthropology is not evolutionary anthropology, but biblical anthropology.

## Biblical Evidence Against Human Evolution

Since there are multitudes of professing Christian people who believe in evolution while also maintaining at least a nominal belief in the Bible as the Word of God, it is well first of all to list a number of biblical arguments against human evolution. In addition to the general "after his kind" doctrine of Genesis 1, as discussed in the previous chapter, the following teachings of Scripture stress the unbridgeable gap between man and the animals.

1. *Man's dominion.* God commanded man to "subdue" the earth and to "have dominion . . . over every living thing that moveth upon the earth" (Gen. 1:28). The animals were all created to serve man, not to compete with him in an evolutionary struggle for survival.

2. *Man's body specially formed.* The land animals were all formed by God "out of the ground" (Gen. 2:19), but only Adam and Eve were individually formed directly by God himself, Adam out of the dust of the ground (Gen. 2:7) and Eve out of Adam's side (Gen. 2:22).

3. *No help-meet among the animals.* When Adam was instructed to name the animals (an instruction that in itself was a testimony to the separation of man from the animals), there were none that were sufficiently like him to be a "helper fit for" him. This indicates there were none whose immediate past ancestry he shared.

4. *Adam's return to the dust.* The curse upon Adam after his sin culminated in a return to the dust from which he had been taken (Gen. 3:19), showing that the "dust of the ground" from which he had been formed (Gen. 2:7) could not have been a long evolutionary development, as theistic evolutionists had alleged.

5. *Eve's unique creation.* It is impossible to explain the special formation of Eve's body out of Adam's side by the Lord in terms of any kind of evolutionary development from an animal ancestry.

6. *Chronology of man's creation.* According to the testimony of Christ himself, "from

the beginning of the creation God made them male and female" (Mark 10:6, quoting Gen. 1:27). That is, man and woman were made, not after four billion years of evolutionary development, but from the beginning of the creation.

7. *Distinctiveness of human flesh.* Supporting the "after his kind" teaching of Genesis, the New Testament stresses the created differences between man and the main divisions of the animal kingdom. "All flesh is not the same flesh: but there is one kind of flesh of men, another flesh of beasts, another of fishes, and another of birds" (1 Cor. 15:39).

For those nominal Christians who do not believe in biblical inerrancy, and who regard Genesis in particular as mythological or allegorical, the above considerations may seem to carry little weight. For those who do believe in the inerrant authority of the Bible, however, they should be conclusive. Man is not a descendant of an animal ancestry, either in body or soul, but was uniquely created, in every respect, "in the image of God."

It is noteworthy that there are at least 60 quotations from, or allusions to, the first three chapters of Genesis in the New Testament. In all of these, it is obvious that the writers regarded these records as absolutely historical, with no slightest hint that they were merely allegorical or symbolical. Especially significant are the following references to Adam and Eve as the first man and woman, parents of all nations, created in God's image but also responsible for the introduction of sin into the world: Matthew 19:3–6; Mark 10:5–9; Acts 17:24–29; Romans 5:12–19; 8:20–22; 1 Corinthians 11:8–12; 15:21–22, 45–47; 2 Corinthians 11:3; Ephesians 5:30–32; Colossians 3:10; 1 Timothy 2:13–15; James 5:9.

Although we shall not discuss these passages here, each would warrant careful study. In addition to their basic doctrinal importance in establishing the universality of sin and the need of the promised Redeemer, they clearly confirm the historicity of the Genesis record of the special creation of the first man and woman.

If man is, after all, merely the product of a billion years of organic evolution, then the biblical record (including its acceptance as history by Christ and the apostles) is wrong. This is true even if we try to think of evolution as somehow directed by God. If the Bible is a false witness with respect to this most basic doctrine of man's origin, then why should we trust it when it treats other doctrines (e.g., sin, salvation, eternal life) that are based on the doctrine of creation?

## No Ape-men in the Fossils

We have already seen in chapter 12 that there are no true transitional forms anywhere in the fossil record. This is even the case with the so-called hominids.[3] Although there has been great media propaganda about various fossil ape-men

---

3. A *hominid* is supposed to be a pre-human form in the line leading to man, whereas *hominoids* include all apes, men, and hominids. *Homo* is the generic name meaning "man." A "pongid" is a true ape (chimpanzees, orangutans, gorillas, siangs, gibbons).

over the years, there is still no real evidence of any such thing. Since man is supposedly the most recent arrival on the evolutionary scene, and since more people are looking for human fossils than any other single type, the evolutionary history of man should be the best-documented evolutionary history of all, but there is nothing! There are many fossils of true apes and many of true men, but nothing in between. There have never been any man-apes or ape-men. Men have always been men, and apes have always been apes, according to the real fossil evidence, and this is exactly what the Bible teaches, too.

But, then, what about such famous "ape-men" as Neanderthal man, Java man, and Peking man? Of more current interest are *Ramapithecus* and the various dryopithecines, *Australopithecus* (which includes such notables as *Zinjanthropus*, *Homo habilis*, and Lucy), and *Homo erectus*. These have been the object of numerous articles, books, and even television specials. These have all been presented to the public as intermediate links between man and the ape, but what are the actual hard facts, in terms of real, unequivocal fossil evidence? The following survey will show that no such evidence exists.

Most of the textbook ape-men of a generation ago are no longer cited in modern textbooks. Nebraska man turned out to be a peccary, Piltdown man was exposed as a hoax, the original Peking man was lost, and the original Java man was acknowledged as a composite of two separate individuals, man and gibbon. A fascinating comment on the Java man (also called *Pithecanthropus erectus*, found in the Trinil gravel beds of Java) is found in the following exposition by J.B. Birdsell: "Virtually all of the Pithecanthropine relics from these beds have been washed out and found by native collectors. Not only is their original location in the beds uncertain, but there is a possibility that they reached the Trinil beds by being redeposited from earlier ones."[4]

Creationists for decades had pointed out this secondary, transported character of the Pithecanthropine fossils, but evolutionists continued to cite them as proof of evolution until recent years, when new candidates came along that they thought were better. Birdsell pointed out another interesting aspect of the skull of the so-called Java man: "Most of the Trinil crania have lost their basal portions in such a fashion as to suggest that they were murdered, and then their brains eaten."[5] Actually, it eventually became accepted — even by the discoverer of *Pithecanthropus*, Dr. Eugene Dubois — that the skullcap was that of a giant gibbon and the thigh bone truly human. Quite probably the gibbons were hunted and eaten by men. This also was found most likely to be the case with many of the Peking skulls as well.

As a sidelight, another very interesting observation was made by Birdsell in connection with the dating of the Trinil fossils. "In the last two years an absolute date has been obtained for the Ngandong beds (above the Trinil beds), and it has

---

4. J.B. Birdsell, *Human Evolution* (Chicago, IL: Rand-McNally, 1975), p. 294.
5. Ibid.

the very interesting value of 300,000 years plus or minus 300,000 years."[6] At least the geochronologist who originally recorded such a date was more realistic than most in thus recognizing that these dates are essentially meaningless.

Although the original Peking man and Java man are rarely offered today as evidence of human evolution, there have been other fossils found since — all the way from Africa to Australia — that have been placed in the same category as previously assigned to these fossils, using the name *Homo erectus* for the entire group. The name itself (meaning "erect man") indicates that these fossils probably were all true men, though of an extinct tribe or tribes that were significantly different from existing tribes in certain respects. Most notably the cranial capacity (from about 800 to over 1100 cubic centimeters) was much less than the modern average of about 1500 cubic centimeters.

Nevertheless, even this small brain size is definitely within the range of modern man. Similarly, their larger tooth size does not indicate any kinship to the apes, but merely a more rigorous diet requiring heavy chewing.

> In modern populations . . . there is such a wide range in variation that the lower end of the range is well below the capacity for certain fossil hominids, yet there is no evidence that these individuals are any less intelligent than persons with larger cranial vaults. . . . Variation of plus or minus 400 c.c. about the mean is seen in most European populations. These individuals with larger or smaller cranial capacities are normally functioning and intellectually competent individuals; in fact, there are many persons with 700 to 800 cubic centimeters.[7]

> It has long been suspected that as human populations grew in technological elaboration, they shrank in tooth dimension. . . . C. Loring Brace of Michigan University has applied the theory to populations in Australia and found that it holds true, with the largest teeth being those of Australian aborigines. Differential reduction of chewing surface gradually led to the varying facial forms of living populations.[8]

Although the *Homo erectus* evidence is still fragmentary and equivocal, it seems probable at this time that these were true human beings, descendants of Adam and even of Noah. There is certainly no basis for believing that they were evolutionary intermediates of any kind.

A more recently repudiated hominid was *Ramapithecus* ("Rama's ape," Rama being one of the gods of India, where the fossils were found), which was promoted for a long time as the first evolutionary stage in the line leading to man after it had diverged from the line leading to the pongids. The evidence, however, was always extremely tenuous and it has now finally been rejected. It should

6. Ibid., p. 295.
7. Stephen Molnar, *Races, Types and Ethnic Groups — the Problem of Human Variation* (Englewood Cliffs, NJ: Prentice-Hall, 1975), p. 56–57.
8. The Shrinking Tooth," *Science News* (Dec. 13, 1975): 375.

never have been used in the first place (exactly as had been true with *Hesperopithecus*, *Pithecanthropus*, *Eoanthropus*, and other so-called ape-men, which once were widely publicized as proof of evolution but were later recognized as based on insufficient and misinterpreted evidence), but it was eagerly appropriated by eager evolutionists. "Human nature abhors a vacuum, particularly a genealogical one. There have always been gaps in the fossil record of human evolution but never a shortage of speculative 'missing links.' "[9] This desire to fill the unfillable gap between ape and man led to a much too hasty acceptance of the minimal fossil evidence of *Ramapithecus*.

> There are still no skulls, no pelvic or limb bones unequivocally associated with the teeth to show whether *Ramapithecus* had a brain like a hominid, swung through trees like an ape, or walked upright like a human. . . . the pelvis is probably the most diagnostic bone of the human line. . . . Yet an entire *Ramapithecus*, walking upright, has been "reconstructed" from only jaws and teeth. The prince's ape latched onto the position by his teeth and has been hanging on ever since, his legitimacy sanctified by millions of textbooks and *Time-Life* volumes on human evolution.[10]

One of the leading proponents of *Ramapithecus* had been Dr. David Pilbeam of Yale University, one of the nation's top physical anthropologists. When he reluctantly had to abandon the evolutionary scenario he had been promoting, Pilbeam wrote the following fascinating confession.

> In the course of rethinking my ideas about human evolution, I have changed somewhat as a scientist. I am aware of the prevalence of implicit assumptions and try harder to dig them out of my own thinking. I am also aware that there are many assumptions I will get at only later, when today's thoughts turn into yesterday's misconceptions. I know that, at least in paleoanthropology, data are still so sparse that theory heavily influences interpretations. Theories have, in the past, clearly reflected our current ideologies instead of the actual data.[11]

The confession of Pilbeam, of course, did not mean that he was questioning the "fact" of human evolution. It just meant that there was no meaningful evidence that he knew how to interpret. "All this makes a more complex picture of hominoid evolution than we once imagined. It no longer resembles a ladder but is, instead, more like a bush."[12] Many other anthropologists today, and possibly most, would echo such a state of confusion in their discipline.

At the upper end of the evolutionary ladder is Neanderthal man, who was regarded as an ape-man in the days of Charles Darwin, but now is often accepted

---

9. Adrienne L. Zihlman and Herold M. Loewenstein, "False Start of the Human Parade," *Natural History,* 88 (Aug.–Sept. 1979): 86.

10. Ibid., p. 89.

11. David Pilbeam, "Rearranging Our Family Tree," *Human Nature* (June 1978): 45.

12. Ibid., p. 44.

as fully human. Note the reconstruction pictured in figure 31. A leading evolutionist had acknowledged, "The cranial capacity of the Neanderthal race of *Homo sapiens* was, on the average, equal to or even greater than in modern man."[13]

Similarly, Dr. Francis Ivanhoe of London has shown that Neanderthal man, while suffering from the disease of rickets because of his residence too near the great ice cap of the Pleistocene epoch, nevertheless was very intelligent and skillful. "He had a brain with a capacity sometimes larger than that of modern man. He was a talented and successful hunter, even dabbled in art and most importantly from a cultural standpoint, developed a rudimentary social and religious consciousness."[14] Although the evolutionary bias of Ivanhoe is still evident, it is clear that Neanderthal was a skilled toolmaker, hunter, and artist. It is also known that he raised flowers and buried his dead. His successor, Cro-Magnon, was even more highly advanced than Neanderthal, probably physically and intellectually superior to modern man.

More recent evidence is beginning to indicate that Neanderthal man and his supposed predecessors even had a form of written language!

> Communication with inscribed symbols may go back as far as 135,000 years in man's history, antedating the 50,000-year-old Neanderthal Man. Alexander Marshack of Harvard's Peabody Museum made this pronouncement recently after extensive microscopic analysis of a 135,000-year-old ox rib covered with symbolic engravings. . . . This bone, Marshack feels, is an indirect indicator that Neanderthal Man must have talked and could well have communicated in a reasonably sophisticated manner."[15]

A fascinating study of the various Neanderthal skulls has been made and published by a dental scientist, Jack Cuozzo.[16] A careful study of their dentition led him to the strong conviction that the form of teeth and skull shape was due to great age. Dr. Cuozzo was able to argue from this evidence that their indicated longevity correlated with the record in Genesis 11 that early post-diluvian men were still living for hundreds of years.

Another remarkable study on the Neanderthals was made by an anthropologist at the University of Texas.

> Other data show that archaic *Homo* had a more strongly constructed skeleton than all but the very earliest modern humans, and the pronounced muscle markings on the bones are believed to indicate great strength.[17]

As a matter of fact, it almost seems that practically every anthropologist dealing with the various *Homo* fossils has his own unique interpretation of the data —

---

13. Theodosius Dobzhansky, "Changing Man," *Science,* 155 (Jan. 27, 1967): 410.

14. Francis Ivanhoe, *Nature* (Aug. 8, 1970), cited in *Prevention* (Oct. 1971): 117.

15. "Use of Symbols Antedates Neanderthal Man," *Science Digest,* 73 (Mar. 1973): 220.

16. Jack Cuozzo, *Buried Alive* (Green Forest, AR: Master Books, 1998), 349 p.

17. John Kappelman, "They Might Be Giants," *Nature,* 387 (May 8, 1997): 126.

*FIGURE 31 — Neanderthal Man*
*This standard reconstruction of Neanderthal man, based on a wealth of fossil evidence,*
*makes it evident that this was a true example of* Homo sapiens. *Other fossil hominid*
*forms, including those identified as* Australopithecus *and* Homo erectus, *are based on*
*fragmentary and equivocal evidence.*

both the physical data and the molecular data derived from the study of living apes and humans.

Many evolutionists today are trying to sort out these evolutionary relationships by using DNA studies and other molecular dating concepts, but these tend not only to contradict the paleontological data but also to be inconsistent with themselves. It is all rather confusing, not only to outsiders but even to the specialists.

> Even with DNA sequence data, we have no direct access to the processes of evolution, so objective reconstruction of the vanished past can be achieved only by creative imagination.[18]

A question here is whether "creative imagination" can truly be objective! An eminent anthropologist and linguist at Stanford University has made the following observation.

> But fossil material was scant, and even today we must content ourselves with a very small number of incomplete skulls and bones. These few fragments are the only random pieces left of a giant jigsaw puzzle — how can we hope to reconstruct the whole from such limited clues? Often a new fossil, or the revision of a single date, forces a major reassessment of our understanding of human evolution — the discovery of a million-year-old mandible may take up entire pages in the scientific and popular presses."[19]

---

18. N. Takahata, "A Genetic Perspective on the Origin and History of Humans," *Annual Review of Ecology and Systematics,* 26 (1995): 344.

19. Luigi L. Cavalli-Sforza, *Genes, People, and Languages* (New York, NY: North Point Press, 2000), p. 33.

The most serious remaining candidate for an evolving hominid is *Australopithecus* ("southern ape"). These creatures are now recognized in terms of several species — *Australopithecus africanus, Australopithecus robustus*, and *Australopithecus afarensis*, in particular — and each of them has both proponents and denigrants in terms of its candidacy as a possible ancestor of *Homo sapiens*. Most notorious has been the widely publicized controversy between Carl Johanson and Richard Leakey (with their respective colleagues and followers) as to whether or not "Lucy" is man's ancestor.

Although the fossil collections of the australopithecines are considerably more extensive than those of *Ramapithecus* and the other dryopithecines, any real evidence for human evolution is still altogether lacking. *Australopithecus* admittedly had fully ape-like cranial features and brain capacity (500 cubic centimeters), and its dentition was likewise far more ape-like than human. However, some of the very limited pelvic and limb fossils of *Australopithecus*, especially the remains of one creature named "Lucy" by its discoverer, Carl Johanson, have been interpreted by a number of anthropologists as indicating an erect posture and bipedal walking; this is the main reason why many of these scientists are promoting it as an important evolutionary ancestor of man.

The popular media, however, rarely give the other side of the question. There is no good evidence that the australopithecines were erect walkers at all.

> Multivariate studies of several anatomical regions, shoulder, pelvis, ankle, foot, elbow, and hand are now available for the australopithecines. These suggest that the common view, that these fossils are similar to modern man or that on those occasions when they depart from a similarity to man they resemble the African great apes, may be incorrect. Most of the fossil fragments are in fact uniquely different from both man and man's nearest living genetic relatives, the chimpanzee and gorilla. . . . To the extent that resemblances exist with living forms, they tend to be with the orangutan.[20]

The author of the above exposition, Dr. Charles Oxnard, has been dean of the graduate school and professor of anatomy at the University of Southern California. Prior to that, he was on the faculty at the University of Chicago, and before that he was a member of a large research team in England under the direction of Sir Solly Zuckerman (later named Lord Zuckerman), one of England's top scientists. The Zuckerman team conducted long and intensive research on the skeletal structure of both living apes and fossil hominoids and hominids, in comparison with that of modern man, making detailed three-dimensional measurements and then a computerized multivariate statistical analysis of all pertinent relationships. No investigators before or since have obtained more detailed or more accurate information on the relationships of the australopithecines to other primates. As noted above, the conclusion was that the australopithecines were not related to

---

20. Charles Oxnard, *University of Chicago Magazine* (Winter, 1974): 11.

man, did not walk erect, and were more like the orangutan than any other living animal.

Lord Zuckerman himself had the following to say about the evidence for human evolution. ". . . [in] the interpretation of man's fossil history, where to the faithful anything is possible . . . the ardent believer is sometimes able to believe several contradictory things at the same time."[21] ". . . [if man] evolved from some ape-like creature . . . [it was] without leaving any fossil traces of the steps of the transformation."[22] Zuckerman and Oxnard, of course, still believe in human evolution, but this belief is obviously not because of the evidence, since there is no evidence.

Gould had an interesting comment about Oxnard. "Oxnard is our leading expert on the quantitative study of skeletons. . . . [he] has spent years studying the australopithecines. . . . In short, he sees australopithecines as uniquely different from apes and humans, not as imperfect people on the way up."[23]

A very fascinating development in the pseudoscience of anthropological evolutionary speculation was the sudden incorporation of the modern pygmy chimpanzee, Pan paniscus, first discovered in 1928, into the body of evolutionary theory. The remarkable fact is that the pygmy chimpanzee (or the "bonobo") seems to fit all or most of the specifications previously drawn up by evolutionists for their hypothetical common ancestor of man and the apes. Furthermore, the bonobo seems strangely similar to Lucy, the famous australopithecine whose fairly complete fossil skeleton has been so widely promoted by its discoverer, Carl Johanson.

> Along with Sarich, Zihlman and Cramer have become the champions of the bonobo model, and they have based their claims primarily on studies of the anatomy of living apes and fossilized hominids.[24]

> To make her point; Zihlman compares the pygmy chimpanzee to "Lucy," one of the oldest fossil hominids known, and finds the similarities striking. They are almost identical in body size, in stature and in brain size, she notes.[25]

Not only do they match Lucy in size and appearance, but also in mode of locomotion. Modern chimps, as well as other apes, are essentially knuckle-walkers, but the australopithecines are thought by many to have had some ability to walk erect, and this is the main reason for believing they might have been ancestors of man. As we have seen, this hypothetical upright gait has been a serious bone of contention between advocates and skeptics relative to Australopithecus.

---

21. Solly Zuckerman, Beyond the Ivory Tower (New York, NY: Taplinger, 1970), p. 19.

22. Ibid., p. 64.

23. Stephen Jay Gould, "A Short Way to Big Ends," Natural History, 93 (Jan. 1986): 28.

24. Herbert Wray, "Lucy's Uncommon Forebear," Science News, 123 (Feb. 5, 1983): 89.

25. Ibid. The scientists named here are three top evolutionists, very influential in evolutionary anthropology. Vincent Sarich is at the University of California (Berkeley), Adrienne Zihlman at the University of California (Santa Cruz), and Douglas Cramer at New York University.

Now we find that the present-day pygmy chimpanzee seems to have such an ability, though other modern apes do not. "Susman also discovered that pygmy chimps have a unique style of locomotion. Like modern gorillas they tend to be knuckle-walkers on the ground, yet they seem to be natural bipeds, too, frequently walking upright both on the ground and in the trees."[26] Thus, for all we can tell, Lucy and the other australopithecines might well have been nothing but pygmy chimpanzees, or some type of creature very much like them.

Anthropologists have been searching all these years for the ape-like ancestor of man, and here it turns out to be nothing but an ape, and an ape contemporary with man at that! This is an odd sort of family tree, to say the least.

The chronological aspects of these evolutionary developments are also quite confusing. We have already noted that published dates are subject to great errors and are frequently being revised. Furthermore, fossils of *Homo erectus* have been found that are apparently contemporaneous with those of *Australopithecus* and *Homo sapiens*. Louis Leakey once found remains of a circular stone hut (obviously manmade) at a lower level than that at which remains of *Australopithecus* had been found.[27]

With no intermediate forms available, with the supposed ancestor of all apes and men maybe still living, and with the chronology all confused, some scientists have actually wondered whether man descended from the apes at all, or whether it may have been the other way around. The evidence, such as it is, could fit either model!

> So the anatomical similarities of man and apes could have come about because they share a common ancestor, or they could be the result of so-called parallel evolution. The problem, for the paleontologists, is that they lack the evidence to decide.[28]

> To translate our suggestion into that form of speech, we think that the chimp is descended from man, that the common ancestor of the two was more man-like than ape-like.[29]

> Certainly we would not want to defend it to the death, but the very fact that it is entirely within the confines of the evidence that we have points up the frailty of the conventional history of man and the apes.[30]

This, of course, is exactly the point we made at the beginning of this section. There has been much sound and fury about the evolutionary history of man, but it still signifies nothing. There is absolutely no evidence that man evolved from any other creature.

---

26. Ibid., p. 92.
27. Richard Leakey, "Hominids in Africa," *American Scientist* (Mar.–Apr. 1976): 177.
28. John Gribbin and Jeremy Cherfas, "Descent of Man = Ascent of Ape?" *New Scientist*, 91 (Sept. 3, 1981): 592.
29. Ibid., p. 594.
30. Ibid.

## Ape-like Men

One of the myths fostered by evolutionary thinking is that some tribes and "races" are more "primitive" than others, less advanced from the "brutes" along the evolutionary ladder. Conversely, certain races or nations are claimed to be more highly evolved and thus justified in subjugating those who are still "stone-age" peoples, or "aborigines." This type of thinking was especially pronounced among the white nations of Europe and America during the decades immediately following Darwin.

In fact, this idea was a strong motivator of Charles Darwin himself. On the famous voyage of the *Beagle*, his attitude toward the natives of Tierra del Fuego was indicative. "[Darwin's] air was 'to show that there is no fundamental difference between man and the higher mammals [monkeys] in their mental faculties.' "[31] This evaluation was taken from his *Voyage of the Beagle*, describing what Darwin called "the miserable inhabitants of Tierra del Fuego," whom he portrayed as benighted cannibals, still almost as much beasts as men. Darwin's biased account of these South American Indians had a profound and baleful effect on the Europeans of his day, conditioning them to think in terms of human evolution and the "descent of man" (as Darwin would entitle his later book) from some ape-like ancestor. However, as the British Catholic scholar Paul Kildare points out, "Darwin hardly saw an Indian at all, and could not speak one word of their language, yet his description of the Fuegians is still quoted as authoritative over a century later in countless so-called scientific works."[32]

How a young "naturalist" like Charles Darwin, with no degree except in theology — and with a poor record as well as disbelief, even in that — could presume to pass such broad anthropological judgments based on such flimsy evidence, and how people could believe him if he did, remains a sad testimony to human pride and gullibility. "But these superficial comments of a passing tourist in 1832 were entirely without foundation. They were completely demolished by the findings of two missionary priests, both highly qualified scientists . . . on the staffs of American and European universities. . . . Darwin had no scientific qualifications at all."[33] The findings of these priest-scientists included the following: "The Fuegian Indians were not cannibals; they believed in one Supreme Being, to whom they prayed with confidence; they had 'high principles of morality' and they rightly regarded the white people who exploited them as morally inferior to themselves."[34]

During more recent years, many other missionaries, both Protestant and Catholic, have found this same characteristic to be true almost everywhere.[35] The so-

---

31. Paul Kildare, "Monkey Business," *Christian Order,* 23 (Dec. 1982): 591.
32. Ibid.
33. Ibid.
34. Ibid., p. 592.
35. See also the exposé of anthropologist Margaret Mead's unfortunate treatment of Samoan cultures, *Margaret Mead and Samoa*, by Derek Freeman (Cambridge, MA: Harvard University Press, 1982).

called primitive tribes of the jungles and other remote areas universally have highly developed languages and social systems, as well as complex religious practices and moral principles. When given the opportunity, many in their numbers have the ability to succeed in higher education and even in graduate schools. To the extent that they now seem to fall short of western standards, the evidence always seems to point to a "fall" from a higher state of civilization in the past, not to a rise from an ancient animal ancestry. Further, their present animalistic religions system can usually be shown to represent a deterioration from primitive monotheism and higher moral standards now only dimly preserved in their traditions.

Untold damage has been wrought, especially during the past century, by this dismal doctrine that man is merely an evolved animal. Racism, economic imperialism, communism, Nazism, sexual promiscuity and perversions, aggressive militarism, infanticide, genocide, and all sorts of evils have been vigorously promoted by one group or another on the grounds that, since they were based on evolution, they were "scientific" and, therefore, bound to prove beneficial in the long run. Even cannibalism, of all things, is beginning to receive favorable attention by certain evolutionists. A professor of anthropology at Columbia University cites the example of the Aztecs, who supposedly ate the flesh of enemy soldiers to overcome the protein deficiency in their diet after the depletion of their faunal resources. "Surely there can be no special pride in the practice of letting millions of soldiers rot on the battlefield because of a taboo against cannibalism. One can even argue that, nutritionally, the best source of protein for human beings is human flesh because the balance of amino acids is precisely that which the body requires for its own proper functioning."[36]

But the clinching argument supporting the practice of cannibalism is that animals do it, and it must therefore have been favorable to evolution. Philip Tobias, one of the chief authorities on human evolution, in a speech at the University of Alberta, described the overwhelming evidence of cannibalism among man's supposed pre-human evolutionary ancestors. "An exhaustive survey by biologist Gary Polis showed cannibalism in more than 1,300 species, including some human societies where human flesh was the single great source of protein."[37]

Commenting on this, the Canadian columnist Paul Tisdall made the following astounding observation: "Among the experts, cannibalism is a hotly debated and emotion-charged issue. Still, given its obvious advantages plus our own history of cannibalism and its prevalence in nature, the wonder seems to be that modern humans have developed a repugnance for eating each other and have largely discontinued the practice."[38]

One would almost suspect such writers are indulging in some kind of warped

---

36. Marvin Harris, "Our Pound of Flesh," *Natural History* 88 (Aug.–Sept. 1979): 36.
37. Philip Tobias, as reported by Paul Tisdall, in "Cannibalistic Taboos a Recent Development," *Edmonton Journal* (Jan. 2, 1983).
38. Ibid.

and grisly humor. But they seem to want to be taken seriously, as rational scientists, arguing logically from the "known facts" of human evolution.

To the biblical writers (see Deut. 28:53, 57; 2 Kings 6:28–29), on the other hand, the very idea of cannibalism was such an unspeakable practice as to be conceivable only in times of the severest famine, and then only in great shame.

Actually the idea that "primitive" tribes have practiced cannibalism may be another evolutionary myth. Dr. William Arens, professor of anthropology at the State University of New York (Stony Brook) has shown that there is no good evidence that any tribe was ever cannibalistic as a part of its culture. Occasional instances of people eating human flesh have been recorded (even in civilized nations), but always only in an extreme starvation emergency, or as a crime, never as a regular cultural practice.[39]

Cannibalism, though perhaps the most repugnant, is certainly not the most harmful practice that has been justified in the name of evolution. Right at the end of Darwin's epochal book, *The Origin of Species by Natural Selection*, appears his own summary of the ugly character of evolution (though he saw it as good!). "Thus, from the war of nature, from famine and death, the most exalted object which we are capable of conceiving, namely, the production of the higher animals, directly follows."[40] In Darwinism, war, famine, and death are good because they have generated the higher animals and finally man himself from lower animals. One might paraphrase this grotesque concept as: "By death, came man!"

In sharpest contrast, on the other hand, the Word of God says that "by man came death" (1 Cor. 15:21). These practices that evolutionary theory considers natural, contributing to the survival of the fittest and to evolutionary progress, the Bible considers sinful, the result of man's rebellion against his Creator and estrangement from His fellowship. If men behave (or even look) like apes or other animals today, it is not because of any evolutionary throwback to an animal ancestry, but because of sin and its destructive effects on mind and body, bringing them down from the image of God in which they were created to an animalistic style of life and thought. "But these, as natural brute beasts, made to be taken and destroyed, speak evil of the things that they understand not; and shall utterly perish in their own corruption" (2 Pet. 2:12).

## Science and the Nature of Man

The Bible, of course, emphatically teaches that human beings are more than complex physical and chemical machines. "Is not the life more than meat, and the body than raiment?" Jesus said (Matt. 6:25).

The body and soul are clearly distinguished in the New Testament; even when

---

39. See Dr. Arens's book *The Man-Eating Myth: Anthropology and Anthropophagy* (Cambridge: Oxford University Press, 1979). Also see Elizabeth Rosenthal, "Myth of the Man-Eaters," *Science Digest*, 91 (Apr. 1983): 10–14, for a fascinating interview with Arens.

40. Charles Darwin, *The Origin of Species by Natural Selection*. This is the next-to-last sentence (any edition) of Darwin's famous book.

the body dies, the soul survives (Matt. 10:28; Rev. 6:9; et al.). Similarly, the Scriptures teach that a man's spirit survives the death of his body (Acts 7:59; 1 Cor. 5:5; 1 Pet. 3:18; et al.). Thus, both soul and spirit are distinct from the body and therefore cannot be analyzed and described, as the body can, in terms of mere biochemical systems and relationships. As we have seen previously, the human body is composed of some of the same chemical elements — "the dust of the earth" — that make up the rest of God's physical creation (note Gen. 2:7; 3:19; 1 Cor. 15:47), and therefore his bodily structure and functions can, in principle at least, be fully specified in terms of biophysics and biochemistry. This is not true, however, of man's soul and spirit. These nonmaterial entities — though just as real as his physical body — cannot be understood by the laws that describe material objects, even those material bodies that are indwelt and energized by soul and spirit.

This is not the view of modern evolutionary humanism, however. One of the chief tenets of humanism is the following: "Holding an organic view of life, humanists find that the traditional dualism of mind and body must be rejected."[41] This is the more or less official view of modern intellectual unbelievers, by whatever name they are called — humanists, atheists, materialists, naturalists, or various others. But for such people to claim that this position is supported by science is quite out of order. Science, by its very nature, deals with material phenomena, seeking to establish relationships that describe the behavior of matter and energy in space and time. It does not deal with "nonmaterial" entities. Even though such entities have real existence, they do not conform to mechanical laws and so are beyond reach of the scientific method as applied to natural science.

Some outstanding modern scientists are willing to recognize that there is, indeed, more to human life than the life of the flesh. Dr. Lewis Thomas, for example, chancellor of the Sloan Kettering Memorial Cancer Center in New York City, says, "We know a lot about the structure and function of the cells and fibers of the human brain, but we haven't the ghost of an idea about how this extraordinary organ works to produce awareness; the nature of consciousness is a scientific problem, but still an unapproachable one."[42] With respect to what happens after death, Thomas frankly admits that natural scientists have no way of determining this. "We do not understand the process of dying, nor can we say anything clear, for sure, about what happens to human thought after death."[43]

One of the world's outstanding scientists in the field of human biology has long been Sir John Eccles, winner of the 1963 Nobel Prize in Physiology or Medicine for his research on how nerve cells communicate with each other. "Eccles

---

41. American Humanist Association, "Humanist Manifesto I," *The New Humanist,* 6 (May–June 1933). This is tenet 3, following the tenets asserting the self-existence of the universe and the naturalistic evolution of man.
42. Lewis Thomas, "On Science and Uncertainty," *Discover,* 1 (Oct. 1980): 59.
43. Ibid.

strongly defends the ancient religious belief that human beings consist of a mysterious compound of physical matter and intangible spirit. . . . Boldly advancing what for most scientists is the greatest heresy of all, Eccles also asserts that our non-material self survives the death of the physical brain."[44] Despite what almost seems to be a conspiracy of silence in the scientific journals on such issues, there are many other scientists of similar persuasion. "Eccles is not the only world-famous scientist taking a controversial new look at the ancient mind-body conundrum. From Berkeley to Paris, and from London to Princeton, prominent scientists from fields as diverse as neurophysiology and quantum physics are coming out of the closet and admitting they believe in the possibility, at least, of such unscientific entities as the immortal human spirit and divine creation."[45] Eccles himself gives the following testimony about his own scientific and personal conclusion. "If I say that the uniqueness of the human self is not derived from the genetic code, not derived from experience, then what is it derived from? My answer is this: from a divine creation. Each self is a divine creation."[46]

One of the most obvious and unequivocal proofs of the uniqueness of man in contrast to the animals is the ability to communicate in terms of intelligible, abstract, symbolic human language. Animals bark and grunt and chatter, but this attribute is completely and qualitatively different from human speech. Noam Chomsky, one of the world's top experts of linguistics, has said, "Human language appears to be a unique phenomenon, without significant analogue in the animal world. . . . There is no reason to suppose that the 'gaps' are bridgeable. There is no more of a basis for assuming an evolutionary development of 'higher' from 'lower' stages, in this case, than there is for assuming an evolutionary development from breathing to walking."[47] Similarly, Lewis Thomas comments: ". . . but we do not understand language itself. Indeed, language is so incomprehensible a problem that the language we use for discussing the matter is itself becoming incomprehensible."[48] The question of the origin of language in general and the different languages in particular will be discussed further in the next chapter.

The use of language to express concepts is mysteriously related to the way our consciousness translates visual images we see with our eyes to percepts we comprehend with our minds. All of this seems quite beyond the possibility of analysis in terms of the criteria of natural science.

> No matter how deeply we probe into the visual pathway, in the end we need to posit an "inner man" who transforms the visual image into a percept. And, as far as linguistics is concerned, the analysis of language appears to be

---

44. John Gliedman, "Scientists in Search of the Soul," *Science Digest,* 90 (July 1982): p. 77.
45. Ibid.
46. Ibid.
47. Noam Chomsky, *Language and Mind* (New York, NY: Harcourt, Brace, Jovanovich, 1972), p. 67–68. Dr. Chomsky is professor of linguistics at Massachusetts Institute of Technology.
48. Lewis Thomas, "On Science," p. 59.

heading for the same conceptual impasse as does the analysis of vision. . . . That is to say, for man the concept of "meaning" can be fathomed only in relation to the self, which is both ultimate source and ultimate destination of semantic signals. But the concept of the self, the cornerstone of Freud's analytical psychology, cannot be given an explicit definition. Instead, the meaning of "self" is intuitively obvious. It is another Kantian transcendental concept, one which we bring *a priori* to man, just as we bring the concepts of space, time, and causality to nature.[49]

Thus, even though "self" or "consciousness" or "inner man" is a concept that everyone intuitively understands and accepts in practice, it is extremely difficult (in fact, impossible) to define and pinpoint scientifically, at least in the currently recognized categories of naturalistic science.

A rather amazing expression of this paradox was given by Dr. George Wald, long-time professor at Harvard and winner of the 1967 Nobel Prize for Physiology or Medicine, as well as many other honors. His primary field of research had been in the physiology and biochemistry of vision, but he also had a broad range of scientific interests, with special concern for evolution and natural selection. He was a thoroughgoing evolutionary humanist, but his studies finally led him to the conclusion that consciousness is an entity not explicable in material terms. "There are two major problems rooted in science but unassimilable as science, consciousness and cosmology. . . . The universe wants to be known. Did the universe come about to play its role to empty benches?"[50]

Thus, Wald concluded that the universe itself must be conscious and is somehow feeding the necessary information into its own evolutionary processes to enable it to evolve consciousness in living organisms! This is a strange circumlocution to avoid the concept of creation by a conscious, personal God, but Wald had often said that he did not even like to make sentences containing the world "God." According to Wald, as reported by Thomsen:

> Seeing is related to self-consciousness. Consciousness seems to be characteristic of higher organisms, and a particular self-awareness connected with the ability to plan future actions on the basis of past experience of human beings.
>
> He concedes that nothing one can do as a scientist identifies the presence or absence of consciousness. . . . Consciousness lies outside the parameters of space and time.[51]

Wald then came to the following remarkable conclusion, especially for a man who had always been at best agnostic in relation to the existence of God. "Believing

49. Gunther S. Stent, "Limits to the Scientific Understanding of Man," *Science*, 187 (Mar. 21, 1975): 1057. Dr. Stent is professor of molecular biology at the University of California at Berkeley.
50. George Wald, in a lecture at a Orbis Scientiae meeting in Miami, as quoted by Dietrick E. Thomsen in "A Knowing Universe Seeking to Be Known," *Science News,* 123 (Feb. 19, 1983): p. 124.
51. Ibid.

in the importance of consciousness, he now tries to put consciousness and cosmology together. Perhaps consciousness, rather than being a later evolutionary development, was there all the time. Consciousness formed the material universe and brought out life and overt forms of consciousness."[52]

Wald may not have liked to use the name of God, but it is obvious that "God" could easily be substituted for "consciousness" as the subject of the last sentence. God, like consciousness, is "outside the parameters of space and time," and a universe containing conscious life, by the fundamental principle of causality, can be explained only in terms of its formation by a "conscious" Creator, who also created space and time, as well as the material universe.

Although the more or less "official" scientific view of man is the reductionist view that he is merely a complex physical machine, science as such can never "explain" consciousness and the real essence of human nature.

## Spirit and Soul and Body

Since the scientific method is completely incapable of dealing with the non-material components of man's nature, it is presumptuous for humanists to reject the biblical testimony on this vital subject. The scriptural doctrine of man is reasonable to the mind and satisfying to the heart, but, most important, it is centered in the person and work of the Son of Man, Jesus Christ, the only man who knows by direct experience the independent existence of human soul and spirit. As man, his human body died and was in a tomb for three days, while His "quickened" spirit (1 Pet. 3:18) was triumphing over death and hades. His spirit then returned to His resting body and raised it from the grave. The Bible clearly teaches that the soul and spirit of man survive the death of the body, but it also teaches that the body itself is destined for resurrection and life in eternity. The experience and triumph of the Lord Jesus Christ constitute our proof and promise of both.

The bodily resurrection of Christ is supported by many compelling proofs of its real occurrence, and many volumes have been written setting forth these evidences and refuting the objections.[53]

Nevertheless, the exact character of this component of human nature is difficult to ascertain even from Scripture. Many theologians over the years have insisted that man is a tripartite being of body, soul, and spirit. Others have contended strongly that his nature is dichotomous, that his soul and spirit are actually the same, both terms having references to his "inner man," everything beyond his bodily structure and functions.

That the soul and spirit are indeed distinct is the clear teaching of two passages of Scripture in particular.

---

52. Ibid.
53. For a summary by this writer of the case for the resurrection, see the book *Many Infallible Proofs* (Green Forest, AR: Master Books, 1974), p. 88–96.

And the very God of peace sanctify you wholly; and I pray God your whole spirit and soul and body be preserved blameless unto the coming of our Lord Jesus Christ (1 Thess. 5:23).

For the word of God is quick, and powerful, and sharper than any twoedged sword, piercing even to the dividing asunder of soul and spirit, and of the joints and marrow, and is a discerner of the thoughts and intents of the heart (Heb. 4:12).

Although such passages show that the spirit and soul cannot be synonymous, it is not easy to define each term individually. The Scripture itself says that only the Word of God can distinguish between them. We are not likely, therefore, to get much assistance from natural science, which can deal only with the material, bodily component of human nature.

The biblical data on the subject, however, are abundant. "Soul" in the Old Testament (Hebrew *nephesh*) occurs over 425 times in addition to over 250 times when it is translated by some other word ("life," "heart," "person," etc.). Its New Testament equivalent (Greek *psuche*) is translated "soul" 50 times plus over 40 other occurrences ("life," etc.).

Similarly, the Old Testament *ruach* is translated "spirit" 232 times, "breath" 28 times, "wind" 90 times, plus various others. The New Testament equivalent is the Greek *pneuma*, which is translated as "spirit" 288 times and "ghost" 91 times,[54] plus once each as "life" and "wind."

The problem, therefore, is not a lack of data to go by, but the variety of ways in which the two concepts are applied, often seeming to overlap with each other. The difficulty is compounded by the fact that both *nephesh* and *ruach* are said in the Old Testament to be possessed by animals as well as people. For example: "God created great whales, and every living creature [*nephesh*] that moveth, which the waters brought forth abundantly" (Gen. 1:21). "And they went in unto Noah into the ark, two and two of all flesh, wherein is the breath [*ruach*] of life" (Gen. 7:15). Thus, even the marine animals have "souls" and all land animals have "spirits."

In fact, the soul seems to be connected physically somehow with the blood supply apparatus and the spirit with the air supply, at least while the person or the animal is alive. For example, when speaking of animals to be offered in sacrifice on the altar, God spoke through Moses as follows: "For the life [*nephesh*] of the flesh is in the blood: and I have given it to you upon the altar to make an atonement for your souls" (Lev. 17:11). Perhaps it is merely figurative speech to say that the "soul" that indwells the flesh is somehow doing so by means of the circulating bloodstream (though, certainly, the shedding of a creature's blood is followed by the death of his flesh), but in any case it is clear that animals, as well as people, have souls of a sort, whatever precisely that soul might be.

---

54. The above numbers refer specifically to use in the King James Version.

This is the case in New Testament usage as well. In the coming period of worldwide judgment on the earth, we are told in the Book of Revelation that "every living soul (Greek *psuche*] died in the sea" (Rev. 16:3). This again is a reference (as in Gen. 1:21) to the marine animals.

Also, as noted above, the "spirit," especially in the Old Testament, often refers to the physiological function of breathing, both in man and animals. It is often translated "breath." For example: "Thou takest away their breath [Hebrew *ruach*], they die, and return to their dust" (Ps. 104:29). In the context, this verse is speaking of the death of animals. Then, in the very next verse, *ruach* is translated "spirit," this time referring to the energizing and quickening breath of God. "Thou sendeth forth thy spirit, they are created: and thou renewest the face of the earth" (Ps. 104:30). This usage does not seem to occur in the New Testament, but *pneuma*, the usual word for "spirit" is also translated "wind." "The wind bloweth where it listeth . . . so is every one that is born of the Spirit [also *pneuma*]" (John 3:8).

Although animals are said to have souls and spirits (in the physiological sense, as discussed above) and although human beings, like the animals, also live by the blood supply and air supply systems which these terms entail, there is no doubt whatever that the human soul and human spirit are far more complex than their rudimentary counterparts in the animals.

We are commanded, for example, to "love the Lord thy God . . . with all thy soul" (Matt. 22:37), and to "worship God in the spirit" (Phil. 3:3), capacities and abilities that go far beyond those of the animals. Furthermore, at least from what Scripture tells us, when an animal dies, its soul and spirit die along with its body. As noted in the previous section, on the other hand, man's soul and spirit both survive the death of the body and are thus essentially independent thereof.

Many Bible teachers have suggested that the soul is the seat of man's self-consciousness and emotions, whereas the spirit is that part of his nature that thinks and wills. This is probably too simplistic, however, as the terms often seem to be used almost synonymously and interchangeably. One can verify this by noting how easily and naturally each term can be substituted for the others in verses where they occur. For example, look at the two following verses, both referring to the Lord Jesus. "Now is my soul troubled" (John 12:27). ". . . he was troubled in spirit" (John 13:21). It is difficult to discern why it was Jesus' soul that was troubled at the contemplation of His coming crucifixion, while it was His spirit that was troubled at the contemplation of His coming betrayal.

Or consider an Old Testament example, in two consecutive verses of Psalm 77: ". . . my soul refused to be comforted" (v. 2) ". . . and my spirit was overwhelmed" (v. 3). Again it is hard to discern the difference.

Nevertheless, there is a subtle difference, even though it may be hard to express in words, or else such verses as Acts 17:25 would be redundant: ". . . he giveth to all life, and breath, and all things." In this key reference to God's work of creation, the words "life and breath" are actually the same as "soul and spirit." We have already noted the emphasis on soul and spirit as separate entities in such verses as 1 Thessalonians 5:23 and Hebrews 4:12.

Furthermore, both soul and spirit are the objects of the Lord's great work of salvation: "Receive with meekness the engrafted word, which is able to save your souls" (James 1:21); ". . . that the spirit may be saved in the day of the Lord Jesus" (1 Cor. 5:5).

It often may be appropriate to speak of the "soul/spirit complex," almost as if these constituted a single entity, the "inner man," the nonmaterial part of human nature. In other situations, however, one or the other may be more appropriate. In fact, the "soul" usually seems to correspond more to the person, the "spirit" more to his or her personality. The one connotes what he is, as a living individual; the other relates more to what he does, through attitude, action, and influence, by virtue of what he is. "And so it is written, The first man Adam was made a living soul; the last Adam was made a quickening spirit" (1 Cor. 15:45).

There seems, in fact, to be a striking analogy between the tripartite nature of man and the triune nature of God. It is significant that there is a strong hint of the Trinitarian character of the Creator in the account of man's creation, when God made man in His own image. "And God said, Let *us* make man in *our* image, after *our* likeness. . . . So God created man in *his* own image, in the image of God created *he* him, male and female created *he* them" (Gen. 1:26–27, emphasis added). Three times God refers to himself in the plural; three times the narrative also refers to God in the singular. God is both one and three. He is a triunity.

We have already noted (in chapter 2) the amazing reflection of the triune Creator in the tri-universe which He created. If the physical universe of space/time/matter is a model of the godhead (and, whatever the reason, it is indeed a great Trinity of trinities, as we have seen),[55] it is not surprising to find that His greatest creation, man, likewise reflects His nature.

In the biblical doctrine of the divine Trinity, the Father is the unseen essence of the godhead, the Son is the visible expression of the godhead, and the Spirit is the invisible but powerful influence of God in His creation. So it is with man: his soul is the unseen essence of the man, his person; his body is the visible manifestation of his presence; and his spirit is the unseen, but energizing, personality of the man.

Since the person and personality, though real and distinct, are themselves invisible (as are the Father and the Holy Spirit), it is not surprising that it is difficult to distinguish between them or even (for materialists, at least) to believe in them at all. Nevertheless, they are real, and they are distinct, though it takes the Word of God to discern both their separate existence from the body and their individual interrelationships and functions.

And it must not be forgotten that, though they are three, they are fundamentally

---

55. See chapter 3.

one — a truism that is true both for the triune God and for triune man. Even in salvation they are one, for not only does God (in Christ, from the Father, by the Spirit) save man's soul and spirit, but also his body, through the great coming resurrection event, when Christ "shall change our vile body, that it may be fashioned like unto his glorious body, according to the working whereby he is able even to subdue all things unto himself" (Phil. 3:21).

It was beautifully appropriate, therefore, for the apostle Paul to write, "And the very God of peace sanctify you wholly, and I pray God your whole spirit and soul and body be preserved blameless unto the coming of our Lord Jesus Christ" (1 Thess. 5:23).

# 15

# BABEL AND THE WORLD POPULATION

*Biblical Demography and Linguistics*

In our study of biblical anthropology, we have thus far focused particularly on the nature of man himself, showing that human beings are created in the image of God, uniquely distinct from the animal creation. Man's origin is in no way an evolutionary development from ape-like progenitors, but a special creation, destined for eternity.

The same applies to human societies and interrelationships. The families, nations, and so-called races of mankind are not to be analyzed in an evolutionary context, as though they were somehow like hives of bees or colonies of prairie dogs, but in the light of God's distinct purposes. He told the first man and woman, "Be fruitful, and multiply, and replenish the earth, and subdue it: and have dominion over the fish of the sea, and over the fowl of the air, and over every living thing that moveth upon the earth" (Gen. 1:28). Similarly, after the Flood He renewed this primeval command to Noah saying, "Be fruitful, and multiply, and replenish the earth. And the fear of you and the dread of you shall be upon every beast of the earth, and upon every fowl of the air, upon all that moveth upon the earth, and upon all the fishes of the sea; into your hand are they delivered" (Gen. 9:1–2).

In the next two chapters, therefore, we wish to deal with those sciences related to human societies, especially their historical development. To some degree, this discussion must touch on the social sciences, which are really outside the intended scope of this book. However, the treatment will be limited to the available facts from the historical sciences (cultural anthropology, ethnology, archaeology, etc.) in relation to their bearing on the biblical or evolutionary views concerning the development of human societies. First of all, it will be appropriate to consider the growth of the total human population and its fundamental divisions. The latter, as we shall see, are essentially linguistic rather than racial divisions.

## Demography of the Bible

The first field we should consider is the field of demographics, the study of populations. As a matter of fact, it was largely the population studies of Thomas Malthus, in the early 19th century, that led Charles Darwin to his ideas about natural selection and survival of the fittest in nature. Malthus had argued that human populations tend to increase geometrically, or exponentially (with the population doubling at constant intervals), whereas food supplies and other necessities could only be increased arithmetically (that is, linearly, the increase per unit time being a constant). Thus, the population was perpetually increasing more rapidly than available supplies could warrant, with the result that multitudes would have to be in poverty and might be better off if allowed to die. This same attitude is widely prevalent among ecologists and environmentalists today, who believe that the world population is already too great for its resources and that it is still rapidly increasing. Donald Mann said, "There is a growing consensus that further population growth in our already vastly overpopulated world threatens to destroy man's ancient dream of a good life for all, free from material want. . . . More and more, informed individuals believe that the only possible solution lies in halting and then reversing population growth so that population size can eventually be stabilized at some reasonable fraction of today's numbers."[1]

The world population in 2001 is estimated to be over six billion, although the accuracy of this estimate is open to question. Furthermore, it is a matter of considerable controversy whether the earth's optimum "carrying capacity" is about two billion (as Mann believed), or far more than even the present population. Many have argued the world could satisfactorily support more than 50 billion.

Our discussion here, however, must center not on future population trends, but on historical growth rates. It does seem difficult to explain why, if man has been on the earth for a million years or so, his populations have proliferated only in modern times. How could it be that the planet only now is experiencing a population crisis — why not several hundred thousand years ago, soon after man first appeared on earth?

As a matter of fact, this is a strong argument in favor of the short biblical chronology. At first one might suppose that a few thousand years of human history beginning with Adam and Eve (or, better, with Noah and his wife) could not possibly suffice to explain the present world population of about six billion. The fact is, however, that the difficulty really lies in explaining why the population, after such an interval, is *only* six billion!

---

1. Donald Mann, "The Population Debate: Growth Means Doom," *Science Digest,* 91 (Apr. 1983): p. 79–80. Mann was president of Negative Population Growth, Inc.

That being the case, think how much more unlikely it is that the hypothetical million-year evolutionary history of the human race would only have resulted in the present population.

Although we have no truly reliable population data to work with until modern times, it is possible to study population growth in terms of some reasonable model, to compare that model's implications with respect to modern trends, and then to extrapolate backwards into the past on that basis. There are several possible models that might be used for this purpose, and these will all indicate the reasonableness of a short chronology. Population statistics can be made to fit an evolutionary chronology only by extreme manipulations of the model, in effect only by using an arbitrary model, designed to fit evolution, rather than by using a rational model that at least fits the population data available. All this can be illustrated by the following mathematical examination of population growth rates.[2]

## Rapid World Growth of Population

Assume that the earth had an initial population of 2 people, ready to assume their responsibilities as husband and wife and then as parents. Assume also that the average number of children per family (growing to maturity and marriage) was 2c with c boys and c girls. In the first succeeding generation, then, there would have been c families (and 2 individuals, plus the first 2 still living). The second generation, on the same basis, would contain c x 2c, or $2c^2$, individuals. In the third generation, there would be $2c^3$ individuals, and so on. The total number of individuals in the world at the end of n generations, assuming no deaths, could be calculated as:

$$S_n = 2 + 2c + 2c^2 = 2c^3 + \ldots + 2c^n \tag{1}$$

The sum, $S_n$, can be calculated directly. Multiply both sides of equation (1) by c:

$$S_n(c) = 2c + 2c^2 + 2c^3 = 2c^4 + \ldots + 2c^n + 2c^{n+1}$$

Subtracting the first equation from the above:

$$S_n(c) - S_n = 2c^{n+1} - 2,$$

$$\text{or } S_n(c - 1) = 2c^{n+1} - 2$$

Dividing through by $(c - 1)$ yields the sum $S_n$ as:

$$S_n = \frac{2c^{n+1} - 2}{(c - 1)}$$

---

2. Although nothing more difficult than simple algebra is employed here, any readers who find this section hard to follow can skip the math and only examine the results of the calculations.

Thus,

$$S_n = \frac{2(c^{n+1} - 1)}{(c - 1)} \tag{2}$$

However, the number of people represented by $S_n$ would have to be reduced by the number who had died since the first generation in order to get the actual population. Now, let the average life-span be represented by x generations. The people who had already died by the time of the nth generation, therefore, would be those who were in the $(n - x)^{th}$ generation, or earlier. This number is:

$$S_{(n-x)} = \frac{2(c^{n-x+1} - 1)}{(c - 1)} \tag{3}$$

The total population at the $n^{th}$ generation, then, combining equations (2) and (3), becomes:

$$P_n = S_n - S_{n-x} = \frac{2(c^{n+1} - c^{n-x+1})}{(c - 1)}$$

Thus,

$$P_n = \frac{2(c^{n-x+1})(c^x - 1)}{(c - 1)} \tag{4}$$

Equation (4), in summary, will give the world population n generations after the first family, for an average life-span of x generations and an average number of children growing to maturity and marriage of 2c per family. The equation clearly demonstrates how rapidly populations can grow under favorable conditions.

For example, assume that c = 2 and x = 2, which is equivalent to saying that the average family has 4 children who later have families of their own, and that each set of parents lives to see all their own grandchildren. For these conditions, which are not at all unreasonable, table 8 indicates the population at the end of the indicated numbers of generations, as calculated by equation (4).

| TABLE 8 — *Extended Population Calculation for 6-member Family* | |
|---|---|
| **Generations** | **Population** |
| 5 | 96 |
| 10 | 3,070 |
| 15 | 98,300 |
| 20 | 3,150,000 |
| 30 | 3,220,000,000 |

This last number is almost equal to the present world population, so that only 30 generations under these conditions would suffice to produce a population almost equal to that in the world today. The population at 31 generations would be 6.5 billion.

The next obvious question is: How long is a generation? Again, a reasonable assumption is that the average marriage occurs at age 25 and that the 4 children have been born by age 35. Then the grandchildren will have been born by the time the parents have lived their allotted span of 70 years. A generation thus is about 35 years. Many consider a generation to be only 30 years.

This would mean that practically the entire present world population could have been produced in approximately 31 x 35, or 1,085 years!

The fact that it has actually taken considerably longer than this to bring the world population to its present size indicates that the average family size is less than 4 children, or that the average life span is less than 2 generations, or both. For comparison, let us assume then that the average family has only 3 children and the life-space is 1 generation (i.e., that c = 15 and x = 1). Then, equation (4) yields the figures in table 9.

| TABLE 9 — *Extended Population Calculation for 5-member Family* | |
|:---:|:---:|
| **Generations** | **Population** |
| 10 | 106 |
| 20 | 6,680 |
| 30 | 386,000 |
| 52 | 4,340,000,000 |

It would thus take 52 generations under these conditions to produce almost the present world population. At 35 years per generation, this would still be only 1,820 years. Evidently even 3 children per family is too many to assume for human history as a whole.

However, the average would have to be more than 2 children per family; otherwise, the population would have remained static. *It begins to be glaringly evident that the human race cannot be very old!* The traditional biblical chronology is infinitely more realistic than is the million-year history of mankind assumed by the evolutionist. If the above very conservative assumptions were made (x = 1 and c = 1.5) for the over 28,600 generations assumed in a supposed million years of man's life on earth, the world population should now be over $10^{5000}$ people! This number, which could be written as 1 followed by 5,000 zeros, is inconceivably large. Even if we eventually were able to colonize other worlds and to build space cities everywhere in the interstellar spaces, it can be shown that a maximum of no more than $10^{100}$ people could be crammed into the entire known universe!

The Ussher chronology, on the other hand, based on a literal acceptance of the biblical histories, gives the date of the Flood as about 4,300 years ago.[3] The present population of the world has come originally from Noah's three sons (Gen. 9:19). To be ultraconservative, assume that a generation is 43 years and thus that there have been only 100 generations since Noah. To produce a world population of 6 billion persons (still assuming x = 1), equation (4) is solved for c as follows:

$$6,000,000,000 = 2 (c)^{100}$$

from which:

$$c = (6,000,000,000).01 = 1.244 \text{ (approximately } 1\text{-}1/4)$$

Thus, the average family must have had 2.5 children in order to bring the population to its present magnitude in 100 generations. This is eminently reasonable, though conservative, and is strong support for at least the order-of-magnitude accuracy of the Ussher chronology. However, a period of human history much greater than indicated by the post-Deluge chronology of the Bible is evidently rendered improbable in a very high degree by the facts of population. A million years even at this rate would produce a population of $10^{2700}$ people.

## Effects of Disease and Wars

But what about the possibility that the great plagues and wars of the past may have served to keep the population from growing at the indicated rates? Could the population have remained static for long ages and only in modern times have started to expand?

We are unable to answer these questions dogmatically, of course, since population data are not available for earlier times. We can only say that all that we know about population growth is based on data from the past two centuries. There are no reliable census figures, of course, except in modern times.

If the earth's population started with 2 people just 4,300 years ago, it would only have to have increased at the rate of 0.5 percent each year in order to reach the present population. This is significantly less than the present known rate of population growth of almost 2.0 percent per year. Thus, there is ample provision for long periods when the growth rate may have been less than the average of 0.5 percent.

Furthermore, there is no real evidence that the growth of population has been retarded by wars or disease epidemics. The past century, which has experienced the greatest mushrooming of populations, has also witnessed the most destructive wars in all history, as well as the worst plagues and famines.

---

3. This assumes there are no gaps in the genealogies of Genesis 11. Since it may be possible there are such gaps, especially at the time of Peleg, our calculations are conservative at this point.

It is interesting to note that the best secular estimates of the world population at the time of the birth of Christ yield a probable figure of about 200 million. If we apply our formula, using the very conservative figures of 2.75 children per family, an average life span of only one 40-year generation, and the beginning of population growth with 2 people in 2340 B.C., the calculations yield a probable population of 210 million at that time.

Or, to take another example, consider the nation Israel, which began with the patriarch Jacob about 3,700 years ago. Despite tremendous persecutions over the centuries, and despite the lack of a national homeland for much of their history, the people of Israel have maintained their national identity and now number probably about 14 million people.

This population could have been produced in 3,700 years if we assume the average family size was only 2.4 children (instead of 2.5, to allow for the losses due to the above-mentioned factors), but still assuming a life span of one 43-year generation. Using these figures, the formula yields a present world population of 13,900,000 Israelites.[4]

Thus we conclude that all that is actually known about present or past populations can be explained very reasonably and logically on the basis of a beginning only about 4,300 years ago, making ample allowance for the effects of wars and natural catastrophes. However, the evolutionist assumption that man first appeared a million or more years ago is absurd in light of population statistics.

## Antediluvian Populations

According to the genealogical records of Genesis 5, there were 1,656 years from Adam to the Flood. However, the population constants were significantly different then from what they now are. Men lived to great ages and evidently had large families. Excepting Enoch, who was taken into heaven without dying at 365 (Gen. 5:23–24), the average of the recorded ages of the nine antediluvian patriarchs was 912 years. Recorded ages at the births of their children ranged from 65 years (Mahalaleel, Gen. 5:15; Enoch, Gen. 5:21) to 500 years (Noah, Gen. 5:32). Every one of them is said to have had "sons and daughters," so that each family had at least 4 children, and probably many more.

As an ultraconservative assumption, let $c = 3$, $x = 5$, and $n = 16.56$. These constants correspond to an average family of 6 children, an average generation of 100 years, and an average life span of 500 years. On this basis, the world population at the time of the Flood would have been 235 million people. This probably represents a gross underestimate of the numbers who actually perished in the Flood.

Multiplication was probably more rapid than assumed in this calculation, especially in the earliest centuries of the antediluvian epoch. For example, if the

---

4. These assumptions are obviously far too conservative for the first several generations of Israelites at least, for Jacob had 12 sons, and his descendants numbered probably over two million by the time of the exodus from Egypt (Num. 1:45–47).

average family size were 8, instead of 6, and the length of a generation 93 years, instead of 100, the population at the time of Adam's death, 930 years after his creation, would already have been 2,800,000. At these rates, the population over 700 years later at the time of the Deluge would have been 137 billion! Even if we use rates appropriate in the present world (x = 1 and c = 1.5), over 3 billion people could easily have been on the earth at the time of Noah. These numbers follow directly from equation (4) when the assumed values are inserted in the equation.

Two obvious conclusions appear from these calculations. First, there is no problem whatever in the reference to Cain, Adam's son, as taking a wife, building a city, or fearing avengers (Gen. 4:14–17).[5] Second, the Flood would certainly have to be a global catastrophe if its purpose of destroying all mankind were to be accomplished.

The fact that many hundreds of millions of people may have perished in the Flood does not of course mean that we could now expect to find any of their remains. There is no doubt that, as the Flood waters rose, men would flee to the highest hills and would be the last of all living creatures on the dry land to be overtaken by the waters and drowned. They would thus not be buried in the sediments of the Deluge.

It is possible, of course, that occasional individuals would be trapped and buried, and their bones thus eventually fossilized, but even most of these would never be discovered later. A few fossils possibly of antediluvian men have been found and others may be unearthed in the future, but these are found to be very rare.

The absence of antediluvian human fossils is of course not nearly as serious a problem for the creationist as is the absence of human fossils for the evolutionist. If man has actually been living on the earth for a million or more years, there have been uncounted billions upon billions of people who have lived and died. But only a scant handful of the remains of prehistoric men have ever been found! Surely the bones of a fair number of these multitudes must have been preserved somewhere, if they ever really existed.

## Population Growth from Noah to Abraham

After the Flood, antediluvian conditions of longevity continued to prevail for a while, with life spans only gradually being reduced. Noah lived 950 years (350 of them after the Flood, Gen. 9:28–29). Noah's 3 sons had a recorded total of 16 sons and, presumably, about the same number of daughters, with each family thus averaging about 10 children. From the Flood to the birth of Abraham a total of 292 years and 8 generations are recorded.

---

5. Either Cain or one of his brothers must have married a sister in the first generation after Adam. There is no other way the command to multiply could have been implemented. Some have sought to avoid this inference by suggesting Cain married a woman of a "pre-Adamite" tribe, only semi-human perhaps, and that this explains the degeneration of Cain's descendants. But then the question would only be shifted to "Where did Seth get his wife?"

By the time Abraham journeyed into Canaan, about 400 years had elapsed since the Flood. There were then apparently a number of well-populated cities and nations in the world, as mentioned in Genesis 12–25 (Egypt, Chaldea, Philistia, etc.). Abraham died at age 175, leaving 8 sons (Gen. 25:1–8).

It seems reasonable to assume, for this 400-year period of history, say, 10 generations and an average family size of 8, with an average life span of 5 of the 40-year generations, or 200 years. That is, in our population formula, assume $c = 4$, $n = 10$, and $x = 5$. The world population at the time of Abraham (neglecting any possible gaps in the genealogies of Genesis 11) is then calculated as 2,800,000, a figure that more than adequately explains the biblical and archaeological population inferences for this period of earth history.

The Tower of Babel seems to have been built about the time of the birth of Peleg (whose name, meaning "division," probably was given by his father Eber in commemoration of that event; Gen. 10:25) 101 years after the Flood. Using the same constants as above, the population at this time would have been only 85 people (using equation 2). It is possible that at least 1 generation is missing in the genealogy of Peleg as given in Genesis 10:21–25 and 11:10–16. In the corresponding record in Luke 3:35–36, the name of Cainan is inserted between those of Arphaxad and Salah.

If we assume that, in the course of transcribing the lists in the Old Testament, Cainan's name somehow was omitted from the received text, but that his name was preserved in the Septuagint version from which Luke obtained his data, this would mean 1 more generation in the interim from the Flood to Babel. On this basis, the population would be 340.

This is probably still too small, but the assumed family size of 8 may very well be too small for the early centuries after the Flood. Assuming an average family of 10 children gives a population at Babel of over 700. An average of 12 children gives 1,250. Both these figures assume 40-year generations with, therefore, 3.5 generations from the Flood to Babel.

Since there are 70 nations mentioned in Genesis 10 as resulting from the "division" at Babel, it is reasonable to infer that there were 70 families at Babel, representing probably the generation of Noah's grandsons and great-grandsons. Seventy families containing 800 or 1,000 individuals altogether seem to fit the situation described at Babel very adequately.

We conclude, therefore, that the biblical chronologies are all eminently reasonable in the light of population statistics, and that any significant departures from these chronologies, as required to meet evolutionary speculations, are highly unreasonable and improbable.

## Totals Since the Beginning

Although it is not possible to determine accurate totals, it is of interest to try to estimate how many people have been born into the human family since the beginning of time. Formula (2) is appropriate in this case, provided we can estimate n and c reasonably well. We noted that, if the Ussher chronology is correct, the present world population would have developed from 2 people with n = 100 and c = 1-1/4. If these values are inserted in equation (2), the total number of people born in the postdiluvian world turns out to be about 16 billion.

To this should be added the people in the antediluvian world, but we can only make a guess in this case. It might be fairly reasonable to assume n = 11 (length of a generation 150 years) and c = 6 (average family size of 12). Then the sum $S_n$ is 870 million. We also need to allow for individuals who lived and died but did not have children of their own. Again we have no adequate data, but it would seem reasonable to increase the above figures by about 20 percent for this factor.

The total number of men and women who have ever lived since God created Adam, therefore, is probably on the order of, say, 20 billion people.

We have been assuming, of course, the general accuracy of the Ussher chronology. As we have noted, there may be certain gaps in the genealogies of Genesis 5 and 11. These cannot be stretched very far, however. The outside limit would be to place the creation at about 10,000 years ago, with most of the "gaps" probably occurring since the Flood. In this case, if we assume the Flood occurred 8,000 years ago and assume 40-year generations, then n = 200. The present population would then have been attained with c only about 1.11, or an average family of $2^{2/9}$ children. Placing these values (n = 200 and c = 1.11) in equation (2), the total post-Flood inhabitants would number 30 billion, and we could probably increase this, for reasons noted before, to about 38 billion.

Now, if we go further and consider the possibility that man may have arisen by evolution and reached a truly human status about a million years ago, then again assuming 40-year generations, equation (4) indicates the required value of c to be only 1.001 or less. Thus, the average number of children per family would only have had to be 2.002 in order to attain the present world population in a million years. There would be no population growth at all, of course, if the average family had exactly 2 children. On this basis the total number of people living in the past million years would be the fantastically high number of 3,000 billion!

The evolutionist may object and say that the rate has drastically accelerated only in recent centuries. So, let us consider that the "normal" growth was such as to produce only the earth's population as it was at the time of Christ, about 200 million people. This is the oldest date for which anyone has even a reasonable guess as to the population.

The value of c necessary to give 200 million people in 25,000 generations can be calculated as 1.0007 and the corresponding number of people who had lived and died in that period would still be over 300 billion.

Therefore, using the most conservative figures for which we have even the remotest justification, if the theory of human evolution is true, there have been at least 300 billion people who have lived and died on the earth — almost all of them a long time before Christ came into the world and before any other revelation was given to man about God!

It is interesting that, even using evolutionary assumptions, one can come up with a very large number of people who have lived and died on the earth. A.H. Westing concludes his detailed study of this subject as follows: Thus, approximately 50 billion humans have inhabited the earth at one time or another during our 300,000-year existence."[6] This is apparently the smallest number any kind of evolutionary model could allow.

A good question to consider is: Where were they buried and what happened to their bones? An even more disturbing question is: What happened to their souls?

It may be claimed that none of these calculations really prove anything, since no one really has any way of knowing exactly what birth and death rates and what population figures existed in prehistoric times. This is quite true, of course, but the known facts of population growth do fit the biblical chronology very well and they do not fit the assumed evolutionary chronology at all.

Scientists work in terms of "models" and try to evaluate each proposed model of a particular process in terms of the "degree of fit" of the known data into that model. On this basis, we are abundantly justified in concluding that the creationist model with its brief chronology fits the actual known data of population statistics far better than does the million-year evolutionary model. In terms of scientifically-accepted standards of evaluation, this can only mean that, on this issue at least, creationism is much more "scientific" than evolutionism.

Other population models could be used, of course, and no one knows which is best, nor that the assumed rates have been constant. A simpler approach (as used by Malthus and Darwin) would be to assume a simple geometric increase in population, and to assume that only one generation is living at any one time. That is, in equation (4), assume that $x = 1$. Then, equation (4) becomes simply:

$$P_n = 2c_n \qquad (5)$$

The results obtained from equation (5) are practically the same as from equation (4), when $n$ becomes large.

If one wishes to think in terms of a constant annual percentage increase in population, the population equation can be written as:

$$P_y = 2(1 + \frac{G}{100})^Y \qquad (6)$$

where $G$ is the annual percentage increase in population and $P_y$ is the population after $Y$ years. From this equation, one can calculate that $G$ would have to be about

---

6. Arthur H. Westing, "A Note on How Many Humans That Have Ever Lived," Bioscience, 31 (July–Aug. 1981): 523.

0.5 percent per year to produce the present world population in the assumed 4,300 years since the Flood. This is only one-fourth the present growth rate of 2 percent per year.

It is possible, of course, to specify changing growth rates of family sizes on any arbitrary basis one chooses, in order to make the results come out to any predetermined value. This is what evolutionists have to do in order to account for such a small present world population after such a long imagined evolutionary history. Nevertheless, the simplest and most straightforward population models, based upon all the real population statistics that are available, clearly correlate with the biblical chronology as the true framework of human history.

The total world population, of course, has long since been subdivided into various nations and other groupings, even though the original population was all in one small group. When, and on what basis did these subdivisions take place? The development of different nations is in the domain of ethnology.

## The Origin of Language

Before considering the origin of different cultures, nations, and races, how-ever, we need to consider the remarkable phenomenon of the various human languages, for the former depend on the latter. Evolutionary theorists are inca-pable of presenting a plausible model, either of the origin of human language in general or of the different language groups in particular. The biblical record is far more realistic on this score than anything developed by evolutionists.

In the preceding chapter we discussed briefly, in connection with our analy-sis of human nature and the distinctive entity of human consciousness, the unique character of human language as distinct from animal noises. The only realistic way of accounting for man's unique ability to think and communicate in abstract, symbolic, intelligible speech is that this is a created gift of God. Man was created in God's image, and this requires that there be such a means of communication between God and man and, therefore, also between man and man.

That is, God deigns to speak to man, and man is thus expected to respond in praise to God and in testimony and fellowship to other men. This is the exalted purpose and function intended by God for the created gift of human speech and language. "And the LORD said unto him, Who hath made man's mouth? . . . have not I the Lord? Now therefore go, and I will be with thy mouth, and teach thee what thou shalt say" (Exod. 4:11–12).

But how did man ever acquire such an ability, according to evolutionary specu-lations? This most important of all imagined evolutionary steps, presumably quite recent in geologic time, the step that changed an ordinary animal into a human being, is still completely shrouded in mystery as far as evolutionists are concerned. No less convinced an evolutionist than George Gaylord Simpson has admitted:

> Human language is absolutely distinct from any system of communica-tion in other animals. That is made most clear by comparison with other ani-

mal utterances, which most nearly resemble human speech and are most often called "speech." Non-human vocables are, in effect, interjections. They reflect the individual's physical or, more frequently, emotional state. They do not, as true language does, name, discuss, abstract, or symbolize.[7]

A great deal of study has been devoted to the nature of the chatterings of monkeys and apes, attempting to gain some clue as to how these noises may have evolved into human language. The efforts have been futile. One of the leading workers in this field has concluded, "The more that is known about it, the less these systems seem to help in the understanding of human language."[8]

One would suppose that if man's speech has really evolved upward from that of animals, the most "primitive" tribes would today still have the most simple, animal-like languages. But this is not the case. Missionary linguists, such as the Wycliffe Bible Translators,[9] as well as practically all cultural anthropologists, have univocally pointed out that the languages of such tribes are invariably at least as complex and intricately structured as those of the more civilized nations of the world. Simpson himself has admitted, "Even the peoples with least complex cultures have highly sophisticated languages, with complex grammar and large vocabularies."[10]

The same conclusion applies to all known languages. There is not the slightest evidence, modern or ancient, of the evolution of language. "The oldest language that can reasonably be reconstructed is already modern, sophisticated, complete from an evolutionary point of view."[11]

A few writers have tried to discuss the origin of language by comparison of human and ape jaw structure and by use of the famous "recapitulation" theory. Such naive speculations merely serve to emphasize the barrenness of this entire line of reasoning.

The invention of intelligible speech depends on the brain and central nervous system, not on the shape of the jaw and hard palate, and it is only the latter that can be studied in the fossils. Not only mammals, but even birds, can produce sounds similar to human words, but they have no comprehension of their meaning.

As far as the "recapitulation theory" is concerned, the notion that a baby, in learning to speak, recapitulates the evolution of language in his ancestors, hardly deserves refutation. According to Simpson:

7. George G. Simpson, "The Biological Nature of Man," *Science,* 152 (Apr. 22, 1966): 476.
8. J.B. Lancaster in *The Origin of Man,* symposium ed. by P. L. Devore (New York, NY: Wenner-Gren Foundation, 1965).
9. The author's daughter, Dr. Kathleen Bruce, and her husband, Dr. Leslie Bruce, were Wycliffe missionary linguists in one such supposedly primitive tribe, the Alamblak, along the Sepik River in northwest New Guinea. By evolutionary definitions, the Alamblak people are "stone-age" people, but they are very intelligent and personable, with a very complex social structure.
10. George G. Simpson, "Biological Nature," p. 477.
11. Ibid.

Still another attempt, which now seems very naive, is through the ontogeny of language, that is, the acquisition of language by children. This relies on the famous but, as it happens, quite erroneous saying that ontogeny repeats phylogeny. In fact, the child is not evolving or inventing primitive language but is learning a particular modern language, already complete and . . . different from any possible primitive language.[12]

It is also significant that there is no tribe, no matter how apparently "primitive" it is thought to be, that does not have a distinctive and complex language of its own.

No language-less community has ever been found.[13]

Even that most doctrinaire and anti-theistic of all evolutionists, Richard Dawkins, probably England's leading evolutionary biologist, has found it impossible to explain the origin of human language.

Nobody knows how it began. . . . Equally obscure is the origin of semantics: of words and their meaning.[14]

Dawkins even has noted the impossibility of explaining the high complexity of the languages of what appear to be primitive tribes.

. . . all the thousands of languages in the world are very complex (some say they are all exactly *equally* complex, but that sounds too ideologically perfect to be wholly plausible). I am biased toward thinking it was gradual, but it is not quite obvious that it had to be. Some people think it began suddenly, more or less invented by a single genius in a particular place at a particular time.[15]

With respect to Dawkins admitted bias against the idea that all languages are equally complex, the authoritative *Atlas of Languages* confirms that his bias is just that and nothing more.

It would seem likely that further light could be thrown on the evolution of human language by studying more and less complex human languages spoken today. However . . . no evidence has ever been produced that would suggest that one particular language as spoken by modern humans is more or less complex than any other.[16]

Thus, all human languages, though now having differentiated into "over 6,000 languages" now being "spoken in the world,"[17] are all equally complex (although

12. Ibid. Note, incidentally, Simpson's admission that the nineteenth-century recapitulation theory (which, regrettably is still taught today in many classrooms) is "quite erroneous."
13. Stephen Matthews, Bernard Comrie, and Marcia Polinsky, eds., *Atlas of Languages: The Origin and Development of Languages Throughout the World* (New York, NY: Facts on File, Inc., 1996), p. 10.
14. Richard Dawkins, *Unweaving the Rainbow* (Boston, MA: Houghton-Mifflin Co., 1998), p. 294.
15. Ibid., p. 295.
16. Matthews, Comrie, and Polinsky, *Atlas of Languages*, p. 11–12.
17. Ibid., p. 13.

all do tend to deteriorate with time). Furthermore, despite numerous efforts to teach chimpanzees or other animals to talk, there is an absolutely unbridgeable gap between human language and animal chatterings.

> But though animal trainers and investigators have tried since the seventeenth century to teach chimpanzees to talk, no chimpanzee has ever managed it. . . . To do this, they would have to have our brains.[18] [Not to mention the same sound-producing anatomies.]

From whatever direction the origin of language is studied, therefore, one comes to a dead end. There is simply no satisfactory evidence or theory to explain it.

With one exception, that is! The concept that man was originally created as man, with the unique ability for personal communication with His Creator and with other men, does fit all the facts, simply and directly. According to the biblical record, not only was man created with the unique ability to converse with his Creator and with his wife, but was even instructed to examine and then name all the animals. Man, alone among living creatures, was thus able to evaluate their distinctive characteristics and to recognize that none of them were equipped to be a "help meet for him" (Gen. 2:20).

## The Confusion of Tongues

As far as the great proliferation of *different* languages among men is concerned, the biblical account is likewise the only satisfactory explanation. If all men came from one ancestral population, as most evolutionary anthropologists believe today, they originally all spoke the same language. As long as they lived together, or continued to communicate with one another, it would have been impossible for the wide differences in human languages to have evolved.

Therefore, if anthropologists insist on an evolutionary explanation for the different languages, then they must likewise postulate extremely long periods of isolation and inbreeding for the different tribes, practically as long as the history of man himself. This in turn means that each of the major language groups must be identical with a major racial group. Therefore, each "race" must have had a long evolutionary history, and it is natural to assume that some races have evolved more than others. This natural association of racism with evolutionary philosophy is quite significant and has been the pseudoscientific basis of a wide range of racist political and religious philosophies that have wrought untold harm and misery over the years.

On the other hand, it does seem obvious that all the different nations, tribes, and languages among men do have a common origin in the not-too-distant past. People of all nations are all freely interfertile and of essentially equal intelligence and potential educability. Even the so-called "aborigines" of Australia are as capable

---

18. Philip Lieberman. "Peak Capacity," *The Sciences,* 37 (Nov.–Dec. 1997): 27.

as the so-called "upper classes" in Great Britain of acquiring Ph.D. degrees, and some have done so. Even though their languages are widely different from each other, all can be analyzed in terms of the science of linguistics, and all can be learned by men of other languages, thus demonstrating an original common nature and origin. There is really only one *kind* of man — namely mankind! In actuality there is only one *race* among men — the *human* race.

The source of the different languages cannot be explained in terms of evolution, though the various dialects and similar languages within the basic groups are no doubt attributable to gradual diversification from a common source tongue. But the major groups are so fundamentally different from each other as to defy explanation in any naturalistic framework.

Only the Bible provides an adequate explanation. Originally, after the great Flood, "the whole earth was of one language, and one speech" (Gen. 11:1). Because of man's united rebellion against God, however, refusing to scatter throughout the world as He had commanded, and concentrating instead in the vicinity of the original Babylon, "the LORD did there confound the language of all the earth: and from thence did the LORD scatter them abroad upon the face of all the earth" (Gen. 11:9).

Presumably about 70 families were involved in this dispersion, as suggested by the enumeration of 70 original national groups and tongues in the so-called Table of Nations in Genesis 10. These were represented originally by perhaps a thousand or so individuals,[19] divided into three main ancestral family bodies, the Japhetic, Hamitic, and Semitic. "These are the families of the sons of Noah, after their generations, in their nations: and by these were the nations divided in the earth after the flood" (Gen. 10:32).

The rebellion at Babel was not some impossible undertaking, such as attempting to reach heaven with a manmade tower, as one might infer from the King James translation of Genesis 11:4. The words "may reach" are not in the original; the correct sense of the passage may suggest "a tower, whose top [is dedicated] unto the heavens," that is, the erection of a great temple-tower dedicated to the worship of the "host of heaven," uniting all mankind in worshiping and serving the creature rather than the Creator (Rom. 1:25). A number of ancient ziggurats and similar structures did have a shrine at the apex with the signs of the zodiac emblazoned around the periphery. The most effective way of halting this blasphemy and of enforcing God's command to fill the earth was that of confounding their languages.

If people could not communicate with each other, they could hardly cooperate with each other. This primeval confusion of tongues emphasizes what modern man often fails to realize: the real divisions among men are not racial or physical or geographic, but linguistic. When men could no longer understand each other, there was finally no alternative for them but to separate from each other.

---

19. See discussion of probable population at Babel earlier in this chapter.

If anyone is inclined to question this explanation of the origin of the major differences among languages, then let him offer a naturalistic explanation that better accounts for all the facts. No one has done so yet. Obviously a miracle was involved, but the gravity of the rebellion warranted God's special intervention.

Although the major language groups are so different from each other as to make it inconceivable that they could have evolved from a common ancestral language group (except, as noted above, by such a long period of racial segregation as to cause the corresponding races to evolve to different levels themselves), the very fact that all the languages can be evaluated by common principles of linguistics, and that people can manage to learn other languages than their own, implies an original common cause for all of them.

It is significant that traditions similar to the Babel story exist in various other ancient nations and even in some modern so-called "primitive tribes." Although not as frequently encountered as traditions of the great Flood, many tribes do have a tradition of a former age when all people spoke the same language until the languages were confused as a judgment by the gods.

Thus, there is good reason to accept the biblical record of the confusion of tongues at Babel as the true account of the origin of the different major language groups of the world. Evolutionists certainly have no better answer, and the only reason why modern scientists tend to reject it is because it was miraculous. To say that it would have been impossible, however, is not only to deny God's omnipotence but also to assert that scientists know much more about the nature of language than they do.

No one yet adequately understands the brain and its control of human speech. Therefore, no one understands what manner of physiologic changes in the brain and central nervous system would be necessary to cause different groups of people to associate different sounds with any given concept. Perhaps future research will throw light on this phenomenon but, in the meantime, there is no better explanation than that it was God who did "there confound their language, that they may not understand one another's speech" (Gen. 11:7).

## Language, Race, and Evolutionism

Contrary to common opinion among Christians, the three sons of Noah — Shem, Ham, and Japheth — did not form three "races," but three streams of nations. There are, for example, both light-skinned peoples and black-skinned peoples to be found among all three groups. The various tribal or national (not "racial") characteristics could have developed rather quickly as the tribal units were separated and forced to propagate to considerable extent by an inbreeding process among themselves.

It is reasonable to believe that God implanted in the first man and woman genetic "information" from which could be specified a wide variety of physiological characteristics among their descendants. These characteristics would be distributed more or less at random, as described by Mendelian statistical principles of inheritance, among all the population as long as there was more or less free intermarriage among the members of this population. In fact, those genes that geneticists now denote as "dominant" would tend to maintain the appearance of all men as more or less uniformly structured along the lines of those dominant genes. "Recessive" traits would tend to be submerged together, even though still potentially available in the gene pool.

When, however, men were forced to break up into very small population groups, by the miraculously induced language barriers erected at Babel, many of these recessive genes would have opportunity to be expressed openly for the first time in distinct physical characteristics corresponding to each tribe.

It is in fact known experimentally that small populations vary more quickly and widely than do large populations, at least in genetic observations on animals. In particular, studies on the drosophila fruit fly have demonstrated this phenomenon. One of the top authorities in this field, Theodosius Dobzhansky, has said:

> The founder principle is "establishment of a new population by a few original founders . . . that carry only a small fraction of the total genetic variation of the parental population." Founder events are inevitably followed by inbreeding for one or several generations. . . . Natural selection in experimental populations derived from small numbers of founders resulted in a greater variety of outcomes than in comparable populations descended from numerous founders.[20]

Man has of course accomplished the same sort of thing on numerous kinds of plants and animals by artificial selection and reproductive isolation. The tremendous number of varieties of domesticated dogs, for example, has evidently all been derived by selective breeding processes from one ancestral dog, in just the past few thousand years. Yet when these various breeds of dogs are allowed to mix freely in a wild state, interbreeding soon results in a reversion to some kind of more or less homogenized mongrel type. The same is true of other "pure" breeds of plants or animals. This phenomenon of rapid variation in small, inbreeding populations was first (and most appropriately) called the "founder principle" by the Harvard biologist and taxonomist Ernst Mayr. "The fundamental fact on which my theory was based is the empirical fact that when in a superspecies or species group there is a highly divergent population or taxon, it is invariably found in a peripherally isolated location. . . . My conclusion was that any drastic reorganization of the gene pool is far more easily accomplished in a small founder population than in any other kind of population."[21]

Such rapid variation, or "reorganization of the gene pool," is not evolution, of course, but simply a recombination of genetic factors already present and, in fact,

---

20. Theodosius Dobzhansky, "Species of Drosophila," *Science*, 177 (Aug. 25, 1972): p. 667.
21. Ernst Mayr, "Speciation and Macroevolution," *Evolution*, 36, no. 6 (1982): p. 1122.

part of God's created genetic variational potential for the particular kind. The small population of each animal kind after the Flood undoubtedly led to rapid development of new varieties of animals. Similarly, the small inbreeding family groups of humans emigrating from Babel could each quickly develop new physical attributes — even so-called "racial" characteristics — that would characterize their respective descendants. "More precisely, evidence has been steadily accumulating that, other factors being equal, rate of speciation is inversely correlated with population size. This is why speciation can be so rapid in founder populations, while widespread populous species may be totally inert evolutionarily."[22]

There is thus adequate genetic variation in the human genetic code to allow the development of a great number of distinctive characteristics in only a few generations by the very mechanism described in Genesis 11 — namely, enforced segregation by a confusion of languages.

If, however, one is committed to an evolutionary interpretation of the origin of "races,"[23] it is necessary to assume a long evolutionary history of racial segregation, mutations, and natural selection to develop each distinctive set of racial characteristics.

> It is not hard to assess the origin of an individual with respect to the major racial subdivisions: the straight-haired, tan Orientals, the wiry-haired dark Africans, and the lank-haired, pale Caucasians. If we analyze our impressions in detail, we find that they come down to a few highly visible characteristics: the color of the skin, the color and form of the hair and the gross morphology of the face, the eye folds, the nose and the lips.[24]

These are obviously all rather superficial distinctions and can be easily accounted for in terms of the biblical record of small, separated, inbreeding family groups following the Babel dispersion. If these genetic features were all latent in the created gene pool of mankind, it would only take a few generations of such isolation to allow such latent characteristics to emerge and become dominant in a given tribe.

To require each tribe to develop distinctiveness by the typical Darwinian procedure of mutation, struggle, and selection, on the other hand, would require immense amounts of time in such isolation. Authorities estimate at least 50,000 years[25] of segregation for this to be accomplished, and such vast periods (ten times as long as the known existence of civilization and reliable written records) would surely mean that mental and moral faculties would be evolving as well as physical features, so that the resultant "races" would be eventually differentiated from each other in terms of intelligence and morality also.

---

22. Ibid., p. 1129.
23. As far as the Bible is concerned, there is no such thing as a "race." This is strictly an evolutionist concept, a subspecies supposedly evolving into a new species.
24. L.L. Cavalli-Sforza, "The Genetics of Human Populations," *Scientific American*, 231 (Sept. 1974): 85.
25. Ibid., p. 89.

As a result, evolution — especially of the Darwinian and Lamarckian varieties — has long been used as the supposedly scientific basis of racism. All of the 19th-century evolutionists, in fact — Darwin, Huxley, and all the rest, well up into the first quarter of the 20th century — were convinced proponents of white supremacy.

> Since Darwin's death, all has not been rosy in the evolutionary garden. The theories of the Great Bearded One have been hijacked by cranks, politicians, social reformers — and scientists — to support racist and bigoted views. A direct line runs from Darwin . . . to the extermination camps of Nazi Europe.[26]

The most vicious of the racist philosophies that were built on evolutionism, however, was probably Adolph Hitler's Nazism. The background for this is found especially in the teachings of Darwin's contemporary propagandist in Germany, Ernst Haeckel, who was probably the most influential evolutionist in continental Europe. "Along with his social Darwinist followers, [Haeckel] set about to demonstrate the 'aristocratic' and non-democratic character of the laws of nature . . . up to his death in 1919, Haeckel contributed to that special variety of German thought which served as the seed-bed for national Socialism. He became one of Germany's main ideologists for racism, nationalism, and imperialism."[27] When Hitler came along, he used Haeckel's so-called scientific evolutionism as the basis of his own racist philosophy. "[Hitler] stressed and singled out the idea of biological evolution as the most forceful weapon against traditional religion and he repeatedly condemned Christianity for its opposition to the teachings of evolution. . . . For Hitler, evolution was the hallmark of modern science and culture, and he defended its veracity as tenaciously as Haeckel."[28]

It is hardly possible to overestimate the baleful influence of this man, Professor Ernst Haeckel, in the 19th century development and triumph of evolutionary biology, racism, and Nazism in Germany and other countries.

> Nineteenth-century German morphologist, embryologist, natural philosopher, and artist Ernst Haeckel must surely be counted as one of the most influential and controversial figures in the history of evolutionary biology. . . . Haeckel was arguably, next to Darwin, the dominant intellectual figure of his time. . . . his overall influence on biological research was enormously stimulating. . . . He treated evolutionary biology almost as a religion and believed that just as one could apply the concept of natural selection to animals and plants, one could also determine which groups of humans were superior. Offering intellectual justification and "scientific" support for racism, anti-Semitism,

---

26.  Martin Brookes, "Ripe Old Age," *New Scientist,* 161 (Jan. 30, 1999): p. 41.

27.  Daniel Gasman, *The Scientific Origins of National Socialism: Social Darwinism in Ernst Haeckel and the German Monist League* (New York, NY: American Elsevier Press, 1971), p. xvi, xvii. Haeckel is also famous for popularizing the now-repudiated "recapitulation theory" relating ontogeny to phylogeny and for his fraudulent drawings of supposed embryo similarities.

28.  Ibid., p. 168.

and eugenics, his ideas were later a major ideological influence on the National Socialist German Workers' Party, better known as the Nazis.[29]

Largely as a result of Haeckel's teachings, not only did the German scientific and military establishments under Germany's Kaiser Wilhelm play a vital role in fomenting World War I, but they also contributed to the rise of Adolph Hitler, with his own almost religious commitment to evolutionism and racism.

Hitler was so enamored of evolutionary theory that he was willing to commit the lives of the German people to the struggle for racial supremacy. "Hitler believed in struggle as a Darwinian principle of human life that forced every people to try to dominate all others; without struggle they would rot and perish. . . . Even in his own defeat in April 1945 Hitler expressed his faith in the survival of the stronger and declared the Slavic people to have proven themselves the stronger."[30] Hitler's campaign to destroy the Jews was, in his thinking, merely good science, applied Darwinism. A Jewish biology professor at Purdue University has commented on this: "I don't claim that Darwin and his theory of evolution brought on the holocaust; but I cannot deny that the theory of evolution, and the atheism it engendered, led to the moral climate that made a holocaust possible."[31]

Because of the worldwide moral revulsion to Hitler's racism, modern evolutionists, with few exceptions, now reject the racist connotations of Darwinian evolution, and this has been one important reason for the recent resurgence of belief in catastrophism and rapid evolution in place of uniformitarianism and gradual evolution. This development, as we have already seen, is not based on evidence, but is merely an attempt to explain the lack of evidence without resorting to the biblical record. The biblical account, however, centered in the primeval period of special creation, the Flood, and the dispersion at Babel, satisfactorily explains all the known phenomena of language and the differences in physical appearance that have been erroneously magnified into the evolutionist concept of different races of mankind.

29. James Hanken, "Beauty Beyond Belief," *Natural History*, 107 (Dec. 1998–Jan. 1999): p. 56.
30. P. Hoffman, *Hitler's Personal Security* (London: Pergamon, 1979), p. 264.
31. Edward Simon, "Another Side to the Evolution Problem," *Jewish Press* (Jan. 7, 1983): p. 24-B.

# 16

# GOD AND THE NATIONS
*Biblical Ethnology*

The science of ethnology (from Greek *thenos* — "nation") is very broad, embracing the origin and development of the various nations, peoples, and languages of the world. It may also include such disciplines as archaeology and cultural anthropology, as well as the fields of demographics and linguistics, which were briefly treated in the preceding chapter. The tools and methods of the natural scientist, the social scientist, and the historian must all be utilized in trying to decipher the ancient history of the tribes and cultures of the primeval world. This chapter will focus especially on the early post-Flood nations and the beginnings of civilization in their biblical context.

This book has, of course, focused primarily on the relationship of Scripture to the natural sciences — that is, the physical sciences and the life sciences — and, since ethnology occupies a sort of borderland area between the natural sciences, the social sciences, and the humanities, it is sufficient for present purposes simply to survey the field, leaving it to the interested student to pursue further on his own.

Unfortunately, the literature of all of these ethnologically related fields, dealing with human societies as they do, has been pervasively saturated with evolutionary humanism. This makes it difficult to sift facts from evolutionary speculations concerning those facts.

Because of this evolutionary bias in the social sciences, biblical revelation has not been taken nearly as seriously as it should have been in tracing out these ancient developments. The purpose of this chapter, therefore, will be primarily just to summarize the biblical record of the development of the world's peoples, cultures, and nations, supporting it as appropriate with data from the broad field of ethnology.

## Figure 32 — The World's First Nations After the Flood

*The three sons of Noah became the progenitors of three streams of nations after the Babel dispersion. Although there are uncertainties, the identifications in the Table of Nations, as shown on the map below, are at least approximately correct.*

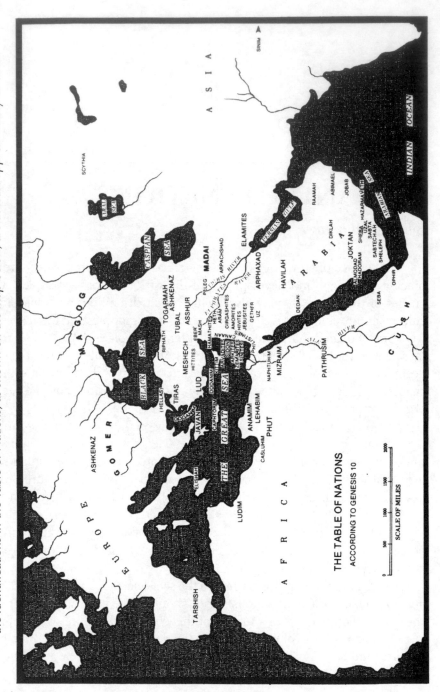

THE TABLE OF NATIONS
ACCORDING TO GENESIS 10

SCALE OF MILES
0   500   1000   1500   3000

Although there are many different nations in the world, all their peoples are members of the same human race. Biologically speaking, they are all still the same *kind!* "[God] hath made of one blood all nations of men for to dwell on all the face of the earth, and hath determined the times before appointed, and the bounds of their habitation" (Acts 17:26). After Babel, people could still inter-breed freely as opportunity afforded, especially as the new language gaps were gradually bridged through commerce and education, and there has been a great amount of such mixing and shifting of national identities through the course of history. Ethnologists, linguists, archaeologists, and cultural anthropologists can to some extent trace these movements as they study the various groups of men, ancient and modern.

## Origin of the Nations

The Table of Nations in Genesis 10 gives the most important information on the origin of the nations. Scientists in the above-mentioned fields would do well to use it as a guide in their studies, instead of using the fallacious philosophy of evolution. Although some have scoffed at the Table, the truly qualified scientists who have studied it have been amazed at its accurate insight into ancient history. For example, the man who has been almost universally acknowledged as the greatest of modern archaeologists, Dr. William F. Albright, has given this evaluation: "It stands absolutely alone in ancient literature without a remote parallel even among the Greeks. . . . The Table of Nations remains an astonishingly accurate document. . . . (It) shows such remarkably 'modern' understanding of the ethnic and linguistic situation in the modern world, in spite of all its complexity, that scholars never fail to be impressed with the author's knowledge of the subject."[1]

The most obvious fact derived from these records in Genesis is that civilization began in the Middle East, in the general vicinity of Mount Ararat (now in Turkey) and Babylon (now in Iraq). The post-Babel dispersion of the nations can be traced to some extent in the names of Noah's descendants as given in Genesis 10. These primeval nations are tentatively identified as shown on the map in figure 32. The Japhetic tribes in general migrated north and west into Europe. The Hamitic tribes mainly journeyed south and west into Africa and the eastern Mediterranean area, although one of them, the Hittites, became a great empire in Turkey and western Asia, and others may well have gone to the Far East. The Semites concentrated more or less in the Middle East.

The Japhetic nations listed in this Table of Nations (Gen. 10:2–5) that have been more or less firmly identified are Javan (Greece); Magog, Mesheck, and Tubal (Russia); Gomer (Cimmeria, Germany); Tiras (Thrace, Etrusca); Madai (the Medes); Ashkenaz (Germany); Togarmah (Armenia); and Dodanim (Dardanians). Most of these peoples seem to have migrated into Europe and to

---

1. W.F. Albright, *Recent Discoveries in Bible Lands* (New York, NY: Funk and Wagnalls, 1955), p. 30, 70.

have become, in general, the ancestors of the so-called Caucasian and Aryan "races." One branch settled in India and others, later, in the Americas, Australia, and New Zealand.

The descendants of Shem (Gen. 10:21–31) include especially Eber (the Hebrews), Elam (Persia), Aram (Syria), Asshur (Assyria), and later through Ishmael, Esau, and other descendants of Abraham (as well as Moab and Ammon, sons of Lot), all the Arab nations.

Some of the Hamites (Gen. 10:6–20) are fairly well identified, especially Mizraim (Egypt), Cush (Ethiopia), Canaan (the Canaanites, Phoenicians, Hittites), and Put (Libya). The first Babylonians, the Sumerians, were also Hamites, under Nimrod.

The ancestry of the Mongol peoples is more difficult to identify. However, several considerations seem to favor a Hamitic origin for these nations as well. First, by a process of elimination, since the Semites and Japhethites are fairly well identified, all others are presumably Hamitic. Second, the Sinites (Gen. 10:17) are listed as descendants of Canaan, and it is possible this name is etymologically related to China. Third, Cathay was the ancient name for China, and there is some evidence this name is derived from Khetae, which in turn may have come from the Hittites, the children of Heth, the son of Canaan. Fourth, there seem to be greater similarities in language and physical characteristics of the Mongols to those of other known Hamites than to those of known Semites and Japhethites. However, a long-time Chinese missionary, Dr. Ethel Nelson, in collaboration with several Chinese scholars, has discovered strong evidence that the very characters of the Chinese language itself reflect the primeval revelation of Genesis 1–11, and therefore possibly relate to the Semites.

These deductions are admittedly tenuous and there is surely room for much fruitful research in tracing out the origin of these and other early peoples. If ethnologists would use Genesis 10 and 11 as their guide, instead of the evolutionary speculations of most modern anthropologists and archaeologists, they would no doubt be able to clear up many of these uncertainties. One anthropologist who has written extensively and effectively on this subject is Dr. Arthur Custance.[2] Other insightful discussions on these earliest nations can be found in the writings of the first-century Jewish historian Josephus, as well as W.F. Albright[3] and most Bible dictionaries.

The famous Noahic prophecy (Gen. 9:25–27) is of great interest in this connection. Noah, knowing that all nations in the new world after the Flood were to be descended from his three sons, was led to make an inspired prediction concerning the main contributions they would make to the future corporate life of mankind.

---

2. Arthur Custance, *Noah's Three Sons* (Grand Rapids, MI: Zondervan, 1975), 368 p.; *Genesis and Early Man* (Grand Rapids, MI: Zondervan, 1975), p. 331.

3. Albright, *Recent Discoveries in Bible Lands*.

Perhaps this prophecy was based in part upon the character development he had observed in his sons, knowing that their respective progeny would, both by genetic inheritance and parental teachings, manifest to some extent their father's particular characteristics. Man has a tripartite nature — physical, mental, and spiritual — and in every man one or another of these three seems to predominate. In the case of Noah's sons, it had become evident that the interests of Ham were primarily physical, those of Japheth were intellectual, and those of Shem were religious. Therefore, it was both genetically and environmentally logical that these attributes would become respectively predominant in the nations descended from them.

It was probably with Shem's deeply spiritual nature and concerns in mind that Noah said concerning Shem, "Blessed be the Lord God of Shem," no doubt thereby prophesying that Shem would be the one through whom the knowledge of the true God would be maintained and transmitted. The great monotheistic religions of Judaism, Islam, Zoroastrianism, and Christianity have, of course, been propagated by Semites (other world religions have all been pantheistic and polytheistic). Of paramount importance is the fact that it was from Shem that, according to human inheritance, Christ came.

Japheth was, according to Noah's prediction, to be "enlarged" by God and to "dwell in the tents of Shem." The "enlargement" probably had a mainly intellectual connotation, with Japheth's descendants due to expand in cultural, philosophical, and scientific influence through the world. Such intellectual influence would, of course, have to be supported first of all by political expansion and influence as well.

During the subsequent course of world history, however, it was a long time before this prophecy began to be fulfilled. The Hamitic nations of Sumeria and Egypt dominated the known world for centuries, to be succeeded by the Semitic nations of Assyria, Babylonia, and Persia. Finally, however, Greece, under Alexander the Great, conquered the Persian hordes, and Japhetic nations have largely dominated world affairs ever since.

The ancient Greeks acknowledged "Iapetos" (Japheth) as their progenitor, and they seem to have constituted the archetype of Japhetic culture. It is universally acknowledged that the western world is founded intellectually on the scientific and philosophical legacy of the Greeks. It was Greek science, pure and applied — not their manpower or physical resources — that led to their enlargement. The same has been true ever since, successively of Rome, France, Germany, England, and America.

Furthermore, Japheth was to "dwell in the tent of Shem." Such an expression can only mean that, in some sense, Japheth was to become a part of the family of Shem, living in his own household. This union, however, could not mean an actual organic merger. Obviously it means that Japheth was to share in Shem's spiritual life, even though his own contribution to mankind would be predominantly that of intellectual enlargement. It has been fulfilled abundantly in the commitment of the Japhetic nations to the God of Abraham and the Messiah of Israel.

If the characters and contributions of Shem and Japheth were mainly spiritual and intellectual, respectively, that of Ham has been primarily physical. However, "physical" does not mean either "trivial" or "menial," and Ham's contributions have been most impressive. Among his descendants, many believe, have been the Sumerians, Egyptians, Phoenicians, Hittites, Dravidians, Chinese, Japanese, Ethiopians, Incas, Aztecs, and Mayans, as well as the modern-day African-Americans, Native Americans, Eskimos, and Pacific island tribes.

These peoples have not been primarily noted for either spiritual or scientific contributions, but they have made innumerable advances in the technological and "creature comfort" aspects of civilization. For example, they were the original pioneers in the exploration and settling of the geographical regions remote from Ararat and Babel. Neither Columbus nor Leif Ericson discovered America — the Native Americans  did! Very likely many of the Native Americans  came across the land bridge at the Bering Strait during the Ice Age, after the Flood, and are descendants of various Mongol tribes. Evidence is accumulating that others came by sea, perhaps from Phoenicia or Egypt. In any case, all of these are probably descendants of Ham.

Similarly, among the Hamitic peoples were the first mariners, the first city builders, the first printers, and probably the first to develop agriculture, animal domestication, and metallurgy, as well as many other technological contributions. The invention of writing, whether Sumerian cuneiform, Egyptian hieroglyphics, or Phoenician alphabetic writing, seems also to have been a Hamitic contribution, at least insofar as the "new" languages dating from Babel are concerned. (Shem himself presumably did not participate in the rebellion of Nimrod at Babel and thus probably perpetuated the one written language with which he was already familiar from pre-Flood times.) The art of printing is due to the Chinese, as is that of navigation by magnetic compass. In general, provisions for all the basic physical needs associated with organized human societies — exploration, food, shelter, clothing, transportation, communication, metal working, and similar functions — seem probably to have been primarily Hamitic in origin.

## Origin of Civilization

The evolutionary system has traditionally included human societies, as well as human physiology, in its scope. It has been assumed that man's biological evolution from an ape-like ancestor has been followed by his social and cultural evolution from primitive food-gathering and hunting groups through various stages up to civilized urban complexes.

As a matter of fact, the hard evidence is all against this evolutionary belief, both in the Bible and in true science. Wherever one finds firm evidence of human societies, he finds evidence of a high order of intelligence and technology very early in the history of that site.

Archaeologists and anthropologists have attempted to divide early human history into several periods, more or less as the geologists have done for prehuman evolutionary history, supposedly identifiable by the tools and other artifacts found in association with those periods. Various more or less parallel nomenclatures have been employed, as follows:

1. Paleolithic
   (Old Stone Age)      = Savagery    = Food Collecting Stage
2. Mesolithic
   (Middle Stone Age)   = Barbarism   = Incipient Cultivation
3. Neolithic
   (New Stone Age)      = Civilization = Village Economy

After the Stone Ages, man supposedly learned how to use metals, and the Bronze Age followed, and then the Iron Age. The artificiality of such divisions when employed as chronologic sequences is obvious from the fact that there are "savages" living in a "Paleolithic" hunting-and-gathering type of culture in various parts of the world today. If such is true today, it probably has likewise been true in all previous periods of man's history. Furthermore, much evidence indicates these "primitive tribes" have deteriorated from a more sophisticated culture in the past, now preserved only in their traditions. Such evolutionary divisions therefore are meaningless when interpreted on a time basis. One can, by providing proper training and opportunity, convert a "stone-age" savage into a 20th-century college graduate in just a few years. Evolutionary stage has nothing to do with it.

In any case, the evolutionary criteria by which anthropologists recognize the "civilized" state are worth investigating briefly. They have called the development of this state the "Neolithic Revolution." The crude stone tools gave way to polished stone axes and finely shaped arrowheads; pottery was employed; agriculture was developed; and animals were domesticated. Furthermore, metallurgy was soon developed and then civilization was supposedly here in earnest. Urbanization soon accompanied all these developments.

A discussion of the origin of civilization thus must deal primarily with the origin of these five accoutrements of civilization: (1) pottery; (2) agriculture; (3) animal husbandry; (4) metallurgy; and (5) cities. As these are each discussed briefly below, one should take *cum grano salis* the dates mentioned, as these are based largely on certain key radiocarbon and tree-ring measurements and attempted corrections. This dating question will be discussed shortly. In the meantime, it is important to note merely that all of these attributes of civilization appear at about the same time, in the Near East, exactly as the Bible has said all along.

For example, consider the art of ceramics and the invention of pottery as well as the use of baked clay for building and sculpture, etc. Dr. Cyril S. Smith, of Massachusetts Institute of Technology, says:

Figurines were certainly being fired by 9000 B.C. in the Middle East. . . .
Ceramics was well on its way to becoming the noblest of the pyrotechnical
arts once the pot was seen to be not only useful but pleasing to the eye and
potters found that both the beauty and the utility of their product could be
increased by firing at higher temperatures and by admixing various minerals
to give rich color and textural effects. . . . Even today we understand only "in
principle" the whole range of physical and chemical properties and their interrelationships that were effectively used in making ceramics.[4]

Evidently these "primitive" people had somehow learned a great deal about
the highly complex science of ceramics and other materials at a very early date.
Pottery has become the stock in trade of the archaeologist, whose entire system of
dating is built largely around the various potsherds he finds at his excavations.

The achievement of a practical science of agriculture and of animal husbandry
was essential for organized human societies. Man must somehow learn how to
produce more food than he could merely collect or kill for the needs of his family
if he was ever to do more than just survive. The domestication of animals and of
food plants, especially wheat, was therefore of paramount importance, and archaeologists have devoted much study to this question. "Thus we may conclude
from present distribution studies that the cradle of Old World plant husbandry
stood within the general area of the arc constituted by the western foothills of the
Zagros Mountains (Iraq-Iran), the Taurus (southern Turkey), and the Galilean
uplands (northern Palestine)."[5] As far as the date of the first agriculture and animal domestication is concerned, Robert Braidwood, of the Oriental Institute at
the University of Chicago, one of the 20th century's foremost archaeologists, and
Halet Cambel, of Istanbul University, note the following: "In very rough outline
the available evidence now suggests that both the level of incipient cultivation
and animal domestication and the level of intensive food-collecting were reached
in the Near East about 9000 B.C."[6]

Note especially the contemporaneity in time and place, not only of the first
domestication of plants and animals, and even of ceramics, but also of so-called
intensive food collecting, which previously had been considered an earlier evolutionary stage. "Our older notion that villages had to mean farmers has gone by
the board."[7]

Robert Dyson, of the University of Pennsylvania, confirms the contemporaneous and complex origin of domesticated plants and animals. "Current research,
however, is making it clear that the problem is far more complex than these

4. Cyril Stanley Smith, "Materials and the Development of Civilization and Science," *Science,* 148
   (May 14, 1967): p. 908.
5. Hans Helbaek, "Domestication of Food Plants in the Old World," *Science*, 130 (Aug. 14, 1959): p.
   365.
6. Halet Cambel and Robert J. Braidwood, "An Early Farming Village in Turkey," *Scientific American,*
   222 (Mar. 1970).
7. Ibid.

simple questions suggest. There may be, in fact, no priority of plants over animals; they may have been domesticated separately in both space and time. Nor is there any longer a question of simple priority between plants and animals: the domestication of each species is now seen as a problem in itself."[8]

In other words, many different communities of the Near and Middle East attained "civilized" status at about the same time.

The domestication of animals was almost as important as that of plants for a stable civilized society. Dogs were needed for hunting, cattle and sheep for food and clothing, horses and camels for transportation. It is a significant correlation with biblical implications to note that apparently the first animal domesticated was the sheep. "The sheep, on the basis of statistics found at Shanidar Cave and at the nearby site of Zawi Chermi Shanidar, now appears to have been domesticated by around 9000 B.C., well before the earliest evidence for either the dog or the goat."[9]

It will be remembered that Abel, the son of Adam, was a keeper of sheep, and thus there is little doubt that the sheep taken on the ark by Noah were domestic sheep and that at least some of Noah's immediate descendants would likewise have kept sheep for sacrifice as well as for food and clothing.

However, not only sheep, but also cattle, dogs, and other animals were apparently first domesticated in the same part of the world, the Near or Middle East. Erich Isaac writes, "The archaeological evidence supports the view that cattle were first domesticated in western Asia."[10] And Dyson tells us, "Asses were domesticated in Egypt and spread eastward, occurring in Mesopotamia in the third millennium B.C."[11]

A similar story could be told for the dog, goat, camel, horse, pig, and most other domestic animals.

The use of metals also occurred very early in man's history, exactly as the Bible says. Smith notes, "The oldest known artificially shaped metal objects are some copper beads found in northern Iraq and dating from the beginning of the 9th millennium B.C."[12]

Similarly, ancient metal objects have been found in Turkey, indicating considerable skill in metal working. "The fact remains that sometime just before 7000 B.C., the people of Cayonu Tepsi not only were acquainted with metal but also were shaping articles out of native copper by abrading and hammering."[13]

Although copper was apparently the first metal used, others were known almost as early. "These metal finds reveal that by the 5th millennium copper, lead,

---

8. Robert H. Dyson, Jr., "On the Origin of the Neolithic Revolution," *Science,* 144 (May 8, 1964): p. 673.
9. Ibid., p. 674.
10. Erich Isaac, "On the Domestication of Cattle," *Science,* 137 (July 20, 1962): p. 196.
11. Dyson, "On the Origin," p. 675.
12. Smith, "Materials," p. 910.
13. Cambel and Braidwood, "Early Farming Village," p. 56.

silver, and gold were known at various sites in the Middle East."[14]

The coming of the so-called Iron Age was also very early. Even the use of steel goes back into antiquity.

> At some point in time — not well established but probably shortly after 5000 B.C., and in the mountains that form the northern boundary of the Fertile Crescent — it was found that heating certain greenish or bluish minerals in the proper kind of fire would produce metal — in other words, something had been discovered.[15]

> Bits of man-made iron appeared in the first half of the third millennium B.C., and iron was not uncommon in the Hittite empire around 1500 B.C. . . . Good steel was certainly being made by the smiths of Luristan (in the mountains in western Iran) at a date within two centuries (plus or minus) of 1000 B.C.[16]

Thus, although remains of iron have not been found as far back as those of brass and bronze and other metals, they do go back to before the time of Moses (about 1400 B.C.). Furthermore, it does seem strange that copper should have been known and used for about seven thousand years before iron. It seems probable either than iron was used earlier but has not yet been recovered in the excavations, or else that the dates of the older archaeological sites have been exaggerated through too much reliance on radiocarbon dating. More will be discussed concerning the dating techniques in the next section.

Another major aspect of civilization is that of urbanization. The development of organized communities was undoubtedly stimulated by the development of the other civilized practices discussed above, but whether it was a cause or consequence is not very clear, as cities seem to have arisen essentially contemporaneously with the others. Thus, some towns and cities are very ancient.

On the other hand, some cultures of a high order of technological attainment seem to have existed without real cities. The most notable of these was the Mayan civilization in Guatemala and Yucatan that produced magnificent temples and art and even a complex hieroglyphic writing system but that apparently had no cities.

In most situations, however, urbanization was of critical importance. Once again, this development occurred first in the Bible lands and at about the same time as the other aspects of civilization discussed above. Dr. Robert Adams of the Oriental Institute at the University of Chicago, in a popular review of this subject says, "In most civilizations urbanization began early. There is little doubt that this was the case for the oldest civilization and the earliest cities: those of ancient Mesopotamia."[17]

---

14.  Theodore A. Wortime, "Man's First Encounters with Metallurgy," *Science,* 146 (Dec. 4, 1964): p . 1259.
15.  Smith, "Materials," p. 910.
16.  Ibid, p. 913.
17.  Robert M. Adams, "The Origin of Cities," *Scientific American,* 203 (Sept. 1960): p. 154.

This oldest civilization, with the earliest cities, is of course that of the Sumerians, the first inhabitants of Babylon. The greatest modern authority on these people is Samuel N. Kramer whose book[18] is the definitive description of their civilization. Dr. William F. Albright, discussing Kramer's works, says, "The Sumerians . . . created the oldest urban society with an advanced higher culture during the fourth millennium B.C."[19]

As far as smaller and less complex communities are concerned, the origin of farming and hunting villages is essentially synonymous with the origin of plant and animal domestication. This, as we have already noted, was also in the Near East and is dated about 9000 B.C. "We now know that somewhat earlier than 7500 B.C. people in some parts of the Near East had reached a level of cultural development marked by the production, as opposed to the mere collection, of plant and animal foodstuffs and by a pattern of residence in farming villages."[20]

Such villages included cobbled streets, imposing stone buildings, plows and wheeled vehicles, and a variety of clay and stone ornaments and implements. Their technology was apparently not much more primitive than that of many similar farming villages in all parts of the world down to modern times.

Very shortly after the appearance of cities, we have the appearance of undisputed forms of written languages. Sumerian cuneiform texts have been found dated as early as 4000 B.C. "Following this the first written records appeared during the Protoliterate period, which spanned the remainder of the fourth millennium."[21]

Thus, we conclude that civilization, as defined in terms of agriculture, animal husbandry, ceramics, metallurgy, urbanization, permanent structures, and written languages, had its beginning in the Bible lands all at about the same time, well before the days of Abraham.

## The Problem of Human Chronology

The origin of civilization thus took place in the Near East, exactly as indicated in the Bible. However, the dates commonly cited for these developments (ranging between 9000 B.C. and about 4000 B.C.) do involve an apparent conflict with the Bible. The Ussher chronology indicates that the great Flood took place approximately 2350 B.C.), and all the relevant archaeological data must certainly apply to post-Flood civilizations.

And, of course, there is the so-called Paleolithic Age supposed to be even earlier, occupying all the vast spans of time during which man was only a hunter and food gatherer, using crude chipped-stone implements and weapons. Man, in essentially modern physical form, at least, has been dated by evolutionists at from 1 million to 3 million years in age.

---

18. Samuel N. Kramer, *The Sumerians* (Chicago, IL: University of Chicago Press, 1963), p. 355.
19. William F. Albright, "Sumerian Civilization," *Science*, 141 (Aug. 16, 1963): p. 623.
20. Cambel and Braidwood, "Early Farming Village," p. 51.
21. Robert M. Adams, "Origin of Cities," p. 160.

Most such human remains and artifacts have been attributed, geologically speaking, either to the Pleistocene or Recent epochs, and these, we believe, must all be post-Flood. The sediments and fossil deposits of the Flood itself correspond to the great geologic formations of the Paleozoic and Mesozoic eras, together with probably most of the Tertiary as well.

Is there any way of harmonizing the millions of years, or even 11,000 years, of human post-Flood history, with the Ussher date of 2350 B.C. for the Flood? We are convinced that the biblical chronology, while not yet worked out in satisfactory detail, is far closer to the truth than is the evolutionary chronology.

Paleolithic and earlier dates are based largely on potassium-argon dating, and Neolithic dates primarily on radiocarbon dating. These methods, when critically examined, can be shown to be seriously in error for all dates earlier than about 2000 B.C. Radiocarbon dates for events more recent than 2000 B.C. may be fairly good, but all earlier dates are invalid due to fallacious assumptions involved in these and other radiometric age calculations. See the discussion[22] of radiometric dating in chapter 9.

The science of dendrochronology (tree-ring dating) has also become increasingly important in recent years. The oldest living trees are the bristlecone pines of the American Southwest, found especially in California's White Mountains. One of these trees, found in the Snake Range of Nevada, has actually been estimated by its rings to be 4,900 years old. Several others have been dated over 4,000 years old. By comparison with patterns of rings between living and dead trees, a bristlecone-pine chronology has been developed at Arizona University supposedly covering almost 8,200 years. If this chronology is valid, the Ussher chronology of about 4,300 years since the Flood is obviously incorrect.

One need not discard Ussher too hastily, however. Although tree-ring counting seems like a very simple, almost mistake-proof method of figuring time back from the present, there are still a number of uncertainties involved. In the first place, it is quite possible for a tree to produce two or more growth rings in one year, especially trees in lower elevations or southern latitudes. Charles Ferguson, the leading worker in this field, notes this: "In certain species of conifers, especially those at lower elevations or in southern latitudes, one season's growth increment may be composed of two or more flushes of growth, each of which may strongly resemble an annual ring."[23] Ferguson feels this question does not apply to the bristlecone pine because of the aridity and high elevation of its present habitat. Even if he is correct with regard to its behavior in recent years, however,

---

22. See also Henry M. Morris, editor, *Scientific Creationism* (San Diego, CA: Creation-Life, 1974), p. 161–167, and also John D. Morris, *The Young Earth* (Green Forest, AR: Master Books, 1994), p. 64–71.

23. C.W. Ferguson, "Bristlecone Pine: Science and Esthetics," *Science,* 159 (Feb. 23, 1968): 840. The tree-ring chronology, which has become widely accepted, and which has even been used to revise upward the previously accepted radiocarbon chronology, is largely the work of one man, Charles Ferguson, in his Laboratory of Tree-Ring Research at the University of Arizona.

this certainly would not be true in the early centuries, or even millennia, after the Flood. It is well known that the present arid regions of Nevada and the Great Basin generally were, until relatively recently, subject to much more rainfall and much higher lake levels (e.g., Lake Lahontan, Lake Bonneville, etc.) than they are at present. The climate then quite probably was very erratic and would surely have been conducive to producing two or more rings annually for many or most of the years in those centuries. Thus a "4,900-year-old" tree need not actually be more than, say, 4,000 years or less in true age.

The practice of extending the chronology by comparing ring patterns in living and dead trees is even more questionable, especially as the growth rings approach closer and closer to the time of the Flood. Furthermore, such comparisons are bound to be highly subjective, even when analyzed statistically on a computer. Each dead tree section contains only from 50 to a few hundred suitable rings, at most, to be incorporated into the chronology, and there is always the question as to where it actually fits relative to the previously established sequences. In the bristlecone pine, the rings are exceedingly thin, averaging only a few hundredths of a millimeter each, and thus similar patterns are very hard to recognize from tree to tree. The very fact that statistical methods and computer analyses have to be used, and that the final correlation coefficients are low, is proof enough that comparisons of this type are far from obvious. For some reason the older living trees have not been used as the starting point in building up this chronology, but rather only living trees going back less than 1,200 years. Erected on this foundation have been successive portions from about 20 different dead trees, to come out with a chronology extending back 8,200 years.

Maybe so, but one has to wonder whether, with only a relatively small number of rings usable on each tree, isn't it possible that there is more than one section of the "master chronology" that they might fit, considering the low correlation that is characteristic of these studies? There are other problems, too. "The validity of the bristlecone pine-sequoia time scale has been questioned for a number of reasons. To us, the most serious concern is that for periods earlier than 3,000 years ago, it is based entirely on one species of tree that grows, or grew, under rather atypical conditions — namely, at elevations of 10,000 to 11,000 feet."[24]

The fact that tree-ring dating is not nearly as reliable as many people think is indicated by the following: "For those who are neither radiocarbon physicists nor 'dendrochronologists,' it is essential to know that all trees are not of equal value for tree-ring dating. It probably would be safe to say that the great majority of trees are of little or no value."[25] Many, like Ferguson, believe that the bristlecone pine is the best tree for dendrochronology, but even this tree is very questionable.

24. Elizabeth K. Ralph and Henry M. Michael, "Twenty-five Years of Radiocarbon Dating," American Scientist, 62 (Sept.–Oct. 1974): p. 556.
25. Harold S. Gladwin, "Dendrochronology, Radiocarbon and Bristlecones," Anthropological Journal of Canada, 14, no. 4 (1976): p. 4.

Among the pines, *Pinus aristata* (i.e., the bristlecone pine) is, if anything, even more undependable than the junipers. . . . We have many cones at the Santa Barbara Botanic Garden that were collected from Bristlecones growing in the White Mountains of California east of the Sierra Nevada, at altitudes of 10,000 feet, where the rainfall is low and erratic. There are also a number of cones from Bristlecones growing at high altitudes in southwestern Utah and on the San Francisco Peaks at Flagstaff, Arizona. Comparison of charts of measured rings show no similarity whatever.[26]

Thus, both radiocarbon dating and tree-ring dating are unreliable. Yet these are the best methods developed so far for estimating dates in prehistoric human chronology. Once we get beyond the beginnings of actual written records, there is simply no way to determine dates with accuracy. There is, thus, no real reason to reject or even question the traditional Ussher chronology of the Bible. It does seem there is an inordinate desire on the part of evolutionists to stretch dates as far into the past as they can, almost as though they were consciously trying to discredit the Bible. "There are also many sites which have yielded Carbon-14 dates that are clearly too recent to be correct. Often these spuriously young dates are not published, though every archaeologist is aware of some examples. Those that are published rarely receive the special attention they deserve. The significance of these inexplicably recent dates is that they also are often quite secure and no flaw can be found in their determination."[27]

The objectivity of scientists is a nice image, but the facts often tarnish it. "Archaeological confirmation is more difficult. Dating the initial occupation of each area would be crucial, but this effort is often clouded by the headline-hunting tendencies of many workers who want to find dates older than anyone else's."[28]

The writer of the above had reference to the problem of dating the earliest settlements in North America, but the desire to stretch out any age-dating calculation is apparently practically universal among evolutionary geochronologists. The older things can be made to appear, the less reliable the Bible seems to be, and the further back God is pushed from any meaningful connection with the world He created. This motivation may not apply to all biblical archaeologists, or even to all Christian geologists. But it does seem to be a real, sometimes subconscious, factor involved in the interpretations of secular evolutionists and even those of many liberal Christians.

In any case, we are well justified in rejecting any evidences of this sort that seem to question the chronology of biblical events before the beginning of recorded history. In tree-ring chronologies, it seems highly probable that, when one of two or more ring-correlations might be chosen, the one selected will be the

---

26. Ibid., p. 5.
27. Grover S. Krantz, "The Populating of Western North America," *Society for California Archaeology Occasional Papers in Method and Theory in California Archaeology*, 1 (Dec. 1977): 7.
28. Ibid., p. 55.

one yielding the oldest dates. The various "fits" have low correlations at best, so it is somewhat arbitrary as to which should be chosen.

As a matter of fact, dendrochronologists have commonly used radiocarbon dating of the wood to determine first about where a given set of rings in a dead-wood sample should fit, and then they search in that vicinity for a possible correlation. Ferguson says, "Occasionally, a sample from a specimen not yet dated by tree rings is submitted for radiocarbon analysis. The date obtained indicates the general age of the sample; this gives a clue as to what portion of the master chronology should be scanned, and thus the tree-ring date may be identified more readily."[29]

But such dependence upon radiocarbon is bound to lead one wrong. When corrected for nonequilibrium conditions, as the radiocarbon equation should be, it gives ages much less, by thousands of years, than the popularly used equilibrium model of radiocarbon, on which practically all radiocarbon datings are based.

It is very doubtful, therefore, that tree-ring dating really justifies abandonment of the 2350 B.C. date for the Flood. But what about radiocarbon itself?

Prior to the application of radiocarbon dating to archaeological studies, it was believed that the village life of the Neolithic evolved quite recently. Radiocarbon vastly enlarged this time span. "Instead of yielding the expected dates of around 4000 or 4500 B.C., the earliest villages in the Near East proved to date back to as early as 8000 B.C."[30]

Radiocarbon dating, however, was based on the assumption that the ratio of radiocarbon to natural carbon was in a steady state in time and space. It had been checked reasonably well against dates in Egyptian history that supposedly could be documented by written records, but these only extended back to Egypt's first dynasty. "Everyone had always been aware that, for the period before 3000 B.C., which is when the Egyptian chronology begins, all dates were guesswork."[31]

For earlier dates, however, the assumption of the steady state becomes quite important. Dr. Melvin Cook has shown[32] that the actual present radiocarbon ratio fits much better in a nonequilibrium model than it does in the standard equilibrium model and that, when this change is made, the resulting equation yields about 7000 to 12,000 B.C. as the time when the process began, which presumably would coincide approximately with the time of the Flood. Prior to the Flood, a vast invisible canopy of water vapor above the stratosphere is believed to have prevented the formation of radiocarbon in significant amounts. The radiocarbon dates prior to about 1000 B.C. (when the nonequilibrium and equilibrium models essentially converge) thus should be recalculated to fit the more accurate nonequilibrium model. An equilibrium radiocarbon date of, for example, 8000 B.C., would be revised to about 3000 B.C., and so on.

---

29. Charles W. Ferguson, "Bristlecone Pine," p. 845.
30. Colin Renfrew, "Carbon-14 and the Prehistory of Europe," *Scientific American*, 225 (Oct. 1971): 67.
31. Ibid.
32. Melvin A. Cook, *Prehistory and Earth Models* (London: Max Parrish, 1966), p. 1–10.

Even with this correction, the radiocarbon method still yields some dates well in excess of 4,300 years ago. However, the nonequilibrium question is only one of the problems in radiocarbon dating. Another is the question of the changing magnetic field. If the magnetic field had been significantly stronger in the period shortly after the Flood, it would have inhibited the formation of radiocarbon even after the vapor canopy had been dissipated. This effect would still further modify the radiocarbon equation, to allow not only for a gradual increase with time of total radiocarbon decay in the world but also for a gradual increase with time of total radiocarbon formation in the atmosphere.

As discussed earlier, it has been demonstrated by Dr. Thomas G. Barnes[33] that the earth's magnetic field is decaying exponentially with a half-life of 1,400 years. Thus, at the time of the Ussher date for the Flood (approximately 2350 B.C.), the field was eight times stronger than it is at present. Although the exact effect has not yet been calculated, as far as we know, there is no question but that much more of the cosmic radiation would have been deflected and therefore much less radiocarbon would have been formed, than is the case at present. The overall result would be still further shortening of the radiocarbon chronology.

We would predict that, once all the calculations have been worked out, the date for the initiation of radiocarbon formation after the Flood will be found to be no earlier than 4000 B.C., and quite possibly as late as 2350 B.C.

## Inaccuracies in Recorded History

The question still remaining is whether actual recorded history conflicts with the Ussher chronology. In view of the many untestable assumptions in all physical dating methods, it is never possible to be sure about any date prior to when man first began recording dates. And, in view of man's innate tendency to exaggerate things, even these are not always reliable.

In general, the two oldest civilizations, those of Egypt and Sumeria, have been the source of our accepted chronology.

> Prehistoric finds are of course by their nature unaccompanied by written records. The only possible recourse was to work from the known to the unknown: to try to move outward toward the unlettered periphery from the historical civilizations of Egypt and Mesopotamia, where written records were available. For example, the historical chronology of Egypt, based on ancient written records, can be extended with considerable confidence back to 1900 B.C. because the records noted astronomical events. The Egyptian "king lists" can then be used, although with far less confidence, to build up a chronology that goes back another 11 centuries to 3000 B.C.[34]

---

33. Thomas G. Barnes, *Origin and Destiny of the Earth's Magnetic Field*, 2nd ed. (San Diego, CA: Institute for Creation Research, 1983).

34. Colin Renfrew, "Carbon-14 and the Prehistory of Europe," *Scientific American,* 225 (Oct. 1971): p. 63. Also see Renfrew's book, *Before Civilization* (New York, NY: Alfred Knopf, 1974), p. 25–28.

This date, 3000 B.C., is not too far from Ussher's date for the Flood. Menes, the first king of Egypt, could well be equivalent to Mizraim, grandson of Noah and probable founder of Egypt (the name "Mizraim" is essentially synonymous with "Egypt" in the Bible, used dozens of times in that way).

However, the beginning of Egypt, as well as that of other nations, must date after the dispersion at the Tower of Babel, one hundred or more years after the Flood, according to the Bible.

Both Mizraim and his father, Ham, probably were still living for a long time after the dispersion and so may have spent a considerable period of time migrating to the Nile and laying the foundation for a kingdom there. Egypt is also called in the Bible "the land of Ham" (Ps. 106:21–22).

Egypt was long divided into two kingdoms, Upper and Lower Egypt. Upper Egypt was known as Pathros, evidently from the Pathrusim, listed in Genesis 10:14 as descended from Mizraim, whereas Lower Egypt continued to be associated especially with Mizraim himself. The "king lists" referred to above, especially those of Manetho (around 290 B.C.), provide the chief basis for Egyptian chronology, which in turn has been the foundation for developing chronologies of other nations throughout the ancient world. There is some indication, however, that his lists include contemporary dynasties from the two kingdoms, with their durations mistakenly added together. Furthermore, the figures on which Manetho based his histories may well have been derived from exaggerated claims of earlier kings and their scribes. It is thus possible that the 3000 B.C. date for the first dynasty should be considerably reduced.

The same questions apply to king lists and other chronological records in Sumeria. The earliest dynasties in Babylon, Ur, Kish, Ebla, and other cities of this region apparently began at roughly the same time as the first dynasty in Egypt. Like that in Egypt, it is possible that similar forces may have been acting to enlarge these other chronologies by several hundred years, as a number of scholars believe.

In any case, the beginning of actual chronological records goes back no further than about 3000 B.C., and these may well have been exaggerated. Donovan Courville,[35] as well as Immanuel Velikovsky[36] and various other scholars, have argued cogently and persuasively that these ancient chronologies should all be reduced by about eight hundred years or more.

It is thus quite possible to defend the Ussher date of about 2300 B.C. for the Flood. On the other hand, many conservative biblical archaeologists argue for a date of, say, 3500 to 4000 B.C. for the Flood, as advocated by a number of careful Old Testament scholars, not only because of such things as king lists, radiocarbon, and tree rings, but also because of the complex and well-inhabited world of Abraham's time, usually dated at about 2000 B.C.

---

35. Donovan Courville, *The Exodus Problem, Volumes I and II* (Loma Linda, CA: Challenge, 1971).
36. Immanuel Velikovsky, *Age in Chaos* (New York, NY: Doubleday, 1952), p. 350.

It has been advocated by many conservative Old Testament scholars that there may have been one or more gaps in the genealogies of Genesis 11. The name of Cainan, for example, is inserted between those of Arphaxad and Sala, in the corresponding genealogy of Luke 3:35–36. The most likely location for a significant gap is at the time of Peleg, "for in his days was the earth divided" (Gen. 10:25). The life spans of the three men preceding Peleg in the lists of Genesis 11 were 438, 433, and 464 years, respectively; that of Peleg and his two successors was 239, 241, and 230 years. Thus, there may have been a long interval between Eber and Peleg, in which the average longevity was decreasing by almost a factor of 2.

Could there have been a gap of, say, 1,500 years between the time of Eber and Peleg? In such a case, the translation of Genesis 11:16 might be: "And Eber lived four and thirty years, and begat [the ancestor of] Peleg." In those days, such a gap would represent the life spans of four of five successive generations. The reason for the long period of silence might be the disruption in recordkeeping, occasioned by the confusion of tongues at Babel. Then, when Peleg's unknown father undertook once again, over a millennium later, to pick up the record (interrupted at the time of Shem's death some four hundred years after the birth of Eber's son, Peleg's ancestor), he named his son Peleg (meaning "division") in commemoration of the tragic rebellion at Babel and its outcome.

Whether this suggestion is reasonable or not the reader may judge for himself. Whether it is more reasonable to reinterpret the archaeological and historical data to correspond to Ussher's chronology, following Velikovsky and Courville, is also still an open question. In any case, it is certainly possible, by some such explanation, to bring the biblical and archaeological chronologies for the history of civilization into full correlation. Further research should resolve the question as to which possible explanation is correct.

## Before Civilization

Thus, the Bible account of early human history is fully supported by the actual facts of archaeology of the Neolithic and later periods. But what about the Paleolithic and Mesolithic periods? Who were these "men of the old Stone Age" — Neanderthal man, Cro-Magnon man, *Homo erectus*? What about the Native Americans, the South Sea islanders, the Eskimos, the African pygmies, and other supposed primitives? How did they get to the islands and the jungles, the Arctic, and the interior mountains?

Evolutionary anthropologists usually claim to find evidence of a "stone-age" culture at lower levels, even on the same site at which a civilized culture is found at higher levels. To them, this speaks of human evolution.

However, there is another interpretation of these data, fully consistent with all the discovered facts and also in full accord with the Bible. The great Flood was worldwide and was so cataclysmic and devastating that, as Peter says, "The world that then was, being overflowed with water, perished" (2 Pet. 3:6). All the antediluvian peoples and their civilizations were washed away, destroyed, and disintegrated. No city or village would be left intact anywhere in the world.

Thus, if any human bones or human artifacts were to be preserved at all, they would almost certainly be buried so deeply and randomly in the flowing sediments as to make their later excavation most unlikely. People often ask why, if the Flood destroyed the antediluvian world, we don't find more human fossils. Actually, since the geography of the continents and oceans was completely different before the Flood, many antediluvian human remains might well now be deep in the sediments at the bottom of the sea; others may be buried deeply in the stratified rocks of the earth's crust. However, because of human mobility, most of the antediluvians probably escaped burial altogether, drowning when finally overtaken by the waters, with their bodies disintegrating when the surface dried.

For the sake of argument, however, we might assume that as many as one billion human beings may have been trapped, buried, and fossilized in the Flood sediments. The earth is approximately $5 \times 10^{15}$ square feet in surface area and its sediments average at least a mile (5,280 feet) in thickness. Therefore, the volume of sediments per human buried would be:

$$\frac{5(10^{15})(5280)}{(10^9)} = \text{over 26 billion cubic feet.}$$

Therefore, one would have to excavate, on the average, over 26 billion cubic feet of sedimentary rock (or a body of rock, one mile by one mile in surface area, and 947 feet deep) to find one antediluvian human fossil. One would hardly expect to find, therefore, except by providential accident, fossils of antediluvian man.

Thus, the hundreds of archaeological sites all over the world do not in any case represent pre-Flood cultures. Without exception they represent post-diluvian migrations and settlements. This conclusion is consistent also with their universal dating in the Pleistocene or late Pliocene epochs, which, in terms of biblical geology, certainly means post-Flood.

Even though the antediluvian civilization was of a high order (Gen. 1–11 speaks of cities, metallurgy, agriculture, musical instruments, jewelry, animal husbandry, and other aspects of organized civilization), it all perished in the Flood. Only the materials that could have been stored in the ark and only the technical skills that Noah and his three sons could have stored in their brains could have been used to found a new civilization after the Flood.

The post-Flood world was initially barren and inhospitable, stormy and rugged, in stark contrast to the beautiful worldwide greenhouse environment in which they had lived before. For years, perhaps centuries, it would take most of their efforts merely to survive.

Noah and his family could not use metals at first, for the simple reason that they must first locate sources from which to mine and refine metallic ores, and they had little time for prospecting. Their implements would necessarily have been of wood and stone, with vessels of clay, as these were the only materials available. Much of their food necessarily would have to be obtained initially by hunting and gathering, especially as they moved out to explore and colonize new sites, until in each case they had time to plant and raise crops and establish herds of cattle and sheep.

Thus when, at a given site, archaeologists seem to find evidence, at successively higher levels, of a chipped-stone culture, then a polished-stone farming village culture, then a metal-working culture, etc., these do not represent a naturalistic evolutionary process at all. Rather, they speak of the difficulties encountered by a small group of post-Flood people in trying to establish a viable community in a difficult environment, with little equipment except their own ingenuity. The situation would be quite analogous to a "Swiss Family Robinson" inadvertently being forced to survive by their wits and hands in an isolated wilderness. Rather than castigation as "primitives" and "savages," these early men deserve respect and admiration for their amazing accomplishments, not only in surviving and multiplying, but also in establishing so early the basic essentials for civilization, which culminated relatively quickly in the great nations and technologies of the ancient world.

The people strongly resisted separating and moving into new areas as God had commanded, preferring instead to stay together in the most fertile and pleasant place they could find in the regions around Ararat, in the land of Shinar (equivalent to "summer") in the southerly portion of Mesopotamia, the "land between the rivers." These rivers they named Tigris and Euphrates, in memory of two of the beautiful rivers that had flowed from the Garden of Eden.

The result of their resistance was God's judgment at Babel, the confusion of their languages, which forced them to disperse. The history that followed this event is what archaeologists are gradually reconstructing (although most of them do not realize it) as they excavate the caves these people occupied, the villages they constructed, and other evidences of their migrations and settlements throughout the world.

As populations grew, so did competition for the most desirable locations. The strongest and most technologically minded families and tribes (initially certain of the Hamites) thus acquired and developed the best sites, in Sumeria and along the valley of the Nile. The Canaanites settled along the eastern and northeastern shores of the Mediterranean. The Japhethites moved into the less hospitable northern and western regions, especially into Europe. The Shemites stayed closer to Ararat, but gradually spread southward and eastward into Arabia, Assyria, Persia, and elsewhere.

Further population growth and competition resulted in warfare and successive waves of migration by those who were defeated into more and more distant regions. In general, as each defeated tribe was forced to move onward, the survivors would have to go once again through the periods of stone culture, metal working, city building, and so on.

Rarely would a defeated tribe be able to return and wrest territory from an already settled and civilized community. They could only go on to some new region, again living as hunters and gatherers until they could settle in one region long enough to develop their own culture and resources. "In general, the rule is that if hunting peoples expand their area, it is only into essentially empty territories, and never at the expense of previously settled inhabitants. The obvious application of this rule is to the initial occupation of a continent like North America, which must have been a single event and not a series of waves of immigration."[37]

It is not surprising that anthropological studies of the earliest of the so-called "primitive men" (such as Neanderthal, Cro-Magnon, and perhaps Homo erectus) have centered on western Europe, eastern Asia, and southern Africa. These are the regions far from Babylon, the outer limits of human habitation in the earliest centuries after the dispersion, where the tribes being forced to move away from their more successful cousins had to survive as best they could in caves and mountains and jungles. In some cases, through inbreeding, inadequate diets (e.g., Neanderthal man with his rickets), and general degeneracy, they acquired a more-or-less deformed physical appearance, and may even finally have become extinct.

In most cases, however, they settled new regions containing good resources and gradually were able to build some form of stable and viable community.

All of these events were probably taking place during the Ice Age. At the same time that Neanderthal man was trying to survive near the ice cap in Europe, and Siberian tribes in Asia, the great civilizations of Egypt, Sumeria, and others were developing in the lower latitudes, where the ice did not extend, but where there was much more rainfall and the climate was more pleasant.

We believe that all the real data of archaeology and anthropology harmonize with some such sequence of events as outlined above. In Siberia, for example, the migrating tribes have left records of their cultures in the form of drawings on rocks in the river villages all across that northern land. "These discoveries are ancient rock drawings that have been found at river sites over the length and breadth of the northern continent all the way from Scandinavia to the Amur River basin in extreme eastern Siberia."[38]

The artifacts at these sites follow the usual pattern of stone, then metal, etc. Also, they reflect the changing environmental conditions as the Ice Age gradually waned.

The same phenomena are noted in Africa. In Egypt the dynastic period was preceded by a rapid growth of technology by the tribes settling the Nile Valley. "It is now known that these assumptions of Nilotic conservation and scarcity were

37. Grover S. Krantz, "The Populating of Western North America," Society for California Archaeology Occasional Papers in Method and Theory in California, 1 (Dec. 1977): p. 5.
38. A.P. Okladnikov, "The Petroglyphs of Siberia," Scientific American, 221 (Aug. 1969): p. 75.

grossly in error. . . . Furthermore, there is convincing evidence that these sites were occupied by groups whose lithic technology and typology were fully as complex and progressive as those known from other parts of the world."[39]

Further south in Africa, the migrations and settlements are best traced, as in Siberia, through rock art. "Africa uniquely contains tens of thousands of paintings and engravings on the surfaces of rocks. . . . The sites of these pictures range from the northern fringe of the Sahara to the Cape of Good Hope. . . . They date from a possible 8000 B.C. until recent times, and exhibit a continuity of art styles from one end of the continent to the other."[40]

It is fairly easy to see how people could radiate out from Babel into Europe, Africa, and Asia. But how did they get into North and South America and the Pacific islands?

The answer is that they did so by both land and sea. During the Ice Age, the sea level was probably lower and there were land bridges across the Bering Strait and down the Malaysian archipelago into New Guinea and Indonesia. "From this rich supply of evidence it has been determined that the Wisconsin glacier reached its maximum 40,000 years ago and lowered the sea level by as much as 460 feet. . . . At 450 feet the entire width of the undersea plain from one edge of the continental shelf to the other must have been exposed, providing a corridor 1,300 miles wide for the flow of biological commerce between the no longer separate continents."[41]

There is little doubt that many of the Native Americans, as well as most of the American fauna, arrived from Siberia via this land bridge. On the other hand, it is also quite possible that some of the Central and South American settlers first came by boat. After all, the technique of shipbuilding was certainly one skill possessed by the survivors of the Flood! There is much evidence that the ancient Phoenicians, as well as others, were such excellent mariners that they sailed south around Africa and all over the globe.

The islands of the sea were also undoubtedly first settled by people arriving on boats. It is significant that these were the last areas of the earth to be inhabited, just as the Near East was the first. A computer analysis of the earth's present land masses indicated that the earth's geographical center is near Ankara, Turkey, and it's "anticenter" (the point most distant from all the earth's land areas) is in the South Pacific, about halfway between New Zealand and South America.[42] It is providential that God arranged for the ark to land near the earth's geographical center, thus expediting its repopulation by both man and animals.

The South Pacific islands were not reached by man until quite late in time.

39. Fred Wendorf, Rushdi Said, and Romuald Schild, "Egyptian Prehistory: Some New Concepts," *Science,* 169 (Sept. 18, 1970): 1161.
40. Carleton S. Coon, "The Rock Art of Africa," *Science,* 142 (Dec. 27, 1963): 1642.
41. William G. Haag, "The Bering Strait Land Bridge," *Scientific American,* 206 (Jan. 1962): 120.
42. Andrew J. Woods and Henry M. Morris, *The Center of the Earth* (San Diego, CA: Institute for Creation Research, 1973), p. 6.

A date of 122 B.C. has been established for human occupation in the Marquesas at the eastern edge of Polynesia, while a date of A.D. 9 has been obtained for Samoa, at the western extremity. An early date of occupation of 46 B.C. has been obtained for neighboring Fiji, and it seems reasonable to expect at least temporally comparable evidence on Samoa. Far to the north, in Hawaii, a possibly valid date of A.D. 124 may indicate that this outpost of Polynesia was settled at about the beginning of the Christian era. To the south, in New Zealand, where 38 radiocarbon samples have been obtained, the earliest date of occupation so far obtained is about A.D. 1000.[43]

The above dates are based on radiocarbon, but this method seems adequate enough for dates this recent. The islanders seem to have reached the islands from a wide variety of mainland starting points, both from Asia and South America.

This relatively brief survey could be expanded considerably. Every new find in anthropology and archaeology seem to illustrate and support the biblical record of man's origin and early history. Man has not slowly "evolved" from an animal ancestry over millions of years; he has always been man, highly intelligent and skillful, capable of exploration and settlement all over the world, and also capable of rapidly developing viable and complex civilizations wherever he has gone.

---

43. Edwin N. Ferdon, Jr., "Polynesian Origins," *Science,* 141 (Aug. 9, 1963): 500.

# BIBLE-BELIEVING SCIENTISTS OF THE PAST

## Scientific Disciplines Established by Bible-believing Scientists

| Discipline | Scientist |
| --- | --- |
| Antiseptic Surgery | Joseph Lister (1827–1912) |
| Bacteriology | Louis Pasteur (1822–1895) |
| Calculus | Isaac Newton (1642–1727) |
| Celestial Mechanics | Johann Kepler (1571–1630) |
| Chemistry | Robert Boyle (1627–1691) |
| Comparative Anatomy | Georges Cuvier (1769–1832) |
| Computer Science | Charles Babbage (1792–1871) |
| Dimensional Analysis | Lord Rayleigh (1842–1919) |
| Dynamics | Isaac Newton (1642–1727) |
| Electrodynamics | James Clerk Maxwell (1831–1879) |
| Electromagnetics | Michael Faraday (1791–1867) |
| Electronics | Ambrose Fleming (1849–1945) |
| Energetics | Lord Kelvin (1824–1907) |
| Entomology of Living Insects | Henri Fabre (1823–1915) |
| Field Theory | Michael Faraday (1791–1867) |
| Fluid Mechanics | George Stokes (1819–1903) |
| Galactic Astronomy | William Herschel (1738–1822) |
| Gas Dynamics | Robert Boyle (1627–1691) |
| Genetics | Gregor Mendel (1822–1884) |
| Glacial Geology | Louis Agassiz (1807–1873) |
| Gynecology | James Simpson (1811–1870) |
| Hydraulics | Leonardo da Vinci (1452–1519) |
| Hydrography | Matthew Maury (1806–1873) |
| Hydrostatics | Blaise Pascal (1623–1662) |
| Ichthyology | Louis Agassiz (1807–1873) |
| Isotopic Chemistry | William Ramsay (1852–1916) |
| Model Analysis | Lord Rayleigh (1842–1919) |
| Natural History | John Ray (1627–1705) |
| Non-Euclidean Geometry | Bernard Riemann (1826–1866) |
| Oceanography | Matthew Maury (1806–1873) |
| Optical Mineralogy | David Brewster (1781–1868) |
| Paleontology | John Woodard (1665–1728) |
| Pathology | Rudolph Virchow (1821–1902) |
| Physical Astronomy | Johann Kepler (1571–1630) |

| | |
|---|---|
| Reversible Thermodynamics | James Joule (1818–1889) |
| Statistical Thermodynamics | James Clerk Maxwell (1831–1879) |
| Stratigraphy | Nicholas Steno (1631–1686) |
| Systematic Biology | Carolus Linnaeus (1707–1778) |
| Thermodynamics | Lord Kelvin (1824–1907) |
| Thermokinetics | Humphry Davy (1778–1829) |
| Vertebrate Paleontology | Georges Cuvier (1769–1832) |

## Notable Inventions, Discoveries, or Developments by Bible-believing Scientists

| Discipline | Scientist |
|---|---|
| Absolute Temperature Scale | Lord Kelvin (1824–1907) |
| Actuarial Tables | Charles Babbage (1792–1871) |
| Barometer | Blaise Pascal (1623–1662) |
| Biogenesis Law | Louis Pasteur (1822–1895) |
| Calculating Machine | Charles Babbage (1792–1871) |
| Chloroform | James Simpson (1811–1870) |
| Classification System | Carolus Linnaeus (1707–1778) |
| Double Stars | William Herschel (1738–1822) |
| Electric Generator | Michael Faraday (1791–1867) |
| Electric Motor | Joseph Henry (1797–1878) |
| Ephermeris Tables | Johann Kepler (1571–1630) |
| Fermentation Control | Louis Pasteur (1822–1895) |
| Galvanometer | Joseph Henry (1797–1878) |
| Global Star Catalog | John Herschel (1792–1871) |
| Inert Gases | William Ramsay (1852–1916) |
| Kaleidoscope | David Brewster (1781–1868) |
| Law of Gravity | Isaac Newton (1642–1727) |
| Mine Safety Lamp | Humphry Davy (1778–1829) |
| Pasteurization | Louis Pasteur (1822–1895) |
| Reflecting Telescope | Isaac Newton (1642–1727) |
| Scientific Method | Francis Bacon (1561–1626) |
| Self-induction | Joseph Henry (1797–1878) |
| Telegraph | Samuel F. B. Morse (1791–1872) |
| Thermionic Valve | Ambrose Fleming (1849–1945) |
| Transatlantic Cable | Lord Kelvin (1824–1907) |
| Vaccination and Immunization | Louis Pasteur (1822–1895) |

# BIBLICAL MIRACLES OF CREATION

| Miracle | Reference |
|---------|-----------|
| **Creation of Matter** | |
| 1. Creation of the physical cosmos | Gen. 1:1; 2:4; Col. 1:16; et al. |
| 2. Fire and brimstone from heaven | Gen. 19:24 |
| 3. The unconsumed burning bush | Exod. 3:3 |
| 4. Daily bread from heaven | Exod. 16:35 |
| 5. Water from the rock | Exod. 17:6 |
| 6. Unfailing oil and meal | 1 Kings 17:14 |
| 7. Elijah's meal in the wilderness | 1 Kings 19:6 |
| 8. Increase of the widow's oil | 2 Kings 4:2–6 |
| 9. Feeding of one hundred men | 2 Kings 4:42–44 |
| 10. Feeding five thousand men | Matt. 14:21; Mark 6:44; Luke 9:14–17; John 6:10–11 |
| 11. Feeding four thousand men | Matt. 15:34–38; Mark 8:4–9 |
| **Creation of Energy, Force, or Power** | |
| 1. Energizing the created cosmos | Gen. 1:2–3 |
| 2. Translation of Enoch | Gen. 5:24 |
| 3. Smoking furnace and burning lamp | Gen. 15:17 |
| 4. Pillar of cloud and fire | Exod. 13:21 |
| 5. Wall of water at the Red Sea | Exod. 14:29 |
| 6. Giving of the law on Sinai | Exod. 24:12–18; 31:18 |
| 7. Glory cloud in the tabernacle | Exod. 40:35 |
| 8. Burning of Nadab and Abihu | Lev. 10:1–2 |
| 9. Fire of the Lord at Taberah | Num. 11:1–2 |
| 10. Sun and moon standing still | Josh. 10:11–14 |
| 11. Consumption of Gideon's offering | Judg. 6:21 |
| 12. Glory cloud in the temple | 1 Kings 8:10–11; 2 Chron. 7:1–2 |
| 13. Fire on Elijah's sacrifice | 1 Kings 18:37–39 |
| 14. Elijah's deliverance by fire from heaven | 2 Kings 1:10–14 |
| 15. Parting of the waters by Elijah's mantle | 2 Kings 2:8 |
| 16. Translation of Elijah | 2 Kings 2:11 |
| 17. Parting of the waters by Elisha | 2 Kings 2:14 |
| 18. The floating axhead | 2 Kings 6:6 |
| 19. Reversing shadow on the sun dial | 2 Kings 20:11; Isa. 38:8 |
| 20. Translation of Ezekiel | Ezek. 3:14–15 |
| 21. Protection in the fiery furnace | Dan. 3:20–26 |
| 22. Voice from heaven at Christ's baptism | Matt. 3:17; Mark 1:11; Luke 3:22 |
| 23. Walking on the water | Matt. 14:25; Mark 6:48; John 6:19 |
| 24. Transfiguration of Christ | Matt. 17:2–3; Mark 9:2–3; Luke 9:29–31 |
| 25. Darkness at the Cross | Matt. 27:45; Mark 15:33; Luke 23:45 |
| 26. Rending of the temple veil | Matt. 27:51; Mark 15:38; Luke 23:45 |
| 27. Ascension of Christ | Mark 16:19; Luke 24:51; Acts 1:9 |
| 28. Translation of Philip | Acts 8:39 |
| 29. Rapture of Paul to paradise | 2 Cor. 12:2–4 |
| **Creation of Order, Information, or Complexity** | |
| 1. Formation of atmosphere and hydrosphere | Gen. 1:6–8 |
| 2. Formation of lithosphere and biosphere | Gen. 1:9–13 |
| 3. Formation of astrosphere | Gen. 1:14–19 |

| Miracle | Reference |
|---|---|
| 4. Formation of air and water animals | Gen. 1:20–23 |
| 5. Formation of land animals | Gen. 1:24–25 |
| 6. Formation of man and woman | Gen. 1:26–27 |
| 7. Formation of new tongues at Babel | Gen. 11:9 |
| 8. Restoration of Moses' leprous hand | Exod. 4:7 |
| 9. Turning of rivers into blood | Exod. 7:20 |
| 10. Balaam's ass enabled to speak | Num. 22:28 |
| 11. Healing of Naaman's leprosy | 2 Kings 5:14 |
| 12. Healing the leper | Matt. 8:3; Mark 1:40–41, Luke 5:12–14 |
| 13. Healing of the centurion's servant | Matt. 8:13; Luke 7:1–10 |
| 14. Healing of two blind men | Matt. 9:29–30 |
| 15. Healing a withered hand | Matt. 12:13; Mark 3:5; Luke 6:10 |
| 16. Healing of the blind and dumb demoniac | Matt. 12:22; Luke 11:14 |
| 17. Healing of two blind men at Jericho | Matt. 20:30–34 |
| 18. Healing of the ten lepers | Luke 17:12–14 |
| 19. Turning water into wine | John 2:9–11 |
| 20. Healing of the nobleman's son | John 4:46–52 |
| 21. Healing of the crippled man at Bethesda | John 5:9 |
| 22. Sight for the man born blind | John 9:1–7 |
| 23. The great catch of fishes | John 21:11 |
| 24. Healing at the beautiful gate of the temple | Acts 3:6–8 |
| 25. Healing of the cripple at Lystra | Acts 14:8–10 |

### Creation of Biological Life

| Miracle | Reference |
|---|---|
| 1. Creation of life (*nephesh*) | Gen. 1:21 |
| 2. Conception of Isaac | Gen. 21:1–2 |
| 3. Transformation of rod into serpent | Exod. 4:2–4 |
| 4. Budding of Aaron's rod | Num. 17:8 |
| 5. Raising of Samuel by the witch of Endor | 1 Sam. 28:11–12 |
| 6. Raising the widow's son | 1 Kings 17:22 |
| 7. Raising the Shunammite's son | 2 Kings 4:33–36 |
| 8. Raising at the tomb of Elisha | 2 Kings 13:21 |
| 9. The handwriting on the wall | Dan. 5:5 |
| 10. Raising of Jairus's daughter | Matt. 9:25 |
| 11. Bodies of the saints rising | Matt. 27:52 |
| 12. Raising of the widow's son | Luke 7:15 |
| 13. Raising of Lazarus | John 11:43–44 |
| 14. Raising of Tabitha by Peter | Acts 9:40–41 |
| 15. Raising of Paul after stoning | Acts 14:19–20 |
| 16. Raising of Eutychus by Paul | Acts 20:9–12 |

### Creation of Spiritual Life, or Spiritual Renewal

| Miracle | Reference |
|---|---|
| 1. Creation of man in the image of God | Gen. 1:27 |
| 2. Entering of the Holy Spirit into Ezekiel | Ezek. 2:2 |
| 3. Virgin birth of Christ | Matt. 1:18–25; Luke 1:26–38 |
| 4. Resurrection of Christ | Matt. 28:6; Rom. 8:11; 1 Cor. 15:42–45 |
| 5. Coming of the Holy Spirit at Pentecost | Acts 2:2–6 |
| 6. Reception of the Holy Spirit by laying on of hands | Acts 8:17 |
| 7. Conversion of Saul | Acts 9:3–7 |
| 8. Holy Spirit received at the house of Cornelius | Acts 10:44–46 |
| 9. Holy Spirit received by the disciples of John | Acts 19:6 |

# BIBLICAL MIRACLES OF PROVIDENCE

| Miracle | Reference |
|---|---|
| *Control of Physical Process Rates or Timing* | |
| 1. Simultaneous eruption of fountains of the deep | Gen. 7:11 |
| 2. Forty-day global rain | Gen. 7:12 |
| 3. Global wind to assuage the Flood | Gen. 8:1 |
| 4. Establishment of the rainbow | Gen. 9:13 |
| 5. Removal of the plague of flies | Exod. 8:31 |
| 6. Plague of hail and fire | Exod. 9:23–24 |
| 7. Stopping of the hail and fire | Exod. 9:33 |
| 8. Wind to remove the locusts | Exod. 10:19 |
| 9. Plague of thick darkness | Exod. 10:23 |
| 10. Sweetening of the waters of Marah | Exod. 15:25 |
| 11. Wind to bring the quails | Num. 11:31 |
| 12. Earthquake to swallow Korah | Num. 16:31–33 |
| 13. Water from the rock at Meribah | Num. 20:10–11 |
| 14. Non-aging raiment | Deut. 8:4 |
| 15. Drying of the Jordan | Josh. 3:15–17 |
| 16. Collapse of the walls of Jericho | Josh. 6:20 |
| 17. Stars fighting against Sisera | Judg. 5:20–21 |
| 18. Wet fleece and dry ground | Judg. 6:38 |
| 19. Dry fleece and wet ground | Judg. 6:40 |
| 22. Consumation of Manoah's offering | Judg. 13:19–20 |
| 23. Thunder on the Philistines | 1 Sam. 7:10 |
| 24. Thunder and rain for Samuel | 1 Sam. 12:18 |
| 25. The great trembling among the Philistines | 1 Sam. 14:15–16 |
| 26. Going sound in the mulberry trees | 2 Sam. 5:24 |
| 27. Elijah's three-and-one-half-year drought | 1 Kings 17:1 |
| 28. End of the drought | 1 Kings 18:42–45 |
| 29. Wind, earthquake, and fire | 1 Kings 19:11–12 |
| 30. Healing of the waters | 2 Kings 2:21 |
| 31. Water seen as blood | 2 Kings 3:22 |
| 32. Meal to heal death in the pot | 2 Kings 4:40–41 |
| 33. Jonah's ship and the tempest | Jon. 1:4 |
| 34. Star of Bethlehem | Matt. 2:2–9 |
| 35. Stilling of the waves | Matt. 8:26; Mark 4:39; Luke 8:24 |
| 36. Earthquake at Calvary | Matt. 27:51 |
| 37. Earthquake at the tomb | Matt. 28:2 |
| 38. Opening of the tomb | Matt. 28:2; Mark 16:4; Luke 24:2; John 20:1 |
| 39. Shaking in the disciples' room | Acts 4:31 |
| 40. Opening of prison doors | Acts 5:19 |
| 41. Release of Peter from prison | Acts 12:5–7 |
| 42. Earthquake in Philippian prison | Acts 16:25–26 |
| *Control of Biological Process Rates or Timing* | |
| 1. Migration of animals to Noah's ark | Gen. 6:20 |
| 2. Transmutation of Lot's wife into salt | Gen. 19:26 |
| 3. Plague of frog multiplication | Exod. 8:6 |

| Miracle | Reference |
|---|---|
| 4. Death of frogs | Exod. 8:13 |
| 5. Plague of lice | Exod. 8:17 |
| 6. Plague of flies | Exod. 8:24 |
| 7. Plague of murrain on cattle | Exod. 9:3 |
| 8. Plague of locusts | Exod. 10:13–15 |
| 9. Non-swelling feet | Deut. 8:4 |
| 10. Jonah preserved in the whale | Jon. 2:10 |
| 11. The gourd and the worm | Jon. 4:6–7 |
| 12. Withering of the fig tree | Matt. 21:19; Mark 11:20–21 |
| 13. Heavy draught of fishes | Luke 5:6 |

*Acceleration of Decay Processes in Human Bodies*

| Miracle | Reference |
|---|---|
| 1. Mark on Cain | Gen. 4:15 |
| 2. Plague on pharaoh's house | Gen. 12:17 |
| 3. Blindness of the Sodomites | Gen. 19:11 |
| 4. Barrenness of Abimelech's wives | Gen. 20:18 |
| 5. Shrinking of Jacob's thigh | Gen. 32:25 |
| 6. Leprosy in Moses' hand | Exod. 4:6 |
| 7. Plague of boils | Exod. 9:10 |
| 8. Plague of firstborn death | Exod. 12:29 |
| 9. Plague of eating quail | Num. 11:33 |
| 10. Miriam's leprosy | Num. 12:10 |
| 11. Plague from following Balaam | Num. 25:8–9 |
| 12. Destruction of Samson's strength | Judg. 16:17–19 |
| 13. Plague from presence of the ark | 1 Sam. 5:2–12; 6:19 |
| 14. Death of Uzzah from touching the ark | 2 Sam. 6:6–7 |
| 15. Plague from David's census | 2 Sam. 24:15–16 |
| 16. Leprosy on Elisha's servant | 2 Kings 5:27 |
| 17. Blindness of the Syrians | 2 Kings 6:18 |
| 18. Slaying of Sennacherib's army | 2 Kings 19:35 |
| 19. Uzziah's leprosy | 2 Chron. 26:19–20 |
| 20. Madness of Nebuchadnezzar | Dan. 4:31–33 |
| 21. Death of Christ | Matt. 27:50; Mark 15:37; Luke 23:46; John 19:30 |
| 22. Dumbness of Zacharias | Luke 1:20 |
| 23. Death of Ananias | Acts 5:5 |
| 24. Death of Sapphira | Acts 5:10 |
| 25. Death of Herod | Acts 12:23 |
| 26. Blindness of Elymas | Acts 13:11 |

*Acceleration of Healing Processes in Human Bodies*

| Miracle | Reference |
|---|---|
| 1. Removal of plague from Pharaoh's house | Gen. 12:17 |
| 2. Healing of wombs of Abimelech's wives | Gen. 20:17 |
| 3. Rebekah's barrenness healed | Gen. 25:21 |
| 4. Rachel made fertile | Gen. 30:22 |
| 5. Healing of the serpent bites | Num. 21:8 |
| 6. Restoration of Samson's strength | Judg. 16:28–30 |
| 7. Conception of Samuel | 1 Sam. 1:27 |
| 8. Stopping of the numbering plague | 2 Sam. 24:16 |
| 9. Conception by the Shunammite | 2 Kings 4:17 |
| 10. Healing of Hezekiah | 2 Kings 20:5–7 |
| 11. Removal of Nebuchadnezzar's madness | Dan. 4:34–36 |

| Miracle | Reference |
|---|---|
| 12. Healing of Peter's mother-in-law | Matt. 8:15; Mark 1:31; Luke 4:39 |
| 13. Healing of the palsied man | Matt. 9:6; Mark 2:12; Luke 5:25 |
| 14. Stopping the issue of blood | Matt. 9:22; Mark 5:29; Luke 8:47 |
| 15. Healing of the deaf and dumb man | Mark 7:32–35 |
| 16. The blind man at Bethsaida | Mark 8:22–25 |
| 17. Blind Bartimaeus | Mark 10:46–52; Luke 18:35–43 |
| 18. Conception of John the Baptist | Luke 1:24 |
| 19. Removal of Zacharias's dumbness | Luke 1:64 |
| 20. Man with the dropsy | Luke 14:4 |
| 21. Restoration of the severed ear | Luke 22:51 |
| 22. Removal of Saul's blindness | Acts 9:18 |
| 23. Healing of Aeneas | Acts 9:33–34 |
| 24. Healing of viper bite | Acts 28:3–6 |
| 25. Healing of Publius's father | Acts 28:8 |

### Casting Out Demons

| | |
|---|---|
| 1. Evil spirit in Saul | 1 Sam. 16:23 |
| 2. Two men in the Gaderene tombs | Matt. 8:28–32; Mark 5:2–13; Luke 8:26–33 |
| 3. Dumb man in Capernaum | Matt. 9:32–33 |
| 4. Blind and dumb man | Matt. 12:22; Luke 11:14 |
| 5. Syro-Phoenician woman's daughter | Matt. 15:22–28; Mark 7:25–30 |
| 6. Demon-possessed child | Matt. 17:14–18; Mark 9:17–27; Luke 9:38–42 |
| 7. Capernaum synagogue demoniac | Mark 1:23–26; Luke 4:31–37 |
| 8. Mary Magdalene | Luke 8:2 |
| 9. Woman with spirit of infirmity | Luke 13:11–13 |
| 10. Damsel at Philippi | Acts 16:18 |

### Providential Timing of Events

| | |
|---|---|
| 1. Meeting of Rebekah and the servant | Gen. 24:14–15 |
| 2. Growth of Jacob's flocks | Gen. 31:9 |
| 3. Holding up Moses' hands | Exod. 17:11 |
| 4. Identification of guilty Achan | Josh. 7:18 |
| 5. Blessings on house of Obed-Edom | 2 Sam. 6:12 |
| 6. Prophet slain by the lion | 1 Kings 13:24 |
| 7. Elijah fed by ravens | 1 Kings 17:6 |
| 8. Elisha and the bears | 2 Kings 2:24 |
| 9. Deliverance of Jehoshaphat | 2 Chron. 20:22–24 |
| 10. Daniel in the lions' den | Dan. 6:22 |
| 11. Preparation of Jonah's fish | Jon. 1:17 |
| 12. Tribute money and the fish | Matt. 17:27 |

# SATANIC AND DEMONIC MIRACLES

| Miracle | Reference |
| --- | --- |
| *Counterfeit Miracles of Creation* | |
| 1. Giants in the earth | Gen. 6:4 |
| 2. Magicians making rods seem as serpents | Exod. 7:11–12 |
| 3. Giants in the land | Num. 13:33 |
| 4. Evil spirit in Saul | 1 Sam. 16:23 |
| 5. Lying spirits of Ahab | 1 Kings 22:23; 2 Chron. 18:22 |
| 6. Spirit message to Eliphaz | Job 4:15–16 |
| 7. Translation of Christ to temple pinnacle | Matt. 4:5; Luke 4:9 |
| 8. Translation of Christ to high mountain | Matt. 4:8; Luke 4:5 |
| *Counterfeit Miracles of Providence* | |
| 1. Magicians making water as blood | Exod. 7:22 |
| 2. Magicians causing frogs to multiply | Exod. 8:7 |
| 3. Destruction of Job's oxen | Job 1:14–15 |
| 4. Destruction of Job's sheep | Job 1:16 |
| 5. Death of Job's servants | Job 1:17 |
| 6. Death of Job's children | Job 1:19 |
| 7. Boils on Job's body | Job 2:7 |
| 8. Paul's thorn in the flesh | 2 Cor. 12:7 |

# APPENDIX 5
# ZODIACAL CONSTELLATIONS AND THE SUGGESTED PRIMEVAL REVELATION

1. Virgo. A deliverer will come into the human family some day, born as a man, yet supernaturally conceived of a virgin, Seed of the Woman, yet Son of God.
2. Libra. Since man is a sinner and under the curse, an adequate price must be paid to redeem him and balance the scales of divine justice.
3. Scorpio. The price of redemption must be the death of the Deliverer, since man is under the condemnation of death, and yet, in dying, He must also destroy the Serpent who led man into sin.
4. Sagittarius. To prevent the coming of the Deliverer in the human family, the great Dragon will seek to corrupt mankind into a race of demon-possessed monsters and murderers.
5. Capricorn. Man will finally become so sinful as to leave no remedy but complete inundation of his entire world.
6. Aquarius. The floodgates of heaven will pour forth waters to cleanse an evil world, but representatives of the land animals will survive to fill the earth again.
7. Pisces. From the waters will emerge the true people of God, as God retains His kingly throne despite all the attacks of Satan.
8. Aries. In the fullness of time, the Seed of the Woman will come, ready to die as the sacrifice for man's sins, paying the great price to redeem His bride and destroy the works of the Dragon.
9. Taurus. Having paid the price, the slain Ram will rise as the mighty Bull, to execute judgment on all ungodliness and to rule supreme.
10. Gemini. As both Son of God and Son of man, the second Adam will claim His bride as did the first Adam, taking her to Himself forever.
11. Cancer. All the redeemed will come to Him from all times and places, secure eternally in His presence, enjoying His love and fellowship.
12. Leo. As eternal King and Lord of Lords, He will utterly vanquish and destroy the Serpent and all his followers, reigning forever and ever.

# APPENDIX 6
# GLOBAL PROCESSES INDICATING RECENT CREATION

## Uniformitarian Estimates — Age of the Earth

(Unless otherwise indicated, these estimates are based on standard assumptions of (1) zero initial "daughter" component; (2) closed system; and (3) uniform rate. Reference numbers refer to documentation cited on pages immediately following this table.)

| Process | Indicated Age of Earth in Years | Reference |
|---|---|---|
| 1. Decay of earth's magnet field | 10,000 | 1 |
| 2. Influx of radiocarbon to the earth system | 10,000 | 2 |
| 3. Continuous rapid deposition of geologic column | too small to calculate | 3 |
| 4. Influx of juvenile water into oceans | 340,000,000 | 3 |
| 5. Influx of magma from mantle to form crust | 500,000,000 | 3 |
| 6. Growth of oldest living part of biosphere | 5,000 | 3 |
| 7. Origin of human civilizations | 5,000 | 3 |
| 8. Efflux of helium-4 into the atmosphere | 1750–175,000 | 4 |
| 9. Development of total human population | 4,000 | 5 |
| 10. Influx of sediment to the ocean via rivers | 30,000,000 | 6 |
| 11. Erosion of sediment from continents | 14,000,000 | 6 |
| 12. Leaching of sodium from continents | 1,000,000 | 7 |
| 13. Leaching of chlorine from continents | 1,000,000 | 7 |
| 14. Leaching of calcium from continents | 12,000,000 | 7 |
| 15. Influx of carbonate into the ocean | 100,000 | 7 |
| 16. Influx of sulphate into the ocean | 10,000,000 | 7 |
| 17. Influx of chlorine into the ocean | 164,000,000 | 7 |
| 18. Influx of calcium into the ocean | 1,000,000 | 7 |
| 19. Influx of uranium into the ocean | 1,260,000 | 8 |
| 20. Efflux of oil from traps by fluid pressure | 10,000–100,000 | 9 |
| 21. Formation of radiogenic lead by neutron capture | too small to measure | 9 |
| 22. Formation of radiogenic strontium by neutron capture | too small to measure | 9 |
| 23. Decay of natural remanent paleomagnetism | 100,000 | 9 |
| 24. Parentless polonium halos | too small to measure | 10 |
| 25. Decay of uranium with initial "radiogenic" lead | too small to measure | 11 |
| 26. Decay of potassium with entrapped argon | too small to measure | 11 |
| 27. Formation of river deltas | 5,000 | 12 |
| 28. Submarine oil seepage into oceans | 50,000,000 | 13 |
| 29. Decay of natural plutonium | 80,000,000 | 14 |
| 30. Decay of lines of galaxies | 10,000,000 | 15 |
| 31. Expanding interstellar gas | 60,000,000 | 16 |
| 32. Decay of short-period comets | 10,000 | 17 |
| 33. Decay of long-period comets | 1,000,000 | 18 |
| 34. Influx of small particles into the sun | 83,000 | 18 |
| 35. Maximum life of meteor showers | 5,000,000 | 18 |
| 36. Instability of rings of Saturn | 1,000,000 | 18 |
| 37. Escape of methane from Titan | 20,000,000 | 18 |

| | | |
|---|---|---|
| 38. Accumulation of dust on the moon | uncertain | 19 |
| 39. Deceleration of earth by tidal friction | 500,000,000 | 20 |
| 40. Cooling of the earth by heat efflux | 24,000,000 | 20 |
| 41. Accumulation of calcareous ooze on sea floor | 5,000,000 | 21 |
| 42. Influx of sodium into the ocean via rivers | 62,000,000 | 22 |
| 43. Influx of nickel into the ocean via rivers | 9,000 | 23 |
| 44. Influx of magnesium into the ocean via rivers | 45,000,000 | 23 |
| 45. Influx of silicon into the ocean via rivers | 8,000 | 23 |
| 46. Influx of potassium into the ocean via rivers | 11,000,000 | 23 |
| 47. Influx of copper into the ocean via rivers | 50,000 | 23 |
| 48. Influx of gold into the ocean via rivers | 560,000 | 23 |
| 49. Influx of silver into the ocean via rivers | 2,100,000 | 23 |
| 50. Influx of mercury into the ocean via rivers | 42,000 | 23 |
| 51. Influx of lead into the ocean via rivers | 2,000 | 23 |
| 52. Influx of tin into the ocean via rivers | 100,000 | 23 |
| 53. Influx of aluminum into the ocean via rivers | 100 | 23 |
| 54. Influx of lithium into ocean via rivers | 20,000,000 | 23 |
| 55. Influx of titanium into ocean via rivers | 160 | 23 |
| 56. Influx of chromium into ocean via rivers | 350 | 23 |
| 57. Influx of manganese into ocean via rivers | 1,400 | 23 |
| 58. Influx of iron into ocean via rivers | 140 | 23 |
| 59. Influx of cobalt into ocean via rivers | 18,000 | 23 |
| 60. Influx of zinc into ocean via rivers | 180,000 | 23 |
| 61. Influx of rubidium into ocean via rivers | 270,000 | 23 |
| 62. Influx of strontium into ocean via rivers | 19,000,000 | 23 |
| 63. Influx of bismuth into ocean via rivers | 45,000 | 23 |
| 64. Influx of thorium into ocean via rivers | 350 | 23 |
| 65. Influx of antimony into ocean via rivers | 350,000 | 23 |
| 66. Influx of tungsten into ocean via rivers | 1,000 | 23 |
| 67. Influx of barium into ocean via rivers | 84,000 | 23 |
| 68. Influx of molybdenum into ocean via rivers | 500,000 | 23 |

## Documentation for Age Estimates

1. Thomas G. Barnes, *Origin and Destiny of the Earth's Magnetic Field* (San Diego, CA: Institute for Creation Research, 1983), 132 p.
2. Melvin A. Cook, "Do Radiological Clocks Need Repair?" *Creation Research Society Quarterly* 5 (Oct. 1968): p. 70. See also *Radiocarbon and the Age of the Earth*, by Gerald Aardsma (San Diego: Institute for Creation Research, 1991).
3. Henry M. Morris, editor, *Scientific Creationism* (Green Forest, AR: Master Books, 1985).
4. Melvin A. Cook, "Where is the Earth's Radiogenic Helium?" *Nature* 179 (Jan. 26, 1957): p. 213. See also *The Age of the Earth's Atmosphere*, by Larry Vardiman (San Diego, CA: Institute for Creation Research, 1990).
5. Henry M. Morris, Evolution and the Population Problem," ICR Impact Series, *Acts and Facts*, no. 21 (Nov. 1974).
6. Stuart E. Nevins, "Evolution, The Ocean Says No," ICR Impact Series, *Acts and Facts* 2, no. 8 (Oct. 1973).
7. Dudley J. Whitney, *The Face of the Deep* (New York, NY: Vantage, 1955).
8. Salman Bloch, "Some Factors Controlling the Concentration of Uranium in the World Ocean," *Geochimica et Cosmochimica Acta* 44 (1980): p. 373–377. See also — *What Is Creation Science?* by Henry M. Morris and Gary Parker (Green Forest, AR: Master Books, 1987), p. 283–284.
9. Melvin A. Cook, *Prehistory and Earth Models* (London: Max Parrish, 1966).
10. Robert Gentry, *Creation's Tiny Mystery* (Knoxville: Earth Science Associates, 1988).

11. Harold S. Slusher, *Critique of Radiometric Dating* (San Diego, CA: Institute for Creation Research, 1980), 58 p.
12. Benjamin F. Allen, "The Geologic Age of the Mississippi River," *Creation Research Society Quarterly,* 9 (Sept. 1972): 96–114.
13. R.D. Wilson et al., "Natural Marine Oil Seepage," *Science,* 184 (May 24, 1974): p. 857–865.
14. "Natural Plutonium," *Chemical and Engineering News,* 49 (Sept. 20, 1971): 29.
15. Halton Arp, "Observational Paradoxes in Extragalactic Astronomy," *Science,* 174 (Dec. 17, 1971): 1189–1200.
16. V.A. Hughes and D. Routledge, "An Expanding Ring of Interstellar Gas with Center Close to the Sun," *Astronomical Journal* 77, no. 3 (1972); 210–14.
17. Harold S. Slusher, "Some Astronomical Evidences for a Youthful Solar System," *Creation Research Society Quarterly* 8 (June 1971): 55–57.
18. Harold S. Slusher, *Age of the Cosmos* (San Diego, CA: Institute for Creation Research, 1980), 76 p.
19. John D. Morris, *The Young Earth* (Green Forest, AR: Master Books, 1994), p. 87–88.
20. Thomas G. Barnes, "Physics, a Challenge to Geologic Time," ICR Impact Series, *Acts and Facts,* 16 (July 1974).
21. Maurice Ewing, J.I. Ewing, and M. Talwan, "Sediment Distribution in the Oceans — Mid-Atlantic Ridge," *Bulletin of the Geophysical Society of America,* 75 (Jan. 1964): 17–36.
22. Steven A. Austin and Russell D. Humphries, "The Sea's Missing Salt: A Dilemma for Evolutionists," *Proceedings of the Second International Conference on Creationism,* vol. 2 (1991), p. 17–33.
23. J.P. Riley and G. Skirrow, editors, *Chemical Oceanography,* Vol. 1 (London: Academic Press, 1965), p. 164. See also Harold Camping, "Let the Oceans Speak," *Creation Research Society Quarterly,* 11 (June 1974): 39–45. Uniformitarian geologists, making the unwarranted assumption that ocean chemicals are all in a steady state, have noted that the same method of calculation would give the so-called "residence time" of each element in the ocean, if the influx and efflux of the elements are assumed to be equal. This assumption is wrong, however, as shown in References 8 and 22, for uranium and sodium in particular.

# CHAPTER BIBLIOGRAPHIES

The following bibliographies do not constitute an exhaustive compilation of books dealing with the respective topics, but they are representative, and should at least give an entrance into the relevant literature. In general, only books are listed which tend to support the biblical point of view advocated in the particular chapter, since such books are much more difficult to find than books with contrary viewpoints. Most of the books are of fairly recent publication, with older books included only if they are believed to be of particular importance. All of the books listed are significant and well worth reading. Each book has been listed only under the chapter to which it is believed to make the most significant contribution.

## Chapter 1. Biblical Theology

Barnes, Thomas G. *Science and Biblical Faith*. CRS Books, 1993. 191 p.

Geisler, Norman H. *Christian Apologetics*. Baker, 1976. 393 p.

Geisler, Norman H. *Philosophy of Religion*. Zondervan, 1981. 416 p.

Hooykaas, R. *Religion and the Rise of Modern Science*. Eerdmans, 1972. 162 p.

Houghton, S.M., ed. *Truth Unchanged, Unchanging*. Bible League, 1984. 503 p.

Johnson, Philip E. *Reason in the Balance*. Inter-Varsity Press, 1995. 245 p.

Klaaren, Eugene M. *The Religious Origins of Modern Science*. Eerdmans, 1977. 244 p.

Morris, Henry M. *History of Modern Creationism*. Master Books, 1993. 444 p.

Morris, Henry M. *Men of Science/Men of God*. Master Books, 1988. 107 p.

Morris, Henry M. *The God Who is Real*. Master Books, 1988. 119 p.

Noebel, David A. *Understanding the Times*. Summit Press, 1991. 896 p.

Pearcey, Nancy R., and Charles B. Thaxton. *The Soul of Science: Christian Faith and Natural Philosophy*. Crossway Books, 1994. 298 p.

Schaeffer, Francis A. *The God Who is There*. Inter-Varsity, 1968. 191 p.

Singer, C. Gregg. *From Rationalism to Irrationality*. Presbyterian and Reformed, 1981. 490 p.

Sire, James W. *The Universe Next Door*. Inter-Varsity, 1976. 238 p.

Thompson, Bert, and Wayne Jackson. *The Case for the Existence of God*. Apologetics Press, 1996. 82 p.

Wilder-Smith, A.E. *God: To Be or Not to Be?* Telos-International, 1975. 117 p.

## Chapter 2. Biblical Cosmology

Andrews, E.H. *From Nothing to Nature*. Welwyn, 1978. 120 p.

Blanchard, John. *Does God Believe in Atheists?* Evangelical Press, 2000. 655 p.

Crossley, Robert. *The Trinity*. Inter-Varsity, 1978. 45 p.

Fortman, Edmund J. *The Triune God*. Baker, 1978. 400 p.

Johnson, Philip E. *Darwin on Trial*. Regnery, 1991. 195 p.

MacArthur, John. *The Battle for the Beginning*. Thomas Nelson, 2001. 232 p.

Morris, Henry M., and John D. Morris. *Modern Creation Trilogy, Vol. I, Scripture and Creation*. Master Books, 1996. 228 p.

Morris, Henry M. *The Defender's Study Bible*. World Bible, 1995. 1628 p.

Morris, Henry M. *The Genesis Record*. Baker Book House, 1976. 716 p.

Morris, Henry M. *The Revelation Record*. Tyndale, 1983. 528 p.

Morris, Henry M. *Science and the Bible*. Moody Press, 1986. 154 p.

Van Bebber, Mark, and Paul S. Taylor. *Creation and Time*. Eden Communications, 1996. 128 p.

Wood, Nathan R. *The Trinity in the Universe*. Kregel, 1978. 220 p.

## Chapter 3. Biblical Supernaturalism

Aalders, G. Charles. *The Problem of the Book of Jonah*. Tyndale, 1948. 30 p.

Andrews, E.H. *God, Science and Evolution*. Evangelical Press, 1980. 129 p.

Geisler, Norman L. *Miracles and Modern Thought*. Zondervan, 1982. 168 p.

Gordon, Ernest. *The Fact of Miracle*. Marshall Jones, 1955. 126 p.

Lockyer, Herbert. *All the Miracles of the Bible*. Zondervan, 1961. 311 p.

McDowell, Josh. *Evidence that Demands a Verdict*. Campus Crusade for Christ, 1972. 387 p.

McIver, Robert S. *Star of Bethlehem*. Overland Press, 1998. 207 p.

Morris, Henry M., and Martin Clark, *The Bible Has the Answer*. Master Books, 1987. 394 p.

Morris, Henry M. *Christian Education for the Real World*. Master Books, 1991. 295 p.

Morris, Henry M., and Henry M. Morris III. *Many Infallible Proofs*. Master Books, 1996. 396 p.

Rimmer, Harry. *The Harmony of Science and Scripture*. Eerdmans, 1976. 283 p.

Smith, Wilber M. *The Supernaturalness of Christ*. W. A. Wilde, 1944. 235 p.

Warfield, Benjamin B. *Counterfeit Miracles*. Banner of Truth, 1972. 327 p.

Wilson, Clifford, and John Weldon. *Occult Shock and Psychic Forces*. Creation-Life, 1980. 482 p.

## Chapter 4. Biblical Evolutionism

Bowden, Malcolm. *The Rise of the Evolution Fraud*. Creation-Life, 1982. 227 p.

Clark, Harold W. *New Creationism*. Southern, 1980. 128 p.

Gish, Duane T., and Henry M. Morris. *The Battle for Creation*. Creation-Life, 1976. 321 p.

Gitt, Werner. *Did God Use Evolution?* Hanssler-Verlag, 1993. 152 p.

Jordan, James B. *Creation in Six Days*. Canon Press, 1999. 265 p.

Kelly, Douglas F. *Creation and Change*. Christian Focus, 1997. 272 p.

Lammerts, W.E., ed. *Scientific Studies in Special Creation*. Presbyterian and Reformed, 1971. 343 p.

Lammerts, W.E., ed. *Why Not Creation?* Presbyterian and Reformed, 1970. 388 p.

Lubenow, Marvin. *From Fish to Gish*. Creation-Life, 1983. 304 p.

MacBeth, Norman. *Darwin Retried*. Gambit, 1971. 178 p.

Moore, John N. *Questions and Answers on Creation and Evolution*. Baker, 1976. 110 p.

Morris, Henry M. *Biblical Creationism*. Master Books, 1993. 276 p.

Morris, Henry M., and Donald Rohrer. *Creation: The Cutting Edge*. Creation-Life, 1982. 240 p.

Morris, Henry M., and Donald Rohrer. *Decade of Creation*. Creation-Life, 1980. 316 p.

Overton, Basil. *Evolution in the Light of Scripture, Science, and Sense*. J.C. Choate, 1981. 165 p.

Patten, Donald W., ed. *Symposium on Creation, I, II, III, IV, V.* Baker, 1969, 1970, 1971, 1972, 1975.

Thompson, Bert. *The History of Evolutionary Thought*. Star Bible and Tract, 1981. 192 p.

Thompson, Bert. *Theistic Evolution*. Lambert, 1977. 235 p.

Wysong, R.L. *The Creation-Evolution Controversy*. Inquiry, 1976. 455 p.

## Chapter 5. Biblical Cosmogony

Bird, Wendell R. *The Origin of Species Revisited* (Two Volumes). Philosophical Library, 1991. 1114 p.

Fields, Weston W. *Unformed and Unfilled*. Presbyterian and Reformed, 1976. 245 p.

Hughes, Philip E. *Christianity and the Problem of Origins*. Presbyterian and Reformed, 1964. 44 p.

Humphries, D. Russell. *Starlight and Time*. Master Books, 1994. 137 p.

Moore, John N. *How to Teach Origins*. Mott Media, 1983. 382 p.

Morris, Henry M. *Defending the Faith*. Master Books. 1999. 256 p.

Rehwinkel, Alfred M. *The Wonders of Creation*. Baker, 1974. 288 p.

Setterfield, Barry. *The Velocity of Light and the Age of the Universe*. Creation Science Publishing, 1981. 48 p.

Slusher, Harold S. *Age of the Cosmos*. Institute for Creation Research, 1980. 76 p.

Slusher, Harold S. *Origin of the Universe*. Institute for Creation Research, 1980. 90 p.

Slusher, Harold S., and Stephen Robertson. *Age of the Solar System*. Institute for Creation Research, 1982. 131 p.

White, A.J. Monty. *What About Origins?* Dunestone, 1978. 170 p.

## Chapter 6. Biblical Astronomy

Bliss, Richard B. *Voyage to the Stars*. Institute for Creation Research, 1991. 111 p.

Bliss, Richard B., and Donald B. DeYoung. *Voyage to the Planets*. Institute for Creation Research, 1994. 128 p.

Bullinger, E.W. *The Witness of the Stars*. Kregel, 1967. 204 p.

Burgess, Stuart. *He Made the Stars Also*. Day One Publications, 2001. 186 p.

Chatfield, Gene. *The Heavens Declare*. Sonlight Publishers, 1997. 167 p.

Cottrell, Ronald G. *The Remarkable Spaceship: Earth*. Accent, 1982. 62 p.

Curtis, William M. *Specific Revelation: The Gospel Prior to Moses*. Brentwood Christian Press, 1993. 155 p.

DeYoung, Donald B. *Astronomy and the Bible*. Baker Book House, 1989. 146 p.

Gitt, Werner. *Stars and Their Purpose*. Hannsler-Verlag, 1986. 217 p.

Henry, Jonathan. *The Astronomy Book*. Master Books, 1999. 80 p.

Morris, Henry M. *Creation and the Modern Christian*. Master Books, 1985. 298 p.

Mulfinger, George, ed. *Design and Origins in Astronomy*. CRS Books, 1984. 150 p.

Patten, Donald W., Ronald R. Hatch, and Loren C. Steinhauer. *The Long Day of Joshua and Six Other Catastrophes*. Baker, 1973. 328 p.

Seiss, Joseph A. *The Gospel in the Stars*. Kregel, 1972. 188 p.

Showalter, Lester E. *Discovering God's Stars*. Rod and Staff, 1968. 70 p.

Steidl, Paul B. *The Earth, the Stars and the Bible*. Presbyterian and Reformed, 1979. 250 p.

Whitcomb, John C. *The Bible and Astronomy*. BMH Books, 1984. 32 p.

Whitcomb, John C. *Origin of the Solar System*. Presbyterian and Reformed, 1964. 34 p.

Whitcomb, John C., and Donald B. DeYoung. *The Moon: Its Creation, Form, and Significance*. BMH Books, 1978. 180 p.

## Chapter 7. Biblical Thermodynamics

Bowden, Malcolm. *Science Vs. Evolution*. Sovereign Publications, 1991. 238 p.

Campbell, Jeremy. *Grammatical Man*. Simon and Schuster, 1982. 319 p.

Clark, Robert E.D. *Darwin: Before and After.* Moody, 1967. 192 p.

Coppedge, James. *Evolution: Possible or Impossible?* Zondervan, 1973. 276 p.

Couch, Mal, ed. *The Fundamentals for the Twenty-First Century.* Kregel Publishing, 2000. 656 p.

Gish, Duane T. *The Amazing Story of Creation.* Institute for Creation Research, 1990. 112 p.

Gitt, Werner. *In the Beginning Was Information.* Hannsler-Verlag, 1998. 256 p.

Morris, Henry M. *King of Creation.* Creation-Life, 1980. 239 p.

Morris, Henry M., and John D. Morris. *Modern Creation Trilogy, Vol. II, Science and Creation.* Master Books, 1996. 343 p.

Morris, Henry M., and Gary E. Parker. *What is Creation Science?* Master Books, 1987. 332 p.

Perloff, James. *Tornado in a Junkyard.* Refuge Books, 1999. 322 p.

Sharp, G. Thomas. *Science According to Moses.* Creation Truth Publishers, 1992. 442 p.

Sewell, Curt. *God at Ground Zero.* Master Books, 1997. 278 p.

Siegler, H.R. *Evolution or Degeneration—Which?* Northwestern, 1972. 128 p.

Wilder-Smith, A.E. *The Natural Sciences Know Nothing of Evolution.* Master Books, 1981. 166 p.

Wilder-Smith, A.E. *The Scientific Alternative to Neo-Darwinian Evolution.* TWFT Publishing, 1987. 198 p.

Williams, Emmett L., ed. *Thermodynamics and the Development of Order.* Creation Research Society, 1981. 141 p.

## Chapter 8. Biblical Chemistry and Physics

Aw, S.E. *Chemical Evolution: An Examination of Current Ideas.* Creation-Life, 1982. 206 p.

Barnes, Thomas G. *Physics of the Future.* Institute for Creation Research, 1983. 208 p.

Behe, Michael. *Darwin's Black Box.* Free Press, 1996. 192 p.

Bliss, Richard B., and Gary E. Parker. *Origin of Life.* Institute for Creation Research, 1979. 70 p.

Chittick, Donald E. *The Controversy.* Multnomah Press, 1984. 280 p.

Clark, R.E.D. *The Universe: Plan or Accident?* Paternoster, 1949. 192 p.

Croft, L.R. *How Life Began.* Evangelical Press, 1988. 120 p.

Denton, Michael. *Evolution: A Theory in Crisis.* Burnett Books, 1985. 368 p.

DeYoung, Don B. *Physical Science and Creation.* CRS Books, 1997. 81 p.

Gish, Duane T. *Speculations and Experiments on the Origin of Life.* Institute for Creation Research, 1972. 41 p.

Morris, Henry M. *The Remarkable Record of Job.* Master Books, 1988. 146 p.

Rosevear, Donald. *Creation Science.* New Wine Press, 1991. 158 p.

Sarfati, Jonathan. *Refuting Evolution.* Master Books, 1999. 144 p.

Spetner, Lee. *Not by Chance.* Judaica Press, 1997. 272 p.

Thaxton, Charles, Walter L. Bradley, and Roger Olson. *The Mystery of Life's Origin.* Philosophical Library, 1984. 228 p.

Wilder-Smith, A.E. *The Creation of Life.* Creation-Life, 1970. 269 p.

Wilder-Smith, A.E. *Man's Origin, Man's Destiny.* Creation-Life, 1968. 320 p.

Williams, Emmett L., and George Mulfinger. *Physical Science for Christian Schools.* Bob Jones University Press, 1974. 628 p.

## Chapter 9. Biblical Geophysics

Ackerman, Paul D. *It's A Young World After All.* Baker Book House, 1986. 131 p.

Arndts, Russell, and William Overn. *Isochron Dating and the Mixing Model.* Bible-Science Association, 1983. 36 p.

Barnes, Thomas G. *Origin and Destiny of the Earth's Magnetic Field.* Institute for Creation Research, 1983. 132 p.

Brown, Walter T. *In the Beginning: Compelling Evidence for Creation and the Flood.* Center for Scientific Creation, 1995. 230 p.

Cook, Melvin. *Prehistory and Earth Models.* Max Parrish, 1966. 353 p.

Gentry, Robert V. *Earth's Tiny Mystery.* Earth Science Association, 1992. 364 p.

Morris, Henry M. *Scientific Creationism.* Master Books, 1985. 294 p.

Morris, Henry M., and John D. Morris. *Science, Scripture and the Young Earth.* Master Books, 1989. 95 p.

Morris, Henry M., William W. Boardman, and Robert F. Koontz. *Science and Creation.* Creation-Science Research Center, 1971. 206 p.

Morris, John D. *The Young Earth.* Master Books, 1994. 206 p.

Mulfinger, George, and Donald E. Snyder. *Earth Science for Christian Schools.* Bob Jones University Press, 1979. 469 p.

Reed, John. *The North American Mid-Continent Rift System.* Creation Research Society Books, 2000. 155 p.

Showalter, Lester E. *Investigating God's Orderly World.* Rod and Staff, 1970. 453 p.

Vardiman, Larry. *Ice Cores and the Age of the Earth.* Institute for Creation Research, 1993. 93 p.

Vardiman, Larry. *Sea-Floor Sediment and the Age of the Earth.* Institute for Creation Research, 1996. 94 p.

Vardiman, Larry, Andrew Snelling, and Eugene F. Chaffin. *Radioisotopes and the Age of the Earth: A Young Earth Research Initiative.* Institute for Creation Research, 2000. 667 p.

Whitney, Dudley J. *Face of the Deep.* Vantage, 1955. 102 p.

Woodmorappe, John. *The Mythology of Modern Dating Methods.* Institute for Creation Research, 1999. 108 p.

Woods, Andrew J., and Henry M. Morris. *The Center of the Earth.* Institute for Creation Research, 1973. 18 p.

## Chapter 10. Biblical Hydrology and Meteorology

Boyd, Bob. *Scientific Facts in the Bible.* Author, 1983. 72 p.

Corbin, B.J. *The Explorer's of Ararat.* Great-Commission Books, 1999. 482 p.

Daly, Reginald. *Earth's Most Challenging Mysteries.* Craig, 1980. 405 p.

DeYoung, Donald B. *Weather and the Bible.* Baker Book House, 1996. 162 p.

Dillow, Joseph C. *The Waters Above: Earth's Pre-Flood Canopy.* Moody, 1982. 479 p.

Morris, Henry M., and James M. Wiggert. *Applied Hydraulics in Engineering.* John Wiley and Sons, 1972. 629 p.

Morris, John D. *Adventure on Ararat.* Creation-Life, 1973. 128 p.

Morris, John D. *Noah's Ark and the Ararat Adventure.* Master Books, 1994, 62 p.

Morris, John D., and Tim F. LaHaye. *The Ark on Ararat.* Thomas Nelson, 1976. 275 p.

Morton, Jean. *Science in the Bible.* Moody, 1978. 272 p.

Oard, Michael. *An Ice Age Caused by the Genesis Flood*. Institute for Creation Research, 1990. 243 p.

Oard, Michael. *The Weather Book*. Master Books, 1997. 80 p.

Patten, Donald W. *The Biblical Flood and the Ice Epoch*. Pacific Meridian, 1966. 336 p.

Vardiman, Larry. *The Age of the Earth's Atmosphere*. Institute for Creation Research, 1990. 32 p.

Vardiman, Larry. *Climates Before and After the Genesis Flood*. Institute for Creation Research, 2001. 116 p.

Woodmorappe, John. *Noah's Ark: A Feasibility Study*. Institute for Creation Research, 1996. 306 p.

## Chapter 11. Biblical Geology

Austin, Steven. *Catastrophes in Earth History*. Institute for Creation Research, 1984. 318 p.

Brand, Leonard. *Faith, Reason and Earth History*. Andrews University Press, 1997. 332 p.

Clark, Harold. W. *Fossils, Flood, and Fire*. Outdoor Pictures, 1968. 239 p.

Froede, Carl. *Field Studies in Catastrophic Geology*. CRS Books, 1998. 120 p.

Howe, George, ed. *Speak to the Earth*. Presbyterian and Reformed, 1975. 463 p.

Metcalf, John. *Noah and the Flood*. John Metcalfe, 1976. 95 p.

Morris, Henry M., and John C. Whitcomb. *The Genesis Flood*. Presbyterian and Reformed, 1961. 518 p.

Morris, John D. *The Geology Book*. Master Books, 2000. 80 p.

Nelson, Byron C. *The Deluge Story in Stone*. Bethany, 1968, 204 p.

Oard, Michael J. *Ancient Ice Ages or Gigantic Submarine Landslides*. CRS Books, 1997. 130 p.

Price, George McCready. *The New Geology*. Pacific Press, 1923. 726 p.

Price, George McCready. *Common-Sense Geology*. Pacific Press, 1946. 239 p.

Price, George McCready. *Evolutionary Geology and the New Catastrophism*. Pacific Press, 1926. 352 p.

Rehwinkel, Alfred A. *The Flood*. Concordia, 1951. 372 p.

Roth, Ariel A. *Origins, Linking Science and Scripture*. Review and Herald, 1998. 384 p.

Von Fange, Erich A. *Noah to Abram: The Turbulent Years*. Living Word Services, 1994. 372 p.

Whitcomb, John C. *The Early Earth*. Baker Book House, 1986. 174 p.

Whitney, Dudley J. *Genesis Versus Evolution*. Exposition, 1961. 61 p.

Woodmorappe, John. *Studies in Flood Geology*. Institute for Creation Research, 1993. 240 p.

## Chapter 12. Biblical Paleontology

Anderson, J. Kerby, and Harold G. Coffin. *Fossils in Focus*. Zondervan, 1980. 96 p.

Austin, Steven A., ed. *Grand Canyon: Monument to Catastrophe*. Institute for Creation Research, 1994. 284 p.

Baugh, Carl E. *Against All Odds*. Hearthstone Publications, 1999. 160 p.

Bliss, Richard B., Duane Gish, and Gary Parker. *Fossils—Key to the Present*. Creation-Life, 1980. 80 p.

Coffin, Harold G. *Creation: Accident or Design*. Review and Herald, 1969. 512 p.

Davis, Buddy, Mike Liston, and John Whitmore. *The Great Alaskan Dinosaur Adventure*. Master Books, 1998. 137 p.

Dewar, Douglas. *Difficulties of the Evolution Theory*. Edward Arnold, 1931. 192 p.

Dewar, Douglas. *The Transformist Illusion*. DeHoff, 1955. 305 p.

DeYoung, Donald B. *Dinosaurs and Creation*. Baker Book House, 2000. 141 p.

Gish, Duane T. *Creation Scientists Answer Their Critics*. Institute for Creation Research, 1993. 451 p.

Gish, Duane T. *Dinosaurs by Design*. Institute for Creation Research, 1992. 88 p.

Gish, Duane T. *Evolution—The Fossils Still Say No!* Master Books, 1995. 391 p.

Morris, Henry M. *Evolution in Turmoil*. Creation-Life, 1982. 190 p.

Morris, Henry M. *That Their Words Might be Used Against Them*. Master Books, 1997. 496 p.

Morris, Henry M. *The Twilight of Evolution*. Master Books, 1998. 91 p.

Morris, John D. *Tracking Those Incredible Dinosaurs—and the People Who Knew Them*. Creation-Life, 1980. 240 p.

Read, John G. *Fossils, Strata and Evolution*. Scientific-Technical Presentations, 1979. 64 p.

Sutherland, Luther. *Darwin's Enigma*. Master Books, 1998. 192 p.

Tilney, A.G. *The Case Against Evolution*. Evolution Protest Movement, 1964.

Von Fange, Erich A. *Genesis and the Dinosaur*. Living Word Services, 1990. 311 p.

Whitcomb, John C. *The World That Perished*. Baker Book House, 1988. 178 p.

## Chapter 13. Biblical Biology

Bergman, Jerry, and George Howe. *Vestigial Organs Are Fully Functional*. CRS Books, 1990. 97 p.

Booth, Ernest S. *Biology, the Story of Life*. Pacific Press, 1950. 710 p.

Burgess, Stuart. *Hallmarks of Design*. Day One Publishers, 2000. 200 p.

d'Abrera, Bernard. *The Concise Analysis of Butterflies of the World*. Hill House Publishers, 2001. 353 p.

Davidheiser, Bolton. *Evolution and Christian Faith*. Craig, 1969. 372 p.

Davis, Percival, and Dean Kenyon. *Of Pandas and People*. Haughton Publishers, 1993. 170 p.

Frair, Wayne, and Percival Davis. *A Case for Creation*. Moody, 1983. 155 p.

Klotz, John W. *Genes, Genesis and Evolution*. Concordia, 1970, 544 p.

Lester, Lane. *Cloning: Miracle or Menace?* Tyndale, 1980. 156 p.

Lester, Lane, and Raymond G. Bohlin. *The Natural Limits to Biological Change*. Zondervan, 1988. 207 p.

Marsh, Frank L. *Variation and Fixity in Nature*. Pacific Press, 1976. 150 p.

Moore, John N., and Harold S. Slusher, eds. *Biology: A Search for Order in Complexity*. Zondervan. 1974. 595 p.

Nelson, Byron C. *After Its Kind*. Bethany, 1967. 200 p.

Parker, Gary E. *Creation: The Facts of Life*. Creation-Life, 1994. 216 p.

Pinkston, William S., Jr. *Biology for Christian Schools*. Bob Jones University Press, 1980. 741 p.

Ridlon, Elizabeth J., and Robert R. Ridlon. *Creation Science Made Easy*. Jordan Hall Research Association, 1997. 136 p.

Romine, Walter J. *The Biotic Message*. St. Paul Science, 1993. 538 p.

Wells, Jonathan. *Icons of Evolution*. Regnery Publishers, 2000. 338 p.

## Chapter 14. Biblical Anthropology

Bowden, Malcolm. *Ape-Men: Fact or Fallacy*. Sovereign Publications, 1977. 258 p.

Cousins, Frank W. *Fossil Man*. Evolution Protest Movement, 1966. 106 p.

Cuozzo, Jack. *Buried Alive.* Master Books, 1998. 349 p.

Custance, Arthur C. *Evolution or Creation?* Zondervan, 1976. 329 p.

Custance, Arthur C. *Genesis and Early Man.* Zondervan, 1975. 331 p.

Custance, Arthur C. *Man in Adam and in Christ.* Zondervan, 1975. 350 p.

Custance, Arthur C. *The Mysterious Matter of Mind.* Zondervan, 1980. 105 p.

Gillen, Allen, Frank J. Sherwin, and Alan C. Knowles. *The Human Body: An Intelligent Design.* CRS Books, 1999. 155 p.

Johnson, Phillip E. *Darwin on Trial.* Inter-Varsity Press, 1993. 220 p.

Lubenow, Marvin. *Bones of Contention.* Baker Book House, 1992. 295 p.

Marsh, Frank L. *Life, Man and Time.* Outdoor Pictures, 1967. 238 p.

Rendle-Short, John. *Man: Ape or Image.* Creation-Science, 1981. 195 p.

Taylor, Ian T. *In the Minds of Men.* TFE Publishers, 1992 498 p.

White, A.J. Monty. *Wonderfully Made.* Evangelical Press, 1989. 128 p.

## Chapter 15. Biblical Demography and Linguistics

Booker, Harold R. *Origins, Icons and Illusions.* Warren H. Green, 1998. 474 p.

Camping, Harold. *Adam When?* Frontiers for Christ, 1974. 297 p.

Chittick, Donald E. *The Puzzle of Ancient Man.* Creation Compass, 1998. 182 p.

Clark, Gordon H. *Language and Theology.* Presbyterian and Reformed, 1981. 152 p.

Ham, Ken, Carl Wieland, and Don Batten. *One Blood.* Master Books, 2000. 174 p.

Kang, C.H., and Ethel R. Nelson. *The Discovery of Genesis.* Concordia, 1979. 139 p.

Manley, Isaac V. *God Made.* College Press Publishers, 1994. 209 p.

Matrisciana, Caryl, and Roger Oakland. *The Evolution Conspiracy.* Harvest House, 1991. 221 p.

Nelson, Ethel R., and Richard Broadberry. *Genesis and the Mystery Confucius Couldn't Solve.* Concordia Publishing House, 1994. 182 p.

Nelson, Ethel R., Richard Broadberry, and Samuel Wang. *The Beginning of Chinese Characters.* Read Books Publishers, 2001. 268 p.

Reed, John K. *Plain Talk About Genesis.* Word Ministries Inc., 2000. 199 p.

Rose, Seraphim. *Genesis, Creation and Early Man.* St. Herman of Alaska Brotherhood, 2000. 709 p.

Rushdoony, Rousas J. *The Myth of Over-Population.* Craig, 1969. 64 p.

Wilson, Clifford. *Monkeys Will Never Talk — or Will They?* Creation-Life, 1978. 183 p.

## Chapter 16. Biblical Ethnology

Adam, Ben. *The Origin of Heathendom.* Bethany, 1963. 128 p.

Cooper, Bill. *After the Flood.* New Wine Press, 1995. 256 p.

Corliss, William R. *Ancient Man: A Handbook of Puzzling Artifacts.* The Sourcebook Project, 1978. 786 p.

Courville, Donovan. *The Exodus Problem and its Ramifications.* Two vols. Challenge, 1971. 687 p.

Custance, Arthur C. *Noah's Three Sons.* Zondervan, 1975. 368 p.

Ham, Ken. *Genesis and the Decay of the Nations.* Master Books, 1991. 81 p.

Ham, Ken. *One Blood.* Master Books, 1999. 176 p.

Ham, Ken. *The Lie: Evolution.* Master Books, 1987. 164 p.

Hyma, Albert, and Mary Stanton. *Streams of Civilization,* Creation-Life, 1976. 411 p.

Morris, Henry M. *The Long War Against God.* Master Books, 1989. 344 p.

Morris, Henry M. *The Twilight of Evolution.* Baker, 1964. 103 p.

Morris, Henry M., and John D. Morris. *Modern Creation Trilogy, Vol. III, Society and Creation.* Master Books, 1996. 203 p.

Nelson, Byron C. *Before Abraham.* Augsburg, 1948. 124 p.

Peterson, Dennis R. *Unlocking the Mysteries of Creation.* Christian Equippers International, 1990. 204 p.

Richardson, Don. *Eternity in Their Hearts.* Regal, 1981. 176 p.

Von Fange, Erich A. *Time Upside Down.* Erich A. Von Fange, 1981. 41 p.

Wilson, Clifford. *Ebla Tablets: Secrets of a Forgotten City.* Creation-Life, 1977. 128 p.

Wang, Samuel, and Ethel R. Nelson. *God and the Ancient Chinese.* Read Books Publishers, 1998. 305 p.

Zwemer, Samuel M. *The Origin of Religion.* Loizeau, 1945. 156 p.

# INDEX OF SUBJECTS

454

460

# INDEX OF NAMES

# INDEX OF SCRIPTURE REFERENCES

470

472

# Men of Science, Men of God

## Henry M. Morris

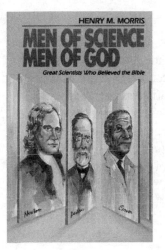

Because of the evolutionary dogma that dominates America's teaching institutions, most people are unaware that many of the world's greatest scientists were Christians and ardent creationists who believed the Book of Genesis. This book presents the facts.

ISBN: 0-89051-080-6
Trade Paperback • $7.99

# Many Infallible Proofs

## Henry M. Morris

Studying closely the internal and external evidences for the divine nature of Scripture, *Many Infallible Proofs* is perfect for both the academic skeptic and Christian struggling with hard questions about faith. A fascinating look at science, archaeology, and prophecy.

ISBN: 0-89051-005-9
Trade Paperback • $11.99

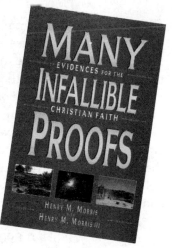

*Available at Christian bookstores nationwide*

# The Remarkable Record of Job

## Henry M. Morris

Far from a myth or fable, the majestic Book of Job stands forever as a genuine historical account of a man assaulted by the accuser, Satan, and redeemed by a loving God. The author asserts further that Job's ancient account (possibly the oldest book in the Bible, apart from Genesis) is scientifically reliable, touching on aspects of nature that prove man's early knowledge of the universe was more highly sophisticated than many believe today.

ISBN: 0-89051-292-2
Paperback • 6 x 9 • $8.99

# The Remarkable Wisdom of Solomon

## Henry M. Morris

Isn't it amazing that a man who had 700 wives and 300 concubines and ruled a country for 40 years still had time to write three of the most profound books of the Bible? Proverbs, Ecclesiastes, and Song of Solomon all show marks of divine inspiration, and each can be a blessing to the reader, but why would God choose a man who turned to idolatry to write these books? Dr. Morris addresses the enigma of Solomon and presents a verse-by-verse commentary on his writings.

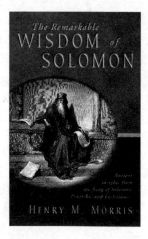

ISBN: 0-89051-356-2
Paperback • 6 x 9 • $11.99

*Available at Christian bookstores nationwide*

# Treasures in the Psalms

## Henry M. Morris

This marvelous look at the author's favorite book of the Bible gives the reader insights not commonly taught in the church today.

This devotional, focusing on the spiritual, physical, and scientific dimensions of the Psalms, starts with the conviction that the Bible is a supernaturally transmitted collection of the books, with Psalms leading the parade of the world's greatest literature. From the book's definite nod to scientific concepts, to the groanings of King David, *Treasures in the Psalms* promises to be a gift beyond measure.

ISBN: 0-89051-298-1
Trade Paperback • $13.99

# Defending the Faith

## Henry M. Morris

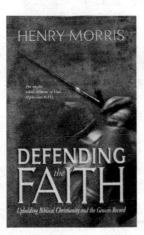

A brand-new book from "the father of the modern creation movement," this insightful work offers a fresh look at Satan's age-old war against God. by exposing the fragility of evolutionary theory, and the real harm it has had for society and the Church, Dr. Morris gives pause to those who believe evolution and Christianity can co-exist.

For over six decades, Dr. Morris has explored the evil fruits of evolution. In *Defending the Faith*, he shows Christians the danger in compromising with a philosophy so contrary to the love of God. Dr. Morris's unique ability to puncture evolutionary fallacies, and show the relevance to Christians is on display once again. This book is a shattering apologetics read.

ISBN: 0-89051-324-4
Trade Paperback • $11.99

*Available at Christian bookstores nationwide*

# The Modern Creation Trilogy

Volume I - Scripture and Creation
Volume II - Science and Creation
Volume III - Society and Creation

## *Dr. Henry M. Morris and Dr. John D. Morris*

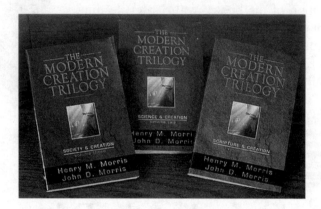

The definitive work on the study of origins, from a creationist perspective, *The Modern Creation Trilogy* examines the evidences for both evolution and special creation. Authored by the prolific father-son research team of Henry and John Morris, this three-volume gift set is a "must-have" for those who believe the Bible is God's plain-spoken Word.

Volume I looks at what the Bible says about origins — man, animal, planet, and universe. Volume II studies the scientific evidences for evolution and creation, contending that the evidence favors creation, since none of us were there in the beginning. Volume III sheds light on the fruits of each worldview — which stance produces better results for all creation? Interest level: Adult.

ISBN: 0-89051-216-7
Gift-boxed set of three • Paperback • 5-1/4 x 8-1/2 • $34.95

*Available at Christian bookstores nationwide*

# Biblical Creationism

## Henry M. Morris

Critics of the doctrine of creation often attempt to marginalize the great truths of God's creative acts. The reality, however, is that creation is mentioned in each of the Bible's 66 books. This is one of the great ignored truths of the modern Church.

Far from being a trivial issue, or one that can be interpreted many different ways, God's record of creation displays a marvelous and clear consistency throughout. From the symphony of the creation week in Genesis to the promise of a new heaven and a new earth in Revelation, the Bible speaks of a recent, six-day creation of the universe.

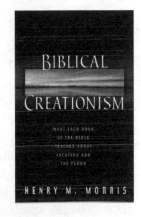

Respected scholar Henry Morris has spent six decades studying God's Word, and his commentaries have enriched the faith of many. In this remarkable book, Dr. Morris examines the famous creation account in Genesis, as well as lesser-known references such as Ezra and Colossians.

ISBN: 0 89051-293-0
Paperback • 6 x 9 • $12.99

# Scientific Creationism

## Dr. Henry M. Morris

This book provides an in-depth examination of the research for creation. Covers dating methods, geology, biology, and other areas. Interest level: High school - adult.

ISBN: 0-89051-003-2
Paperback • 5-1/4 x 8-1/4 • $10.95

*Available at Christian bookstores nationwide*

# That Their Words May Be Used against Them

## Henry M. Morris

The most complete guide to evolutionists' quotes available anywhere. Compiled from a half-century of research into the creation/evolution debate, this book looks at the contradictory statements made by evolutionists in the various fields of science.

Discover the rancorous debates over "ape-men," the geologic column, fossilization, astronomy, and much more. Contained in 15 chapters, these quotes are taken from a wide variety of sources including technical journals, popular magazines, and books.

See for yourself that the united front presented to the public by the evolutionary community is often a facade.

ISBN: 0-89051-228-0
Casebound • $21.95

# The God Who Is Real

## Henry M. Morris

Written really for the unbeliever or person whose faith is weak, this book is a fresh look at the author's love of apologetic works, emphasizing the amazing design of the created world.

An easily read book, *The God Who Is Real* reiterates that, quite different from the god of deism, the true God of the universe is also very near to each of us. Dr. Morris's unique commentary on God's Word will make a powerful witnessing tool for anyone with a burden for the lost, while serving as a guide for the believer.

ISBN: 0-89051-299-X
Paperback • 6 x 9 • $9.99

*Available at Christian bookstores nationwide*